BY THE EDITORS OF CONSU

HOW TO
FIX
EVERYTHING
IN YOUR
HOME

BEEKMAN HOUSE
New York

Contents

Library of Congress Catalog Card Number:
80-84046

ISBN: 0-517-324458

BEEKMAN HOUSE
A Division of Crown Publishers, Inc.
One Park Avenue
New York, New York 10016

Cover Design: Frank E. Peiler
Illustrations: Clarence A. Moberg
Front Cover Illustrations: Tim Burkhardt

Manufactured in the United States of America
1 2 3 4 5 6 7 8 9 10

Electricity 57

Appliances 91

Heating and Cooling 163

Furniture 206

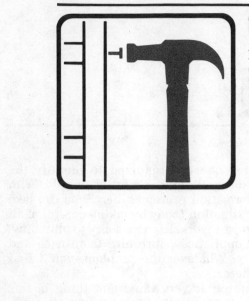

Structural **238**

Introduction

Wherever you live—house or apartment, city or country, large home or small—keeping your home in shape is a constant challenge, and a constant expense. There's always something—the faucets leak, the drains back up, the electrical system fails, appliances don't work right, the furnace or the air-conditioner breaks down, furniture gets scratched or broken, the walls crack, the roof leaks. It's a never-ending battle to keep everything in your home looking good and working right. If you have to call a professional to fix everything that goes wrong, you find yourself paying and paying again. And in a time when inflation has raised the cost of living astronomically and cut deep into your paycheck's buying power, you can't afford that.

Taking Control: How to Beat the System

Short of sudden riches, there's really only one way to cope with this situation, and that's to take care of your home yourself. It doesn't take any great skill or mechanical genius to make most home repairs—all you really need is time, patience, some basic knowledge, and a little common sense. *How To Fix Everything In Your Home* gives you that basic knowledge, with simple, step-by-step procedures and complete troubleshooting charts, organized to identify the problem fast and spell out the solution exactly. With the repair information presented here, you can take control of the situation today by taking control of all your home's repair work, from masonry to plumbing, electricity to appliances, furniture to furnace and air-conditioner. Whatever the problem, you'll find the solution here.

There is one other very important thing in this book, and it's a vital part of taking control: confidence. Principles and procedures that you don't understand are intimidating, and if you're intimidated by the materials or the assembly of your home, you can't take control of it. *How To Fix Everything In Your Home* is designed to give even the unhandiest homeowner or apartment-dweller a solid, easy to understand grasp of the systems and components that make up a home—what they do, how they work, and how to fix them when they fail. With the confidence of this knowledge, you're in charge.

Learning the Basics: How Your Home Works

Everyone would agree that the first essential for a home is simple: four walls and a roof. Beyond this elementary requirement, we've come to demand

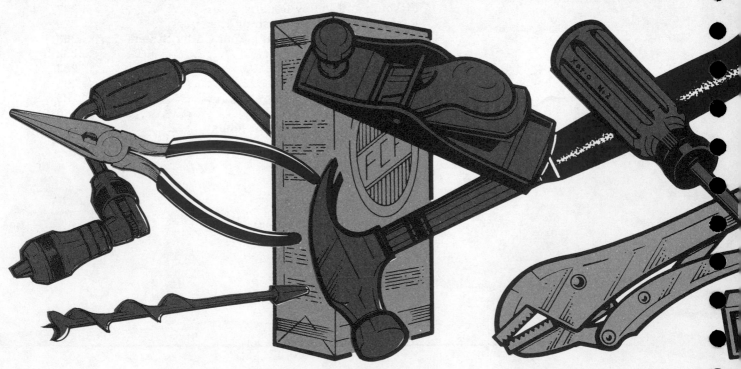

much more of the places we live in. Indoor plumbing and electric light and power, once unheard-of, are now not luxuries but necessities. A battery of appliances takes much of the drudgery out of housekeeping, and gives us time to enjoy our homes and our families. Central heating and air-conditioning keep us warm in winter and cool in summer. In simple terms, your home consists of several different systems, each one working with the others to keep you comfortable.

The plumbing and electrical systems are probably the most intimidating of these basic systems; they're the systems we depend on most, and the ones that seem to need attention most often. They work on similar principles — water enters your home under pressure, from the municipal water source; power enters your home under electrical pressure, from the municipal power source. Water flows through pipes, and electricity through wires. Both systems operate very simply; both are very dependable. And both are easy to repair when problems occur.

Appliances, the service-providers, are not a system in themselves, but together they act as a reliable corps of helpers — heating water, washing clothes and dishes, refrigerating and cooking food. They're all different, but they all operate on the same basic principles — and with care and determination, you can usually fix them when they fail. Heating and cooling systems are similar in concept, but they're connected to the structure of the house itself, and the work they do — heating and cooling — affects your entire home.

The structure of your home—the physical shelter itself—is probably the most important of the parts of your home. The effectiveness of all the other systems depends on the building that encloses them. Your home's structure is made up of several components — the foundation, the outside walls, the roof, the ventilation and drainage systems, the inside walls and floors, the windows and doors. All of these components need attention periodically to correct all kinds of problems, from a burned rug to a leaky roof or basement. Here, more than in any other system of your home, successful repairs depend largely on care and common sense. Some major repairs should be professionally taken care of, but in most cases you can—and should—do the work yourself. And when you know how the components go together, repairing them is easy.

One other essential part of your home must be maintained and, sometimes, repaired: the furniture. Furniture, unlike the other systems or components of your home, is movable and nonmechanical. It's often used and enjoyed for generations. Furniture is a part of you, an expression of your personality, more than any of the other major parts of your home. And with the techniques given here, you can keep it in top condition for generations to come.

The Payoff: Take Action Today!

In all of these basic parts of your home—plumbing, electricity, appliances, heating and cooling, structure, and furniture—you can start realizing savings today, with the first service call this book eliminates. *How To Fix Everything In Your Home* is the best way yet to protect your investment in your home and protect your paycheck too. Next time something goes wrong with your home, don't pay someone else to do a job you can do yourself. Take control of the situation — with *How To Fix Everything In Your Home*. You can't afford not to.

Plumbing

Few things strike such terror in our hearts, homeowner and apartment-dweller alike, as the word "plumbing." Cartoonists have played on this fear for years, picturing the victim of a plumbing calamity floating on the rising waters of a flooded basement. Naturally, there is some truth in all this. Severe plumbing emergencies do arise, and there is probably no one so lucky as never to be plagued by some type of plumbing problem.

Most likely, though, it's not really the calamities that bother you. With most of us, the feeling is rooted in fear of the unknown. Plumbing, for most of us, is a mysterious system, which works in ways known only to those who belong to the union, who never seem to be available when you need them the most. Fortunately, this isn't true: plumbing works according to the basic laws of nature—gravity, pressure, water seeking its own level—and you can understand it in no time. There is little mystery about how your plumbing system works, but there is often a great deal of misunderstanding. Once you know the basics, you can take care of many plumbing problems yourself—and save yourself time, trouble, and money in the process.

How the Plumbing System Works

The plumbing in your home is one system composed of two complementary but entirely separate subsystems. One subsystem brings fresh water in, and the other subsystem takes wastewater out. Naturally, if you and your family are to stay healthy, you must avoid any cross-connection between the supply and disposal lines.

The Supply System

The water that comes into your home is under pressure. It makes no difference whether your water supply is public or private; water that comes from either a storage tank or a well enters your home under enough pressure to allow it to travel upstairs, around corners, or wherever else it's needed.

In urban and suburban areas, the community water department pumps water into a tank or tower that's higher than the surrounding homes; the force of gravity supplies the water pressure. If you have your own well,

you probably have a pump to bring water into your home under pressure.

From the supply tank or tower, water travels through a water main to the supply line for your home. Before you actually use the water for drinking, bathing, washing clothes and dishes, and so on, it may pass through a meter that registers the number of gallons or cubic feet you use. The water meter may be somewhere on your property outside the house, or it may be inside, at the point where the supply pipe enters. The outside type of meter has a metal cover over it; you can lift the cover for access to the meter.

Even if you never look at the water meter itself, you should be familiar with one device that's generally located close to the meter. This is the main shutoff or stop valve. In a plumbing emergency, it's vital that you close the main shutoff valve as fast as you possibly can. When a pipe bursts, for example, it can flood your house in no time, but you can minimize damage by closing the main shutoff valve to shut off all the water coming into the house. The shutoff may be a stop-and-waste valve, which drains the water from the pipes as well as shutting off the supply. Naturally, if the emergency is confined to a sink, tub, or toilet, you may not want to turn off your entire water supply. Therefore, most fixtures have—or should have—individual stop valves.

Once the water has passed from the public facility's tower or tank through the main supply line to your individual supply line, and through your home water meter and main shutoff valve, it travels to the different fixtures in the house for your use. Water must be heated for your hot-water supply, but the water from the main supply is immediately ready for your cold-water needs.

The hot-water supply requires another step. One pipe carries water from the cold-water system to your water heater. From the heater, a hot-water line carries the heated water to all the fixtures, outlets, and appliances that require hot water. You can adjust the water temperature by raising or lowering the temperature setting on the water heater. A thermostat on the heater maintains the temperature you select by turning the device's heating elements on and off as required. The normal temperature setting for a home water heater is between 140° and 160° F, but 120° F is usually adequate, and is also more economical.

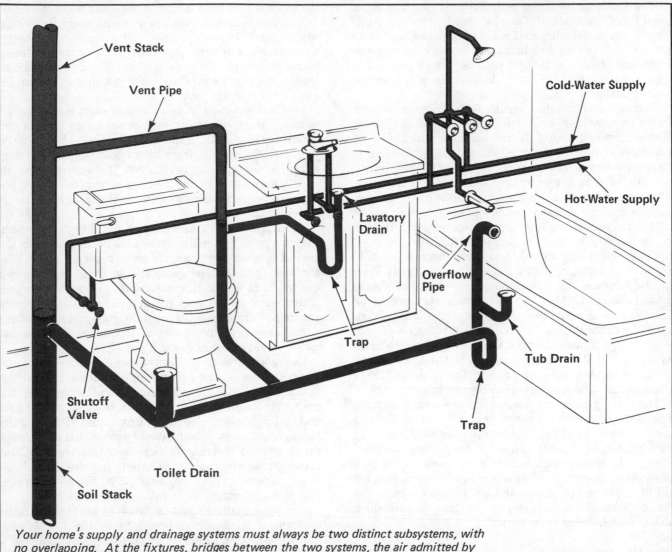

Vent Stack

Vent Pipe

Cold-Water Supply

Hot-Water Supply

Lavatory Drain

Overflow Pipe

Trap

Tub Drain

Trap

Shutoff Valve

Toilet Drain

Soil Stack

Your home's supply and drainage systems must always be two distinct subsystems, with no overlapping. At the fixtures, bridges between the two systems, the air admitted by the vent stack and vent pipes keeps the traps sealed and prevents sewer gases from backing up through the drains.

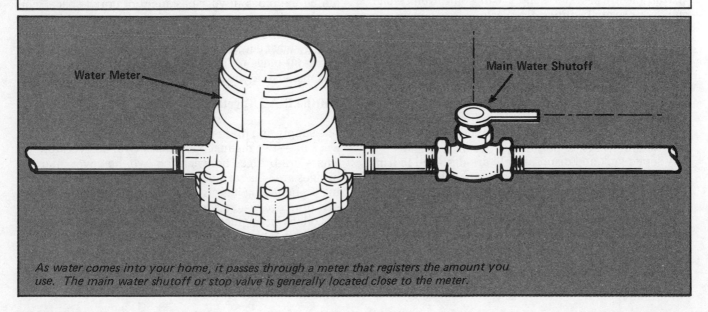

Water Meter

Main Water Shutoff

As water comes into your home, it passes through a meter that registers the amount you use. The main water shutoff or stop valve is generally located close to the meter.

The water pressure in your home is like any other good thing; too much of it can be very bad indeed. Residential water pressure that reaches or exceeds 70 to 80 psi (pounds per square inch) can cause your pipes to bang and faucets to leak. It can also break pipe joints and connections. At the very least, excessive pressure wastes water.

You can measure the average water pressure in your home by attaching a pressure gauge to the cold-water faucet nearest the main shutoff valve. Be sure to test the pressure at several different times during the day to find an average. Water pressure does fluctuate, but it shouldn't fluctuate greatly or you'll have an uncomfortable time trying to take a shower. One other thing to remember when measuring the water pressure: make sure no water is running from any other outlet in your home besides the one the gauge is attached to.

If the gauge registers 70 to 80 psi or more, you should install a pressure-reducing valve. This is a fairly inexpensive device, and a do-it-yourselfer should be able to install one easily. Most of these valves work best when installed on a horizontal pipe; the valve can be connected into the supply line with union fittings—fittings used to join pipes—without much difficulty. Once the valve is installed, you can simply set it to the water pressure that best suits your needs. The valve will lower the pressure and maintain it at that setting.

Decreasing excessive water pressure is easy; increasing inadequate water pressure is much harder. You can reduce the 70-to-80-psi flow for the relatively small cost of a pressure-reducing valve, but increasing the pressure could involve such major projects as building your own water tower, installing a pump, or even ripping out all the pipes in your home and installing new ones. For those reasons, too little water pressure is something many people learn to live with.

The Drainage System

Just as the fresh-water supply can come from either public or private facilities, the wastewater drainage can go to either a public sewer line or private septic tank. Like the public supply facilities, collective sewer systems are much more convenient than private waste disposal methods. After the waste drains from individual houses into a network of pipes, it's carried to a sewage treatment plant, where it's aerated to hasten bacteriological breakdown. Solids are settled out and used for fertilizer, while the liquid is chlorinated and discharged into natural water supplies like rivers and lakes.

A septic tank and disposal field are designed to handle the waste of a single home. The tank, like the public facility, separates solids from liquid. The solids settle to the bottom of the tank, while the liquid runs out through a network of pipes into the disposal field. The tank, of course, must be cleaned every few years, and the disposal field—composed of pipes in underground trenches or pits—must be enlarged as it becomes clogged with waste matter.

No matter which method of waste disposal is used,

the drainage systems in homes are essentially the same. Drainage systems do not depend on pressure, as do supply systems. Instead, waste matter leaves your house because the drainage pipes all pitch or angle downward; gravity pulls the waste along. The sewer line continues this downward flow to the sewage treatment facility or the septic tank.

While the system sounds simple—and it is—there's more to waste drainage than pipes tilted downward. There are also vents, traps, and clean-outs. You can see the vents sticking up from the roof of your house; they allow air to enter the drainpipes. If there were no air supply coming from the vents, wastewater would not flow out properly, and the water in the traps could be siphoned away.

Traps are vital components of the drainage system. You can see a trap under every sink or lavatory; it is the curved or S-shaped section of pipe under the drain. Water flows from the basin with enough force to go through the trap and on out through the drainpipe, but enough water stays in the trap to form a seal that prevents sewer gas from backing up into your home. If there were no seal at the drain, bad odors and dangerous gases would back up through the pipes.

Every fixture must have a trap. Toilets are self-trapped; they do not require an additional trap at the drain. Bathtubs frequently have drum traps; these not only form a seal against sewer gas, but also collect hair and dirt to prevent clogged drains. Some kitchen sinks have grease traps, which collect grease that goes down the sink drain that might otherwise cause clogging. Because grease and hair are generally the causes of drain clogs, traps often have clean-out plugs that give you easier access to remove or break up any clogs.

Since the drainage system involves all of these components, it is usually referred to as the DWV—the drain/waste/vent system. If water is to flow out freely and waste is to exit properly, all components of the DWV must be present and in good working order. Examine the pipes in your basement or crawl space. The larger and heavier pipes are for drainage. It's always a good idea to tag as many pipes as possible, and to know exactly what each one does. In addition, try to locate the clean-out plugs on the traps and in the drainage lines, and make sure you know where all the vents are.

Putting It All Together

The supply and drainage subsystems are—and must always be—two distinct operations, with no overlapping. There are bridges between the two, however, and the bridges are what make the plumbing system worth having. In plumbing jargon, any bridge between the supply and drainage systems is a fixture.

Toilets, sinks, tubs—these are all fixtures; but there are plenty more. An outside hydrant is a fixture, and so is an automatic washing machine. All devices that draw fresh water and discharge wastewater are fixtures, and all are designed to keep the supply and drainage systems strictly segregated.

Pipe Repairs

Take a look at the pipes in your home's plumbing system. How much do you know about them? Can you tell what they're made of? Do you know how to remove a broken section of pipe and install a replacement? Can you stop a leak, thaw a pipe that's frozen solid, or eliminate the noise caused by banging pipes? Pipes are the lifelines of your plumbing system, and you should know all you can about how they work and how to fix them.

Types of Pipe

Unless you're building a new home, there's not much chance that you can determine the type of pipe used in your house. Your choice of replacement or additional pipe in an existing home is limited by what's there at present and by the local plumbing code. The code, of course, also dictates what can and cannot be used in new construction. Despite the fact that your choice is limited, you should at least know how each type is used.

Copper Pipe. One type of pipe that's on the approved list in nearly every local plumbing code is rigid copper pipe. Relatively lightweight and easy to handle, copper pipe is one of the most popular types of pipe. It resists corrosion and scaling; in fact, it's so durable that under normal conditions the copper pipe you have today will probably outlast both you and your house. Moreover, the smooth inside surface of copper pipe offers little resistance to water, a property that allows a copper pipe of smaller diameter to handle the same job performed by larger pipes made of some other metals.

Rigid copper pipe or "plumbing tube" comes in three different wall thicknesses for different plumbing purposes. Type K is the heaviest and, therefore, the type used mainly for underground installations. Type L is a medium-weight copper pipe; it's used for interior plumbing. Type M is the lightest copper pipe; it is also used—where local plumbing codes permit—for interior plumbing. Even though some local codes do not allow the use of Type M copper pipe, it is adequate for most above-ground home plumbing requirements. Nevertheless, if your local plumbing code prohibits Type M, use some other weight of copper or another kind of pipe.

There is one more kind of rigid copper pipe. It is called DWV, and it is used only for drain, waste, and vent applications. DWV is even thinner-walled than Type M copper pipe, and some plumbing codes forbid its use just as they do Type M. Unlike Type M, however, DWV copper pipe does not have to withstand any pressure. In a supply system, wall thickness is very important, but it is not as crucial in the drainage system. Nevertheless, if the local plumbing code says no to copper DWV, use another type of pipe.

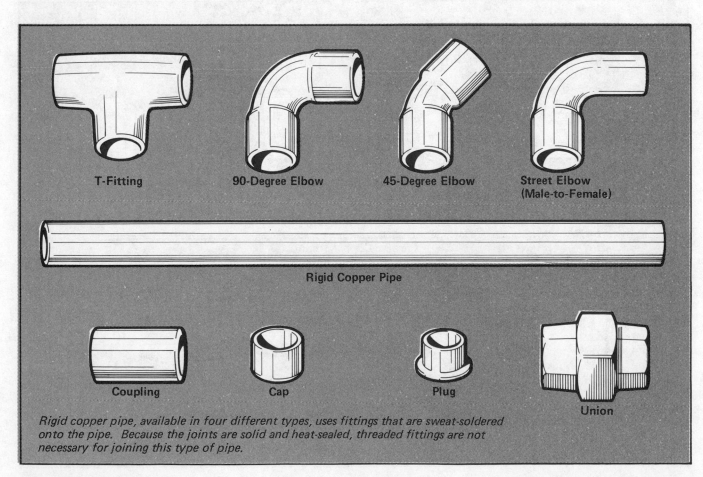

T-Fitting 90-Degree Elbow 45-Degree Elbow Street Elbow (Male-to-Female)

Rigid Copper Pipe

Coupling Cap Plug Union

Rigid copper pipe, available in four different types, uses fittings that are sweat-soldered onto the pipe. Because the joints are solid and heat-sealed, threaded fittings are not necessary for joining this type of pipe.

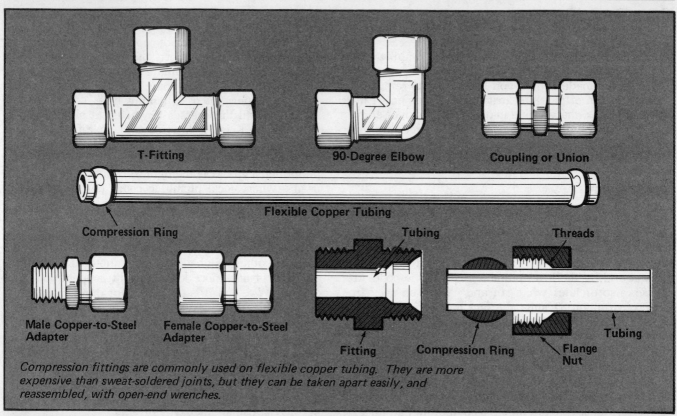

T-Fitting

90-Degree Elbow

Coupling or Union

Flexible Copper Tubing

Compression Ring

Tubing

Threads

Male Copper-to-Steel Adapter

Female Copper-to-Steel Adapter

Fitting

Compression Ring

Flange Nut

Tubing

Compression fittings are commonly used on flexible copper tubing. They are more expensive than sweat-soldered joints, but they can be taken apart easily, and reassembled, with open-end wrenches.

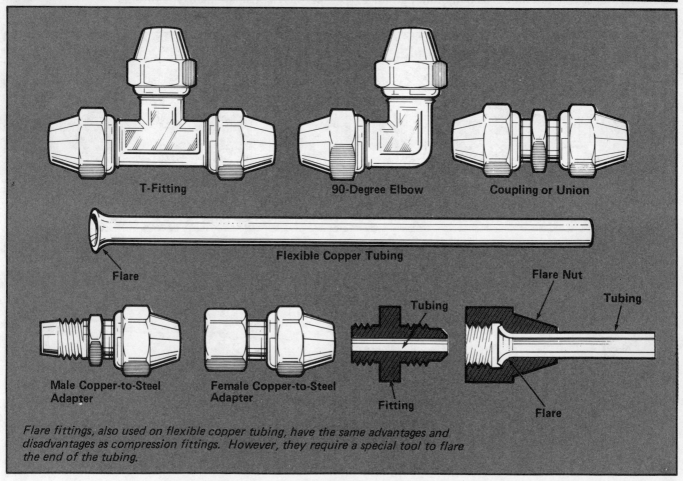

T-Fitting

90-Degree Elbow

Coupling or Union

Flexible Copper Tubing

Flare

Flare Nut

Tubing

Male Copper-to-Steel Adapter

Female Copper-to-Steel Adapter

Tubing

Fitting

Flare

Flare fittings, also used on flexible copper tubing, have the same advantages and disadvantages as compression fittings. However, they require a special tool to flare the end of the tubing.

Flexible Copper Tubing. You can buy flexible copper tubing only in Type K (designed for hard use) and Type L (for most other applications), but that disadvantage is about the only one you will encounter. Flexible copper tubing can do just about anything rigid copper pipe can do, and plenty more besides. You can bend the tubing around corners or snake it through walls and over ceilings more easily than you can maneuver rigid copper pipe. However, installations made with flexible copper tubing are not as neat as those made with rigid copper pipe, so flexible tubing is usually used where it will be concealed from view. The biggest advantage of flexible copper tubing is that it comes in rolls of up to 100 feet or more. When you work with rigid copper pipe, you must usually sweat-solder sections to be joined, and every connection is a potential source for a leak. With flexible copper tubing, you just unroll the length you need; the only connections you have to make are at each end of the run. Fewer joints, of course, mean fewer chances for a leak, and allow a better water flow.

Keep in mind that the larger the diameter of the tubing, the easier it is to get a kink—which is the last thing you want to have happen to copper tubing. The tube doesn't have to stay perfectly round, but a kink will restrict water flow and form a weak spot in the pipe. You can form gradual bends in flexible copper tubing just by using your hands. If you need to make a sharp turn, don't try to do it by hand; use a tube bender, a spring-like tool that's designed specifically for this purpose.

Galvanized Steel Pipe. Although copper pipe and tubing have replaced galvanized steel pipe as the most popular type for new-home water supply lines, galvanized pipe—which used to dominate the supply pipe market—still offers some distinct advantages. For example, suppose your pipes run through a garage or basement, or any other area where they're exposed to blows from cars or tools. For such situations, you would be much smarter to use galvanized steel pipe, because it's very tough and much better able to withstand damaging shocks.

Galvanized steel pipe is much less expensive than copper pipe at the time of initial purchase; on the other hand, galvanized pipe is much more expensive to repair. It takes so much longer to cut, thread, and join galvanized pipe than copper pipe or tubing that labor costs will be very high if you have to call in a professional plumber.

Another disadvantage is that galvanized steel pipe does not resist corrosion from either alkaline or acidic deposits in the water. Lime and scale can build up in galvanized steel pipe, restricting the flow of water. Even at its best, galvanized pipe can't match copper for water-flow properties. The surface inside a galvanized steel pipe is not as slick as the inside surface of a copper pipe, and the fittings that must be used with galvanized pipe also tend to reduce the water flow.

Plastic Pipe. There's only one problem with plastic pipe—many building codes prohibit some or all uses of

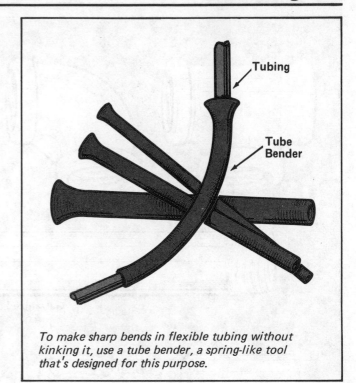

To make sharp bends in flexible tubing without kinking it, use a tube bender, a spring-like tool that's designed for this purpose.

it. However, these codes are likely to change in the future because plastic pipe possesses so many fine features. It's hard to say which one of the many aspects of plastic pipe is its most advantageous. Plastic pipe is not subject to corrosion, scaling, or rust; it is virtually self-cleaning; it will not rot, and usually it does not sweat; it can withstand freezing temperatures much better than metal pipe can; and it is so light that it's easier to handle than just about any other kind of pipe. In addition, because plastic is more flexible than metal, plastic supply lines virtually eliminate water hammer and the need for installing air chambers; plastic pipe damps vibrations and does not carry sound. Plastic pipe also has low resistance to water flow and, consequently, excellent flow rates; it is the easiest of all piping to install, especially for the do-it-yourselfer. Finally, plastic pipe is less expensive than even galvanized steel pipe.

There are several types of plastic pipe in use today, for various home plumbing applications. CPVC (chlorinated polyvinyl chloride) pipe is rigid; it is used for hot- and cold-water distribution systems. PB (polybutylene) pipe is a new, highly flexible tubing used for the same purpose as CPVC pipe, as well as for water supply lines. One form of rigid PVC (polyvinyl chloride) pipe is made for water supply lines, another for DWV systems, and a third for sewer lines and underground drainage systems. PVC is also used for cold-water distribution and for drainage traps and their assorted parts. Rigid ABS (acrylonitrile-butadiene styrene) pipe is made for the same applications as PVC pipe, except for water supply or distribution uses. For water supply lines, lawn sprinkling, and irrigation purposes, the most popular type is flexible PE (polyethylene) pipe, which

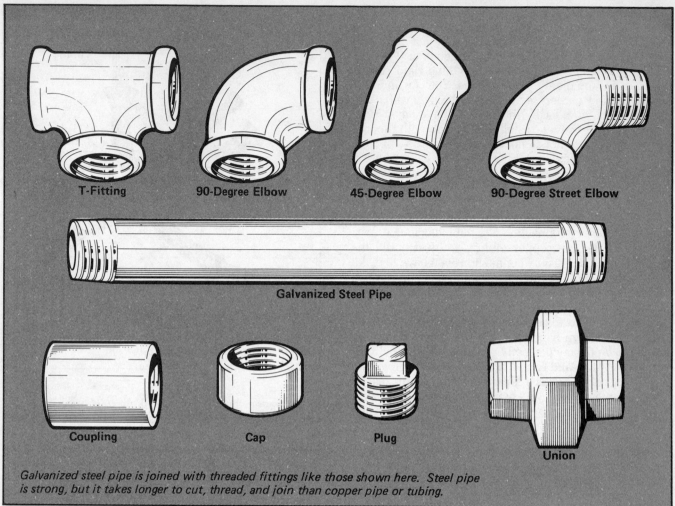

Galvanized Steel Pipe

T-Fitting　　90-Degree Elbow　　45-Degree Elbow　　90-Degree Street Elbow

Coupling　　Cap　　Plug　　Union

Galvanized steel pipe is joined with threaded fittings like those shown here. Steel pipe is strong, but it takes longer to cut, thread, and join than copper pipe or tubing.

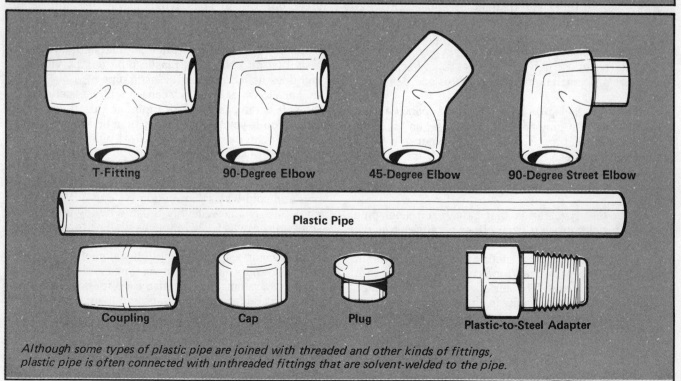

Plastic Pipe

T-Fitting　　90-Degree Elbow　　45-Degree Elbow　　90-Degree Street Elbow

Coupling　　Cap　　Plug　　Plastic-to-Steel Adapter

Although some types of plastic pipe are joined with threaded and other kinds of fittings, plastic pipe is often connected with unthreaded fittings that are solvent-welded to the pipe.

is available in several grades. SR (styrene rubber) pipe is used primarily for underground drainage systems, while PP (polypropylene) pipe is available in plumbing fixture traps, tailpieces, and trap extensions and their associated parts. PP pipe is by far the best choice for new or replacement gear of this nature. Both SR and PP are rigid pipe.

All of these types of plastic pipe can be used in new installations, in additions to existing systems made up of metallic piping, or for repair work, because adapters are available to allow you to connect just about any type of pipe to just about any other type. However, check your local plumbing code carefully. If the code does not prohibit plastic pipe, or if it does but you can obtain a variance, give plastic pipe serious consideration for your next plumbing installation or repair.

Cast-Iron Pipe. When it comes to soil and waste pipes, the traditional favorite is cast iron. Cast iron is so very durable and corrosion-free that it can be used for underground installations with no problems. In most home drainage systems, cast-iron pipe is used for the soil and waste stacks (and for the main drains), while copper tube of the DWV type is used for the branches to the fixture drains. Cast-iron pipe comes in two weights: service (standard) and extra heavy. Unless your local plumbing code demands otherwise, opt for the lighter service-weight version when buying cast-iron pipe.

Other Types of Pipe. When weight is a factor and underground installation is not, steel drainpipes are often used in place of cast-iron ones. Much lighter than cast-iron pipe, steel pipe can never be used underground because it could collapse under the weight of the earth. Lead pipe is rarely used any more except sometimes as a "closet bend"—the pipe that joins the toilet to the soil pipe. Septic tank systems occasionally employ a perforated type of fiber pipe for releasing waste liquids into

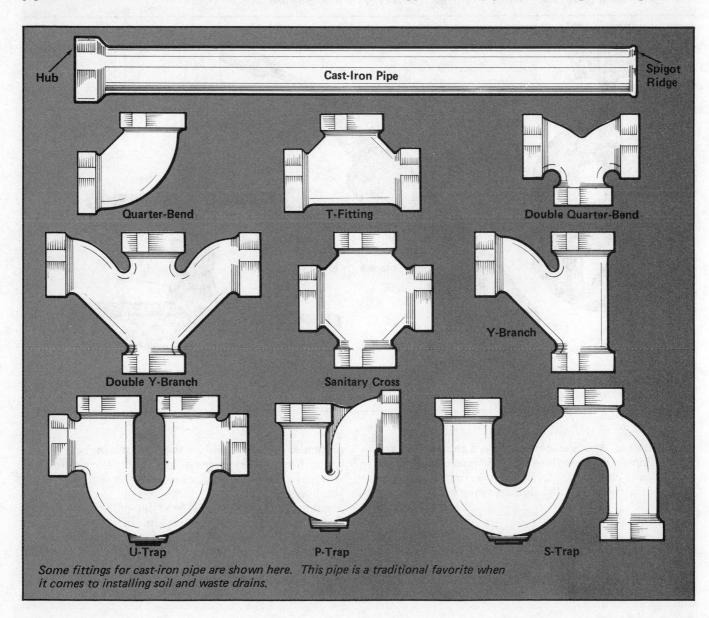

Some fittings for cast-iron pipe are shown here. This pipe is a traditional favorite when it comes to installing soil and waste drains.

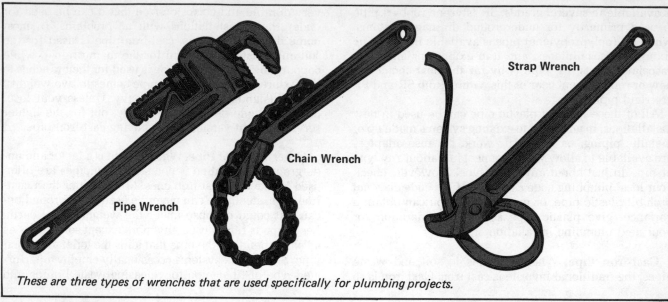

These are three types of wrenches that are used specifically for plumbing projects.

Pipe Wrench

Chain Wrench

Strap Wrench

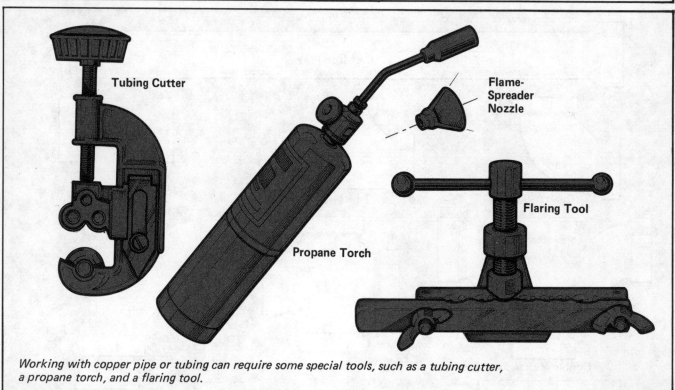

Tubing Cutter

Propane Torch

Flame-Spreader Nozzle

Flaring Tool

Working with copper pipe or tubing can require some special tools, such as a tubing cutter, a propane torch, and a flaring tool.

the drain field. Asbestos-cement pipe is sometimes used for underground sewer lines in septic tank installations, and brass is common in traps and was once widely installed in home water distribution systems.

Pipe Tools

If you plan to do a fair amount of plumbing, your tools are very important. Many plumbing tools, of course, can be used for other do-it-yourself tasks around the house; but no matter how much or how little you plan to use a particular tool, it should be the best of its type that you can afford. Often a good tool will last a lifetime, whereas a poor tool may not make it through the project you bought it for.

Although the tools you'll need depend on how deeply you're involved in home repairs in general and in plumbing projects in particular, there are certain basic tools that any self-respecting do-it-yourself plumber should have. For working with cast-iron or galvanized steel pipes, you'll need pipe wrenches. These wrenches are generally used in pairs; one holds like a vise while the other turns a fitting or a pipe. A chain wrench is designed for larger galvanized steel or cast-iron pipes, and a strap wrench—which works on the same principle as the chain wrench—can be used on polished or plastic pipe without damaging it.

Copper pipe and copper tubing require some special tools. You should avoid using a hacksaw on copper pipe, so be sure you have a tubing cutter in your toolbox. A small-size cutter makes it much easier to work in close quarters, and you'll be amazed at how many plumbing chores are performed in cramped surroundings. You'll also need a propane torch for sweat-soldering, and a flaring tool for making flare connections at pipe joints.

Just like copper pipes, galvanized steel pipes also require some special tools. When cutting steel pipe, you should have a combination vise—one that has a section with pipe jaws—or a yoke or chain vise, both of which are made especially for pipe work. A pipe-cutter tool is easier to use than a hacksaw, but be sure that the cutter is designed for galvanized steel pipes; the tubing cutter for copper is very similar in appearance, but not suitable for cutting steel. You must also be prepared to remove the burrs created by cutting. Outside burrs can be removed with a file, but you'll need a reamer to remove any burrs inside the pipe.

Although you can generally buy the galvanized steel pipe you need already threaded, you may want to do your own threading. If so, you'll need special dies that come in sizes for threading all standard pipe diameters. Whenever you're cutting or threading pipe, use cutting oil as you work. And, speaking of oil, a can of penetrating oil can come in handy when you tackle any plumbing repair.

Very few tools—none of them special—are needed for working with plastic pipe. Rigid plastic pipe can be cut with a fine-toothed hacksaw (or, if you prefer, a plastic-tubing cutter); flexible types can be cut with a sharp knife. On most common types of plastic pipe, fittings are joined with solvent cement. On other types, compression or threaded fittings are usually used; they are simply tightened with an adjustable open-end wrench.

For sealing large cast-iron drainpipes against leaks, you'll need a yarning iron for packing the oakum into the joint, a melting pot for heating the lead, a ladle for pouring the molten lead over the oakum, and a caulking tool for packing the lead down. When you work on horizontal drainpipes, you face the problem of keeping the molten lead in the joint and preventing it from running while it hardens. The answer to this problem is a special tool called an asbestos joint runner, which is clamped onto the pipe to mold the molten lead around the joint.

Working With Copper Pipe and Tubing

Cutting copper pipe or tubing without kinking it takes care, so avoid sawing copper, if possible; use a tubing cutter instead. Of course, a tubing cutter will be of little use on large copper pipes. For these, use a hacksaw, but

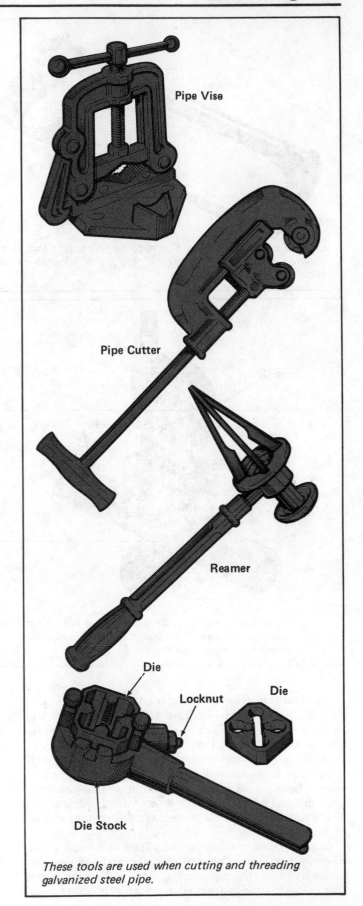

These tools are used when cutting and threading galvanized steel pipe.

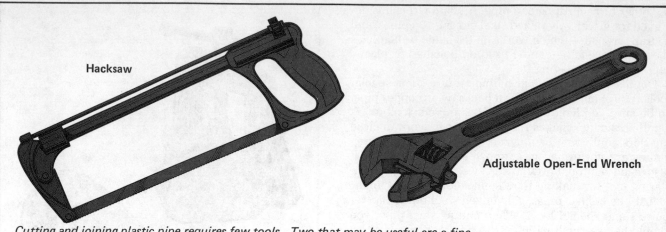

Cutting and joining plastic pipe requires few tools. Two that may be useful are a fine-toothed hacksaw for cutting rigid pipe and an adjustable wrench for plastic pipe with certain types of fittings.

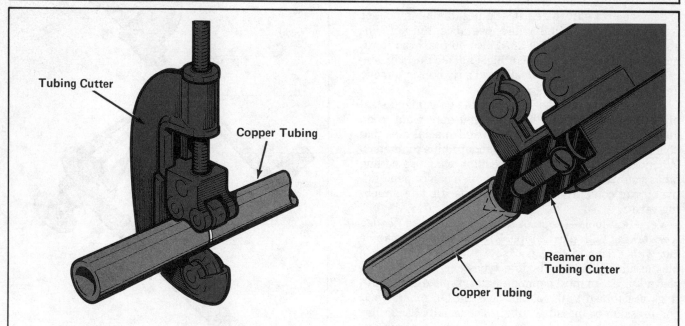

To avoid damaging the ends of copper pipe, a tubing cutter should be used (left). Any burrs inside the cut end of the pipe must be removed (right); the outside can be cleaned with sandpaper or emery cloth.

equip it with the finest-toothed blade you can find. Saw as straight as possible—using a miter box will help you make a square cut. Eliminate any irregularities in the edge—as well as any burrs, both inside and out—with a file. If you must put the copper pipe in a vise to hold it while you saw, clamp the vise on the pipe as far away from where you're cutting as possible, so that you don't dent the end of the tubing or pipe. Anything but a perfectly round end will not connect well to another section of pipe or tube.

Copper pipes or tubes can be joined in several ways. Sweat-soldering is the most common and least expensive way of joining copper pipe, while flare fittings and compression fittings are used mainly for flexible tubing.

Flare Fittings. The advantages of a flare fitting are that it can be taken apart easily with a pair of open-end wrenches and that it can be used in situations where sweat-soldering is either dangerous (fire hazard) or impossible (uncontrollably wet conditions). The disadvantage is that flare fittings are much more expensive than sweat-soldered joints.

To make a flare connection you need a flaring tool and a special fitting that includes a flare nut. First, slip the flare nut over the cut copper tubing, making sure that the open end of the nut faces out. Then insert the tubing into the proper-size hole in the flaring tool vise. Make sure the cut edge of the tube is flush with the edge of the vise. Turn the flaring cone down to flare the end of the tube. Inspect the flared end to make sure that it's even, that there are no burrs or cracks, and that the tube surface is completely clean.

Put the fitting into the flared end of the tube, pull the flare nut up to it, and turn the nut down tightly. When you get the flare nut as tight as you can by hand, use a pair of open-end wrenches—one to hold the fitting and the other to turn the flare nut—to complete the connection.

Compression Fittings. The compression fitting offers the same advantages—and the same price disadvantage in relation to sweat-soldering—as the flare fitting, but it does not require a flaring tool. Actually, compression fittings are much like flare fittings, but without the flare. A compression fitting has the same two parts as the flare fitting, but the compression fitting also has a compression ring or ferrule. You slip the flange nut onto the tubing, and slip the ring over the tube. Then insert the tube into the fitting as far as it will go. Hand-tighten the flange nut, and then use two open-end wrenches—one to turn the nut and the other to hold the fitting—to seal the ring against the fitting and against the tube.

Sweat-Soldering. Sweat-soldering is the most popular method of connecting copper pipes. Done properly, with sweat fittings and well-cut pipe, sweat-soldering is both effective and inexpensive. If not done right, however, sweat-soldering certainly is not effective—and it can be disastrously expensive.

Unlike conventional soldering with an iron or gun,

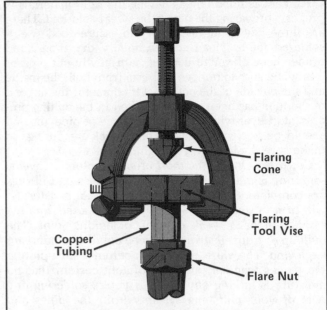

To flare the end of copper tubing, slip the flare nut over the end of the tubing, insert the tubing into the flaring tool vise, and turn down the flaring cone.

sweat-soldering is done with a torch. Most people use a propane torch, which is easier and safer to operate than a blowtorch. In addition to the heat source, you need nonacid paste flux, emery cloth, and 50-50 lead-tin solid-core solder.

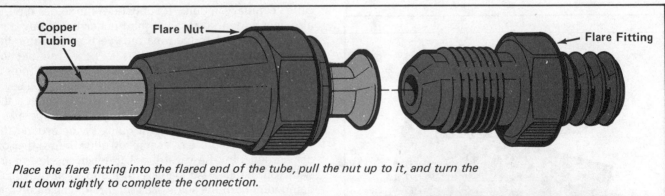

Place the flare fitting into the flared end of the tube, pull the nut up to it, and turn the nut down tightly to complete the connection.

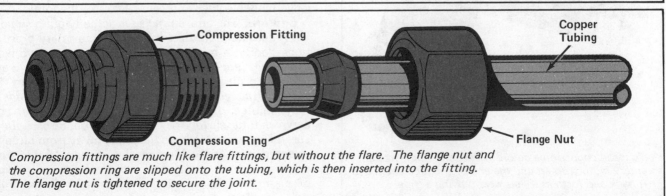

Compression fittings are much like flare fittings, but without the flare. The flange nut and the compression ring are slipped onto the tubing, which is then inserted into the fitting. The flange nut is tightened to secure the joint.

At least as important as having the right materials is properly preparing the pipe to be sweat-soldered. There are three key factors necessary to assure good sweat-soldered joints: clean copper, totally dry pipes, and proper heat. If you're dealing with newly cut pipe or tubing, be sure to remove all burrs from both the inside and the outside of the cut end. Of course, if the cut end of the tube has been bent or crushed in the cutting process, start over with a freshly cut piece of pipe; the end should be perfectly round. Then check the fittings to make sure the joint will be tight.

Caution: One of the most crucial factors in sweat-soldering is making sure that all the pipes and fittings are completely dry. If there is any residual moisture, it will turn to steam when the pipes are heated, and the result will be a weak or even a leaking joint. The buildup of trapped steam in a pipe could also cause an explosion. Therefore, before you actually start putting the pieces together, make absolutely certain that no moisture is lurking anywhere. If you're soldering any part of your plumbing system, drain the pipes and leave the faucets open so steam can escape.

There are a couple of techniques that will help you to dry the pipes thoroughly. If you're sweat-soldering on a vertical pipe, you can use a rag to remove any moisture. If the connection is to be made on a horizontal run of pipe, try this plumbing trick. Wad a piece of soft bread into a ball, poke the bread ball into the pipe, and push it back beyond the area you'll be soldering. The bread will absorb moisture that might otherwise reach the joint and ruin your sweat-soldering. When the job is done and you turn the water back on, the bread will dissolve; the residue will come out through the nearest open tap.

Now, clean all the metal surfaces you plan to join. Fine steel wool or fine sandpaper can be used for this job, but the best way to clean the outside of a pipe is to wrap an emery-cloth strip around the tubing or pipe and go back and forth as if you were buffing a shoe. You want the metal to shine, but be careful not to overdo it. The last thing you want is to take away so much metal that you lose the snug fit. Clean every surface that will be part of the sweat-soldered joint, including inside the fitting where the pipe will go.

When you've cleaned the pipe and fitting, coat all the cleaned metal surfaces with a paste flux that's especially made for soldering copper. Spread the flux on both the pipe and the fitting with your fingers, an old toothbrush, or a small, stiff paintbrush. Insert the pipe into the fitting and rotate the pieces a bit to distribute the paste evenly around the joint.

Once you've applied the flux and joined the pipe to the fitting, you're ready to solder. Light your propane torch and get the solid-core solder ready in your other hand. You'll have to heat the copper to about 400° F. Play the flame over the fitting, not the pipe. Do *not* put the flame on the solder; the solder should melt when it's brought into contact with the hot fitting and pipe. Be careful not to overheat the fitting and pipe; test by touching the joint with the solder to see if the solder melts.

As you continue to play the flame over the fitting, bring the end of the solder into contact with the lip of the fitting. When the metal gets hot enough to melt the solder, you will witness the results of a natural process called capillary action. Not only does the solder melt, it also gets drawn up into the joint under the fitting; this happens even when the pipe runs vertically up into the fitting. When the solder begins to flow, remove the flame, and keep applying solder until the entire joint is filled. You know that point is achieved when you see a continuous bead of solder form all the way around the lip of the fitting. For neater joints, you can wipe away any excess solder by taking a quick swipe around the fitting lip with a piece of coarse toweling before the solder hardens, but be careful not to touch the hot metal with your hand. Also, be careful not to disturb the soldered joint until the solder has solidified; you could dislodge molten solder and cause leaks in the joint.

Caution: The entire process is actually quite simple, but it does demand that you keep some safety precautions clearly in mind. If you're working close to a wall or ceiling, place a scrap of asbestos or gypsum wallboard or a piece of heavy aluminum foil between the pipe and the wall or ceiling. Otherwise, if you accidentally pointed the torch in the wrong direction, you could char the surface or even start a fire. Be especially careful, of course, to keep the flame away from already soldered joints or valves nearby. Wrapping wet rags around soldered joints and valves is one good way of dissipating heat and preventing the flame from doing any damage. One other safety rule: when you

To clean copper pipe before sweat-soldering, wrap an emery cloth strip around the end of the pipe and move it back and forth as if you were buffing a shoe.

finish sweat-soldering the joint, turn off the torch immediately.

Many amateur plumbers are so proud of their first sweat-soldered joints that they immediately turn on the water. This is a big mistake. You must let the joint cool naturally; the sudden cooling effect of rushing water can weaken the joint or even cause it to crack. If, when you finally do turn on the water, you discover a leak in the sweat-soldered joint, start the whole job over from scratch: cut off the water, drain the line, melt the solder, remove the fitting, dry and reclean the fitting, reflux, and finally resolder. There are instances when you can get away without starting over, but it is generally easier, quicker, and more effective to sweat-solder the joint again.

Good sweat-solderers acquire expertise through practice. Why not buy a few short pieces of copper pipe and some fittings and try your hand at it before you're faced with a genuine sweat-soldering situation? After you do a few joints, you'll be sweat-soldering like a professional.

Working With Galvanized Steel Pipe

Galvanized steel pipe is pipe that has been treated with zinc to slow corrosion. Despite this zinc treatment, steel pipe is still the most corrosion-prone type of pipe used for water supply systems.

Some hardware stores and plumbing supply outlets will cut and thread galvanized pipe for you, if you tell them what sizes you need. Short pieces can be bought in stock sizes, already threaded. However, if you plan to cut and thread pipe yourself, you'll need some special equipment.

Galvanized steel pipe can be cut with a hacksaw, but a steel-pipe cutter—if you have one—makes the job much easier. To cut the pipe with a hacksaw, clamp the piece of pipe in a vise that's equipped with a set of pipe jaws, and use a hacksaw with a 24- or 32-tooth-per-inch blade. While cutting, use generous amounts of cutting oil. To use the pipe cutter, secure the pipe in the vise and clamp the cutter onto the pipe, with the cutting wheel on the mark where the cut is to be made. Rotate the cutter completely around the pipe once, then tighten the cutter and rotate the cutter again. Repeat this procedure until the pipe has been cut through.

After cutting the pipe, remove the burrs on both the inside and the outside end of the pipe. Outside burrs can be removed with a file; inside burrs should be removed with a pipe reamer.

Since galvanized steel pipe is connected with threaded fittings, you must thread the pipe end after each cut. This is done with a pipe die. Install the correct size die in the die stock; then fit the pipe threader and die over the end of the pipe and tighten it. Rotate the stock clockwise, exerting some force at first to start the die-cutting action. Apply cutting oil generously while cutting the threads. If metal shavings or chips jam the tool, back it off slightly and brush them away; then resume cutting the threads. Stop cutting when the end

Solder

When sweat-soldering, heat the fitting until it's hot enough to melt the solder and draw it into the joint under the fitting.

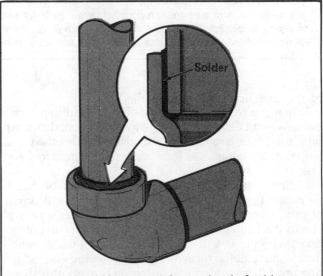

Solder

The joint should have a continuous bead of solder all the way around it.

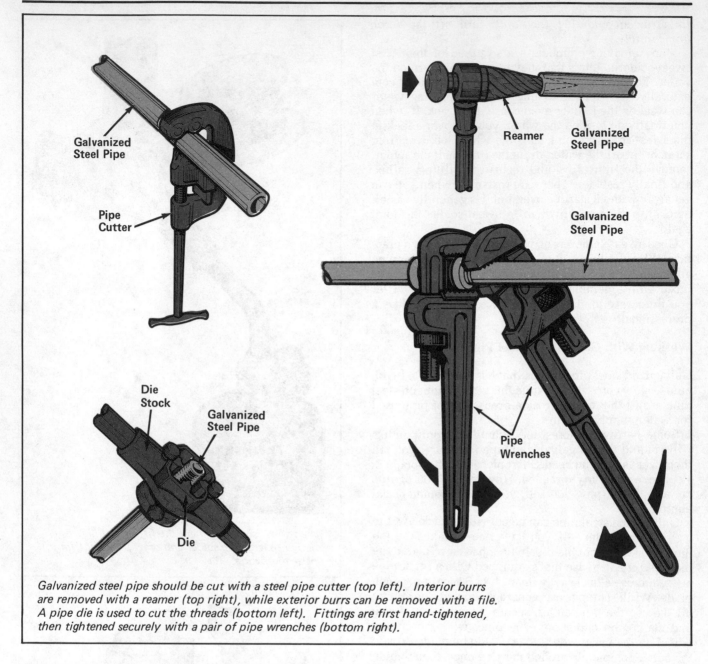

Galvanized steel pipe should be cut with a steel pipe cutter (top left). Interior burrs are removed with a reamer (top right), while exterior burrs can be removed with a file. A pipe die is used to cut the threads (bottom left). Fittings are first hand-tightened, then tightened securely with a pair of pipe wrenches (bottom right).

of the pipe is flush with the die.

When you're ready to join the pipe to its fitting, smear the newly cut threads with pipe joint compound or wrap pipe joint tape around the threads; either method will help seal the completed joint, making it waterproof and leak-free.

Fittings for galvanized steel pipe should be hand-tightened first, and then tightened securely with a pair of pipe wrenches. Apply one wrench to the pipe and one to the fitting. Turn the wrenches in opposite directions, with the jaw of each wrench facing the direction in which it's being turned. Tighten the pipe and the fitting until there are only about three threads still showing outside the fitting. If either the pipe or the fitting is already installed in a run, use one wrench to hold the pipe or fitting stationary; use the second wrench to turn the new fitting or pipe until it's tightened properly.

Working With Plastic Pipe

Although cutting and connecting galvanized steel pipe is not difficult, it cannot match the ease and convenience of working with plastic pipe. Some plastic pipe can be threaded and connected with threaded fittings, much like galvanized steel pipe; other types of plastic pipe are joined by welding sections together with a chemical solvent. Joining plastic pipe with solvent is almost as simple as gluing photographs in an album. And plastic is a joy to cut as compared to cutting steel pipe.

Plastic pipe can be cut with a plastic-pipe cutter, but

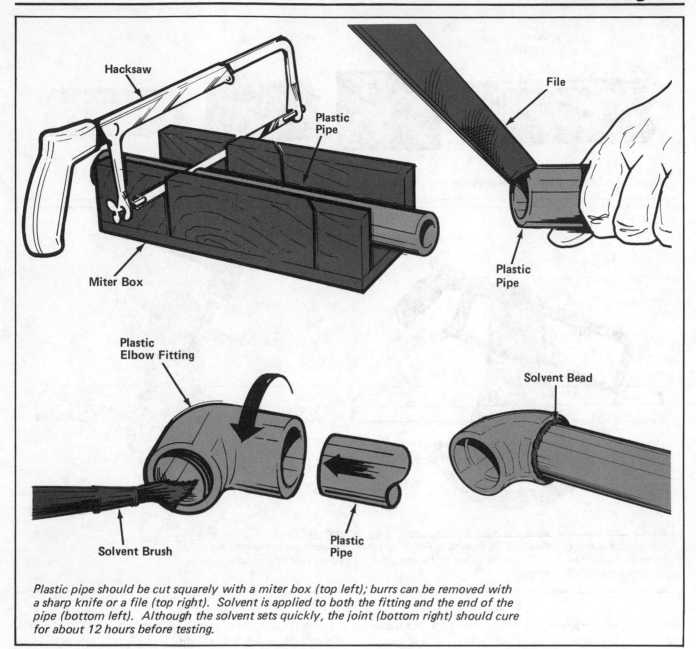

Plastic pipe should be cut squarely with a miter box (top left); burrs can be removed with a sharp knife or a file (top right). Solvent is applied to both the fitting and the end of the pipe (bottom left). Although the solvent sets quickly, the joint (bottom right) should cure for about 12 hours before testing.

any fine-toothed hacksaw can be used. Sawing plastic requires very little effort, and a file or a sharp knife, along with light sanding, can get rid of all the little burrs both inside and outside the cut end. Of course, plastic pipe—like any other type of pipe—must be cut square. To obtain a square cut, it's best to use a miter box.

After cutting the pipe, remove the burrs, both inside and out. Then apply a special cleaner to remove any oil or wax. Next, brush the solvent on the end of the pipe and inside the fittings. For good results, make sure you use the proper solvent; it's a good idea to buy the correct cleaner and solvent when you buy the plastic pipe. Use a brush with natural bristles to apply the solvent; the solvent will dissolve synthetic bristles.

After applying the solvent to both pieces, insert the

end of the pipe into the fitting and twist the pipe a quarter-turn; this distributes the solvent more evenly. Do this quickly and without hesitation, because the solvent goes right to work in forming the bond; it actually welds or fuses the two parts together. Hold the fitting in its correct position for about 15 seconds to prevent any slippage, and then clean off any excess solvent. Despite the fact that the solvent sets quickly, do not turn on the water or otherwise test the solvent-welded joint for about 12 hours.

Some types of plastic pipe must be connected differently. With PE (polyethylene) pipe, for example, ringed insertion fittings are slipped into the pipe and secured with stainless-steel worm-drive clamps around the outside of the pipe. PB (polybutylene) pipe can be joined

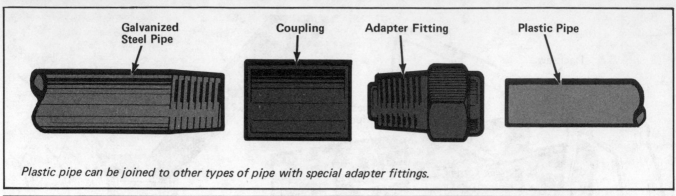

Galvanized Steel Pipe   Coupling   Adapter Fitting   Plastic Pipe

Plastic pipe can be joined to other types of pipe with special adapter fittings.

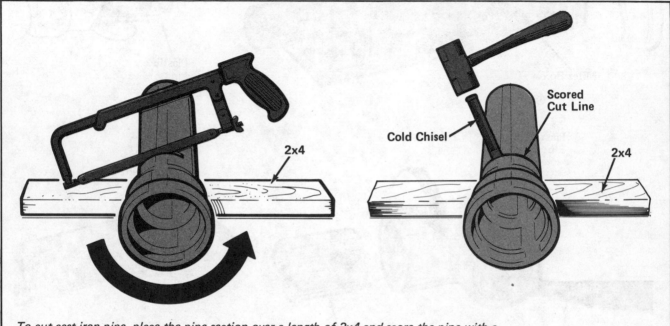

2x4   Scored Cut Line   Cold Chisel   2x4

To cut cast-iron pipe, place the pipe section over a length of 2x4 and score the pipe with a hacksaw, making a shallow cut all around it (left). On service-weight pipe, use a heavy hammer to tap near the cut on the piece to be removed; on heavier pipe, tap a cold chisel along the scored line (right).

the same way, but special mechanically gripping transition adapter fittings are used.

Where local codes permit, plastic pipe can be joined to other types of pipe by special adapter fittings. For example, suppose you want to use plastic pipe for an underground sprinkler system. At some point, you must attach the plastic pipe to your existing plumbing, which is galvanized steel pipe. You can make the connection easily with an adapter designed specifically for linking plastic to galvanized steel pipe.

Working With Cast-Iron Pipe

Cast-iron pipe is more difficult to work with than copper, galvanized steel, or plastic pipe. Smart do-it-yourself plumbers always plan ahead when it comes to dealing with cast iron, and try to arrange as few cuts as possible.

If you don't have access to a soil-pipe cutter, follow these steps to cut cast-iron pipe. Draw a line around the pipe with chalk where the cut will be. From this point on, the pipe requires support—it should not rest on the joint. Place the pipe crosswise on a piece of 2×4, with the chalk line directly over the wood. Score the pipe with a hacksaw, making a shallow cut all the way around at the chalk mark. Be sure the cut is square, and score the pipe to a depth of about 1/16 inch. Then move the pipe so that the scored line slightly overhangs the 2×4. If you're cutting the lighter service-weight pipe, use a heavy hammer to tap near the cut line on the piece of pipe to be removed; tap gently until the pipe breaks cleanly. If you're cutting the heavier grade of cast-iron pipe, place the tip of a cold chisel in the scored line, and tap the chisel gently with a heavy hammer. Apply the hammer and chisel all the way around the scored line.

Cast-iron pipe can be joined with one of three methods: the bell-and-spigot joint, the gasket-type or compression connection, and the no-hub or hubless system.

Bell-and-Spigot Joints. The bell-and-spigot joint is the oldest method of joining cast-iron pipe, and it is still in widespread use. In this type of joint, one end of the pipe has a bell-shaped hub into which the slightly ridged end (the spigot) of the connecting pipe fits. You will find that there is space to spare between the two sections of pipe; you caulk this space with an oily rope fiber called oakum. The strands of oakum are wrapped around the pipe, and then packed down into the gap between the two sections of pipe with a hammer and a tool called a yarning iron. When the oakum fills the void to within an inch of the edge of the hub—different plumbing codes specify different depths—molten lead is poured over it to fill the joint completely.

Caution: Working with molten lead can be hazardous. Make sure the pipes you're working on are clean and dry; moisture can cause molten lead to splatter out from the joint and seriously injure you. Always wear protective safety goggles and heavy gloves when you work with lead.

Here is the general procedure for joining vertical pipes. First heat the lead. Also heat the ladle; dipping a cold ladle into hot lead could cause an explosion. While you're waiting for the lead to melt, pack oakum into the joint with a yarning iron. When the oakum has been packed down firmly to the proper depth to form a solid bed for the lead, carefully and cautiously pour the molten lead into the joint. The lead should be poured continuously and evenly into the joint until the level of the lead is even with the top of the hub.

When the lead cools and begins to harden, tap the lead with a caulking iron and a hammer, packing it tight against the bed of oakum and the sides of the joint to make an airtight and leakproof seal. First work all the way around the inner edge of the joint; then work around the outer edge.

This procedure is followed whether you're connecting two sections of cast-iron pipe or a section of pipe to a fitting. The only time you do anything different is when you're working on a horizontal joint. On horizontal pipes, you must use a device called an asbestos joint runner to keep the lead from running out of the hub.

After the oakum has been packed into the joint, the joint runner is placed around the pipe just above the hub, with its clamp at the top. The clamp forms a funnel for pouring the lead. Before pouring, make sure the joint runner is tightly against the top of the hub so lead does not seep out. After the lead begins to harden, remove the joint runner and tap down the lead in the joint, as with vertical joints.

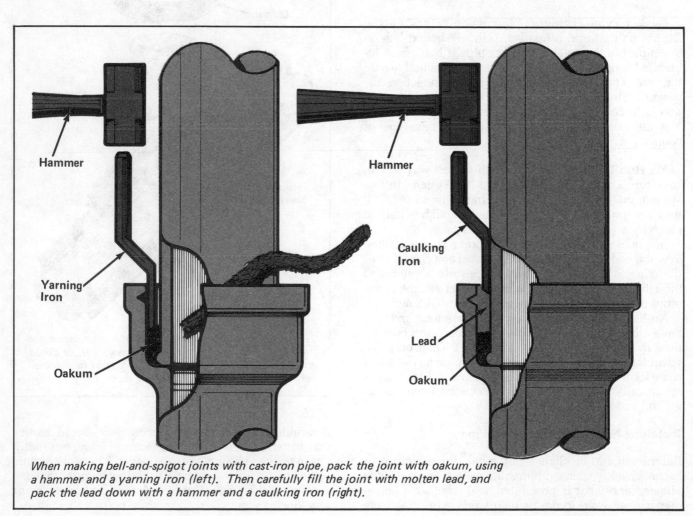

Hammer

Yarning
Iron

Oakum

Hammer

Caulking
Iron

Lead

Oakum

When making bell-and-spigot joints with cast-iron pipe, pack the joint with oakum, using a hammer and a yarning iron (left). Then carefully fill the joint with molten lead, and pack the lead down with a hammer and a caulking iron (right).

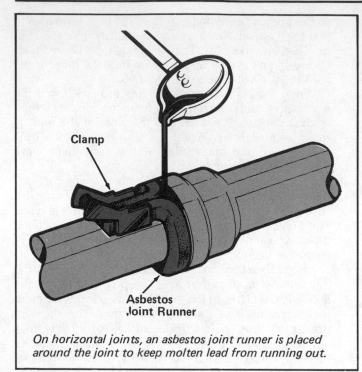

On horizontal joints, an asbestos joint runner is placed around the joint to keep molten lead from running out.

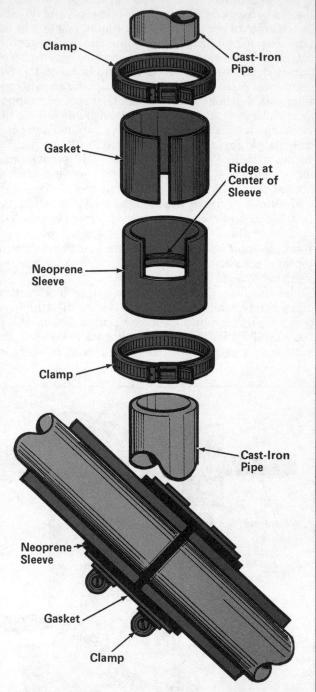

The no-hub system of joining cast-iron pipe uses a neoprene sleeve that is held in place by a gasket, or shield, and clamps. No-hub joints are easy to put together and take apart, but some codes forbid them.

Gasket-Type Fittings. Compression or gasket-type fittings on cast-iron pipe also include a belled hub on one pipe, but the end of the other pipe is hubless. A lubricated neoprene gasket is inserted into the bell to hold the connection together. In this type of connection, the gasket is first fitted into the hub; then the hubless section is forced into the gasket to form a leakproof seal. Not all local plumbing codes approve this type of connection.

No-Hub Joints. The newest and easiest way to join cast-iron pipe is the hubless or no-hub system. In this system, the ends of all the pipes and fittings are plain; they are joined by a neoprene sleeve, which is held in place by a gasket, or shield, and clamps.

In a hubless connection, the neoprene sleeve is fitted over the end of one pipe, and the gasket and clamps over the other. The ends of the two pipes are aligned and brought together. The sleeve and gasket are then centered over the joint, and the clamps are tightened.

No-hub connections are easy to put together, and they have a definite advantage over other cast-iron connections in that they are easy to take apart. Their only disadvantage—the same one that plastic pipe has—is that some local plumbing codes forbid their use. Many codes specifically exclude no-hub connections from underground installations.

Installing New or Replacement Pipe

Before you add or change any pipe anywhere in your house, check your local plumbing code to learn what is allowed and what is prohibited, and whether a homeowner is allowed to do his own work. After you have determined that you can proceed, you should realize that installing new plumbing is never easy, but that it doesn't have to be a nightmare either. There are certain basic ground rules and many useful techniques that any do-it-yourselfer should know before adding or replacing any kind of pipe.

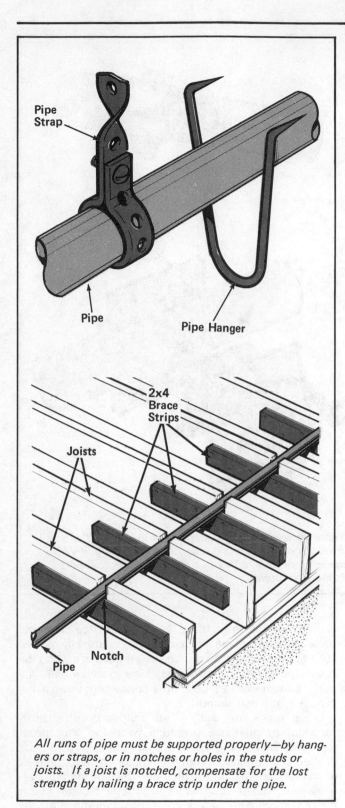

All runs of pipe must be supported properly—by hangers or straps, or in notches or holes in the studs or joists. If a joist is notched, compensate for the lost strength by nailing a brace strip under the pipe.

Remember that drainage lines work on the basis of gravitational pull, not water pressure. Therefore, when you are adding or replacing drainpipes, the pipes must be pitched so that the downward flow will carry out the waste. The normal degree of pitch is 1/4 inch per foot.

All runs of pipe must be supported properly—by hangers or straps, by notches cut or holes drilled in the studs or joists, or by whatever method is best for the given situation. If you notch a joist, be sure to compensate for lost strength by nailing a brace strip under the pipe. This should be a steel brace or a 2×4 about 4 feet long. Notches in studs should be reinforced with metal mending plates. It's always best to run the pipe across the upper half of the studs, because the higher the notches, the less the studs are weakened. Also, do not notch a joist or stud more than a quarter of its depth. Keep in mind that drilling holes for a pipe run weakens joists or studs less than cutting notches does. The diameter of the hole should be less than a quarter of the joist or stud depth.

Plan the entire run of pipe carefully before you start doing any work. If you must tear into floors or walls to correct pipe problems, consider substituting a new run over an entirely different course. Naturally, there are questions of aesthetics, but even pipe run along the outside of an interior wall may—when properly boxed— be preferable to ripping into the walls themselves. Frequently, you can hide a visible stretch of pipe by running it through a closet.

Once you decide exactly how to install your new or replacement pipe, you must know how to order the length of pipe you'll need. To measure pipe properly, you must consider two factors in addition to the length of the pipe you can see. One of these is "fitting gain," or the distance added by the fitting itself. The other is "make-up," the length of each end of the pipe where it goes into the fitting. Since pipes in most fittings do not butt up against each other, the fitting gain must be added to the length for the overall run, and the make-up must be added to each individual section of pipe. Threaded fittings are so standardized that your hardware or plumbing supply store can show you a table that tells you the screw-in distance; then you should have no problem in measuring the pipes and fittings you plan to install.

With most rigid copper or plastic pipe fittings, you can see from the outside just how much of the pipe goes inside. With flexible copper or plastic tubing, precise measuring is not critical, because you can generally make the tubing fit—provided you have sufficient length—with a little gentle bending. Bell-and-spigot connections for cast-iron pipe, however, require that you measure the distance from the bell lip down to the place where the spigot will rest. Since no-hub fittings butt up against each other, there is neither gain nor make-up to consider with these joints.

Whenever possible, connections or joints should be kept to a minimum in every run of pipe, because each joint represents a possible source for a leak and is a point of flow resistance. Use only as many joints as you have to.

Stopping Leaks in Pipes and Joints

There are all kinds of leaks; some can flood your home, while others are not nearly so damaging. Your approach

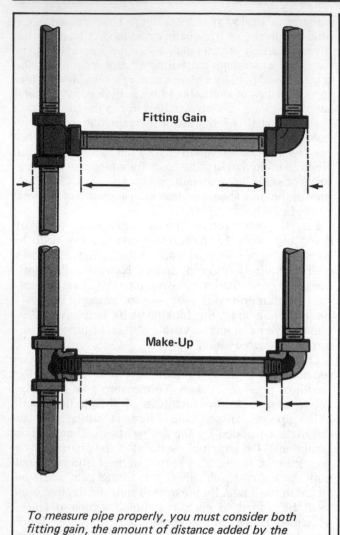

To measure pipe properly, you must consider both fitting gain, the amount of distance added by the fitting itself, and make-up, the amount of each end of the pipe that goes into the fitting.

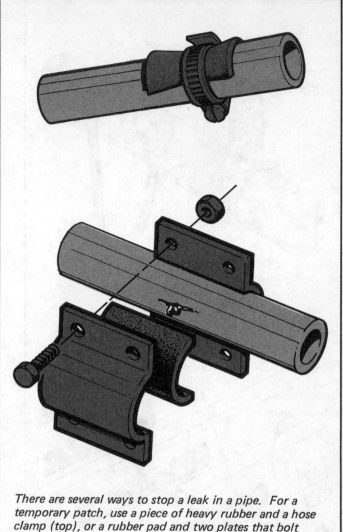

There are several ways to stop a leak in a pipe. For a temporary patch, use a piece of heavy rubber and a hose clamp (top), or a rubber pad and two plates that bolt together (bottom).

to stopping a particular leak depends on the type of leak it happens to be.

If the leak is at a joint, the answer is to tighten or re-make the joint. If the leak is in a pipe, the safest and surest way is to remove the section that has the leak in it and replace it with a new section. But this is more easily said than done. When you turn a threaded galvanized steel pipe, for instance, to unscrew it from its fitting at one end, you tighten the pipe into its fitting at the other end. There is, of course, a solution to this dilemma; but before going into that, consider another alternative: the pipe patch.

You'll find patch kits for plumbing leaks at the hardware store, or you can rig up your own with a piece of heavy rubber from an old inner tube and a C-clamp. Another possibility is to use a hose clamp with the rubber patch. The factory-made kits generally contain a rubber pad that goes over the hole in the pipe and metal plates that bolt tightly together to compress the rubber pad over the hole. The homemade rubber patch and the

C-clamp do the same thing, but to spread the clamping pressure better, place a block of wood against the pad or cut a tin can along its seam and wrap the can around the rubber patch. A quick and easy way to stop a leak, the patch kit can even be used on a permanent basis if the pipe is otherwise sound.

Other quick and easy—but temporary—measures for stopping pipe leaks include wrapping waterproof tape over the bad spot and rubbing the hole with a stick of special compound. Applying epoxy paste to the leak or inserting a self-tapping plug into the hole are other alternatives. When using waterproof tape, be sure to dry the pipe thoroughly before you start wrapping. Start the tape about two to three inches from the hole and extend it the same distance beyond. For tiny leaks in pipes, there is probably no easier cure than the compound sticks that are available at most hardware stores. You just rub the stick over the hole to stop the leak; it can even stop small leaks while the water is still running in the pipe. Epoxy paste can be applied only to dry pipes,

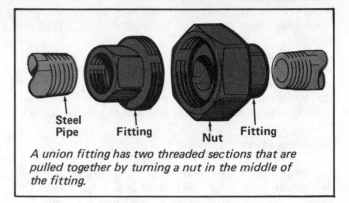

and the water must be turned off. Self-tapping plugs are best used for leaks in large pipes or tanks; they impede the flow of water in smaller pipes. When tightened down, the screw of a self-tapping plug applies enough pressure to stop the leak.

The problem with all of these solutions is that a pipe that's bad enough to spring one leak often starts leaking in other places too; you may fix one spot only to see the pipe burst somewhere else. Especially in cases where the leak results from substantial corrosion, the chances are that the whole section of pipe needs replacing.

Replacing Galvanized Steel Pipe. This gets us back to the dilemma of removing the threaded steel pipe that gets tighter at one end when you loosen the other end. The solution to this seemingly impossible situation is to cut the pipe at a point midway between the joints. Before you do any cutting, however, you must turn off the water. In addition, drain all the water out of the system, by opening the faucets *below* the pipe or by opening the drain valve that's built into the system. You must also be exceedingly careful in sawing and removing so you don't put undue strain on other parts of the pipe system. Before sawing, make sure the pipe is properly braced; the two stubs left by the cut will be heavy, and unless you have them propped up they will sag and pull on the joints. The last thing you want is for your sawing to break the seal at an otherwise perfect joint in your plumbing system.

Saw straight through the pipe with a fine-toothed, 24- to 32-tooth-per-inch blade in a hacksaw. Now, by gripping the fitting at one end of the section with one wrench and the cut section of pipe with another, turn the pipe stub out of its fitting. Do the same for the other stub section of pipe. Once you've removed both stubs, you can install the new pipe.

Replace the leaky pipe with two sections of good pipe connected by a union fitting. A union fitting has two threaded sections that are pulled together by turning a special nut in the middle of the fitting; it allows you to fasten the pipes together without having to twist the pipes themselves. Measure the sections of pipe carefully to assure a proper fit, and be sure to add in the length of the union when figuring the overall run of pipe. The two new sections of pipe must be threaded on both ends, and—as is true of all threaded metal connections—the ends should be coated with pipe joint compound or joint tape to make the joints watertight. To install the two sections of new pipe, screw each piece into its fitting at one end of the run. Then join the sections with the union fitting.

Replacing Copper Pipe and Tubing. When you must replace a section of soldered copper pipe or tubing, melt the solder in the joints at each end of the section. Remove the old section of pipe, and clean the solder out of the fittings. To install the new section of pipe, prepare the fittings and pipe and sweat-solder the joints, following the procedures outlined in "Sweat-Soldering" earlier in this chapter.

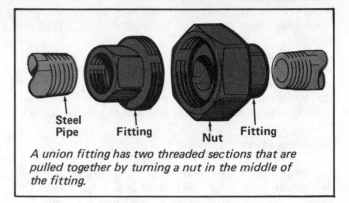

A union fitting has two threaded sections that are pulled together by turning a nut in the middle of the fitting.

Caution: *Before working on the pipe, don't forget to turn off the water and drain all the water out of the system by opening the faucets below the pipe or by opening the drain valve that's built into the system. Dry the pipes as thoroughly as you can and stuff balls of soft bread into the cut ends to absorb any moisture when you solder.*

If there's not enough give in the run to remove an old section of rigid pipe from its fittings in one piece, you can use a tube cutter to cut the pipe midway between the two joints. Then remove the pipe stubs from their fittings. Replace the old pipe with two new sections of pipe connected by a copper-to-copper union fitting.

Replacing Plastic Pipe. If you have a problem with a leaky section of plastic pipe that has been solvent-welded to fittings, you can't remove the section from its fittings; instead, you must cut the section just *outside* the fittings at each end of the section you plan to replace. First, turn off the water, and drain all the water out of the system by opening the faucets below the pipe or by opening the drain valve that's built into the system.

Use a fine-toothed hacksaw to cut completely through the plastic pipe outside the two fittings. Then carefully measure the amount of plastic pipe you'll need to replace that section, keeping in mind that the run of pipe will be a bit longer because you've removed the fittings as well. You will also need two new plastic fittings to replace the ones you've removed, plus a union fitting. To install the new section of pipe, follow the procedure outlined in the section "Working With Plastic Pipe" earlier in this chapter.

Repairing Leaking Joints. What do you do if there's a leak in a joint? That depends on what type of joint it is. If there's a leak in a sweat-soldered joint in copper pipe or tubing, you should melt the solder in the joint, take it apart, clean it, and sweat-solder it all over again. Leaky joints in plastic pipe must be cut out and replaced, because the solvent that fuses pieces of plastic pipe together does such a good job that there's no way to get the pieces apart.

A threaded joint in galvanized steel pipe or cast-iron pipe may only need retightening when it starts to leak. If retightening doesn't stop the leak, try applying epoxy paste to the joint. First cut off the water and dry the pipe thoroughly; then follow the directions for applying the epoxy.

One of the easiest ways to solve a leaking joint problem is to install a nylon fitting; this type of fitting requires no solvent, no solder, and no tools. Such fittings are available for use with plastic, copper, and other types of pipe, and for either hot- or cold-water service.

Sweating Pipes

Sometimes there's so much water dripping from a pipe that you're sure there must be a leak somewhere. On closer examination, however, you may discover that there is no leak, even though your floors and furnishings have suffered as much damage as if there were. What you are witnessing is a natural phenomenon called condensation or sweating.

Sweating occurs when the water inside the pipe is much colder than surrounding humid air, a situation that exists nearly year-round in many homes. During the summer, the surrounding air is naturally hot; during the winter, the air is heated by the furnace. In either case, when warm humid air reaches cold pipes—and water that comes from below-ground is always fairly cool— drops of moisture form and drip as if there were a tiny hole in the pipe.

One good way to control the moisture problem of a sweating pipe is to insulate the pipes. There are several types of thick "drip" tape in rolls of self-sticking material, made to adhere easily to problem pipes. Before applying the tape, wipe the pipes as dry as you can. Wind the tape so that it completely covers the pipe and the fittings; you should see no further signs of sweating.

Another sweat-fighter is asbestos tape, but you must use this tape with a special asbestos cement. Soak the tape in the cement until it becomes like papier-mâché for molding around odd-shaped fittings. For straight runs of pipe, ready-made asbestos or fiberglass pipe jackets are excellent. There are also no-drip compounds that you can brush on pipe to form a coating of insulation.

It is well worth your time, effort, and expense to eliminate condensation problems. The moisture that drips from sweating pipes can harm your floors, encourage mildew, and cause other damage.

Thawing Frozen Pipes

You may think that your entire plumbing system is in perfect working order, and that there's little or no chance of a pipe bursting and flooding your house. Yet there is one situation that you may not have considered. Water that freezes during the winter in an unprotected pipe expands, and that expansion can rupture an otherwise sound pipe. Of course, a frozen pipe is always an inconvenience, but it can result in a much more serious situation than just a temporary loss of water. If there is one example of how a little prevention is superior to a lot of cure, fighting frozen pipes is it. By taking the

proper preventive steps, you may never need to worry about thawing frozen pipes, or—worse yet—repairing a pipe that bursts when the water in it freezes solid.

If you're building a new house or adding pipes underground, follow these freeze-fighting tips. Bury the pipes *below* the frost line. Since this depth varies in different regions, check with the local National Weather Service office to learn about the frost line in your area. Make sure the new pipes are as well insulated as practical, and run as many pipes as you can along your home's inner walls instead of along its outside walls. If you have pipes on outside walls leading to outside faucets, make sure the faucets are the frost-free type. When cold weather sets in, shut off the water to the outside faucets and open the faucet to drain the exposed pipe. Finally, if you know you have a stretch of pipe that's subject to freezing, wrap the pipe with heat tape (sometimes called heat cable) or pipe insulation. You can buy heat tape that has an automatic thermostat to start the heat when the outside temperature drops to about 38° F.

What happens, though, when you wake up some frigid winter morning to find a water pipe frozen solid? What you need then are not freeze-fighting tips, but directions on the best way to thaw frozen pipes.

Before doing anything else, *open the faucet* so that the steam produced by your thawing activities will be able to escape. In addition, start thawing the pipe *at the faucet* and work back toward the other end of the frozen section. As you melt the ice, the water and steam will come out the open faucet. If you started in the middle, the steam produced by the melting ice could get trapped and build up enough pressure to burst the pipe.

You can use any of several pipe-thawing heat sources. Probably the most popular—and certainly the safest—is hot water. Wrap and secure a heavy towel or a burlap bag around the pipe to concentrate and hold the heat against the pipe. Pour hot or boiling water over the towel, but be careful because most of the water will run off the towel onto you or the floor. A properly positioned bucket can save you both a scalding and a mess.

A less messy but far more dangerous heat source for thawing frozen pipes is a propane torch equipped with a flame-spreader nozzle. With this heat source, you must be extremely careful to prevent the torch flame from damaging or igniting the wall behind the pipe. A scrap of asbestos siding or some other fireproof material between the pipe and the wall is a good precautionary measure, but the way you use the torch is the main ingredient in safe pipe thawing. Keep the flame moving back and forth; never leave it very long in one spot. Be especially careful if you're near any soldered pipe joints—pass over them very quickly or they may melt and cause leaks, and you'll find that you have a much more serious plumbing problem on your hands than a frozen pipe. *Never* use a torch or other direct high heat on plastic pipe.

If you want to avoid the messiness of thawing with hot water and the danger of melting soldered joints with a propane torch, you can use a heat lamp, a hair dryer, or an electric iron as the heat source. These are slower-

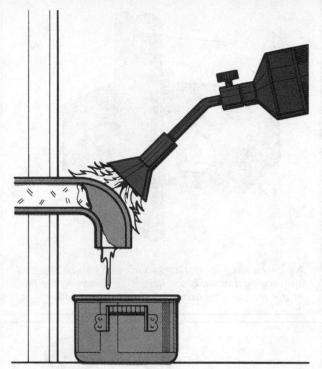

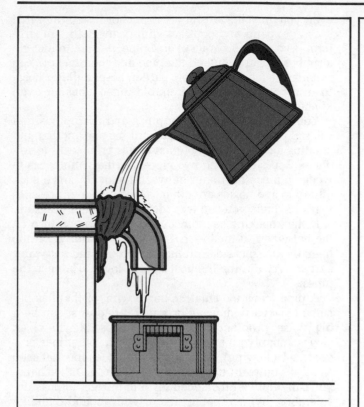

The safest and most popular method of thawing a frozen pipe is pouring boiling water over a towel wrapped around the frozen section. Catch the runoff in a pan.

A propane torch can also be used to thaw a frozen pipe. This method is much faster, but it could melt soldered pipe joints or cause a fire. Don't use a torch on plastic pipe.

working, but much safer to use.

There is a special technique for thawing a frozen drainpipe. Actually, all it involves is melting the blockage with hot water; but if the ice is some distance from the drain opening, the hot water you pour in could cool considerably before it reaches the trouble spot. For more effective thawing, remove the trap and insert a length of garden hose into the drainpipe. When the hose reaches the ice—that is, when you can't push it in any farther—raise your end of the hose and feed hot water in through a funnel. This way, the hot water is sure to get to the problem area. You must be careful when using this technique. Until the ice melts and drains down the pipe, the hot water you pour in will back up toward you. Have a bucket ready to catch the overflow, and be careful not to scald yourself.

Quieting Noisy Pipes

Most people refer to the sound of banging pipes as water hammer, but water hammer is only one of several different noises that can come from your plumbing system. If you hear the sound whenever you turn on the water, then the problem is certainly not water hammer; it probably results from the pipes striking against something.

Banging pipes are much easier to cure if you can see

them. Turn on the water and start looking for movement; once you find the trouble, you should have no problem in stopping the pipe or pipes from hitting against whatever is in the vicinity. Even if the moving pipe is between the walls, you may be able to silence it without tearing your house apart. Just place stops—rubber or other padding—at each end where the pipe emerges from behind the wall.

Generally, you'll find that the moving pipe is loose within its strap or U-clamp, and is banging against the wall it's supposed to be secured to. To eliminate the noise completely, just slit a piece of old garden hose or cut a patch of rubber and insert it behind the strap or clamp to fill in the gap. Pipes that strike against a masonry wall can be silenced by wedging a block of wood between the pipe and the wall. Nail the block to the wall with masonry nails—or with a screw installed in a masonry wall anchor—and attach the pipe to the block with a pipe strap.

In a basement or crawl space, you will frequently find galvanized steel pipes suspended from the joists by perforated pipe straps. While this is a perfectly proper installation, a long run of suspended pipe can move within the straps, strike against something, and create a racket. A block of wood strategically wedged along the run can eliminate the pipe's movement—and, of course, the noise. Whenever you secure a pipe, how-

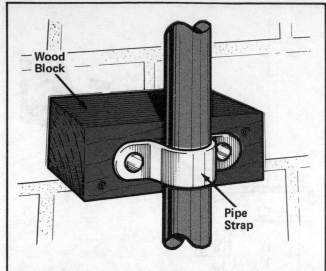

A pipe banging against a masonry wall can be silenced by wedging a wood block behind it, fastening the block to the wall, and securing the pipe to the wood.

Wood Block

Pipe Strap

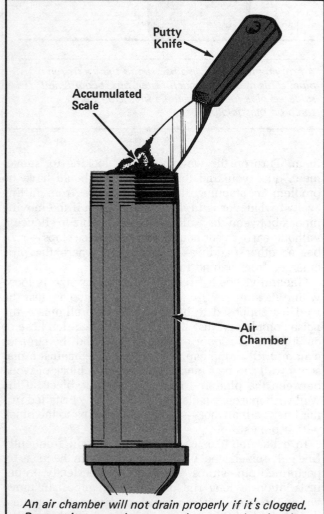

Putty Knife

Accumulated Scale

Air Chamber

An air chamber will not drain properly if it's clogged. Remove its cap and ream out the accumulated scale inside the chamber.

ever, you must be careful not to anchor it so tightly that it can't expand and contract with changes in temperature. If you place a bracket on a pipe, be sure to include a rubber buffer between the pipe and the bracket. You can make such buffers from garden hose, radiator hose, foam rubber, rubber cut from old inner tubes, or even kitchen sponges.

You may find that supply pipes and drainpipes that run right next to each other are striking one another and creating a clatter. One solution to this problem is to solder—if possible—the two pipes together; another is to wedge a piece of rubber between them. Or, since such vibration and noises are often caused by water pressure that's too high, you can try reducing the water pressure.

If the knocking sound occurs only when you turn on the hot water, it means that the water heater is set too high; the noise is steam rumbling through the hot-water system. Try turning the heat setting down to silence the pipes.

A pipe that's too small to begin with, or that has become clogged with scale or mineral deposits, can be a big noise problem. It's almost impossible to clean clogged supply pipes (a water filter can sometimes prevent such clogging), and you must replace pipe that's too small if you want to stop the noise. On the other hand, you can diminish the sound level of clogged pipes considerably by wrapping them with sound-damping insulation.

Drainpipes rarely clatter, but they can make a sucking noise as the water leaves the sink or basin. This kind of sound means that a vent is restricted, or perhaps that there's no vent at all attached to the drain. In either case, you have a potentially serious plumbing problem on your hands—not because of the noise, but because a nonfunctioning or nonexistent vent could result in the water seal being siphoned from the fixture's trap, allowing sewer gas to back up into your home. Run a plumbers' snake through the vent from the fixture, if possible, or from the roof vent, to eliminate any clogging. If there is no vent on the drain, install an antisiphon trap (available at the hardware store) to quiet the noise and to prevent any problem with sewer gas.

Water hammer is a particular type of plumbing noise, not a generic name for any kind of pipe clatter. It occurs when you shut off the water suddenly, and the fast-moving water rushing through the pipe is brought to a quick halt—creating a sort of shock wave and a hammering noise. Plumbing that's properly installed has air chambers or "cushions" that compress when the shock wave hits, softening the blow and preventing this hammering. The chambers can fail, though, because water under pressure gradually absorbs the air. If you formerly experienced no hammering and then it suddenly started, most likely your plumbing system's air chambers have become waterlogged.

You can cure water hammer by turning off the water behind the waterlogged chambers (perhaps even at the main shutoff), opening the offending faucet, and permitting the faucet to drain thoroughly. Once all the water drains from the chamber, air will fill it again and

Pipe Troubleshooting Chart

PROBLEM	POSSIBLE CAUSE	SOLUTION
Leaking pipe	1. Joint not watertight.	1. Tighten threaded joint, if possible. Apply epoxy paste to joint. Disassemble and resolder sweat-soldered joint in copper pipe or tubing. Cut out and replace joint in plastic pipe.
	2. Hole in pipe.	2. Repair by patching hole, using best available method, or replace section of pipe. If section is inaccessible, disconnect it from system and route new section of pipe.
	3. Burst pipe.	3. Immediately turn off water at main shutoff. Repair or replace pipe or joint. Avoid electrical shock due to contact between electrical devices or equipment and water.
Pipe drips, but there is no leak	1. Condensation.	1. Apply insulation to pipe.
Noise in pipes—hot water only	1. Steam causing rumbling in hot-water pipes.	1. Turn down thermostat setting on water heater or replace faulty thermostat.
	2. Pipe creaks against surroundings from expansion and contraction.	2. Rehang pipe on slip hangers or in larger notches or holes.
Water makes sucking noise when draining	1. Improper venting.	1. Clean roof vent. If there is no vent, add antisiphon trap.
Hammering noise when water is shut off	1. Air chambers waterlogged.	1. Shut off and drain supply line to allow air to reenter air chambers.
	2. No air chamber.	2. Install air chamber.
Banging noise while water is running	1. Loose pipe.	1. Track down loose pipe and brace, cushion, or strap it.
No water supply	1. Frozen pipes.	1. Open faucets. Start at closest point to faucet and work back.
	2. Main shutoff valve closed.	2. Open main shutoff valve.
	3. Broken or closed main.	3. Call water department.
	4. Well pump failure.	4. Check and repair pump.

restore the cushion. If the air chamber is located below the outlet, you may have to drain the main supply lines to allow the chamber to fill with air again.

The air chamber will not drain properly if it's clogged with scale or residue from chemicals or minerals in the water. The chamber should be a bit larger than the supply pipe to preclude such clogging. Since the chamber is simply a capped length of pipe, however, all you have to do to clear it is remove the cap and ream out the scale.

What do you do if there are no air chambers built into your plumbing system? You must do something, because water hammer pressures are often sufficient to cause eventual damage—failure of fittings or burst pipes. The problem is most often caused by water pressure that's too high, so the first step is to reduce the water pressure if possible. Sometimes this isn't feasible, because a reduction in pressure may result in only a dribble of water at an upper-floor faucet if one on the first floor is turned on. Where the idea is a workable one, you can reduce pressure by installing a pressure-

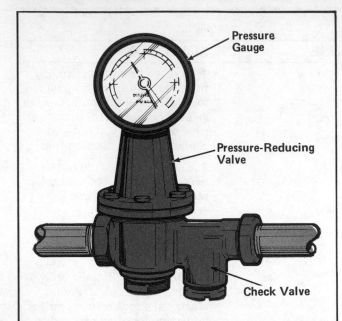

If you must reduce the water pressure in your home's plumbing system, a pressure-reducing valve can be installed in the supply pipe coming into the house.

Labels in image: Pressure Gauge, Pressure-Reducing Valve, Check Valve

that are designed for such problem areas. Many of these devices have a valve that makes it easy for air to reenter the system.

Toilet Repairs

The toilet is one of the most important fixtures in your home. Although toilets are—if not mistreated—sturdy and reliable components of the plumbing system, it's a rare homeowner or apartment-dweller who never has any problems with a toilet. Clogging is perhaps the most serious toilet trouble, but it is far from the only one. The tank, for example, can make all sorts of strange noises, or water can run continuously. Fortunately, most toilet troubles can be fixed by any do-it-yourself plumber.

Specialized Tools

Few special tools are required for toilet repairs. For changing a toilet seat, you'll need a wrench, or perhaps a deep socket wrench, or a hacksaw. Of course, the most frequently used toilet tool is the plumbers' friend, also known as a plunger, a force cup, or a pump. Get one with a long handle, and be sure the suction cup is large enough to cover the toilet's drain opening.

A closet auger is a version of the plumbers' snake, but it's designed specifically for clearing clogs in toilets. The closet auger is shorter than a regular snake, and it comes encased in a metal housing with a crank.

If you really plan to get involved in plumbing chores and you decide to remove a toilet for replacement or repairs, you may well need a spudwrench. Older toilets frequently have a large pipe that connects the tank to the bowl; this pipe is called a spud, and it is held to the bowl and tank by extra-large hexagonal slip nuts. A spudwrench is designed to remove these slip nuts. The

reducing valve in the supply line that comes into the house. The same purpose is served by installing a globe valve (a valve that halts water flow with a washer) at the head of the affected pipeline, but this too may result in pressure too low for proper operation when other faucets are open. If pressure reduction is infeasible or ineffective, you must install the necessary air chambers to prevent water hammer. If you have no room to make the installation without tearing into a wall, go to a plumbing supply dealer and find out about the substitute devices

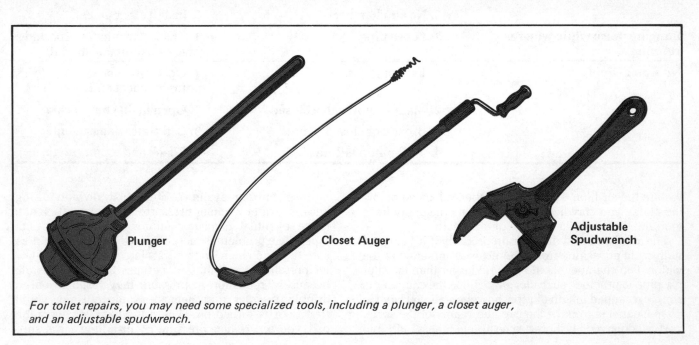

For toilet repairs, you may need some specialized tools, including a plunger, a closet auger, and an adjustable spudwrench.

Labels in image: Plunger, Closet Auger, Adjustable Spudwrench

adjustable type of spudwrench is far more versatile than the nonadjustable type, which has a fixed opening at each end.

Replacing a Toilet Seat

Undoubtedly, the easiest toilet repair task is replacing the lid and seat. There are so many styles of replacement seats available that you should have no trouble finding one to match any bathroom color scheme or motif. Most modern toilets are manufactured in two standard sizes, and replacement seats are made to fit them. If your toilet is extra wide or very old, however, you may not be able to use one of the standard replacement seats. In this case, you may have to place a special order for the seat with a company that deals in plumbing fixtures.

Once you have the right size seat, remove the old one. Removal sounds simple; all you have to do is remove two nuts and lift your old toilet seat up and out. You may wonder what's so hard about that—but wait until you try to loosen those nuts. Consider yourself lucky if the nuts that secure the toilet seat are not rusted or corroded; sometimes, in fact, they are recessed and practically inaccessible.

If you can get to the fasteners relatively easily, apply some penetrating oil to help loosen them. Give the oil plenty of time to soak in. Use a wrench or, if you can't reach the nuts with a regular wrench, a deep socket wrench. Be sure you don't use too much force; if the wrench slipped off a stubborn nut, it could strike and crack the tank or the bowl or anything else it happened to hit.

When all else fails, you'll have to cut off the bolts with a hacksaw. To protect the bowl's finish, apply tape to the bowl at the spots the hacksaw blade is likely to rub against. Then insert the blade under the hinge, and saw through the bolts. Sawing is a measure of last resort; try every other procedure to loosen the nuts first. Then, if you're convinced that nothing is going to break the nuts loose, be extremely cautious in using the saw. A careless slip with a hacksaw can crack the fixture just as easily as a blow with a wrench can.

With the nuts removed or the bolts cut, you can remove the old seat without further difficulty. Clean the area before installing the new seat. The new one can be fastened simply by inserting the bolts and tightening the nuts, but be careful not to overtighten the nuts—you may want to replace this seat too some day. If you live in an apartment and put on a new seat, be sure to keep the old one. When you're ready to leave, you can replace the new one with the original and take the new seat with you.

If the toilet lid and seat are still in good condition, but the small rubber bumpers on the bottom are in bad shape, you can buy replacement bumpers at the hardware store. Some bumpers screw in; others must be nailed into place. Whichever type you have, try to install the new ones in holes that are close enough to conceal the original holes.

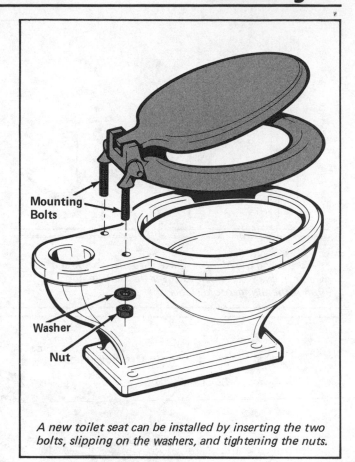

Mounting Bolts

Washer

Nut

A new toilet seat can be installed by inserting the two bolts, slipping on the washers, and tightening the nuts.

Clearing a Clogged Toilet

You can generally clear a clogged toilet with the plumbers' friend, or plunger. Just make sure that there's enough water in the toilet bowl to cover the rubber suction cup, and then work the handle of the plunger up and down. There are two types of plungers, and the one with a bulb-type head is especially effective. Some types have a fold-out head that's designed for toilet use. If there isn't enough water in the bowl, do *not* flush the toilet; flushing a clogged toilet will just cause the bowl to overflow. Instead, bring a pan or pot of water from another source to supply the water you need to cover the plunger cup.

Usually, whatever is blocking the toilet drain is not very far away. If the plunger's action doesn't dislodge the clog, you can try to hook the blockage and pull it free. A wire coat hanger can sometimes do the job. The coat hanger, however, is really a substitute for the closet or toilet auger. This tool has a long sleeve or tube to guide the snake and auger hook into the trap. A crank on the end enables you to turn the hook in the drain or trap.

Insert the auger into the toilet trap and turn the crank until it feels tight. This means that the snake has twisted its way to and into the blockage. Pull in the auger and you should be able to remove whatever is clogging the toilet. If you aren't successful, try the closet auger sev-

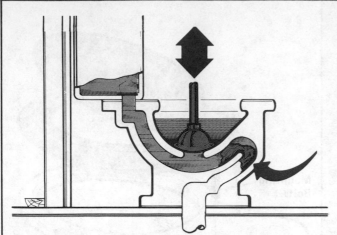

Before using the plunger, make sure there's enough water in the toilet bowl to cover the suction cup. Pump the plunger to dislodge the clog.

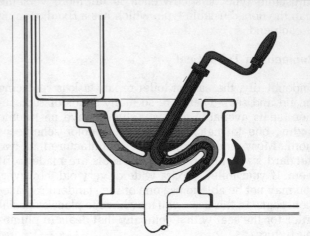

The closet auger has a long sleeve to guide the snake and auger hook into the trap. A crank enables you to turn the hook and dislodge the blockage.

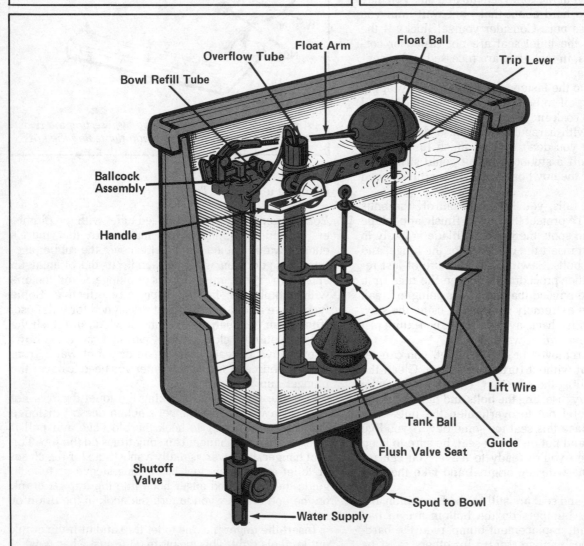

Overflow Tube

Float Arm

Float Ball

Bowl Refill Tube

Trip Lever

Ballcock Assembly

Handle

Lift Wire

Tank Ball

Guide

Flush Valve Seat

Shutoff Valve

Spud to Bowl

Water Supply

Toilet tank troubles are both common and annoying, and they could be costing you money in wasted water. Most problems, however, can be eliminated quickly and easily. Above is a cross-section of a typical toilet tank and its components.

eral more times. In some cases, you may have to resort to pushing a regular plumbers' snake through the blockage if you can't pull it out with the auger.

When all else fails, the toilet may have to be removed from the floor and turned upside down so you can get at the blockage. This is not what anyone would call an easy job, so you should give the simpler methods as good a try as you can before you remove the toilet. But removing the toilet is not beyond the capabilities of the average do-it-yourselfer, and this procedure is explained below in the section "Removing and Replacing a Toilet."

Toilet Tank Problems

Compared with a clogged toilet, tank troubles can seem relatively insignificant. Yet these problems—strange noises or water running continuously—can be more than annoying; they can also be costing you money in wasted water. Fortunately, you can eliminate most toilet tank troubles quickly and easily.

Do you know how the toilet works—what happens between the time you push the handle and the time the toilet is ready for further use? Before you can solve tank problems, you must know exactly how this fixture operates.

When you trip the handle on the tank to flush the toilet, a trip lever is raised inside the tank. This lever lifts wires which, in turn, raise the tank ball (or rubber flap) out of the flush valve opening at the bottom of the tank.

When the flush valve opening is clear, the water in the tank rushes out past the raised tank ball and into the toilet bowl below. This raises the level of water in the bowl above the level of water in the toilet trap. While the water is rushing out of the tank, the float ball, which floats on top of the water in the tank, drops down. This pulls down on the float arm, raising the valve plunger in the ballcock assembly and allowing fresh water to flow into the tank. Since water seeks its own level, the water from the tank pushes the bowl water out into the drain, causing a siphoning action that cleans everything out of the bowl. When all the water is gone from the toilet bowl and air is drawn into the trap, the siphoning stops. Meanwhile, the tank ball falls back into place, closing the flush valve opening at the bottom of the tank.

As the water level rises in the tank, the float ball rises until the float arm is high enough to lower the valve plunger in the ballcock assembly and shut off the incoming water. If, for some reason, the water should fail to shut off, there is an overflow tube that carries excess water down into the bowl to prevent the tank from overflowing.

Lift the lid off your toilet tank, and you should be able to follow this procedure quite easily. Once you know how the toilet works, you can start to look for the source of toilet tank problems.

Suppose your toilet never stops running—water flows continuously out of the tank to the bowl and down the drain. What should you do? Try lifting up on the

float arm. If the water stops, you know the problem is that the float ball doesn't rise far enough to lower the valve plunger in the ballcock assembly. One reason could be that the float ball is rubbing against the side of the tank. If this is the case, bend the float arm slightly to move the ball away from the tank side.

The problem could also be in the float ball itself. If the ball doesn't touch the tank, continue to hold the float arm, and remove the ball from the end of the arm by turning it counterclockwise. Then shake the ball to see if there's water inside it; the weight of water inside could be preventing the ball from rising normally. If there is water in the ball, shake it out and put the ball back on the float arm; if the ball is corroded, replace it with a new one. If there is no water in the ball, put the ball back on and bend the float rod down—very gently—to lower the level the float ball must reach to shut off the flow of fresh water into the tank.

What do you do if, when you lift the float arm, the water doesn't stop running? You know then, of course, that the problem is not in the float arm at all. The next logical place to check for trouble is the tank ball at the flush valve seat. Frequently, chemical residue from the water can prevent this ball from seating properly, or the ball itself may have decayed. In either case, the result is the same—water will seep through the flush valve opening into the toilet bowl below.

Turn off the water at the toilet shutoff valve, and flush the toilet to empty the tank. You can now examine the tank ball for signs of wear, and install a new ball if necessary. If the problem is chemical residue on the lip of the flush valve opening, take some wet-dry emery cloth, steel wool, or even a knife and clean away the debris. You can retard any further formation of such residue by putting a few slivers of soap into the tank.

There are still other possible causes for a toilet's running continuously. The guide or the lift wire that raises and lowers the tank ball may be out of line or bent. Make sure the guide is in place so that the wire is directly above the flush valve opening. Rotate the guide until the tank ball falls straight down into the opening. If a lift wire is bent, try to bend it back to the correct position, or install a new one. Make sure the trip lever rod is not rubbing against anything, and the lift wire is not installed in the wrong hole of the rod; either situation could cause the tank ball to fall at an angle and not block the opening as it should. If neither the float ball nor the tank ball is at fault, then the problem must be in the ballcock assembly.

Working With the Ballcock Assembly

The ballcock assembly looks far more complicated than it really is. Just make sure the water shutoff valve for the toilet is in the "off" position, and you're ready to go to work.

With many ballcock assemblies, you'll find a pair of thumbscrews that hold the valve plunger; but if the unit in your toilet tank has a different linkage arrangement, you should still be able to determine how to remove the

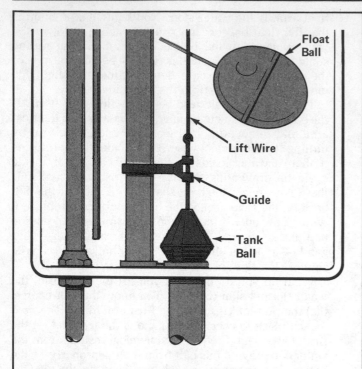

If your toilet runs continuously, check the guide and the lift wire that raises and lowers the tank ball to be sure they are aligned properly.

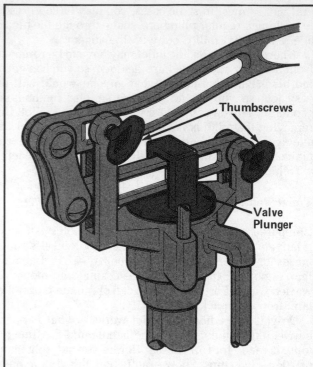

On many ballcock assemblies, a pair of thumbscrews holds the valve plunger. You will have to unscrew them to remove the valve.

valve plunger. Remove the valve plunger, and you'll see one or two washers—sometimes you'll find an O-ring. Naturally, if any of these parts is faulty, water will flow out past the plunger continuously and the toilet will run constantly. Examine all of the washers, and replace any defective ones.

Some ballcock assemblies are completely sealed, and there's no way you can get inside this kind of unit without breaking it. If this is what you find when you lift the lid off the toilet tank, you'll have to buy a replacement ballcock assembly. Most cost only a few dollars. If you discover either a sealed ballcock assembly or a damaged one, the first thing to do is to get all the water out of the tank so that you can remove the old unit and install a new one. Shut off the toilet water supply at the shutoff valve, and flush the tank. Use a sponge to remove whatever water is left inside the tank. Unscrew the float arm from the old ballcock unit, and remove the refill tube from the overflow tube—the refill tube may be clipped on or bent into position.

Now look under the tank. You'll see a coupling or slip nut where the water inlet pipe enters the base of the tank. Loosen the coupling nut to free the water inlet pipe. Then use an adjustable wrench to grip the retaining nut or locknut immediately above the slip nut under the tank, and use another wrench to grip the base of the ballcock assembly shaft inside the tank. Unscrew the locknut under the tank to remove the ballcock assembly. If the nut is stubborn, try using some penetrating oil to loosen it. Lift the old assembly out of the tank, but be

sure to save all the washers from all connections, both inside and outside the tank. You may not need them— most likely all necessary washers will be included with the replacement unit—but it's always smart to keep the old parts until you've installed the new ballcock assembly.

Insert the new ballcock assembly into the hole in the tank, with the inside washer in place. Tighten the locknut on the outside sufficiently to make the inside washer fit watertight against the hole, but don't overtighten it. Replace the coupling nut and water inlet pipe, reinstall the float arm, set the refill tube into the overflow tube, and the job is done. Turn the water back on at the toilet shutoff valve, and check for leaks at all points. Of course, another thing to check is that the float ball does not rub against the back of the tank.

When you go to a hardware or plumbing supply store to buy a new ballcock assembly, you'll find that both plastic and metal units are available. Plastic costs less and will not corrode, but plastic assemblies are not as sturdy as metal ones. In addition, plastic units usually cannot be repaired because many of them are sealed. Nevertheless, you can purchase a different type of unit than the one you're replacing as long as the new assembly has a threaded shank the same size as the old one. If possible, bring the old assembly with you when you go to buy the replacement.

Newer types of ballcock assemblies eliminate the float arm and the float ball. One kind features a plastic cup that floats up to cut off the water as the tank fills.

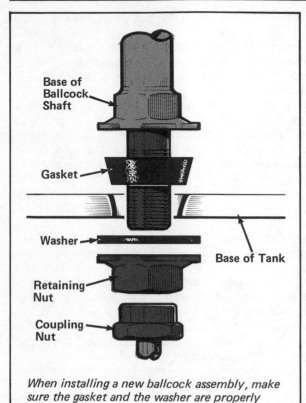

Base of
Ballcock
Shaft

Gasket

Washer

Base of Tank

Retaining
Nut

Coupling
Nut

When installing a new ballcock assembly, make sure the gasket and the washer are properly seated and firmly secured by the retaining nut.

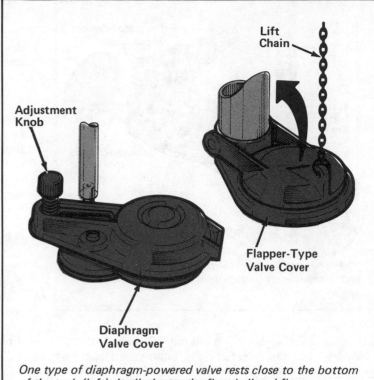

Lift
Chain

Adjustment
Knob

Flapper-Type
Valve Cover

Diaphragm
Valve Cover

One type of diaphragm-powered valve rests close to the bottom of the tank (left); it eliminates the float ball and float arm. Another type (right) uses a flapper cover, lifted by a chain.

You can set the water level in the tank by adjusting the position of the plastic cup on a pull rod. One advantage to this type of ballcock assembly is that it lets the water run full-force until the tank is filled; then it shuts the water off immediately, eliminating the groaning noises some toilets make as a conventional float arm gradually closes the valve.

Another type also eliminates the float ball and float arm. This is a small unit that rests almost on the bottom of the tank; its diaphragm-powered valve senses the level of the water from down there. Moreover, since it requires no tools, this assembly is an easy unit to install. You may need a couple of common tools for the removal of the old assembly.

The first step in installing this type of unit is to turn off the tank's water supply shutoff valve. Then flush the toilet to drain the tank. Sponge up any water remaining in the tank before proceeding. Remove the old ballcock assembly, following the procedure outlined earlier in this section. Slip the parts over the water inlet pipe under the tank in this order: coupling nut, friction washer, cone washer, and retaining or mounting nut.

Now install the new unit inside the tank, fitting the threaded shank down through the hole over the water supply pipe and making sure the gasket fits into the hole. Start the retaining or mounting nut under the tank onto the threaded shank; hand-tighten it only. Push the washers into place, and hand-tighten the coupling nut under the tank.

Inside the tank, attach one end of the refill tube to the tank's overflow pipe, and place the other end on the stem of the replacement unit. Open the water supply valve to fill the tank. The water level in the tank can be adjusted by a knob on the new valve unit.

Inadequate Flushing, Sweating, and Other Problems

What can you do if too little water comes from the tank to flush the toilet bowl clean? The first thing you should check is the water level in the tank; it's probably too low. If the water level doesn't reach within 1½ inches of the top of the overflow tube, try bending the float arm up slightly to let more water enter the tank.

In some cases, the water level may be correct, but there's still not enough water coming from the tank to clean the bowl properly. Most likely, the culprit in this situation is the tank ball at the flush valve seat at the bottom of the tank. The ball is probably dropping too soon because the guide is set too low. Try raising the guide, but make sure it stays in line with the lift wire; if the guide and the wire are out of alignment, the tank ball will not drop straight into the valve seat opening, and the toilet will run continuously.

There is one other possible cause for inadequate flushing. The small ports around the underside of the toilet bowl's rim can get clogged with residue from chemicals in the water and prevent a sufficient amount of tank water from running out into the bowl. A small mirror can help you examine the holes, and a piece of wire coat hanger or an offset Phillips screwdriver—if

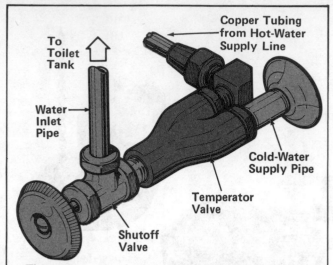

To Toilet Tank

Copper Tubing from Hot-Water Supply Line

Water Inlet Pipe

Cold-Water Supply Pipe

Temperator Valve

Shutoff Valve

The temperator valve, which requires both hot- and cold-water supply connections, can reduce toilet tank sweating.

one is available—can ream out any clogged debris.

Toilet tanks can sweat and drip onto your floors just as pipes can. There are jackets designed specifically to fit over the tank and absorb the moisture. There are also drip pans that fit under the tank to catch the dripping condensation so that it doesn't damage your bathroom floor. A device called a temperator valve is another way to combat tank sweating. The valve provides a regulated mixture of hot and cold water, which lessens the difference between the temperature inside the tank and the temperature of the surrounding air. It is this temperature difference, of course, that causes condensation, or sweating. You might consider installing a temperator valve if the water in the tank is usually below 50° F.

A temperator valve requires you to hook up a hot-water line to the valve, which may be quite inconvenient if there is no such line relatively close to the toilet. Moreover, the temperator valve does not prevent the water inside the tank from cooling between flushings; thus, condensation can still occur even on a temperator-equipped toilet.

If you do have an accessible hot-water line at a lavatory near the toilet, follow this procedure to install a temperator valve. Turn off the water at the main shutoff. Working at the toilet, drain the tank, disconnect the water inlet pipe from the fixture's shutoff valve, and unscrew the valve from the cold-water supply pipe. Attach the "cold" inlet of the temperator valve to the cold-water supply pipe. Screw a short threaded nipple into the temperator valve outlet; the fixture's shutoff valve is screwed onto the other end of the threaded nipple. Reconnect the toilet tank's water inlet pipe to the shutoff valve.

Now, at the lavatory, disconnect the flexible hot-water line leading to the fixture's hot-water faucet from the shutoff valve. Install a compression T-fitting with a takeoff adapter in this flexible line. Then reconnect the

line, with its T-fitting, to the hot-water shutoff valve. Run flexible copper tubing from the T-fitting to the "hot" inlet of the temperator valve. Attach the tubing to the valve with a compression adapter fitting. Finally, secure the copper tubing to the wall, and turn on the water at the main shutoff.

One of the simplest, least expensive, and most effective methods of stopping tank sweating is to glue thin (1/4- to 1/2-inch) panels of foam rubber to the inside surfaces of the tank walls. To install the panels, shut off the fixture's water supply, flush the tank, and sponge it dry. Cut pieces of foam to fit all four sides of the tank, and secure them with silicone glue. Let the glue cure thoroughly—24 hours, if possible—before refilling the tank.

One of the worst effects of a sweating tank is that it can hide a genuine leak in the tank. You may see water on the floor, but fail to attribute it to a leak, believing that it's just condensation from the tank. Fortunately, there is an easy way to check for leaks. Pour enough bluing into the tank to give the water a noticeably blue color; some toilet bowl cleaners also turn the water blue and can be used. If the tank does have a leak, the moisture on the floor will show traces of blue.

The leak may be due to loose connections or defective washers on the spud pipe—if your toilet has an exposed pipe from the tank to the bowl—or where the water inlet pipe and ballcock assembly are attached to the tank. Replace any worn gaskets or washers and tighten all of the nuts; then test with bluing in the water again. It is also possible that water is seeping out from *under* the toilet bowl; the wax ring seal that joins the bowl to the drain outlet may be defective. If this is the case, the bowl—and the tank, if it's supported by the bowl—must be removed, and a new gasket installed. If the leak is due to a crack in the tank or bowl, the whole toilet must be replaced.

Removing and Replacing a Toilet

Removing and replacing a toilet is not a task to be undertaken without good reason, but it is certainly not beyond your capabilities. When you can't unclog the toilet by less drastic means, removing it is the answer. Maybe you want a new, more modern toilet; maybe the bowl or the tank is cracked; maybe the fixture leaks around its base. All of these situations call for removing the old toilet and reinstalling it or installing a new fixture.

Although there's nothing terribly difficult in removing and replacing a toilet, many communities—as stated in the official plumbing code—prohibit anyone but a licensed plumber from doing the job. Check the code for your community. If it doesn't prohibit do-it-yourself toilet replacement—and if you feel confident of your plumbing skill and knowledge—go ahead.

If you're installing a new toilet, the first step is to measure the rough-in distance, the distance from the wall behind the bowl to the center of the toilet floor drain. You can do this with the old bowl in place by measuring from the wall to the center of either of the two hold-down bolts, one on each side of the toilet, that hold the fixture to the floor. If there are two bolts on each side, measure to the center of the rear bolt. Use this measurement when you buy the new toilet so that it will fit properly in your bathroom. You can replace your old toilet with a more modern fixture, but you must make sure that the new unit will fit into the space between the drainpipe and the wall. You can install a smaller unit—one that will leave a space between it and the wall—but you cannot put a larger toilet into the same space that was occupied by a smaller fixture.

Once you have the new toilet, shut off the water supply to the toilet tank, and then remove all the water from both the tank and the bowl. Trip the flush handle to eliminate most of the water from the tank, and then soak up whatever water is left with a sponge. Bail out the water in the bowl with a small container, and then sponge it dry.

If you're unclogging the toilet or fixing a leak at the base, you'll have to remove only the bowl, leaving the tank in place. Look to see whether there's a spud pipe between the bowl and the tank. This is a large pipe, found most frequently on older units, that's connected at both ends by a slip nut similar to the nuts that hold a sink trap. The nuts that hold the spud, however, are much larger than those on a sink. Use a spudwrench to remove the slip nuts. Once you loosen the slip nuts, slide them onto the spud itself. You should have just enough room now to remove the connecting pipe and then the bowl while the tank is still fastened to the wall.

What if there is no spud pipe, or if you want to remove the tank as well as the bowl? First, disconnect the water supply inlet pipe at the base of the tank. Older tanks are probably connected to the wall; newer tanks are most likely supported by the bowl. If the tank is connected to the wall, remove the hanger bolts inside the tank that secure the tank to the wall. Then remove the pair of bolts—if present—at the bottom of the tank that connect the tank to the bowl. Remove the tank and set it out of the way. Be sure to keep the rubber gaskets you find under all the bolts; you'll need them if you reinstall the old tank. With the tank removed from the wall mounting or the bowl support, you're ready to work on the bowl itself.

Remove the toilet seat; otherwise, it will get in your way as you work on the bowl. If there are caps over the hold-down bolts at the base of the bowl, take them off. Most of these caps are made of ceramic to match the bowl. Some types are held on by plumbers' joint compound and can be pried off with a putty knife; others are threaded and can be unscrewed. If you don't know which kind of caps are on your toilet, wrap the caps with masking tape to protect their finish, and try to unscrew them. If they don't come off this way, you'll have to pry them off. After removing the caps, brush away the dried compound before proceeding.

With the caps off, remove the hold-down nuts or bolts. These may be extremely stubborn, but some penetrating oil should make removal much easier. Be sure to save the washers and bolts if you will be rein-

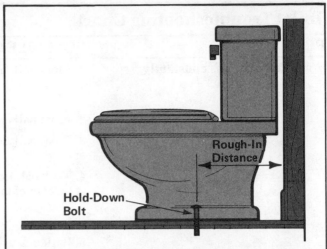

The rough-in distance can be measured with the toilet in place by measuring from the wall to the center of the hold-down bolt, or to the center of the rear bolt if the fixture is held by two pairs of bolts.

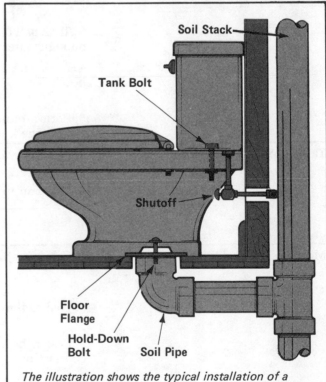

The illustration shows the typical installation of a two-piece floor-mounted toilet.

stalling the bowl. Once the hold-down nuts or bolts are out, there's nothing else holding the bowl to the floor. Because the bowl and the tank can crack from just one sharp blow to the porcelain, it's a good idea to spread an old piece of carpeting to put the fixtures on. You should also have a bucket and sponge handy to soak up the water you couldn't bail out earlier. With your work surface prepared, rock the bowl gently back and forth to loosen it, and then lift it straight up—it weighs about 60 or 70

Toilet Troubleshooting Chart

PROBLEM	POSSIBLE CAUSE	SOLUTION
Water in tank runs constantly	1. Float ball or rod is misaligned.	1. Bend float rod carefully to move ball so it will not rub against side of tank.
	2. Float ball contains water.	2. Empty or replace float ball.
	3. Float ball not rising high enough.	3. Carefully bend float rod down, but only slightly.
	4. Tank ball not sealing properly at bottom of tank.	4. Remove any corrosion from lip of valve seat. Replace tank ball if worn. Adjust lift wire and guide.
	5. Ballcock valve does not shut off water.	5. Replace washers in ballcock assembly or, if necessary, replace entire assembly.
Toilet does not flush or flushes inadequately	1. Drain is clogged.	1. Remove blockage in drain.
	2. Not enough water in tank.	2. Raise water level in tank by bending float rod up slightly.
	3. Tank ball falls back before enough water leaves tank.	3. Move guide up so that tank ball can rise higher.
	4. Leak where tank joins toilet bowl.	4. Tighten nuts on spud pipe; replace spud washers, if necessary.
	5. Ports around underside of bowl rim clogged.	5. Ream out residue from ports.
Tank whines while filling	1. Ballcock valve not operating properly.	1. Replace washers or install new ballcock assembly.
	2. Water supply is restricted.	2. Check shutoff to make sure it's completely open. Check for scale or corrosion at entry into tank and on valve.
Moisture around fixture	1. Condensation.	1. Install foam liner, tank cover, drip catcher, or temperator valve.
	2. Leak at flange wax seal.	2. Remove toilet and install new wax ring seal.
	3. Leak at bowl-tank connection.	3. Tighten spud pipe nuts; replace worn spud washers, if necessary.
	4. Leak at water inlet connection.	4. Tighten locknut and coupling nut; replace washers and gasket, if necessary.
	5. Crack in bowl or tank.	5. Remove bowl, tank, or entire fixture.

pounds. Set the bowl on the piece of carpeting.

With the toilet bowl out of the way, you'll find yourself looking down into an uncovered soil pipe. If you're dealing with a clog, the obstruction is probably somewhere in this pipe; you can now go on to clear the drain, as detailed below in the section "Clearing Clogged Drains." Once the pipe is clear, you can proceed with the replacement of the toilet. *Caution: To prevent sewer gas from backing up the soil pipe, you should plug the opening while you work. Tie a cord around an old towel so it won't fall through into the opening, and jam this plug into the soil pipe.*

As long as you're going to all the trouble of removing the toilet from its moorings, you might as well take the opportunity to consider any other work that might make your toilet function better than it does. For example, if the ballcock assembly has been malfunctioning, this is a good time to install a new one—especially since you've already done a great deal of the work in disconnecting the tank for removal.

Putting in a new toilet and reinstalling the old one are done in the same way. With a putty knife, scrape away all the old putty (or other sealing material) from both the bottom of the bowl and the metal or plastic floor flange. Inspect the floor where the toilet was. If the floor has rotted, it will have to be rebuilt before the toilet can be installed. Depending on how bad the damage is, the rebuilding may involve the floor, the subfloor, and even the joists. In this case, have a carpenter rebuild the damaged area before you install the toilet. Also inspect the flange and the bolts that come up from the flange. If the flange is damaged or the bolts are stripped, replace the faulty part or parts before you go any further. All of these parts are inexpensive, and it's far better to replace them than to try to get by with parts of doubtful quality.

The next step is to put a new sealer ring on the water outlet opening on the bottom of the new bowl; the best and easiest type to install is the wax toilet bowl gasket. With the fixture upside down, set the wax ring into place on the bottom of the bowl. If the floor flange is recessed, you'll need a gasket with a plastic sleeve in the wax; this sleeve faces toward you as you position it, since it will go into the soil pipe. Now apply a uniform layer of toilet-bowl setting compound—about 1/8 inch thick—around the edge of the bowl at the base. You can buy the compound at most hardware stores, and at all plumbing supply stores. With the gasket and the compound in place, remove the plug from the soil pipe. Turn the bowl right side up and place it down over the flange, guiding the bolts into place. Press down firmly, and give the bowl a slight twist to make sure the wax ring seats properly against the flange. It is very important that the bowl be level; check this by placing a level across the bowl. Either press down on any higher portion or insert thin wedges (you can hide them with toilet bowl compound) under any lower portion of the bowl to even it. Whatever you do, however, make sure you don't disturb or break the seal of the wax ring; if this seal is broken, the toilet will leak.

Once you get the bowl positioned properly, you can install the nuts to hold the bowl to the floor. Do *not* overtighten the nuts; if you do, you can crack the fixture. Hand-tightening is all that's required. Coat the holddown nuts and bolts with toilet bowl setting compound and reinstall the caps.

This completes the installation of the bowl; now you're ready to attach the tank. Rebolt a wall-mounted tank, or reinstall the bolts and washers that connect a bowl-supported tank. Naturally, before you put them

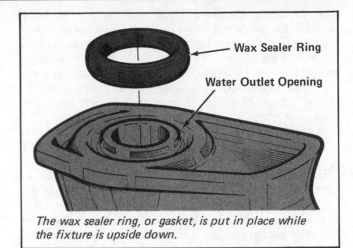

The wax sealer ring, or gasket, is put in place while the fixture is upside down.

back, make sure all washers, gaskets, and bolts are still in sound condition, and replace any damaged parts. If the tank and bowl are connected with a spud pipe, apply pipe joint compound to the threads of the spud slip nuts and tighten them in place. Finally, reconnect the water supply inlet pipe to the tank, make sure the ballcock assembly is properly attached, and turn the water back on.

Sink, Tub, and Drain Repairs

Many people who rush to call a plumber when a pipe springs a leak or a toilet clogs draw the line at calling in professional help when it comes to sinks and tubs. They feel that it takes no great expertise to fix a dripping faucet or to clear a slow drain—and they are right. Hopefully, you won't hesitate to tackle pipe problems and toilet troubles; certainly you should be able to take care of most sink and tub problems without paying for a plumber.

Specialized Tools

Most likely, you already own many of the tools necessary for working on sinks and tubs. For the most part, they are tools that can be used for many other do-it-yourself projects besides plumbing chores, or they are tools that are so well-known that no detailed explanation of them is needed. For example, a must for every household is the plumbers' friend, also called a plunger or a force pump. The best models have long handles, and their suction cups are large enough to cover different types of drain openings.

Plumbers' snakes, or drain-and-trap augers, come in various lengths; you should have both a short and a long one. When you buy an auger, look for one that comes encased in a metal housing—it's far less messy to use. A plumbers' tape looks like a long clock spring.

You'll need wrenches for most faucet repairs and for various other connections. A medium-size adjustable wrench is a fine tool to have, because it can be used on nuts of many different sizes; with one adjustable wrench you can handle the same tasks that would otherwise require a complete set of open-end wrenches. Open-end wrenches, however, do have an advantage over an adjustable wrench, because they provide a secure grip on the nut. Of course, you can frequently substitute a pair of long-handled slip-joint pliers for either kind of wrench.

A basin wrench is a specialized tool that allows you to reach tight spots under sinks and basins. The jaws of a basin wrench not only adjust to accommodate nuts of different sizes, but also flip over to the opposite side, so that you can keep turning without first removing the wrench. If you plan to work on tub and shower fixtures, there's a good chance that you'll need a socket wrench set to remove recessed packing nuts. If you don't already own a socket wrench set, it may not pay to buy one for this job; but you can find many uses for a socket wrench set besides plumbing chores.

Eliminating Faucet Drips

Although a dripping faucet is the most common plumbing problem—and one of the easiest to repair—many people try to ignore it, and leave the dripping faucet unrepaired. You may not think that a tiny drip is worth the effort to fix, but you'd be amazed to learn how much that tiny drip costs. A steady drip can add up to so many gallons over a year's time that it can end up costing $50 or more in wasted water. Multiply that figure by the number of faucet drips in your home, and you can calcu-

late how much of your money is literally going down the drain. If that isn't enough to convince you, just think about the drip that comes from a hot-water faucet; in that case, you're also paying to heat the water before you waste it.

A drip is caused by seepage from the water supply. Remember that the water supply enters your house or apartment under pressure. Therefore, there must be a watertight seal holding back the incoming water when the faucet handle is in the "off" position. That seal is usually created by a washer pressed tightly against the faucet seat. Obviously, when the washer or the seat is not functioning properly, a little water can seep through and drip out of the faucet spout. To stop the drip, all you usually have to do is replace the washer or repair the seat.

Naturally, the first thing to do when fixing a faucet drip is to turn off the water supply. You should be able to turn off the supply at a nearby shutoff; but if your house is not equipped with shutoffs for individual fixtures, you'll have to go to the main shutoff and turn off the entire water supply throughout your home.

Compression-Type Faucets. With the water flow stopped, you can start to disassemble the faucet. No matter what the faucet looks like, whether it has separate handles for hot and cold water or just one that operates both hot and cold, it operates according to certain basic principles. The first thing to do is to remove the faucet handle, which is held to the main body of the faucet by a tiny screw—either on the top or at the back of

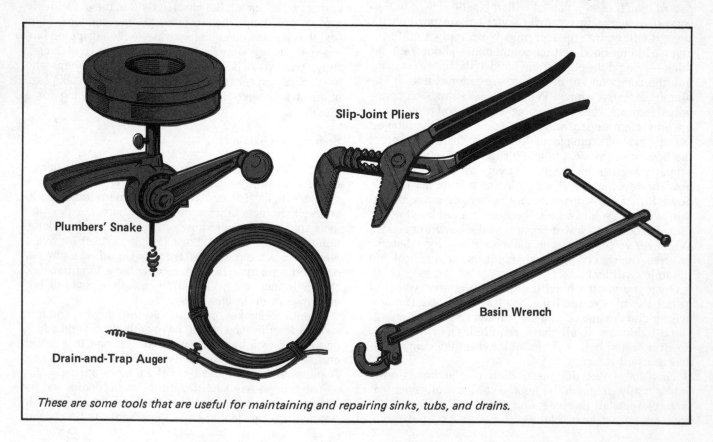

Slip-Joint Pliers

Plumbers' Snake

Drain-and-Trap Auger

Basin Wrench

These are some tools that are useful for maintaining and repairing sinks, tubs, and drains.

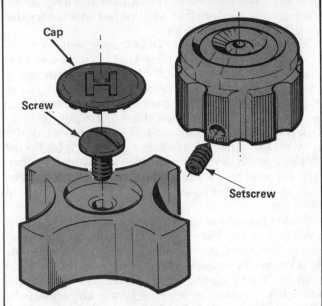

the handle. You may not be able to see a top-mounted screw at first, because some of them are hidden by a metal or plastic button or disc. These buttons usually snap out, although some are threaded. Once you get the button out, you'll see the top-mounted handle screw. If a handle's screw—no matter where it's located—is very hard to turn, use a little penetrating oil to help loosen it. Often, a standard blade or Phillips screwdriver can be used to remove the screw. Sometimes, however, the handle is secured by a setscrew; an Allen wrench (hex-key wrench) is required to loosen this type.

Take the handle off and look at the faucet assembly. You'll see a packing nut (sometimes called the bonnet); remove the nut with either a large pair of slip-joint pliers or an adjustable wrench, but take special care not to scar the metal. It's a good idea to wrap plastic tape around the packing nut to protect it from the teeth of your pliers or wrench. Once you get the packing nut off, twist out the stem (sometimes called the spindle) by turning it in the same direction—counterclockwise— you would to turn on the faucet.

You can see the washer at the base of the stem, but to remove it you must first take out the brass screw that holds it. That can be difficult, but some penetrating oil should make a stubborn brass screw much easier to remove. After you remove the screw, examine it to see whether it should be replaced along with the washer. If you can't get the brass screw out, don't despair; you can buy a whole new stem, if necessary.

Look for the size on the old washer. It is absolutely essential that you put on a replacement washer that is

Some faucets are secured by a screw on top, which may be hidden by a snap-out or threaded cap (left); others are secured by a setscrew (right).

exactly the right size; washers that *almost* fit will *almost* stop the drip. Also note whether the old washer is beveled or flat; the shape is important too. If you can't determine the precise size, take the whole stem with

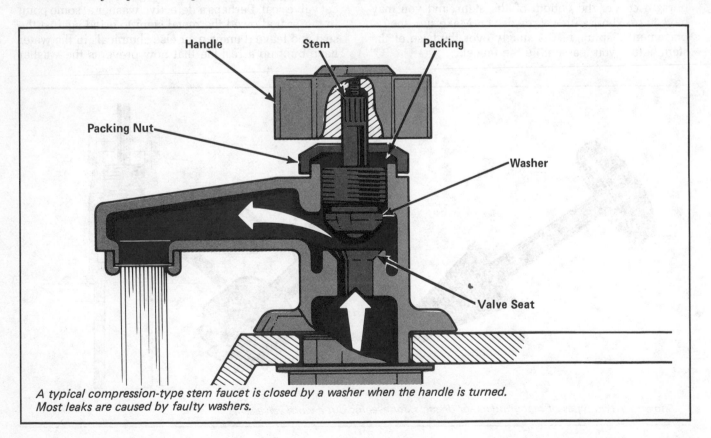

A typical compression-type stem faucet is closed by a washer when the handle is turned. Most leaks are caused by faulty washers.

you to the hardware store. You can also buy a big assortment pack of washers that contains just about every size and shape you might need.

Some washers, however, don't work well on a hot-water faucet. A washer designed only for cold water expands greatly when it gets hot, thereby closing the opening and slowing the flow of hot water. Perhaps you've experienced a hot-water faucet that works fine until the water gets quite hot and then slows to a trickle; its problem is the washer. Be sure to tell your hardware dealer whether the replacement washer you need is for the hot side or the cold side. Some washers will work for either. You can also buy a swivel-head washer with a fitting that snaps into the threaded screw hole in the base of the stem.

Fasten the new washer to the stem, and reinstall the assembly in the faucet. Turn the stem the same way you'd turn the faucet handle to stop the water flow (clockwise). With the stem in place, put the packing nut back on, but be careful not to scar the metal with the wrench. Once you screw on the handle and replace the button or disc, your faucet is completely reassembled. Turn the water supply back on, and you should find that your days of wasting water (and money) are over.

Other Types of Faucets. Instead of washers, some faucets use rubber diaphragms to control the flow of water. If you have this type of faucet, you may have to remove the faucet stem from the faucet body with a pair of pliers. Be sure to wrap the top of the stem with tape to protect it from the teeth of the pliers. The rubber diaphragm covers the bottom of the stem, and you may have to pry it off with a screwdriver. Make sure the replacement diaphragm fits snugly over the base of the stem before you reassemble the faucet.

Another type of faucet uses a rubber seat ring that acts like a washer. To remove it from the stem, hold the end of the faucet stem with pliers while you unscrew the threaded center piece that holds the seat ring in place. Remove the sleeve to insert the new seat ring, but be sure the seat ring's lettering faces the threaded part of the stem.

Cartridge-type stem faucets may have a spring and a rubber washer. To replace these, lift the cartridge out of the faucet body and remove the washer and spring from the faucet body. Insert the new spring and washer, and carefully align the cartridge so it fits correctly into the slots in the faucet body when reassembling it.

There are also faucets with washers that have the faucet seat built into the stem itself. This type of assembly lifts off the base in a removable sleeve, which contains the valve seat. Unscrew the stem nut from the base of the stem and remove the metal washer and the washer retainer, which contains a rubber washer. Insert the new washer—bevel side up—into the washer retainer.

One type of faucet doesn't have washers at all; it works by means of two metal discs. Turning the faucet on aligns holes in the discs and allows water to flow through the faucet. If something goes wrong with this type of faucet, the valve assembly must usually be replaced.

Repairing a Faucet Valve Seat. Sometimes a faucet may still drip after you've replaced a washer. This indicates that there may be something wrong with the faucet valve seat. Perhaps a defective washer at some point in the past allowed the metal stem to grind against the seat and leave it uneven, or else chemicals in the water have built up a residue that now prevents the washer

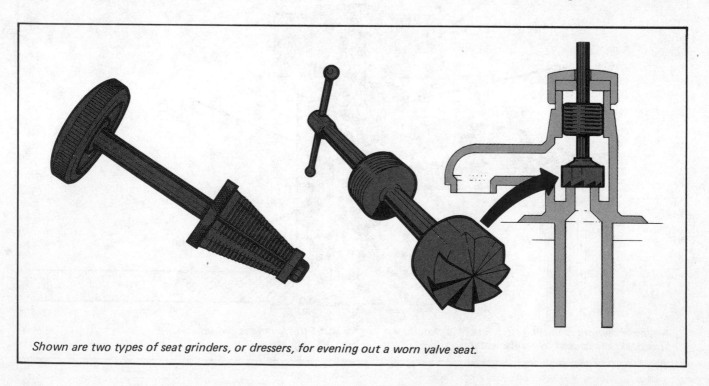

Shown are two types of seat grinders, or dressers, for evening out a worn valve seat.

from fitting tightly against the valve seat.

What do you do to repair a bad faucet seat? You can use a valve seat grinder, or dresser, an inexpensive tool that will even out a worn seat. But you must be careful not to use the tool too long or with too much force, because the seat is made of soft metal and you can grind too much of it away quite easily. To use this tool, remove the faucet stem and insert the seat grinder down to the valve seat in the faucet body. Using moderate pressure, turn the tool clockwise a few times. Then clean the valve seat with a cloth to remove any metal shavings.

The other thing you can do is to replace the seat—a necessity if you grind it down too far with the tool. Removal of the old valve seat is fairly simple if you have the right tool, called a seat wrench. Just insert the seat wrench into the seat and turn it counterclockwise. Once you get the old seat out, be sure the replacement seat you buy is an exact duplicate. On occasion, you may discover that the valve seat is impossible to remove; in this case, you can insert a seat sleeve, which slides into place in the old seat and provides a tight seal.

Stopping Faucet Leaks

A drip occurs when the faucet is turned off; a faucet leak occurs when the water is running. If you see water coming out around the handle, you have a faucet leak.

The first thing to do is make sure the faucet's packing nut is tight, but be careful not to scratch the nut with pliers or a wrench. If you find a loose nut is not causing the leak, you should replace the packing. Faucet packing can be a solid piece of packing; it can consist of one or more rubber O-rings; or it can resemble string or soft wire wrapped around the stem under the packing nut.

To replace the packing, shut off the water supply and remove the faucet handle. Loosen the packing nut and slip both the nut and the old packing up off the stem. Put the new packing on. If you use the string-like packing material, wrap a few turns around the stem; packing that resembles soft wire is wrapped around the stem only once. Before you finish reassembling the faucet, smear a light coat of petroleum jelly on the threads of the stem and on the threads of the packing nut.

Kitchen faucets—the kind where the spout swings from side to side—present a somewhat different situation. These faucets have one or more O-rings to prevent water from oozing out around the spout. If the ring wears out, you'll see water at the base of the spout every time you turn on the water. To replace an O-ring, shut off the water supply and remove the threaded coupling nut that holds the spout in place by turning it counterclockwise. Be sure to wrap the nut with tape to prevent scratching it with pliers or a wrench. With the coupling nut removed, work the spout up and out of its socket, where you will find the ring(s). Replace the defective ring(s); be sure to use exactly the same size. Then reassemble the faucet.

Single-lever faucets are easy to fix too, but there are so many different types that you must buy a specific re-

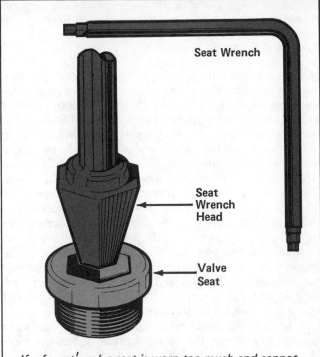

If a faucet's valve seat is worn too much and cannot be evened out with a seat grinder, it can usually be removed with a seat wrench.

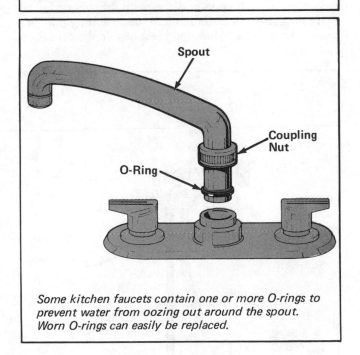

Some kitchen faucets contain one or more O-rings to prevent water from oozing out around the spout. Worn O-rings can easily be replaced.

pair kit for the faucet you have. Generally, a faucet company makes repair kits for its products, and includes detailed instructions and diagrams with the replacement parts. The hardest part of repairing a single-lever faucet may be tracking down the hardware dealer or plumbing supply store that carries the appropriate kit. Once you have the kit, however, you should have little difficulty in eliminating the leak. Just make sure the water supply is shut off before disassembling the faucet, and follow the kit's instructions carefully.

Silencing Noisy Faucets

Faucets can scream, whistle, or chatter when you turn them on or off. There are several possible causes for these ear-shattering phenomena. If your house is newly built, you may have pipes that are too small to allow the water to pass through them properly. Similarly, pipes in older homes can become restricted by the formation of scale, with the same result—a noisy faucet. In either case, you must replace the pipes to get rid of the noise.

Most likely, however, your noisy faucet is caused by a washer, either the wrong size or not held securely to the stem. Turn off the water supply before starting this or any other faucet repair job. Just replace the washer, or tighten it, and you should eliminate the noise. If the faucet still makes noise, check the washer seat; the seat can become partially closed with residue, and the restricted water flow can cause whistling or chattering. If this is the case, clean the seat.

A terrible squealing noise when you turn the faucet handle means that the metal threads of the stem are binding against the faucet's threads. Remove the stem and coat both sets of threads with petroleum jelly. The lubrication should stop the noise and make the handle easier to turn. Of course, if the stem threads or faucet body threads have become worn, the resulting play between them causes vibration and noise in the faucet. In

Stub-Out

Flexible Tube

Basin Wrench

Shutoff Valve

Because there is very little room under the sink, you will probably need a basin wrench to tighten the coupling nuts.

this case, you'll need more than just lubrication to quiet the faucet. Install a new stem and see if the noise stops. If not, the faucet body threads are worn, and the only solution is a completely new faucet. Fortunately, the stem is the part that usually wears first; but even if you must replace the entire faucet, you'll find the job fairly easy.

Replacing a Faucet

Replacing a faucet—for either functional or aesthetic reasons—gets you into a little more work than just changing a washer or putting in a new faucet valve seat. Fortunately, new faucet units are made for do-it-yourself installation, with easy-to-follow instructions included. A new faucet can work wonders for the appearance of your fixtures, and—even better—it will eliminate all the leaks, drips, and other problems you may have had with your old one.

Suppose, for example, you want to replace the old faucet on your kitchen sink with a modern single-handle unit. Just make sure whatever unit you choose will cover the old faucet's mounting holes. Generally this is no great problem, but some sinks—especially older ones—can be somewhat unusual. If you have an unusual sink, look for an adjustable faucet unit that's made to fit many types of sinks. Once you select the faucet model you want, follow this general procedure to install it properly.

Turn off both hot- and cold-water supplies to the sink faucets. Disconnect the old faucets from their water supply lines under the sink. The connections will probably be threaded compression fittings that are held by locknuts. Loosen the nuts with an adjustable wrench or basin wrench, and disconnect the water supply pipes from the faucets.

The old faucets are probably held in place by nuts under the sink. Loosen and remove these nuts. In most cases, the nuts are almost impossible to remove without a basin wrench.

If the old assembly has a spray head and hose, remove the spray head mounting nut under the sink; also disconnect the hose from its spout connection. Now you should be able to completely remove the old faucet assembly from the sink. Clean the sink around the faucet mounting area.

Before you install the new faucet, apply plumbers' putty around its base; if gaskets are supplied with the faucet for this purpose, putty is not necessary. Then insert the new faucet assembly into the mounting holes in the sink.

If the new faucet has a spray hose, it's generally a good idea to attach the hose first, if possible. Run the spray hose down through its opening in the faucet assembly, through its opening in the sink, and up through the sink's center opening. Then attach the hose to the supply stub on the faucet.

With the new faucet assembly in position, place the washers and nuts on the assembly's mounting studs under the sink and hand-tighten them, making sure the assembly is in proper position and any gaskets are correctly aligned. Then tighten the nuts with a basin wrench.

Align the original water supply lines with the flexible supply tubes coming from the new faucet, and connect them with compression couplings. Make sure the hot- and cold-water lines are connected to the proper supply tubes on the faucet assembly. When you attach the lines, be sure to use two wrenches—one to hold the fitting, the other to turn the nut on the water supply line.

If the combined length of the old and new supply lines is inconveniently long, you can cut off a portion of the original lines before attaching the coupling. Conversely, if the new supply tubes reach all the way to the shutoff valves under the sink, the tubes can be connected directly to the valves with a compression fitting. Also, on some installations, you may need adapters or transition fittings to join different size supply lines and tubes or to connect one type of pipe to another.

Now turn on the hot- and cold-water supplies to the fixture, and run both hot and cold water full-force to clear the supply lines and to check the fixture for leaks. If there's any evidence of leakage, go back over the procedure to check for loose or improper connections.

A bathroom lavatory faucet can be replaced using essentially the same procedures. One difference may be the presence of a pop-up drain that's connected by a linkage to a knob or plunger on the old faucet assembly. There should be one or two places in the linkage where it can be easily disconnected from the faucet before removing the original unit from the basin; the instructions provided with the new faucet will tell you exactly how to connect the new drain assembly. Be sure to reconnect the drain linkage when installing the new faucet.

Shower and tub faucets can be a bit more complicated because the connections are made not under a sink but behind a wall. Whoever built your home should have provided an access panel so that you can get at the pipes without ripping the wall apart. If you find that you must cut into the wall, however, be sure to add an access panel for future pipe and faucet repairs.

Actually, once you get to the tub faucet connections behind the wall, the job is no harder than working on your kitchen sink. Just shut off the water supply, remove the faucet handle on the tub side, and then disconnect the old faucet unit from the back. If there's an old shower head pipe, unscrew it from its pipe inside the wall; do the same thing with the tub spout. Now you're ready to install all the new parts. Just follow the directions that are included with the new assembly.

Repairing a Spray Hose

Many modern sink faucets are fitted with spray hose units, and these units occasionally leak or malfunction. The assembly consists of a special diverter valve located within the spout body, a flexible hose connected to the spout under the sink, and a spray head with an activating lever and an aerator assembly. The spray

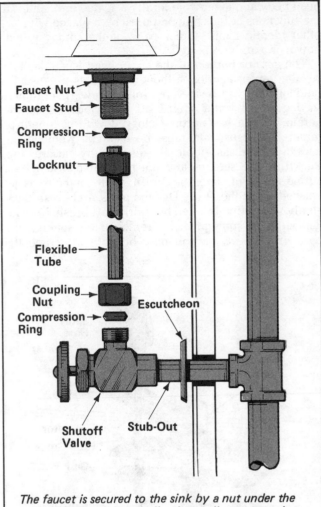

The faucet is secured to the sink by a nut under the basin. The water supply line is usually connected to the faucet with a threaded compression fitting.

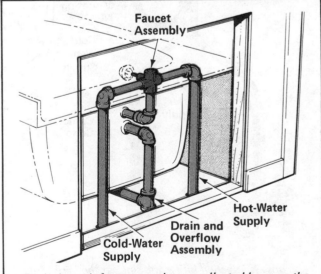

Replacing tub faucets can be complicated because the connections are behind a wall. There may, however, be an access panel so you can reach the connections.

head body and lever is generally a sealed unit, and if it malfunctions or fails, the unit must be replaced with another identical unit. Other parts of the spray system, however, can be repaired.

The aerator portion of the spray head is similar to a regular faucet aerator, although the parts are usually held together with a small retaining screw. If aeration is inadequate or water squirts off at various angles, the aerator screen has become clogged with sediment or mineral deposits, and must be cleaned. Remove the aerator and disassemble it—usually by unscrewing. Backflush the screens and the perforated disc with a strong stream of water; be careful not to let the parts get washed down the drain. Dry the parts, and brush them gently with a fine-bristled but fairly stiff brush. Mineral deposits can sometimes be removed by soaking the parts in vinegar, or you may be able to scrape the

deposits away with a penknife. Reassemble the aerator, making sure that you get all of the parts positioned in the proper order and direction.

Water dripping off the flexible hose beneath the sink indicates a leak at the hose-to-spout connection, the hose-to-spray-head connection, or somewhere in the hose itself. Dry the hose thoroughly and check the head connection; this may or may not be repairable. If the leak is at this point, tighten the connection, disassemble and make repairs, or replace the head and hose assembly. Next, check the spout connection under the sink. Tightening may stop a leak here; otherwise, disconnect the hose, apply plumbers' joint compound or wrap plumbers' joint tape around the threads, and reconnect it. The easiest way to spot a leak in the hose is to inspect it inch by inch under a strong light while water is running through it. Look particularly for tiny cracks, chafes, or indications of some mechanical damage. Temporary repairs can be made by wrapping a slightly damaged section of hose with vinyl electrical tape, but replacement of the hose will eventually be necessary.

Uneven water flow, low pressure when the pressure at other faucets seems all right, or troublesome switching back and forth from spray head to sink spout can be caused by a malfunctioning diverter valve or by a restricted hose. To check the hose, remove the spray head at the coupling—if possible—and disconnect the coupling from the hose by prying off the snap-ring retainer. Turn on the water and let a strong stream of water flow into the hose. If a strong stream of water flows out of the open end of the hose, then you know the diverter valve is the source of the trouble. A weak stream flowing from the open end of the hose may indicate a blockage in the hose itself. Running the water full-force for a brief time may clear the hose. If not, remove the hose from the spout attachment, stretch it out straight, and sight through it toward a strong light source. If the hose appears to be clear, the problem lies in the diverter valve. If the hose is blocked, you may be able to clear it with a wire coat hanger or a length of wire. Failing that, replace the hose; if you can't get an exact replacement, adapters are available for connecting other types and sizes.

To service the diverter valve, you must first remove the sink spout: loosen the screw on top, unscrew the threaded spout ring or nut, and lift the spout out of its socket. This exposes the valve. Some valves are just set in place, and can be lifted straight out by gripping them with a pair of pliers; others are secured by a screw. If there is a screw, turn it enough to free the valve. If possible, disassemble the valve. Flush all the parts with water and clean all the surfaces and apertures with a toothpick—never use metal instruments; they could damage the unit. Reassemble and reinstall the valve, and test the unit. If it still operates poorly, you will probably have to replace the valve. The replacement must be exact, so take the faucet manufacturer's name and the unit model number, or the old valve, along when you buy a new valve.

The hose is attached under the sink, at the base of the spout assembly. The entire spray assembly can be removed from the top of the sink, by unscrewing it and pulling it out through the hose guide.

Fixing Shower Heads

Shower heads are subject to several problems. Leaks, for instance, can occur where the head connects to the shower arm (the curved, chrome-plated pipe that protrudes from the wall), or at the connection between the shower head body and the swivel ball. If the arm connection leaks, unscrew the entire shower head from the pipe, using a pair of strap wrenches if necessary. If you use the other types of wrenches, tape the pipe to avoid scratching it. Clean the arm threads and coat them with plumbers' joint compound or a wrap of plumbers' joint tape. Screw the shower head back and hand-tighten it only. Remove any excess compound or tape. If the leak is at the swivel, unscrew the shower head body from the swivel ball ring; you'll find an O-ring or a similar seal inside. Replace it and screw the shower head back into place.

Problems can also be caused by grit or sediment lodged in the head or by a buildup of scale or mineral deposits. The solution is to remove the shower head body at the swivel ball, take it completely apart, and start cleaning. Soaking in vinegar may be necessary for some parts, scraping for others, but be careful not to scratch or gouge anything. If the shower head is of the adjustable-spray type, examine all of the moving parts carefully for signs of excessive wear. If the adjustment handle binds or does not work smoothly, or the internal cam is fouled up, usually the only solution is to replace the entire head.

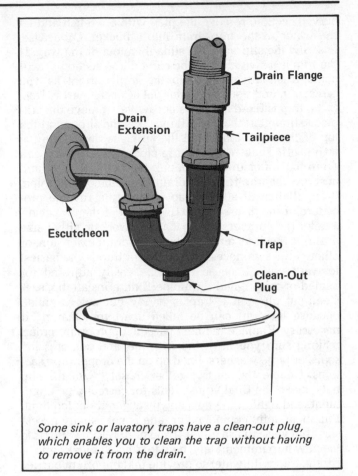

Some sink or lavatory traps have a clean-out plug, which enables you to clean the trap without having to remove it from the drain.

Replacing a Trap

Directly beneath the drain outlet of your kitchen sink, and every bathroom lavatory, is the trap. This element is vital not only to the proper functioning of the drainage system, but to your health and safety as well. Each trap contains, and maintains, a plug of water within its curved section that acts as a seal against the entrance of harmful sewer gases. If the trap leaks, this water barrier may disappear and create a hazardous situation. All traps must be kept in proper working order and good condition. Restrictions and clogging are immediately noticeable, because the drainage flow is slowed or stopped; clearing the blockage takes care of the problem. Leakage or seepage can often go undetected for a time, so check your traps from time to time and make quick repairs if anything seems wrong.

Trap assemblies are comprised of several parts. The short piece of pipe that extends downward from the drain outlet flange in the sink or lavatory is the tailpiece. The curved section of pipe connected to the tailpiece is the trap itself; it may be one piece or two coupled sections. The piece of pipe extending from the end of the trap to the drainpipe outlet in the wall or floor is the drain extension; it may be straight or curved. All of these pieces may be made of rather thin metal—often chrome-plated brass—and they are subject to eventual corrosion, failure of seals, and sometimes, in the case of exposed traps, mechanical damage. Damage

can also result from frequent reaming with a plumbers' auger. Whatever the reasons for failure, a malfunctioning trap should be repaired immediately.

Sometimes the problem is simply that the slip nuts that hold the trap assembly together and secure it to the drain and the drainpipe have loosened; just tightening them may solve the problem. But if the metal has corroded through, the slip-nut threads are damaged, or other damage has occurred, the only solution is replacement. Trap assemblies and parts to fit just about any possible installation requirement are readily available at most hardware and all plumbing supply stores. Chrome-plated thin-wall brass traps are popular, especially where appearance is important. Polypropylene (PP) plastic traps, notable for their ruggedness and longevity, will outperform all other types. ABS plastic traps are also in use, but they deform and eventually fail when handling frequent passage of boiling water and caustic household chemicals—and they may not be allowed by your local plumbing code. Whatever the material, you're likely to encounter two trap diameters—$1\frac{1}{2}$-inch traps for kitchen sinks, and $1\frac{1}{4}$-inch traps for lavatories. Take the old trap with you when you buy the new one; if possible, also take the old tailpiece and drain extension.

In most cases, trap replacement is simple. If the trap is equipped with a clean-out plug on the bottom of the curved section, remove the plug with a wrench and let the water in the trap drain into a bucket. Otherwise, unscrew the slip nuts and slide them out of the way. If the trap is a swivel type, the curved trap section(s) will come free. However, keep the trap upright as you remove it, and pour the water out after the part is free. If the trap is fixed and does not swivel, remove the tail-piece slip nut at the drain flange and the slip nut at the top of the trap, and shove the tailpiece down into the trap itself. Then twist the trap clockwise until you can drain the water in the trap, pull the tailpiece free, and unscrew the trap from the drain extension or drainpipe.

Installation of a new trap is merely a reverse procedure of the disassembly. Buy a trap of the proper diameter (or a universal type that will work on either size drain), as well as a new tailpiece, a drain extension, or other fittings as necessary. A swivel trap is the easiest to work with, because it can be easily adjusted for angled or misaligned drainpipe/fixture installations. A clean-out plug on a trap is handy but not essential, because the trap can be taken apart for cleaning if necessary. Replace the new parts in appropriate order, making sure you have the slip nuts and compression seals, or large washers, lined up on the proper pipe sections. Couple the parts together loosely with the slip nuts, make the final adjustments for correct pipe alignment, and tighten the nuts down snug, but not too tight. Plumbers' joint compound or tape is not usually necessary, but you can use either if you prefer. Run water into the new trap immediately, both to check for leaks and to fill the trap with water to provide that important barrier against sewer gases.

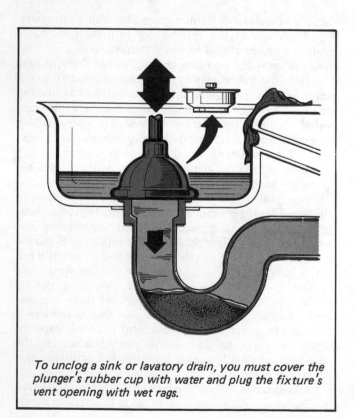

To unclog a sink or lavatory drain, you must cover the plunger's rubber cup with water and plug the fixture's vent opening with wet rags.

Clearing Clogged Drains

Of the two most common plumbing problems—dripping faucets and clogged drains—the latter is undoubtedly the one that receives the most attention. Most people don't realize how much a drip costs them, but everyone knows the inconvenience and mess that accompany a sluggish drain. Even so, many people wait until the drain stops completely before they take corrective action.

When you do take corrective action, you must know what to do, and in most cases that means knowing how to use one of the best drain-clearing tools of them all: the plumbers' friend, or rubber plunger. Working a plunger requires no special training or expertise, but if the plunger is to do its job properly, you must know a few basic facts. Otherwise, you'll follow the familiar pattern: pump up and down two or three times, step back to see what happens, and then go on to other drain-clearing devices—or even call in a plumber—when the water fails to whoosh out the drain.

If you expect to clear a clogged drain with a plunger, the suction cup must be large enough to cover the drain opening completely. Second, the water in the sink or tub must cover the plunger's cup completely. Third—and undoubtedly the most neglected aspect of using this tool—you must block off all the other outlets between the drain and the blockage. If you don't block off the outlets, all the pressure you create will be dissipated long before it can get to the clog.

For clogged lavatory, sink, and tub drains, use this procedure with the plunger. First, cover the overflow opening in the basin or tub with a wet cloth. Most kitchen sinks don't have an overflow vent, but if you're working on one of two side-by-side basins, you'll have to plug the other basin's drain opening with wet cloths. In addition, there may be yet another drain outlet connected to the drain line you're working on, and this outlet must be blocked too—you'll find this out if the water starts backing up in the unsuspected outlet. For example, in homes that have two bathrooms back to back in adjacent rooms, there's a good chance that both are connected to the same drain. In such cases you must block the other basin at both its drain and its overflow vent. Shower facilities seldom have overflow vents, but bathtubs do have vents, and laundry tubs may have two or three. You must cover all of them with wet cloths for your plunger to work properly.

Next, fill the clogged basin with enough water to cover the head of the plunger. Coat the lip of the plunger with petroleum jelly; this assures a better seal. *Slide* the plunger's cup over the drain opening; then rapidly pump the plunger up and down. You should feel the water move in and out of the drain. It is this back-and-forth water pressure that can eventually build up enough force to dislodge whatever is blocking the drain. After about a dozen firm strokes, jerk the plunger up quickly. The water should rush out. If it doesn't, try the same procedure two or three more times before attempting another method.

If the plunger doesn't remove the clog in your drain, you'll have to try another method. Many people often turn to a chemical drain opener, in either dry or liquid form. In a drain that's completely blocked, however, it's best not to use chemicals. For one thing, most chemical drain cleaners contain caustic agents that can harm fixtures. Moreover, if you must later remove a trap or clean-out to free the blockage, you will be exposed to the harmful solution.

Instead, your safest course is to resort to a drain-and-trap auger. To use it, remove the pop-up stopper or strainer from the clogged drain, and insert the auger wire into the opening. As you feed the flexible wire in, crank the handle of the device clockwise, loosening and then tightening the thumbscrew on the handle as you advance the wire. If the wire encounters something, move it back and forth while you turn the auger handle. Then continue to turn the handle while withdrawing the auger slowly.

If the auger has cleared the drain of most of the debris inside, you can pour hot, soapy water into the drain to remove any remaining debris. If the auger didn't work, proceed to the trap to unclog the drain.

If the trap under the basin is equipped with a clean-out, remove the clean-out plug, catching the water in the trap in a bucket. You can use a wire coat hanger with a hook shaped in one end to try to reach the clog. If this

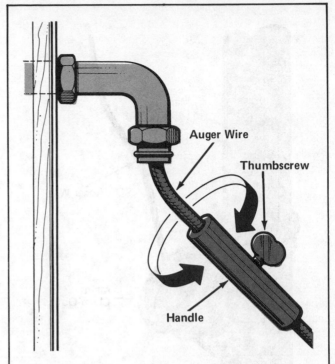

If the clog is not in the fixture's trap, insert a drain-and-trap auger into the drain extension that goes into the wall, and work the auger into the drainpipe.

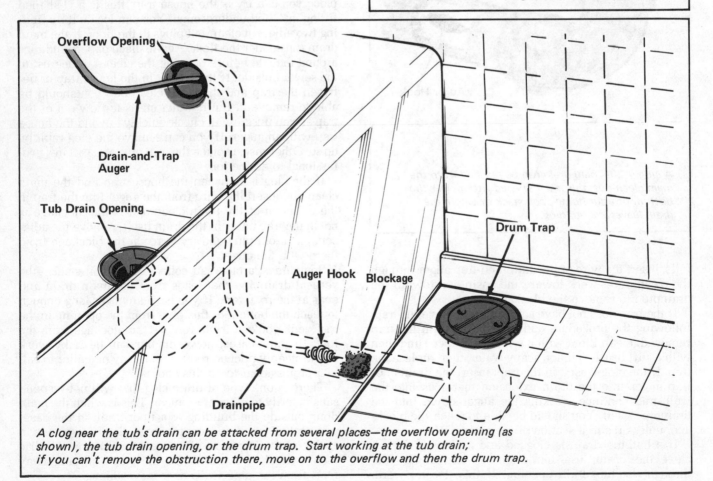

A clog near the tub's drain can be attacked from several places—the overflow opening (as shown), the tub drain opening, or the drum trap. Start working at the tub drain; if you can't remove the obstruction there, move on to the overflow and then the drum trap.

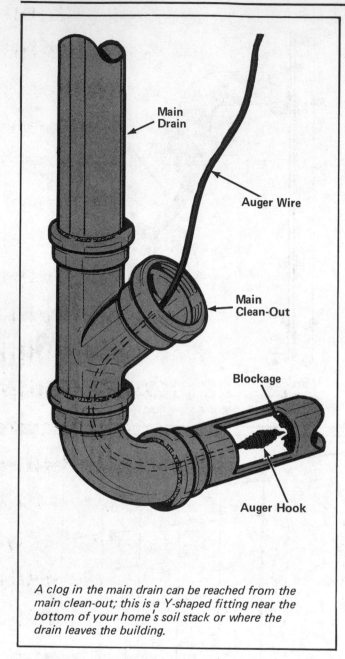

Main Drain

Auger Wire

Main Clean-Out

Blockage

Auger Hook

A clog in the main drain can be reached from the main clean-out; this is a Y-shaped fitting near the bottom of your home's soil stack or where the drain leaves the building.

remove the overflow plate and insert the auger directly into the overflow pipe and down into the drainpipe.

Some older bathtubs have a drum trap. Usually, the drum trap is near the tub at floor level. Unscrew the lid of the drum trap counterclockwise with an adjustable wrench, and clean out the trap. If the debris is elsewhere, try to reach it through the drum trap with the drain-and-trap auger.

For floor drains, such as those in basements and showers, a garden hose can be effective in unclogging drains, especially if the clog is not close to the opening. Attach the hose to a faucet, feed the hose into the drain as far as it will go, and jam rags around the hose at the opening. Then turn the water on full-force for a few moments.

If you suspect a clog is in the main drainpipe, locate the main clean-out; this is a Y-shaped fitting near the bottom of your home's soil stack, or where the drain leaves the building. Set a large pail or container under the clean-out and spread plenty of papers and rags around the site to soak up the backed-up water. Using a pipe wrench, slowly unscrew the clean-out plug counterclockwise, trying to control the flow of water that will seep from the clean-out. Once the flow has stopped and you've cleaned up the flooded site, insert the auger to remove the debris.

If you still haven't located the blockage, another place you can try is the house trap; this is a U-shaped fitting installed underground. You can locate it by finding two adjacent clean-out plugs in the floor, if the main drain runs under the floor. Again, place papers and rags around the site before opening the clean-out nearest to the sewer outside. If the clog is in the house trap or between the trap and the main clean-out, you should be able to remove it. But if water starts to flow out of the trap as you unscrew it, check quickly beyond the house trap with an auger. If you can remove the clog rapidly, do so. Otherwise, replace the trap plug and call in a professional to do the job.

If the clog is between the house trap and the main clean-out, insert the wire from the auger into the trap in the direction of the main clean-out. If the blockage is not in the trap but is in the drain itself, remove the adjacent clean-out plug and try to reach the blockage from there with the auger.

Sometimes, a clog can collect in the soil stack—the vertical drainpipe that leads from the main drain and ends at the roof vent. If you have an auger long enough to reach the bottom of this pipe from the opening in the roof vent, you can try to remove the blockage from the roof. In some cases, however, this can be risky work due to steeply pitched roofs, and it may be better to call in a professional to do this chore.

There is one type of drain clog that will not respond satisfactorily to plunger or auger. This is when the main drain outside the building or a floor drain in the basement gets stopped up from tree roots that have grown in at the joints. The most effective solution is an electric rooter, which is inserted into the pipe and cuts away roots from the pipe walls as it moves along.

fails, insert the wire of the drain-and-trap auger through the clean-out—work toward the basin and toward the drainpipe to remove the blockage.

If the trap does not have a clean-out, remove the trap, following the procedure outlined above. With the trap removed, clean it out with a wire coat hanger and then with a stiff brush and hot, soapy water; then replace the trap. If the clog wasn't in the trap, insert the drain-and-trap auger into the drain extension that goes into the wall, and continue working the auger down into the drainpipe itself. You should be able to reach the blockage, unless it's in a section of the main drain.

If a bathtub drain is clogged and a plunger doesn't clear the drain, use the drain-and-trap auger first through the tub drain opening. If this doesn't work,

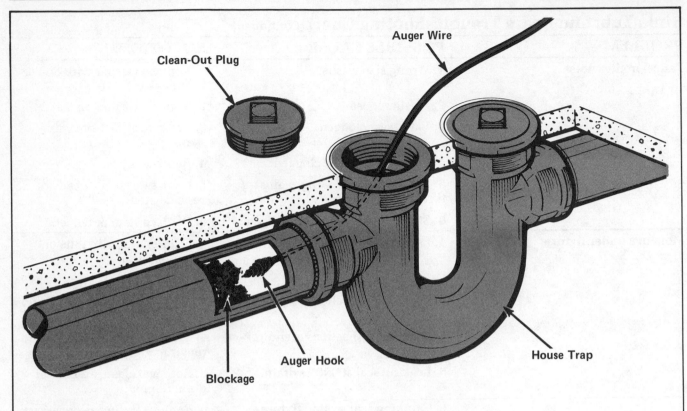

The house trap is a U-shaped fitting installed underground. You can locate it by finding two adjacent clean-out plugs in the basement floor. A blockage between the trap and the main clean-out can be reached by removing the plug closest to the main clean-out.

You can rent one of these power augers at a tool-rental firm. Feed the auger cable into the clean-out opening closest to the blockage. When the device's cutting head encounters roots, you should be able to feel the cable strain. Keep feeding the cable slowly until you feel a breakthrough; then go over the area once again.

Remove the cable slowly and run water from a garden hose through the pipe to wash away the root cuttings. Before you return the power auger to the rental firm, replace the clean-out plug and flush a toilet several times. When you're sure the drain is clear of tree roots, clean the cable and return the machine.

Sink, Tub, and Drain Troubleshooting Chart

PROBLEM	POSSIBLE CAUSE	SOLUTION
Faucet drips	1. Faulty washer.	1. Replace washer. For single-handled faucet, install all parts in repair kit.
	2. Uneven valve seat.	2. Use valve seat grinder to even seat, or replace seat.
	3. Worn stem or cartridge parts.	3. Replace stem assembly.
Hot water slows to trickle	1. Washer expands when hot.	1. Replace with proper nonexpanding washer.
Leaks around faucet handle	1. Packing nut loose.	1. Tighten packing unit.
	2. Inadequate packing.	2. Replace packing.
Leaks around faucet spout	1. Faulty O-ring.	1. Replace O-ring.

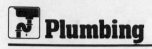

Sink, Tub, and Drain Troubleshooting Chart (Continued)

PROBLEM	POSSIBLE CAUSE	SOLUTION
Faucet makes noise	1. Wrong size washer.	1. Replace washer with one of proper size.
	2. Washer loose.	2. Tighten washer on stem.
	3. Valve seat clogged.	3. Clean residue from valve seat.
	4. Pipes too small or clogged.	4. Replace pipes.
	5. Stem threads binding against threads in faucet body.	5. Lubricate stem threads or replace stem.
	6. Stem or body threads damaged.	6. Replace stem or faucet.
Moisture under fixture	1. Leaking trap joints.	1. Tighten trap slip nuts or clean-out plug.
	2. Leaking trap.	2. Replace trap.
	3. Leaking connections at fixture.	3. Tighten, or disassemble and repair.
	4. Leaking connections at shutoff valves.	4. Tighten, or disassemble and repair.
	5. Leaking seal at fixture drain.	5. Remove, clean, and reseal drain flange.
	6. Caulking seal around fixture rim faulty—splash water seeping.	6. Remove fixture as necessary and recaulk.
Spray hose does not function properly	1. Spray head body or level malfunction.	1. Replace spray head.
	2. Spray head aerator clogged.	2. Disassemble and clean aerator.
	3. Hose damaged or connection loose.	3. Repair or replace hose; tighten connections.
	4. Hose clogged.	4. Remove blockage; replace hose, if necessary.
	5. Diverter valve clogged or damaged.	5. Disassemble and clean valve; if necessary, replace valve.
Shower head leaks	1. Connection at arm loose or corroded.	1. Tighten; or remove head from arm, clean, coat with plumbers' joint compound, and retighten.
	2. Swivel connection O-ring or other seal in poor condition.	2. Replace O-ring or other seal and retighten.
Shower head water flow restricted	1. Shower head clogged.	1. Disassemble and clean head.
Shower head adjustment handle binds or does not operate	1. Internal cam broken or other mechanical damage.	1. Replace shower head.
Drains overflowing	1. Pipes or trap clogged.	1. Use plunger or auger to clear pipes or trap.
Drain sluggish with sucking noises	1. Drain flow restricted.	1. Clean drain.
	2. Vent restricted.	2. Clean vent.
	3. Improper venting.	3. Install vent or larger vent.

Electricity

Nothing seems to draw the line between primitive and advanced living conditions quite so clearly as the possession of such electrically powered devices as lamps, appliances, and home entertainment systems. We depend on electricity for more than just luxury and convenience items; we look to our electric system to maintain our high standard of modern living.

Despite our dependence on electricity, many of us would be hard pressed to explain just how our home power systems work. We plug appliances into outlets, flip switches, adjust dials, slide levers—and do all of

this without a moment's thought as to how an electrical system actually functions. Most of us would be totally confounded if we had to fix an electrical component that doesn't work the way it should.

This is a shameful situation. Although electricity and electrical theory can be difficult to learn in depth, practical electricity, as it applies to a residential wiring system, is neither hard to understand nor hard to work with. Indeed, there are plenty of good reasons for learning how your home's electrical system works, how you can fix it, and how you can improve its usefulness. You

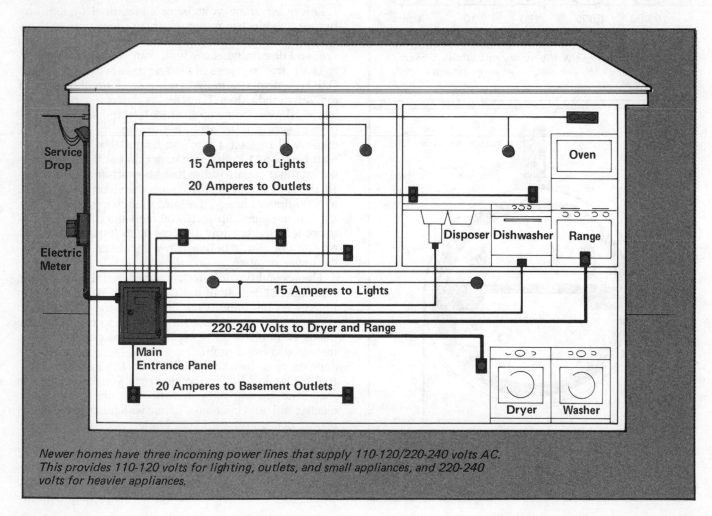

Newer homes have three incoming power lines that supply 110-120/220-240 volts AC. This provides 110-120 volts for lighting, outlets, and small appliances, and 220-240 volts for heavier appliances.

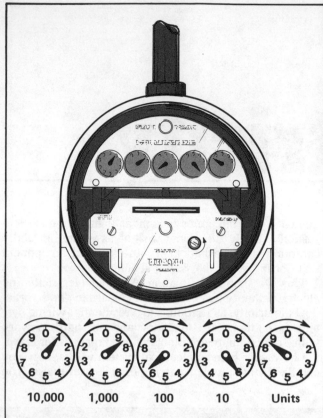

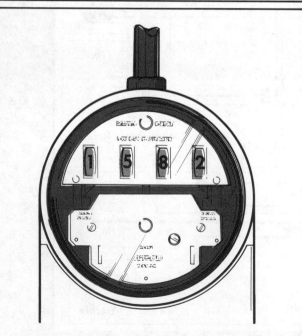

| 10,000 | 1,000 | 100 | 10 | Units |

One common type of electric meter displays a series of dials; they register the number of kilowatt-hours used. Some dials run clockwise, some counter-clockwise.

Another type of electric meter works like a car's odometer; numerals in a series of slots register the kilowatt-hours used. This type of meter reads from left to right.

can save yourself plenty of money by making your own repairs. In addition, your family's safety could well depend on your knowledge.

How the Electrical System Works

On the surface, your home's plumbing and electrical systems may seem as different as any two things could be. But there are significant parallels. Water enters your home through a pipe, under pressure (hydraulic pressure, measured in pounds per square inch), and when you turn on a tap, the water flows at a certain rate (gallons per minute). Electricity enters your home through copper (or aluminum, and sometimes both) wires, also under pressure—electrical pressure, called electromotive force or voltage, measured in volts. When you turn on an electrical device, the electricity flows at a certain rate; this is current, measured in amperes, or amps. But unlike water, which is used as it comes from the tap, electricity is meant to do work; it is converted from energy to power, measured in watts. Since household electrical consumption is relatively high, the unit of measure most often used is the kilowatt, 1,000 watts. The total amount of electrical energy that you use in any period is measured in terms of kilowatt-hours (kwh).

Before we trace your home's electrical system any further, the electric meter deserves consideration. This is the instrument that records how much electricity you use, and determines how high your electric bill is.

There are two types of electric meters in general use. One type displays on its face a row of small dials with individual indicators. Each dial registers a certain number of kilowatt-hours of electrical energy. For example, if you leave a 100-watt bulb burning for 10 hours, the meter will register 1 kilowatt-hour (10 × 100 = 1,000 watt-hours, or 1 kwh). The meter dial at the far right is the one that counts individual kilowatt-hours from 1 to 10; the next one to the left counts the electricity from 10 to 100 kilowatt-hours; the third dial counts up to 1,000; the fourth counts up to 10,000; and the dial at the extreme left counts kilowatt-hours up to 100,000. If the arrow on the dial is between two numbers, always read the lower number.

The second type of electric meter performs the same function, but instead of individual dials, it has numerals in slots on the meter face, much like the odometer in your car. This meter is read from left to right, and the numbers indicate total electrical consumption. Some meters also use a multiplying factor—the number that appears must be multiplied by 10, for instance, for a true figure in kilowatt-hours. Once you know how to read your meter, you can verify the charges on your electric bill, and become a better watchdog of electrical energy consumption in your home.

The electrical service drop, or supply line, and the meter are as far as the local utility company is involved in your home's electrical system. From that point on, the system is the homeowner's responsibility. Electricity passes from the meter to the service equipment by means of three lines (older houses may have two) that supply 110-120/220-240 volts AC (alternating current). The exact voltage varies, depending on several external factors. This three-wire system gives you 110-120-volt power for lighting, outlets, and small appliances, as well as 220-240-volt power for air conditioning, an electric range, a clothes dryer, a water heater, and, in some homes, electric heating.

The Service Equipment

Electricity enters your home through the power company's service equipment. By strict definition, the service equipment is simply a disconnect device mounted in a suitable approved enclosure. Its purpose is to disconnect the service from the interior wiring system. This disconnect might be a set of pull-out fuses, a circuit breaker, or, in a few instances, a large switch. The disconnect device is usually called a main fuse, main breaker, or main disconnect, and often simply "the main." It can be in a separate enclosure, and though it's usually installed inside the building, it can be mounted outdoors in a weatherproof box.

In practice, main disconnects are nearly always inside the house, in a large enclosure that also contains the fuses or circuit breakers, which handle the distribution of power throughout the house. This is called a main entrance panel, main box, or entrance box. The three wires from the meter enter this box. Two of them—the heavily insulated black and white lines—are secured in lugs to the tops of a parallel pair of exposed heavy copper bars, called busses, that are positioned vertically toward the center of the box. These two lines are the "live" or "hot" wires. The third wire, generally bare, is the neutral. It is attached to a separate grounding bar or bus, a silver-colored strip usually found at the bottom or to one side of the main box. In most homes this ground bus is actually connected to the ground—the earth—by a heavy solid copper wire, clamped to a cold-water pipe or to an underground bar or plate.

Overload Protection

Power is distributed through your house through various electrical circuits that originate in the main entrance panel. The 110-120-volt circuits have two conductors—one neutral (white) wire and one hot (black) wire. Occasionally, three conductors may be used inside one jacket to serve as two circuits, with one red (hot) wire, one black (hot) wire, and a common neutral or white wire. The 220-240-volt circuits may consist of two hot wires alone, or a third, neutral wire may be added. In all cases, the hot lines are attached directly to the hot main busses. The neutral wire is always connected to the ground bus, and *never*, under any circumstances, passes through a fuse or circuit breaker.

Fuses and circuit breakers are safety devices built into your electrical system. Since the typical homeowner probably does not know about wire current-

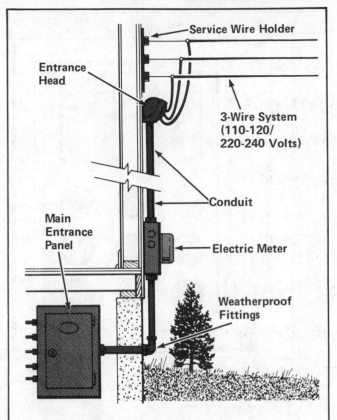

The electrical service drop, or supply line, and the meter are as far as the local utility company is involved in your home's electrical system. From that point on, the system is your responsibility.

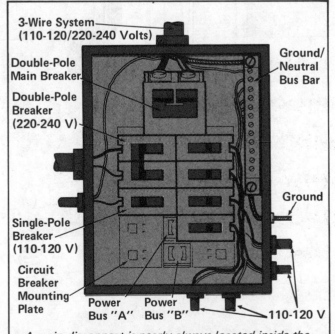

A main disconnect is nearly always located inside the house in the top part of a large enclosure also containing the fuses or circuit breakers. This is the main entrance panel, main box, or entrance box.

Fuse Panel

In addition to screw-in fuses, a typical main fuse panel has a main disconnect and other pull-out blocks with cartridge-type fuses.

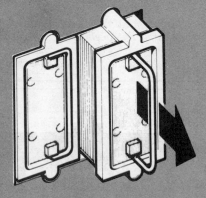

To reach cartridge fuses, simply pull the fuse blocks out of the main entrance panel.

Cartridge Fuses

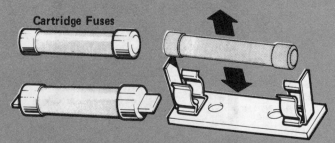

Cartridge fuses, which can be checked with a continuity tester, are held in place by spring clips.

Type S Fuse and Adapter

Remove by Turning Counterclockwise

Unless an adapter base is used, a Type S fuse cannot be inserted into a fuse panel.

Standard Fuse   **Time-Delay Fuse**

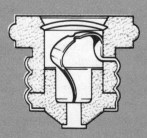   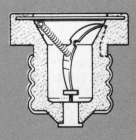

The standard fuse and the time-delay are other common types used. A time-delay does not blow if the current overload is only a momentary surge.

To protect against serious overloads, fuses and circuit breakers are designed to blow or trip, stopping the flow of current to the overloaded cable. A 15-ampere fuse, for example, should blow when the current passing through it exceeds 15 amperes.

carrying capacity, the fuses or circuit breakers are there to prevent overloading of the circuits. If there were no fuses or circuit breakers, and if you operated too many appliances on a single circuit, the cable carrying the power for that circuit would get extremely hot and short-circuit—and, quite possibly, start a fire.

To prevent electrical overloads, fuses and circuit breakers are designed to blow or trip, stopping the flow of current to the overloaded cable. For example, a 15-ampere fuse should blow when the current through it exceeds 15 amperes; a 20-ampere circuit breaker should trip when the current through it exceeds 20 amperes. A fuse that blows or a circuit breaker that trips is not faulty; it is doing its job properly, indicating that there is trouble somewhere in the circuit. When a fuse blows or a circuit breaker trips, either there are too many appliances plugged in, or some malfunctioning device—like an appliance with an internal short—is connected to the circuit.

A blown fuse or a tripped circuit breaker is the signal that you should look for trouble. It makes no sense to replace a blown fuse or reset a tripped circuit breaker until you've located and eliminated the cause of the trouble. *Caution: Never try to defeat this built-in safety system by replacing a fuse with one of a larger current-carrying capacity.* The fuse or circuit breaker capacity should equal, or be less than, the current-carrying capacity (or ampacity) of the conductors. The older Edison-base type of plug fuses can be interchanged in certain sizes, as can some cartridge fuses. But if you replaced a 15-ampere fuse with a 25-ampere version, you could be placing yourself in a highly dangerous situation. Placing a copper penny behind a blown fuse is also sure to lead to disaster. Certain types of circuit breakers can also be interchanged, but like fuses, they never should be. The newer Type S fuses are not interchangeable.

Branch and Feeder Circuits

From the fuses or circuit breakers, circuits go to all the devices in your home that require electrical power. There are two types of circuits: branch and feeder. Feeder circuits, which are not found in every house, are relatively heavy cables that travel from the main entrance panel to other, smaller distribution panels called subpanels or load centers. These auxiliary panels are located in remote parts of the house or in outbuildings, and are used for redistribution of "bulk" power, such as in a garage or workshop.

All of the circuits that run from either the main entrance panel or other, smaller panels to the various points of use are branch circuits. For 110-120-volt needs, a circuit branches out through a circuit breaker from one of the main busses and from the ground bus. For 220-240 volts, many circuits use only the two main busses. But all three wires are needed for devices that operate on both 110-120 and 220-240 volts, such as an electric range, and for 220-240-volt appliances that require the third wire for a neutral.

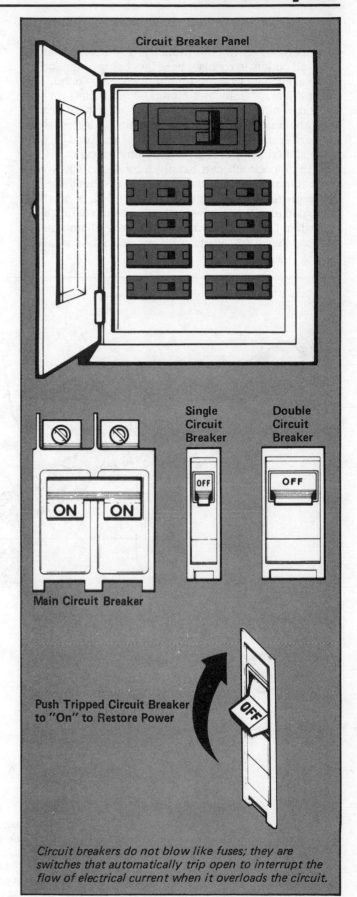

Circuit Breaker Panel

Main Circuit Breaker

Single Circuit Breaker

Double Circuit Breaker

Push Tripped Circuit Breaker to "On" to Restore Power

Circuit breakers do not blow like fuses; they are switches that automatically trip open to interrupt the flow of electrical current when it overloads the circuit.

The 110-120-volt branch circuits go through fuses or circuit breakers, which are labeled either 15 amperes or 20 amperes. The 15-amp branches go to ceiling lamps and wall outlets in rooms where less energy-demanding devices, such as floor and table lamps, are found. The larger 20-amp branch circuits go to outlets in the kitchen, dining, and laundry areas—anywhere heavy-duty appliances like washing machines, dryers, dishwashers, refrigerators, and toasters are used. Every home should have at least two 20-amp circuits.

A 15-amp circuit can handle a total of 1,800 watts, and a 20-amp circuit a total of 2,400 watts; but these figures represent circuits that are fully loaded. In practice, it's a good idea to limit the load on a 15-amp circuit to no more than 1,440 watts, and the load on a 20-amp line to no more than 1,920 watts. Add up the individual watt-ages for all lamps and appliances plugged into each circuit to make sure there's no overload anywhere in your home.

When computing the load on each branch circuit, be sure to allow for the fact that many motor-driven appliances draw more current when the motor is just starting up than when it's running. A refrigerator, for example, might draw up to 15 amps initially, but quickly settle down to around 4 amps. Suppose the refrigerator is plugged into a 20-amp branch circuit, and a 1,000-watt electric toaster—which draws a little more than 8 amps—is also plugged into that circuit. If the refrigerator motor starts while the toaster is toasting, the total current load exceeds the current-carrying capacity of the circuit, and the fuse blows or the circuit breaker trips.

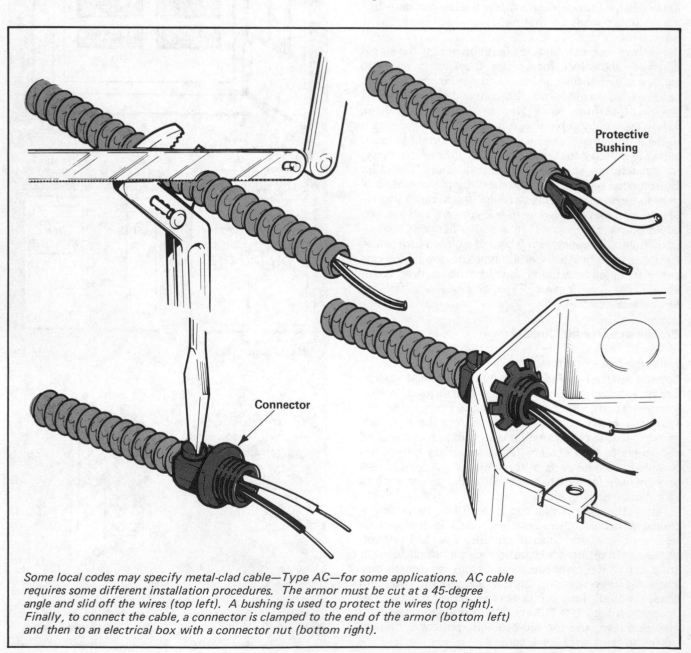

Some local codes may specify metal-clad cable—Type AC—for some applications. AC cable requires some different installation procedures. The armor must be cut at a 45-degree angle and slid off the wires (top left). A bushing is used to protect the wires (top right). Finally, to connect the cable, a connector is clamped to the end of the armor (bottom left) and then to an electrical box with a connector nut (bottom right).

Wire Types and Capacities

Several types of wires have been used over the years in residential electrical circuits. Some older homes may still have circuits wired with the knob-and-tube system, which employs separate individual conductors, surface-mounted and running on or through porcelain insulators. Such wiring should be replaced.

There are numerous types of cables used in modern wiring systems, and each is designed for particular purposes. In residential applications, however, only three types of wire are widely used in branch circuits. One is the metal-clad Type AC cable, which is installed wherever local electrical codes specify that the cables must be metal-clad. Type NM cable is by far the most commonly used type; it is a plastic-sheathed cable. Unless local codes specify otherwise, this is the cable to choose for all indoor, dry-location residential wiring, except for certain kinds of appliance circuits that may require other types. The somewhat similar Type UF cable replaces Type NM where the circuit must be buried underground or located in wet or corrosive spots; it must not, however, be exposed to sunlight. Most home electricians will need only Type NM cable, two- or three-wire, in conductor sizes #14 and #12—perhaps occasionally #10—all with a ground wire, an extra bare conductor.

The size of an electrical conductor is determined by its diameter in mils (or thousandths of an inch), measured at 68° F. In this country, that size is translated into trade sizes expressed as gauge numbers that follow the American Wire Gauge (AWG) system. For wiring outdoor lighting circuits and receptacles, and running buried branch circuits, use Type UF in the same sizes; both types are handled in much the same way. A few circuits, such as a range hookup, might require Type SE or some other kind of cable; check the specific requirements with your electrical inspector or electrical supply dealer, or in applicable electrical codes.

Type NM cable is found inside the walls of nearly all recently constructed homes. It has a tough outer plastic sheath, which covers two or more plastic-insulated copper conductors and a bare copper grounding conductor. The insulated wires are color-coded as follows:
- Two-wire cable: one white, one black, one bare.
- Three-wire cable: one white, one black, one red, one bare.
- Four-wire cable: one white, one black, one red, one blue, one bare.

Type NM cable can be run free through spaces in floors, ceilings, or walls. Or it can be fastened to the sides of exposed joists and studs, secured at least every 4½ feet with approved electrical staples, and also at a point no more than 12 inches from the entrance point into any electrical box. Type NM can also be run through holes bored in structural members, spaced at least two inches up from the outside edge, or centered in 2×4's. Staples used to secure the cable should not compress its outer sheath; corner bends should be gentle, with a radius of no less than about three inches. The ca-

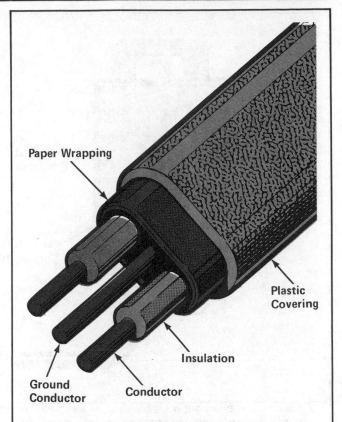

Type NM cable is a plastic-sheathed cable, used for almost all indoor, dry-location residential wiring.

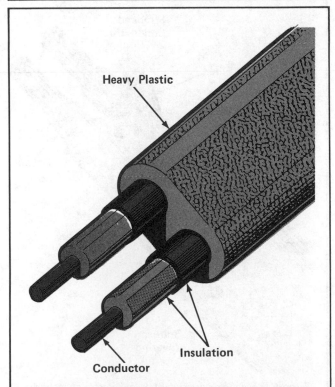

Type UF cable is similar to Type NM; it is used in wet or corrosive areas, and for cable laid underground.

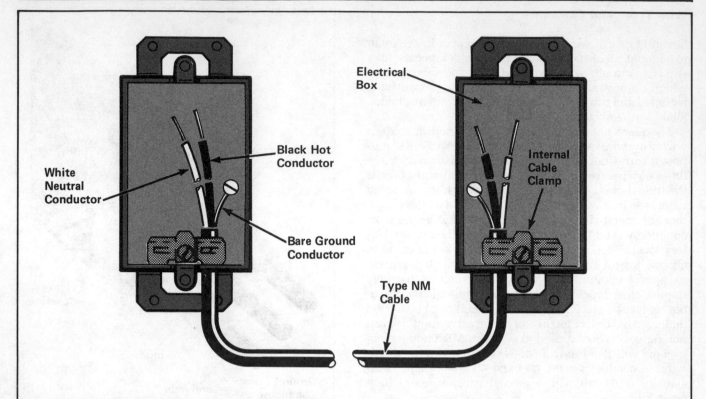

White Neutral Conductor

Black Hot Conductor

Bare Ground Conductor

Electrical Box

Internal Cable Clamp

Type NM Cable

All cable must be a continuous, unbroken run from box to box; a splice or connection can only be made within a box—never in the open. And a cable end must be clamped in place within any electrical box.

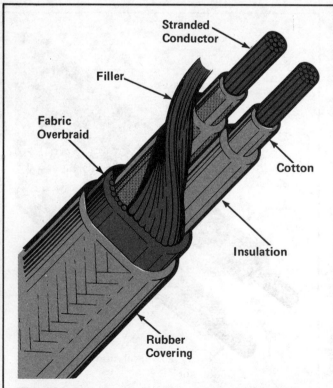

Stranded Conductor

Filler

Fabric Overbraid

Cotton

Insulation

Rubber Covering

Type SJ cable is a tough rubber- or plastic-sheathed cord, used for heavy-duty appliances that don't produce heat.

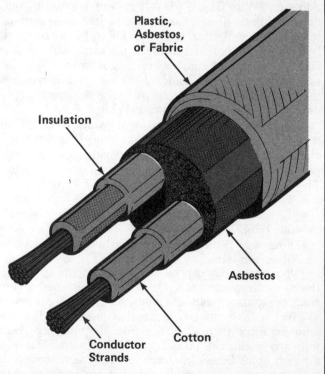

Plastic, Asbestos, or Fabric

Insulation

Asbestos

Cotton

Conductor Strands

Type HPD cable, insulated with asbestos and covered with cloth or plastic, is used for cords on heat-producing appliances.

ble must be clamped in place within any electrical box, with a minimum of six inches of free conductor left within the box. The cable must also be a continuous, unbroken run from box to box; a splice or connection can be made only within a box—never out in the open.

As you might expect, one type of wire cannot handle all electrical wiring situations. Fixtures and appliances call for other kinds of wire. Look at the wire on your washing machine, refrigerator, or any other heavy-duty appliance, and most likely you'll see a tough rubber- or plastic-sheathed cord called Type SJ. Type SJ is one of the workhorse cords, for appliances that require a great deal of current but do not produce heat.

If you need a heater cord, you can choose between Type HPD and Type HPN. For many years, the cloth-covered HPD—with a packing of asbestos around its inner conductors—was used for all heating cords. With the development of temperature-resistant thermoplastics, however, Type HPN (which looks like heavy lamp cord) is replacing Type HPD on many appliances.

The most common lamp cord—also used on radios, television sets, electric clocks, and so forth—is called Type SPT. Each plastic-insulated conductor is composed of many individual strands; that's what makes lamp cord so flexible. Since Type SPT features a molded groove between the two wires for easy splitting, it is often referred to as zip cord.

Wire that's used properly—that is, only for the purpose for which it was designed—and not loaded beyond its capacity should last the lifetime of a high-quality home or other structure, except for some fixture wires. You must not, however, exceed a particular wire's current-carrying capacity. All wire is rated for capacity; #14 Type NM, for example, has an allowable current-carrying capacity of 15 amperes.

What happens if wire is loaded beyond its capacity? An occasional quick excess load would probably do no damage at all—except perhaps to blow a fuse or trip a circuit breaker. The wire would not evaporate, disintegrate, or suffer any other sort of immediate damage. Over the long term, however, wire that continuously carries excessive current will deteriorate; the copper will degrade and the insulation will dry out, flake, or crack long before it has served its normal useful life. A wire's capacity, therefore, refers to the amount of current it can conduct continuously—day in and day out—without suffering any damage.

Electrical Safety

It is the insulation around a conductor that protects you from danger. An electric shock is always distressing, always hazardous, and often fatal. The idea behind electrical safety is that you must avoid physical contact with any live or hot part of the circuit. All electrical devices and electrical wires are designed to provide the greatest measure of safety, but you can defeat any built-in safeguards through carelessness and ignorance. If you are to work safely with electricity, you must understand both the hazards and the precautions those

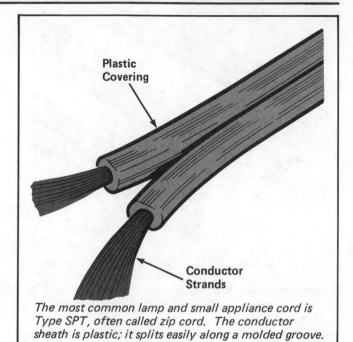

The most common lamp and small appliance cord is Type SPT, often called zip cord. The conductor sheath is plastic; it splits easily along a molded groove.

hazards require you to practice.

Never do anything that would break the conductor's insulation. Do not, for example, staple an extension cord to a baseboard or to a wall (an illegal practice). The staple can cut through the insulation and create a short circuit, which, in turn, can start a fire. Moreover, you should examine all wiring regularly and discard any cord that has brittle insulation. Replace old cord with new cord that has good insulation.

There is one wire in the electrical system that you can theoretically touch without fear of getting shocked (if the circuit is correctly connected), and that is the neutral

For safety, examine wiring regularly. Replace cords that have brittle or damaged insulation.

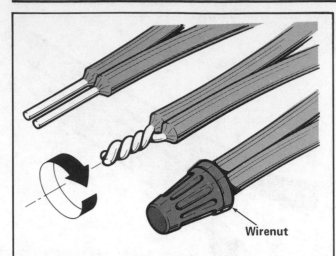

One of the most popular ways to join wires is to use solderless connectors called wirenuts. The conductor ends are twisted together and the wirenut is screwed onto the twisted ends; make sure no bare conductor is exposed.

Wirenut

wire. The problem is, though, that you can't always be sure without testing which wire is the neutral. The equipment grounding circuit, present only in later wiring systems, should also be dead, but there is always the possibility that it might not have been properly installed. Nor are identifying marks or colors on the wires always reliable. Therefore, it's always a good idea to avoid *any* kind of contact whatsoever with *any* part of a live circuit. This is particularly true when working with poorly done or jury-rigged systems, and with an old type of wiring like BX armored cable. The latter can be particularly hazardous, since the casing itself may well be hot. Even if the circuit to be worked on has been disconnected or turned off, the casing may *still* be hot because of feedback, so check carefully with a circuit tester or volt meter before starting work.

If you plan to work on a portable electrical device, unplug it. If you want to work with a household circuit, remove the fuse or trip the circuit breaker to its "off" position. These two safety rules seem almost too obvious to mention, but many people forget to obey them and wind up as casualties of their do-it-yourself electrical repairs.

About the only thing you can do relatively safely without first unplugging is changing a light bulb. Never start to repair an appliance until you disconnect the power cord from the circuit. Do all appliance work with the unit "cold," and do not plug it in again until all your work is finished. Then, if it blows a fuse, disconnect the appliance immediately. Don't plug it in again until you locate and eliminate the cause of the trouble.

When you replace an outlet or a switch, or do any other work on a circuit, always turn the power off first. If your system operates with fuses, remove the fuse for the circuit you're working on, and slip the fuse into your pocket or toolbox. If you leave it nearby, there's a

chance that someone might put the fuse back in while you're working on the circuit. If your home's electrical system uses circuit breakers, trip the appropriate circuit breaker to its "off" position. Then, to make sure no one accidentally flips the circuit breaker back on while you're working, put a piece of tape—and a sign telling people what you're doing—over the circuit breaker's handle. The sign is a good idea for a fuse box too.

What do you use for light once you deenergize the circuit you want to work on? If deenergizing the circuit plunges the area into darkness, use a flashlight—a portable fluorescent lantern works very well—or a trouble light with a long cord that you can plug into another circuit that's still energized.

When you work on an electrical circuit, you must—for a safe installation—make all wire joints and connections inside an approved electrical box. There are several ways to join wires, but the best way is to use solderless connectors of either the crimp-on or the screw-on (wirenut) kind. Never connect wires together in a behind-the-wall or in-the-ceiling location that is not accessible by simply opening an electrical box. In addition, when joining insulated wires to one another or when fastening them under terminal screws, make sure no uninsulated (bare) wire extends beyond the connection. The insulation should go right up to the solderless connector or the terminal screw.

Electrical Grounding

Proper grounding of your electrical system is essential to your safety. Electricity always follows the path of least resistance, and the path could be *you* whenever an appliance or another electrical component is not grounded.

The idea behind grounding is simply to direct electrical energy into the earth by providing a conductor that is less resistant than you are. This is frequently accomplished by attaching one end of the wire to the frame of an appliance and fastening the other end to a cold-water pipe.

Most non-metal-sheathed cable contains a bare wire, which carries the grounded connection to every electrical box, outlet, and appliance in your home. You can usually tell whether your electrical system is grounded by checking the outlets. If you have the kind that accepts plugs with two blades and one prong, your system should have three wires—one of which is a grounding wire. The prong carries the safety ground to the metal frame of any appliance that has a three-wire plug and cord.

It's the metal frame, of course, that can pose the safety hazard. Suppose, for example, some of the insulation on the power cord of a major appliance (refrigerator, dishwasher, washing machine, or dryer) wears away just at the point where the cord enters the frame. The contact between the metal current conductor and the metal frame could make the whole appliance alive with electricity. If you touched a charged metal frame while simultaneously touching a water faucet or

HOW DANGEROUS IS ELECTRICITY?

How much electricity is dangerous? For comparison, average household voltage is about 115 or 230 volts, alternating at 60 cycles per second. A standard 100-watt bulb draws a little less than 1 ampere of current, a toaster about 7 amperes. A doorbell operates on about 10 to 12 volts. In tests, some people were found to tolerate no more than 7/1000 of 1 ampere at 12 volts AC before having to let go of test leads. Others were able to withstand anywhere from 20 to 40 volts at the same current with leads held in dry hands, but lost control of arm muscles after only a few seconds. Some, with thicker-skinned, calloused, dry hands, could stand momentary jolts of up to 120 volts, but within seconds the current broke down the skin, caused blisters, and greatly increased conductivity.

Shock sensation occurs at as little as 1/1000 of 1 ampere, and 7 to 8 milliamperes causes severe discomfort. If conditions are right, a current of only 30 milliamperes can be fatal.

When a person receives an electrical shock, two things can happen. One, current interferes with the nerves of the breathing control center at the back of the neck. Respiration ceases, and artificial respiration must be started immediately; the nerves may or may not recover. Two, current may stop the heart completely or cause it to fibrillate; the heart may or may not recover. So take all possible precautions and proceed with care and thought when working with electricity. In the interest of electrical safety, follow these precautions:

1. Before working on any electrical circuit or apparatus, deenergize the circuit by removing the appropriate fuse or tripping the circuit breaker to the "off" position.
2. When deenergizing a circuit, remove the plug fuse entirely and put it in your pocket or toolbox, or securely tape the circuit breaker handle in the "off" position. This will prevent the circuit from being turned back on by someone else. In both cases, post a sign at the main entrance panel to notify everyone that electrical work is in progress.
3. Always assume that an electrical outlet or apparatus is energized until you prove otherwise with a circuit tester or by pulling a disconnect plug. Deenergizing the wrong circuit is easy to do, with unhappy results.
4. Do not work on an outlet or lighting fixture with a switch, even when the switch is turned off, without first deenergizing the circuit. In many switching systems, parts of the circuit are still energized when the switch is off.
5. When working in a main entrance panel, always trip the main circuit breaker to the "off" position or remove the main fuses before removing the panel cover. If possible, cover the top main line connecting lugs, which remain energized, with a piece of corrugated cardboard (a good insulator) wedged into the panel box, to prevent accidental contact.
6. When working in a main entrance panel located over a dirt or concrete surface, or any other surface that might be damp, always lay down a piece of plywood or plank to stand on to isolate yourself from the ground.
7. When working in a load center or subpanel, always deenergize the entire panel by tripping the appropriate circuit breaker in the main entrance panel to the "off" position or by removing the appropriate fuses.
8. Always use tools with insulating handles—wood- or plastic-handled screwdrivers, diagonal cutters with plastic grips, etc.
9. In making electrical repairs or installations, always follow safe, accepted practices, procedures, and techniques, and use proper, approved materials and devices. Never overload circuits, make open splices or connections, mount inaccessible junction boxes, break conductor insulation, use improper materials or equipment, or otherwise make a potentially hazardous situation possible. Ignorance is no excuse; make sure you know what you're doing and why. You might not get a second chance.

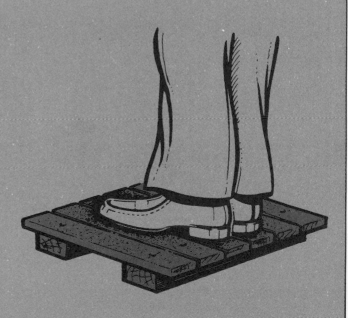

When working at the main panel over a surface that might be wet or damp, always use a piece of plywood or a wooden platform to isolate yourself from the ground.

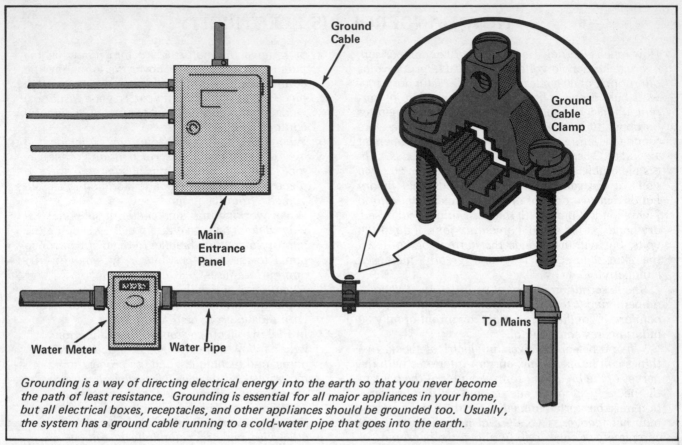

Ground
Cable

Ground
Cable
Clamp

Main
Entrance
Panel

Water Meter

Water Pipe

To Mains

Grounding is a way of directing electrical energy into the earth so that you never become the path of least resistance. Grounding is essential for all major appliances in your home, but all electrical boxes, receptacles, and other appliances should be grounded too. Usually, the system has a ground cable running to a cold-water pipe that goes into the earth.

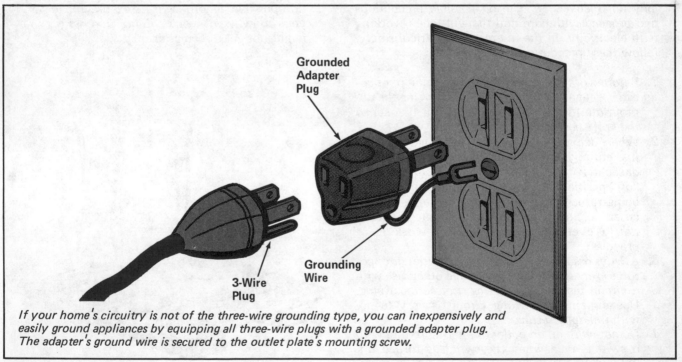

Grounded
Adapter
Plug

Grounding
Wire

3-Wire
Plug

If your home's circuitry is not of the three-wire grounding type, you can inexpensively and easily ground appliances by equipping all three-wire plugs with a grounded adapter plug. The adapter's ground wire is secured to the outlet plate's mounting screw.

a radiator, the current would surge through you, and could kill you.

There are other places throughout the electrical system where conductor/metal contact is a distinct possi-

bility—wherever wires enter a metal pipe (conduit), where the cord enters a lamp or lamp socket, where in-wall cable enters an electrical box. Surfaces at these points must be free of burrs that could chafe the wire and damage its insulation. Washers, grommets, and special fittings have been devised to protect wire at these various points of entry, but the best thing you can do is to make sure that the whole system is grounded and that the ground circuit is electrically continuous, without breaks.

If your circuitry is not of the three-wire grounding type, you should ground all of your appliances. You can do this without going to the expense of installing completely new wiring. An inexpensive and easy way to ground appliances is to equip all three-prong appliance plugs with a grounded adapter plug. Some adapter plugs have a metal tab near the prongs; some have a short grounding wire, or pigtail, with a metal tab at the end. The plug fits into any two-blade outlet; with the pigtail type, the small grounding wire connects under the screw of the outlet plate. *Caution: Never remove the prong from a three-wire plug to make it fit a two-slot receptacle. Always use an adapter.*

Even if appliances are properly grounded, dampness can cause a potential shock hazard. If you touched a charged metal frame in a damp location, or while touching a water faucet or radiator, the current would surge through you, and could kill you. There are three things you can do to eliminate this hazard. First, make sure your appliances are properly grounded, and follow all electrical safety rules. Second, make sure that appliance cords are in good repair, and that they are not chafing against burrs or rough spots where they enter the appliance frame. And third, add a ground-fault circuit interrupter (GFI or GFCI) to the circuit. Ground-fault circuit interrupters are monitoring devices that instantly shut off a circuit when a current leak occurs; they are required by the National Electrical Code on all new 15- and 20-amp outdoor outlets, and for wiring in bathrooms, where dampness is a common problem. GFIs are available to plug into existing outlets, to replace outlets, and to replace circuit breakers in the electrical entrance panel. A professional electrician should install the circuit-breaker type; you can install the other types yourself. Ground-fault circuit interrupters are available at electrical supply and home center stores.

Electrical Codes

Residential electrical installations—and, for that matter, other kinds as well—are usually regulated by an electrical code. The best-known, and the one in most widespread use today, is the National Electrical Code (NEC). In addition, there are any number of local electrical codes, based in large measure on the NEC, and shortened, amplified, or revised as necessary to suit local conditions and requirements. Most governmental authorities, at all levels, have adopted either the NEC (in whole or in part) or some similar code, to which all electrical installations under their jurisdiction must conform.

Where an electrical code is in force, and particularly where it is *enforced*, it is the responsibility of the home electrician to be familiar with its provisions as they ap-

ply to residential wiring and his own electrical work, and to follow them *exactly*. This involves obtaining a copy of the applicable code and becoming familiar with it, drawing up whatever plans and specifications are required for the proposed work, obtaining a permit (and paying the attendant fee) to do the work, and, finally, having the completed job inspected by the proper authority. In most cases, simple repair work requires no permit or inspection, but circuit additions, rewiring, and such may. Note, too, that in some areas the homeowner cannot do *any* electrical work, even in his own home; all work must be done by a licensed electrician. This is the first point to check before you make any electrical repair.

In areas where no code is in force, following the provisions of the NEC is an excellent idea. Though this by no means ensures an installation that is fully efficient and fault-free, it is a good step in the right direction. The NEC is based on many years of field experience, testing, research, and study, and by following its regulations and recommendations—required or not—you will greatly lessen your chances of going astray. Though it is definitely not an electrical wiring manual, the NEC provides good guidelines for the proper application and installation of electrical equipment of all sorts and in practically all circumstances, and does so with one principal point in mind—safety. The code is the recognized authority for electrical installations everywhere, and following it makes good sense. Knowing the code will stand you in good stead, especially if you plan to go beyond simple fix-it projects to become your own resident electrician.

Copies of local electrical codes can be obtained from your building department or electrical inspector, and may be available at your library. Copies of the NEC can be found in the same places in areas where that code is used; or purchase it direct from the National Fire Protection Association (NFPA).* The code is revised every four years; ask for the current edition. Other helpful publications, such as the *Handbook of the National Electrical Code,* which interprets the NEC, are also available from the NFPA.

Repairing and Replacing Electrical Components

With prices skyrocketing for nearly everything in sight, it's a rare homeowner or apartment-dweller who doesn't feel the pinch of inflation. Nearly everyone, it seems, is trying to avoid unforeseen expenses like those occasioned by an electrical breakdown. But electrical components, even good ones, don't last forever. Lamps stop lighting, doorbells stop ringing, and outlets stop holding plugs; these failures occur in the normal course of events.

What options are available to someone faced with a

---

*Publication Sales Department, 470 Atlantic Ave., Boston, MA 02210.

malfunctioning electrical component? An electrician can be called in, of course, but then the cost of repair or replacement gets really steep. The logical solution for many simple repairs is to do it yourself. Generally speaking, these electrical tasks require only tools you're likely to have around the house, and they demand no more technical expertise than reading and following directions. Just be sure you make safety your first priority, and you'll be amazed at what you can do to maintain and upgrade the electrical devices in your home.

Equipping Your Workshop

To make simple electrical repairs, you'll need a few simple hand tools. The more extensive and complex your repair work, and the more rewiring you eventually do, the more tools you'll need. Most, however, are inexpensive, and can be found in your home workshop; there are a few specialized tools you might want or eventually need, but these are also usually inexpensive.

The first requisite is a selection of screwdrivers. These should be good-quality tools with insulated handles. You'll need at least three sizes for slotted screws, as well as at least one Phillips-type screwdriver. You will also want a hammer—a claw hammer will do—slip-joint, long-nose, and adjustable slip-joint, or water-pump, pliers. One or two adjustable wrenches will come in handy. Your electrical toolbox should also contain a measuring rule, a putty knife, a keyhole saw, perhaps a wood chisel, a small level, either a hand brace or a 3/8-inch electric drill, and a good selection of drill bits. Keep electrical tape and wirenuts on hand.

You'll need some specialized tools, too, which you can obtain at any electrical supply house or at a hardware store. Equip yourself with a pair of electricians'

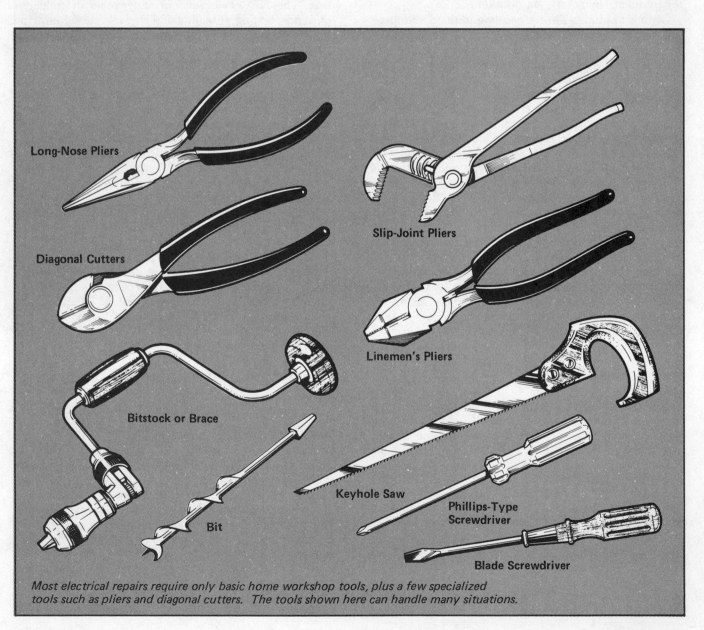

Long-Nose Pliers

Diagonal Cutters

Slip-Joint Pliers

Linemen's Pliers

Bitstock or Brace

Bit

Keyhole Saw

Phillips-Type Screwdriver

Blade Screwdriver

Most electrical repairs require only basic home workshop tools, plus a few specialized tools such as pliers and diagonal cutters. The tools shown here can handle many situations.

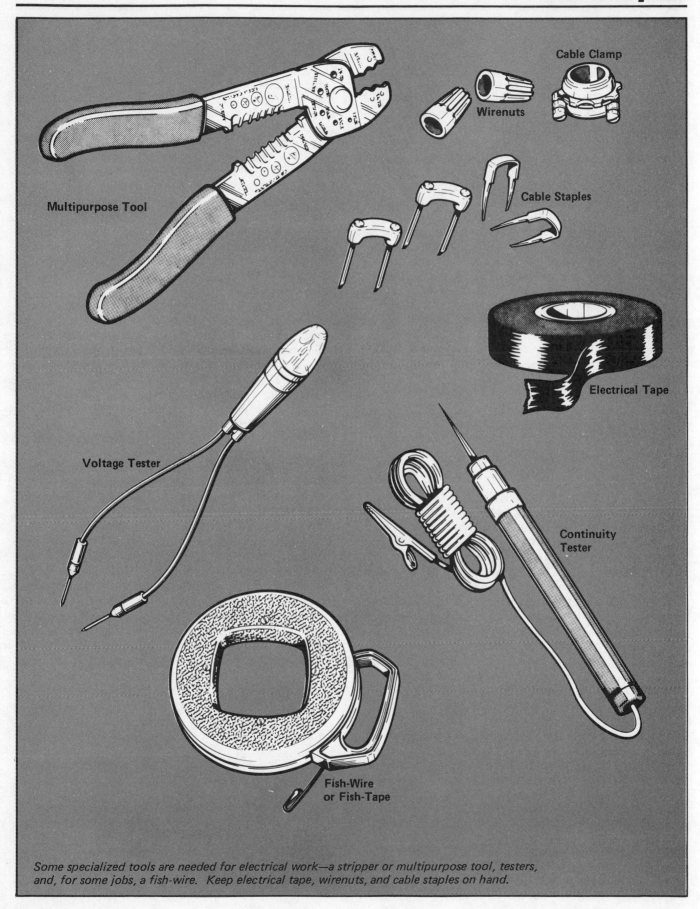

Multipurpose Tool

Wirenuts

Cable Clamp

Cable Staples

Electrical Tape

Voltage Tester

Continuity Tester

Fish-Wire or Fish-Tape

Some specialized tools are needed for electrical work—a stripper or multipurpose tool, testers, and, for some jobs, a fish-wire. Keep electrical tape, wirenuts, and cable staples on hand.

diagonal cutters with insulated handles—the kind that has stubby, wide jaws works better than one with long, narrow jaws. An ordinary utility knife is fine for slitting the outer plastic jacket of Type NM or Type UF cable, but for stripping the insulation off the conductors, you should use a wire stripper made for this purpose. Another special tool you'll need is a voltage tester, used to determine whether a circuit is live or dead. Or you can buy a more sophisticated—and more expensive—tester that will actually measure voltages and currents in the circuit.

If you'll be working with metal-clad cable, a special armored-cable cutter will save you a lot of time. Installing EMT (electrical metallic tubing) or rigid conduit requires a hacksaw or a pipe cutter, a pipe or tubing bender, and a file and a reamer for smoothing cut ends. Conduit work also calls for pipe-threading equipment. If you'll be working with modern circuits that have three-slot outlets and an equipment grounding loop, a polarity-checking device is very useful. You may also need an electricians' snake or fish-wire for pulling cables behind walls and ceilings, and a continuity tester for determining whether a dead circuit is open or closed and checking ground loops.

Restoring a Circuit

The overload devices—fuses or circuit breakers—in your electrical system are there for a purpose, to blow or trip if the circuit is overloaded. When that happens, as it does from time to time in almost every home, what do you do?

The first step should be taken *before* a circuit trips off. If you haven't already done so, make a list of all the branch circuits in your home, by number and by what area each one controls. Then you can figure out which outlets and fixtures are on each branch circuit. If you aren't sure the list is accurate and complete, you can verify it through a very simple procedure. Just remove a fuse or trip a circuit breaker to its "off" position, and check to see what equipment or devices are deenergized. Of course, it's easy to see when a ceiling light goes out; but you can check an outlet just as easily by plugging in a lamp—a small night-light is an ideal indicator. Once you know exactly which outlets, fixtures, and appliances are connected to each branch circuit, write all the information on a card and attach the card to the inside of the main entrance panel's door.

When a circuit goes off, there may be some visual or audible indication of the trouble spot, such as a bright flare from a lamp or a sputtering, sparking sound from an appliance, that will immediately lead you to the source of the trouble. If so, disconnect the faulty equipment. If not, arm yourself with a flashlight, if necessary, and go to the main entrance panel. Check to see which fuse is blown or which breaker has tripped, and determine from your information card which outlets, appliances, and lighting fixtures are on the circuit. Then disconnect everything on that circuit that you can, and inspect those fixtures that you can't easily disconnect

for signs (or smells) of malfunction.

Replace the fuse or reset the breaker. If the circuit holds, perhaps something you disconnected is faulty; check for short circuits or other problems. If there's no evidence of electrical fault in the fixtures, the problem may be an overload—too much current draw for the circuit to handle. In this case, remove some of the load from the circuit.

If the new fuse blows or the circuit breaker refuses to reset, the problem lies in equipment that's still connected, or in the circuit cable itself. The greater likelihood of malfunction lies with the still-connected items, so tackle those first, examining each for faults until you find the offending equipment. If the circuit still goes out when there are no loads connected to it, the wiring itself is faulty, probably because of a short in a junction or outlet box, or possibly in the cable itself. With the circuit dead, start at the far end of the line and inspect all of the connections.

If there's no visible evidence of a problem, you'll have to check each segment of the circuit, section by section, with a continuity tester. Make sure the circuit is still deenergized, because a continuity tester must never be used on a live circuit. Be sure nothing is connected to the circuit segments during this procedure; otherwise you may get a false reading.

Start at the panel end of the circuit and touch the probe leads of the tester to the bare ends of the wires. If the tester lights up, or you get a reading on the meter dial, the circuit has continuity and there are no breaks or loose connections in the line; that part of the circuit is all right. If the tester doesn't register, there's a break somewhere; you'll have to disconnect each segment of the circuit, section by section, and check each section until you get a clear reading (no light or meter reading). This procedure will isolate the fault, which you can then repair to permanently clear the circuit.

A circuit breaker is a remarkably trouble-free device, but once in a while a breaker does fail. The result is that the circuit will not energize, even when it's fault-free. When a circuit goes out, if the circuit breaker itself has a distinctive, burnt-plastic smell, the trip handle is loose and wobbly, the reset mechanism seems all afloat internally, or the breaker rattles when you shake it, it has probably failed. You can make certain by checking it with a continuity tester. The only remedy, of course, is to replace the circuit breaker; they are not repairable.

Coping With a Power Outage

What do you do when all the power in the house goes off? Usually this is due to a general power outage in the entire neighborhood or district, but sometimes the problem lies in the individual residential wiring system.

The first step is to see whether the outage is a general one or yours alone. If it's night, look around the neighborhood to see if everyone else's lights are off. During the day, call a neighbor to see if others are affected. Or, if you have a circuit breaker main disconnect, check to see whether it has tripped to the "off" position. If the

EMERGENCY BLACKOUT KIT

1. Candles or oil lamps and matches for lighting.
2. Flashlight, battery lantern, or other auxiliary light source for troubleshooting.
3. Correct and up-to-date circuit directory posted on main entrance panel door.
4. Tool kit with appropriate tools for making electrical repairs.
5. Circuit tester, preferably the voltage-readout type of tester.
6. Spare parts:

For Fuse Boxes
- Two each replacement plug fuses of each amperage rating in use, preferably Type S.
- Four each replacement cartridge fuses, including main fuses, of each amperage rating in use.

For Circuit Breaker Boxes
- One replacement single-pole circuit breaker of a rating equal to the smallest size in use or one of each size in use.
- One replacement double-pole circuit breaker of each amperage rating in use.

General Parts
- Selection of light bulbs.
- One replacement duplex outlet (receptacle) to match existing units.
- One replacement single-pole switch to match existing units.
- One replacement three-way or other special switch to match existing units.
- Miscellaneous supplies—wirenuts, electricians' tape, etc.

main entrance is wired with fuses, pull the fuse block out and slip the fuses free. Check them with a continuity tester to see if they're blown or still good; with a probe lead touched to each end of the fuse, the tester light will come on if the fuse is good.

If the trouble is a general power outage, all you can do is call the power company; by this time, other people probably already have. If your main breaker is still in the "on" position or both main fuses are good, but your neighbors have power and you don't, the fault lies between your main entrance panel and the power transmission lines. The reason could be a downed service drop, a faulty or overloaded pole transformer, or some similar problem; call the power company, because this part of your system is their responsibility.

If you find a tripped main breaker or blown main fuses in your main entrance panel, the problem lies within the house, and may be serious. *Do not* attempt to reset the breaker or replace the fuses; this would probably be futile. The difficulty may be a general overload—you're simply using more total current than the main breaker can pass. Or there may be a dead short somewhere in the house.

The first step is to go back through the house and turn off everything you can. Then, if you have a circuit breaker panel, flip all the breakers to the "off" position, and reset the main breaker to the "on" position. One by one, trip the branch circuit breakers back on. If one of them fails to reset, or the main breaker again trips off as you trip the branch breaker on, the source of the trouble lies in that circuit, and the circuit will have to be cleared of the fault.

If all the breakers go back on and the main breaker stays on, you're faced with two possibilities. One is that something you disconnected earlier is faulty. Go back along the line, inspect each item for possible fault, and

plug each one back in. Sooner or later you'll discover which one is causing the problem, either visually or by the fact that a breaker trips out when you reconnect it. The other and more likely possibility is a general, system-wide overloading. This is characterized by recurrent tripping-out of the main breaker when practically everything in the house is running but there are no electrical faults to be found. There are two remedies for this problem. One is to lessen the total electrical load; this should be done in any case as at least a short-term measure. The other is to install a new, larger main entrance panel, with new branch circuits to serve areas of heavy electrical usage and help share the total load.

The troubleshooting approach is much the same if the main panel has fuses, except that you'll need a supply of fuses on hand. First, pull all the cartridge fuses and unscrew all the plug fuses in the panel. Replace the main fuses and put the fuse block back into place. Then, one by one, replace each fuse or set of fuses until the one that's causing the outage blows out again. This is the circuit that must be cleared. General overloading, however, will cause the main fuses to go out again.

Specific testing for general overload is easy. This is most easily done with a snap-around volt-ohm-ammeter, an instrument that snaps around the cable and provides you with a direct amperage reading while the line is under load—no interconnections are needed. Use the test instrument according to the manufacturer's instructions, and take readings at each of the two main incoming lines in the main entrance panel at various times of day, or after turning on all of the power-consuming devices in the house that might normally be operating at the same time. Note the highest reading obtained from each line, and compare it to the capacity rating of the main disconnect. If, for instance, your main panel is rated at 100 amps and is equipped with a 100-amp main breaker, and if your readings show a maximum draw of 97 amps, that line is running right on the verge of trouble—just a bit more load and the main disconnect is sure to go out. On the other hand, if the greatest draw you can manage is 90 amps, you're safe enough. But you won't be able to add another circuit or a major appliance without running into trouble, unless the other main line is only lightly loaded and you can shuffle circuits around to effect a better balance between the two.

Checking Outlet Polarity

Residential wiring systems installed a few years ago or earlier use a two-wire system in the 110-120-volt branch circuits. One conductor is hot and the other is neutral, and the neutral may also serve as a ground. But, unfortunately, it usually does not; the system is ungrounded, and the situation is potentially hazardous. You can easily tell if your circuits are of this type by looking at your outlets—there are only two slots for each plug in ungrounded outlets. Modern wiring calls for the installation of a third conductor, a bare wire called the equipment grounding conductor. Outlets used with this system have three openings: two vertical slots and a third, rounded hole centered above them. Either two-prong or three-prong plugs can be plugged into these outlets, but only the three-pronged kind will carry the equipment grounding line to the electrical equipment. Also, one of the vertical slots is different in size from the other, so that the newer types of two-pronged plugs can be inserted in only one direction. This ensures that the equipment being connected will be properly polarized, hot side to hot side and neutral to neutral.

For proper operation and safety, it is essential that all outlets on each circuit be installed with the individual conductors going to the correct terminals, so that there are no polarity reversals along the line that would negate the effectiveness of the system. Unfortunately, outlets are not always connected this way, even in new wiring systems installed by professional electricians. You can easily and quickly check out your outlets with a small, inexpensive tester called a polarity checker, designed for this purpose. It looks like a fancy three-pronged plug, and contains three neon bulb indicators. Simply plug the checker into an outlet; the lights will tell you if the polarity is correct—and, if not, which lines are reversed. If there is a reversal, turn the circuit off, pull the outlet out of the electrical box, and switch the wires to the proper terminals. Or, if the equipment-grounding circuit is open (discontinuous), trace the circuit until you find the disconnection or missing link, and reconnect it to restore the effectiveness of the circuit.

Rewiring a Lamp

There's no reason why you have to live with lamps that don't work properly, and may be dangerous too. The plug, cord, and socket—the parts that are probably causing the lamp to malfunction—are easy and inexpensive to replace. You can get them at any well-stocked hardware store, and certainly at any store that specializes in electrical parts. Why, for example, should you put up with a plug that's misshapen or broken, or that doesn't make a good electrical connection in the outlet? With a quick-clamp plug—the kind that eliminates the need for fastening wires under terminal screws—you can have a new one on in seconds.

You can install a new socket almost as easily. Replacement sockets come in various finishes—brass or nickel metal, and black or brown plastic—so you should be able to find a socket that approximates the color tone of the existing socket. And if you plan to replace a socket, why not put in a three-way socket for greater lighting versatility? Wiring a three-way socket is as simple as wiring the standard on/off version.

Lamp cord is known as Type SPT, but if you ask for zip cord at a hardware or electrical supply store, you'll get what you need. The #18 size is satisfactory for most lamp applications. Zip cord is available in many colors, the most common being black, brown, white, and transparent. Match the cord color to the lamp, and order a sufficient length for your needs. The customary length is six feet, but you can use as much cord as you need to reach from the lamp to the outlet; add the length of the cord hidden in the lamp, plus one foot for attachments to socket and plug, and for some slack. In terms of safety and appearance, it's better to have an adequate length of cord than to compensate for a short one with an ex-

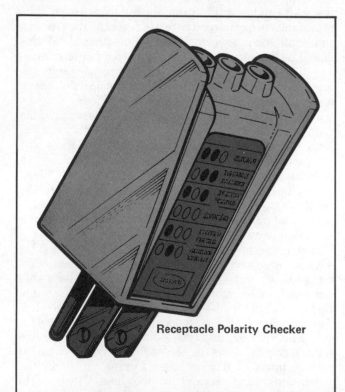

Receptacle Polarity Checker

To make sure outlets are installed properly—with the individual conductors going to the correct terminals— you can use a plug-in analyzer to check polarity.

tension cord; but keep all cords as short as possible.

To rewire a lamp, first pull the plug out; never do any work while the lamp is connected. Remove the shade, unscrew the bulb, and squeeze the socket shell at the switch to separate the shell and the cardboard insulator from the socket cap. *Do not* use a screwdriver to pry the socket apart if you plan to reuse the socket. Pull the socket out of the shell as far as the attached wire permits. If this doesn't give you enough wire to work with, push some of the cord up from the bottom of the lamp for additional slack.

Loosen the socket's terminal screws, and remove the cord wires from under them. If the lamp is a small one and the cord goes through in a fairly straight path, you should be able to slide the old wire out and easily feed the new wire through from one end or the other. But if the lamp is large and the cord twists inside it, your job can be more difficult. If the old cord offers any resistance at all, don't tug on it; check to see if you can disassemble the lamp to make removal easier. Also check to see if the cord is tied in a knot to keep it from being pulled out at its base. To remove a tight cord, cut the wire off about 12 inches from the lamp's base, slit the cord's two conductors apart, and strip about an inch of insulation off the ends; do the same to one end of the

Socket Shell

Cardboard Insulator

Socket

Socket Cap

Type SPT Cable (Zip Cord)

Lamp Base

Fixing a lamp is not difficult; the electrical components are inexpensive and easy to replace. The parts that are most often responsible for lamp failure are the socket, the cord, and the plug.

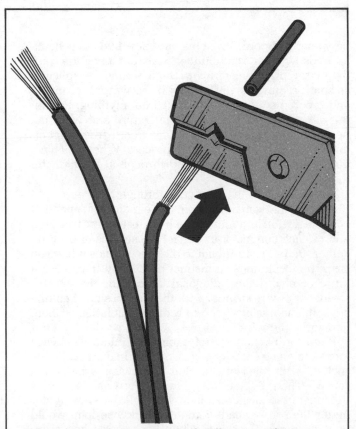

Before connecting the lamp cord, split the conductors apart for about three inches. Then, with a wire stripper, remove about 3/4 inch of insulation from each conductor end. Do not use a knife for this job.

Twist the exposed conductor strands to form a solid prong (top); then loop the prong clockwise around the terminal screw. The loop is snugged in as the screw is tightened.

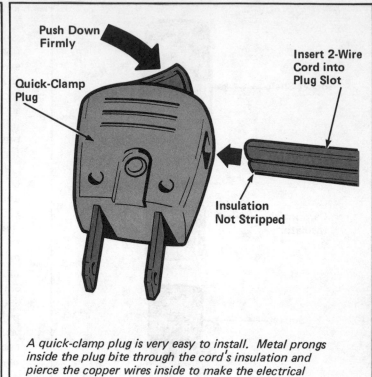

Push Down Firmly

Quick-Clamp Plug

Insert 2-Wire Cord into Plug Slot

Insulation Not Stripped

A quick-clamp plug is very easy to install. Metal prongs inside the plug bite through the cord's insulation and pierce the copper wires inside to make the electrical connection.

new length of cord. Twist the bare new and old conductor ends together and fold the twists flat along the cord; then wrap plastic electricians' tape around the splice in as small a lump as you can, with the wrapping smooth and tapered so that it won't catch on anything. Pull on the old cord from the top of the fixture and work the new cord through; push on the new cord from the bottom at the same time to aid the process. When you have a sufficient length of new cord through at the top, clip the old cord off.

Once you pass the new cord through the lamp, split the end so that you have about three inches of separated conductors. Strip about 3/4 inch of insulation from the end of each conductor and twist the strands of each together. Be very careful not to nick the strands when you strip the insulation—a distinct possibility if you use a knife or electricians' diagonal cutters for the job. Instead, use a wire stripper with the correct size of cutting slots; this tool is designed to remove insulation without damaging the wire.

Bend the twisted end of each wire into a clockwise loop, and place each loop under a terminal screw on the socket, with the loop curled clockwise around the screw. Then tighten the screws. As each screw is tightened, the clockwise loop will pull the wire tighter under the screw head; a counterclockwise loop would tend to loosen the wire. When both screw heads are snugged firmly over the bare conductor ends, clip off any excess bare wire with your diagonal cutters. It is important that all the uninsulated wire be under the screw heads, with no loose strands or exposed bare

wire. If the bare wire is visible beyond the screw heads, unscrew the terminals, remove the wires, and make the connection again.

Now slide the socket shell over the cardboard insulator, and slip shell and insulator over the socket. Then snap the shell and socket into the cap. That's all there is to it at the socket end of the lamp. A new cord, of course, requires a new plug. A quick-clamp plug is the easiest kind to connect; you merely stick the end of the cord into a slot on the side of the plug and push down on the lever at the top. Metal prongs inside the plug will bite through the cord's insulation, piercing the copper wires to make the electrical connection.

If you use a screw-type plug, however, you must prepare the wire ends just as you did when making the socket screw connections. Loop each wire around a prong of the plug before tightening the bare end under the screw head. The loops keep the wires apart and also make it more difficult to loosen the connections by pulling on the cord. Of course, you should never disconnect a lamp—or any other electrical device—by yanking the cord out of the wall socket, but the loops will give some strain support if the cord is jerked. Tighten the wires under the screw heads, and clip off any excess uninsulated conductor before you plug in the lamp.

Incandescent Wall and Ceiling Fixtures

As far as the electrical work is concerned, replacing a lighting fixture is relatively simple. You can even put in fluorescent lighting where you now have incandescent

Lamp Troubleshooting Chart

PROBLEM	POSSIBLE CAUSE	SOLUTION
Lamp does not light	1. Lamp unplugged.	1. Plug lamp in.
	2. Circuit dead.	2. Restore circuit.
	3. Bulb loose.	3. Tighten bulb.
	4. Bulb burned out.	4. Replace bulb.
	5. Loose connection at plug or socket.	5. Trace and repair.
	6. Defective wall switch.	6. Replace switch.
	7. Defective socket switch.	7. Replace socket.
	8. Defective center contact in socket.	8. Pry contact up or replace socket.
	9. Broken conductor in line cord.	9. Replace line cord.
Lamp blows fuse or trips circuit breaker	1. Overloaded circuit.	1. Check total load on circuit. If overloaded, transfer some equipment to different circuit.
	2. Short circuit in socket, in cord, or in lamp wiring.	2. Replace socket and cord. Rewire carefully to make sure no bare wires touch each other or any metal parts of lamp.
Lamp flickers when moved or touched	1. Lamp bulb loose in socket.	1. Tighten bulb.
	2. Loose connection, usually where line cord wires are fastened under terminal screws on lamp socket.	2. First make sure lamp is unplugged; then take socket apart and inspect wire connections under screws. Tighten screws or, if necessary, cut off a short piece of cord and reattach wire ends.
	3. Defective contacts or faulty switch in socket.	3. First make sure lamp is unplugged; then remove socket and replace it with new one.
	4. Defective lamp cord.	4. Replace cord. Rewire so no bare wires touch each other or any metal parts of lamp.

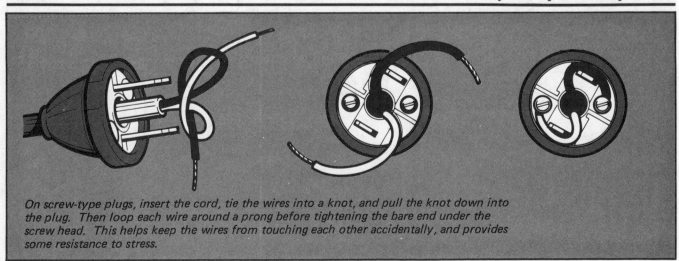

On screw-type plugs, insert the cord, tie the wires into a knot, and pull the knot down into the plug. Then loop each wire around a prong before tightening the bare end under the screw head. This helps keep the wires from touching each other accidentally, and provides some resistance to stress.

fixtures without encountering any great problems. In fact, the worst difficulties you'll probably encounter involve not the electrical connections but the mechanical complexities of attaching a new fixture to older mounting hardware. If you need more light, use a trouble light plugged into another circuit.

Caution: Before you replace or repair any lighting fixture, you must deenergize the appropriate electrical circuit. In a house that's properly wired (with switching done in the hot wire), turning off the wall switch deenergizes the fixture. Nevertheless, if you have any doubts at all regarding the wiring in your house, deenergize the entire circuit by pulling the appropriate fuse or tripping the proper circuit breaker.

With the fixture or the entire circuit deenergized and your alternate light source in position, take off the globe, unscrew the bulb(s), and disassemble all mounting hardware. Usually there are just screws holding the fixture against the wall or ceiling, but you may discover that a particular lighting fixture possesses no visible mounting hardware at all. If you don't see any screws or bolts, look for a decorative feature that could double as a fastener. Take off the mounting hardware and withdraw the fixture from the electrical box.

Disconnect the lamp fixture wires from the circuit wires. You may find that the wire joint is fused together with old insulating tape that defies easy removal. In this case, you'll find it simpler to cut the wires close to the tape. *Caution: If the wire insulation, or the conductors, coming into the electrical box are brittle or frayed, that part of the circuit or switch loop should be rewired.*

Once you remove the old fixture, examine the electrical box—as well as the new fixture—to determine which of the following installation procedures you should use.

Standard Electrical Box. Make sure you have about ³⁄₄ inch of bare copper conductor on the end of each line wire before you start to connect the wires of your new lighting fixture. If necessary, remove enough insulation from the line wires so that you can twist each line wire end together with the end of each light fixture wire, white wire to white and black to black. Screw a wirenut tightly over each pair of twisted ends. Hold onto the fixture to support its weight until you attach the mounting screws; otherwise, you might break a connection or damage the fixture wires.

If the fixture has more than one socket, connect the black wire from each socket to the black line wire, and the white wire from each socket to the white line wire. In other words, connect all the sockets in parallel to both line wires. Naturally, three or four socket wires joined to a line wire would require that you use a larger wirenut.

That's really all there is to do as far as the electrical connections are concerned. Now all you have to do is

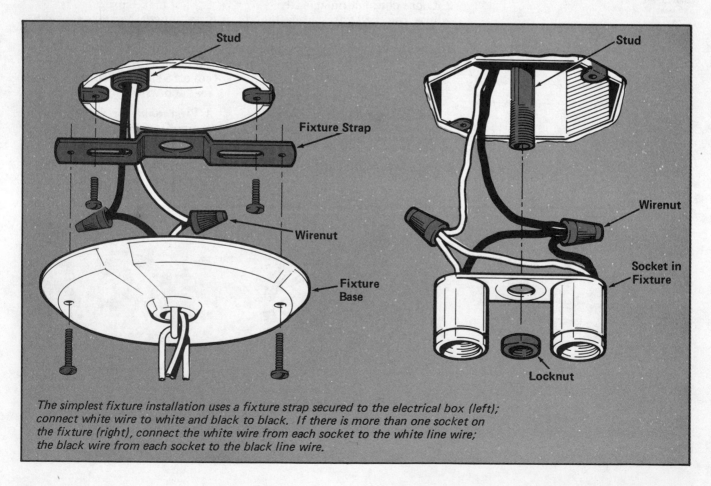

The simplest fixture installation uses a fixture strap secured to the electrical box (left); connect white wire to white and black to black. If there is more than one socket on the fixture (right), connect the white wire from each socket to the white line wire; the black wire from each socket to the black line wire.

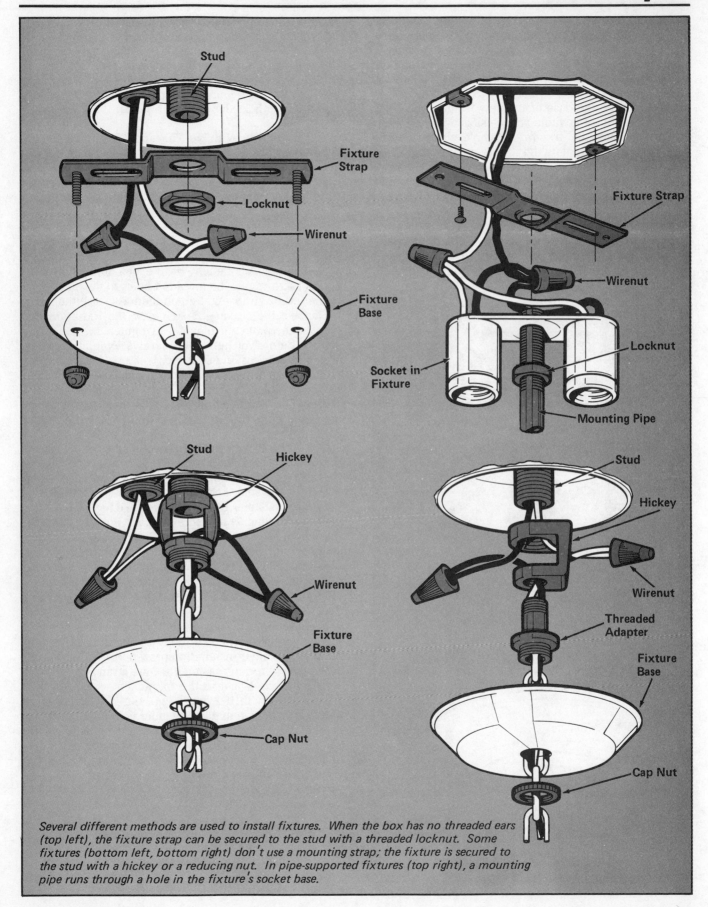

Stud

Fixture Strap

Locknut

Wirenut

Fixture Base

Fixture Strap

Wirenut

Socket in Fixture

Locknut

Mounting Pipe

Stud

Hickey

Wirenut

Fixture Base

Cap Nut

Stud

Hickey

Wirenut

Threaded Adapter

Fixture Base

Cap Nut

Several different methods are used to install fixtures. When the box has no threaded ears (top left), the fixture strap can be secured to the stud with a threaded locknut. Some fixtures (bottom left, bottom right) don't use a mounting strap; the fixture is secured to the stud with a hickey or a reducing nut. In pipe-supported fixtures (top right), a mounting pipe runs through a hole in the fixture's socket base.

mount the fixture. Usually, mounting screws of the proper length will be included with your new lamp fixture; screws 2 or 2½ inches long should take care of most fixtures. Insert the screws into the attachment screw holes in the electrical box, and tighten each screw four or five turns—just enough so that it holds in place. Examine the base of the new fixture; you'll see two or more sets of keyhole-shaped slots. Mount the fixture by passing the fixture's keyhole slots over the screw heads. Then rotate the fixture enough so that the screws go into the narrow parts of the keyhole slots.

Tighten the screws, but don't overtighten them; they should be just snug enough to hold the fixture firmly in place. If you tighten the mounting screws too much, you may distort and misalign the fixture. With the fixture mounted properly, screw in the bulbs, attach the globe or cover, and replace the fuse or trip the circuit breaker back on. Flip the wall switch. If the fixture lights, the

job is finished. If nothing happens, go back and figure out which connection needs remaking.

Some fixtures are mounted with a short piece of threaded pipe, called a nipple. To mount this type of fixture, screw the nipple into the center hole of the strap and set the fixture onto the nipple. Screw a cap nut onto the nipple to hold the fixture in place.

Electrical Box With No Threaded Ears. The electrical connections in a box with no threaded ears are exactly the same as those in the standard electrical box. The only difference is in mounting the new fixture. After you remove the old fixture, fasten a fixture strap to the threaded stud inside the electrical box, using a locknut that fits the stud threads. Frequently, the manufacturer packages a strap with the fixture, but if you have to buy one, make sure the screw holes are spaced so that they match the new fixture's mounting holes. Insert the screws into the threaded holes at the outer ends of the fixture strap, and tighten them two or three turns.

Connect the circuit line wires to the fixture wires, mount the fixture in place, and tighten the mounting screws. Before you tighten the screws completely, make sure all the wires and solderless connectors are tucked up inside the fixture and the electrical box. They should never be squeezed between the fixture strap and the fixture. Screw in the bulb(s), attach the globe or cover, and replace the fuse or trip the circuit breaker back on.

Box With No Mounting Strap. Some light fixtures are not strap-mounted. Instead, a nipple is connected to the box stud with a reducing nut—a nut threaded at one end to fit the stud, and at the other end to fit the nipple—or an adapter called a hickey. To mount a fixture that uses a reducing nut, screw the nut onto the stud and the nipple onto the nut, set the fixture onto the nipple, set the fixture into place, and screw a cap nut onto the nipple to hold the fixture in place. To mount a fixture with a hickey, screw the hickey onto the stud, and then mount the fixture the same way.

Pipe-Supported Fixtures. A replacement fixture that includes a globe held by a pipe running through its center demands other installation procedures. After you remove the old fixture, fasten a fixture strap firmly to the electrical box. Usually, the manufacturer packages a fixture strap with the new lamp, but if you must buy one, ask for a strap that has a center hole threaded to accommodate a ⅛-inch pipe. Connect the line wires to the fixture wires, and turn a locknut onto one threaded end of the mounting pipe. Now, while holding the fixture body up in its final mounting position, run the pipe through the hole in the fixture and thread it into the fixture strap far enough so that it holds the fixture firmly in place.

Screw a bulb into the fixture socket and turn the circuit on to make sure you installed everything properly. Then attach the globe with the threaded cap that comes with the fixture. You may find that the globe doesn't fit properly, but you can remedy this situation easily; just

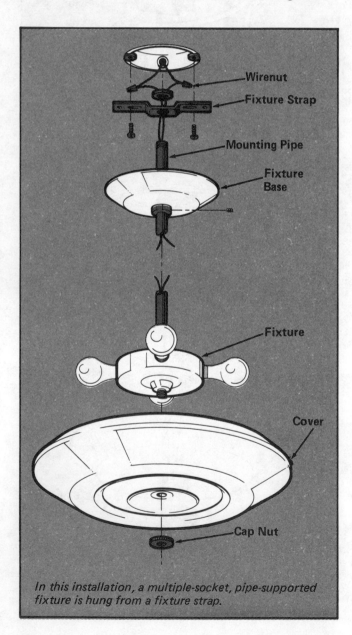

Wirenut

Fixture Strap

Mounting Pipe

Fixture Base

Fixture

Cover

Cap Nut

In this installation, a multiple-socket, pipe-supported fixture is hung from a fixture strap.

tighten or loosen the pipe a few turns from the fixture hanger. Be sure to adjust the position of the locknut to keep the fixture secure against the ceiling. Keep working with the pipe and locknut until precisely the right length of pipe hangs down to accommodate the globe and its mounting knob.

Fluorescent Lamps

Consider replacing some of your old incandescent fixtures with fluorescent lamps. Fluorescent light provides even and shadow-free illumination, but best of all, fluorescent bulbs produce much more light—watt for watt—than incandescent bulbs. In an incandescent bulb, much of the electric power is discharged as heat instead of light; the fluorescent bulb, in contrast, remains fairly cool.

In a fluorescent circuit, beginning at the left-hand prong of the plug, current goes through the ballast, then through one of the lamp filaments, through the closed switch in the starter, through the other filament in the lamp, and out the right-hand prong of the plug. The current heats the two small elements in the ends of the fluorescent tube; then the starter opens, and current flows through the lamp.

The ballast is a magnetic coil that adjusts the current through the tube. It makes a surge of current arc through the tube when the starter opens, and then keeps the current flowing at the right rate once the tube is glowing. In most fluorescent fixtures, the starter is an automatic switch. Once it senses that the lamp is glowing, it stays open. The starter closes whenever you deenergize the fixture.

Many fluorescent fixtures have more than one tube, to provide more light. These lamps must have individual starters and ballasts for each tube. The fixture may appear to have two tubes working off one ballast, but actually there are two ballasts built into one case. Fixtures with four tubes, similarly, have four starters and four ballasts. In some kinds of fixtures, the starters are built in and cannot be individually replaced.

Since there are only three principal parts in a fluorescent lamp—tube, starter, and ballast—you can usually take care of any repairs yourself. All fluorescent lamps grow dimmer with age, and they may even begin to flicker or flash on and off. These are warning signals, and you should make the necessary repairs as soon as you notice any change in the lamp's normal performance. A dim tube usually requires replacement, and failure to replace it can strain other parts of the fixture. Likewise, repeated flashing will wear out the starter, causing the insulation at the starter to deteriorate.

Fluorescent fixtures can be serviced quite simply by the replacement method. If you suspect that a part may be defective, install a new part. Start with the fluorescent tube or bulb. You can either install a new one or, if you're not sure the tube is burned out, test the old tube in another fluorescent fixture. Doing both gives you double verification. Remove the old tube by twisting it out of its sockets in the fixture. Install the new tube the

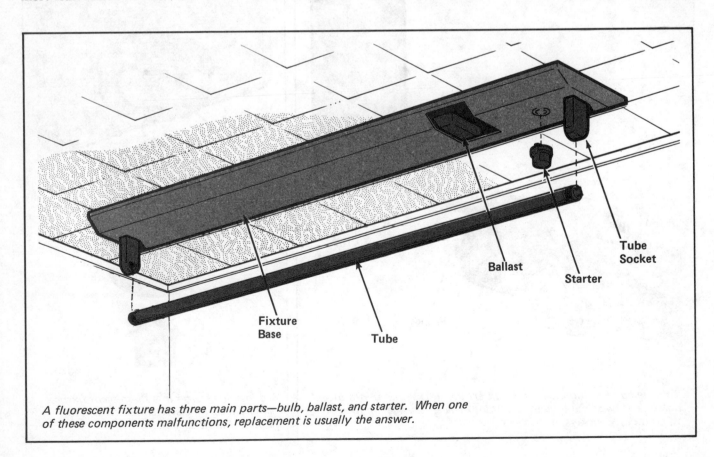

Ballast

Tube Socket

Starter

Fixture Base

Tube

A fluorescent fixture has three main parts—bulb, ballast, and starter. When one of these components malfunctions, replacement is usually the answer.

same way; insert the tube's prongs into the socket and twist the tube to lock it into place.

Caution: *Discard old fluorescent tubes carefully.* You may already be aware of the possible hazards in throwing away fluorescent tubes: youngsters have been injured by glass cuts and chemical effects when they pull discarded tubes from trash containers. To avoid problems, hide an old tube at the bottom of the trash or destroy the tube before you put it in the trash container. Wrap it in heavy paper (a grocery bag is fine), smash the tube with a hammer, and put the wrapped broken glass in another bag before disposing of it properly.

If the problem is not in the tube, change the starter, if possible. Fluorescent lamp starters are rated according to wattage, and it's important that you use the right starter for the tube in your fixture. Remove the old starter the same way you removed the old tube, by twisting it out of its socket in the fixture. Install the new one by inserting it into the socket and twisting it to lock it into place.

The ballast is also rated according to wattage, and a replacement ballast—like a replacement starter—must match the wattage of the tube and the type of fixture. The ballast is the least likely part to fail, and it is the most difficult to replace, so leave the ballast for last when you start replacing parts. But if neither the tube nor the starter is defective, the problem must be the ballast. To replace a faulty ballast, you must deenergize the circuit, disassemble the fixture, transfer wires from the old ballast to the new one—one at a time, to avoid an incorrect connection—and, finally, reassemble the fixture.

If the tube, the starter, and the ballast are all working properly, and the lamp still doesn't light, the only other possibility (if the lamp is receiving power) is a defective switch. If the lamp is controlled by a wall switch, replace the switch, as detailed below. If the lamp has a push-button switch, the old switch can be replaced by a new one of the same type. You must deenergize the circuit before working on the switch; if you're not sure about the wiring, remove the circuit's fuse or trip the circuit breaker.

In most cases, the switch screws into a threaded mounting nut on the inside of the lamp. Two wires from the switch are connected, usually with wirenuts, to four wires from the fluorescent tube. Disassemble the fixture as far as necessary to gain access to the back of the switch, and unscrew the old switch. Then screw in the new switch and transfer wires from the old switch to the new one, one at a time to avoid an incorrect connection. Finally, reassemble the fixture and reenergize the circuit.

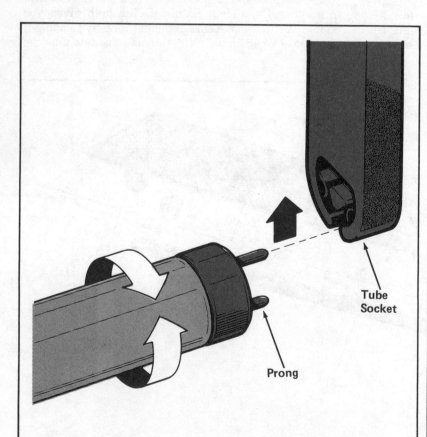

To install a new fluorescent tube, insert the tube's prongs into the holder and twist the tube to lock it into place. Change the tube when it dims, flickers, or flashes on and off.

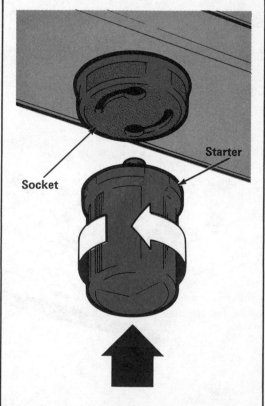

To install a starter in a fluorescent fixture, simply insert the starter and twist it to secure it in its socket.

Fluorescent Lamp Troubleshooting Chart

PROBLEM	POSSIBLE CAUSE	SOLUTION
Lamp will not light	1. Burned-out tube.	1. Replace with new fluorescent tube of correct dimensions and wattage.
	2. Defective starter.	2. Replace starter with new one of appropriate wattage.
	3. Defective ballast, sometimes accompanied by the odor of burning insulation.	3. Replace ballast; before replacing, consider cost of new ballast in comparison to value of lamp fixture.
	4. Defective switch.	4. Replace switch.
	5. Tube not seated correctly in sockets.	5. Reseat tube in sockets.
	6. No power to lamp.	6. Check power circuit.
Lamp glows dimly	1. Defective tube.	1. Replace tube. If lamp has been flashing on and off repeatedly for extended period, also replace starter.
	2. Defective starter.	2. Replace starter with one of correct wattage.
Tube ends lit but middle dim or dark	1. Wiring incorrect.	1. Check wiring.
	2. Shorted starter.	2. Replace starter with new one of appropriate wattage.
	3. Tube burned out.	3. Replace tube.
Spiraling or flickering lamp	1. Tube burned out.	1. Replace with new fluorescent tube of correct dimensions and wattage.
	2. Defective or wrong starter.	2. Replace starter with one of appropriate wattage.
	3. Low line voltage.	3. Check voltage; it must be within 10 percent of 120 volts.
	4. Wrong ballast.	4. Replace ballast.
Lamp flashes on and off repeatedly	1. Defective tube.	1. Replace tube and starter.
	2. Defective starter.	2. Replace starter with one of appropriate wattage.

If you're considering going to all the trouble involved in installing a new ballast, or switch, give some thought to putting in an entirely new fixture. An old fluorescent fixture suffers the same aging effects—in both appearance and performance—that an outmoded incandescent fixture does. Of course, you can also replace an old incandescent lamp with a new fluorescent model. Either replacement is well within the capabilities of the do-it-yourselfer.

Caution: Before you start, be sure to deenergize the old fixture. If your home is wired properly (with switching done only in the hot wire), simply turning off the wall switch will deenergize the fixture. If you're uncertain about the wiring, however, be sure to remove the circuit's fuse or trip the circuit breaker.

Remove the old hardware that holds the existing lamp fixture—either incandescent or fluorescent—in place, and disconnect the lamp wires from the circuit line wires. Then disassemble the new fluorescent lamp as far as necessary to gain access to the fixture wires, and connect the fixture wires to the line wires with wirenuts or crimp-type solderless connectors. Match the wires by color: white wire to white, black to black.

Position the fixture against the ceiling, and fasten it with the screws that are packaged with the new lamp. You may have to reassemble the fixture, either before

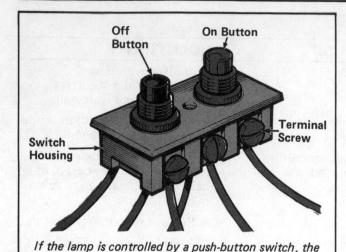

Off Button

On Button

Switch Housing

Terminal Screw

If the lamp is controlled by a push-button switch, the switch can also be replaced. Transfer the wires one at a time from the old switch to the new one.

or after mounting it; this depends on its style. Once you get the lamp back together, restore the power and turn on your new fluorescent lighting fixture.

Replacing a Wall Switch

Sometimes a lamp that's in perfect operating condition doesn't work because the wall switch is faulty. There are four primary symptoms of switch failure:

1. When the switch loses its snap, when the handle hangs loosely in any position, or when there is no clear distinction between the "off" and "on" positions.
2. When flipping the switch no longer turns the light on or off.
3. When flipping the switch makes the light flicker, but doesn't make it stay on or off.
4. When the switch may work occasionally, but you have to jiggle the handle back and forth several times to keep the light on.

If you spot any of these symptoms of switch failure, install a replacement wall switch as soon as you can. *Caution: First deenergize the electrical circuit that controls the switch.*

After deenergizing the circuit, remove the switch cover plate. If the cover plate doesn't come off easily, it is probably being held in place by several layers of paint. Use a razor blade or a craft or utility knife to cut the paint closely around the edge of the plate to free it. Then inspect the old switch to determine the type of replacement model you must buy; you must use the same type, but in most cases you can install a better grade of switch than the one you had before. All work on the same general principles, and you can usually choose a switch to get the features you like best.

The traditional single-pole toggle switch is still the most popular. When the toggle switch is mounted properly, the words "On" and "Off" are upright on the toggle lever, and the light goes on when you flip the switch

up. You can also buy a silent toggle switch. Although it costs more, the silent toggle switch is a pleasure to use, and is generally quite durable. One version contains a capsule of mercury that the toggle handle tilts to make electrical contact. It's especially important that you mount this type of switch properly; otherwise, the mercury will not make the correct contact.

A variation of the traditional toggle switch is the lever-action switch. The lever-action switch is designed to lie almost flush with the wall. It turns the fixture on when someone pushes the top of the switch in. Another type, the push-button switch, has a single button that turns the light on when pressed, and off when it's pressed again. Some switches, including the mercury type and the push-button type, are available with the extra feature of a built-in neon lamp that glows when the switch is off, making it easy to locate the switch in the dark. And dimmer switches, which have a dial to control the brightness of the light, turn the light off when the dial is turned all the way down or pushed in. You can install these switches as replacements for nearly any type of switch in your home.

Some kinds of wall switches have no terminal screws for conductor attachments. Instead, the switch has small holes that are only slightly larger than the bare copper conductors. After removing about ½ inch of insulation from the ends of the wires, you push the bare ends into the holes. Locking tabs make the electrical connection and grip the wires so that they can't pull out. To release the wires from the switch, all you have to do is insert a narrow-bladed screwdriver in the slots next to the wire-grip holes.

After you buy the type of replacement switch you want to install—and turn off the electric current to the old switch—you're ready to go to work. Remove the mounting screws on the switch cover plate and take off the plate. With the plate removed, you'll see two screws holding the switch in the switch box. Remove the screws and carefully pull the switch out of the box as far as the attached wires allow. If there are two screws with wires attached, the switch is a simple on-off (single-pole) type. If there are three screws with wires attached, you're working with a more complicated type called a three-way switch. The new switch must be the same type—single-pole or three-way—as the old one.

Three-way switches allow you to turn a light on and off from two different locations—such as at the top and the bottom of a stairway. Look carefully at the three terminal screws; you'll see that two are one color, while the third is a different color. *Do not* disconnect any wires until you compare the old switch with the replacement switch to make sure you know which wire goes to which terminal screw.

Loosen one of the old terminal screws, remove the wire, and attach the wire to the corresponding terminal screw on the new switch. Then do the same with the remaining wires. Take care to connect the wires so that all the bare wire is safely under the screw heads, and clip off any excess uninsulated wire. The procedure is the same whether you're working with a simple on-off

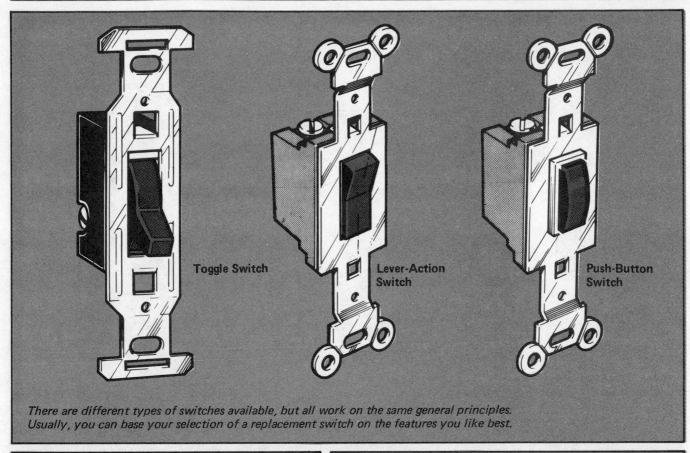

Toggle Switch   Lever-Action Switch   Push-Button Switch

*There are different types of switches available, but all work on the same general principles.
Usually, you can base your selection of a replacement switch on the features you like best.*

*Dimmer switches have a dial that controls the
brightness of the light, from bright to off.
A dimmer can be used to replace almost any
existing switch.*

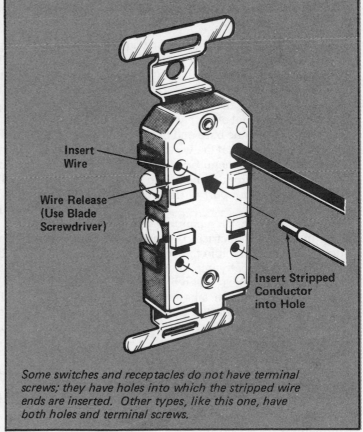

Insert Wire

Wire Release
(Use Blade
Screwdriver)

Insert Stripped
Conductor
into Hole

*Some switches and receptacles do not have terminal
screws; they have holes into which the stripped wire
ends are inserted. Other types, like this one, have
both holes and terminal screws.*

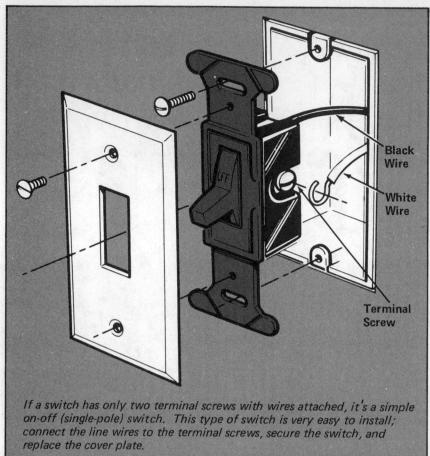

Black Wire

White Wire

Terminal Screw

If a switch has only two terminal screws with wires attached, it's a simple on-off (single-pole) switch. This type of switch is very easy to install; connect the line wires to the terminal screws, secure the switch, and replace the cover plate.

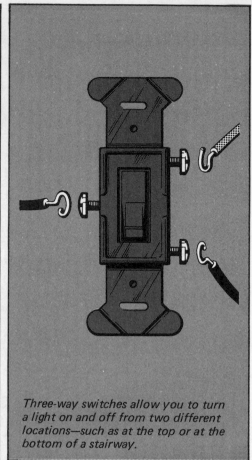

Three-way switches allow you to turn a light on and off from two different locations—such as at the top or at the bottom of a stairway.

switch or a three-way switch, but you must be more careful with the latter. Verify your wiring by comparing it with the diagram on the package your new switch came in.

If you're installing the modern wire-grip type of wall switch, cut off the end of each wire to leave only $1/2$ inch of bare wire. Push one bare end of wire into each wire-grip hole, and check that the wires have caught properly by tugging gently on them. *Caution: If the wire insulation, or the conductors, coming into the switch box are brittle or frayed, that part of the circuit or switch loop should be rewired.*

Now the only tasks remaining are to replace the switch in the wall electrical box and install the cover plate. Push the switch into the box carefully, and make sure the wires fit neatly into the box behind the switch. There are small tabs extending from the switch's mounting bracket; these tabs are supposed to lie flat against the wall outside the electrical box. They hold the switch flush with the wall no matter how the electrical box is angled inside.

Put the switch back into place, using the two mounting screws provided with the new switch. Oval holes in the mounting bracket allow you to fasten the switch so that it's straight up and down even when the screw holes in the electrical box are tilted. Finally, attach the cover plate with the screws you took out earlier, and re-

place the circuit fuse or trip the circuit breaker back on. Then enjoy the convenience of a switch that works the way it should.

Replacing a Broken Outlet

Few people call an electrical outlet by its proper name, a receptacle, but nearly everyone has come across an outlet that doesn't work as well as it should—or, perhaps, one that doesn't work at all. How does it happen that an outlet fails to do its job efficiently and safely? There are two possible explanations.

As you would expect, an electrical outlet can be permanently damaged through improper use. Sticking a hairpin or a paper clip in it, for example, is a sure way to shorten an outlet's—and your—life. You may never do anything so foolish as sticking hairpins or paper clips in an outlet, but you can do the same damage when you plug in an appliance with a short circuit. No matter how it happens, the damaged outlet must be replaced.

The other possible explanation for an outlet that doesn't work efficiently and safely is that it's just so old, and has been used so often, that it's worn out. There are two clear indications of a worn-out outlet: the cord drops of its own weight, pulling the plug out of the outlet; or the plug blades do not make constant electrical contact within the outlet slots. At that point, the old out-

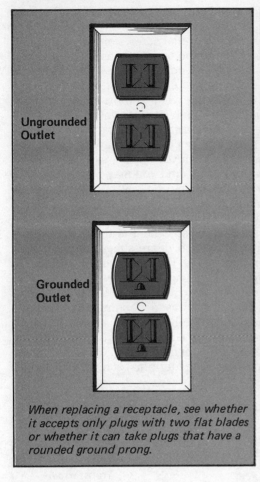

When replacing a receptacle, see whether it accepts only plugs with two flat blades or whether it can take plugs that have a rounded ground prong.

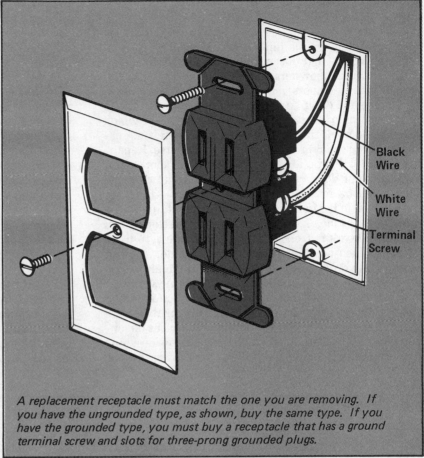

A replacement receptacle must match the one you are removing. If you have the ungrounded type, as shown, buy the same type. If you have the grounded type, you must buy a receptacle that has a ground terminal screw and slots for three-prong grounded plugs.

let must be replaced. This is not difficult, but you must follow the correct installation procedures precisely.

First, inspect the old outlet to see whether it accepts only plugs with two flat blades or whether it can take a plug that has a round prong (for grounding) in addition to two flat blades. Buy a new outlet with a 20-amp rating of the same type—grounded or ungrounded—as the one you're replacing. *Caution: Before working on the outlet, deenergize the circuit that controls it.*

After deenergizing the circuit, take off the plate that covers the outlet. This should be an easy task; the cover plate should fall off when you remove the center screw. If it doesn't, it's probably being held in place by several coats of paint. Cut the paint closely around the edge of the cover plate with a razor blade or a craft or utility knife.

Remove the two screws holding the outlet in the electrical box and carefully pull the outlet out of the box as far as the attached line wires allow. Loosen the terminal screws on the outlet and remove the line wires. *Caution: If you find that the wiring is quite old and that the insulation is brittle, that part of the circuit should be rewired.*

Connect the wires to the new outlet, with the white wire under the silver-colored screw and the black wire under the dark-colored screw. If there's a green or bare wire in the box, fasten it under the screw with the dab of green color on it, and then fasten it to the box with a grounding screw or clip. Be sure to loop the line wires in a clockwise direction under the heads of the terminal screws so that the screw heads will pull the wire loops tighter. Take care to connect the wires so that all the wire without insulation is safely under the screw heads. Clip off any excess uninsulated wire.

Carefully fold the wires into the space in the electrical box behind the outlet, and then push the outlet into the box. Although there's no such thing as right side up for a two-blade outlet, there is a correct position for outlets designed to handle three-prong grounding plugs. Grounding plugs often attach to their cords at a right angle; you should position the outlet so that the cord will hang down without a loop.

You'll also notice that the slots in an outlet are not identical; one is wider than the other. The wider one connects to the white or neutral wire while the narrower slot connects to the black or hot wire. Some plugs, in fact, are designed with one wide and one narrow blade, and these plugs will fit into the outlet in only one way. The idea behind such a polarized plug is to continue the hot and neutral wire identity from the circuit to the appliance.

Tighten the two screws that hold the receptacle in the outlet box, replace the cover plate, and your work is done. Restore the fuse or trip the circuit breaker.

Repairing a Broken Doorbell

A broken doorbell ranks as one of those electrical repairs that many people think a professional is required for, and yet one that doesn't need immediate attention. Thus, some homeowners simply put up a sign to tell friends and neighbors that the doorbell doesn't work, and then settle down to wait until the electrician has to be called in for some other pressing task—at which time the doorbell finally gets fixed too. There's no reason why you should follow this familiar course. Repairing a broken doorbell is a job you can do in short order.

When your doorbell or door chime doesn't ring, the fault could be in any part of the circuitry—from the push button to the bell or chime to the transformer. The transformer is the electrical component that steps down the 110-120-volt current to the approximately 10 to 18 volts at which doorbells and chimes operate. You can work safely on all parts of the doorbell circuit except the transformer without disconnecting the power.

If you don't know which part of the circuit is faulty, start by removing the screws that hold the doorbell push button to your house. Pull the button as far out as the circuit wires allow, and then detach the wires by loosening the terminal screws on the button. Now bring the two bare wire ends together. If the bell rings, you know the fault is in the button. Install a new one by connecting the two wires to the terminal screws of the new button and reattaching the button to your house. The doorbell button is a single-pole switch (two wires attached), and you can place either wire under either screw.

If the bell doesn't ring when you bring the two bare wire ends together, the fault lies elsewhere—in the bell or chime assembly, the wiring, or the transformer. Go to the bell or chime and remove the snap-on cover. Removal may be harder than you expect; there are several different types of covers, and you may have to try several procedures. Try lifting the cover upward slightly and then pulling it out. If this doesn't work, pull it straight out without first lifting it up. Or look to see whether the snap-on cover is held to the bell or chime assembly with prongs; if so, depress the prongs and then pull the cover to release it. Whatever you do, never pull so hard that you risk damaging the cover.

When you remove the cover, you will see two, three, or more terminals and wires, depending on how many tones ring in your doorbell system. A standard bell or buzzer has two wires. Detach the wires by loosening the terminal screws, and connect them to a 12-volt circuit tester or attach them to the terminal screws on a substi-

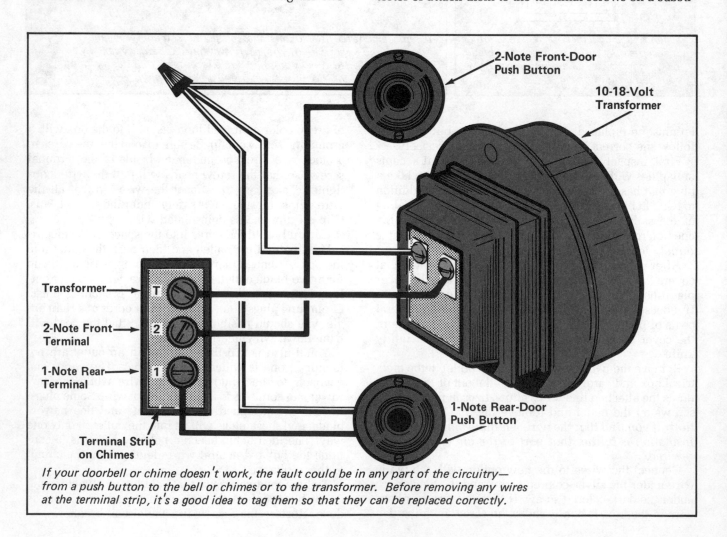

If your doorbell or chime doesn't work, the fault could be in any part of the circuitry— from a push button to the bell or chimes or to the transformer. Before removing any wires at the terminal strip, it's a good idea to tag them so that they can be replaced correctly.

tute bell or chime. An inexpensive bell or buzzer or a 12-volt car lamp bulb in a socket with two wires can be used for testing purposes. If the test bell or buzzer sounds or the bulb lights when you push the doorbell button, you'll have to install a new bell or chime.

If you have a chime assembly with three or more wires, tag them with masking tape: "T" for transformer, "2" for the front-door chime, and "1" for the back-door chime. Loosen the terminal screws, remove all the wires, and connect the wires labeled "T" and "2" to the screw terminals on the test bell or bulb. If the test bell rings or the bulb lights when you push the front door button, your old chime set is faulty. To check this conclusion, connect the wires labeled "T" and "1" to the screw terminals on the test bell. If the bell rings when you push the back-door button, then you're doubly certain that the chimes must be replaced.

What if the bell doesn't ring or the bulb doesn't light at the button or at the bell or chime box? In this case, neither the button nor the bell is defective; by the process of elimination, you now know that the problem must be in the transformer or the wiring. You'll usually find the transformer mounted on an electrical junction box, a subpanel, or the main entrance panel. Generally, the transformer connections to the power lines are hidden from view within the box. The bell wires are attached to exposed terminal screws on the transformer. Connect the test bell directly to the exposed low-voltage transformer terminals; don't touch any other screws. If

the bell doesn't ring, you can be sure that the transformer is defective or not getting power.

Caution: Unlike the other parts of the circuit, the transformer is connected directly to the power supply, and carries current that can hurt you. Before working on the transformer, you must deenergize the branch circuit that supplies power to the transformer. Remove the appropriate fuse or trip the correct circuit breaker, or—if you don't know which circuit controls the doorbell—throw the main switch to shut off all the electricity in your home.

Before replacing the transformer, check to make sure that it's getting power from the 110-120-volt circuit. With the circuit deenergized, disconnect the transformer from the line wires. One easy way to make a line circuit test is to attach a spare screw-terminal lamp socket, fitted with a 110-120-volt bulb, to the line wires. If the terminals are exposed, wrap a piece of electrical tape around the socket to cover them. You can also use an old lamp; remove the plug, and connect the lamp wires to the line wires with wirenuts. Then turn the circuit back on again. If the lamp lights, the circuit is fine; the transformer is faulty, and must be replaced.

An alternative and easier method of testing, if you're sure of your electrical skills, is to separate the two line wires so that they *cannot* touch each other or any part of the electrical box. Turn the circuit back on, and gently touch the probes of a 110-120-volt circuit tester to the bare wire ends. If you get a positive indication from the

Doorbell or Chime Troubleshooting Chart

PROBLEM	POSSIBLE CAUSE	SOLUTION
Bell or chime does not ring	1. Defective button.	1. Test by removing button and touching wires together. If bell rings, button is defective; replace button.
	2. Defective bell or chimes.	2. Detach wires from bell or chimes and connect them to a test bell or light. If bell rings or bulb lights when doorbell button is depressed, bell is defective; replace bell.
	3. Defective transformer.	3. Connect test bell to transformer and press door button. If bell does not ring, transformer is defective; replace transformer.
	4. Loose connection or break in circuit.	4. Trace and check all wiring; tighten loose connections or replace damaged wiring.
	5. No power at transformer.	5. Check to see that circuit is turned on; check for loose connection at transformer primary. If transformer is defective, replace.

tester (tester light glows, or indicator reads 110-120 volts), the circuit is all right. **Caution:** *Always keep in mind that you're working with hot wires; don't touch them!*

If the transformer is defective, deenergize the circuit and remove the transformer. Buy a replacement transformer of the same voltage and wattage (or VA—volts/amps). You can find the electrical information stamped on the transformer, and you should find installation instructions on the package. Follow the instructions carefully. Use crimp-on connectors or wirenuts to attach the new transformer to the circuit line wires of your electrical system. Then connect the bell wires to the low-voltage screw terminals on the transformer, turn the power back on, and press the doorbell button. If you've installed the transformer properly, you should hear the bell or chime.

If the transformer and its power circuit prove to be all right, the only possibility left is a break or a loose connection somewhere in the bell wiring. Since a loose connection is more likely, trace the entire bell circuit from transformer to bell or chime to push buttons, and search for a loose terminal screw or wire joint. If this proves unsuccessful, you'll have to check each segment of the circuit with a continuity tester.

Disconnect the bell wires at the transformer to de-energize the bell circuit—a continuity tester can never be used on an energized circuit. Then disconnect the transformer wires at the bell or chime, and twist them together just enough so that they make good contact with one another. Go back to the transformer, and touch the probe leads of the continuity tester to the bare ends of the bell wires. If the tester lights up, or you get a reading on the meter dial, the circuit has continuity and there are no breaks or loose connections in the line; that part of the circuit is all right. If the tester does not register, there's a break somewhere.

If there is a break, you must try to locate it and make repairs. Sometimes, however, especially where much of the bell circuit wiring is hidden within walls or is otherwise inaccessible, the easiest course is to run a new segment of bell wire along whatever path is easiest, and forget about the old wiring segment.

If that particular segment of the bell circuit proves to be fault-free, go on to the next segment and check it the same way. Make sure both ends of the segment are disconnected; twist the two wires together at one end of the line and touch the tester leads to the two separated wire ends at the other end of the line. Continue this process with each segment or leg of the circuit, and eventually you'll locate the break. Once repairs are made or new wire is run, the bell or chime system will be operational.

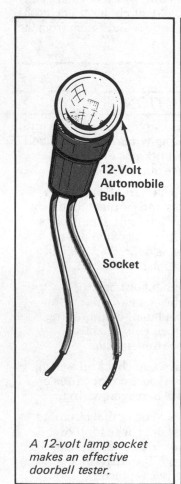

12-Volt Automobile Bulb

Socket

A 12-volt lamp socket makes an effective doorbell tester.

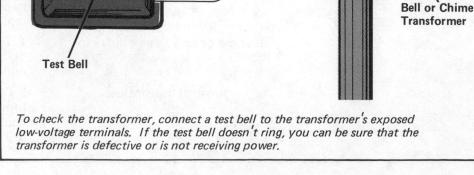

Test Bell

Low-Voltage Terminals

Bell or Chime Transformer

To check the transformer, connect a test bell to the transformer's exposed low-voltage terminals. If the test bell doesn't ring, you can be sure that the transformer is defective or is not receiving power.

Appliances

Like all the conveniences of modern living, appliances have become not a luxury but a necessity. Major appliances provide comfort and convenience; they keep your home working smoothly and efficiently; they save time and trouble and work. They don't make up a single system, but together they act as one of the most important components of your home: the service-providers, the mechanical gadgets that do the drudge work and simplify all your housekeeping chores.

Appliances are built to perform. They work hard, year after year—and, usually, without too many problems. They're easy to take for granted. The result is that when an appliance breaks down, you may be completely at a loss—you don't know how it works or why it's stopped working, much less how to fix it. In this situation, you're at the mercy of the professionals—and professional repairs are expensive.

Actually, appliances are not anything you should be afraid of. All appliances work on the same fundamental principles, and all appliance repairs are based on these principles.

How Appliances Work

Most appliances operate on your home's electrical system; they use AC current from the circuit wiring in your home. Small appliances work on 110-120-volt circuits; the plugs on their cords have two blades. Large appliances, such as air conditioners, dryers, and ranges, usually require 220-240-volt wiring, and cannot be operated on 110-120-volt circuits. Large appliances are wired with a grounding wire; their plugs have two blades and a prong. This type of appliance must be plugged into a grounded outlet—one with openings to accept both blades and grounding prong — or grounded with a special adapter plug. All appliances are labeled, either on a metal plate or on the appliance casing, to show their power requirements in watts and volts, and sometimes in amps.

Small appliances are usually fairly simple machines. They may consist of a simple heating element, or of a fan, a set of blades, or rotating beaters attached to a drive shaft; or they may have two or three simple mechanical linkages. Repairs to these appliances are usually correspondingly simple. Large appliances are more complex—one major appliance, such as a washing machine, may have a motor, a timer, a pump, and various valves, switches, and solenoids. In this type of appliance, problems can occur in either the control devices or the mechanical/power components. Failure of a control device may affect one operation or the entire appliance; failure of a mechanical/power device usually affects only the functions that depend on that device. When a large appliance breaks down, knowing how to diagnose the problem is as important as knowing how to fix it.

Because large appliances are so complex, it usually isn't obvious where a malfunction is. The first step is to decide whether the problem is in a control device or a mechanical device. In a dryer, for example, the control devices govern the heat; the mechanical components turn the drum. Which system is affected? If the drum turns but the dryer doesn't heat, the problem is in the control system; if the dryer heats but the drum doesn't turn, the problem is mechanical. This kind of analysis can be used to pinpoint the type of failure — control system or mechanical system—in all large appliances.

To find out exactly what the problem is, you must check each part of the affected system to find the malfunctioning part. This isn't as difficult as it sounds, because appliance components work together in a logical sequence; starting with the simplest possibilities, you can test the components one by one to isolate the cause of the failure. The troubleshooting charts in this chapter will help you diagnose the problem. Each chart also describes the measures you should take to repair the appliance once you've found the problem.

Key Appliance Repair Principles

There are three very important rules to follow in making appliance repairs:

- *Always* — with no exceptions — make sure the electric power and/or the gas supply to the appliance is disconnected *before* you test the appliance to diagnose the problem, or make any repairs. If you turn the power on to check your work after making a repair, do not touch the appliance; just turn the power on and observe. Never touch the appliance while it is running. If adjustments are needed, turn the power off before you make them.

- If the parts of an appliance are held together with screws, bolts, plugs, and other take-apart fasteners, you can probably make any necessary repairs. If the parts are held together with rivets or welds, don't try to repair the appliance yourself; call a professional service person.

- In most cases, broken or malfunctioning appliance parts can be replaced more quickly and inexpensively than they could be repaired, by you or by a professional. Replace broken or malfunctioning parts with new parts made especially for the appliance. Appliance parts are available from appliance service centers, appliance repair dealers, and appliance parts stores. You don't *always* have to go to a specific brand-name appliance parts service center to obtain the parts and service you need for brand-name appliances, so you have some shopping/service choice. If you can't locate a parts service center in your area, order the part you need directly from the manufacturer; give the manufacturer all the model and parts data possible for the appliance. The name and address of the appliance manufacturer are usually printed on the appliance.

These three basics are essential for safe and successful appliance repairs. Don't ever try to save time or money by ignoring them — you won't save anything at all, and you could end up hurting yourself or ruining the appliance.

Before you make any appliance repair, make sure the appliance is receiving power — lack of power is the most common cause of appliance failure. Before you start the testing and diagnosis process, take these preliminary steps:

- Check to make sure that the appliance is properly and firmly plugged in, and that the cord, the plug, and the outlet are working properly. To determine whether an outlet is working, test it with a voltage tester, as detailed below in the section on electrical testing tools.

- Check to make sure the fuses and/or circuit breakers that control the circuit have not blown or tripped. There may be more than one electrical entrance panel for your home, especially for 220-240-volt appliances such as ranges and air conditioners — check for blown fuses or tripped circuit breakers at both the main panel and the separate panel. If necessary, restore the circuit.

- Check to make sure fuses and/or breakers in the *appliance* are not blown or tripped. Push the

reset buttons to restore power on such appliances as washers, dryers, and ranges. Some ranges have separate plug-type fuses for oven operation; make sure these fuses have not blown.

- If the appliance uses gas or water, check to make sure it is receiving an adequate supply.

- Check your owner's manual; many manufacturers include very helpful problem/solution troubleshooting charts. If you don't have a manual for an appliance, you can probably get one — even for an old or obsolete appliance — from the manufacturer's customer service department.

Disassembling and Reassembling Appliances

Before you can repair an appliance, you'll almost always have to disassemble it to some extent. All appliances are different, but the disassembly procedure is always the same: basically, you must remove the parts in reverse of the way the manufacturer put them together. Remember that you'll have to put the appliance back together again. Lay the parts out in order as you remove them, with fasteners at hand. If you aren't sure you'll be able to put the appliance back together, take notes and make drawings as you work. Label all terminals and wires if you must disconnect more than one wire at a time. Check your owner's manual for assembly diagrams and instructions.

To disassemble an appliance, start with the obvious knobs and fasteners. Many knobs and dials are push-fit; simply pull them off their control shafts. Knobs may also be held in place by setscrews, springs or spring clips, or pins; or they may be screwed on. All of these types are easy to release. Housing panels are usually held by screws or bolts; they may also be held in place by tabs. Sometimes parts are force-fitted, and may be hard to remove. Never force parts apart; look for hidden fasteners. For instance, there may be no obvious fasteners holding the top of a washer in place. You can locate the clips that hold the top down by sticking the blade of a putty knife into the seam where the top panel meets the side panel; run the knife along the seam until you hit an obstruction. This is a spring clip. To release the clip, push the blade of the knife directly into the clip, at a right angle to the seam, while pushing up on the top panel. Repeat this procedure to locate and remove any other spring clips holding the top panel; then lift the panel off.

Fasteners may also be hidden under a nameplate or company logo, behind a scarcely visible plastic plug or under a cork pad on the bottom of the appliance, or under an attachment plate. Carefully pry up the part that's hiding the fastener. When you reassemble the appliance, snap the concealing part back over the fastener, or, if necessary, glue it into place. If you can't find hidden fasteners on force-fitted parts, warm the parts gently with a heating pad; the heat may make disassembly easier. Inside the appliance,

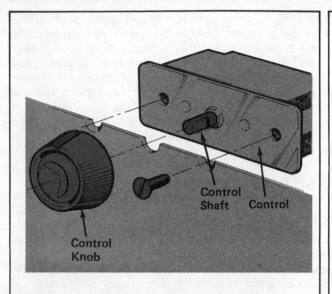

To disassemble an appliance, start with the obvious knobs and fasteners. Knobs and dials either pull right off or are held by setscrews, pins, or clips.

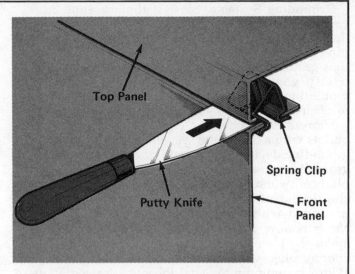

Spring clips are often hidden. To remove a panel held by spring clips, use a putty knife to find each clip; then push in against it to release the panel.

watch for clips holding parts to the housing panels.

After making the repair, and before reassembling the appliance, vacuum inside the appliance to remove all dust and lint. Check for other problems and make any necessary repairs or adjustments. If the appliance has a motor, lubricate the motor; check carbon brushes in universal motors for wear, and replace them if necessary, as detailed below in the section on motor maintenance and repairs. Lubricate moving parts sparingly, and make sure electrical contacts are clean.

Reassemble the appliance in reverse of the way you took it apart; never force parts together or overtighten fasteners. Make sure moving parts, such as armatures or gears, don't bind. After reassembly, connect the appliance and turn it on. If it makes noise, smells, or overheats, turn it off and disconnect the power. Then go back over your repair.

Mechanical and Electrical Safety

You may be tempted to work on an appliance while it's running, or to test an appliance while the power is on. This is something you can never do safely. *Never* work on any running appliance that's had its access or service panels removed; *never* stick your hands or your tools into moving parts such as gears, belts, pulleys, and other moving components. When you turn the power on to check your work after making a repair, *do not* touch the appliance; simply turn the power on and observe. If adjustments are needed, turn the power off before you make them.

There's one more very important safety factor to remember in making appliance repairs: electricity can be dangerous, and you should *never* allow yourself or your tools to make contact with an electrical current. You must be extremely careful when making repairs to appliances powered by electricity. Before you start work on an appliance, unplug it from its power source. If it can't be unplugged, turn off the power to the circuit that supplies electricity to the appliance by removing the fuse or tripping the circuit breaker to the circuit at the main entrance panel in your home, or, in some cases, at a separate entrance panel. After turning off the power, test the appliance to make sure it's off. If the appliance doesn't work, *do not* assume that the power is off. Instead, check the leads to a motor, convenience light, or other component of the appliance that can be tested with a voltage tester. If the light of the tester does not come on, you can assume that the electricity to the appliance is off. If it does come on, the appliance is still connected, and you must locate the power source and turn it off before proceeding further.

Large appliances often have electrical circuits separate from the main power panel. This is especially true in older homes where appliances such as washers, dryers, ranges, and air conditioners have been added after the original wiring was done. Because large appliances require more power than many old wiring systems can supply, a separate fuse or circuit-breaker system is sometimes installed to handle the extra electrical load. These auxiliary power entrances are usually—but not always—located near the main entrance panel. Make a thorough check for additional fuse or breaker boxes before you assume that you've turned off the power to the appliance.

Grounding Systems. Most stationary appliances (washers, dryers, ranges) are grounded by a wire that's attached to a cold-water pipe. The cold-water pipe runs into the ground outside your home, and thus grounds the appliance so that any leaking electricity goes into the ground. Disconnect this grounding wire before you make repairs, and be sure to reconnect it before you turn the power back on.

Many homes today are equipped with electrical outlets with a three-wire system. The third wire is a grounding device, and operates the same way as the grounding wire on stationary appliances. Large appliances, whose plugs have two blades and a prong, should be plugged into a grounded outlet, or grounded with a special adapter plug. *Caution: Never remove the prong from a three-wire plug to make it fit an ungrounded outlet; always use an adapter plug.*

Proper grounding is vital for metal-framed appliances. If the insulation on the power cord of a metal-framed appliance (such as a washer or dryer) is broken or worn away just at the point where the cord enters the frame, contact between the current conductor and the metal frame could charge the whole appliance with electricity — obviously a dangerous situation. When this happens, even if the appliance is properly grounded, dampness can cause a shock hazard. If you touched a charged metal frame in a damp location, or while touching a water faucet or radiator, the current would surge through you, and could kill you.

There are three things you can do to eliminate this hazard. First, make sure your appliances are properly grounded, and follow the electrical safety rules presented in the chapter on electrical repairs. Second, make sure that appliance cords are in good repair, and that they are not chafing against burrs or rough spots where they enter the appliance frame. And third, add a ground-fault circuit interrupter (GFI or GFCI) to the circuit. Ground-fault circuit interrupters are monitoring devices that instantly shut off a circuit when a current leak occurs; they are required by the National Electrical Code on all new 15- and 20-amp outdoor outlets, and for wiring in bathrooms, where dampness is a common problem. GFIs are available to plug into existing outlets as adapters, to replace outlets, and to replace circuit breakers in the electrical entrance panel. A professional electrician should install the circuit-breaker type; you can install the other types yourself. Ground-fault circuit interrupters are available at electrical supply and home center stores.

Double-Insulated Appliances. In double-insulated appliances and power tools, the electrical components are isolated from any parts of the appliance that could carry electrical current. These appliances are not completely shock-safe, of course; you should use caution with any electrical device — never operate an electric drill, for example, while standing on a wet surface; never drill into a wall where power lines may be present. Double-insulated appliances and tools should almost always be repaired by a professional, because the double-insulation depends on a plastic housing and a plastic buffer between parts that carry electricity. If these plastic parts are not properly positioned, the appliance or tool could produce a harmful electrical shock. Appliances and tools that are double-insulated are usually labeled as such.

The Appliance Repair Workshop

For most appliance repair jobs, you'll need only simple tools, both mechanical and electrical. These tools are inexpensive, readily available, and easy to use; you may well have most of them in your workshop already. There is some very sophisticated equipment needed for complex repair work, and this equipment is expensive — but it's still, in the long run, less expensive than professional service. For most jobs, however, simple tools are adequate.

Buy your appliance repair tools as you need them, if you don't already own these basics. The necessities are simple. First, you'll need a selection of good-quality screwdrivers — at least three sizes for standard slotted screws, and at least one Phillips-type screwdriver. For small appliances, you may need smaller screwdrivers. You'll also need a hammer—a claw hammer is fine—an adjustable wrench and a socket wrench set, a pump-type oil can, a utility knife, and a trouble light. Some simple electrical equipment is also necessary — a fuse puller, a multi-purpose tool for stripping the insulation off conductors and crimping solderless connectors, a test wire or jumper wire with an alligator clip on each end, and a 20,000-ohm, 2-watt wire-wound resistor, for work on capacitor-type motors. Resistors are not expensive; they're available at most appliance and television parts stores. All of your electrical tools should have insulated handles.

Tools for Electrical Testing

Many appliance repairs also require electrical testing for accurate diagnosis of the problem. At least 80 percent of the time, you'll be able to pinpoint an appliance malfunction from the troubleshooting charts included in this chapter, and proceed from them to make the repair. But the other 20 percent of the time, you'll need one of three electrical testing devices to spot the problem: a voltage tester, a continuity tester, or a volt-ohm-milliammeter (VOM). With this equipment you'll be able to tell whether the electrical current is reaching and flowing through the part of the appliance you suspect.

Voltage Tester. The voltage tester is the simplest of these three tools. It consists of a small neon bulb

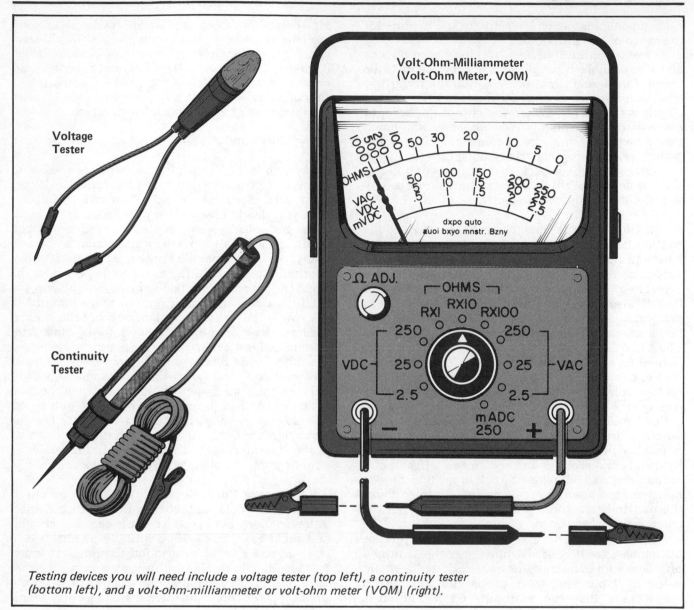

Testing devices you will need include a voltage tester (top left), a continuity tester (bottom left), and a volt-ohm-milliammeter or volt-ohm meter (VOM) (right).

with two insulated wires attached to the bottom of the bulb housing; each wire ends in a metal test probe. The voltage tester is used with the current turned on, to determine whether there is current flowing through a wire and to test for proper grounding. It is also sometimes used to determine whether adequate voltage is present in a wire. Look for a tester rated for up to 500 volts.

To use a voltage tester, touch one probe to one wire or connection and the other probe to the opposite wire or connection. If the component is receiving electricity, the light in the housing will glow; if the light doesn't glow, the trouble is at this point. For example, if you suspect that an electrical outlet is faulty, insert one probe of the tester into one slot in the outlet, and the other probe into the other slot. The light in the tester should light; if it doesn't, the outlet may be bad. To further test the outlet, pull it

out of the wall. Place one probe of the tester on one terminal screw connection and the other probe on the other terminal screw. If the tester bulb lights, you know the outlet is malfunctioning—there is current flowing to the outlet, but it isn't flowing *through* the outlet to provide power to the appliance plugged into it. If the test bulb doesn't light, there is no current coming into the outlet. The problem may be a blown fuse or tripped circuit breaker, or the wire may be disconnected or broken behind the outlet.

Continuity Tester. The continuity tester, the primary diagnosis tool for many appliance repairs, consists of a battery in a housing, with a test probe connected to one end of the battery housing and a test wire with an alligator clip connected to the other end. The continuity tester is used with the current turned off, to determine whether a particular electrical component is carrying electricity and to pinpoint the cause of a malfunction.

To use a continuity tester, unplug the appliance and disassemble it to get at the component to be tested. *Caution: Do not use a continuity tester unless the appliance is unplugged or the power to the circuit is turned off.* Fasten the clip of the tester to one wire or connection of the component and touch the probe to the other wire or connection. If the component is receiving electricity and transmitting it, the tester will light or buzz; the circuit is continuous. If the tester doesn't light or buzz, or if it reacts only slightly, the component is faulty.

Volt-Ohm Meter (VOM). The voltage tester and the continuity tester are adequate for many diagnostic jobs, and they're fairly inexpensive. But for serious appliance troubleshooting and repairs, you should invest in a volt-ohm-milliammeter or volt-ohm meter (VOM), also known as a multitester. VOMs range in price from $10 to more than $100; you can buy one that's adequate for appliance testing for about $35. The VOM is battery-powered and is used with the current turned off. It's used to check continuity in a wire or component and to measure the electrical current — from 0 to 250 volts, AC or DC — flowing through the wire or component. *Caution: Do not use a VOM unless the appliance is unplugged or the power to the circuit is turned off.* The VOM is used with plug-in test leads, which may have probes at both ends or a probe at one end and an alligator clip at the other. An adjustment knob or switch is set to measure current on the scale desired, usually ohms; the dial indicates the current flowing through the component being tested.

The VOM is particularly useful for appliance testing because it is used while the power is turned off; there's no danger of electric shock while you're using it. It provides more precise information, in many cases, than the continuity tester, and so is preferable for testing many components. Learning to read a VOM is very easy, and manufacturers provide complete operating instructions with the meters. You can also buy information sheets on test readings of various electrical components used in appliances and in other applications, such as lights, switches, and outlets. Where a standard reading is available, this information has been included in the appliance repairs covered here. All readings are given in ohms; make sure you read the VOM dial on the ohms scale.

Repairing and Replacing Basic Components

Regardless of how complex they are, appliances are put together with the same basic electrical components—electrical conductors, a cord and a plug, and various switches, sensors, and elements. All of these components can malfunction, and what looks like a total breakdown in an appliance is often traceable to the failure of a very simple component. For this reason, it's important to know how these basic electrical components work, why they fail, and how to repair or replace them. With this information, you can take care of many appliance problems very simply, with the minimum of effort and inconvenience.

Power Cords and Plugs

Many appliance "breakdowns" are really due to worn, frayed power cords or plugs that no longer make good electrical contact. To ensure safe operation, you should check all appliance cords for problems periodically, and replace frayed or broken cords immediately. When you suspect a cord is faulty, remove it from the appliance and test it with a continuity tester. Clip the tester to one blade of the plug, and touch the probe to one of the two wires — or, if it's a plug-in cord, insert the probe into one of the two holes — at the appliance end of the cord. If the tester lights or buzzes, move it to the other wire or hole and test again. Repeat this procedure to test the other blade of the plug. If the tester lights or buzzes at every test point, the cord is not faulty; if it fails to light or buzz at any point, the cord or the plug is faulty. You can pinpoint the defect by cutting off the plug and testing the cut end of the cord; if the tester lights or buzzes at all test points now, the plug is the defective part. The damaged component — cord or plug, or both—should be replaced.

Replacing a Cord. Replacing the cords on appliances, power tools, and other equipment is generally a simple chore. Some special cords can, and should, be bought as complete sets, with a plug attached to one end and special connection terminals attached to the other end. General-purpose cords can be fashioned from a separate plug, a length of an appropriate type of cord, and perhaps connection terminals as well. Electric ranges and clothes irons, for example, use complete-set-type cords; table saws and mixers use general-purpose cords. Always make sure you replace the old cord with a new one of the same type.

Often, the hardest part of the job is trying to determine how the appliance comes apart so that you can remove the old cord and attach a new one. Sometimes all you have to do is remove the cover from a connection box, as on a water pump. In other cases, as with a small hair dryer, the unit itself must be partially disassembled before you can reach the terminals. In nearly all cases, the cord is held in place by a clamp or by a fitted strain-relief device. To remove the cord, unscrew the terminal screws or pull the pressure connectors apart, loosen the clamp or remove the strain-relief device, and pull the cord out. Installation of the new cord is simply a reverse procedure. Be sure to save the strain-relief device and replace it on the new cord. If you have to destroy the strain-relief device to remove it, replace it with a new one of the same type.

In some equipment, the conductor ends are looped around terminal screws, and making new connections is easy. Carefully strip off the outer insulation—not the insulation on the inner wires—for about three inches at the end of the cord. Then, with a wire stripper, remove about ½ inch of insulation from the end of each conductor wire. Twist the exposed filaments of each wire, clockwise, into a solid prong. Loosen the terminal screws and loop each bare wire end clockwise around a screw; then tighten the screws firmly. Connect the wires at the appliance end of the new cord the same way the old ones were connected.

In some appliances, solderless connection terminals may be clamped to the old cord, and you'll have to fit replacement terminals to the new cord. This requires terminals of a matching kind, and a tool called a staker or crimper. You can find this tool at automotive or electrical supply stores. In a few cases, the terminals may be soldered to the conductor ends. You can replace them with solderless connectors.

Replacing a Plug. If only the plug of an appliance is faulty, you can attach a new plug to the old cord. Male plugs, with two blades or with two blades and a grounding prong, plug into an outlet. Female plugs, often used at the appliance end of the cord, have terminal holes instead of blades. Male plugs can usually be taken apart so you can get at the terminal screws. Female plugs may be held together by rivets or by screws; screw-held plugs can be taken apart, but rivet-held plugs cannot be repaired. When a plug malfunctions, open the plug, if possible, and check to make sure the conductor wires are properly attached to the plug's screw terminals. If the wires are loose, tighten the screw terminals. This may solve the problem; otherwise, the plug should be replaced.

To attach a new male plug, insert the cord end through the plug opening, and pull it through for about five or six inches. Carefully strip off the outer insulation—not the insulation on the inner wires—for about three inches, and then, with a wire stripper, remove about ½ inch of insulation from the end of each conductor wire. Twist the exposed filaments of each wire, clockwise, into a solid prong. After twisting the conductor ends, tie a tight underwriters' knot with the inner wires of the cord—follow the diagrams here to tie the knot. Then pull the plug down over the knot, leaving the exposed ends of the conductor wires sticking out. Loosen the terminal screws in the plug.

On a two-wire plug, loop each wire around one prong and toward a screw terminal. Loop the bare wire end clockwise around the screw terminal, and tighten the screw. If the screws are different colors (metals), connect the white wire to the white screw and the black wire to the yellow screw. On a three-wire plug, use the same technique to connect each of

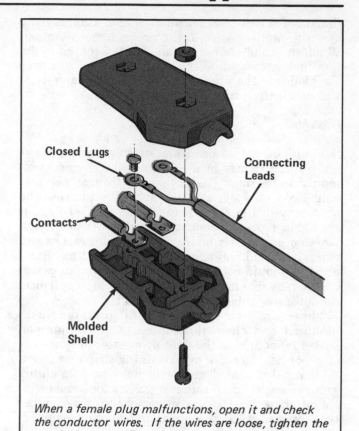

Closed Lugs

Connecting Leads

Contacts

Molded Shell

When a female plug malfunctions, open it and check the conductor wires. If the wires are loose, tighten the terminal screws. For other problems, replace the plug.

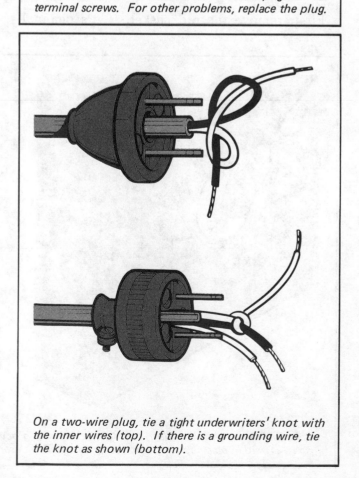

On a two-wire plug, tie a tight underwriters' knot with the inner wires (top). If there is a grounding wire, tie the knot as shown (bottom).

the three wires to a terminal screw. Connect the green grounding wire to the green screw terminal. When the conductor wires are firmly secured to the terminal screws, slide the cardboard insulator over the blades of the plug. If the plug has a clamp-type sleeve, clamp it firmly around the cord.

Gaskets

All appliances that use water or cold to do a job — and some that use heat — have gaskets, most commonly on the door. Gaskets do two things: they prevent leaks of water and air, and they increase the efficiency of the appliance. When a gasket fails, it should be replaced as soon as possible. To determine whether a gasket is faulty, inspect it for cracks and tears. It should feel spongy; if the gasket has hardened, it should be replaced. Replace a faulty gasket with a new one made specifically for the appliance; do not use a universal, fit-all gasket.

There are two basic types of gaskets, flush-mounted and channel-mounted. A flush-mounted gasket is secured to the door by a series of screws or clips, or held in place by a retaining strip or a panel. A channel-mounted gasket is held in a retaining groove; a special splining or gasket tool makes installation easier. Use gasket cement to install either type of gasket, as recommended by the manufacturer.

First, remove the old gasket. If it's channel-mounted, pull it carefully out of the channel; if it's flush-mounted, remove the fasteners, retaining strip, or panel to release the gasket. Clean the gasket area thoroughly with warm water and liquid detergent, or, if necessary, with mineral spirits. Dry the door and then install the new gasket, smoothing it evenly into place and easing it around corners; use gasket cement if specified by the manufacturer. If you're installing a channel-mounted gasket, press it into place with a splining tool. Make sure the gasket is properly and smoothly positioned, with no part sticking up or curled under. Finally, replace the fasteners or the retaining strip or panel and its fasteners. Remove any excess gasket cement with mineral spirits; be careful not to damage the appliance's finish.

Wiring

Many appliance repair tasks involve wiring — connecting individual wires or groups of wires to install a new electrical component. The electrical wires in appliances may be connected in one of several ways, including the basic screw terminal connection, the push-in terminal, and sometimes the sleeve-type lug terminal. Wires may also be joined with the solderless connectors called wirenuts. Components that have many wires — washer timers, for instance, which control several operating cycles — are often connected in a wiring harness, a group of wires en-

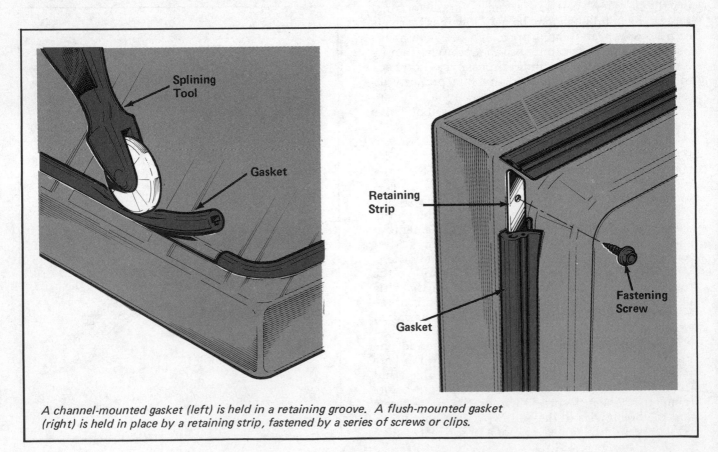

A channel-mounted gasket (left) is held in a retaining groove. A flush-mounted gasket (right) is held in place by a retaining strip, fastened by a series of screws or clips.

closed in a plastic sleeve. Each type of wire connection must be properly made when you install a new component, for each individual wire and each wire of a harness. Before you disconnect any wiring in an appliance, make sure you know how it's attached; when you install the new component, attach its wires the same way.

Switches

Switches operate by making contact with the conductor of an electrical circuit. When an appliance is plugged in, it's connected to a circuit in your home; power runs through the wires of the circuit to the appliance. When the appliance's on/off switch is turned on, the conductors of the appliance cord are moved into contact with the circuit conductors, and electricity flows through the switch to operate the appliance. The current flows in a loop through the appliance, making a complete circuit back through the switch to the line wires. Other basic appliance components are actually various types or variations of switches—rheostats, thermostats, solenoids, and timers, for example, are all switches or secondary switches. These components operate inside appliances, to turn on motors, open and close valves, control heating elements, and turn on different parts of the appliance during different cycles, such as the rinse and spin cycles of a washer. There are several common types of switches—push buttons, toggles, rockers, slides, throw switches, and so on.

All switches are made up of electrical contacts in a mechanical housing, and switch failure can be caused by problems with either the contacts or the housing. When a switch malfunctions, turn it to the "on" position and watch to see if the contacts are moved into position so that they touch. If the contacts are not operating properly, the switch housing is faulty, and the switch should be replaced. If the switch's mechanical operation is all right, its contacts may be dirty or misaligned; if it has terminal screws, they may be loose. If the contacts are dirty or corroded, rub them gently with a fine emery board, and then with a soft cloth; if they're misaligned, bend them gently back into place. Tighten any loose terminal screws. If the contacts or screws are badly corroded, the switch should be replaced.

To determine whether a switch is working properly, disassemble the appliance to get at the switch, and test it with a continuity tester or a VOM, set to the R × 1 scale. With the appliance unplugged, hook the clip of the continuity tester to one lead of the switch and touch the probe to the other; or touch one probe of the VOM to each terminal. Turn the switch on. If the switch is functioning, the continuity tester will light or buzz, and will stop glowing or buzzing when the switch is turned off; or the VOM will read zero. If the tester doesn't light or buzz, or the VOM reads higher than zero, the switch is faulty, and should be replaced. Some switches should have a

higher reading than zero, as detailed for each appliance. Use a new switch of the same type as the old one, and connect it exactly the same way.

Thermostats

A thermostat is a switch that controls temperature, in a heating element or a cooling device. Thermostats used in appliances may use a bimetal strip, bimetal thermodiscs, or a gas-filled bellows chamber to control the electrical contact. Faulty bimetal-strip and thermodisc thermostats should be replaced. Gas-filled thermostats can sometimes be professionally repaired; where repair is feasible, it is much less expensive than replacement.

To determine whether a thermostat is functioning, disassemble the appliance to get at the thermostat, and test it with a continuity tester, or a VOM set to the R × 1 scale. With the appliance unplugged, hook the clip of the continuity tester to one lead of the thermostat and touch the probe to the other; or touch one probe of the VOM to each terminal. The continuity tester should light or buzz; or the VOM should read zero. Turn down the temperature control dial; you'll see the contact points open at the thermostat. The tester should stop glowing or buzzing when the contacts open. If the thermostat is faulty, replace it with a new one.

Switch Control Devices

Many appliances perform several functions, such as the various cycles of a washer or dishwasher. These appliances operate automatically; once the on-off switch is turned on, switch components inside the appliance take over to control heat, water or fuel flow, motor speed, and other variables. The most important of these devices, used to operate switches, levers, and valves automatically, are solenoids, relays, and sensor/responder pairs.

Heating Elements

Heating elements work very simply. Unlike conductors, they are made of metal with high electrical resistance — usually a nickel-chrome alloy called nichrome. When current flows through the element, this high resistance prevents it from flowing easily; it must do work to get through the element, and this work is converted into heat. When the current is turned off, the element gradually cools. There are three types of heating elements: wire, ribbon, and rigid.

To determine whether a heating element is functioning, disassemble the appliance to get at the element, and test it with a continuity tester or a VOM, set to the R × 1 scale. With the appliance unplugged, hook the clip of the continuity tester to one terminal of the heating element and touch the probe to the other terminal; or touch one probe of the VOM to each terminal. If the element is functioning, the tester will light or buzz; or the VOM will read from 15 to 30 ohms. If the tester doesn't light or buzz, or the VOM reads higher than 30 ohms, the element is faulty, and should be replaced. If you use a continuity tester, however, look closely at the tester, especially if it's the light-up type — some heating elements have an extremely high resistance factor, and the light may produce only a dim glow or a faint buzz. This reaction does not mean that the element is faulty, but that it converts current to heat efficiently.

Timers

The operation of an appliance that has several cycles — a washer, a dishwasher, a dryer, a frost-free refrigerator, a range—is controlled by a timer, a complex rotary switch powered by a small synchronous motor. The timer consists of a shaft, gears, and a series of notched cams, one for each circuit or cycle. The timer itself is powered by the timer motor; the appliance is powered by the much larger appliance motor. When the switch is turned on, electrical contact is made with the timer motor, and a spring on a trip arm is coiled. The arm trips when the spring is tight, releasing the spring and moving the cam of the switch to the next circuit. At the last cycle, contact with the motor is broken, and the timer turns the appliance off.

When a timer malfunctions, it should usually be replaced; professional rebuilding is sometimes possible, but this is likely to be more expensive than replacement. Many timers are sealed units. Some timers have an adjustment shaft, which can be turned with a screwdriver blade. To replace a timer, disconnect its wires one at a time, connecting the

corresponding wires of the new timer as you go to avoid the chance of a misconnection.

To determine whether a timer is functioning, test it with a continuity tester or a VOM, set to the R × 1 scale. Make a sketch of the timer wires and then, with the appliance unplugged, disconnect all timer wires from their terminals. Make sure you'll be able to reconnect the wires exactly the same way. Touch or clip one probe of the tester or the VOM to the common terminal, and touch the other probe to each cycle terminal in turn; rotate the timer control knob as you work. The continuity tester should light or buzz at each circuit; the VOM should read zero. If one or more circuits do not give these results, the timer is faulty, and should be replaced.

Pilot Lights and Thermocouples

Gas-fired appliances often have pilot lights to provide instant ignition when the gas is turned on. The pilot light is a small open flame fed by a steady flow of gas.

Problems occur when the gas flow is obstructed or misdirected, or when the pilot is blown out. In newer appliances, ignition may be achieved by a sparking device or a glow bar instead of a pilot light. In furnaces and water heaters, and in some ranges and dryers, the pilot light is accompanied by a safety device called a thermocouple, a heat sensor that turns the gas off if the pilot flame is extinguished. *Caution: Some older appliances may not have a safety device to turn the gas off when the pilot is extinguished. With any gas-fired appliance, if a strong smell of gas is present, do not try to relight the pilot or turn the appliance on, or turn any lights on or off. Get out of the house, leaving the door open, and go to a telephone; call the gas company or the fire department immediately to report a leak.*

A correctly adjusted pilot flame is steady and blue, and between ¼ and ½ inch high. If the flame goes out repeatedly, it may be getting too little air; if it's yellow at the tip, it's getting too much air. To correct either condition, turn the pilot adjustment screw slightly, as directed by the manufacturer.

When a pilot goes out, relighting it is simple. If there is a gas valve at the pilot, turn the valve to "off" and wait at least three minutes to let any built-up gas dissipate; after three minutes, turn the valve to "pilot." If there is a safety or reset button, push the button, and keep it depressed. Hold a lighted match to the pilot orifice, and turn the gas valve to "on"; then, when the pilot is burning brightly, release the reset button. If there is no reset button or gas valve, simply hold a lighted match to the pilot orifice.

If the pilot flame won't stay lit after several tries, it should be adjusted by a professional; don't try to adjust the mechanism or tamper with the gas line. In an appliance that has a thermocouple, the problem may be a faulty thermocouple. You can replace this component to correct the problem.

Blue-Green Inner Flame

Blue Outer Flame

Pilot Gas Supply Line

Gas-fired appliances have pilot lights to provide ignition when the gas is turned on. The pilot is a small, open flame fed by a steady flow of gas.

Thermocouples. The thermocouple operates as a safety device, to turn the gas supply off when the pilot light goes out. It consists of a heat sensor connected to a solenoid; when the sensor is not heated by the pilot flame, the solenoid closes the gas supply line. When a thermocouple fails, the pilot light won't stay lighted; the thermocouple may be burned out or broken. A faulty thermocouple should be replaced.

Motor Maintenance and Repairs

Depending on how much work it has to do, an appliance may be powered by one of several types of motors. Small appliances are usually powered by a universal motor, or, where less power is needed, by a shaded-pole or a synchronous motor. Larger appliances are usually powered by a split-phase or a capacitor motor. Direct-current motors are used for small appliances that use batteries as the power source. Universal and direct-current motors have two blocks of carbon, called brushes, that function as electrical contacts. The other motors do not have brushes; they are all types of induction motors, in which a solid rotor spins inside a stationary piece called a stator. Both brush motors and induction motors are powered by the electromagnetic force created when electrical current passes through them.

Whatever their size and horsepower, appliance motors are usually dependable and long-wearing. You can prolong their life and increase their efficiency by keeping them clean and well lubricated. Use motor-driven appliances sensibly — don't overload them, don't abuse them, and don't ignore problems until they become serious.

There are several basic rules for operating motor-driven appliances:

- Always connect an appliance to an adequate power source; a 220-240-volt appliance must be connected to a 220-240-volt outlet. If the outlet for a major appliance is not grounded, use a grounded adapter plug to ground the appliance.
- Never use a small appliance that's wet, or operate any appliance while your hands are wet. If a large appliance, such as a washer or dryer, gets wet, *do not* operate it or try to unplug it. Have the motor examined by a professional before you use the appliance again.
- Never overload an appliance. Overloading causes inefficient operation and motor overheating, and can cause excessive wear. If a motor turns off because it's overloaded, reduce the load before restarting the appliance.

Regular maintenance can forestall many motor problems. To prevent overheating and jamming, vacuum the motor housing periodically to remove dirt and lint. Make sure ventilation to the motor is adequate. At least once a year, oil the motor — if it

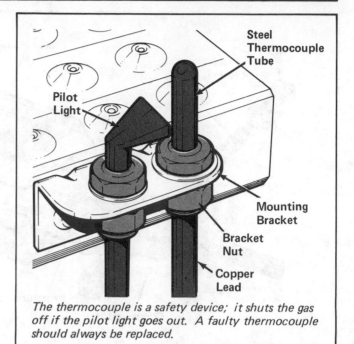

The thermocouple is a safety device; it shuts the gas off if the pilot light goes out. A faulty thermocouple should always be replaced.

has oil ports — with No. 30 nondetergent motor oil (not all-purpose oil).

If the motor has belts, examine them periodically for wear and damage; damaged belts should be replaced. To quiet a squeaky belt, spray it with fan belt dressing, available at automotive and hardware stores and some home centers. Also check the tension of all belts, about halfway between the motor shaft and the nearest pulley. The belt should give about ½ inch when you press on it. If it's too loose, increase the tension by tightening the adjustment bolt; if it's too tight, decrease the tension by loosening the bolt. If pulleys are misaligned, carefully bend them back into alignment, or call a professional service person. Procedures for specific appliances are detailed below.

When a motor malfunctions, you may or may not be able to fix it — motors are complex pieces of machinery, and serious problems should be handled by a professional. Many motors are sealed units, and should not be opened for any reason. But motor failure or malfunction is often caused by minor operational problems, and these are easily dealt with.

The simplest problem is lack of power — the appliance may be unplugged; the circuit may not be receiving power; a fuse or circuit breaker in the appliance may have blown or tripped. Before you go any further, make sure power is reaching the appliance. Correct any electrical problems, as discussed in the chapter on electricity.

If the appliance is receiving power, the problem may be caused by a faulty power cord or plug, or a faulty outlet. Check the cord and plug visually and then test them with a continuity tester, as detailed above; use a voltage tester, as detailed above, to make

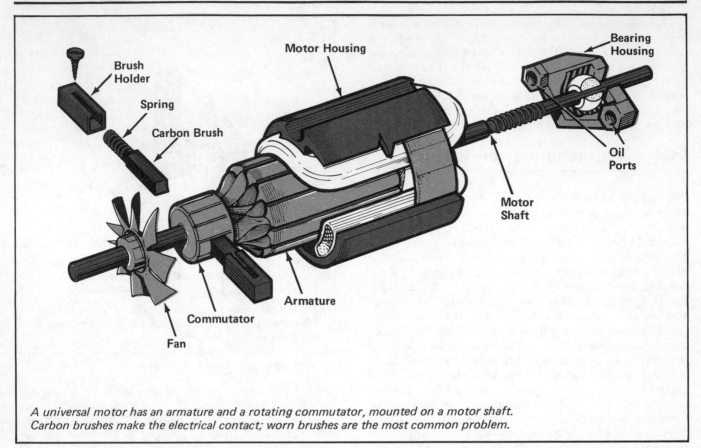

A universal motor has an armature and a rotating commutator, mounted on a motor shaft. Carbon brushes make the electrical contact; worn brushes are the most common problem.

sure the outlet is functioning. Another possibility is that the motor's on/off switch is defective. If the switch is accessible, test it for continuity, as detailed above. If the cord, the plug, or the switch is faulty, replace it with a new one of the same type.

Universal Motors. These motors consist of a rotor called an armature, with coils of wire wound around it, and a rotating cylinder called a commutator, with alternating strips of conducting and nonconducting material. The armature and the commutator are both mounted on the motor shaft. On each side of the commutator, a carbon brush carries current from the circuit. When the carbon brushes press against the commutator, the armature is magnetized and rotates. Most universal motors also have a cooling fan at the end of the shaft. Universal motors are used in many small and medium-size appliances; they provide strong power at both low and high speeds. Universal motors can operate on either AC or DC current. Their speed is controlled by a rheostat, a tapped-field control, a rectifier, or a governor, or by physical movement of the carbon brushes away from the armature.

Most universal motors are permanently lubricated and sealed by the manufacturer, and require no further attention. Some universal motors, however, have covered lubrication ports, usually marked "oil," at the ends of the motor shaft. This type of motor should be oiled every six months, or accord-

ing to the manufacturer's instructions. Lift each port's lid and apply a drop or two of No. 30 nondetergent motor oil (not all-purpose oil); do not overlubricate.

Many universal motor malfunctions are caused by wearing down of the carbon brushes, the soft blocks of carbon that complete the electrical contact to the motor's commutator. When these brushes become worn, the motor will spark, and electrical contact may be incomplete. You can solve both problems by replacing the brushes.

Brushes can be checked visually or tested with a continuity tester. To sight-check them, remove the screws that hold the brushes and brush springs into the brush holders at the sides of the commutator. The screws will pop out of the screw holes; turn the motor over to tap out the brushes. The ends of the brushes should be curved to fit the commutator; if they're worn down short, new brushes are needed. To check carbon brushes with a continuity tester, remove the motor lead wires from the circuit. Tag the wires as you disconnect them so that you'll be able to reconnect them properly. Hook the tester clip to one motor lead and touch the probe to the other lead; the tester should light or buzz. Slowly revolve the motor shaft, keeping the tester in position. If the tester doesn't light or buzz, or if it flickers or stutters when you turn the motor shaft, the brushes should be replaced. If the springs behind the brushes are damaged, they should be replaced too.

Replace worn carbon brushes and damaged springs with new ones made specifically for the motor; the model information (number and make) is stamped on a metal plate fastened to the motor, or embossed on the metal housing of the motor. If you can't find the model information, take the worn brushes and springs with you to an appliance parts store to make sure you get the right kind. Insert the new springs and brushes in the brush holders, replace the brush assemblies, and secure the new brushes with the mounting screws that held the old brushes.

No other repairs should be attempted to a universal motor; if a serious malfunction occurs, buy a new motor or take the faulty motor to a professional for repairs. Most large universal motors are fastened to plate-type mountings; to remove the motor, disconnect the wires and remove the holding bolts and any belts that are present. If the faulty motor is in a small appliance, take the entire appliance to the repair shop. It may, however, be less expensive to buy a new appliance than to have the old one repaired.

Split-Phase Motors. These motors consist of a rotor turning inside a stator that has two wire coils, a starting winding and a running winding. Current flows through both windings when the motor is starting up, but when the rotor has reached about 75 to 80 percent of its top speed, the starting winding is turned off, and only the running winding receives current. Split-phase motors operate on AC current; they are fairly powerful, and are used in washing machines, dryers, and dishwashers.

These motors require no maintenance except cleaning and lubrication, as detailed above. Split-phase motors have a special auxiliary winding, the starting winding; don't try to make any repairs yourself. When a motor malfunctions, buy a new motor or take the faulty motor to a professional service person, whichever is less expensive. You can save the expense of a service call by removing the old motor from its mounting and installing the repaired or new motor yourself.

Capacitor-Start Motors. This type of motor is a shaded-pole motor with a capacitor — an energy-storing device—wired into the starting winding. The capacitor stores current, and releases it in bursts to provide extra starting power. When the motor reaches about 75 percent of its top speed, the starting winding is turned off. Capacitor-start motors operate on AC current. They are very powerful, and are used in appliances that require a high starting torque or turning power, such as air conditioners and furnaces. *Caution: Capacitors store electricity, even after the power to the appliance is turned off. When working with a capacitor-start motor, you must discharge the capacitor with a 20,000-ohm, 2-watt wire-wound resistor, as detailed for each appliance.*

These motors require regular cleaning, as detailed above, to keep them free of lint and oil. Ventilation to the motor must be adequate. If the motor has oil ports, lift each port's lid and apply a drop or two of No. 30 nondetergent motor oil (not all-purpose oil); do not overlubricate. Finally, make sure the belts attached to the motor are not too tight. Press down on each belt, about halfway between the motor shaft and the nearest pulley; the belt should give about ½ inch. If necessary, adjust the belt tension, as detailed above.

Capacitor-start motors are usually hard to get at, and have a capacitor and special auxiliary windings; don't try to make any repairs yourself. When a motor malfunctions, call a professional service person.

Permanent-Split-Capacitor (PSC) Motors. This type of capacitor motor has a large running capacitor wired in series with the starting windings. In this motor, the starting winding does not turn off when the motor approaches its top speed. Instead, the capacitor makes a phase shift as the motor approaches top speed, causing the starting winding to act as a running winding, and thus increasing the efficiency of the motor. PSC motors operate on AC current. They are used in large appliances that don't require as high a starting torque as capacitor-start motors provide, such as large air-conditioning systems. *Caution: PSC motors, like capacitor-start motors, store electricity, even after the power to the appliance is turned off. When working with a PSC motor, you must discharge the capacitor with a 20,000-ohm, 2-watt wire-wound resistor, as detailed for each appliance.*

These motors require regular cleaning and lubrication, as detailed for capacitor-start motors. Make sure belts are properly adjusted and ventilation to the motor is adequate. PSC motors, like capacitor-start motors, are very complex; don't try to make any repairs yourself. When a motor malfunctions, call a professional service person.

Repairing Major Appliances

Because major appliances constitute a major investment, their maintenance and repair is very important. Most appliances of the same type operate on the same basic principles, so repairs to most models are similar or identical, no matter what brand or make is involved. Although different makes of appliances generally operate alike, however, they don't conform to the same design; major brand-name appliances may look quite different. To make it even more complicated, manufacturers, in order to beat their competition, build their appliances with all sorts of extra features. Many of these extras are real value-added innovations; others, unfortunately, are not. Because of the differences among brand-name appliances, you should use the repair and replacement tech-

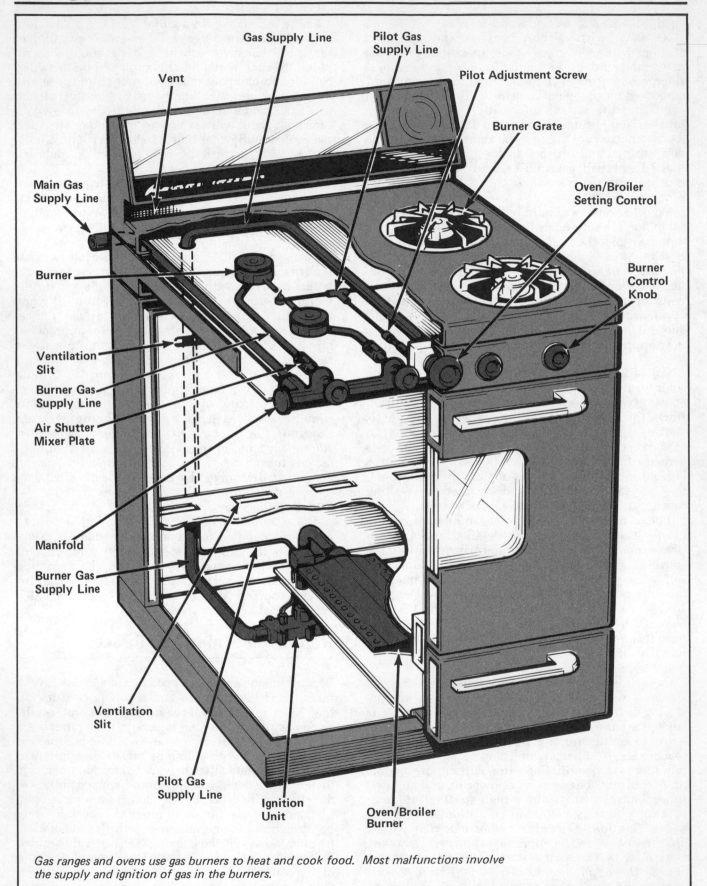

Vent

Gas Supply Line

Pilot Gas Supply Line

Pilot Adjustment Screw

Burner Grate

Main Gas Supply Line

Oven/Broiler Setting Control

Burner

Burner Control Knob

Ventilation Slit

Burner Gas Supply Line

Air Shutter Mixer Plate

Manifold

Burner Gas Supply Line

Ventilation Slit

Pilot Gas Supply Line

Ignition Unit

Oven/Broiler Burner

Gas ranges and ovens use gas burners to heat and cook food. Most malfunctions involve the supply and ignition of gas in the burners.

niques in this chapter as general guidelines, not as absolute standards for specific models.

Because appliance operation does follow the same principles, it's easy to be tempted into buying repair parts that look alike or "fit all." This is not a good idea — replacement parts must match the make and model of the appliance being repaired. Most appliances have a metal tag, attached to the back service panel, that provides the model, make, and other identification information. If the tag is missing, look for this information embossed or stamped onto a service panel. If you can't find this information, take the malfunctioning part to an appliance parts store or an appliance repair shop that sells replacement parts. The dealer should be able to identify the part for you and provide the proper replacement. If the appliance is riveted or welded together, don't try to disassemble it; you could do more harm than good. Call a professional service person, or, if possible, take the entire appliance in to a professional service center.

While you will be able to handle many parts *replacement* jobs yourself, you probably won't be able to handle many parts *repair* jobs — you probably don't have the skill or own the specialized equipment necessary for them, and it isn't recommended that you invest in such specialized equipment. Moreover, it's often less expensive to replace a part than to repair it. If you aren't sure replacement is worth it, call a repair shop for an estimate. You can save the expense of a service call, though, by removing the malfunctioning part yourself and taking it in to be tested and/or repaired. You can save the cost of installation by installing the part yourself.

Gas Ranges and Ovens

Gas ranges and ovens operate fairly simply, and they're usually easy to repair, mainly because the components are designed for quick take-apart. Most of the malfunctions that affect gas ranges involve the supply and ignition of gas in the burners and the oven. *Caution: Before doing any work on a gas range or oven, make sure it's unplugged, or turn off the electric power to the unit by removing a fuse or tripping a circuit breaker at the main entrance panel or at a separate panel; if there is a grounding wire to the range, disconnect it. Also close the gas supply valve to shut off the unit's gas supply.*

Disassembly. A gas range cabinet comes apart very easily. Take out the screws that hold the panels, and pull off the control knobs. On the control panel the knobs are friction-fit; pull them straight off. Some knobs may have setscrews in the base of the knobs; back out these screws and pull off the knobs.

Many ranges have a back service panel on the control panel; remove this panel by backing out a series of screws around the edge of the panel. To remove the front panel, take off the control knobs, and remove a series of screws that holds the decorative panel to the frame. These screws may be hidden by decorative molding or trim; pry off the molding or trim with a screwdriver, or take out several screws.

To gain access to the burner assemblies, remove the burner grates and then the top of the range; the entire range top lifts up and off the range or opens up and back on hinges. The oven door can usually be removed by pulling it straight up off the hinges on both sides of the door. Some hinges have a latch that must be unlocked before the door can be removed.

If the surface light of the range burns out, remove retaining screws and panels as necessary to gain access to the bulb, and remove the bulb. Replace the burned-out bulb with a new one of the same type and wattage; check the ends of the old bulb for this information. Then replace any retaining panels. If the oven light burns out, unscrew it and remove it from the oven. Replace the burned-out bulb with a new one of the same wattage, made for oven use.

Door Gasket. If the oven won't heat to the desired temperature or heats unevenly, the problem could be a defective door gasket. The best way to test for this is to pass your hand around the door, being careful not to touch it, while the oven is turned on. If you can feel heat escaping, the gasket needs replacement. Replace it with a new gasket made for the range.

On most ovens, the gasket—made of asbestos—is located on the frame of the oven, and the door closes against it. This gasket is generally friction-fit in a channel, and can be replaced. In other units, the oven door is in two sections, and the gasket is not mounted on the door frame, but installed between the front and back sections of the door. Don't try to replace this type of gasket; call a professional service person.

To replace a frame-mounted gasket, pull the old one out of the channel, and then clean the channel and the door frame with a solution of mild household detergent and water. To install the new gasket, start the replacement at the top of the door frame and work down the sides; ease the gasket around corners. Finish the installation along the bottom; butt the ends of the gasket firmly together. On some oven door frames the gasket is held in place with screws. To get at the screws, bend back the exposed edge of the gasket.

Cleaning. Clogged burners are a very common problem with gas ranges, because food spilled on the burners blocks the gas ports and prevents ignition. On some gas ranges you can remove the top ring of the burner to expose the ports. With a cloth moistened with water and household detergent, clean the burner. Then, with a straight pin or needle, clean out the gas ports. *Caution: Do not use a toothpick or matchstick to clean the gas ports. If the tip of the wood gets stuck in the burner ports, it could cause a serious blockage.*

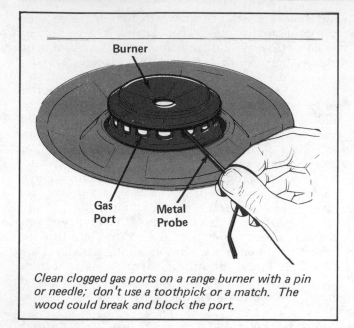

Clean clogged gas ports on a range burner with a pin or needle; don't use a toothpick or a match. The wood could break and block the port.

If the burner is thickly encrusted with burnt food, turn off the power supply, both gas and electric, to the range; then remove the burner. Soak the burner in a solution of mild household detergent and water, and then clean the burner with a soft cloth. Clear the gas ports with a pin or needle, rinse the burner, and let it dry. When the burner is completely dry, replace the burner and turn on the power and the gas supply.

Burner Switches. The switches that control the burners of the range are similar to the oven thermostat; there is a sensing bulb connected to the switch. If you suspect a switch is faulty, don't try to fix it yourself; remove it from the range and take it to a professional. The bulb is usually clipped to the range cabinet; pry it off with a screwdriver. Take the entire unit to a professional service person for testing; if the switch is faulty, replace it with a new one made for the range. Connect the new switch the same way the old one was connected.

If the range can be adjusted to control the simmer setting at the burners, you can make this adjustment by removing the control knob to the burner. Inside the knob shaft, locate a screw slot. Turn this screw, usually counterclockwise, and test the burner. If it doesn't work properly, turn the screw clockwise and test the burner again. Repeat this procedure until the simmer setting is correct.

Oven Setting Control. When this component, located on the control panel, malfunctions, the oven won't heat. To remedy the situation, remove the control knob. Then remove the back service panel or the front panel, if necessary. Remove other control knobs as needed to remove the panel. The oven setting control is located directly in back of the control knob, and is usually held to the control panel by two screws. Testing the control with a VOM is not recommended, because the results will not always be conclusive. The best procedure is to substitute a control that you know is working, if you suspect that the setting control is faulty. Or simply replace the faulty control with a new one made for the oven. Disconnect the electrical lead wires from the control terminal and lift out the control. Connect the new control the same way the old one was connected.

Oven Thermostat. If the oven doesn't heat evenly, or doesn't heat at all, the oven thermostat may be malfunctioning. First, determine how much the temperature in the oven is off from the control setting. Put an oven thermometer inside the oven and turn the oven on for about 20 minutes, with the thermostat set at 350° F. Or set the oven at any range between 300° and 400° F. If the oven thermometer reads 25° or more lower or higher than the oven control setting, the thermostat should be recalibrated.

To calibrate the thermostat on some ranges, pull off the thermostat knob on the control panel. Behind the knob are two screws holding a round, notched plate. Loosen these screws, but do not remove them. With a screwdriver, change the notch setting on the notched plate by turning the plate counterclockwise; for every eighth of a turn, the oven temperature goes up about 25° F. To turn the heat down, move the plate clockwise.

Some thermostats can be adjusted by turning a screw inside the control knob shaft housing. To do so, remove the knob and insert a screwdriver into the shaft so that the screwdriver blade engages a screw slot. Turn the screwdriver counterclockwise about one-eighth of a turn to raise the heat about 25° F.

If a malfunctioning thermostat cannot be recalibrated, it should probably be replaced. Test the thermostat with a VOM, set to the R × 1 scale; instructions for using the VOM are given earlier in this chapter. The thermostat is located directly in back of the control knob that regulates the heat; to gain access to it, remove the back service panel to the control panel. Disconnect one electrical lead wire from a terminal of the thermostat, and clip one probe of the VOM to each thermostat terminal. If the thermostat is in working order, the meter will register zero; if the needle jumps to a higher reading, the thermostat is faulty, and should be replaced. Replace the thermostat with a new one of the same type.

First disconnect the terminal wires to the thermostat and pull off the control knob. The thermostat is usually held to the control panel with retaining screws. On some ranges, there is a wire running from the thermostat into the oven. This wire operates a sensing bulb that controls the thermostat. The sensing bulb is usually held by a bracket; unscrew this bracket to remove the bulb. Then carefully slip out the wire, the bulb, and the thermostat. Install the new thermostat in reverse of the way the old one came out.

Timer. The range timer is usually located in the control panel on top of the range. If you suspect the timer is faulty, don't try to fix it yourself; remove it and take it to a professional service person for testing. To take out the timer, remove the back service panel to the control panel and release the spring clips that hold it in position, or remove the retaining screws. Then push the timer forward to release it. Then remove the electrical lead wires from the timer housing.

If, when disassembling the timer, you notice that the electrical wire terminals look burned, remove these leads and buff the leads and the terminal points with fine steel wool. Burned and/or dirty terminals can cause the timer to malfunction; cleaning can solve this problem.

Replace the old timer or install a new one of the same size and type, if this is necessary. Connect the new timer the same way the old one was connected.

Fuel Mixture Adjustments. The flame of gas range burners should be steady and slightly rounded, with a light blue tip. The flame should be quiet, and should respond to adjustments made at the control knobs. Most burner troubles can be quickly solved by adjusting the air shutter mixer plate, which is located at the end of the burner tube near the knob controls. Turn a small screw on the plate and slide the plate open or closed; then tighten the setscrew. If the flame is yellow, it's not receiving enough air; open the plate slightly. If the flame is high, or makes a roaring noise, it's getting too much air; close the plate slightly.

Pilot Lights. One pilot light usually serves all the top burners of a gas range; on some ranges there are two pilot lights, one for each side of the range. A correctly adjusted pilot flame is steady and blue, between ¼ and ½ inch high. If the flame goes out repeatedly or if it's yellow at the tip, it's getting too little air; if there's a space between the flame and the pilot feed tube, it's getting too much air. To correct either condition, turn the pilot adjustment screw on the gas line slightly, as directed by the manufacturer of the range.

When the pilot goes out, relighting it is simple. If there is a gas valve at the pilot, turn the valve to "off" and wait at least three minutes to let any built-up gas dissipate; after three minutes, turn the valve to "pilot." If there is a safety or reset button, push the button, and keep it depressed. Hold a lighted match to the pilot orifice, and turn the gas valve to "on;" then, when the pilot is burning brightly, release the reset button. If there is no reset button or gas valve,

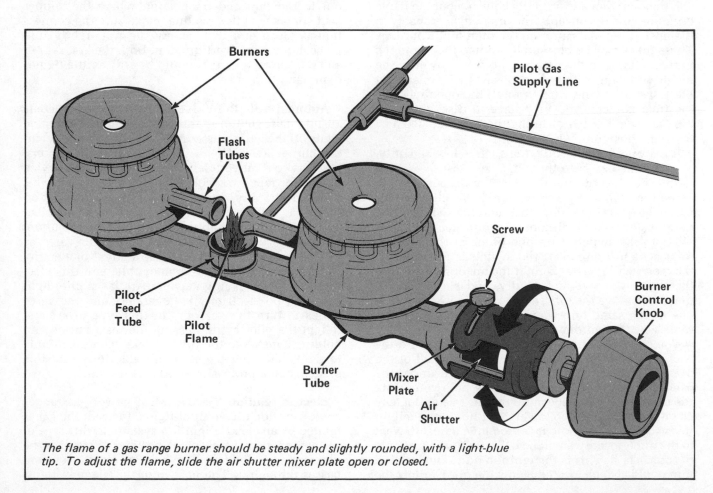

The flame of a gas range burner should be steady and slightly rounded, with a light-blue tip. To adjust the flame, slide the air shutter mixer plate open or closed.

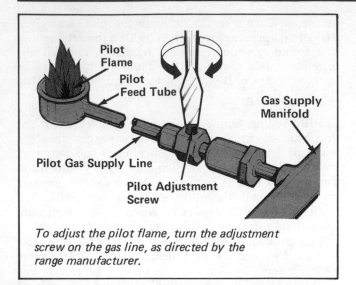

To adjust the pilot flame, turn the adjustment screw on the gas line, as directed by the range manufacturer.

simply hold a lighted match to the pilot orifice.

If the pilot flame won't stay lit after several tries, it should be adjusted by a professional; don't try to adjust the mechanism or tamper with the gas line. If the range has a thermocouple, the problem may be a faulty thermocouple. You can replace this component to correct the problem, as detailed below.

If the pilot flame is properly adjusted but the flame doesn't ignite the burners, the problem is probably in the flash tubes that run from the pilot to the burners. These tubes may be blocked by spilled food from the burners. If this is the case, turn off the power to the range, and then, with a short piece of wire, clean out the tubes. Push the wire through the opening until the tube is clear; you may have to disconnect the tube to clear it. After cleaning the tube, replace it in the same position.

If the pilot has a switch, the switch may be faulty. Turn off the power to the range, and test the switch with a VOM, set to the R × 1 scale; instructions for using the VOM are given earlier in this chapter. Remove the retaining screws that hold the switch in the range cabinet, and disconnect both electrical lead wires to the switch. Clip one probe of the VOM to each switch terminal. If the switch is functioning, the meter will register zero; if the meter reads higher than zero, the switch is faulty, and should be replaced. Remove the switch and replace it with a new one of the same type; connect the new switch the same way the old one was connected.

The oven pilot light is usually located toward the back of the oven, or under the bottom panel of the oven box. If the range has a drawer unit under the oven, pull out the drawer; this may help you locate the pilot. If the oven doesn't light, the oven pilot may be out or may be set too low. If the pilot is out, relight it, as above. If the flame is set too low, adjust it. Next to the pilot, locate a small box-like unit with a couple of screws in it. This is the ignition unit. The ignition unit could also be located below the pilot; follow the

gas line down until you locate the ignition unit. Turn one of these screws on the ignition. Experiment, turning the screws a little at a time, until the flame is adjusted properly. It should not be as high as the top pilot flame; leave it as low as possible. On some oven pilots, turn the control to "off" and light the pilot; then turn the oven dial to "broil." The pilot will heat the controls to the ignition switch.

Thermocouple. On some ranges, the pilot assembly includes a thermocouple, a safety device that turns the gas supply off when the pilot light goes out. The thermocouple consists of a heat sensor connected to a solenoid; when the sensor is not heated by the pilot flame, the solenoid closes the gas supply line. When the thermocouple fails, the pilot light won't stay lighted; the thermocouple may be burned out or broken. A faulty thermocouple should be replaced.

To replace a thermocouple, unscrew the copper lead and the connection nut inside the threaded connection to the gas line. Under the mounting bracket at the thermocouple tube, unscrew the bracket nut that holds the tube in place. Insert a new thermocouple into the hole in the bracket, steel tube up and copper lead down. Under the bracket, screw the bracket nut over the tube. Push the connection nut to the threaded connection where the copper lead connects to the gas line; make sure the connection is clean and dry. Screw the nut tightly into place, but do not overtighten it. Both the bracket nut and the connection nut should be only a little tighter than hand-tightened.

Automatic Shutoff Valve. On some ranges, there is an automatic shutoff in the pilot assembly; this valve shuts off the gas to the burner any time the pilot and the burner are both off. If this unit malfunctions, don't try to fix it yourself; call a professional service person for repair or replacement.

An electrically operated shutoff valve used on some gas ranges has two facing valves, an electromagnet, and a manually activated reset button. The thermocouple fitting is next to the pilot valve, as in most burner systems. A small amount of electricity is generated in the thermocouple, and this electricity holds the facing valves apart. If the pilot light goes out, no electricity is generated, and the valve closes to turn the gas off. On this type of system, relight the pilot by depressing the reset button and holding a match to the pilot. It takes about a minute to light this pilot. If you aren't able to relight this system, call a professional service person.

Electric Ignition System. Most newer gas ranges and ovens don't have pilot lights; instead, the gas is ignited by an electric ignition system. In this type of system, an element becomes hot and glows like the filament in a light bulb when an electric current passes through it. The heat from the filament lights

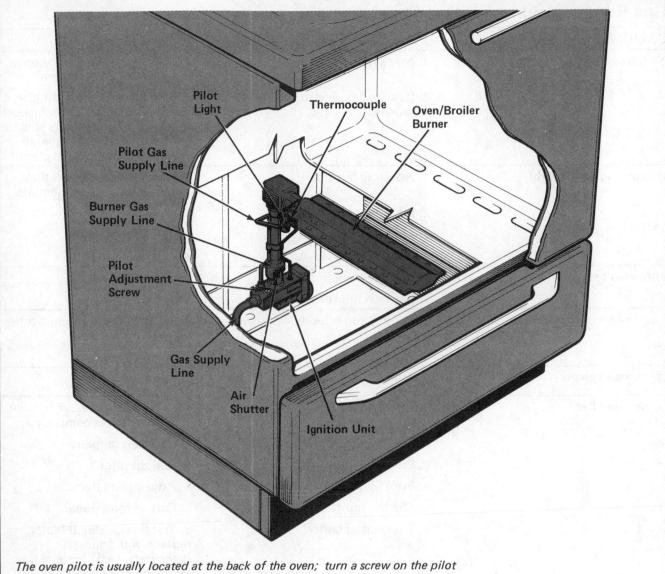

Pilot
Light

Thermocouple

Oven/Broiler
Burner

Pilot Gas
Supply Line

Burner Gas
Supply Line

Pilot
Adjustment
Screw

Gas Supply
Line

Air
Shutter

Ignition Unit

The oven pilot is usually located at the back of the oven; turn a screw on the pilot ignition unit to adjust the pilot flame height.

the gas. As a rule, these ignition systems are sealed; they cannot be repaired or adjusted. When an electric ignition device fails, don't try to fix it; call a professional service person for replacement.

Self-Cleaning Ovens. There are two types of self-cleaning ovens, pyrolytic and catalytic. Pyrolytic ovens use very high heat — usually 1,000° F — to incinerate food on the oven's surface, leaving only a fine ash. The smoke produced by the burning is vented from the oven. When the cleaning process is complete, the fine ash left in the oven is wiped off the surface. Catalytic self-cleaning ovens are also called continuous-clean ovens. These ovens are coated with a special finish that allows most dirt to burn away at normal cooking temperatures. With these ovens, major food spills and spatters must be cleaned away immediately or the special finish will not work. *Caution: Never use a commercial oven cleaner to clean a catalytic or a pyrolytic oven.*

Most problems with pyrolytic ovens occur because procedures are not properly carried out. In most cases, the oven heat selector must be set to "clean," and the oven door must be firmly closed and, sometimes, latched. When the oven reaches a predetermined temperature — about 600° F — the door automatically locks shut so that it can't be opened during the cleaning cycle. If you've followed the correct procedures for using a self-cleaning oven but the oven is not coming clean, call a professional service person. Before you call, though, make these basic checks:

• Check for a blown fuse or tripped circuit breaker

 **Appliances**

Gas Range Troubleshooting Chart

PROBLEM	POSSIBLE CAUSE	SOLUTION
No burners light	1. No gas.	1. Make sure gas valve is open. If open, call gas company.
	2. If range has electric ignition, no power.	2. Check power cord, plug, and outlet. Check for blown fuses or tripped circuit breakers at main entrance panel or at separate entrance panel; restore circuit.
One burner won't light	1. No gas to burner.	1. Test other burners; if they light, clean burner assembly.
	2. Pilot light out.	2. Relight pilot.
	3. Electric ignition faulty.	3. Call a professional.
	4. Defective gas valve.	4. Call gas company.
Pilot won't stay lit	1. Pilot light set too low.	1. Adjust pilot light.
	2. Gas feed tube blocked.	2. Clean feed tube.
Burners pop when lighted	1. Conduction tubes misaligned.	1. Reposition conduction tubes on holding bracket.
	2. Pilot light set too low.	2. Adjust pilot light.
Light won't go on	1. Bulb burned out.	1. Replace bulb.
Oven won't heat	1. No gas to range.	1. Make sure gas valve is open. If open, call gas company.
	2. Defective gas valve.	2. Call gas company.
	3. Pilot light out.	3. Relight pilot.
	4. Pilot light set too low.	4. Adjust pilot light.
	5. Electric ignition system faulty.	5. Call a professional.
	6. Thermostat faulty.	6. Test thermostat; if faulty, replace. If thermostat inaccurate, recalibrate; if no result, call a professional.
	7. Timer faulty.	7. Clean timer terminals; set timer to "manual" and turn clock on control panel 24 hours ahead. If no result, call a professional.
Oven heat uneven	1. Door gasket faulty.	1. Make sure door is closed tightly and hinges operate smoothly; if gasket damaged, replace, or call a professional.
Burner won't simmer	1. Simmer nut needs adjustment.	1. Adjust simmer nut on burner.
Flame yellow	1. Not enough air in gas mixture.	1. Adjust air shutter.
Flame noisy	1. Too much air in gas mixture.	1. Adjust air shutter.
Flame too high	1. Too much air in gas mixture.	1. Adjust air shutter.
Soot forms on burner	1. Air shutter clogged.	1. Clean air shutter.
	2. Air shutter needs adjustment.	1. Adjust air shutter.

Gas Range Troubleshooting Chart (Continued)

PROBLEM	POSSIBLE CAUSE	SOLUTION
Gas smell		Leave the house immediately; do not try to turn off the gas, or turn any lights on or off. Go to a telephone and call the gas company or the fire department immediately to report a leak. Do not reenter your home.

at the entrance panel controlling the unit.

- Make sure the heat selector is set to "clean," and the timer is set to "manual."
- Be sure to allow the prescribed amount of time for the oven to clean itself. If the oven is only partially cleaned, more cleaning time may be required.
- Make sure the oven door is tightly closed and latched.

Electric Ranges and Ovens

Electric ranges and ovens are generally easy to repair, because there's not much to go wrong and there's not much you can do. Most repairs are replacements, a matter of unplugging the old and plugging in the new. Most of the malfunctions that affect electric ranges involve faulty heating elements. *Caution: Before doing any work on an electric range or oven, make sure it's unplugged, or turn off the power to the unit by removing one or more fuses or tripping one or more breakers at the main entrance panel or at a separate panel. If the range is fused at a separate panel, this panel may be located adjacent to the main panel or in a basement, crawl space, or other location. If there is a grounding wire to the range, disconnect it. Make sure the power to the unit is off.*

Fuses. If the range or oven is receiving power, but doesn't work, the unit may have its own fuse or circuit breaker assembly. This assembly is usually located under the cooktop of the range. Inside the oven, look back to spot the fuse assembly. In some units, lift the top of the range to gain access to the fuse assembly; or lift the elements, remove the drip pans, and look toward the sides of the cabinet.

If the unit has this additional fuse or breaker system, components such as the oven light, the range heating elements, the timer, and a self-cleaning feature may be separately fused. If these components or features fail to work, don't overlook the possibility that the fuses have blown. To replace a blown fuse, unscrew the old fuse and install a new one of the same type and electrical rating. *Caution: Do not use a fuse with more than a 15-amp rating.* If the unit has circuit breakers, push the breaker or reset button. This button is usually on the control panel.

Disassembly. To take an electric range cabinet apart, take out the screws that hold the panels, and pull off the control knobs. On the control panel the knobs are friction-fit; pull them straight off. Some knobs may have setscrews in the base of the knobs; back out these screws and pull off the knobs.

Many ranges have a back service panel on the control panel; remove this panel by backing out a series of screws around the edge of the panel. To remove the front panel, take off the control knobs and remove a series of screws that holds the decorative panel to the frame. These screws may be hidden by decorative molding or trim; pry off the molding or trim with a screwdriver, or take out several screws to remove it.

The elements on an electric range are fastened to terminal blocks with screws; you can remove the elements by removing the screws that hold the power wires in position. On some models the terminal block is fastened to the element. Unscrew the fasteners that hold the block in position. The oven door can usually be removed by pulling it straight up off the hinges on both sides of the door. Some hinges have a latch that must be unlocked before the door can be removed.

If the surface light of the range burns out, remove retaining screws and panels as necessary to gain access to the bulb, and remove the bulb. Replace the burned-out bulb with a new one of the same type and wattage; check the ends of the old bulb for this information. Then replace any retaining panels. If the oven light burns out, unscrew it and remove it from the oven. Replace the burned-out bulb with a new one of the same wattage, made specifically for oven use.

Door Gasket. If the oven won't heat to the desired temperature or heats unevenly, the problem could be a defective door gasket. The best way to test for this is to pass your hand around the door, being careful not to touch it, while the oven is turned on. If you can feel heat escaping, the gasket needs replacement. Replace it with a new gasket made for the range. On most ovens, the gasket — made of asbestos — is located on the frame of the oven, and the door closes against it. This gasket is generally friction-fit in a channel, and can be replaced. In other units, the oven door is in two sections, and the gasket is not mounted on the door frame, but installed between the front and back sections of the door. Don't try to replace this type of gasket; call a professional service person.

To replace a frame-mounted gasket, pull the old one out of the channel, and then clean the channel

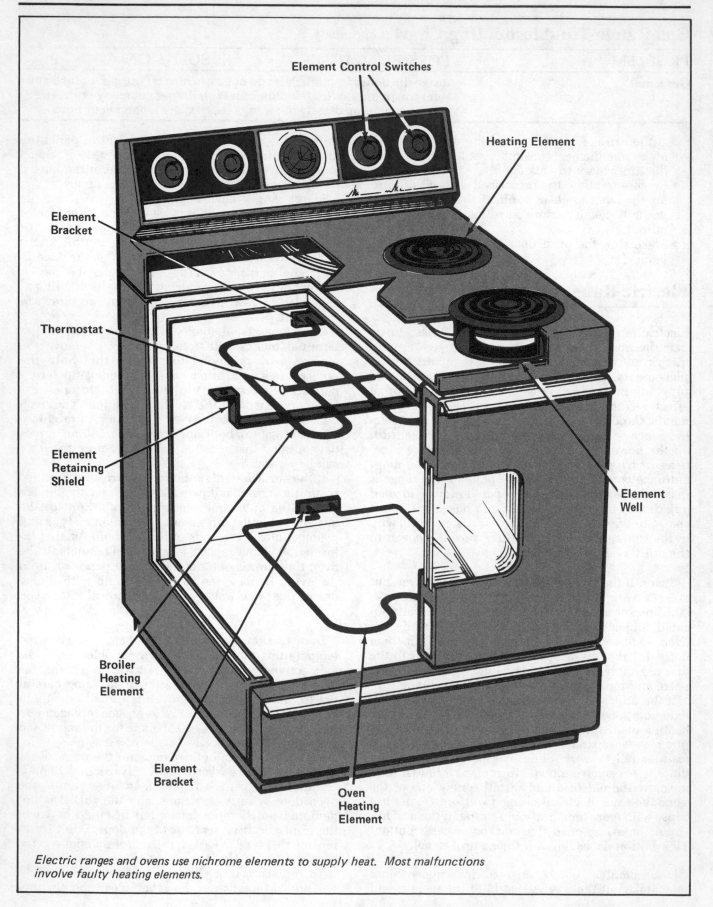

Element Control Switches

Heating Element

Element Bracket

Thermostat

Element Retaining Shield

Element Well

Broiler Heating Element

Element Bracket

Oven Heating Element

Electric ranges and ovens use nichrome elements to supply heat. Most malfunctions involve faulty heating elements.

and the door frame with a solution of mild household detergent and water. To install the new gasket, start the replacement at the top of the door frame and work down the sides; ease the gasket around corners. Finish the installation along the bottom; butt the ends of the gasket firmly together. On some oven door frames the gasket is held in place with screws. To get at the screws, bend back the exposed edge of the gasket.

Element Switches. When an element doesn't work, the problem may be the element or the element switch. Procedures for element replacement are detailed below. A faulty element switch cannot be repaired; call a professional service person for replacement.

Oven Setting Control. This component is located on the control panel; when it malfunctions, the oven won't heat. To correct the problem, remove the control knob. Then remove the back service panel or the front panel, if necessary. Remove other control knobs as needed to remove the panel. The oven setting control is located directly in back of the control knob, and is usually held to the control panel by two screws. Testing the control with a VOM is not recommended, because the results will not always be conclusive. The best procedure is to substitute a control that you know is working, if you suspect that the setting control is faulty. Or simply replace the faulty control with a new one made for the oven. Disconnect the electrical lead wires from the control terminal and lift out the control. Connect the new control the same way the old one was connected.

Oven Thermostat. If the oven doesn't heat evenly, or doesn't heat at all, the oven thermostat may be to blame. First, determine how much the temperature in the oven is off from the control setting. Put an oven thermometer inside the oven and turn the oven on for about 20 minutes, with the thermostat set at 350° F. Or set the oven at any range between 300° and 400° F. If the oven thermometer reads 25° or more lower or higher than the oven control setting, the thermostat should be recalibrated.

To calibrate the thermostat on some ranges, pull off the thermostat knob on the control panel. Behind the knob are two screws holding a round, notched plate. Loosen these screws, but do not remove them. With a screwdriver, change the notch setting on the notched plate by turning the plate counterclockwise; for every one-eighth turn, the oven temperature goes up about 25° F. To turn the heat down, move the plate clockwise.

Some thermostats can be adjusted by turning a screw inside the control knob shaft housing. To do so, remove the knob and insert a screwdriver into the shaft so that the screwdriver blade engages a screw slot. Turn the screwdriver counterclockwise about one-eighth of a turn to raise the heat about 25° F.

If a malfunctioning thermostat cannot be recalibrated, it should probably be replaced. Test the thermostat with a VOM, set to the R × 1 scale; instructions for using the VOM are given earlier in this chapter. The thermostat is located directly in back of the control knob that regulates the heat; to gain access to it, remove the back service panel to the control panel. Disconnect one electrical lead wire from a terminal of the thermostat, and clip one probe of the VOM to each thermostat terminal. If the thermostat is in working order, the meter will register zero; if the needle jumps to a high reading, the thermostat is faulty, and should be replaced. Replace the thermostat with a new one of the same type.

First, disconnect the terminal wires to the unit and pull off the control knob. The thermostat is usually held to the control panel with retaining screws. On some ranges, there is a wire running from the thermostat into the oven. This wire operates a sensing bulb that controls the thermostat. The sensing bulb is usually held by a bracket; unscrew this bracket to remove the bulb. Then carefully slip out the wire, the bulb, and the thermostat. Install the new thermostat in reverse of the way the old one came out.

Timer. The range timer is usually located in the control panel on top of the range. If you suspect the timer is faulty, don't try to fix it yourself; remove it and take it to a professional service person for testing. To take out the timer, remove the back service panel to the control panel and release the spring clips that hold it in position, or remove the retaining screws. Then push the timer forward to release it. Then remove the electrical lead wires from the timer housing.

If, when disassembling the timer, you notice that the electrical wire terminals look burned, remove these leads and buff them and the terminal points with fine steel wool. Burned and/or dirty terminals can cause the timer to malfunction; cleaning can solve this problem.

Replace the old timer or install a new one of the same size and type, if this is necessary. Connect the new timer the same way the old one was connected.

Range Heating Elements. When a range heating element burns out, it's easy to replace. But before any disassembly to check or replace an element, make sure the range is receiving power. First check the power cord, the plug, and the outlet; then look for blown fuses or tripped circuit breakers at the main entrance panel or at a separate panel. Finally, check the fusing system inside the range. If the circuit is broken, restore it; if the range is receiving power, go on to check the element.

In most ranges, each top heating element is connected to a terminal block in the side of the element well. To get at the terminal block, lift the element and remove the metal drip pan that rests below it. The element is held by two retaining screws or is

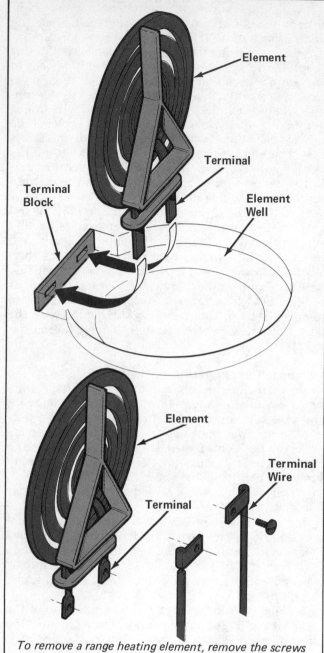

To remove a range heating element, remove the screws holding the terminal wires, or pull the element straight out of its connection.

and should be replaced with a new one.

To test a range element without a VOM, remove a working element from its terminal block and connect it to the malfunctioning element terminal. Don't let the test element overlap the edges of the element well; keep the element inside the well, even if it doesn't fit perfectly. Then turn on the power to the range. If the working element heats, the suspected element is bad, and should be replaced. If the working element doesn't heat, chances are the terminal block wiring or the switch that controls the element is faulty. In this case, call a professional.

Replace a burned-out range element with a new one made specifically for the range. Take the old element to the appliance parts store to make sure you get the right type; if possible, take the make and model information, too. This data will probably be on a metal tag attached to the back service panel of the range. To install the new element, connect it the same way the old one was connected.

Oven and Broiler Heating Elements. Electric oven and broiler elements are often even easier to test and replace than range elements. If the oven element doesn't work, first check to see if the range is receiving power; don't overlook the fusing system inside the range. If the range is receiving power, set the timer on the range to "manual." If the element still doesn't heat, turn off the power to the range, and test it with a VOM, set to the R × 1 scale; instructions for using the VOM are given earlier in this chapter.

The oven and broiler heating elements are connected almost the same way as the range elements. Remove the screws or plugs that connect the element to the power. Remove a retaining shield, which is usually held by two screws, and remove the element from the brackets that hold it in the oven. The element is usually held in these brackets by screws. Clip the probes of the VOM to each element terminal. If the element is in working order, the meter will read from 15 to 30 ohms. If the meter reads higher than 30 ohms, the element is faulty, and should be replaced. If the element tests all right but doesn't work, the problem may be at the terminals; make sure the terminals are clean and tight at the element connections.

Oven and broiler elements cannot be tested without a VOM. If you don't have a VOM, take the element to a professional service person for testing. The problem is usually a malfunctioning element, however; you aren't risking much by replacing the element without a professional test.

Replace a burned-out element with a new one made specifically for the oven or broiler. Take the old element to the appliance parts store to make sure you get the right type; if possible, take the make and model information, too. To install the new element, place it in the same position as the old one. Connect it the same way the old one was connected, and use the same screws to hold it in place.

push-fit into the terminal block. To remove a screw-type element, remove the screws holding the wires. To remove a push-type element, pull the element straight out of its connection.

Test the element with a VOM set to the R × 1 scale; instructions for using the VOM are given earlier in this chapter. Disconnect one of the electrical leads to the element, and clip one probe of the VOM to each element terminal. If the element is functioning properly, the meter will read between 40 and 125 ohms; if the meter reads extremely high, the element is faulty

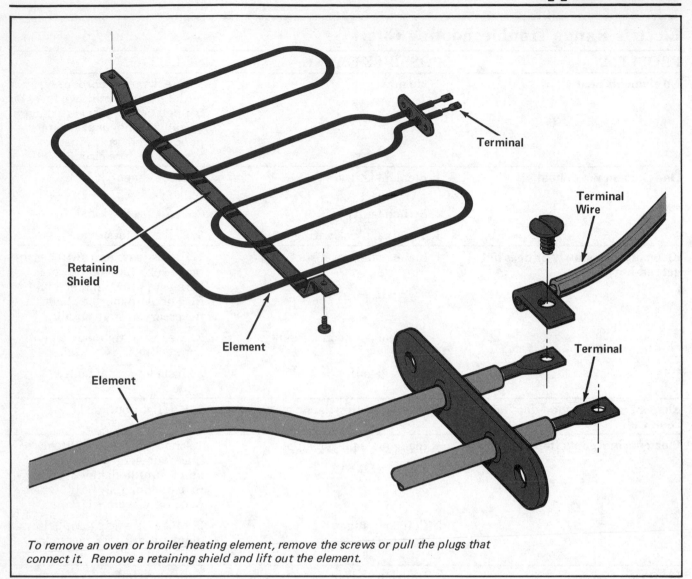

To remove an oven or broiler heating element, remove the screws or pull the plugs that connect it. Remove a retaining shield and lift out the element.

Self-Cleaning Ovens. There are two types of self-cleaning ovens, pyrolytic and catalytic. Pyrolytic ovens use very high heat — usually 1,000° F — to incinerate food on the oven's surface, leaving only a fine ash. The smoke produced by the burning is vented from the oven. When the cleaning process is complete, the fine ash left in the oven is wiped off the surface. Catalytic self-cleaning ovens are also called continuous-clean ovens. These ovens are coated with a special finish that allows most dirt to burn away at normal cooking temperatures. With these ovens, major food spills and spatters must be cleaned away immediately or the special finish will not work. *Caution: Never use a commercial oven cleaner to clean any part of either a catalytic or a pyrolytic oven.*

Most problems with pyrolytic ovens occur because cleaning procedures are not properly carried out. In most cases, the oven heat selector must be set to "clean," and the oven door must be firmly closed and, sometimes, latched. When the oven reaches a predetermined temperature — about 600° F — the door automatically locks shut so that it can't be opened during the cleaning process. If you've followed the correct procedures for using a self-cleaning oven but the oven is not coming clean, call a professional service person. Before calling, though, make these basic checks:

- Check for a blown fuse or tripped circuit breaker at the panel controlling the oven, or check the fuse panel in the oven.
- Make sure the heat selector is set to "clean" and the timer is set to "manual."
- Be sure to allow the prescribed amount of time for the oven to clean itself. If the oven is only partially cleaned, more cleaning time may be required.
- Make sure the oven door is tightly closed and latched.

Electric Range Troubleshooting Chart

PROBLEM	POSSIBLE CAUSE	SOLUTION
No elements heat	1. No power.	1. Check power cord, plug, and outlet. Check for blown fuses or tripped circuit breakers at main entrance panel or at separate panel, and in range fuse system. Restore circuit.
One element won't heat	1. Element faulty.	1. Test element; if faulty, replace.
	2. Switch faulty.	2. Call a professional.
	3. Terminal block wiring faulty.	3. Call a professional.
Element heats slowly or does not get red-hot	1. Inadequate power supply.	1. Check fuses and switches to make sure 220-volt power is being supplied; half of double-fuse hookup may be blown. If necessary, restore circuit.
	2. Element connections faulty.	2. Clean and tighten element connections.
	3. Element faulty.	3. Test element; if faulty, replace.
Element heats but food does not cook well	1. Pan not resting flat on element.	1. Use flat-bottomed pan.
Elements burn out often	1. Inadequate power supply.	1. Check fuses and switches to make sure 220-volt power is being supplied; half of double-fuse hookup may be blown. If necessary, restore circuit.
	2. Foil covering pan below element.	2. Make sure drip pans below elements are not covered by aluminum foil.
Light won't go on	1. Bulb burned out.	1. Replace bulb.
Oven won't heat	1. No power.	1. Check power cord, plug, and outlet. Check for blown fuses or tripped circuit breakers at main entrance panel or at separate panel, and in range fuse system. Restore circuit.
	2. Oven element faulty.	2. Test element; if faulty, replace.
	3. Control switch faulty.	3. Call a professional.
	4. Timer faulty.	4. Clean timer terminals; set to "manual" and turn clock on control panel 24 hours ahead. If no result, call a professional.
Broiler doesn't work	1. No power.	1. Check power cord, plug, and outlet. Check for blown fuses or tripped circuit breakers at main entrance panel or at separate panel, and in range fuse system. Restore circuit.

Electric Range Troubleshooting Chart (Continued)

PROBLEM	POSSIBLE CAUSE	SOLUTION
Broiler doesn't work (continued)	2. Broiler element faulty.	2. Test element; if faulty, replace.
	3. Control switch faulty.	3. Call a professional.
	4. Timer faulty.	4. Clean timer terminals; set to "manual" and turn clock on control panel 24 hours ahead. If no result, call a professional.
Oven temperature uneven	1. Door gasket faulty.	1. Make sure door is closed tightly; if gasket damaged, replace or call a professional.
	2. Thermostat faulty.	2. Test thermostat; if faulty, replace. If thermostat inaccurate, recalibrate; if no result, call a professional.
Timer won't work	1. Terminals loose or corroded.	1. Clean and tighten terminals; if no result, call a professional.
Element smokes and smells	1. Food spills; soap residue.	1. Clean element and drip pan with steel-wool soap pad; some odor is normal after cleaning.
Oven sweats	1. Preheating necessary.	1. Preheat oven.
	2. Exhaust vent closed or blocked.	2. Make sure vent is open; clean vent.
	3. Door gasket faulty.	3. Check gasket for leaks; if damaged, replace or call a professional.
	4. Hinges faulty.	4. Check hinges to make sure door shuts tightly; if hinges damaged, call a professional.
	5. Temperature setting too high.	5. Start oven at low temperature; increase to desired temperature.

Refrigerators and Freezers

Refrigerators and freezers, like air conditioners, consist of two basic components—a condenser coil and an evaporator coil. A liquid coolant is circulated through these coils by a compressor and a motor. The refrigerant liquid is cooled in the condenser; it then flows to the evaporator. At the evaporator, the air in the unit is cooled by contact with the liquid-filled coil. The condenser of a refrigerator or freezer is the coil on the outside of the unit; the evaporator is the coil on the inside. The coolant is circulated through the system by a compressor.

Some refrigerators and freezers have a manual defrosting system. In this type of unit, the temperature control is turned to the defrost setting to raise the temperature, and frost inside the unit melts slowly.

After the unit has been defrosted, the control is turned back to the cooling cycle. Some refrigerators and freezers have an automatic defrost system. With this system, a heater in the refrigerator melts frost in the unit. A control switch must be turned to set the thermostat that controls this defrost heater; then, when the heater reaches the set point and the unit has defrosted, the switch automatically shuts off the heater and turns the unit back to the cooling cycle.

Most newer refrigerators and freezers are frost-free. In this type of unit, a heater is automatically turned on by a timer to melt the frost inside the unit. Frost is melted by the heater at several different spots in the unit, in a series, starting at the coldest and most frosted areas. When the frost is completely melted, the thermostat automatically switches to a cooling cycle. Because this process is automatic, frost does not build up inside the box.

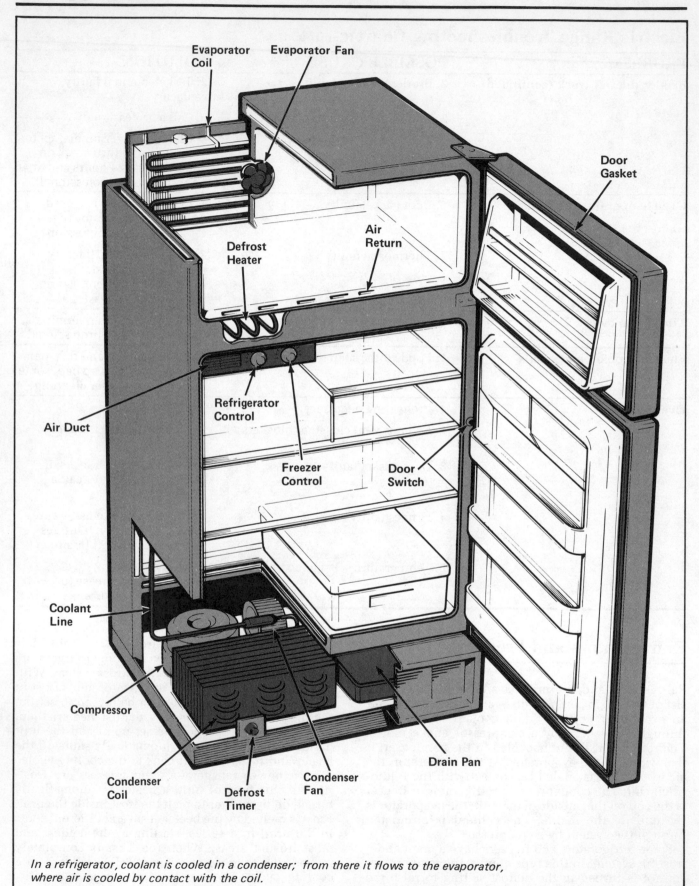

Evaporator Coil

Evaporator Fan

Door Gasket

Air Return

Defrost Heater

Refrigerator Control

Air Duct

Freezer Control

Door Switch

Coolant Line

Compressor

Condenser Coil

Defrost Timer

Condenser Fan

Drain Pan

In a refrigerator, coolant is cooled in a condenser; from there it flows to the evaporator, where air is cooled by contact with the coil.

The unit's compressor system, which forces the coolant through the coil system, is driven by a capacitor-type motor. Other basic parts of the cooling/defrosting system include switches, thermostats, heaters, condensers, and fans. You can test and replace many of these refrigerator components. However, there are exceptions, as noted in the procedures below, which are best left to a professional repair person. *Caution: Before doing any work on a refrigerator or freezer, make sure it's unplugged. After unplugging the unit, check to see if the motor/ compressor has a capacitor; this component is located in a housing on the top of the motor. Capacitors store electricity, even when the power to the unit is turned off. Before you do any work on a capacitor-type refrigerator or freezer, you must discharge the capacitor, or you could receive a severe shock.*

First, unplug the refrigerator or freezer. To gain access to the capacitor, remove the service panel over the back rear portion of the unit, or the service panel on the front of the unit below the door, as detailed below for disassembly. The capacitor is located in a housing on the top of the motor/ compressor unit; it looks like a large dry cell battery. To discharge the capacitor, use a 20,000-ohm, 2-watt resistor, an inexpensive wire unit available at most electrical supply stores. Fasten the probes of the resistor to the terminals of the capacitor; this discharges the capacitor. If the capacitor has three terminal posts, connect the resistor to one outer terminal and the center terminal, then to the other outside terminal and the center terminal. After discharging the capacitor, you can proceed to make the repairs.

Disassembly. The control components of a refrigerator are usually located in the top or upper section of the unit. The motor, compressor, condenser coil, and condenser fan are located in the bottom section. To get at the components in the upper section, remove the retaining screws or pry out the clips that hold plastic or metal panels over the parts. These fasteners may be hidden by trim or molding; pry off the trim or molding with the tip of a screwdriver or a stiff-bladed putty knife. Protruding controls may also serve as retainers for the various panel sections. In most refrigerators, the shelves—except in the freezer—can be removed to allow access to some of the panels.

To gain access to the lower section of the refrigerator, remove a service panel held by retaining screws at the back of the unit below the condenser coils. The unit may also have a front access panel below the door. This panel may be held by retaining screws or may slip up and off two side brackets. On some models, you can tip over the refrigerator and test and service parts from the bottom. In this case, the refrigerator must be defrosted, unplugged, and emptied before any servicing can be done.

The condenser and evaporator coils and the compressor are sealed units on most refrigerators. If a malfunction occurs within these parts, call a professional service person. Other parts can usually be unscrewed or pried loose from mounting brackets.

Cleaning and Positioning. The condenser and evaporator coils of a refrigerator collect dust and dirt over a period of time. This decreases their efficiency. Thus, one of the most important maintenance procedures is to clean these coils with a vacuum cleaner, a soft cloth, and/or a whisk broom, *at least* once a year.

Positioning also affects the efficiency of the unit. Refrigerators or freezers with exposed condenser coils on the back panel should be at least two inches from the wall, and the back of the refrigerator or freezer should not be placed against a heat register or a window or door where heat or sun could affect the temperature of the coil. To keep your refrigerator or freezer working properly, make sure it is clean and well positioned at all times.

Power Cord. If the cord of the unit looks frayed, or you see burn marks on the prongs of the plug or at the terminal screws—on the terminal block, under the rear access panel of the unit—the cord may be faulty. Test the cord with a VOM set to the R × 1 scale; instructions for using the VOM are given earlier in this chapter. Clip a test wire across the terminals; then clip the probes of the VOM to the prongs of the plug. If the cord and plug are in working order, the meter will read zero; if the needle moves, replace the cord, as detailed above in the section on repairing basic components.

Door Gaskets. When a refrigerator gasket becomes hard or cracked, its seal is broken, and the unit's efficiency drops sharply. Test the door gasket for leaks by placing a dollar bill between the gasket and the door jamb, and closing the door. Pull the bill out. If it offers some resistance, chances are the gasket fits properly. If the bill comes right out, or falls out, the gasket is faulty, and should be replaced. Test the gasket at several locations around the door.

To replace a gasket, buy a gasket made specifically for the model refrigerator you own. "Fit-all" gaskets may fit after a fashion, but tailoring them to the door's configuration can be a tough job. If you aren't sure about the model number of your refrigerator, cut out a small section of the gasket and take the sample to an appliance dealer for matching. If the gasket has to be ordered, you can glue the section back into the gap with rubber cement for a make-do repair until the new gasket comes in.

Let the new gasket set for about 24 hours in the room with the refrigerator to bring it to the correct temperature and humidity. Or soak the gasket in warm water to make it pliable.

Door gaskets are held by screws, clips, or adhesives, and the gasket may have a retaining strip, which helps shape it and provides a fastening tab or guide. On some units, the gasket may be held in place by the edge of the door panel; the panel is fastened with spring-steel pressure clips, bolts, or screws. The gasket may also be held by adhesive. To remove the gasket, remove the fasteners that hold it, and remove any retaining strips; or remove the fasteners that hold the door panel.

Remove the fasteners on one side of the door at a time; do not remove the entire door panel. If the gasket is held by spring clips, be careful not to pry too hard on the clips; they're under tension and could spring out of their mountings. If the gasket is held by adhesive, pry it off with a putty knife. When the old gasket is off, clean the mounting area throughly with mild household detergent and water. Remove stubborn adhesive with mineral spirits and fine steel wool, followed by a detergent/water rinse.

Start the replacement at one side of the top of the door, and work down the sides to replace the entire gasket. Smooth the gasket evenly into place, easing it around corners; use gasket cement to secure it if the manufacturer specifies this step. Make sure the gasket lies flat, with no lumps or curled edges. Then replace the fasteners, retaining strips, or panel that held the old gasket.

It may take some time for the new gasket to conform to the door. After the gasket is in place, tighten or loosen the mounting bolts as necessary to adjust the gasket to the door jamb. If the gasket is glued in place, there isn't much you can do but wait for the gasket to conform to the door jamb.

Test the gasket on a freezer door with the same dollar-bill procedure; if the gasket is faulty, replace it with a new gasket made especially for the freezer.

To replace the freezer gasket, follow the procedure outlined above. Do not remove the freezer door to replace the gasket. Freezer doors are often tensioned with spring devices, which can be very troublesome to replace after the door has been removed; and on some models wiring has to be disassembled, too.

Door Hinges. A worn or broken door gasket may not be the cause of door leaks. Misaligned and loose door hinges can cause the door to rock or sag slightly, making even a well-fitted gasket ineffective.

If the door won't shut tightly, try tipping the refrigerator *slightly* backward by propping up the front of the unit or unscrewing the front leveling legs two complete turns. Experiment with this adjustment until the door stays closed, but don't tip the unit very far out of front-to-back level.

If leveling doesn't work, tighten the hinge screws. You may have to open the door (especially freezer doors) to turn these screws. On some units, you may have to remove a hinge cap or trim to reach the screws; pry off cap or trim with a screwdriver. Sagging and looseness can be corrected by shimming the door hinges. Loosen the hinge and place a cardboard shim — the shape of the hinge — between the hinge and the door; then tighten the hinge again.

Sagging may also be caused by a wrongly placed shim; in this case, you can correct the problem by removing the shim. Experiment with the shims; you may be able to eliminate the sagging.

If the door is warped, tighten the screws that hold the inner door shell to the outer door shell. You may have to change or adjust the door gasket after making this adjustment.

On some older refrigerators, the door is held shut by a latch. This latch can become misaligned or worn, so that it fails to engage and the door does not close tightly. In this case, remove the screws that hold the latch plate to the door jamb, and shim out the latch plate with thin cardboard so that the latch engages properly.

Newer units — and especially freezers and freezer compartments — have a magnetic catch on the door. If the door doesn't latch properly, remove the magnetic strike and shim it slightly with a piece of thin cardboard. You may have to adjust the gasket to conform with the new shim.

Door Switch. On the refrigerator door jamb, locate a small push-button switch. This component operates the light inside the refrigerator or freezer. If the switch is malfunctioning, the light in the unit may stay on, and the heat from the light bulb can cause cooling trouble in the box.

If you suspect the door switch is faulty, first make sure the bulb is not burned out; then depress the push button. If the light stays on, remove the switch from the jamb. Remove retaining screws hidden by a plastic trim piece, pry the switch out of the jamb with a screwdriver, or pry off the jamb trim to expose the switch. Then test the switch with a VOM, set to the R × 1 scale; instructions for using the VOM are given earlier in this chapter.

Clip one probe of the VOM to each terminal of the switch, and press the push button. The meter should read zero; if the needle on the scale moves above zero, replace the switch with a new one of the same type. Connect the new switch the same way the old one was connected.

Limit Switch. The limit switch is found only on frost-free refrigerators and freezers; its function is to keep the defrost heating element from exceeding certain set temperatures. If a refrigerator has lots of frost in the freezer compartment, the problem may be the limit switch. However, other components — the evaporator fan, the defrost timer, and the defrost heater — can cause the same problem. Check these parts for malfunctions, as detailed below. If these parts are in working condition, the problem is most likely in the limit switch. Don't try to fix the limit switch yourself; call a professional service person for replacement.

Thermostat Control. This component is usually mounted inside the refrigerator; the visible control

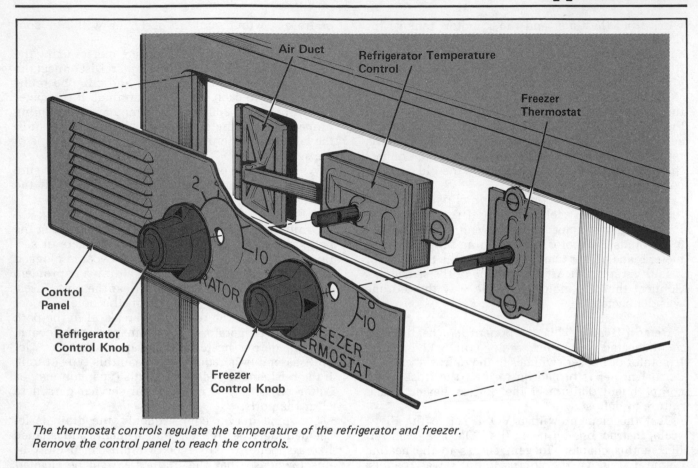

Air Duct

Refrigerator Temperature
Control

Freezer
Thermostat

Control
Panel

Refrigerator
Control Knob

Freezer
Control Knob

*The thermostat controls regulate the temperature of the refrigerator and freezer.
Remove the control panel to reach the controls.*

knob is turned to regulate the refrigerator/freezer temperature. The workability of this control can be tested in various ways, depending on the problem.

If the compressor runs all the time, turn the control knob to the "off" position. If the compressor still runs, unplug the unit; then pull off the control knob and remove the screws holding the thermostat in place. Pull out the thermostat, and remove either the red or the blue wire from its terminal. Plug in the unit. If the compressor doesn't run, the thermostat is faulty; replace it with a new one of the same type. Connect the new thermostat the same way the old one was connected.

If the compressor runs after the wire is removed from its terminal, there is probably a short circuit somewhere in the unit's wiring. In this case, don't try to fix the problem yourself; call a professional service person.

If the refrigerator or freezer runs but the box doesn't cool, unplug the unit; then, with a screwdriver, remove the thermostat. Disconnect both wires from the thermostat, and tape the ends of the wires together with electrical tape. Plug in the appliance. If the refrigerator starts and runs normally, the thermostat is faulty; replace it with a new one of the same type. Connect the new thermostat the same way the old one was connected.

If the freezer compartment is normal but the re-

frigerator box doesn't cool, set the dials that control both compartments to mid-range. Remove these knobs; they're usually friction-fit. Then unscrew the temperature control housing; you'll see an air duct near the control. Replace the knob on the freezer thermostat, and turn the control to "off." Open the refrigerator door and look closely at the air duct. If this duct doesn't open wider in about 10 minutes, the control is faulty; replace it with a new one of the same type. Connect the new control the same way the old one was connected.

Evaporator Fan. In some cases, a faulty thermostat may not be the cause of a warm refrigerator or freezer. A warm box may also be caused by a defective fan, a blocked fan, or broken or bent fan blades. If the blades are jammed, try to free them; if they're bent, straighten them with pliers. If this doesn't solve the problem, call a professional service person.

On some refrigerators, the door switch operates the evaporator fan; if the fan seems to be malfunctioning, the door switch could be faulty. Test the switch as detailed above, and replace it if necessary.

Defrost Timer. If the compressor doesn't run, chances are the defrost timer is malfunctioning. This part is located near the compressor. To test the defrost timer, unplug the refrigerator. Disconnect the wires from the timer and timer motor; remove the timer from its brackets by backing out two retaining screws. Test the defrost timer with a VOM, set to the R × 1 scale; instructions for using the VOM are given earlier in this chapter. Clip one probe of the VOM to each defrost timer—not motor—wire, and turn the timer control screw shaft until it clicks. If the defrost timer is functioning, the meter will read zero. If the needle jumps, the defrost timer is faulty; replace it with a new one of the same type. Connect the new defrost timer the same way the old one was connected.

To check the defrost timer motor, clip one probe of the VOM to each motor wire, and set the scale to R × 100. If the meter reads between about 500 and 3,000 ohms, the motor is functioning properly. If the meter reads higher than 3,000 ohms, the timer motor is faulty; replace it with a new one of the same type. Connect the new motor the same way the old one was connected.

Defrost Heater. This component is a heating element located on the evaporator coil; when the refrigerator or freezer switches to the defrost cycle, the defrost heater is turned on to melt the frost in the compartment. Failure of the defrost heater causes failure to defrost.

Test the element with a VOM, set to the R × 1 scale; instructions for using the VOM are given earlier in this chapter. To gain access to the heating element, remove the compartment's wall panels. Clip one probe of the VOM to each element terminal. The meter should read between 5 and 20 ohms; if it doesn't, the heating element is faulty, and should be replaced. Replace the heater with a new one of the same type and electrical rating; connect the new heater the same way the old one was connected.

Condenser Fan. This component is located under the unit. If the fan is malfunctioning, the refrigerator

or freezer won't cool properly, or will run continuously or not at all.

Test the fan with a VOM; instructions for using the VOM are given earlier in this chapter. Disconnect the electrical wires to the fan motor and clip one probe of the VOM to each fan motor terminal. If the meter reads from 50 to 200 ohms, the motor is functioning properly. If the meter reads higher than 200 ohms, the fan motor is faulty; replace it with a new one of the same type.

While you're working on the fan motor, make sure the fan blades are clean and unobstructed. If the blades are bent, straighten them with pliers.

Drain Ports. The drain ports are located along the bottom of both the freezer and the refrigerator sections of the unit. These holes can become clogged with debris or with ice, causing a drainage problem when the unit is defrosting. To clear the ports, use a short section of wire that will fit the holes. Do not use a toothpick; the wood may break off in the port. On some refrigerators, the drain ports are located near the defrost heater at the evaporator coils. A lot of disassembly is required to clean this type of unit; if the refrigerator or freezer is this type, you may be better off calling a professional service person to clear the ports.

On some freezer compartments, the drain is located under the freezer compartment, and shaped like a shoehorn. This type of drain can usually be unscrewed so that the drain area can be cleaned.

Drain Pan. This component is located under the bottom of the refrigerator. During the defrosting cycle, water runs through a small hose into the drain pan, and then is naturally evaporated. On some refrigerators, the drain hose is rubber instead of metal. This type of hose can become cracked, causing leaks. Examine the hose; if it's damaged, replace it with a new one of the same type. If you spot water on the floor, the drain pan may be tipped on its brackets, or the pan may be cracked or rusted. To eliminate the leak, realign or replace the pan.

Ice-Makers. Freezers with automatic ice-makers sometimes malfunction because the water inlet valve strainer that feeds water to the ice-maker becomes clogged. To correct this problem, unplug the appliance and disconnect the water supply. Then remove the water line where it enters the valve—usually at the bottom edge of the unit. Locate the wire strainer and remove it, and clean the strainer with a stiff brush and mild household detergent. Reassemble the component in reverse fashion.

Wet Insulation. When condensation appears on the outer shell of a refrigerator or freezer in a specific and confined area, the insulation inside the unit is probably wet. This problem is usually caused by moisture penetrating the insulation through a

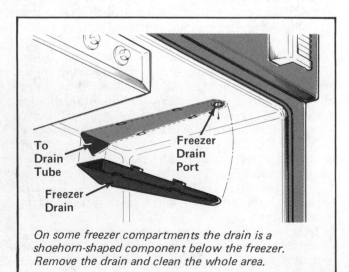

To Drain Tube

Freezer Drain Port

Freezer Drain

On some freezer compartments the drain is a shoehorn-shaped component below the freezer. Remove the drain and clean the whole area.

Refrigerator/Freezer Troubleshooting chart

PROBLEM	POSSIBLE CAUSE	SOLUTION
Unit doesn't run	1. No power.	1. Check power cord, plug, and outlet. Check for blown fuses or tripped circuit breakers at main entrance panel; restore circuit.
	2. Controls not set properly.	2. Set controls properly. If no result, test controls; if faulty, replace.
	3. Compressor fan faulty.	3. Call a professional.
	4. Timer faulty.	4. Call a professional.
	5. Compressor faulty.	5. Call a professional.
Fuses blow	1. Circuit overloaded.	1. Put on different circuit.
	2. Voltage low.	2. Call a professional or the power company.
Unit doesn't cool	1. Very hot weather.	1. Set thermostat several degrees lower.
	2. Door gasket faulty.	2. Check gasket for leaks; if faulty, replace.
	3. Condenser coil dirty.	3. Pull unit away from wall and vacuum condenser coil; or remove bottom access panel and clean coil.
	4. Unit needs defrosting.	4. Defrost, reset, and test unit.
	5. Unit in bad location.	5. Move unit at least 2 inches away from wall; keep away from heat registers and windows.
	6. Light stays lit when door is shut.	6. Replace switch.
	7. Wet insulation around unit.	7. Take unit out of service so insulation can dry; locate and mend leak.
	8. Door doesn't close tightly.	8. Level unit so door closes by itself. Check door alignment; if necessary, reset or replace hinges.
	9. Unit overloaded.	9. Store less food in unit.
	10. Condenser fan clogged.	10. Clean fan assembly. If no result, replace if possible; otherwise, call a professional.
	11. Timer faulty.	11. If timer is not complex, test and replace. If timer is complex, disconnect and take to a professional.
	12. Coolant leak.	12. Call a professional.
	13. Defrost heater faulty.	13. Call a professional.
	14. Frost on evaporator coil.	14. Defrost; then defrost frequently.

 **Appliances**

Refrigerator/Freezer Troubleshooting Chart (Continued)

PROBLEM	POSSIBLE CAUSE	SOLUTION
Frost forms quickly or unit doesn't defrost	1. Controls set incorrectly.	1. Reset thermostat control to higher temperature.
	2. Defrost heater faulty.	2. Test heater; if faulty, replace.
	3. Defrost limit switch faulty.	3. Call a professional.
	4. Door opened too often.	4. Open door less often.
	5. Door gasket faulty.	5. Check gasket for leaks; if faulty, replace.
	6. Door sagging.	6. Level unit so door closes by itself. Check door alignment; if necessary, reset or replace hinges.
	7. Drain clogged (frost-free unit).	7. Defrost freezer; clean drain port.
Noisy operation	1. Unit not level.	1. Level unit from front to back and side to side.
	2. Drain pan vibrating.	2. Reposition pan; if damaged or warped, replace.
Condensation	1. Controls set incorrectly.	1. Set thermostat control to higher temperature.
	2. Door opened too often.	2. Open door less often.
	3. Door gasket faulty.	3. Check gasket for leaks; if faulty, replace.
Water leaks	1. Drains clogged.	1. Defrost and clean drain ports.
	2. Drain hose cracked or split.	2. Replace drain hose.
	3. Drain pan cracked.	3. Replace drain pan.
Unit runs continuously	1. Door gasket faulty.	1. Check gasket for leaks; if faulty, replace.
	2. Controls set incorrectly.	2. Set thermostat control to higher temperature.
	3. Condenser coil dirty.	3. Pull unit away from wall and vacuum condenser coil; or remove bottom access panel and clean coil.
	4. Unit in bad location.	4. Move unit at least 2 inches away from wall; keep away from heat registers and windows.
	5. Door opened too often.	5. Open door less often.
	6. Coolant leak.	6. Call a professional.
Cycles too frequent	1. Condenser coil dirty.	1. Pull unit away from wall and vacuum condenser coil; or remove bottom access panel and clean coil.
	2. Compressor faulty.	2. Call a professional.

Refrigerator/Freezer Troubleshooting Chart (Continued)

PROBLEM	POSSIBLE CAUSE	SOLUTION
Light won't light	1. Bulb burned out.	1. Replace bulb.
	2. Door switch faulty.	2. Test switch; if faulty, replace.
Ice-maker won't work	1. Blockage in strainer unit.	1. Defrost; clean strainer.
Bad smell in unit	1. Spoiled food in unit.	1. Remove spoiled food and clean unit.
	2. Drains clogged.	2. Defrost, clean drain ports.
	3. Drain pan dirty.	3. Clean drain pan.

broken jamb or trim strip that covers the gap between the outer and inner shells of the unit.

To correct the problem, unplug the refrigerator or freezer and empty it. Prop the door open. Leave the unit off, with its door open, for 36 to 48 hours; this should be ample time for the insulation to dry. During this period, examine the trim strips. If you find any cracks in them, pry out the strips with the tip of a screwdriver or the blade of a putty knife, and replace them with new ones. If this treatment doesn't work, the insulation may be thin in spots. In this case, call a professional service person to replace or repack the insulation.

Wet insulation may also be due to broken shelf supports. Broken brackets also cause shelf leveling problems. The supports—metal or plastic—are easy to replace; don't try to repair them. Lift the broken support up and off its mounting bracket, and replace it with a new one of the same type.

Refrigerant Leak. Coolant leaks are identifiable by their acrid smell. There is nothing you can do to repair a coolant leak; call a professional service person to deal with the problem.

Motor/Compressor. The compressor and motor of a refrigerator or freezer are contained in a sealed unit. If you trace problems to either of these components, do not try to fix the unit yourself; call a professional service person.

Dishwashers

The control panels on the latest dishwashers can look intimidating — they're loaded with so many dials, push buttons, lights, clocks, and other features that the machine looks too complex to repair. But this is actually not the case. With the exception of the control panel, dishwashers haven't changed much in basic design over the last 10 years. You can repair most dishwasher malfunctions.

As in many appliances, dishwasher parts can be replaced as a unit, and this is often easier and less expensive than having a professional service person make repairs. If you aren't sure a part is still usable, remove it from the dishwasher and take it to a professional service person for testing, and decide whether to buy a new part or have the old one repaired on the basis of the repair estimate.

Dishwashers usually run on 115-volt or 120-volt power; the water they use comes directly from the water heater, and wastewater is drained into the sink's drainpipe. The dishwasher is not connected to the cold-water supply. For best dishwashing results, set the temperature control of the water heater to no less than 140° F; water cooler than this usually doesn't get the dishes clean. The water shutoff for the dishwasher is almost always located below the floor underneath the unit; to turn off the water supply, you'll have to go to the shutoff in the basement or crawl space under the kitchen.

Caution: Because the dishwasher is connected to both the plumbing system and the electrical system, you must consider both systems when working on this appliance. Before doing any work on the dishwasher, make sure the unit is unplugged or the power to the unit is turned off; remove the fuse or trip the circuit breaker that controls the circuit, at the main entrance panel or at a separate panel. Shut off the water supply to the dishwasher at the shutoff in the basement or crawl space under the kitchen.

The repair procedures in this section are complete, but for repairs involving the plumbing system, you may need additional information. For a detailed discussion of plumbing procedures and repairs, see the chapter on plumbing.

Basic Operating Checks. If the dishwasher doesn't run, first check to make sure it's receiving power. If the unit plugs into a wall outlet, check the cord, the plug, and the outlet to make sure they're functioning properly. Also check the switch that controls the outlet to make sure it's turned on. Most dishwashers are wired directly into a circuit; check the main entrance panel for a blown fuse or tripped circuit

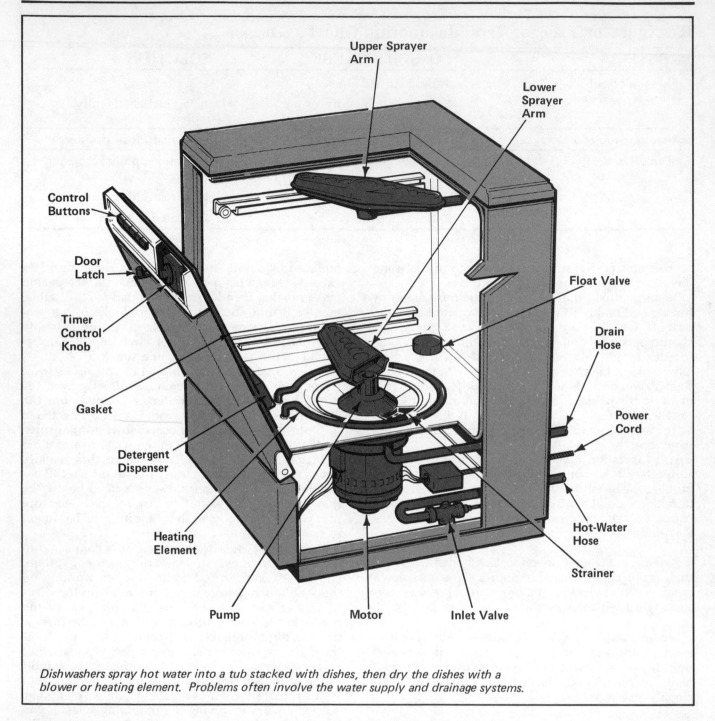

Dishwashers spray hot water into a tub stacked with dishes, then dry the dishes with a blower or heating element. Problems often involve the water supply and drainage systems.

breaker, and restore the circuit. If your home is an older one, the dishwasher may be wired to a separate entrance panel; look for a blown fuse or breaker at this panel, and restore the circuit. If the circuit is receiving power, and the wall outlet is controlled by a switch, the switch may be faulty. Test the switch with a voltage tester. Take off the switch cover plate; place one probe of the tester on one terminal and the other probe on the other terminal. If the tester bulb lights, the switch is functioning; if it doesn't light, the switch is faulty. Replace the switch with a new

one of the same type, as detailed in the chapter on electricity.

Second, make sure the door is tightly closed and latched; the dishwasher will not operate until the latch is properly engaged. To check the latch, close and latch the door, and hold the latch tightly in place. Then, still pressing the latch closed, turn the control knob to "on." If the dishwasher works, the latch is faulty, and should be replaced.

Third, make sure the water is turned on, and the water temperature is high enough. A breakdown in

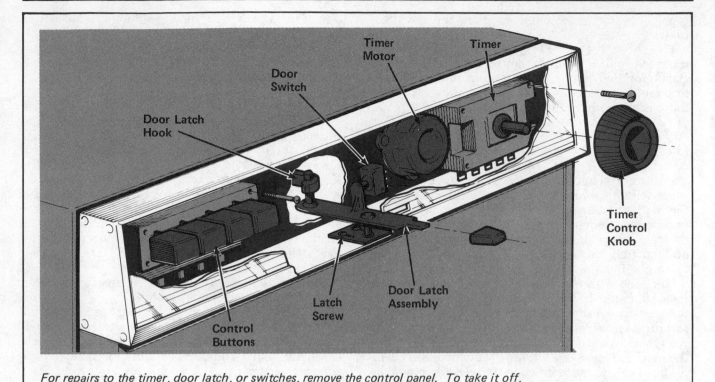

For repairs to the timer, door latch, or switches, remove the control panel. To take it off, remove a series of retaining screws and the control knobs, and lift the panel off.

the water heater could stop the flow of water to the dishwasher. Try the hot water in the kitchen sink or lavatory. If you can draw hot water, the water heater may not be at fault.

Finally, make sure the controls on the control panel are properly set. The newer push-button controls can be very sensitive; make sure the buttons are *firmly* pressed into position.

Disassembly. Access to the working parts of most dishwashers is through the front door of the unit. Many repairs can be made to the machine by simply opening the door and reaching in to the various component parts, such as the sprayers, strainers, float switch, racks, and door latch.

To get to the control panel on the door, remove a series of retaining screws around the panel. These screws may be under molding trim strips, which usually snap onto the metal housing; pry off the strips with a stiff-bladed putty knife or a screwdriver, or remove a setscrew that holds the molding. The control knobs are friction-fit on shafts, or are held by small setscrews in the base of the knobs. In some dishwashers, the entire front door panel must be removed to gain access to the control components. This panel is held to the door by a series of retaining screws, usually found around the edge on the inside back of the door.

On many models, once the control panel is removed the door panel can be removed; unscrew a series of fasteners holding the door panel in place.

Sometimes these retaining screws are covered by trim moldings, which must be pried or slipped off. For access to the motor, pump, hoses, inlet valves, and other parts, remove the lower access panel; this can usually be removed without removing the door. The panel may be held by retaining screws, or may lift up and off metal hangers.

If the dishwasher is portable, tip the machine over on its back or side before removing the control, door, or lower access panels. This may give you a more comfortable working position.

Door Gasket. If water leaks through the dishwasher door, the gasket is probably faulty. Open the door and examine the gasket. It should be soft and resilient; if it's worn, cracked, or hard, it should be replaced. To replace a gasket, buy a gasket made specifically for the model dishwasher you own. "Fit-all" gaskets may fit after a fashion, but tailoring them to the door's configuration can be a tough job. Let the new gasket set for about 24 hours in the room with the dishwasher, to bring it to the correct temperature and humidity. Or soak the gasket in warm water to make it pliable.

There are two basic types of gaskets, flush-mounted and channel-mounted. A flush-mounted gasket is secured to the door by a series of screws or clips, or held in place by a retaining strip or a panel. A channel-mounted gasket is held in a retaining groove; a special splining or gasket tool makes installation easier. Use gasket cement to install either type of gasket, as recommended by the manufacturer.

First, remove the old gasket. If it's channel-mounted, pull it carefully out of the channel; if it's flush-mounted, remove the fasteners, retaining strip, or panel to release the gasket. Clean the gasket area thoroughly with warm water and liquid detergent, or, if necessary, with mineral spirits. Dry the door and then install the new gasket, smoothing it evenly into place and easing it around corners; use gasket cement if specified by the manufacturer. If you're installing a channel-mounted gasket, press it into place with a splining tool. Make sure the gasket lies flat, with no lumps or curled edges. Then replace the fasteners or the retaining strip or panel and its fasteners. Remove any excess gasket cement with mineral spirits; be careful not to damage the dishwasher's finish.

Once the gasket is in place, check it for fit against the door frame. It should fit tightly, with no cracks or bulges between the gasket and the frame. If necessary, tighten or loosen the retaining screws, or refit the gasket in the clips or the door channel. Then run the machine through a washing sequence, and check for leaks. If you spot a leak and the gasket seems to be properly in place, try adjusting the door latch. The trick is to seat the gasket against the frame of the door without flattening the gasket or squeezing it too flat when the door is latched properly. Adjust the latch or the gasket until it fits just right.

Door Latch. The latch on a dishwasher door is opened and closed repeatedly, and this hard use can lead to mechanical problems — the latch may be loose, or may have slipped out of position, throwing the alignment off and preventing the door from closing properly. When this happens, the latch does not engage properly, and the dishwasher will not start. In many cases, you may be able to solve the problem by adjusting the position of the latch. Move the latch slightly by loosening the screws that hold it, and slide the latch with your fingers or pliers. The screw slots are made especially for this purpose. Close and open the door to see whether the latch is properly aligned, and tighten the screws to hold it in place in the correct position.

After repositioning the latch, check to see if it's working properly. Close and latch the door, and turn the control knob to "on." If the dishwasher doesn't start, the latch is faulty. Replace it with a new latch; connect it the same way the old one was connected. You may have to move the new latch back and forth several times before it works properly.

Door Switch. On many dishwashers, the latch engages a switch to activate the timer and other control components; if the latch is not completely engaged or the switch is faulty, the machine will not operate. To determine whether the switch is faulty, latch the door and hold the latch tightly in the closed posi-tion. This works best on a unit with a lever-type latch. Then turn the control to the "on" position. If the unit works, the problem is probably a misaligned lock unit; adjust the lock unit with a screwdriver. If this doesn't solve the problem, the switch may be faulty.

Test the switch with a VOM, set to the R × 1 scale; procedures for using the VOM are detailed earlier in this chapter. Remove the panel covering the door switch, and remove one of the electrical lead wires of the switch from its terminals. Clip one probe of the VOM to each switch terminal, and shut the dishwasher's door. If the meter reads zero, the switch is working. If the meter reads higher than zero, the switch is faulty, and should be replaced. Replace the switch with a new one of the same type; connect the new switch the same way the old one was connected.

Float Switch. Dishwashers are usually protected from overfilling by a float switch. This switch is located in the bottom of the unit; to get at it, open the door and remove the bottom dish rack. If water over-filling is a problem, the float valve may be stuck. Clean away any food debris around the float. With a screwdriver handle, lightly tap the top of the float; this may free it.

If tapping doesn't work, remove the lower access panel and locate the bottom portion of the float and float switch. Test the float switch with a VOM, set to the R × 1 scale; procedures for using the VOM are detailed earlier in this chapter. Unscrew one electrical lead wire to the switch terminal, and clip one probe of the VOM to each terminal. If the meter reads zero, the switch is not faulty; the trouble is probably in the timer. If the meter reads higher than zero, the switch is faulty; replace it with a new one made to fit the dishwasher. The switch is held to a mounting bracket with screws; remove the screws to get the old switch out. Connect the new switch the same way the old one was connected.

Pressure Switch. Although the water level in most dishwashers is controlled by the timer, some machines are equipped with a pressure switch that does this job. You can quickly tell if your unit has one by removing the lower access panel. The pressure switch is mounted under the tub housing, and has a small hose running into it, about the size of a car windshield washer hose. The hose is usually held to the switch by a spring clip.

If the dishwasher won't fill with water, lightly tap the switch housing with a screwdriver handle; this may jar the switch loose. Also make sure that the hose and the spring clip are properly attached, and that the hose is not defective. Tighten the connections and replace the hose, if necessary. If this doesn't solve the problem, test the switch with a VOM, set to the R × 1 scale; instructions for using the VOM are given earlier in this chapter. Disconnect the electrical leads from the switch terminals, and clip one probe of the VOM to each terminal. If the meter reads zero, the switch is functioning; if it reads higher than zero, the switch is faulty, and should be replaced. Replace the switch with a new one made for the dishwasher. The switch is held to the tub with retaining screws; remove the screws to take out the old switch. Connect the new switch the same way the old one was connected.

Timer and Control Switches. The timer controls many operations, and a faulty timer can cause many problems. Because the timer is a complex component, don't try to fix it; if it's faulty, replace it with a new timer made for the dishwasher. Test the timer with a VOM, set to the R × 1 scale; instructions for using the VOM are given earlier in this chapter. To gain access to the timer, remove the front control panel. The timer is directly behind the main timer control knob. Disconnect one of the timer's terminal wires, and clip one probe of the VOM to each terminal. If the meter reads zero, the timer is working; if the meter reads higher than zero, the timer is faulty, and should be replaced. If possible, use the same procedure to test the selector and cycle switches. The wiring hookup, however, may be too complicated to figure out on either of these switches. If you aren't sure you can deal with these switches, call a professional service person. Replace a faulty timer— or a faulty control switch—with a new one made for the dishwasher.

The timer is connected to several wires, which supply power to operate the various functions of the dishwasher. To replace the timer, have a helper hold the new timer next to the old one, and connect the wires of the new timer one by one, removing the old wire and connecting the new, to make sure you connect the wires correctly. The wires may be friction-fit on the terminals; if they are, use long-nosed pliers to remove the wires. Don't pull up on the wires or you may break the connection between the wires and the clips. After connecting the wires, set the new timer in position, secure it the way the old one was secured, and replace the control panel and knobs.

Water Inlet Valve. The water inlet valve controls the amount of water flowing into the dishwasher; it may be activated by the timer or by a solenoid. If the dishwasher doesn't fill with water, first make sure that the water supply to the unit is turned on, and that there's no problem at the water heater—a shutdown of the water heater would cause a shutdown of the water to the dishwasher. Finally, check the timer to make sure it's working through its programmed sequences. If both the water supply and the timer are in working order, the problem is probably in the inlet valve.

The inlet valve is located under the tub of the dishwasher. If the valve is controlled by a solenoid, the solenoid is usually connected to the side of the unit. Tap the solenoid and the valve lightly with the

handle of a screwdriver; then start the dishwasher again. If the dishwasher still doesn't fill, test the solenoid with a VOM, set to the R × 1 scale; instructions for using the VOM are given earlier in this chapter. Disconnect one electrical lead to the solenoid, and clip one probe of the VOM to each solenoid terminal. If the meter reads from about 100 to 1,000, the solenoid is functioning. If the reading is higher than 1,000, the solenoid is faulty, and should be replaced. Replace the solenoid with a new one of the same size and type; connect the new solenoid the same way the old one was connected.

Malfunctions of the inlet valve may also occur when a screen inside the valve becomes clogged with mineral deposits. To solve this problem, pry out the screen with a screwdriver and flush it thoroughly with running water; then replace it in the valve.

Badly worn or misshapen inlet valves cannot be repaired; if the valve is damaged, replace it with a new one made for the dishwasher. The valve is usually held to a mounting bracket with screws. Take apart the connection linking the valve to the water supply; then take out the screws and remove the valve. Install the new valve by making the connections in reverse order. For more detailed information on plumbing connections, see the chapter on plumbing.

Drain Valves. Some dishwashers have drain valves; these valves are used only in dishwashers with nonreversible motors. If you can't tell from the manufacturer's operating instructions whether your dishwasher has a drain valve, or a nonreversible motor, remove the bottom panel of the unit and locate the motor. If the motor has two or three wires running into it, the motor is nonreversible. When the drain valve malfunctions, follow the procedures detailed below for water pumps; if this doesn't solve the problem, call a professional service person.

Heating Element. This component is used to help dry the dishes. In most dishwashers, the heating element fits around the screen in the bottom of the tub housing; it looks like a round version of an electric oven element. The heating element doesn't malfunction often, but it can burn out. If you suspect a faulty element, test it with a VOM, set to the R × 1 scale; instructions for using the VOM are given earlier in this chapter. Remove the dishwasher's bottom access panel and disconnect one of the power leads to the element. Clip one probe of the VOM to each element terminal. If the meter reads between 15 and 30 ohms, the element is working; if the reading is higher than 30 ohms, the element is faulty, and should be replaced. Replace it with a new one made for the dishwasher.

Removing and replacing an element is easy. Disconnect the electrical leads to the element's terminal screws, and remove the nuts or other fasteners that hold the element to the terminals. From inside the tub, lift the element out. It may be held by clips and ceramic blocks in the tub, but you can easily thread it past these spacers. Set the new heating element in position, reconnect the power leads, and replace the fasteners that hold the element in place.

Blower. Some dishwashers use a blower unit instead of a heating element to dry the dishes. The blower forces hot air through the dishwasher tub; it is located under the tub, not in it. If the blower system malfunctions, don't try to fix it yourself; call a professional repair person. Before you call for service, though, make sure that the power is on and the timer is working.

Detergent Dispenser. Accumulated detergent from prior washings can cause problems with the soap dispenser when the soap gets into the spring that triggers the flip-out tray, or slows down the pivot action of the tray. If the dispenser is not opening, first make sure you aren't loading the machine so dishes or pots and pans are touching the dispenser, and that dish racks aren't blocking the dispenser. Also check to make sure the dispenser tray isn't cracked—if the detergent in the tray is almost liquid, rather than just damp, the tray may be damaged.

If you can't solve the problem easily, replace the entire dispenser unit; this is usually easier than trying to disassemble it and replace separate parts. Use a new dispenser made for the dishwasher. The screws holding the dispenser may be on the front of the unit, or you may have to remove the front door panel to get to the screws and make the replacement. Remove the old dispenser and secure the new one, connecting it the same way.

Dish Racks. Problems with the dish racks usually occur because the racks have been jammed back into the tub housing after they're fully loaded. Careless handling can exert enough force to crack or break the roller wheels, or to throw the racks off the tracks. The solution is easy: stop jamming the racks. The repair is easy, too. Remove the racks by pulling out tiny metal pins that hold them in the tracks; or simply lift up on the racks and pull them out of the tracks. Then replace the racks on the tracks so that they roll smoothly. If the rollers are cracked or broken, replace them with new ones of the same type. The rollers may be friction-fit to their hubs; simply pull them off for replacement. Or, if they are held by tiny spring clips, pull the clips out with pliers, or pry them out with the tip of a screwdriver. If you can't pull the rollers off for replacement, remove and replace the entire rack.

Lower Sprayer Arm
Screen
Pump Housing
Bolt
Upper Impeller
Food Disposer Blade
Spacer Plate
Impeller Hood
Flat Plate
O-Ring
Lower Impeller
Washers
Motor Shaft
Motor

To reach the water pump, remove the sprayer arm and screen and then the pump housing. Remove a bolt, and the pump components can be disassembled.

Sprayer Arms. The sprayer arms seldom cause any trouble, but sometimes the spray holes in the arms become crusted with detergent. When this happens, the holes must be cleaned out so that the arms will work efficiently. Remove the lower arm by twisting off the cap that holds it to the motor shaft; wash it thoroughly with water and mild household detergent. Sharpen a lead pencil and break off the lead point; use the tapered end of the pencil to ream out the holes. A wood manicure stick can also be used. Do not use toothpicks, matches, or metal objects for this job—lightweight wooden sticks could break off in the ports, causing blockage; metal could scrape and enlarge the ports. After cleaning, place the sprayer arm back on the motor shaft, and twist the cap back on to hold it in place. Follow the same procedure to clean the upper sprayer arm.

Strainer. The strainer is located directly under the lower sprayer arm. When the strainer becomes clogged with food and detergent debris, the dishwasher may flood or overfill. On some dishwashers, the strainer is a plastic or metal component consisting of two semicircular halves; to remove this type of strainer, pry it up. On other dishwashers, the strainer is a one-piece component; to remove this type, remove the cap that holds the sprayer arm on its shaft, and then remove the sprayer arm and the strainer.

Wash the strainer in the kitchen sink, with water and mild household detergent. Use a fairly stiff brush to get the debris out of the holes and slots in the strainer. Rinse the strainer well and replace it. If part of the strainer lifts out for regular cleaning, check it and clean it, if necessary, after each load of dishes is washed.

Leaks. If the dishwasher leaks and you know the problem is not related to tub overfilling, the pump, or inlet valve problems, the plumbing connections may be faulty. Most dishwashers are connected to the water supply with metal pipe and fittings; the leak could be at these fittings. If the fittings are threaded—not soldered—tighten them with an adjustable wrench. If this doesn't work, chances are the threads are stripped, or the fitting is cracked or otherwise damaged. In this case, replace the fitting;

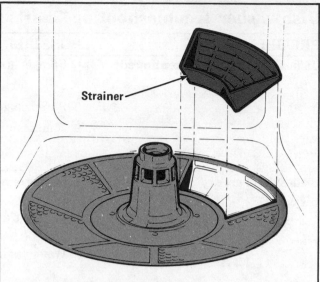

A clogged strainer can cause the dishwasher to flood or overfill. Clean the strainer regularly, or after each load of dishes is washed.

Dishwasher Troubleshooting Chart

PROBLEM	POSSIBLE CAUSE	SOLUTION
Unit doesn't run	1. No power.	1. Check power cord, plug, and outlet. Check for blown fuses or tripped circuit breakers at main entrance panel; restore circuit.
	2. Motor overload or safety shutoff.	2. Press reset button on control panel.
	3. Controls not properly set.	3. Set controls properly.
	4. Door not latched.	4. Close door so latch engages; if latch faulty, replace.
	5. Timer faulty.	5. Make sure timer is properly set. Test timer; if faulty, replace.
	6. Motor faulty.	6. Check motor leads for proper connections. Remove motor and take to a professional, or replace motor.
Dishes don't get clean	1. Inadequate preparation.	1. Scrape and rinse dishes before loading machine.
	2. Water not hot enough.	2. Set water heater thermostat at 140° to 150° F.
	3. Soap dispenser blocked, clogged, or broken.	3. Leave dispenser exposed when loading machine. Clean dispenser; if broken, replace.
	4. Wrong type of detergent.	4. Use detergent recommended for dishwashers.
	5. Detergent ineffective or spoiled.	5. Use new detergent.

Dishwasher Troubleshooting Chart (Continued)

PROBLEM	POSSIBLE CAUSE	SOLUTION
Dishes don't get clean (continued)	6. Sprayer arm clogged.	6. Clean sprayer arm.
	7. Strainer clogged.	7. Clean strainer.
	8. Pump clogged.	8. Clean pump.
	9. Timer faulty.	9. Make sure timer is properly set. Test timer; if faulty, replace.
Dishes don't get dry	1. Dishes removed too soon after end of cycle.	1. Wait until hot water has had time to evaporate from dishes.
	2. Poor stacking.	2. Stack dishes so there is air space around them.
	3. Water not hot enough.	3. Set water heater thermostat to 140° to 150° F.
	4. Heating element faulty.	4. Test element; if faulty, replace.
	5. Wetting agent gone.	5. Check dispenser; if necessary, refill.
	6. Leaky water inlet valve.	6. Clean water inlet valve; if damaged, replace.
	7. Fan motor faulty.	7. Clean fan assembly; check fan terminals for proper connections. If necessary, replace fan.
Dishes have soap spots and film	1. Poor stacking.	1. Stack dishes so there is air space around them.
	2. Not enough detergent.	2. Use amount of detergent recommended by manufacturer.
	3. Wrong type of detergent.	3. Use detergent recommended for dishwashers.
	4. Water not hot enough.	4. Set water heater thermostat to 140° to 150° F.
	5. Inadequate preparation.	5. Scrape and rinse dishes before loading machine.
	6. Water hard.	6. Add rinsing conditioner.
Silverware tarnishes	1. Water contains chemicals.	1. Adding rinsing conditioner, or add water softener to water supply.
Dishwasher doesn't fill	1. Float switch stuck.	1. Clean float and float switch; tap lightly with screwdriver handle. If necessary, replace float switch.
	2. Timer faulty.	2. Make sure timer is properly set. Test timer; if faulty, replace.
	3. Water inlet valve screen clogged.	3. Clean water inlet valve screen.

Dishwasher Troubleshooting Chart (Continued)

PROBLEM	POSSIBLE CAUSE	SOLUTION
Dishwasher doesn't fill (continued)	4. Water inlet valve solenoid faulty.	4. Tap solenoid lightly with screwdriver handle; if no result, replace water inlet valve.
	5. Drain valve stuck open.	5. Call a professional.
	6. Pressure switch faulty.	6. Replace switch.
	7. Water not turned on.	7. Check valve under dishwasher. Open hot water faucet in kitchen sink; if water doesn't flow, check for problems at water heater.
	8. Water pressure low.	8. Call water company.
Water doesn't drain	1. Impeller jammed.	1. Clean impeller; if faulty, replace.
	2. Drain valve solenoid faulty.	2. Tap solenoid lightly with screwdriver handle; if no result, call a professional.
	3. Drain valve clogged.	3. Clean drain valve.
	4. Drain hose kinked.	4. Straighten drain hose.
	5. Strainer clogged.	5. Clean strainer.
	6. Pump faulty.	6. Clean pump; if no result, replace pump.
	7. Motor faulty.	7. Call a professional.
Dishwasher doesn't shut off	1. Timer faulty.	1. Make sure timer is properly set. Test timer; if faulty, replace.
	2. Float switch stuck.	2. Clean float switch; tap switch lightly with screwdriver handle. If no result, replace float switch.
	3. Water inlet valve clogged or stuck open.	3. Disassemble and clean water inlet valve.
Dishwasher runs while door is open	1. Door switch faulty.	1. Replace door switch.
	2. Motor faulty.	2. Call a professional, or remove motor and take to a professional.
Water leaks	1. Poor stacking.	1. Stack dishes so there is air space around them.
	2. Too much detergent.	2. Use amount of detergent recommended by manufacturer.
	3. Door gasket worn or damaged.	3. Replace gasket.
	4. Timer faulty.	4. Make sure timer is properly set. Test timer; if faulty, replace.
	5. Water inlet valve stuck open.	5. Clean water inlet valve; if damaged, replace.

Dishwasher Troubleshooting Chart (Continued)

PROBLEM	POSSIBLE CAUSE	SOLUTION
Water leaks (continued)	6. Pump seal faulty.	6. Call a professional.
	7. Hose loose or damaged.	7. Tighten hose connections; if hose damaged, replace.
	8. Door hinges broken or misaligned.	8. Tighten and realign hinges; if necessary, replace hinges.
Noisy operation	1. Poor stacking.	1. Make sure dishes are properly stacked.
	2. Machine out of level.	2. Level unit with shims; check level from front to back and side to side.
	3. Sprayer arms misaligned.	3. Adjust sprayer arms so they don't scrape against screens or racks.
	4. Water level low.	4. Refrain from using washer, shower, and toilets while dishwasher is operating.
Racks stick	1. Door not open.	1. Make sure door is fully open when racks are pulled out.
	2. Racks off tracks.	2. Guide racks into tracks.
	3. Rack guides and glides dirty or misaligned.	3. Adjust and clean rack bearing points.
	4. Rack guides damaged.	4. Replace rack guides.
Dishwasher smells bad	1. Trapped food particles in unit.	1. Clean inside of washer—especially below sprayer—with household detergent; then run through complete cycle. Rinse dishes before stacking in washer.

see the chapter on plumbing for detailed pipe assembly and repair procedures.

Most dishwashers discharge used water through a pipe or a hose connected to the garbage disposer under the kitchen sink. If the drain line is flexible hosing, it may have cracked from prolonged exposure to hot water. Examine the hose and, if it's damaged, replace it. If the hose is leaking at its connections with the disposer or dishwasher, tighten the fittings or clamps at the connections, or replace the clamps. Also check for water leaks around inlet valves, drain valves, and wherever you see flexible hoses and hose connections. Leaks at clamps can be stopped by tightening or replacing the clamps; leaks in hoses can be eliminated by replacing the hoses. For more detailed plumbing procedures, see the chapter on plumbing.

Water Pump. In most dishwashers, the water pump is located under the lower sprayer arm. This component pumps the water through the dish-washer. The pump has two impellers—top and bottom—and these, as well as other components, can become clogged with food or detergent. To disassemble the pump, remove the cap that holds the sprayer arm on. Then, in sequence, take off the sprayer arm, the screen, the pump housing, a bolt, the upper impeller, the food disposer blade, a spacer plate, the impeller hood, a flat plate, an O-ring, and the lower impeller. Lay the parts out in order as you disassemble them so that you'll be able to put the assembly together properly. Clean the parts throughly with a mild detergent solution, and if any parts are worn, replace them with new ones made for the dishwasher. Replace any seals, such as the O-ring or other washers, with new ones. Then reassemble the pump, being careful to keep the parts in order.

On some dishwashers, the lower impeller serves as a drain pump. This type of system usually has a reversible motor; machines with nonreversible motors have drain valves, as detailed above. If your machine has this impeller pump system and the water will not drain from the dishwasher, clean the lower pump impeller; this may solve the problem. Otherwise, call a professional service person.

Motor. If the dishwasher motor malfunctions, don't try to fix it yourself; call a professional service person to make repairs or replace the motor. Before you call for service, though, check to make sure that the timer is working and that the dishwasher is receiving power. Check for a blown fuse or tripped circuit breaker at the main entrance panel or at a separate entrance panel; if the dishwasher is portable, make sure that it's plugged in, and that the wall outlet, if it is controlled by a switch, is turned on.

Washers

Because they do so many things, washing machines may be harder to diagnose than to repair — mainly because of the special timing cycles that operate valves and motors that turn water on, spin the tub, drain water, and control the water temperature. But diagnosis can be done; all it takes is common sense and patience. *Caution: Before you do any work on a washer, make sure it's unplugged. Disconnect the grounding wire and the water hoses.*

Basic Operating Checks. Before starting a serious appraisal, follow these procedures. First, make sure the washer is receiving power. Check the cord, the plug, and the outlet; if a wall switch controls the outlet, make sure the switch is working. Look for blown fuses or tripped circuit breakers at the main entrance panel; restore the circuit. If the unit is receiving power and still won't run, press a reset button on the control panel, if the washer has one.

Second, make sure the control knob is properly set to the "on" position, and the door is tightly closed. Check the latch to make sure it's free of lint and soap buildup.

Third, make sure that both water faucets are turned on, and that the drain and soap-saver return hoses are properly extended, without kinks. If the washer has a water-saver button, make sure the button is depressed; water may not circulate through the filter nozzle if the basket is not full and the button is not depressed.

Finally, make sure the water is the proper temperature. Check the temperature selector switches on the control panel to make sure they're properly set. Also check the water heater temperature control; it should be set no lower than 120° F.

Cleaning. Regularly wipe the top and door of the washer clean to prevent the buildup of dirt and detergent. When you wash very linty materials, remove lint from the tub after removing the laundry. Soap deposits may cause laundry to smell bad, but this problem is easy to solve. Fill the tub with water and add one pound of water softener or one gallon of white vinegar; then run the machine through the complete wash cycle. If the deposits are really bad, wash the inside of the tub with a solution of household ammonia and mild detergent. Rinse throughly and then wipe the tub with liquid bleach. *Caution: Rinse the tub thoroughly before wiping it out with bleach. Ammonia and bleach can combine to form a very dangerous gas.* Finally, run the machine through a complete wash cycle.

Disassembly. The washer cabinet must usually be disassembled for repairs and maintenance. The control panel is held to the top of the machine with retaining screws spaced around the panel—usually under a piece of molding or trim that can be pried off. On some machines, you'll have to remove the back of the control panel, also held by retaining screws, to get at the working parts of the controls. Knobs on the control panel are usually friction-fit. Some knobs are held by small setscrews at the base of the knob. Loosen the setscrews and pull the knobs straight off the shafts.

Most washers have a removable service panel at the back of the machine. This panel is held by retaining screws. Tip the washer over on its front or side to gain access through the bottom of the machine; spread an old blanket on the floor to protect the washer's finish. The bottom of the machine doesn't have a service panel; generally, the bottom of the washer is open. The top of the cabinet is usually held by spring clips. Insert a stiff-bladed putty knife into the joint between the top and side panels, and give the knife a rap with your fist. This should release the spring clips so that the top can be removed.

The washer is connected both to the electric power and to the water supply. *Caution: Make sure the power cord and water hoses are disconnected before you disassemble the cabinet or tip it over for service.*

Lid Switch. The lid switch often serves as a safety switch; if the switch is not working, or the switch opening in the lid is clogged with detergent, the machine will not run. If you suspect a detergent block, try cleaning out the port with a wood manicure stick after the power is turned off. Clean off any detergent buildup around the rim of the lid; sometimes there's enough detergent crusted on the metal to prevent the lid from closing tightly and keep the washer from operating. If cleaning doesn't help, remove the top of the cabinet to get at the switch. With the switch exposed, check the screws for looseness; loose screws can cause the switch to move when the lid is closed or as the machine goes through its cycles. Check the terminals of the switch to make sure they're tight, and tighten the mounting screws after the switch is in alignment.

To determine whether it's functioning, test the switch with a VOM, set to the R × 1 scale; proce-

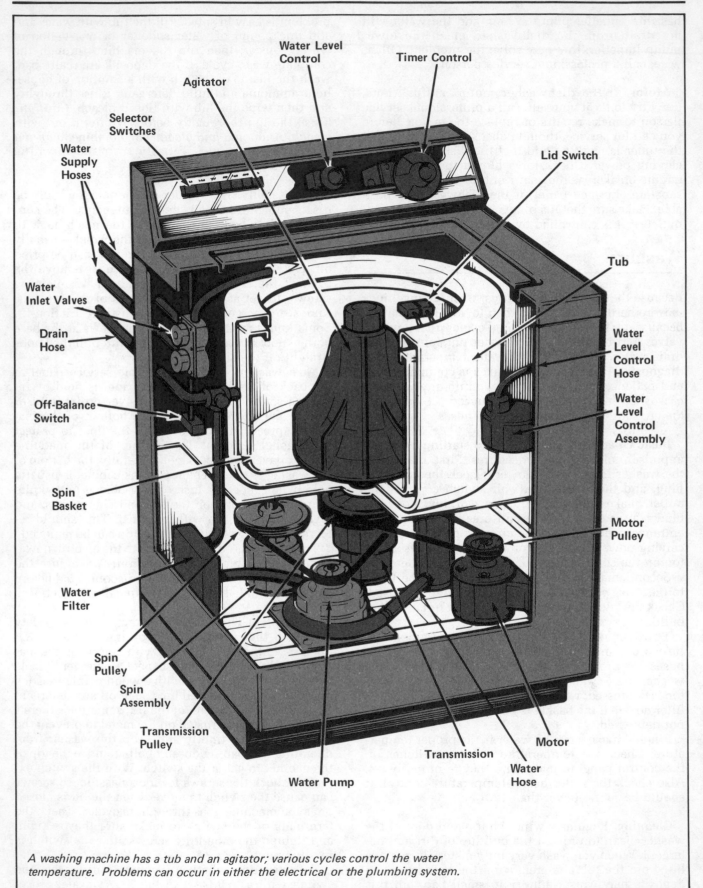

Water Level Control

Timer Control

Agitator

Selector Switches

Water Supply Hoses

Lid Switch

Water Inlet Valves

Tub

Drain Hose

Water Level Control Hose

Off-Balance Switch

Water Level Control Assembly

Spin Basket

Motor Pulley

Water Filter

Spin Pulley

Spin Assembly

Transmission Pulley

Water Pump

Transmission

Motor

Water Hose

A washing machine has a tub and an agitator; various cycles control the water temperature. Problems can occur in either the electrical or the plumbing system.

dures for using the VOM are detailed earlier in this chapter. Disconnect the power leads to the switch terminals and clip one probe of the VOM to each terminal. Close the lid. If the meter reads zero, the switch is working; if not, the switch is faulty, and should be replaced. Replace it with a new one of the same type; connect the new switch the same way the old one was connected.

If the switch still doesn't work, it is probably misaligned. Realign the switch by repositioning the screws holding it in place, testing the switch as you go until it works properly.

Temperature Selector Switch. This control panel switch regulates the temperature of the water in the tub; it also plays a role in controlling the fill cycle. If you suspect this switch is faulty, remove it—back out the screws that hold it in place—and take it to a professional service person for testing; the test takes special equipment. Or hook a test wire across the switch terminals; if water flows, the switch is faulty. If the switch is faulty, replace it with a new one of the same type. Connect the new switch the same way the old one was connected.

If there's a problem with both water temperature and tub filling cycles, both the temperature switch and the timer may be faulty; test both components, and replace them as necessary. Procedures for testing the timer are given below.

Water Level Control Switch. This is another control panel switch, usually located next to the temperature switch. There is a small hose connected to this switch, and sometimes this hose becomes loose and falls off the connection. When this happens, the water in the tub usually overflows. To solve this problem, cut about ½ inch off the end of the hose and reconnect it, with a push fit, to the switch. The switch itself can also malfunction, resulting in tub overflow and other water-level trouble in the tub. If you suspect this switch is faulty, remove it by backing out the screws holding it in place, and take it to a professional service person for testing. If the switch is faulty, replace it with a new one of the same size and type; connect the new switch the same way the old one was connected.

Timer. Most washing machine timers are very complicated. The timer controls most of the operations of the washer: water level, tub filling and emptying, length of cycles, and cycle setting sequences. For this reason, any repairs to the timer should be made by a professional service person. However, there are a couple of checks you can make when you suspect the timer is faulty; and you may be able to install a new timer.

To get at the timer, remove the control knobs and the panel that covers the controls. This may be a front panel, or access may be through a panel in back of the unit. Carefully examine the wires that connect the timer to the other parts of the washer. If the wires are loose or disconnected, try pushing them into position; they usually fit into their terminals like plugs. Use long-nosed pliers to avoid breaking the wire connections—never pull a wire by hand.

To test the timer, use a VOM, set to the R × 1 scale; procedures for using the VOM are detailed earlier in this chapter. Disconnect the power leads to the timer and clip one probe of the VOM to each lead. The VOM should read zero if the timer is working. Since the timer is a multiple switch, turn it through its cycle and test each pair of terminals in turn. The meter should read zero at all of these points. If one or more readings are above zero, the timer is faulty, and should be replaced.

Most timers are single components. To replace the timer, unscrew and disconnect the old one, and install a new timer made specifically for the washing machine. If there are many wires on the timer, have a helper hold the new timer next to the old one as you work, and disconnect the old wires one at a time, connecting each corresponding new wire as you work, to make sure the connections are properly made. Or draw a diagram showing the connections before removing the old timer. After all the wires are connected, check the connections again for correctness, and then screw the timer assembly into place.

Water Inlet Valves. If the washer won't fill or fills very slowly, if it overfills, or if the water is the wrong temperature, the water inlet valves could be faulty. These components are easy to locate and very easy to replace, at little cost. When you suspect an inlet valve is faulty, first check to make sure the water faucets are fully turned on and properly connected to the hot and cold inlets of the valves. Then check the screens in the valves; if they're clogged, clean or replace them. If water doesn't enter the tub, set the temperature control to "hot." If there is no water, set the control to "warm." If all that comes out is cold water, the hot-water inlet valve is faulty. Reverse the procedure to test the cold-water valve, setting the control first on "cold" and then on "warm." If the tub overfills, unplug the washer. If water still flows into the tub, the valve is stuck open. In any of these cases, the valves should probably be replaced.

To gain access to the valve assembly, take off the back service panel and disconnect the hot- and cold-water hoses to the valves. Remove the hoses connected to the valves inside the cabinet, and also disconnect the wires from the terminals. Back out the screws holding the valves to the machine. The inlet valves have solenoids inside the housing. These can be tested, but chances are the valves are simply worn out. Try tapping the solenoids with a screwdriver handle; if this doesn't work, replace the entire inlet valve assembly — repairs usually cost more than a new part. Replace a faulty inlet valve assembly with a new one of the same type; install it in reverse of the way you disconnected the old one.

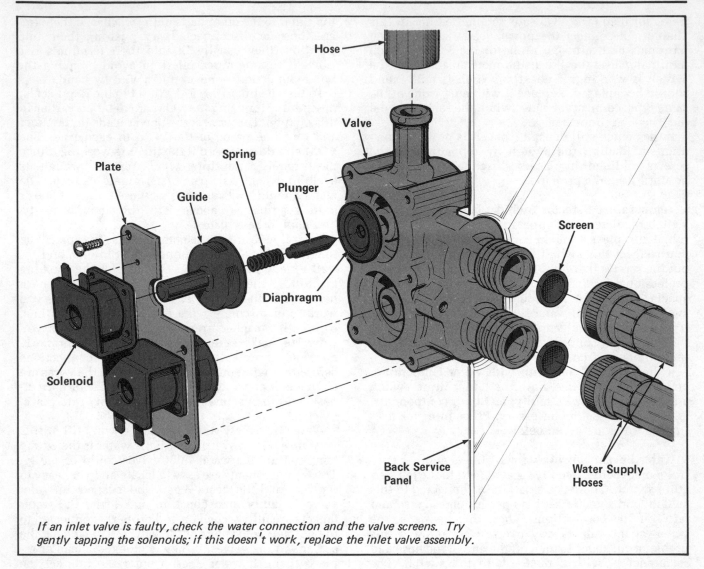

Hose

Valve

Spring

Plunger

Plate

Guide

Screen

Diaphragm

Solenoid

Back Service
Panel

Water Supply
Hoses

If an inlet valve is faulty, check the water connection and the valve screens. Try gently tapping the solenoids; if this doesn't work, replace the inlet valve assembly.

Tub and Agitator. The washing machine tub, or basket, usually doesn't cause problems, but it can cause damage to the laundry, make a lot of noise, vibrate, or stop completely.

If laundry is torn during the wash cycle, feel around the tub. If you find a rough spot, you may be able to smooth it with emery cloth. Sand lightly. If this doesn't work—or if you have to cut to bare metal to remove the roughness — the tub should be replaced, and it's probably much wiser to replace the entire washer.

The agitator—the finned part that fits on the tub shaft—can also tear laundry if the fins are cracked or broken. You may be able to solve the problem temporarily by pinching off the splinters with pliers and lightly filing the plastic smooth, but this is just a stopgap measure; the agitator should be replaced. Replace a damaged agitator with a new one of the same type. To do this, unscrew the cap on top of the agitator. With the cap off, pull straight up on the agitator; it should lift off. If it doesn't move, rap its

side with a hammer. If it still won't lift off, drive wedges under the bottom rim of the agitator to dislodge it. Then set the new agitator into place and replace the agitator cap.

Damage to the snubber, a pad-like device sometimes located under the agitator cap, can cause the machine to vibrate. The snubber is usually part of the agitator cap; it may have a suspension spring in it. Lift off the cap and examine the snubber. If the spring is broken, or the pad is visibly worn, replace the entire snubber. Snubbers might also be found at the splash guard at the top of the tub, under the transmission, or as part of the water pump housing.

If the machine doesn't have a snubber, listen for noise at the suspension unit between the tub and the machine cabinet. The suspension unit has fins or pads that may need replacement; in some cases, the entire unit may have to be replaced. Another noise point is the basket support nut. Tighten the nut, or, if you can't tighten it, replace it.

Sudden tub stops can be caused by a broken motor

belt, but they are usually due to poor tub loading. Check to see if laundry is wadded around the bottom of the tub shaft, under the basket or agitator assembly. Remove the basket or agitator to remove the laundry.

Water Leaks. Water leaks in a washer are often difficult to trace. The problem could be a loose connection, a broken hose, a cracked component, or a defective seal; it could also be a hole in the tub. If a hole in the tub is the problem, it's best to replace the washer.

Most leaks can be eliminated by tightening water connections and replacing deteriorated components. To stop a leak, check these components:

- *Lid seal.* If faulty, replace with new gasket, as detailed earlier in this chapter.
- *Hoses at faucet connections.* Tighten connections or replace hoses.
- *Hoses at water valve connections.* Tighten connections or replace hoses.
- *Drain hoses.* Tighten connections or replace hoses.
- *Inlet nozzles.* Tighten connections or replace nozzles.
- *Splash guard.* Tighten connections or replace.
- *Any plastic valve.* Tighten connections or replace.
- *Outlet hose to drain.* Tighten connections or replace hose.
- *Water pump.* See procedures below.

Oil Leaks. Oil on the floor under the washer could be a sign of problems with the transmission; it could also be caused by a faulty drain plug gasket. First, check the drain plug gasket. Tip the washer over on its front, using a heavy blanket or pad to protect the washer's finish. Remove the drain plug and check the gasket; if it is worn, cracked, or no longer flexible, it should be replaced. The gasket is held in place by a screw, or is slip-fit. Remove the old gasket and replace it with a new one made to fit the washer. Put the drain plug back and stand the washer up. If this stops the oil leak, no further repairs are needed. If it doesn't, oil could be leaking from the oil pump or around the gasket under the transmission. In this case, don't try to fix the machine yourself; call a professional service person.

Water Pump. Of all washing machine parts, the water pump probably takes the most punishment, because it is constantly in use. When the pump fails, you can hear or see the trouble: a loud rumbling inside the machine, or a failure of the water to drain out of the tub. These symptoms can also be caused by kinked or crimped drain hoses, or by blocked inlet screens, so before you start work on the water pump, make sure the drain hoses are draining properly. Remove the water supply hoses from the back of the

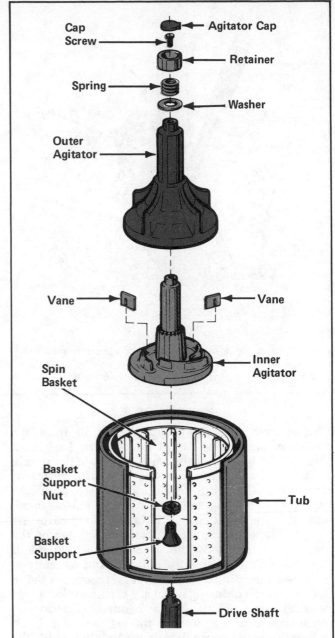

Replace a damaged agitator with a new one of the same type. Unscrew the cap on top of the agitator and pull straight up; the agitator should lift off.

washer. With long-nosed pliers, extract the filter screens from the valve ports in the washer, or from the hoses themselves. Wash the screens thoroughly, and then replace them and reattach the hoses. If the machine still rumbles or doesn't drain, examine the pump.

To gain access to the pump, bail and sponge out any water in the machine's tub, then tip the washer over on its front, using a heavy blanket or pad to protect the washer's finish. Remove the back service panel. The pump is usually along the bottom of the

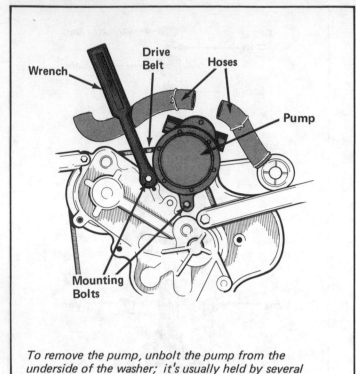

To remove the pump, unbolt the pump from the underside of the washer; it's usually held by several hex bolts on the bottom of the pump housing.

machine, but with the unit tipped on its front, it's easier to remove the pump through the back than through the bottom of the washer. Locate the pump; it has two large hoses attached to it with spring or strap clips. If the clips are the spring type, pinch the ends of the clips together with pliers to release them, and slide the clips down the hoses. If the clips are the strap type, unscrew the metal collar to loosen the clamp, and disconnect the hoses by pulling them off the connections. If the hoses are kinked or crimped at these connections, straighten and reconnect them, and try the machine again to see if this kinking was causing the problem. If the machine still doesn't drain, you'll have to remove the water pump.

To remove the pump, loosen the bolt that holds the drive belt taut and move the washer motor on the bracket to loosen the belt. Move the motor out of the way and unbolt the pump; it's usually held by two or three hex-head bolts located on the bottom of the pump housing. As you loosen the last mounting bolt, support the pump with your hand. Then lift the pump out of the washer.

On some washers, the housing that covers the pump parts can be removed. If you can take the pump apart, do so, because the trouble could be lint or dirt or pieces of cloth or paper clogging the pump impeller. Clean away all debris inside the pump, and clear any debris out of the water tubes; then reassemble the pump. Hook up the pump again and test it. If cleaning the pump doesn't put it back into working order, or if the pump housing can't be re-

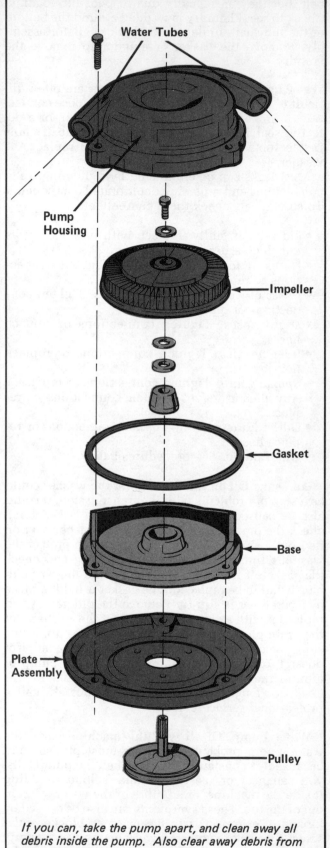

If you can, take the pump apart, and clean away all debris inside the pump. Also clear away debris from the water tubes.

Appliances

moved, replace the pump with a new one.

To install the new pump, set it into position and connect the mounting bolts to the pump housing. Move the motor back into position. Tighten the drive belt on the motor by prying it taut with a hammer handle or pry bar; it should give about ½ inch when you press on it at the center point between the two pulleys. Finally, reconnect the hoses leading to the pump.

Drive Belts and Pulleys. The drive belt (or belts) of a washing machine may become worn or damaged, causing noisy operation or stopping the washer entirely. A damaged drive belt is easy to replace. Remove the back panel of the washer to gain access to the belt.

To remove the belt, loosen the bolt on the motor bracket, and move the motor to put slack in the belt. Remove the old belt and stretch a new one into place on the pulleys. To tension the new belt, use a hammer handle or a short pry bar to push the motor into position while you tighten the bolt in the adjustable bracket. The belt should have about ½ inch deflection when you press on it at the center point, midway between the pulleys. If the belt is too loose, it will slip on the pulleys, causing the machine to malfunction. If the belt is too tight, it will wear very quickly, and will probably become so hot that it will start to smoke or smell.

Loose pulleys can also cause problems. Most pulleys are fastened to shafts with setscrews around the hub of the pulley. These screws must be tight or the pulley or belt will slip. The resultant malfunction may seem to be caused by a faulty motor, but it can be corrected by tightening the pulleys and adjusting the belt. For this reason, always check the belts and pulleys before working on the motor.

Motor. In most cases, motor malfunctions should be handled by a professional; do not try to fix the motor yourself. If the motor is a universal motor, however, you can change worn carbon brushes when sparking occurs, as detailed earlier in this chapter. You can also save the expense of a service call by removing the motor from the washer and taking it to a professional service person, and by reinstalling the repaired or new motor. To gain access to the motor, remove the back panel of the washer. The motor is mounted on an adjustable bracket.

There is one other motor problem you can repair yourself. Washer motors usually have an overload protector clipped to the motor. When this component fails, the motor won't work. Before you take the motor in for service, test the protector with a VOM, set to the R × 1 scale; procedures for using the VOM are detailed earlier in this chapter. Disconnect one electrical lead wire to the protector, and clip one probe of the VOM to each protector terminal. The meter should read zero; if the needle jumps higher, the protector is faulty, and should be replaced. Pry up the protector with a screwdriver, and replace it with a new one made specifically for the motor or washer. Connect the new protector the same way the old one was connected.

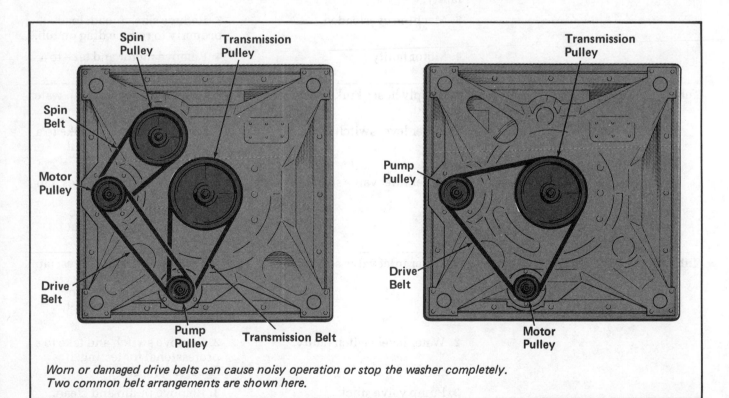

Worn or damaged drive belts can cause noisy operation or stop the washer completely. Two common belt arrangements are shown here.

 **Appliances**

Washer Troubleshooting Chart

PROBLEM	POSSIBLE CAUSE	SOLUTION
Washer doesn't run	1. No power.	1. Check power cord, plug, and outlet. Check for blown fuses or tripped circuit breakers at main entrance panel; restore circuit.
	2. Motor overload or safety shutoff.	2. Press reset button on control panel or motor.
	3. Timer faulty.	3. Make sure timer is properly set. Test timer; if faulty, replace.
	4. Lid switch faulty.	4. Remove detergent buildup from orifice; make sure switch is secure and making contact. Test switch; if faulty, replace. Make sure new switch is properly aligned.
	5. Off-balance switch faulty.	5. Test switch; if faulty, replace.
	6. Water pump clogged.	6. Clean out pump, if possible; otherwise, replace pump.
	7. Motor binding.	7. Remove motor and take to a professional.
Fuses blow	1. Too much detergent.	1. Suds can cause problem; reduce amount of detergent used.
	2. Motor overload protector faulty.	2. Replace overload protector.
	3. Machine overloaded.	3. Reduce size of load; load properly to reduce drag on tub.
	4. Motor faulty.	4. Remove motor and take to a professional.
Tub doesn't fill	1. Supply hoses kinked or clogged.	1. Straighten hoses; clean water inlet valve screens.
	2. Water level switch faulty.	2. Remove switch and take to a professional for testing; if faulty, replace.
	3. Water inlet valve solenoids faulty.	3. Clean water inlet valves; tap solenoids lightly with screwdriver handle; if no result, replace water inlet valves.
Tub fills at wrong cycle	1. Water inlet valve solenoids faulty.	1. Clean water inlet valves; tap solenoids lightly with screwdriver handle; if no result, replace water inlet valves.
	2. Water level switch faulty.	2. Remove switch and take to a professional for testing; if faulty, replace.
	3. Pump valve stuck.	3. Remove pump and clean.

Washer Troubleshooting Chart (Continued)

PROBLEM	POSSIBLE CAUSE	SOLUTION
Water doesn't shut off	1. Hose to water level switch disconnected or faulty.	1. Reconnect or replace hose.
	2. Water inlet valve faulty.	2. Clean inlet valve; if problem persists, replace valve.
Tub won't empty	1. Drain hose kinked.	1. Straighten drain hose.
	2. Pump jammed or clogged.	2. Remove and clean pump; if necessary, replace.
	3. Motor belt slipping or broken.	3. Adjust or replace belt.
	4. Pump pulley loose or worn.	4. Tighten setscrews holding pulley; if necessary, replace pulley.
	5. Pump impeller faulty.	5. Replace pump.
Water too hot or too cold	1. Temperature selector switch set wrong.	1. Make sure water temperature switches on control panel are set properly.
	2. Water heater temperature set wrong.	2. Check water temperature thermostat on water heater; if necessary, reset.
	3. Supply hoses reversed.	3. Switch water hoses at faucets; "hot" hose may be connected to "cold" inlet.
	4. Mixing valve faulty.	4. Check solenoid on valve; if faulty, replace valve.
	5. Temperature selector switch faulty.	5. Test switch; if faulty, replace.
	6. Timer faulty.	6. Make sure timer is properly set. Test timer; if faulty, replace.
Tub fills slowly	1. Water inlet valve screens clogged.	1. Clean water inlet valve screens.
	2. Fill spout clogged.	2. Clean fill spout.
	3. Water pressure low.	3. Call water company.
Water level low	1. Water inlet valve screens clogged.	1. Clean water inlet valve screens.
	2. Fill spout clogged.	2. Clean fill spout.
	3. Water pressure low.	3. Call water company.
High water level or overflow	1. Flow valve washer faulty or wrong size.	1. Replace flow valve washer.
	2. Water pressure too high.	2. Call water company; reduce flow by closing water faucets slightly.
	3. Water level control switch faulty.	3. Check and repair hose connected to switch. Remove switch and take to a professional for testing; if faulty, replace.

 **Appliances**

Washer Troubleshooting Chart (Continued)

PROBLEM	POSSIBLE CAUSE	SOLUTION
Tub spins in wash cycle	1. Timer contacts bad.	1. Test timer; if faulty, replace.
	2. Timer improperly wired.	2. Call a professional.
Oil leaks on floor	1. Drain plug faulty.	1. Replace gasket on drain plug.
	2. Support gasket faulty.	2. Call a professional.
	3. Gasket between washer housing and base faulty.	3. Call a professional.
	4. Oil pump faulty.	4. Call a professional.
	5. Vent tube leaking.	5. Solder tube shut, or call a professional.
Wash tangled	1. Not enough water.	1. See "Water level low."
	2. Improper loading.	2. Follow manufacturer's loading instructions.
	3. Extended washing time.	3. Follow manufacturer's control setting instructions.
	4. Agitator pulsator clearance not properly set.	4. Call a professional.
Wash smells bad	1. Soap deposits.	1. Fill the tub with water and add 1 pound water softener or 1 gallon white vinegar; run machine through complete cycle. Or wash inside of tub with ammonia-detergent solution, rinse with household bleach, and cycle as above.
Excessive washer vibration	1. Machine not level.	1. Adjust leveling legs; check for level front to back and side to side.
	2. Tub unbalanced.	2. Follow manufacturer's loading instructions.
	3. Oversudsing.	3. Reduce amount of detergent used.
	4. Tub faulty.	4. Replace tub, or replace washer.
	5. Snubber plate on water pump dirty.	5. Clean plate.
	6. Tub bolts loose.	6. Tighten nut that holds tub, replace tub, or replace washer.
	7. Cross brace damaged.	7. Call a professional.
	8. Supports loose.	8. Call a professional.
Washer rips laundry	1. Machine overloaded.	1. Follow manufacturer's loading instructions.
	2. Agitator rough or cracked.	2. Inspect agitator for rough spots and cracks; if necessary, replace.

Washer Troubleshooting Chart (Continued)

PROBLEM	POSSIBLE CAUSE	SOLUTION
Washer rips laundry (continued)	3. Rough spot in tub.	3. Smooth rough spot, replace tub, or replace washer.
Water leaks	1. Oversudsing.	1. Reduce amount of detergent used.
	2. Fill nozzle out of alignment.	2. Align fill nozzle so it squirts into tub.
	3. Overflow nozzle out of alignment.	3. Align overflow so it squirts into drain.
	4. Fill tube faulty.	4. Replace fill tube.
	5. Lid seal faulty.	5. Replace lid seal.
	6. Hose connections loose or faulty.	6. Tighten hose connections; if hoses faulty, replace.
	7. Bolts on pump impeller loose.	7. Tighten bolts.
	8. Hole in tub.	8. Replace tub, or replace washer.
	9. Pump gasket faulty.	9. Replace gasket, if possible; otherwise, replace pump.

Dryers

Most dryers operate from their own power supply lines of 220-240 volts. These electrical supply lines are sometimes fused through a separate electrical entrance panel rather than through the main panel. This separate panel is located in the basement or crawl space, or in some other inconspicuous location in your home. Most dryers are grounded; gas dryers are connected to a gas line.

Very simply, a dryer consists of a large drum, into which wet laundry is loaded. A motor with pulleys, connected by a series of belts, turns the drum, and air heated by a gas heater or electric heating element is blown through the drum to dry the laundry. The temperature and speed of the drum are controlled by a series of thermostats operated from a timer device on the control panel of the dryer. As a safety device, a dryer usually has a door switch that activates the working parts. Unless the door is properly closed, the dryer won't work, regardless of the control settings on the control panel. Many dryers are equipped with a reset button on the control panel. If the motor won't run, let the dryer cool for about 10 minutes; then push the reset button. If there are no problems with the motor, switches, or electrical system, this should restart the dryer.

Caution: Before doing any work on the dryer, make sure it's unplugged. Disconnect the grounding wire. If the dryer is gas-fueled, close the gas supply valve to shut off the unit's gas supply.

Disassembly. The components that make up the dryer are contained, except for the power cord and the exhaust vent, in a sheet metal box. Each component acts independently of the others, but all are interrelated in some way. There are several different ways to disassemble the cabinet for tests and repairs, depending on the manufacturer and model of the machine. Basic disassembly procedures are simple. To remove the back panel, remove a series of screws or bolts that hold the panel to the top and sides of the cabinet. To remove the lower front panel, pull it away from the bottom of the cabinet. Remove the springs under each side of the lower panel after lifting the lower panel up and away. To remove the top panel, wedge a stiff-bladed putty knife under the rim of the top and pry the top off. The putty knife helps release several spring fasteners at the top of the cabinet sides and front.

To remove the dryer's control panel, remove the screws that hold it to the cabinet top or front. These screws may be under a piece of metal or plastic trim; pry off or unscrew the trim. Most knobs are friction-fit; pull them straight out. Some knobs may be held to their shafts with setscrews; unscrew the fasteners and pull the knobs straight out. To get at most parts, however, remove just the back panel. Don't disassemble the rest of the cabinet until you're sure you can't make the tests, replacements, or repairs from the back. If the light in the dryer burns out, remove it from the dryer; if necessary, remove any retaining screws and panels to gain access to it. Replace the burned-out bulb with a new one of the same type and

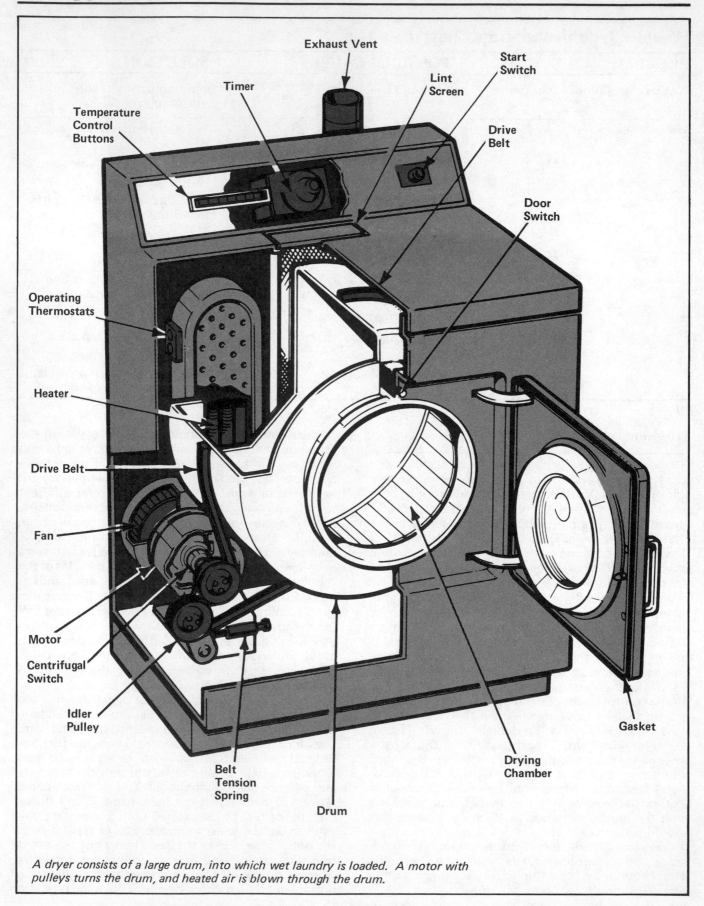

Exhaust Vent

Timer

Temperature Control Buttons

Lint Screen

Start Switch

Drive Belt

Door Switch

Operating Thermostats

Heater

Drive Belt

Fan

Motor

Centrifugal Switch

Idler Pulley

Belt Tension Spring

Drum

Drying Chamber

Gasket

A dryer consists of a large drum, into which wet laundry is loaded. A motor with pulleys turns the drum, and heated air is blown through the drum.

wattage; check the ends of the old bulb for this information. Then replace any retaining panels.

Caution: When testing or repairing the electrical parts of a gas dryer, remember that the dryer is hooked to a gas pipe. Turn off the shutoff valve on the supply pipe before disconnecting the gas supply line or moving the dryer, and before doing any electrical work.

Cleaning. Besides drying clothes, dryers also remove lint. This fine, fuzzy material can cause trouble, because it blocks dryer lint traps, clogs vents, and fills blowers. Lint can also gather around and in the tracks of the drum rollers, or in and under the pulleys and the drive belt. The result is poor clothes drying or, sometimes, no drying. To avoid lint problems, clean out the dryer's lint trap system every time you use the dryer.

To clean the lint screen, remove it from the unit. The screen may be located near or under the door sill, or in the top of the dryer near the control panel; it can usually be removed by pulling it up and out of its housing. Remove the accumulated lint to clear the screen; then replace the screen.

The exhaust vent also collects lint, and vent maintenance involves cleaning the lint from a screen in the dryer's vent exhaust collar and/or at the end of the exhaust vent where it sticks out through a basement window or through an exterior wall. To clean the screen, remove the clamp that holds the vent to the collar, or back out the screws that hold the vent to the collar, or pull the vent straight off an extended collar. Clean the screen thoroughly and then replace it in the vent assembly.

To clean the vent itself, bend the end of a wire hanger into a fairly tight hook. Insert the wire into the vent and pull out any lint deposits. Also check the vent run to make sure that the vent piping or tubing isn't loose at the joints, or, in the case of flexible plastic venting, isn't sagging between hanging brackets. Breaks or sags cause undue strain on the dryer's blower system, and can cause drying problems. If the vent pipe or tubing has become clogged with lint, remove the lint by pushing a garden hose or a drain-and-trap auger through the vent to a convenient joint, and disassemble the joint to remove the debris. With this procedure, it isn't necessary to disassemble the entire vent to find the blockage.

Lint can also get into pulley grooves and roller wheel tracks inside the dryer. Even though the lint traps are cleaned regularly, open the back of the dryer cabinet once a year and vacuum up the dust and lint inside. If the roller wheel tracks are filled with lint, disassemble the cabinet and clean the tracks — especially around the idler arm — with a wood manicure stick; or use the tip of a pencil, with the lead removed, to clean the tracks, grooves, and other recesses. If the wheels look worn — they're usually nylon, plastic, or composition material — replace them with new ones of the same type.

Door Gaskets. The door of the dryer is sealed with one or more gaskets to prevent the cool air in the laundry area from being sucked into the dryer, and the hot air in the dryer from escaping. A deteriorated or damaged gasket greatly lowers the efficiency of the dryer. To check the gasket, hold a sheet of tissue paper near the rim of the door while the machine is running; if the door leaks, the paper will flutter. If the gasket or seal looks worn or warped, and has chunks of material missing or feels hard and nonresilient, it should be replaced.

Some doors, called plug-type doors, are made in two sections; the plug is equipped with a soft rubber gasket. This type of gasket is secured with gasket cement. Some plug-type glass doors have two seals, one on the door and another between the outer and inner sections. Gasketing on this type of door is more or less permanent, but it should be checked occasionally for wear and hardness.

To replace a gasket, buy a gasket made specifically for the model dryer you own. "Fit-all" gaskets may fit after a fashion, but tailoring them to the door's configuration can be a tough job. Let the new gasket set for about 24 hours in the room with the dryer to bring it to the correct temperature and humidity.

Door gaskets are held by screws, clips, or adhesives, and the gasket may have a retaining strip, which helps shape it and provides a fastening tab or guide. On some units, the gasket may be held in place by the edge of the door panel; the panel is fastened with spring-steel pressure clips, bolts, or screws. The gasket may also be held by adhesive. To remove the gasket, remove the fasteners that hold it, or remove the fasteners holding a retaining strip or the door panel.

Remove the fasteners from one side of the door at a time; do not remove the entire door panel or retaining strip assembly. If the gasket is held by spring clips, be careful not to pry too hard on the clips; they're under tension, and could spring out of their mountings. If the gasket is held by adhesive, pry it off with a putty knife. When the old gasket is off, clean the mounting area thoroughly with mild household detergent and water. Remove stubborn adhesive with mineral spirits and fine steel wool, followed by a detergent/water rinse.

Start the replacement at one side of the top of the door, and work down the sides to replace the entire gasket. Smooth the gasket evenly into place, easing it around corners; use gasket cement to secure it if the manufacturer specifies this step. Make sure the gasket lies flat, with no lumps or curled edges. Then replace the fasteners, retaining strips, or panel that held the old gasket.

It may take some time for the new gasket to conform to the door. After the gasket is in place, tighten or loosen the mounting bolts as necessary to adjust the gasket to the door jamb. If the gasket is glued in place, there isn't much you can do but wait for the gasket to conform to the door jamb.

Door Switch. This component is critical to the dryer's operation; if the switch is not working, the dryer will not run unless there's a special grounding problem somewhere in the system. If such a grounding problem occurs, the dryer will run even when the door is open; in this case call a professional service person.

If the dryer has a door latch, make sure the latch is free from dirt or lint and properly adjusted before you make any switch tests or replacements. Sometimes a misaligned latch prevents the door from being closed tightly, and this in turn prevents the switch from being activated.

The switch on the dryer may be accessible from the outside door, or you may have to remove the top of the dryer to get at it. The switch is a simple assembly, with two lead wires running to it. Test the switch with a VOM, set to the R × 1 scale; procedures for using the VOM are detailed earlier in this chapter. Disconnect the switch leads and clip one probe of the VOM to each switch terminal. Press the switch closed with your finger. The VOM should read zero; if the needle jumps, the switch is faulty, and should be replaced. Replace the switch with a new one of the same type.

The switch is held to the dryer with setscrews; remove these screws and disconnect the leads to the switch. Install a new switch and connect the leads; then position the switch and tighten the setscrews to hold it in place.

Start Switch. This switch, located on the control panel, is usually the push-button type. Start switches don't fail often, but it does happen. To check the start switch, remove the control panel and test the switch with a VOM, set to the R × 1 scale; procedures for using the VOM are detailed earlier in this chapter. Disconnect the leads from the switch terminals, and clip one VOM probe to each terminal. Press the switch button. If the meter reads zero, the switch is working; if the needle jumps to a high reading, the switch is faulty, and should be replaced. Replace the switch with a new one of the same type; connect the new switch the same way the old one was connected.

Thermostats. Thermostats, the dryer temperature control switches, are controlled by the temperature inside the dryer, or by the heat of the motor. A temperature control switch, such as those found on dryer control panels, is basically a thermostat that can be adjusted to control the temperature in the dryer. Operating thermostats sometimes stick, causing control problems. These thermostats are usually positioned near the exhaust duct bulkhead or the fan housing of the dryer. Remove the back panel of the dryer to get at them. Before you make any checks, try tapping the housing of the thermostats lightly with the handle of a screwdriver. This may jar the contacts loose. Temperature control switches are located behind the dryer control panel,

and the panel must be removed for switch testing or replacement.

To check the control panel thermostat, test it with a VOM, set to the R × 1 scale; instructions for using the VOM are given earlier in this chapter. Clip one probe of the VOM to each thermostat terminal. If the meter reads zero, the thermostat is working; if the needle jumps to a high reading, the thermostat is faulty, and should be replaced. Replace the thermostat with a new one of the same type. Connect the new thermostat the same way the old one was connected.

Before checking an operating thermostat, make absolutely certain that the power to the dryer has been turned off and the dryer is cool. Then disconnect the leads to one side of the thermostat. Test an operating thermostat with the VOM, set to the R × 1 scale; clip one probe to each terminal of the thermostat. Disconnect the leads to one side of the thermostat so that the meter won't give a false reading. If the meter reads zero, the thermostat is working; if the needle jumps to a high reading, the thermostat is faulty, and should be replaced. Do not repair the thermostat or have the thermostat repaired; replace it with a new one of the same type.

Operating thermostats open and close circuits, turning the heating element on and off. The components of this type of switch are a thermal bulb and capillary tube, a bimetallic disc, a switch, and a control screw. To remove this type of unit, pry out the thermal bulb, which is located in the back part of the dryer, mounted on the exhaust housing. Install the new thermostat so that its bulb fits tightly on the inside of the housing; otherwise, the bulb could collect lint. Connect the new thermostat in the same position and in the same way as the old one.

Timer. The dryer timer, located in back of the control panel, controls several things: the drying time of the clothes in the drum, the flow of electricity to the heating element, and the flow of power to the timer motor and the drum motor in the dryer cabinet. Timers are driven by synchronous motors. Although the contact part of the timer can be cleaned and adjusted on some dryers, this is a job for a professional repair person; timer motor repairs should also be handled by a professional. But you can replace a faulty timer yourself.

To get at the timer, remove the front of the control panel. On some dryers the timer can be removed without removing the panel. In either case, pull the timer knob off the shaft, and slip off the pointer. The pointer is usually keyed to the shaft by two flat surfaces to keep the pointer from slipping when it's turned.

Test the timer with a VOM set to the R × 1 scale; instructions for using the VOM are detailed earlier in this chapter. Turn the timer to the "normal dry" setting, and disconnect one of the timer power leads. Some timers may have several wires connected to them; the power leads are usually larger than the other wires, and this size difference can be spotted under close examination. Clip one probe of the meter to each timer terminal. If the meter reads zero, the timer is working; if the needle jumps to a high reading, the timer is faulty, and should be replaced. Replace the timer with a new one of the same size and type.

To replace the timer, have a helper hold the new timer close to the old one, especially if there are several wires to be changed. Disconnect the old wires one at a time, connecting each corresponding new wire as you work, to make sure the connections are properly made. Or draw a diagram detailing the proper connections. After all the wires are connected, check the connections again for correctness.

The timer is held to the dryer with hex-type screw bolts; unbolt the old timer and secure the new one.

Gas Heater. In a gas dryer, heat is provided by a gas heater, which is controlled by an air shutter. The gas heater is generally the source of no-heat or drying problems. You can often correct such problems by adjusting the air shutter on the gas burner, which is located along the bottom of the dryer.

To adjust the shutter, turn a thumbscrew at the end of the burner, or turn two screws in a slot and bracket that positions the air shutter. Take out the screws and remove the panel that covers the gas flame. Turn on the dryer so the flame is burning. If the flame has a deep blue color and you hear air whistling around the burner, the air/gas mixture is receiving too much air. If the flame has a yellow tip, the mixture is not receiving enough air. Turn the thumbscrew, or loosen the two screws slightly, to cut down the air to the burner. Keep turning until the flame is a light blue color, without any yellow, and the whistling stops.

The gas heater on a dryer has a pilot light to provide ignition when the gas is turned on. The pilot is a small open flame fed by a steady flow of gas. A correctly adjusted pilot flame is steady and blue, and between ¼ and ½ inch high. If the pilot flame goes out repeatedly, it may be getting too little air; if it's noisy, it's getting too much air. To correct either condition, turn the pilot adjustment screw slightly, as directed by the dryer manufacturer.

When a pilot goes out, relighting it is simple. If

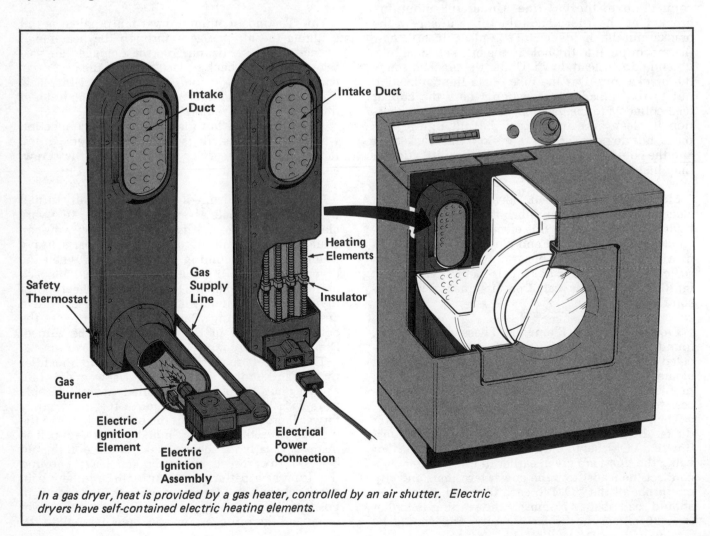

In a gas dryer, heat is provided by a gas heater, controlled by an air shutter. Electric dryers have self-contained electric heating elements.

there is a gas valve at the pilot, turn the valve to "off" and wait at least three minutes to let any built-up gas dissipate; after three minutes, turn the valve to "pilot." If there is no safety or reset button or gas valve, simply hold a lighted match to the pilot orifice.

If the pilot flame won't stay lit after several tries, it should be adjusted by a professional; don't try to adjust the mechanism or tamper with the gas line. If the dryer has a thermocouple, however, the problem may be a faulty thermocouple. You can replace this component to correct the problem, as detailed below.

Thermocouple. The thermocouple operates as a safety device, to turn off the gas supply to the dryer when the pilot light goes out. It consists of a heat sensor connected to a solenoid; when the sensor is not heated by the pilot flame, the solenoid closes the gas supply line. When the thermocouple fails, the pilot light won't stay lighted; the thermocouple may be burned out or broken. A faulty thermocouple should be replaced.

To replace a thermocouple, unscrew the copper lead and the connection nut inside the threaded connection to the gas line. Under the mounting bracket at the thermocouple tube, unscrew the bracket nut that holds the tube in place. Insert a new thermocouple into the hole in the bracket, steel tube up and copper lead down. Under the bracket, screw the bracket nut over the tube. Push the connection nut to the threaded connection where the copper lead connects to the gas line; make sure the connection is clean and dry. Screw the nut tightly into place, but do not overtighten it. Both the bracket nut and the connection nut should be only a little tighter than hand-tightened.

Electric Ignition System. Newer gas dryers use an electric ignition device rather than a pilot light to light the gas heater. In this electric ignition system, an element becomes hot and glows like the filament in a light bulb. These electric systems are always sealed; you can't adjust or repair them. If an electric ignition device fails, call a professional service person for replacement.

Electric Heating Elements. These components, found in electric dryers, are self-contained units located in the back of the dryer. A defective heating element is frequently the source of no-heat or drying problems. Remove the back service panel to gain access to the elements.

The heating elements are located inside the heater ducts. If you think a heating element is faulty, test it with a VOM, set to the R × 1 scale; instructions for using the VOM are given earlier in this chapter. Disconnect the leads from the power terminals and clip one probe of the VOM to each terminal. The meter should read about 12 ohms; if the reading is higher than 20 ohms, the heater is faulty, and should be

replaced. A heater connected to a 115-volt line usually has an 8.4-ohm resistance; a heater connected to a 220-volt line usually has 11 ohms resistance. Replace a faulty heater with a new one of the same type and electrical rating.

The heater may also malfunction because it's grounded. To test for this set the VOM to the R × 1 scale, and remove the leads to the heater. Clip one probe of the VOM to a heater terminal and touch the other probe to the heater housing. The meter needle should jump to a fairly high reading; if the needle flicks back and forth at a low reading, the heater is probably grounded, and should be replaced.

To replace the heater, you may have to remove the cabinet top as well as the back. Disconnect the leads and remove the screws that hold the duct in position; then lift the entire heater unit out of the dryer. Once the heater is out, remove the screws that hold the heating element in the duct. Slip the new heating element into the heating duct the same way the old one came out. Be careful not to damage the resistance coils. Replace the screws that hold the heating element in the duct, reconnect the leads, and screw the unit back into position.

Fan. The most common dryer fan problem is lint clogging the air passages through the heater and through the dryer drum. To clear a clogged air passage, remove the back service panel of the dryer and back out the screws holding the air duct in place. Then reach into the duct and remove all the lint and dirt possible. Reassemble the parts.

Also inspect the fan for a loose screw connection where the motor shaft is set on the dryer's drum. Remove the back service panel, tighten the screw, and replace the panel.

Drum Belt. The drum of the dryer is usually turned by a motor and belt assembly. There are two very clear signs that the belt is malfunctioning: you can easily spin the drum by hand, or you hear a heavy thumping sound coming from the drum when the dryer is running. To get at the belt, remove the back or front service panel. Depending on the type of dryer you own, you may have to prop up the drum to keep it from sagging. Don't let the drum hang; the bolts that hold it in the cabinet could be ruined. Don't remove any more parts than you have to.

The old belt may be threaded around the idler pulley and motor drive shaft. Draw a diagram showing how the pulley is installed, so you'll be able to replace it properly. Then move the idler pulley forward, providing slack in the old belt. Remove the old belt from the pulleys, and stretch a new belt— made especially for the dryer—into place. If the old belt is worn or frayed, but not broken, leave it around the drum as a pattern for positioning the new belt; cut the old belt and remove it when the new belt is in position. The new belt must extend around the dryer drum and the pulleys. The trick here is to align the belt on the drum with the pulleys; the ribs on the new belt should go against the drum.

When the belt is aligned, turn the drum by hand, if possible, to make sure the belt is tracking. You may have to reassemble part of the cabinet to do this.

Some dryers — especially older models — have a V-belt pulley drum drive. With this system, two or three pulleys of different sizes set the speed of the drum. To change this type of belt, decrease the tension on the idler pulley and install the new belt in the V-grooves of all pulleys. Then place the idler pulley back into position.

With any dryer, make absolutely sure that you replace the old belt with a new one made especially for the dryer. Any difference in belts can change the speed of the drum and cause problems with other dryer components.

Drum Bearings. With the back service panel off, check the drum bearing around the dryer drum shaft. You may have to remove the dryer belt to reach it. If the bearing looks worn and dirty, or if it's loose, it should be replaced with a new bearing made for the dryer. A screw in the center of the drum connects the shaft to the drum; remove this assembly and then lift off the drum pulley. Support the drum to prevent it from sagging. The bearing fits around the drum shaft, and is slip-fit. Pull off the old bearing and install the new one; secure it the same way the old one was held. On some dryers, the bearing and shaft are held by a U-bolt, and there are two tapered blocks supporting the bearing and shaft. Remove the bearing by first removing the U-bolt and blocks.

When reassembling the bearing unit, make sure the parts go back together the way they came apart. If the part is assembled with shims, the shims could be placed between the bearing and the support channels. Do not overtighten the screws holding the parts; overtightening could cause damage to the bearing. If the bearing has a lubrication wick, saturate it with auto transmission oil.

Drum Rollers. The front of the dryer's drum is usually supported by two rollers. These wheels are either metal with a rubber rim or pressed nylon. If the rollers squeak, but appear to be in good condition, apply a few drops of No. 20 nondetergent motor oil — not all-purpose oil — to them. If the rollers are worn, you can replace them if the roller assembly is not riveted.

First, remove the front of the cabinet. Rollers are usually held on a metal shaft by a spring clip. To remove the roller, pry the spring clip off with a screwdriver. Under the clip are a washer, the roller, and another washer. You might have to remove a small nut at the back of the shaft, and remove the shaft, in order to reach the roller. Remove the roller from the shaft, and clean away built-up lint and dirt before installing the new roller. This dirt and lint buildup could cause the drum to turn slowly, pre-

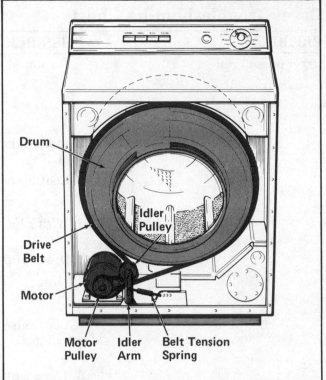

When replacing a belt, you may have to prop up the drum to keep it from sagging. Don't let the drum hang; the bolts that hold it could be ruined.

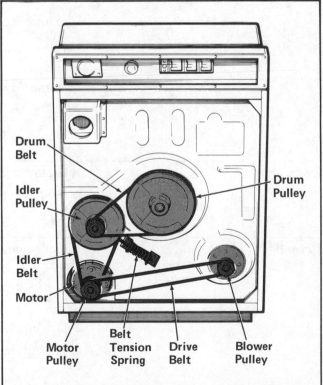

Some dryers employ a series of drive belts to spin the tub instead of just one. A typical three-belt arrangement is shown here.

Dryer Troubleshooting Chart

PROBLEM	POSSIBLE CAUSE	SOLUTION
Dryer doesn't run	1. No power.	1. Check power cord, plug, and outlet. Check for blown fuses or tripped circuit breakers at main entrance panel or at separate panel; restore circuit.
	2. Motor overload or safety shutoff.	2. Press reset button on control panel.
	3. Controls not properly set.	3. Set controls properly.
	4. Door not closed.	4. Close door to activate drum.
	5. Wiring loose or broken.	5. Clean or tighten terminal connections at power inlet.
	6. Door switch faulty.	6. Remove lint and dirt from switch orifice; make sure switch is making contact. Test switch; if faulty, replace.
	7. Door hinges broken or misaligned.	7. Repair hinges so that switch makes contact; if hinges damaged, replace.
	8. Timer faulty.	8. Make sure timer is properly set. Test timer; if faulty, replace.
	9. On/off switch faulty.	9. Make sure switch is properly set. Test switch; if faulty, replace.
	10. Motor faulty.	10. Check motor leads for proper connections. Remove motor and take it to a professional, or replace motor.
	11. Centrifugal switch faulty.	11. If accessible, check switch terminal connections. If inaccessible, call a professional. Or remove switch or entire motor and take to a professional.
Fuses blow	1. Grounding faulty.	1. Call a professional.
	2. Motor bearings worn.	2. Call a professional, or remove motor and take to a professional.
Dryer doesn't heat	1. Inadequate power supply.	1. Check fuses and switches to make sure 220-volt power is being supplied; half of double-fuse hookup may be blown. If necessary, restore circuit.
	2. Lint blockage.	2. Clean lint screen; clean duct.
	3. Thermostat faulty.	3. Lightly tap thermostat housing to jar contacts loose. Test thermostat; if faulty, replace.
	4. Timer faulty.	4. Make sure timer is properly set. Test timer; if faulty, replace.

Dryer Troubleshooting Chart (Continued)

PROBLEM	POSSIBLE CAUSE	SOLUTION
Dryer doesn't heat (continued)	5. Overload protector faulty.	5. Test protector; if faulty, replace. If switch is located inside motor, call a professional.
	6. Centrifugal switch faulty.	6. If accessible, check switch terminal connections. If inaccessible, call a professional. Or remove switch or entire motor and take to a professional.
	7. Electric heating element faulty (electric units).	7. Test heating element; if faulty, replace.
	8. Gas heater faulty (gas units).	8. Check to make sure pilot is lit; if necessary, relight. Adjust air shutter of gas burner.
	9. Thermocouple faulty (gas units).	9. Replace thermocouple.
	10. Electric ignition faulty (gas units).	10. Call a professional.
	11. No gas (gas units).	11. Call gas company.
	12. Motor faulty.	12. Check motor leads for proper connections. Remove motor and take to a professional, or replace motor.
Drying slow or inadequate	1. Machine overloaded.	1. Reduce size of load.
	2. Clogged lint screen.	2. Clean lint screen.
	3. Clothes not adequately wrung out.	3. Make sure spin cycle on washer is spinning clothes dry.
	4. Vent blocked.	4. Clean vent. Make sure vent is not sagging, bent, broken at joints, clogged, or loose where it joins dryer's vent collar.
	5. Door seal defective.	5. Check door for air leaks. Check and tighten gasket screws; if gasket faulty, replace.
	6. Blower faulty.	6. Clean blower assembly; check and tighten blower bolts.
	7. Thermostat faulty.	7. Lightly tap thermostat housing to jar contacts loose. Test thermostat; if faulty, replace.
	8. Timer faulty.	8. Make sure timer is properly set. Test timer; if faulty, replace.
	9. Electric heating element faulty (electric unit).	9. Test heating element; if faulty, replace.
	10. Belt sticking, worn, or broken.	10. Clean belt and pulleys. Check belt; if worn or damaged, replace.

Dryer Troubleshooting Chart (Continued)

PROBLEM	POSSIBLE CAUSE	SOLUTION
Drying slow or inadequate (continued)	11. Drum seal faulty.	11. Check drum seals at front and back of drum; if faulty, call a professional.
	12. Exhaust fan clogged or jammed.	12. Clean fan assembly. Check for frozen bearings by turning; if necessary, lubricate.
Drum doesn't turn	1. Belt misaligned or broken.	1. Adjust or replace belt.
	2. Drum bearings need lubrication.	2. Lubricate bearings.
	3. Exhaust fan needs lubrication.	3. Lubricate fan assembly.
Light won't go on	1. Bulb burned out.	1. Replace bulb.
	2. Door switch faulty.	2. Test switch; if faulty, replace.
Motor runs when door is open	1. Door switch faulty.	1. Remove lint and dirt from orifice; make sure switch is making contact. Test switch; if faulty, replace.
Noisy operation	1. Metal or plastic object in drum.	1. Remove foreign objects from drum. Noise from buttons and clips on clothing is normal.
	2. Duct clogged or out of position.	2. Clean duct; if necessary, reposition.
	3. Belt sticking, worn, or broken.	3. Clean belt and pulleys. Check belt; if worn or damaged, replace.
	4. Pulleys misaligned.	4. Realign pulleys.
	5. Rollers sticking or damaged.	5. Lubricate or replace rollers.
	6. Exhaust fan needs lubrication.	6. Lubricate fan assembly.
	7. Motor bearings worn or need lubrication.	7. Lubricate motor shaft ends. Call a professional, or remove motor and take to a professional, or replace motor.
	8. Centrifugal switch faulty.	8. If accessible, check switch terminal connections. If inaccessible, call a professional. Or remove switch or entire motor and take to a professional.

venting proper drying and straining other dryer components. Put the new roller on the shaft with the washers in the same position.

Motors. Motor malfunctions usually call for service by a professional. There are three main causes of motor failure, and it is recommended that you check these trouble spots before you call a professional service person or take the motor to a repair shop: lack of lubrication, defective motor switch, or worn or frozen bearings.

Humming can be related to a burned-out motor or a defective switch. Remove the back access panel. Then reach behind the drum, motor pulley, and idler arm pulley. If these areas are clogged with dirt and lint, undue strain on the motor may be causing the humming noise. Worn or broken belts can also cause a humming noise. Check the belts for wear and damage, and replace them if necessary, as detailed above. If the belts look all right, you may be able to stop the noise by spraying them with fan belt dressing, available at automotive and hardware stores and home centers.

Next, turn the dryer on. The noise you hear may be the whirl of the spinning drum, not the motor. Some noise is normal.

Most motors are permanently lubricated and sealed by the manufacturer; access to the bearings is not possible. However, force a little No. 20 nondetergent motor oil — not all-purpose oil — around the ends of the motor shaft; this lubrication may stop the humming noise. If this doesn't solve the problem, remove the motor and take it to a professional service person.

The centrifugal switch on the dryer motor may be located on top of the motor. Humming, no motor power, and no heat can be caused by a faulty centrifugal switch. If the switch is externally mounted, check the terminals of the switch to make sure they are tight and not burned. If you spot trouble, remove the switch and take it to a professional service person for testing; the switch will probably have to be replaced. Some centrifugal switches are located inside the motor housing; you won't be able to remove the switch. In this case, remove the entire motor and take it to a professional for repairs.

If the motor hums, but won't run the pulley on the end of the motor shaft, try turning the pulley by hand. *Caution: Before turning the pulley, make sure the power to the dryer is turned off.* If you can't turn the pulley, or the pulley is very hard to turn, the bearings in the motor may be worn. Remove the motor and take it to a professional service person for repairs, or replace the motor. Replacement may be cheaper than repair.

Some motors have overload protectors, which turn off the motor when excess strain is put on it. Often, dryers are equipped with a reset button on the control panel. If the motor won't run, let the dryer cool for about 10 minutes and then press this reset button. The dryer may operate; if it doesn't, check for an overload protector on the motor.

Test the overload protector with a VOM, set to the R × 1 scale; instructions for using the VOM are given earlier in this chapter. Disconnect one lead wire to the protector, and clip one probe of the VOM to each protector terminal. If the meter reads zero, the protector is working; if the needle jumps to a high reading, the overload protector is faulty, and should be replaced. Remove the protector by prying it off or unscrewing it from the motor housing. Replace it with a new one of the same size and type; connect the new protector the same way the old one was connected.

Water Heaters

Water heaters rarely break down, but they do require regular maintenance. Maintenance is largely a matter of cleaning dirt and dust away from the outside of the unit, and draining the tank periodically to prevent sediment buildup. This basic attention is enough to keep most water heaters running trouble-free. When repairs are necessary, it's sometimes easier to replace the entire water heater than to repair it yourself or have it repaired; the cost of a new water heater is surprisingly low.

The water heater consists of an insulated tank and a heat source — electric elements, or a gas or oil burner — surrounded by a cabinet. A water supply pipe carries cold water into the top of the tank, and continues into the tank as a tube called the dip tube to feed cold water in at the bottom of the tank. In some water heaters, the supply line enters the bottom of the tank directly. In both types of water heaters, heated water rises to the top of the tank, and exits via a hot-water supply line at the top of the tank. Because hot water — like hot air — rises, the water that leaves the tank to supply hot water throughout the house is always the hottest water in the tank.

All water heaters have thermostats, which are manually set to control the temperature of the water. A normal setting is between 120° and 160° F, depending on your family's hot-water needs. If your family is large, with lots of laundry, a dishwasher, and a shower/bath combination, a higher setting — 160° F — is best.

Disassembly. For the most part, gas, electric, and oil water heaters cannot be disassembled the way a washer or dryer can. Water heater parts are removed from the heater by unscrewing retaining panels and plugs, and lifting out individual components. When replacing water heater parts, use parts specifically made for the make and model water heater you own. This identifying information is usually embossed on a metal tag fastened to the top of the water heater.

Caution: Before you do any work on a water heater, turn off all power to the unit; at the main entrance panel, remove the fuse or trip the circuit breaker that controls the power to the heater. If the heater is gas- or oil-fueled, close the valve on the supply line that feeds gas or oil to the heater. Finally, turn off the water supply to the heater.

Draining. The water heater should be drained every 30 to 60 days, year-round. If you live in a hard-water area, it's a good idea to drain the tank monthly. To drain the heater, open the drain valve on the lower side of the tank and let the water run into a bucket until it runs clear. This prevents sediment from building up in the bottom of the tank, which helps eliminate noise problems, and keeps the

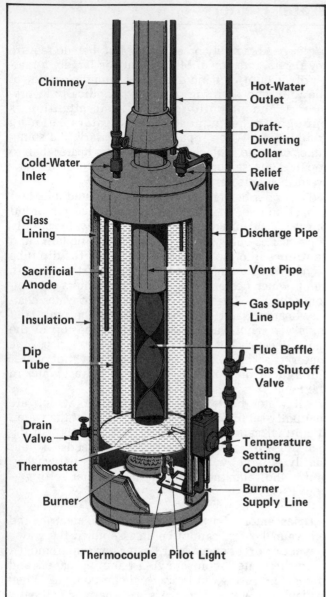

Chimney

Hot-Water Outlet

Draft-Diverting Collar

Cold-Water Inlet

Relief Valve

Glass Lining

Discharge Pipe

Sacrificial Anode

Vent Pipe

Insulation

Gas Supply Line

Dip Tube

Flue Baffle

Gas Shutoff Valve

Drain Valve

Temperature Setting Control

Thermostat

Burner

Burner Supply Line

Thermocouple   Pilot Light

A gas water heater consists of a tank and a gas burner inside an insulated glass-lined cabinet. Clean the chimney at least every other year.

placement of the heater if repairs are necessary; draining the tank for repairs could result in a leaky drain valve. While valve replacement is relatively simple, as detailed below, replacing the valve and repairing the unit may not be worth the trouble.

Cleaning. Both the outside and the inside of the water heater must be kept clean. Vacuum the outside of any water heater—gas, electric, or oil—to remove dirt and improve the unit's running efficiency. If the outside of the tank is very dirty, clean it with a solution of mild household detergent and water. The chimney of a gas water heater should be cleaned at least every other year. This is a messy job, but it can result in fuel savings and cut down on repairs and replacements. The chimney of an oil water heater must also be cleaned, but this job is best left to a professional service person. Electric water heaters, because they do not involve combustion, don't have chimneys, so they don't require the same overall cleaning as gas and oil units.

To clean a gas heater chimney or vent, turn off the power and the gas to the unit, and let the heater cool. Spread newspaper to protect the floor. Open the inspection door at the bottom of the water heater and spread several layers of newspaper over the burner head. As you clean the heater, soot will fall through it onto the newspaper. Work from the top of the water heater down. The chimney of the heater is slipped together in sections; to disassemble it, separate the sections and take them down. The sections are sometimes fastened with sheet metal screws; in this case, remove the sheet metal screws for disassembly.

Start at the top of the chimney where it turns to run horizontally, and remove the sections one by one. Label each section for proper reassembly, and set each section on the newspaper. Clean the inside of each section with a wire brush and a vacuum cleaner or shop vacuum. Chimney brushes, available at home centers and some hardware stores, also work well for this job, or the sections can be cleaned with newspaper, crumpled into a solid ball and pulled through with a piece of string. At the base of the chimney, remove the draft-diverting collar around the chimney, and clean the collar too.

At the top of the water heater, under the collar, look into the vent pipe opening exposed by the removal of the chimney. Inside the vent pipe in the tank is the flue baffle, a twisted metal strip that slows hot air rising through the pipe to transfer as much heat as possible to the water in the tank. To keep the flue baffle working properly, remove all accumulated soot from it—if there's enough room overhead, pull the baffle straight out to clean it; if there isn't, rattle it up and down to dislodge dirt. Use a wire brush and vacuum to clean all exposed baffle surfaces.

If you can pull the flue baffle out, remove it entirely. Then clean the vent pipe in the tank with

heater running more efficiently. When the water runs clear, close the drain valve. Finally, open the relief valve at the top of the tank to flush away accumulated sediment.

Caution: If the water heater has been in service for a long time without being drained, do not drain it. Opening the drain valve could cause leaks. If the heater has never been drained or hasn't been drained in a long time, the drain valve may be corroded; in this case, opening the valve could break it, causing a flood. Before opening the drain valve, check for corrosion. If the valve is corroded, do not open it to drain the tank.

When the drain valve is corroded, consider re-crumpled newspaper and string, as described above. Drop the newspaper into the top of the vent pipe, and pull it through to the bottom of the water heater. Repeat, pulling the ball of newspaper up and down through the pipe, until the pipe is clean.

At the bottom of the water heater, carefully remove the protective newspaper and the dislodged soot from the burner head. Remove dirt from the burner assembly with a vacuum cleaner or a shop vacuum. Examine the burner to make sure all orifices are

Gas-Powered Water Heater Troubleshooting Chart

PROBLEM	POSSIBLE CAUSE	SOLUTION
No hot water	1. No power.	1. Check for blown fuses or tripped circuit breakers at main entrance panel; restore circuit.
	2. Pilot light out.	2. Relight pilot.
	3. No gas.	3. Make sure gas valve is open; if no result, call gas company.
	4. Temperature control set wrong.	4. Make sure temperature is set between 120° and 160° F.
	5. Thermostat faulty.	5. Remove thermostat and take to a professional; if faulty, replace.
Pilot won't stay lit	1. Thermocouple faulty.	1. Replace thermocouple.
	2. Burner dirty.	2. Call a professional.
	3. Gas supply valve not open.	3. Open gas supply valve fully.
	4. Little or no gas.	4. Call gas company.
Water not hot enough	1. Temperature control set too low.	1. Set temperature between 120° and 160° F.
	2. Hot-water faucets dripping.	2. Repair leaky faucets throughout house.
	3. Pipes losing heat.	3. Insulate hot-water pipes.
	4. Thermostat faulty.	4. Remove thermostat and take to a professional; if faulty, replace.
	5. Burner dirty.	5. Call a professional.
	6. Sediment in tank.	6. If unit new, drain; if old, call a professional.
	7. Tank too small.	7. Replace with larger tank.
Water too hot	1. Temperature control set too high.	1. Set temperature between 120° and 160° F.
	2. Thermostat faulty.	2. Remove thermostat and take to a professional; if faulty, replace.
	3. Vent blocked.	3. Check for outward heat draft; if no draft, call a professional.
	4. Hot-water faucets dripping.	4. Repair leaky faucets throughout house.
Tank leaks	1. Rust in tank.	1. Have unit replaced.
Noisy operation	1. Sediment in tank.	1. Drain tank.
	2. Draft on burner.	2. Some burner noise is normal.

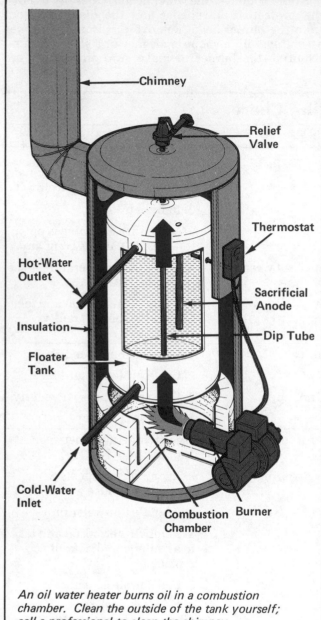

An oil water heater burns oil in a combustion chamber. Clean the outside of the tank yourself; call a professional to clean the chimney.

Labels in figure: Chimney, Relief Valve, Thermostat, Hot-Water Outlet, Sacrificial Anode, Insulation, Dip Tube, Floater Tank, Cold-Water Inlet, Combustion Chamber, Burner

sections; push each section firmly into place to join it to the next one. Replace sheet metal screws section by section as you work. *Caution: Be careful to make the final joint secure, and make sure the entire chimney assembly is firm and stable.* When the chimney is firmly reassembled, turn on the gas to the unit and relight the water heater's pilot light. To make sure the pilot light works, turn the temperature dial down until the burner goes out, and then turn it up again to the proper setting.

Insulation. Most water heaters are glass-lined and insulated. If the tank is not warm to the touch, additional insulation is not needed. If the tank feels warm, heat is being lost that should remain inside, and insulation should be installed on the tank to cut heat loss and conserve energy. Special water heater insulation kits are available at home centers for this purpose; follow the installation instructions provided. *Caution: When applying the insulation, be careful not to cover the vents at the top of the heater.* The tape supplied with the kit to bind the insulation around the tank may not hold long after being subjected to heat; use bands of wire wrapped around the tank to secure the insulation.

Hot-water pipes that run through cold basements and crawl spaces should also be insulated; wrap them with insulation made especially for pipes, available at hardware stores and most home centers. Follow the installation instructions provided.

Relief Valve. The relief valve, fitted into the top of most water heaters, lets water escape through a discharge pipe when the water pressure exceeds a predetermined limit—normally 150 pounds per square inch. To make sure the valve is working, squeeze the lever on it; this should open the discharge pipe. A combination pressure/temperature relief valve also reacts to extreme increases in water temperature; the valve opens to release steam if the temperature in the tank rises to about 210° F. The relief valve should be opened every time the tank is drained to flush away accumulated sediment.

Sacrificial Anode. Inside the heater's tank is a magnesium rod called a sacrificial anode. This component prevents corrosion of tank parts that may not have been completely corrosion-proofed by the manufacturer. In areas where the water supply is very acidic, the anode itself can be eaten away within a few years. To check for corrosion of the anode, turn off the power to the heater and let it cool. Use an open-end wrench to loosen the anode plug at the top of the tank, and lift the anode out. A new anode is about ½ to ¾ inch in diameter; if the anode is badly pitted and very thin, it should be replaced. Replace a corroded anode with a new one specifically made for the water heater; apply pipe sealant to the threads of the plug, lower the anode into place, and tighten the plug with the wrench.

clear; if any opening is clogged by dirt or corrosion, reopen it with a piece of thin wire. *Caution: Do not use a toothpick or any other wood object; wood broken off in a port could block it completely.* If the burner looks extremely clogged, don't try to clean it yourself; call a professional service person.

After cleaning the chimney, the flue baffle, the vent pipe, and the burner, vacuum thoroughly to remove all debris; then replace the flue baffle. Finally, drain the heater as detailed above.

Reassemble the water heater carefully. Make sure the flue baffle is properly positioned; then replace the draft-diverting collar over the chimney opening. Working in reverse order, reassemble the chimney

Temperature Setting Control. The temperature setting control, or thermostat control, is a manual temperature control, and is present on all water heaters. The control has various numbered temperature settings on it, or is labeled "warm," "normal," and "hot," or "W," "N," and "H." The proper setting for the water heater is between 120° and 160° F, or "normal" to "hot." If you have a dishwasher, set the control to at least 140°. If the manual control does not affect the temperature of the water, the problem is probably in the thermostat itself, not in the manual control dial.

Thermostat. The thermostat is the primary water heater control; it regulates the temperature of the water in the tank. The temperature of the water rises until it reaches the setting on the manual thermostat control; at this point the thermostat shuts off the burner or heating element. If the heater won't heat up, or won't heat the water to the set temperature,

Oil-Powered Water Heater Troubleshooting Chart

PROBLEM	POSSIBLE CAUSE	SOLUTION
No hot water	1. No power.	1. Check for blown fuses or tripped circuit breakers at main entrance panel; restore circuit.
	2. No oil.	2. Check oil; if tank is empty, refill.
	3. Oil screens clogged.	3. Call a professional.
	4. Temperature control set wrong.	4. Make sure temperature is set between 120° and 160° F.
	5. Thermostat faulty.	5. Remove thermostat and take to a professional; if faulty, replace.
Water not hot enough	1. Temperature control set too low.	1. Set temperature between 120° and 160° F.
	2. Hot-water faucets dripping.	2. Repair leaky faucets throughout house.
	3. Pipes losing heat.	3. Insulate hot-water pipes.
	4. Thermostat faulty.	4. Remove thermostat and take to a professional; if faulty, replace.
	5. Burner dirty.	5. Call a professional.
	6. Sediment in tank.	6. If unit new, drain on schedule; if old, call a professional.
	7. Tank too small.	7. Replace with larger tank.
Water too hot	1. Temperature control set too high.	1. Set temperature between 120° and 160° F.
	2. Thermostat faulty.	2. Remove thermostat and take to a professional; if faulty, replace.
	3. Vent blocked.	3. Check for outward heat draft; if no draft, call a professional.
	4. Hot-water faucets dripping.	4. Repair leaky faucets throughout house.
Tank leaks	1. Rust in tank.	1. Have unit replaced.
Noisy operation	1. Sediment in tank.	1. Drain tank.
	2. Draft on burner.	2. Some burner noise is normal.

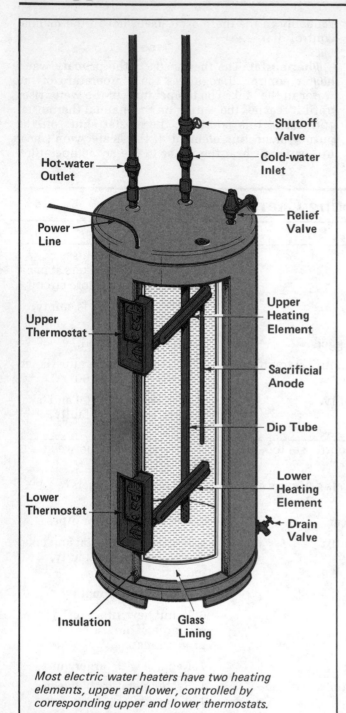

Most electric water heaters have two heating elements, upper and lower, controlled by corresponding upper and lower thermostats.

the thermostat may be malfunctioning.

The thermostat of a gas water heater may be one of two types of switches. One type consists of a tube sensing device that opens and closes a set of electrical contacts. Another type consists of a gas-filled bellows, which expands and contracts in response to temperature changes; it is used to open and close the gas supply valve. In either type, the electrical contacts may become pitted and cause problems. If you suspect the thermostat is faulty, turn off the gas sup-

ply, shut off the water, and drain the tank. Disconnect the gas supply line, burner supply line, pilot supply line, and power wires to the thermostat; then remove the thermostat by backing out several retaining screws. Take the thermostat to a professional service person for testing. If the thermostat is faulty, replace it with one made specifically for the water heater; install the new one the same way the old thermostat was installed.

The thermostat control on an oil-powered water heater operates similarly to the thermostat on a gas-powered heater. A sensing bulb extends into the tank. The heat from the water is transferred to the thermostat, which automatically shuts off the burner when the water reaches the proper temperature. To remove this thermostat, turn off the oil supply and the power to the unit. Disconnect the electrical lead wires to the thermostat, and drain the tank; then remove the thermostat by backing out several retaining screws. Take the thermostat to a professional service person for testing. If the thermostat is faulty, replace it with a new one made specifically for the water heater.

The thermostat on an electric water heater uses a bimetallic control to turn the heating element on and off to maintain the preset temperature. Most electric water heaters have two thermostats, an upper and a lower thermostat, which control corresponding upper and lower heating elements. If an electric water heater won't heat, first check for blown fuses or tripped circuit breakers at the main entrance panel, and restore the circuit if necessary. If the heater is receiving power, let the heater cool; then push the reset button on the thermostat. If the water heater still doesn't operate, test both the upper and the lower thermostats with a continuity tester.

Before testing the thermostats, turn off the power to the unit and the water supply. Let the tank cool; then open the access panels. You may have to pry the panels open or remove several retaining screws. If there is any insulation in the thermostat housing, pull or cut it away, but save it to replace when you replace the thermostats. If the upper thermostat is sealed and not accessible, you will have to call a professional service person to test or replace it, but if you can get to it, test it yourself.

To test the upper thermostat, hook the clip of a continuity tester to the left thermostat terminal and touch the probe to the other terminal on the left side. If the light does not glow or the tester does not buzz, the thermostat is faulty, and should be replaced. To test the lower thermostat, remove the housing or service panel from the thermostat. Hook the clip of the continuity tester to the left terminal and touch the probe to the other terminal. If the light does not glow or the tester does not buzz, replace the thermostat. To replace either of the two thermostats, use a new thermostat made specifically for the water heater. Install the new thermostat the way the old one was installed.

The diagram labels:
- Hot-water Outlet
- Power Line
- Upper Thermostat
- Lower Thermostat
- Insulation
- Shutoff Valve
- Cold-water Inlet
- Relief Valve
- Upper Heating Element
- Sacrificial Anode
- Dip Tube
- Lower Heating Element
- Drain Valve
- Glass Lining

On many electric heaters, a safety interlock device —usually located near the top of the tank and often mounted above the top thermostat — turns off the power to both elements if the water heater overheats. To reset a tripped safety interlock, turn off the power to the heater, remove the front access panel, and push the reset button. If the device kicks out a second time, the elements could be faulty. In this case, follow the procedures below to solve the problem.

Use a thermometer at a nearby faucet to determine whether the water is actually overheating.

Electric Heating Elements. When electricity is the power source for a water heater, the tank contains upper and lower heating elements, corresponding to the upper and lower thermostats, to provide the heat. The heating elements are located in the tank, directly behind and slightly below the thermostat control.

Electric-Powered Water Heater Troubleshooting Chart

PROBLEM	POSSIBLE CAUSE	SOLUTION
No hot water	1. No power.	1. Check for blown fuses or tripped circuit breakers at main entrance panel; restore circuit.
	2. Temperature breaker tripped.	2. Press reset button.
	3. Temperature control set wrong.	3. Make sure temperature is set between 120° and 160° F.
	4. Upper thermostat faulty.	4. If possible, remove and test thermostat; if faulty, replace. Or call a professional.
	5. Lower thermostat faulty.	5. Test thermostat; if faulty, replace.
	6. Upper heating element faulty.	6. If possible, remove and test element; if faulty, replace. Or call a professional.
	7. Lower heating element faulty.	7. Test element; if faulty, replace.
Water not hot enough	1. Temperature control set too low.	1. Set temperature between 120° and 160° F.
	2. Hot-water faucets dripping.	2. Repair leaky faucets throughout house.
	3. Pipes losing heat.	3. Insulate hot-water pipes.
	4. Thermostat faulty.	4. If possible, remove and test thermostat; if faulty, replace. Or call a professional.
	5. Sediment in tank.	5. If unit new, drain on schedule; if old, call a professional.
	6. Tank too small.	6. Replace with larger tank.
Water too hot	1. Temperature control set too high.	1. Set temperature between 120° and 160° F.
	2. Thermostat faulty.	2. If possible, remove and test thermostat; if faulty, replace. Or call a professional.
	3. Hot-water faucets dripping.	3. Repair leaky faucets throughout house.
Tank leaks	1. Rust in tank.	1. Have unit replaced.
Noisy operation	1. Sediment in tank.	1. Drain tank.

The elements are bolted onto a flange mounted to the outside of the tank; a gasket seal protects them against water leakage. If the upper thermostat is sealed and inaccessible, the upper heating element will also not be accessible. Call a professional service person to test or replace this sealed element.

When you suspect a faulty heating element, test it with a continuity tester. Turn off the power to the heater and the water supply, and let the heater cool. Hook the clip of the continuity tester to one terminal of the element and touch the probe to any retaining bolt inside the element housing. If the tester lights or buzzes, the element is faulty, and should be replaced. Replace the element with a new one of the same type.

To replace the element, leave the power and the water off, and drain the water from the tank. Disconnect the power wires to the element, and remove the retaining screws that hold the element to the heater housing. Then pull the element out of the tank. After you remove the element you may discover that it's covered with mineral deposits. In this case, you may be able to clean the element; soak it in vinegar and brush it clean, and reinstall it to see if it works. This procedure isn't always successful, but it's worth trying before you buy a new element.

Replace the faulty element with a new one of exactly the same type; take the element to an appliance parts store to make sure you get the right type. Also buy a new gasket to seal the element where it's mounted to the tank. Install the new element and connect it the same way the old one was connected. Using the new gasket, bolt the element into place on the tank flange. Then, with the new element in place, fill the tank with water. Finally, turn on the power and make the necessary temperature control settings.

Burners. A professional service person should service the burner on a gas or oil water heater; schedule this service annually. If the burner of either a gas or an oil water heater is not operating properly, do not try to clean it or make any repairs—the procedures involved could be hazardous, and special equipment is required. Only a professional should repair, clean, or replace a gas or oil burner.

Pilot Light. Gas water heaters have a pilot light, located next to the burner. The pilot operates like the pilot light on a gas range, and is controlled by the combination temperature control near the bottom of the heater.

If the pilot light goes out, relight it. Turn the gas valve to the "pilot" setting on the control box. Press the reset button next to the gas valve, and hold the button down while holding a lighted match to the pilot orifice. Keep the button depressed until the flame is burning steadily. On most gas heaters, relighting instructions are embossed on a metal tag just above the combination control, or fastened to the top of the heater. Because the reset button shuts off

the gas supply to the burner, there is no danger when lighting the pilot. However, use caution when relighting the pilot light. If possible, use a long fireplace-type match.

If there is an adjustment screw—it will be labeled—on or near the gas valve, you can adjust the height of the pilot light by turning the screw. Turn the screw slightly counterclockwise to open the valve, slightly clockwise to close it. The pilot flame should be about one inch high; it should just touch the thermocouple.

Thermocouple. The thermocouple operates as a safety device, to turn the gas supply off when the pilot light goes out. It consists of a heat sensor connected to a solenoid; when the sensor is not heated by the pilot flame, the solenoid closes the gas supply line. When the thermocouple fails, the pilot light won't stay lighted; the thermocouple may be burned out or broken. A faulty thermocouple should be replaced.

To replace a thermocouple, unscrew the copper lead and the connection nut inside the threaded connection to the gas line. Under the mounting bracket at the thermocouple tube, unscrew the bracket nut that holds the tube in place. Insert a new thermocouple into the hole in the bracket, steel tube up and copper lead down. Under the bracket, screw the bracket nut over the tube. Push the connection nut to the threaded connection where the copper lead connects to the gas line; make sure the connection is clean and dry. Screw the nut tightly into place, but do not overtighten it. Both the bracket nut and the connection nut should be only a little tighter than hand-tightened.

Drain Leaks. All water heaters have a drain valve, similar to a faucet. If this valve is leaking, turn off the water and drain the tank. Then disassemble the faucet by removing the handle, cap, and valve stem; for detailed faucet repair instructions, see the chapter on plumbing. At the bottom of the stem is a washer. Replace this washer with a new one of the same type and size, and reassemble the faucet. If the faucet continues to leak, replace the faucet with a new one of the same type and size. The faucet is connected to a threaded pipe; unscrew the faucet with a pipe wrench to remove it. Coat the threads of the new faucet with pipe joint compound or wrap the threads with plumbers' joint tape; then insert the faucet into the threaded pipe and turn it tightly in with a pipe wrench. Turn on the water supply, and test for leaks. If the joint leaks, tighten it.

Tank Leaks. When the tank of a water heater springs a leak, the entire water heater should be replaced; it doesn't pay to try to repair the tank. Buy a new tank of the same size and the same fuel type, and call a professional service person to handle the replacement.

Heating and Cooling

Most people take heating and cooling for granted. We expect our heating systems to keep us warm during the winter, and depend on air conditioning to keep us cool during the summer. When a problem arises—the house is cold in winter or hot in summer—the natural reaction is to call for service, and professional service is expensive. Fortunately, there is an alternative; you can cut your service costs drastically, and keep your heating and cooling systems working efficiently, by doing regular maintenance chores and simple repairs yourself. Heating and cooling systems can be intimidating, but they are based on simple, easily understood principles. Adjustments and improvements can often be made without much difficulty, and if you take care of your furnace and air conditioner properly, they'll reward you with dependable service.

How Heating and Cooling Systems Work

All climate control devices or systems have three basic components: a source of warmed or cooled air, a means of distributing the air to the rooms being heated or cooled, and a control used to regulate the system (the thermostat). The sources of warm air (the furnace) and cool air (the air conditioner) in a house often use the same distribution and control systems; if your house has central air conditioning, cool air probably flows through the same ducts that heat does, and is regulated by the same thermostat. When a heating or cooling system malfunctions, any one of these three basic components—heat/cold source, distribution system, or thermostat—may be causing the problem.

The Source: Furnaces, Heaters, and Air Conditioners

Both heating and air conditioning work on the principle that heat always moves from a warm object to a cooler one, just as water flows from a higher to a lower level. Furnaces and heaters put heat into the air to make your home warmer; air conditioners remove heat to make your home cooler.

All heating and cooling units burn fuel. Air conditioners use electricity. Some of the most popular home heating systems use natural gas or fuel oil; other sys-

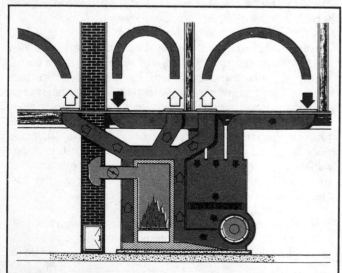

Forced-air heating systems use a fan to move warm air.

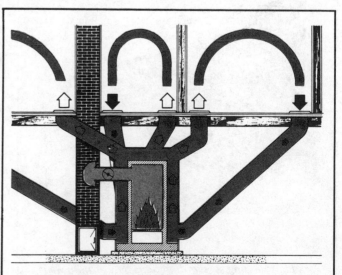

A gravity system relies on warm air rising naturally.

163

tems use electricity. The heat pump, an electrically powered climate control unit, both heats and cools air. In summer it extracts heat from the air inside your home; in winter it extracts heat from the air outside, and uses this heat to warm the air inside. Most homes, however, still rely on conventional gas, oil, or electric systems.

When the furnace is turned on, it consumes the fuel that powers it—gas, oil, or electricity. As fuel is consumed, heat is produced, and is channeled to the rooms and living areas of your home through ducts, pipes, or wires, and out registers, radiators, or heating panels. Some systems use the heat they produce to heat water, which in turn heats the air in your home. These systems use a boiler to store and heat the water supply. When an air conditioner is turned on, electrical power is used to cool a gas in a coil to its liquid state. Warm air in your home is cooled by contact with the cooling coil, and is channeled to the rooms of your home through ducts and out registers, or directly through registers.

Distribution Systems

Once air is warmed or cooled at the heat/cold source, it must be distributed to the various rooms of your home. This can be accomplished with any of three basic systems: forced-air, gravity, or radiant heat.

Forced-Air Systems. A forced-air system distributes the heat produced by the furnace—or the coolness produced by a central air conditioner—by means of an electrically powered fan, called a blower, which forces the air through a system of metal ducts to the rooms in your home. As the warm air from the furnace flows into the rooms, colder air in the rooms flows down through another set of ducts—the cold-air return system—to the

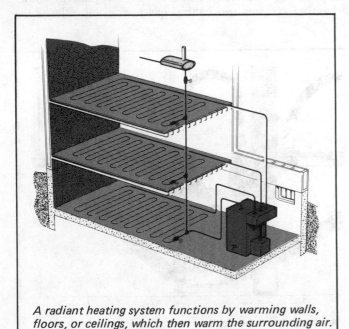

A radiant heating system functions by warming walls, floors, or ceilings, which then warm the surrounding air.

furnace to be warmed. This system is adjustable; you can increase or decrease the amount of air flowing through your home. Central air conditioning systems use the same forced-air system, including the blower, to distribute cool air to the rooms, and to bring back warmer air to be cooled. Problems with this type of system usually involve blower malfunctions. The blower may also be noisy, and it adds the cost of electrical power to the cost of furnace fuel. But because it employs a blower, a forced-air system is probably the most effective way to channel heat throughout a house.

Gravity Systems. Gravity systems are based on the principle that hot air rises and cold air sinks; they cannot be used to distribute cool air from an air conditioner. In a gravity system, the furnace is located near or below the floor—usually in the basement of a house. The warmed air rises, and flows through ducts to registers in the floor throughout the house. If the furnace is located on the main floor of the house, the heat registers are usually positioned high on the walls, because the registers must always be higher than the furnace. Once in a room, the warmed air rises toward the ceiling; as it cools, it sinks, enters the return air ducts, and flows back to the furnace to be reheated.

The big advantage to gravity heating is that it uses no mechanical distribution device; the furnace needs no blower to circulate the heat. Gravity systems use no electric current, and the movement of the heated air is silent. There are disadvantages, though. Gravity-moved air doesn't move with much force, and thus can usually not be filtered. The gravity system doesn't work well if the heated air must travel long distances, and the slow movement of the heated air allows for greater heat loss before the air reaches the rooms of your home. Gravity heating systems are not adjustable, and cannot warm a home as evenly as do most forced-air systems.

Some wall heaters are of the gravity type, with a return air vent at the bottom and a vent for the hot air to go out at the top. These units are used in warmer climates, where heating demands are not extreme.

Radiant Heating. Radiant systems function by warming the walls, floors, or ceilings of rooms, or, more commonly, by warming radiators or convectors in the rooms. These objects then warm the air in the room. The heat source is usually hot water, heated by the furnace and circulated—as steam or as water—through pipes embedded in the wall, floor, or ceiling, or connected to radiators. Some systems use electric heating panels to generate heat, which is radiated into rooms; like gravity wall heaters, these panels are usually installed in warm climates. Radiant systems cannot be used to distribute cool air from an air conditioner.

Radiators and convectors, the most common means of radiant heat distribution in older homes, are used with steam and hot-water heating systems. Steam systems depend on gravity; steam rises into the radiators. Hot-water systems may depend on gravity or on a circulator pump to circulate heated water from the boiler to the radiators or convectors. A system that uses a pump, or circulator, is called a hydronic system.

Modern radiant heating systems are often built into houses constructed on a concrete slab foundation. A network of hot-water pipes is laid within—but near the surface of—the concrete slab. When the concrete is warmed by the pipes, it warms the air that contacts the floor surface. The slab need not get very hot; it will eventually contact all the air throughout the house.

Radiant systems, especially gravity systems, are prone to several problems. The pipes used to distribute the heated water can become clogged with mineral deposits, or slanted to the wrong angle; the boiler, in which water is heated at the heat source, may also malfunction. Steam and hot-water systems are seldom installed now, but they are very reliable.

The Thermostat: Controlling a Heating or Cooling System

The thermostat, a heat-sensitive switch, is the basic control that regulates the temperature of your home. It responds to changes in the temperature of the air where it is located, and turns the furnace or air conditioner on or off as needed to maintain the temperature at a set level. The key component of the thermostat is a bimetallic element that expands or contracts as the temperature goes up or down. All thermostats consist of three sections: a cover, a temperature control section—including the bimetallic element—and a base with switches and electrical connections.

There are two basic types of thermostats. Older thermostats have two exposed contacts; newer ones have contacts sealed in glass to protect them from dirt. On the older version, as the temperature drops, a bimetallic strip bends, making first one electrical contact and then another. The system is fully activated when a second contact closes, turning on the heating system and the anticipator on the thermostat. The anticipator heats the bimetallic element, causing it to bend to break the second electrical contact, turning the heating system off. The first contact is not yet broken, however, and the heater keeps running until the temperature rises above the setting on the thermostat dial.

More modern thermostats have coiled bimetallic strip elements, and the contacts are sealed behind glass. As the temperature drops, the bimetallic element starts to uncoil. The force exerted by the uncoiling of the elements separates a stationary steel bar from a magnet at the end of the coil. The magnet comes down close to the glass-enclosed contact, pulls up on the contact arm inside the tube, and causes the contacts to close, completing the electrical circuit and turning on the heater and the anticipator. As the air in the room heats up, the coil starts to rewind, and breaks the hold of the magnet on the contact arm; the arm drops, breaks the circuit, and turns off the system. At this point the magnet moves back up to the stationary bar, which holds it in place and keeps the contacts open—and the heater turned off—until the room cools down again.

Basic Tools

The basic components of heating and cooling systems are relatively trouble-free and easy to maintain. Efficient operation is a function of good regular maintenance, and no matter what type of system you have, there are several things you can do to keep it in top condition. You'll need very few tools and materials: screwdrivers, a flashlight, pliers, wrenches, a hammer, and a level; newspaper, rags, and brushes; a vacuum cleaner. A few specialized materials are required—motor oil, fan belt dressing, refractory cement, and duct tape. These materials are available at automotive and hardware stores and at some home centers.

How to Keep Your System Running

When a heating or cooling system malfunctions, any one of its three basic components—heat/cold source, distribution system, or thermostat—may be causing the problem. If the furnace or air conditioner doesn't run, the malfunction is probably at the source: the furnace or air conditioner may have lost power; fuel may not be reaching the unit, or—if it's gas or oil—may not be igniting. If the furnace or air conditioner turns on but the warm or cool air isn't reaching the rooms of your home, the problem is likely to involve the blower or the distribution system. And a faulty control, or thermostat, could keep the system from turning on or could cause it to turn on and off repeatedly. Whatever the problem, you should start with the simplest procedures possible. In most cases, all it takes is patience and common sense.

Before you start work on a heating or cooling system, there are several preliminary steps to take:

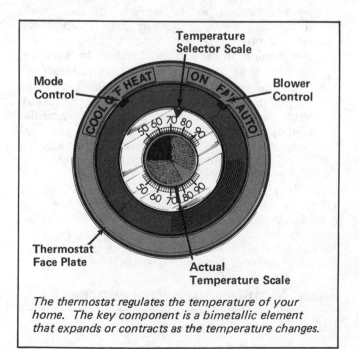

The thermostat regulates the temperature of your home. The key component is a bimetallic element that expands or contracts as the temperature changes.

- Check to make sure the unit is receiving power; look for blown fuses or tripped circuit breakers at the main entrance panel. Some furnaces have a separate power entrance, usually at a separate panel near the main entrance panel. Some furnaces have fuses mounted in or on the unit.
- If the unit has a reset button, marked "reset," near the motor housing, wait 30 minutes to let the motor cool, and then press the button. If the unit still doesn't start, wait 30 minutes and press the reset button again. Repeat at least once more.
- If the unit has a separate power switch, make sure the switch is turned on.
- Check to make sure the thermostat is properly set. If necessary, raise (or, for an air conditioner, lower) the setting five degrees.
- If the unit uses gas, check to make sure the gas supply is turned on; if necessary, turn it on. If the unit uses oil, check to make sure there is an adequate supply of oil. If necessary, have the tank refilled.
- If the unit uses gas, make sure the pilot light is lit. If necessary, relight the pilot.

There are also several important safety factors to remember:

- Before doing any work on any type of heating or cooling system, make sure all power to the system is turned off. At the main electrical entrance panel, remove the fuse or trip the circuit breaker that controls the power to the unit; if you're not sure which circuit that is, remove the main fuse or trip the main circuit breaker to cut off all power to the house. Some furnaces, however, have a separate power entrance, usually at a separate panel near the main entrance panel. If a separate panel is present, remove the fuse or trip the breaker there.
- If the fuse blows or the circuit trips repeatedly when the furnace or air conditioner turns on, there is a problem in the electrical system. In this case, *do not* try to fix the furnace; call a professional.
- If the unit uses gas, and there is a smell of gas in your home, *do not* try to shut off the gas or turn any lights on or off. Get out of the house, leaving the door open, and go to a telephone; call the gas company or the fire department immediately to report a leak. Do not reenter your home.

Finally, to keep your heating and cooling systems in top shape, have them professionally serviced once a year. The best time to have a furnace serviced is at the end of the heating season; because this is the off season, you can often get a discount, and service is likely to be prompt. Have your air conditioner checked then too.

Basic Maintenance Procedures

Dirt is the biggest enemy of your home's heating and cooling system; it can waste fuel and drastically lower efficiency. It affects all three basic components of the system—heat/cold source, distribution, and control. Cleaning is the most important part of regular maintenance, for all three components; lubrication and belt adjustment at the furnace are also important. To keep your system working properly, follow these general procedures. Specific procedures for each type of system are detailed later in this section.

Maintaining the Heat/Cold Source

The heat/cold source is the most complicated part of the heating and cooling system, and the part most likely to suffer from neglect. Problems in the heat/cold source may also lead to distribution problems. Whatever heat/cold source your system uses, give it regular attention to prevent problems.

Cleaning a Furnace. Three parts of the furnace should be cleaned: the filter system, the blower, and the motor. The furnace filter should be replaced—or, if it's the permanent type, cleaned—at the beginning of the heating season, and about once a month during periods of continuous use. Check the filter by taking it out and holding it up to the light; if it looks clogged, replace it regardless of the length of time it's been in service. Use a new filter of the same type and size as the old one.

A disposable furnace filter consists of a fiber mesh in a cardboard frame; the size of the filter is printed on the edge of the frame. An arrow on the edge of the frame indicates the correct direction of air flow through the filter. Air flows from the return-air duct toward the blower, so the arrow on the filter should point away from the return-air duct and toward the blower. A permanent filter is usually sprayed with a special filter-coating chemical, available at hardware stores and home centers. Clean this type of filter according to the manufacturer's instructions; this information is usually attached to the furnace housing.

To gain access to the filter, look for a metal panel on the front of the furnace below the return-air duct, between the duct and the blower system. The panel may be marked "filter," or may form the lid or the front of a box-like projection on the furnace housing. To remove either type of panel, slip the panel off its holding hooks or unscrew the panel from the box or furnace housing. On some heating units, the filters are exposed; just slip the filter up and out of the U-shaped tracks that hold it in place.

After replacing or cleaning the filter, clean the blower assembly, the belts and pulleys to the blower, and the motor housing. *Caution: Before cleaning these areas, make sure the power to the furnace is turned off.* Cleaning the blower is critical if the furnace has a squirrel-cage fan, because the openings in this type of blower often become clogged with dirt.

To clean the blower, turn off the power to the furnace. Remove the panel that covers the filter to gain access to the blower, or remove a panel on the front of the furnace. This panel may be slip-fit on hooks or may be

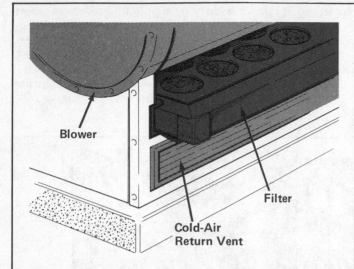

Replace a clogged furnace filter with a new one of the same type. The arrow on the filter, indicating air flow, should point away from the return-air duct and toward the blower.

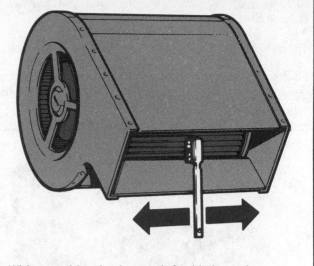

With a toothbrush, clean each fan blade on the blower. Then, with the hose of a vacuum cleaner, remove all the dirt loosened by the brushing.

held by a series of retaining screws. Access to the inside of the blower is usually gained by sliding out the fan unit, which is held on a track by screws. If the power cord to the fan assembly is not long enough to permit the fan unit to slide all the way out, disconnect the cord. Mark the wire connections first so you'll be able to reassemble the unit correctly. With a toothbrush, clean each fan blade and the spaces between the blades. Then, with the hose of a vacuum cleaner, remove all the dirt and debris loosened by the brushing. Also vacuum the belts and pulleys. Wipe the motor housing clean to prevent heat buildup in the motor.

Cleaning a Central Air Conditioner. A furnace used in conjunction with a central air conditioning system should be cleaned as detailed above. In addition, the evaporator—located above the furnace—and the condenser, usually located outside the house, should be cleaned annually. These procedures are detailed below in the section on central air conditioning.

Lubrication. To keep the motor running cool, make sure it's clean. Most motors are permanently lubricated and sealed by the manufacturer; they require no further attention. Some motors, however, have covered oil ports above the bearings, near the motor shaft. If the motor has oil ports, it should be lubricated annually. Apply two or three drops of No. 10 nondetergent motor oil (not all-purpose oil) to each port; do not overlubricate. If the blower shaft has oil ports, it should be lubricated annually too, following the same procedure. You'll probably have to remove an access plate to get at the ports. If the blower has grease cups instead of oil ports, remove the screw caps that cover the cups and fill the cups with bearing lubricant, available at automotive and hardware stores.

Belt Adjustment and Replacement. On furnaces that have a blower, inspect the belts on the blower and motor when you clean and lubricate the furnace. If the belts are worn or frayed, replace them with new ones of the same type and size. To release a worn belt, loosen the mounting bolts on the motor and slide the motor forward toward the blower unit. Remove the old belt and stretch a new one into place on the pulleys; then slide the motor back and tighten the motor mounting bolts to increase the tension. Adjust the bolts so that there's about 1/2 inch deflection when you press on the belt at its center point between the two pulleys.

If the belts are not damaged, adjust the tension as necessary to achieve 1/2 inch deflection. If a belt squeaks when the blower is running, spray it with fan

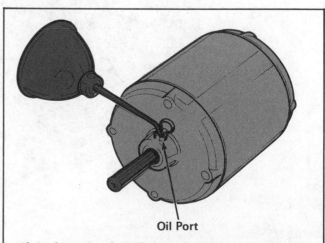

If the fan motor has oil ports, it should be lubricated annually. Apply two or three drops of oil to each port.

belt dressing, available at automotive and hardware stores and at some home centers.

Maintaining the Distribution System

Whatever the heat/cold source, warm or cool air must travel to the various rooms of your home. When the distribution system is dirty or supply and return registers are blocked, the heat or coolness generated by the furnace or air conditioner cannot reach your living spaces. A dirty system wastes energy, and is very inefficient. To keep your system operating at top efficiency, clean it regularly, and make sure supply and return registers are not blocked by draperies, furniture, or rugs.

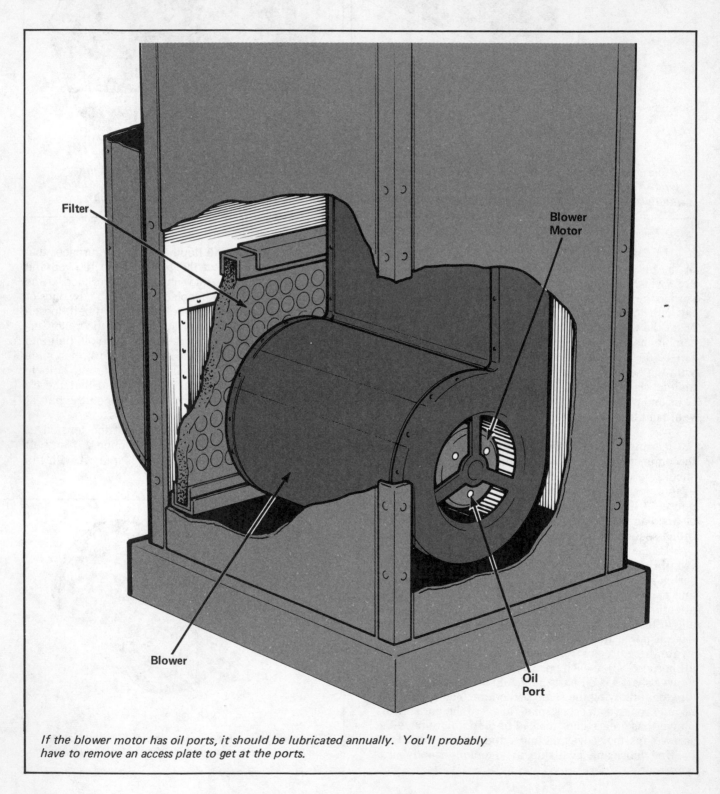

Filter

Blower Motor

Blower

Oil Port

If the blower motor has oil ports, it should be lubricated annually. You'll probably have to remove an access plate to get at the ports.

Forced-Air and Gravity Systems. These two systems use the same type of ducting to distribute heated or cooled air. To maintain the ducting, vacuum supply and return registers thoroughly at least once a month during the heating season. If your home has floor registers, lift the register grilles and clean the ducting below them, as far as you can reach, with a brush and vacuum. Cold-air returns are especially prone to dirt buildup, because air is sucked into them from the rooms back to the furnace. Vacuum cold-air returns at least once a month. In forced-air systems, the blower and motor should also be cleaned and lubricated regularly, as detailed above.

Radiant Systems. The efficiency of radiator or convector systems, either steam or hot-water, depends on free circulation in the radiators or convectors. In both systems, the supply pipes and the radiators/convectors must slope toward the boiler. Check the slope of radiators and pipes with a level, and correct the tilt as necessary to restore proper operation. Lack of heat in a radiator or convector can be caused by air trapped in it; to remove the air, open the air vent until the hissing stops and a few drops of water squirt out, and then close the vent. In steam systems, the boiler should be flushed once a month; in hot-water systems, once a season. All these procedures are detailed below in the sections on steam and hot-water systems.

In radiant systems with distribution pipes embedded in floors, walls, or ceilings, maintenance is usually not possible.

The Control System: Maintaining and Repairing the Thermostat

A thermostat is a highly sensitive instrument, responding to even the slightest changes in temperature. While it has fewer parts to go wrong than the other components of your heating and cooling system, it can be a source of problems. A thermostat cover that's improperly installed or inadvertently bumped can jam the bimetallic element, causing the heater or air conditioner to fail to start. Or the thermostat base may slip out of level, causing it to operate incorrectly. A far more common problem, however, is dirt on the bimetallic element, which can affect the thermostat's calibration and interfere with its operation. If a thermostat set for 70° F, for example, is really maintaining the temperature at 73° F, the additional energy used can add as much as seven percent to your fuel bill. To prevent this, check your thermostat every year before the heating season begins.

Other problems with a thermostat can often be traced to switches on the base and wires near the bimetallic element that loosen and become corroded. Tighten loose connections with a screwdriver; use a cotton swab to clean away corrosion.

Cleaning and Checking Calibration. To check a thermostat's accuracy, tape a glass tube thermometer to the wall a few inches away from the thermostat. Pad the

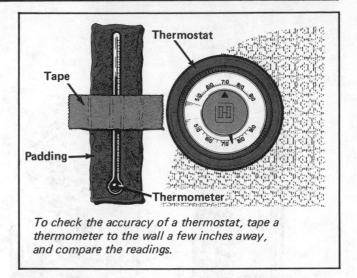

To check the accuracy of a thermostat, tape a thermometer to the wall a few inches away, and compare the readings.

thermometer to prevent it from touching the wall, and make sure that neither the thermometer nor the thermostat is affected by any outside temperature influences. Often the hole in the wall behind the thermostat, through which the wires come, is too large, allowing cold air to reach the thermostat and affect its reading.

After taping the thermometer in place, wait about 15 minutes for the mercury to stabilize; then compare the reading on the thermometer with the reading of the thermostat needle. If the variation is more than a degree, check to see if the thermostat is dirty—dirt can cause inaccuracy. To examine the thermostat, remove the face plate, usually held by a snap or a friction catch. Blow away any dust inside it with your own breath or with a plastic squeeze bottle used as a bellows. *Do not use a vacuum cleaner; its suction is too great.* If the thermostat has open contact points—not sealed within a glass enclosure—rub a new dollar bill between them to clean these spots. *Do not use sandpaper or emery cloth.* If the element is coiled, use a soft brush for cleaning. If the thermostat has a mercury vial inside, make sure the unit is level. Use a level to make sure the unit is straight. If it isn't, loosen the mounting screws and adjust the thermostat until it is level; then retighten the screws.

After cleaning the thermostat, check it again with a glass thermometer, as detailed above. If the thermometer is still not calibrated properly, it should be replaced.

Replacing a Thermostat. Replace a faulty thermostat with a new one of the same voltage as the old one. The thermostat must be compatible with the heating system. *Caution: Before replacing the thermostat, remove the fuse or trip the circuit breaker to turn off the power to the circuit that controls it. If you aren't sure which circuit controls the thermostat, remove the main fuse or trip the main circuit breaker to turn off all the power to the house.*

First, remove the old thermostat. Take the face plate off the old unit and look for the mounting screws. Remove the screws to release the thermostat from the

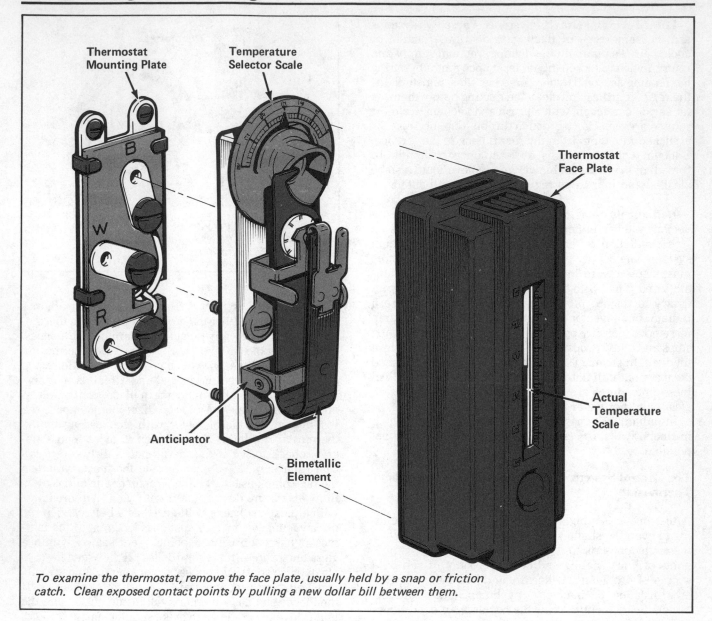

Thermostat Mounting Plate

Temperature Selector Scale

Thermostat Face Plate

Anticipator

Bimetallic Element

Actual Temperature Scale

To examine the thermostat, remove the face plate, usually held by a snap or friction catch. Clean exposed contact points by pulling a new dollar bill between them.

wall. Remove the wires from the back of the old thermostat by turning the connection screws counterclockwise. Be careful not to let the loose wires fall down between the walls. Clean the exposed wires by scraping them with a knife until the wire ends shine; then attach the wires to the new thermostat.

The new thermostat must have the same electrical rating as the old one. To complete the job, push the wires back into the wall and tape up the opening to prevent cold air inside the walls from affecting the thermostat. Install the mounting screws to secure the new thermostat to the wall. If the thermostat has a mercury tube, set the unit against a level during the installation; mercury tube thermostats must be exactly level. Finally, snap the face plate back into place, and make sure the new thermostat turns the heating/cooling system on and off when the temperature setting is adjusted.

Improving Heating and Cooling Efficiency

Although regular maintenance and repair of a central heating and air conditioning system can save you plenty, the system will operate even more efficiently if your home is sealed against the weather. Make sure the structure is properly insulated, weatherstripped, and caulked; install storm windows and doors to prevent heat loss in the winter and heat gain during the summer.

For maximum energy-efficiency, follow these simple procedures:

- Protect the thermostat from anything that would cause it to give a false reading. If the thermostat is in a draft, misplaced on a cold outside wall, or too near a heat-producing appliance or register, its accuracy will be compromised.

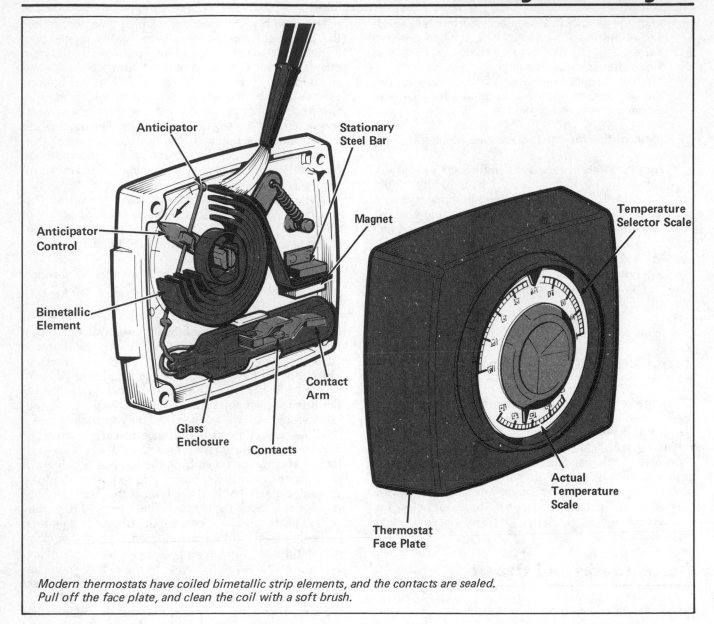

Anticipator

Stationary
Steel Bar

Anticipator
Control

Magnet

Temperature
Selector Scale

Bimetallic
Element

Contact
Arm

Glass
Enclosure

Contacts

Actual
Temperature
Scale

Thermostat
Face Plate

*Modern thermostats have coiled bimetallic strip elements, and the contacts are sealed.
Pull off the face plate, and clean the coil with a soft brush.*

- If you won't be home for a few days, turn the thermostat to its lowest setting. If there's no danger of pipes freezing, turn the heating system off completely.
- Install a thermostat timer to save fuel and money. The timer can be set to automatically raise and lower the temperature during peak and off hours. Installation instructions are usually included with the timer.
- Close the draperies over large windows and glass doors to form a barrier against heat loss during the winter and heat gain during the summer. Insulated draperies or shades are even more effective.
- If your home has rooms that are seldom or never used, close the vents in these rooms and shut the doors. There's no sense in heating and cooling space you don't use.

- Avoid constant thermostat adjustments; they waste fuel in most cases. When coming into the house after the thermostat has been turned down, don't set it higher than the desired temperature. Setting the thermostat up very high generally will not cause the temperature to reach the desired level any faster.
- One adjustment you should make, however, is a reduction in the thermostat setting before you go to bed every night. Cutting back for several hours can make a big difference in fuel consumption.
- Reduce the thermostat setting while you're baking; the heat generated by the oven will compensate.
- Reduce the thermostat setting when you have a large group of people in your home. People generate heat, and a party can quickly raise the temperature.

- Keep the damper in a fireplace or a separate wood- or coal-burning stove closed except when you have a fire going. Otherwise, up-drafts will suck heated air out through the chimney.
- Maintain proper humidity. A house that's too dry can feel uncomfortably cold even when the temperature setting is correct.

Additional tips for efficient air conditioning include:

- Aim the vents of room air conditioners upward for better air circulation; cold air naturally settles downward. On central air conditioning systems, adjust the registers so that the air is blowing up.
- Lighting fixtures can throw off a lot of heat; don't leave lights on unless it's absolutely necessary.
- Make sure the outside portion of the air conditioning system, whether a room unit or a central system, is not in direct sunlight or blocked from free air flow.
- If you have room units, close all heating system vents so that the cool air isn't wasted.

Troubleshooting Heating Systems

There are several types of heating systems in common use: oil, gas, and electric furnaces; gas or electric wall or baseboard heaters; heat pumps; steam or hot-water radiator or convector systems. All of these systems have their own problems, depending on how they're put together and how they work. In any system, the method of distributing the heat is as important as the means of generating it. Specific procedures are given below for maintaining and repairing each type of heat source and distribution system.

Gas Furnaces and Heaters

Although natural gas is more expensive than fuel oil in some parts of the country, it is generally the preferred source for heat. Natural gas burns cleaner than fuel oil, and most natural-gas furnaces present fewer operational difficulties than oil burners do. In fact, the problems that affect natural-gas furnaces usually have little to do with the fuel source. Instead, they typically involve the furnace's thermocouple, the pilot light, or some component of the electrical system. Gas space heaters—either wall units or freestanding units—normally have all of the elements of a central gas heating system built into one compact unit.

Caution: Gas furnaces and heaters have control shutoffs to prevent gas leaks, but they are not fail-safe. If there is a smell of gas in your house, do not turn any lights on or off, or try to shut off the gas leading to the furnace. Get out of the house, leaving the door open, and go to a telephone; call the gas company or the fire department immediately to report a leak. Do not re-enter your home.

Disassembly. On some units, a plug-type door covers the pilot light assembly; to gain access to the pilot burner, pull the door out of the furnace housing. On other units, remove the panel that covers the pilot and gas burners. To service the motor, filters, and blower, remove a front housing access panel, which may be slip-fit on hooks or fastened with a series of sheet metal screws around the edge of the housing. The burners are usually along the bottom of the furnace; slip a metal access panel up and off the furnace housing to expose the burners. This panel may also be held by sheet metal retaining screws.

The pilot light controls, reset buttons, gas valves, and thermocouple are usually contained in an assembly at the front of the furnace. The furnace limit switch is located on the plenum—the main duct junction—on the upper housing of the furnace.

Caution: Before doing any work on the furnace, make sure the power to the furnace is turned off.

Filter. The furnace filter should be changed or cleaned at the start of each heating season, and once a month while the furnace is in continuous use. Furnace filters are almost always positioned between the cold-air return and the blower; most are disposable. To gain access to the filter, look for a metal panel on the front of the furnace near the cold-air return. The panel is usually marked "filter," or the panel may form the lid of a box-like projection on the furnace housing. Both types of panels are removed by slipping the panel off hooks or by unscrewing the panel from the furnace housing. On some heating units the filters are exposed; they are slipped in and out of U-shaped tracks that hold the filter in position. Check the furnace filter every 30 days during the heating season. Remove the filter and hold it up to the light. If the filter looks clogged, replace it or clean it, regardless of the length of time it's been in service.

Use a new filter of the same type and size as the old one. The edge of the filter is marked to indicate size and direction of air flow. Make sure the replacement filter is the same size as the old one, and insert the filter so that the arrow points in the same direction as the air flow, from the return-air duct toward the blower.

Motor. Most motors are permanently lubricated and sealed by the manufacturer; some motors, however, have covered oil ports at each end of the motor housing. If the motor has oil ports, apply several drops of No. 10 nondetergent motor oil (not all-purpose oil) to each port at the beginning of the heating season and midway through it. If there are no oil ports, squirt several drops of oil on the felt pad where the shaft enters the motor. Wipe dirt off the motor housing when you clean the blower unit.

If the motor fails to run, first check for a blown fuse or a tripped circuit breaker at the main electrical service panel. Many furnaces are served by a separate power circuit; look for a separate fuse or breaker box near the main entrance panel. Replace the fuse or reset the breaker. If the fuse blows or the circuit breaker trips

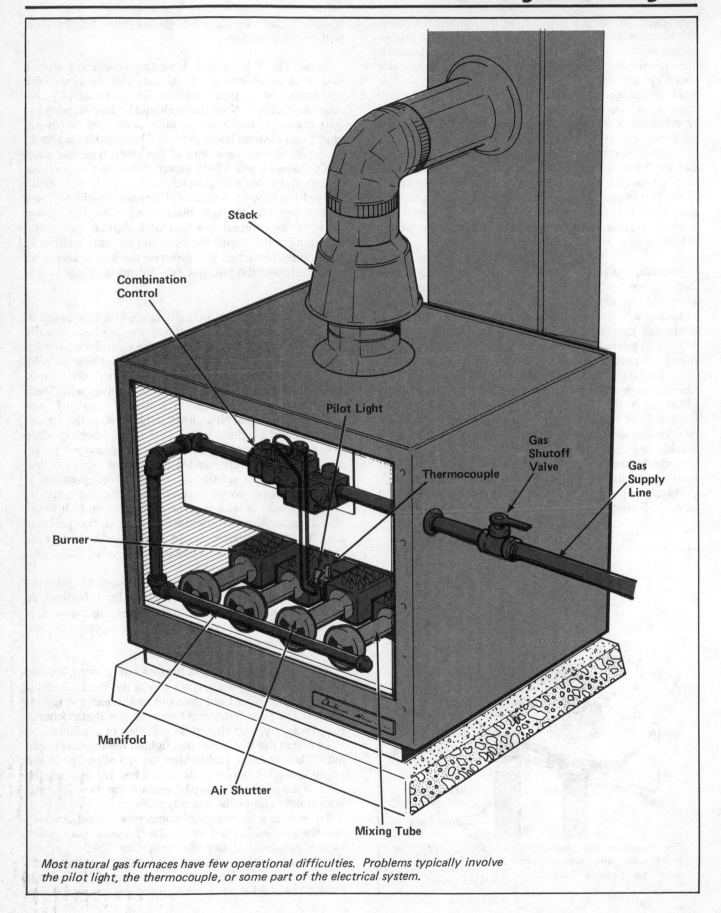

Stack

Combination
Control

Pilot Light

Gas
Shutoff
Valve

Thermocouple

Gas
Supply
Line

Burner

Manifold

Air Shutter

Mixing Tube

Most natural gas furnaces have few operational difficulties. Problems typically involve the pilot light, the thermocouple, or some part of the electrical system.

repeatedly, there is a problem in the electrical system. In this case, *do not* try to fix the furnace; call a professional service person. Some furnaces have a separate power switch on or near the furnace; make sure this switch is turned on.

If the furnace is receiving power, and the motor still won't run, the motor may have shut off because it's overheated or because of a power overload. Most furnace motors have reset buttons (marked "reset") on the housing of the motor, near the electric power terminals. Let the furnace motor cool for about 30 minutes; then firmly press the reset button. If the furnace doesn't start, wait 30 minutes and press the reset button again. You may have to do this several times before a proper connection is made. If the furnace won't start after repeated attempts, call a professional service person.

Blower. Clean the blower at the beginning of the heating season and midway through it. Remove the panel that covers the blower by slipping it off the hooks or taking out the sheet metal screws that hold it in place. Slide out the fan unit, which is held on a track by screws. If the power cord to the fan assembly is not long enough to permit the fan to slide all the way out, disconnect the cord; mark the connections first so you'll be able to reassemble the unit properly. With a toothbrush, clean each fan blade and the spaces between the blades. With the hose of a vacuum cleaner, remove all the dirt and debris loosened by the brushing. Then reassemble the unit.

Some blowers have oil ports above the blower shaft bearings. If the blower has these ports, lubricate each port with several drops of No. 10 nondetergent motor oil (not all-purpose oil) at least twice during the heating season. If the assembly has grease cups, fill the cups with bearing grease.

Belts. The V-belts that drive the blower are often a source of noise, and the belts may also become worn and frayed over a period of time. This is caused by heat from the furnace. Noisy belts should be treated with fan belt dressing, available at auto parts and hardware stores and at some home centers. Damaged belts should be replaced with new ones of the same type and size.

To change a worn belt, loosen the bolts that hold the motor to its mounting bracket, and slide the motor toward the blower assembly. Remove the old belt and stretch the new one into place; then move the blower back to its original position and tighten the motor mounting bolts. Adjust the bolts so that there's about 1/2 inch deflection when you press on the belt at its center point between the two pulleys. Adjust all belts to this deflection.

Pilot Light. The pilot light can go out because of drafts. Instructions for relighting the pilot are usually fastened to the furnace; follow the manufacturer's instructions exactly. If instructions for relighting the pilot are not provided, follow the general procedure below.

The pilot light assembly has a gas valve, with "on," "off," and "pilot" settings. Turn the valve to "off" and wait three minutes. Next, switch the valve to the "pilot" setting. Hold a lighted match to the pilot opening while you push the reset button on the pilot control panel. Keep this button depressed until the pilot flame is burning brightly; then set the valve to the "on" position. If the pilot flame won't stay lit, the opening may be clogged; clean it with a piece of fine wire. If it won't stay lit after several attempts to light it, the problem may be a faulty thermocouple, as detailed below. If the thermocouple is faulty, replace it; otherwise, call a professional service person.

Some furnaces have an electrical system to ignite the gas; in these systems there is no pilot light. Instead, an electric element heats up and ignites the burners. If this electric ignition system malfunctions, call a professional service person.

Thermocouple. This gas furnace component, located near the pilot light burner, is a safety device; it shuts off the gas if the pilot light goes out or the electric igniter fails. If the pilot light won't stay lit, the thermocouple may be faulty, and should be adjusted or replaced.

To adjust the thermocouple, tighten the thermocouple nut with a wrench. Just tighten the nut slightly; do not apply lots of pressure to the nut. Then try lighting the pilot. If the pilot won't stay lit, replace the thermocouple with a new one of the same type.

To replace a thermocouple, unscrew the copper lead and the connection nut inside the threaded connection to the gas line. Under the mounting bracket at the thermocouple tube, unscrew the bracket nut that holds the tube in place. Insert a new thermocouple into the hole in the bracket, steel tube up and copper lead down.

The thermocouple is installed in a bracket, next to the pilot light. A bracket holds it in place, steel tube up and copper lead down.

Gas Furnace and Heater Troubleshooting Chart

PROBLEM	POSSIBLE CAUSE	SOLUTION
Furnace won't run	1. No power.	1. Check for blown fuses or tripped circuit breakers at main entrance panel or at separate entrance panel; restore circuit.
	2. Switch off.	2. Turn on separate power switch on or near furnace.
	3. Motor overload.	3. Wait 30 minutes; press reset button. Repeat if necessary.
	4. Pilot light out.	4. Relight pilot.
	5. No gas.	5. Make sure gas valve to furnace is fully open.
Not enough heat	1. Thermostat set too low.	1. Raise thermostat setting 5 degrees.
	2. Filter dirty.	2. Clean or replace filter.
	3. Blower clogged.	3. Clean blower assembly.
	4. Registers closed or blocked.	4. Make sure all registers are open; make sure they are not blocked by rugs, drapes, or furniture.
	5. System out of balance.	5. Balance system; see section on forced-air systems.
	6. Blower belt loose or broken.	6. Adjust or replace belt.
	7. Burner dirty.	7. Call a professional.
Pilot won't light	1. Pilot opening blocked.	1. Clean pilot opening.
	2. No gas.	2. Make sure pilot light button is fully depressed; make sure gas valve to furnace is fully open.
Pilot won't stay lit	1. Loose or faulty thermocouple.	1. Tighten thermocouple nut slightly; if no results, replace thermocouple.
	2. Pilot flame set too low.	2. Adjust pilot so flame is about two inches long.
	3. Electric pilot faulty.	3. Call a professional.
Furnace turns on and off repeatedly	1. Filter dirty.	1. Clean or replace filter.
	2. Motor and/or blower needs lubrication.	2. If motor and blower have oil ports, lubricate.
	3. Blower clogged.	3. Clean blower assembly.
Blower won't stop running	1. Blower control set wrong.	1. Reset thermostat from "on" to "auto."
	2. Limit switch set wrong.	2. Reset limit switch for stop/start cycling.
	3. Limit control needs adjustment.	3. Call a professional.
Furnace noisy	1. Access panels loose.	1. Mount and fasten access panels correctly.

Gas Furnace and Heater Troubleshooting Chart (Continued)

PROBLEM	POSSIBLE CAUSE	SOLUTION
Furnace noisy (continued)	2. Belts sticking, worn, or damaged.	2. Spray squeaking drive belts with belt dressing; replace worn or damaged belts.
	3. Blower belt too loose or too tight.	3. Adjust belt.
	4. Motor and/or blower needs lubrication.	4. If motor and blower have oil ports, lubricate.
	5. Burner dirty.	5. Call a professional.

Under the bracket, screw the bracket nut over the tube. Push the connection nut to the threaded connection where the copper lead connects to the gas line; make sure the connection is clean and dry. Screw the nut tightly into place, but do not overtighten it. Both the bracket nut and the connection nut should be only a little tighter than hand-tightened.

Limit Switch. The limit switch is a safety control switch, located on the furnace just below the plenum. If the plenum gets too hot, the limit switch shuts off the burner; it also shuts off the blower when the temperature drops to a certain level after the burner has shut off. If the blower runs continuously, either the blower control on the thermostat has been set to "on" or the limit control switch needs adjustment. Check the thermostat first. If the blower control has been set to "on," change it to "auto"; if the blower control is already on "auto," the limit switch needs adjusting.

Remove the control's cover; under it is a toothed dial. One side is marked "limit"; don't touch this side. The other side of the control is marked "fan." There are two pointers on the fan side; the blower goes on at the upper pointer setting and turns off at the lower pointer setting. The pointers should be set about 25 degrees apart. Set the upper pointer at about 115° and the lower one at about 90° F.

Burner Adjustment. The flames on the gas burner should be full and steady, with no sputtering and no trace of yellow. To adjust the flame height on the main burners, call a professional service person. To adjust the height of the pilot flame, turn the flame adjustment screw until the flame is from 1½ to 2 inches high. The adjustment screw is near the gas valve on the pilot assembly, if the control has this adjustment feature.

Gas Leaks. If you suspect leaks around the furnace unit, stir up a mixture of liquid detergent and water. Paint this mixture on the gas supply line along its connections and valves; the soapy water will bubble at any point where there's a leak. If you find a leak, try tightening the leaking connection with a pipe wrench, but be careful not to overtighten the connection. If the pipe connections or valves still leak, don't try to fix them; call a professional service person.

Oil Furnaces

Oil-fired burners are used in many parts of the country as the basic heat source for warm-air, hot-water, and steam heating systems. Most of the home oil systems in use today are called pressure burners. In this type of system, oil is sprayed into a combustion chamber at high pressure, propelled by a blower, and ignited by an electric spark. The oil continues to burn as the mist is sprayed. There are few repairs that you can do yourself with this type of system, so an oil furnace should be inspected by a professional service person once a year.

While there aren't many repairs you can do, good regular maintenance can help eliminate many problems. Regular maintenance should include:

- During the heating season, check the smoke from the chimney. If the smoke is black, the furnace is not burning the oil completely and fuel is being wasted. In this case, call a professional service person for adjustments.
- Clean the blower at the beginning of the heating season and about midway through it.
- Clean the soot from the stack control about midway through the heating season.
- If the blower motor has grease or oil fittings, lubricate the fittings midway through the heating season with cup grease or No. 10 nondetergent motor oil (not all-purpose oil), available at automotive and hardware stores.
- Clean the thermostat before each heating season.

These procedures are detailed below. *Caution: Before doing any work on the furnace, make sure the power to the furnace is turned off.*

Disassembly. An oil furnace is a complex assembly. Your maintenance and repair work is limited to simple parts—the filters, the blower, the motor belts, the switches, the thermostats. The other components of the furnace—electrodes, oil nozzle, air tubes, transformer, and pump—are best left to a professional for service, because they require special tools and testing equipment.

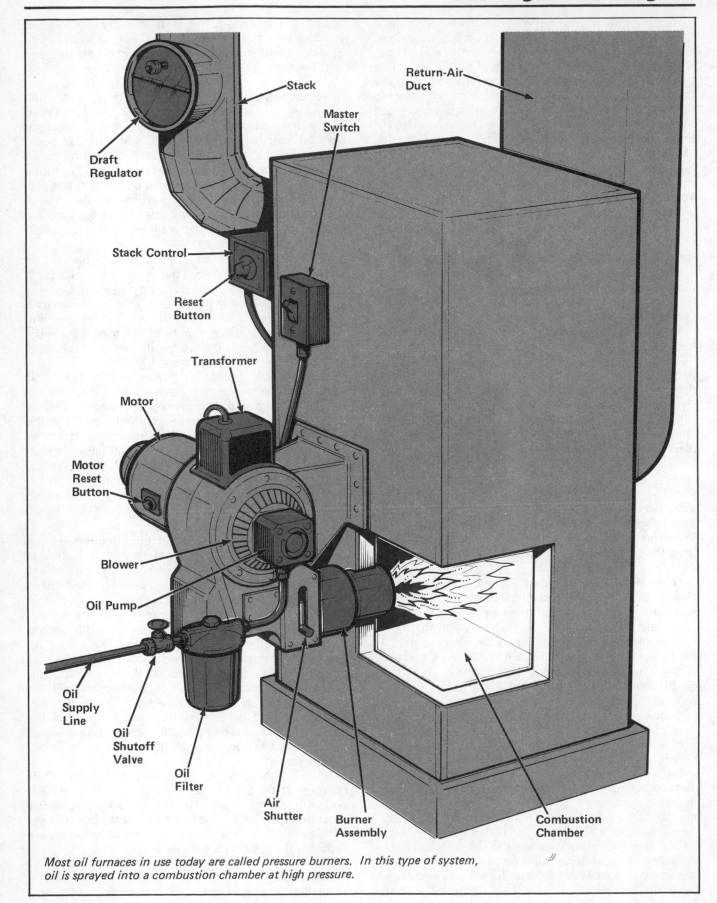

Stack

Return-Air Duct

Master Switch

Draft Regulator

Stack Control

Reset Button

Transformer

Motor

Motor Reset Button

Blower

Oil Pump

Oil Supply Line

Oil Shutoff Valve

Oil Filter

Air Shutter

Burner Assembly

Combustion Chamber

Most oil furnaces in use today are called pressure burners. In this type of system, oil is sprayed into a combustion chamber at high pressure.

Remove the access panel covering the burner blower by backing out a series of retaining screws around the rim of the housing. Access to the air blower and filter is through a metal panel on one side of the furnace. The panel is held by either hooks or retaining bolts; slip the panel up and off the hooks, or remove the bolts and lift the panel off. Most furnaces have switches and reset buttons located on the motor or in a switch box outside the furnace housing. These are usually identified with stampings or labels, such as "disconnect switch," "reset," and so on. The stack control sensor, a safety device that monitors burner operation, is positioned in the stack, and held with a series of retaining bolts.

Air Filter. Change or clean the furnace filter at the start of each heating season, and once a month while the furnace is in continuous use. Furnace filters are almost always positioned between the cold-air return and the blower; most are disposable. To gain access to the filter, look for a metal panel on the front of the furnace near the cold-air return. The panel is usually marked "filter," or the panel may form the lid of a box-like projection on the furnace housing. Both types of panels are removed by slipping the panel off hooks or by unscrewing the panel from the furnace housing. On some heating units the filters are exposed; they are slipped in and out of U-shaped tracks that hold the filter in position. Check the filter for dirt every 30 days or so by taking it out and holding it up to a light. If the filter looks clogged, replace it or clean it, regardless of the length of time it's been in service.

Use a new filter of the same type and size as the old one. The edge of the filter is marked to indicate size and direction of air flow. Make sure the replacement filter is the same size as the old one, and insert the filter so that the arrow points in the same direction as the air flow, from the return-air duct toward the blower.

Oil Filters. The oil filter should be changed or cleaned at the start of the heating season and about midway through the season. To remove the filter, close the oil shutoff valve between the fuel tank and the filter; then unscrew the bottom or cup of the filter housing. If the filter is disposable, remove it and insert a new one of the same size and type. If the furnace has a permanent filter, wash the filter every 45 to 60 days in kerosene, and replace it in the housing. *Caution: Kerosene is flammable; be very careful when cleaning a permanent oil filter.* After installing the filter, replace the old filter gaskets with new gaskets. Finally, screw in the bottom of the housing and open the oil shutoff valve.

Some oil furnaces have a pump strainer, located on the pump attached to the burner/blower unit. Clean this strainer when you clean the oil filter. To get to the strainer, unbolt the cover of the pump housing, where the oil line enters the burner, and lift off the cover. Take off the thin gasket around the rim. Then remove the strainer—a cylindrical or cup-shaped wire mesh screen—and soak it in kerosene for several minutes to loosen the sludge that has built up. Clean the strainer with an old toothbrush; if it's torn or badly bent, replace it with a new one of the same type. Set the strainer into place on the pump, place a new gasket on the rim, and bolt the cover back on.

Motor. Some motors are permanently lubricated and sealed by the manufacturer, and need no oiling. Other motors have oil ports, located at each end of the motor housing over the bearings. If the motor has oil ports, apply several drops of No. 10 nondetergent motor oil (not all-purpose oil) to each port once a month during the heating season. If there are no oil ports, squirt several drops of oil on the felt pad where the shaft enters the motor. Wipe the motor housing clean each time you oil the motor; dirt on the motor's housing can cause heat to build up in the motor.

If the motor fails to run, first check for a blown fuse or tripped circuit breaker at the main electrical service panel. Many furnaces are served by a separate power entrance; look for a separate fuse or breaker box near the main entrance panel. Replace the fuse or reset the breaker. If the fuse blows or the circuit trips repeatedly, there is a problem in the electrical system. In this case, call a professional service person.

If the furnace is receiving power, and the motor still won't run, the motor may have shut off because it's overheated or because of a power overload. Many furnace motors have reset buttons (marked "reset") on the housing of the motor, near the electric power terminals. Let the furnace motor cool for about 30 minutes; then firmly press the reset button. If the furnace doesn't start, wait 30 minutes and press the reset button again. If the furnace won't start after repeated attempts, call a professional service person.

Blower. Clean the blower at the beginning of the heating season and about midway through it. If there is a panel over the filter, remove the panel to gain access to the blower. On some furnaces a panel on the front of the furnace covers the filter. This panel may be slip-fit on hooks or may be held by a series of retaining screws.

Access to the inside of the blower is usually gained by sliding out the fan unit, which is held on a track by screws. If the power cord to the fan assembly is not long enough to permit the fan to slide all the way out, disconnect the cord; mark the connections first so you'll be able to reassemble the unit properly. With a toothbrush, clean each fan blade and the spaces between the blades. With the hose of a vacuum cleaner, remove all the dirt and debris loosened by the brushing. Then reassemble the unit.

Some blowers have oil ports above the blower shaft bearings. If the blower has these ports, lubricate each port with several drops of No. 10 nondetergent motor oil (not all-purpose oil) at the beginning of the heating season and midway through it. If the assembly has grease cups, fill the cups with bearing grease.

Belts. Some blowers are driven by V-belts on pulleys. If the belts are worn or frayed, replace them with new

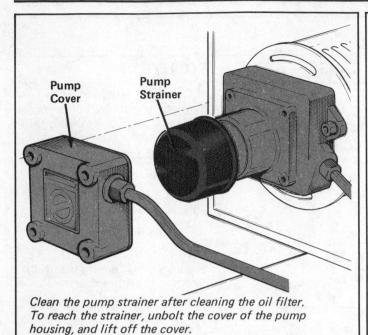

Clean the pump strainer after cleaning the oil filter. To reach the strainer, unbolt the cover of the pump housing, and lift off the cover.

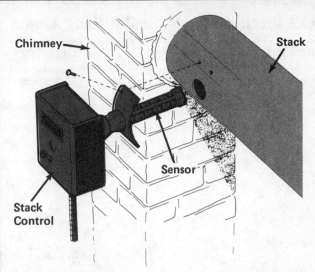

Clean the stack control every month. To remove the control, turn off the power to the furnace; then back out the bolts that hold it in the stack.

belts of the same type and size. To release a worn belt, loosen the mounting bolts on the motor and slide the motor forward toward the blower unit. Remove the old belt and stretch the new one into place; then slide the motor back into position and tighten the motor mounting bolts. Adjust the bolts so that there's about 1/2 inch deflection when you press on the belt at its center point between the two pulleys.

If a belt is squeaking or otherwise noisy, spray it with fan belt dressing, available at auto parts stores, hardware stores, and some home centers.

Switches. Some oil furnaces have two master switches; one is located near the burner unit and the other is near the furnace housing or even at a distance from the furnace. Make sure these master switches are *both* turned to the "on" position.

Stack Control. The stack control, located in the stack, is a safety device that monitors the operation of the oil burner. If the burner fails to ignite, the stack control shuts off the motor. Frequently, however, a furnace shutdown is caused by a malfunctioning stack control rather than by the burner. If the burner fails to ignite, first check the fuel tank; if necessary, refill the tank. If the tank doesn't need to be refilled, press the reset button on the stack control, just once. If the burner doesn't ignite after you've pressed the button once, clean the control, as detailed below, and then press the reset button again. If the burner still doesn't operate, call a professional service person.

The stack control gradually becomes coated with soot during the heating season. To keep it working properly, clean the control every month, or as soon as it becomes soot-covered. To remove the control, turn off the power

to the furnace; then back out the bolts that hold the control in the stack. Pull out the sensor and its housing. With a brush dipped in soapy water, remove all soot from the control. Wipe the control dry with a soft cloth.

Before replacing the control, take the opportunity to clean the stack. Spread newspaper to protect the floor, and disassemble the stack. As you work, remove soot and debris from each section by tapping it firmly on the newspaper-covered floor. After cleaning the sections, reassemble them in reverse order. Make sure that the stack sections are properly aligned and firmly connected. Finally, reposition the stack control in the stack, and reseal the connection to the chimney with refractory cement.

Some oil furnaces have an electric-eye safety switch instead of a stack control. This switch serves the same function as the stack control. If the burner has an electric-eye safety, remove the access cover over the photocell; it is held by hooks or retaining screws. Wipe the cover clean to remove accumulated soot. Reassemble the switch, replace the cover, and turn the power back on. If the burner still doesn't ignite, call a professional service person.

If the stack control or electric-eye safety switch is especially dirty, the furnace may not be properly set to burn the fuel completely. In this case, call a professional service person for adjustment. *Caution: Do not attempt to replace either of these controls yourself.*

Draft Regulator. The draft regulator, located on the stack, is closed when the burner is off, but opens automatically when the burner is running to let air into the chimney. Accumulated soot and rattling are signs that the draft regulator needs to be adjusted. Too much air wastes heat; too little air wastes fuel by failing to burn it

Oil Furnace Troubleshooting Chart

PROBLEM	POSSIBLE CAUSE	SOLUTION
Furnace won't run	1. No power.	1. Check for blown fuses or tripped circuit breakers at main entrance panel or at separate entrance panel; restore circuit.
	2. Switch off.	2. Turn on separate power switch on or near furnace.
	3. Motor overload.	3. Wait 30 minutes; press reset button. Repeat if necessary.
	4. No fuel.	4. Check tank; if necessary, refill tank.
	5. Fuel line blockage.	5. Clean oil filter and oil pump strainer. If problem persists, call a professional.
Burner won't fire	1. No fuel.	1. Check tank; if necessary, refill tank.
	2. No ignition spark.	2. Press reset button on stack control, once; if necessary, clean stack control. If no result, call a professional. If furnace has electric-eye safety, clean safety; if no result, call a professional.
Not enough heat	1. Thermostat set too low.	1. Raise thermostat setting 5 degrees.
	2. Air filter dirty.	2. Clean or replace air filter.
	3. Blower clogged.	3. Clean blower assembly.
	4. Registers closed or blocked.	4. Make sure all registers are open; make sure they are not blocked by rugs, drapes, or furniture.
	5. System out of balance.	5. Balance system; see section on forced-air systems.
	6. Blower belt loose or broken.	6. Adjust or replace belt.
	7. Burner dirty.	7. Call a professional.
Furnace turns on and off repeatedly	1. Air filter dirty.	1. Clean or replace air filter.
	2. Oil filter dirty.	2. Clean or replace oil filter.
	3. Motor and/or blower needs lubrication.	3. If motor and blower have oil ports, lubricate.
	4. Blower clogged.	4. Clean blower assembly.
	5. Stack control faulty.	5. Call a professional.
Blower won't stop running	1. Blower control set wrong.	1. Reset thermostat from "on" to "auto."
	2. Limit switch set wrong.	2. Reset limit switch.
Furnace noisy	1. Access panels loose.	1. Mount and fasten access panels correctly.

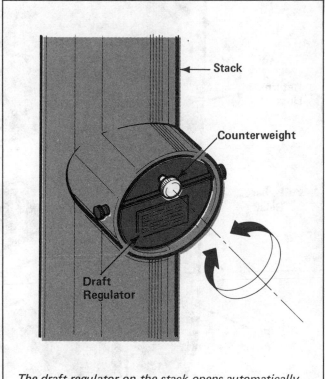

Oil Furnace Troubleshooting Chart (Continued)

PROBLEM	POSSIBLE CAUSE	SOLUTION
Furnace noisy (continued)	2. Belts sticking, worn, or damaged.	2. Spray squeaking belts with fan belt dressing; replace worn or damaged belts.
	3. Blower belt too loose or too tight.	3. Adjust belt.
	4. Motor and/or blower needs lubrication.	4. If motor and blower have oil ports, lubricate.
	5. Burner dirty.	5. Call a professional.

completely. To increase the air flow, screw the counterweight inward; to decrease it, turn the counterweight outward. The draft regulator should be adjusted by a professional service person as part of regular annual maintenance.

Limit Switch. The limit switch is a safety control switch, located on the furnace just below the plenum. If the plenum gets too hot, the limit switch shuts off the burner; it also shuts off the blower when the temperature drops to a certain level after the burner has shut off. If the blower runs continuously, either the blower control on the thermostat has been set to "on" or the limit control switch needs adjustment. Check the thermostat first. If the blower control has been set to "on," change it to "auto"; if the blower control is already on "auto," the limit switch needs adjusting.

Remove the control's cover; under it is a toothed dial. One side is marked "limit"; don't touch this side. The other side of the control is marked "fan." There are two pointers on the fan side; the blower goes on at the upper pointer setting and turns off at the lower pointer setting. The pointers should be set about 25 degrees apart. Set the upper pointer at about 115° and the lower one at about 90° F.

Burner Adjustments. *Caution: Do not try to adjust the burner of an oil furnace; call a professional service person.*

Electric Furnaces

Electric heat is very expensive, whether the unit consists of a central furnace, a boiler system, or baseboard or wall units to heat individual rooms. Although an electric heating system does have advantages, its operating cost generally makes it less desirable than any of the other furnace systems available today. The high cost means that minimizing heat loss caused by improperly installed ducts or inadequate insulation is even more important than with other types of systems. The big advantage of electric heating is that no combustion takes place, so electric heat is cleaner than other fuel-burning types. Moreover, since no flue is required to carry off

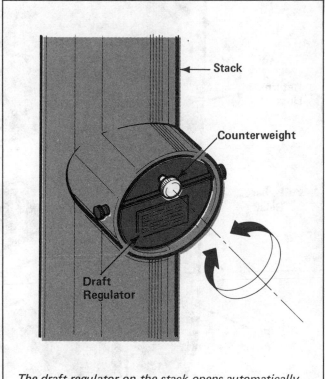

The draft regulator on the stack opens automatically when the burner is running. To increase the air flow, screw the counterweight inward.

undesirable combustion materials, no heat is lost through such venting, as it is in gas and oil systems. The only moving parts in an electric heating system are in the blower assembly.

For maximum energy-efficiency, have a professional service person clean and adjust your electric furnace every year before the beginning of the heating season. *Caution: Before doing any work on the furnace, make sure the power to the furnace is turned off. Do not attempt any repairs to the heating elements, electrical connections, relays, transformers, or similar components of an electric furnace; repairs to these components must be made by a professional service person.*

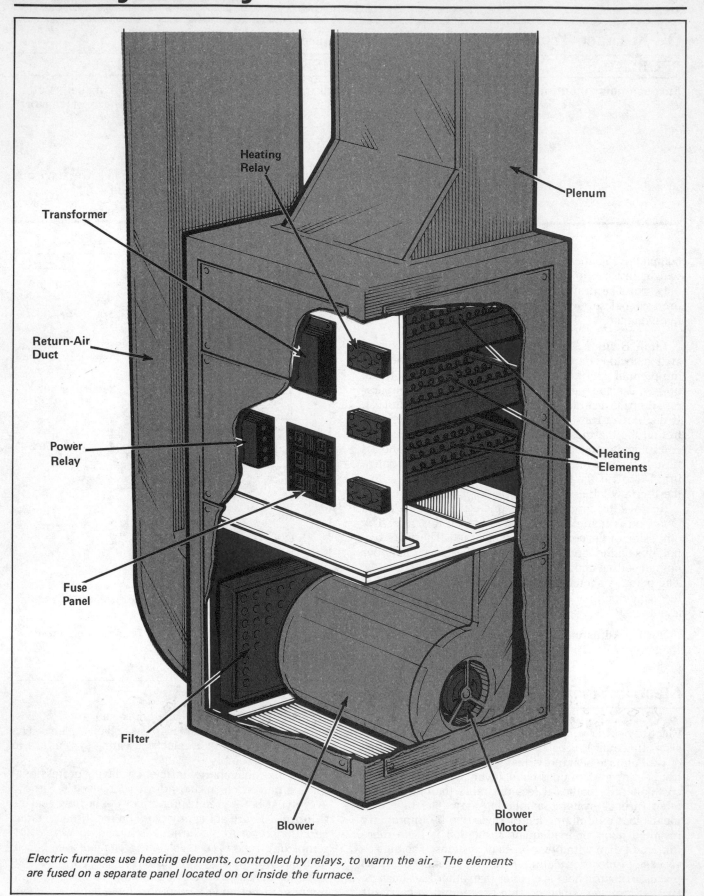

Heating
Relay

Plenum

Transformer

Return-Air
Duct

Power
Relay

Heating
Elements

Fuse
Panel

Filter

Blower

Blower
Motor

Electric furnaces use heating elements, controlled by relays, to warm the air. The elements are fused on a separate panel located on or inside the furnace.

Disassembly. The controls of an electric furnace—fuse panels, switches, and relays—may be mounted on the surface of the housing or installed behind an access panel on the front of the furnace. The access panel may be slip-fit on hooks, or may be fastened to the furnace housing with a series of sheet metal screws. To remove the access panel to the blower, filter, and blower motor, slip the panel up off hooks or remove a series of sheet metal screws.

Fuses. Electric furnaces are fused at the main electrical service entrance to the building. Many electric furnaces are on separate circuits, sometimes located in a separate fuse box away from the main panel. The heating elements of the furnace are also fused, and these fuses are located on a panel on or inside the furnace housing. If changing the fuses or resetting the breakers does not restore power to the furnace, call a professional service person. Do not attempt to repair heating elements, the transformer, heating relays, or power relays; repairs to these components must be made by a professional service person.

Filter. The furnace filter should be changed or cleaned at the start of each heating season, and once a month while the furnace is in continuous use. To gain access to the filter, look for a metal panel on the front of the furnace below the return-air duct. The panel is usually marked "filter," or the panel may form the lid of a box-like projection on the furnace housing. Both types of panels are removed by slipping the panel off hooks or by unscrewing the panel from the furnace housing. On some furnaces, the filters are exposed; they are simply slipped in and out of U-shaped tracks that hold the filter in position. Check the filter every 30 days during the heating season. Remove the filter and hold it up to the light. If the filter looks clogged, replace it or clean it, regardless of the time it's been in service.

Use a new filter of the same type and size as the old one. The edge of the filter is marked to indicate size and direction of air flow. Make sure the replacement filter is the same size as the old one, and insert the filter so that the arrow points in the same direction as the air flow, from the return-air duct toward the blower.

Motor. Most motors are permanently lubricated and sealed by the manufacturer; some motors, however, have covered oil ports at each end of the motor housing. If the motor has oil ports, apply several drops of No. 10 nondetergent motor oil (not all-purpose oil) to each port at the beginning of the heating season and midway through it. Wipe the motor housing clean with a soft cloth; grease, dirt, and other debris on the housing can cause the motor to overheat.

Blower. Clean the blower at the beginning of the heating season and midway through it. Remove the panel that covers the blower by slipping it off the hooks or taking out the sheet metal screws that hold it in place. Slide out the fan unit, which is held on a track by

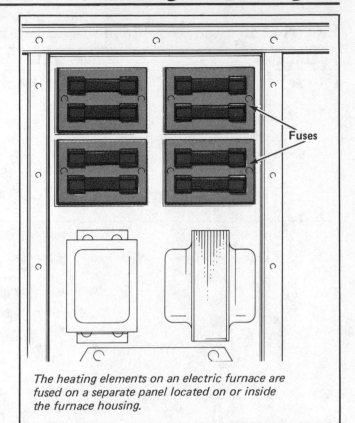

The heating elements on an electric furnace are fused on a separate panel located on or inside the furnace housing.

screws. If the power cord to the fan assembly is not long enough to permit the fan to slide all the way out, disconnect the cord; mark the connections first so you'll be able to reassemble the unit properly. With a toothbrush, clean each fan blade and the spaces between the blades. With the hose of a vacuum cleaner, remove all the dirt and debris loosened by the brushing. Then reassemble the unit.

Some blowers have oil ports above the blower shaft bearings. If the blower has oil ports, lubricate each port with several drops of No. 10 nondetergent motor oil (not all-purpose oil) at the beginning of the heating system and midway through it. If the assembly has grease cups, fill the cups with bearing grease.

Belts. If the blower system is driven by a V-belt, check it for wear; if the belt is worn or frayed, replace it with a new one of the same type and size. To release a worn belt, loosen the mounting bolts on the motor and slide the motor forward toward the blower unit. Remove the old belt and stretch the new one into place; then slide the motor back into position and tighten the motor mounting bolts. Adjust the bolts so that there's about ½ inch deflection when you press on the belt at its center point between the two pulleys. Adjust all belts to this deflection.

If the belt is squeaky but not worn, spray it with fan belt dressing, available at auto parts stores, hardware stores, and some home centers. In most cases, this will stop the noise.

Electric Furnace Troubleshooting Chart

PROBLEM	POSSIBLE CAUSE	SOLUTION
Furnace won't run	1. No power.	1. Check for blown fuses or tripped circuit breakers at main entrance panel, at separate entrance panel, and on or in furnace; restore circuit.
	2. Switch off.	2. Turn on separate power switch on or near furnace.
	3. Motor overload.	3. Wait 30 minutes; press reset button. Repeat if necessary.
Not enough heat	1. Thermostat set too low.	1. Raise thermostat setting 5 degrees.
	2. Filter dirty.	2. Clean or replace filter.
	3. Blower clogged.	3. Clean blower assembly.
	4. Registers closed or blocked.	4. Make sure all registers are open; make sure they are not blocked by rugs, drapes, or furniture.
	5. System out of balance.	5. Balance system; see section on forced-air systems.
	6. Blower belt loose or broken.	6. Adjust or replace belt.
	7. Element faulty.	7. Call a professional.
Furnace turns on and off repeatedly	1. Filter dirty.	1. Clean or replace filter.
	2. Motor and/or blower needs lubrication.	2. If motor and blower have oil ports, lubricate.
	3. Blower clogged.	3. Clean blower assembly.
Blower won't stop running	1. Blower control set wrong.	1. Reset thermostat from "on" to "auto."
	2. Relays faulty.	2. Call a professional.
Furnace noisy	1. Access panels loose.	1. Mount and fasten access panels correctly.
	2. Belts sticking, worn, or damaged.	2. Spray squeaking belts with fan belt dressing; replace worn or damaged belts.
	3. Blower belt too loose or too tight.	3. Adjust belt.
	4. Motor and/or blower needs lubrication.	4. If motor and blower have oil ports, lubricate.

Heat Pumps

A heat pump not only heats your home during the winter, but also cools it during the summer. It does not burn fuel to produce heat, nor does the electricity it consumes go through an element. The heat pump functions on the same principle that refrigerators and air conditioners are based on: a liquid absorbs heat as it turns into a gas, and releases heat as it returns to a liquid state.

During the summer, the heat pump operates as a standard central air conditioner, removing heat from the house and venting it to the outside. A liquid refrigerant is pumped through an evaporator coil of tubing. The liquid expands as it moves through the coil, changing to its gaseous state as it absorbs heat from the air surrounding the coil. A blower then pushes air around the cooled coil through ducts and into the house. The gas—now carrying considerable heat—moves through a compressor, which begins the liquefying process. It then moves to a condenser coil outside the house, where the compressed gas releases its heat and returns to a liquid state.

During the winter, the heat pump reverses this process, extracting heat from the cold air outside and releasing it inside the house. The heat pump is very efficient when the outside temperature is around 45° to 50° F, but it becomes less efficient as the temperature drops. When the outside temperature is very low, an auxiliary electric heater must be used to supplement the heat pump's output. Like standard electric heating systems, this auxiliary unit is quite expensive to operate. Thus, in areas where the winter temperature is consistently below freezing, the heat pump is not usually practical. It has few advantages over conventional heating systems in areas where air conditioning is not necessary, but is very efficient in warm to hot climates.

Heat pump maintenance is important. Small problems that are not promptly and properly taken care of can lead to very expensive compressor problems. Since maintaining a heat pump is more technical than caring for the average heating system, you should call a professional service person when the pump malfunctions. You can, however, keep the system free of dirt, by keeping the filter clean and removing any other obstacles to the flow of air. *Caution: Before doing any work on the heat pump, make sure the power to the pump is turned off.*

General Maintenance. Replace filters and clean and lubricate the components of the heat pump regularly, as detailed above for electric furnaces.

Outdoor Maintenance. Heat pumps, like central air conditioners, have an outdoor unit, which contains a compressor, a coil, a fan, and other components. In order to function properly, this unit should be kept free of debris such as leaves and dirt. The unit should be level

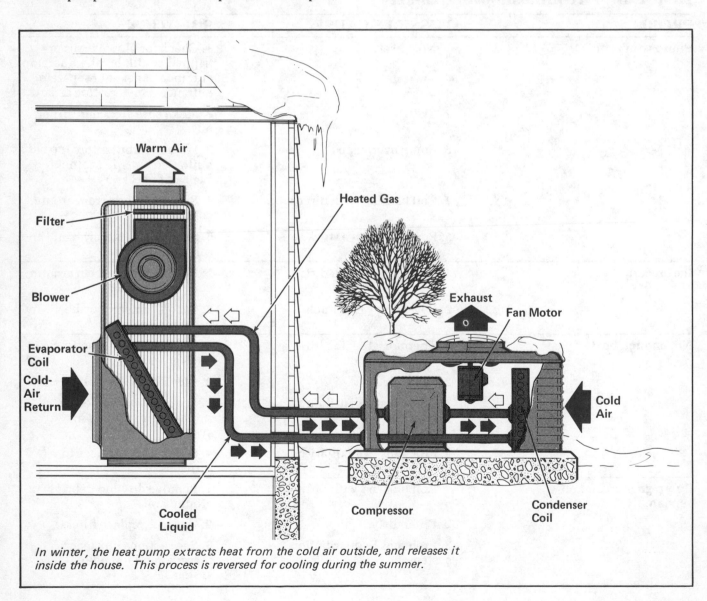

In winter, the heat pump extracts heat from the cold air outside, and releases it inside the house. This process is reversed for cooling during the summer.

on its concrete support pad.

Clean pine needles, leaves, and dirt out of updraft fans by removing the grille, which is held by a series of retaining screws. Make sure the power to the unit is off before this cleaning is done. A vacuum cleaner hose can sometimes be inserted between the fan blades to remove debris from the sides and bottom of the unit. At the beginning of each heating season, set a carpenters' level across the top of the metal cabinet and check the level from side to side and from front to back. If the unit has settled on the pad, lift the pad back to level by prying it up with a pry bar or a piece of 2×4; build up the ground under it with stone or crushed rock. Also check the piping insulation for deterioration. If this insulation is faulty, replace it with new insulation, available at heating supply stores. Installation instructions are usually provided by the manufacturer.

Reversing Problems. A reversing valve on the heat pump automatically switches the pump from the heating mode to the cooling mode and back again, as needed. The process is automatic; when the outdoor temperature drops, the condenser coil starts to ice up. A sensor notes the change and activates the reversing valve, and the heat pump defrosts. If there is a heavy buildup of ice on the condenser coil, the heat pump is not defrosting properly; if there is no ice at all, or if the defrost cycle lasts longer than about 15 minutes, the pump is stuck in the cooling mode. In either case, first check the condenser coil; if leaves, snow, or debris is interfering with the flow of air to the coil, clear it away. If removing obstructions doesn't relieve the problem, and if the ice doesn't disappear after one hour, set the pump on "emergency heat," and call a professional service person immediately.

Heat Pump Troubleshooting Chart

PROBLEM	POSSIBLE CAUSE	SOLUTION
Pump won't run	1. No power.	1. Check for blown fuses or tripped circuit breakers at main entrance panel or at separate entrance panel; restore circuit.
	2. Switch off.	2. Make sure switch is turned on.
	3. Pump overloaded.	3. Wait 30 minutes; press reset button on outside cabinet. Repeat if necessary.
	4. Coil blocked with dirt or ice.	4. Remove debris from around coil.
	5. Reversing valve stuck.	5. Set on "emergency heat" and call a professional.
Ice on coil	1. Coil blocked with dirt.	1. Remove debris from around coil.
	2. Reversing valve stuck.	2. Set on "emergency heat" and call a professional.
Not enough heat	1. Thermostat set too low.	1. Raise thermostat setting 5 to 10 degrees.
	2. Filter dirty.	2. Clean or replace filter.
	3. Problems in distribution system.	3. See sections on electric furnaces and forced-air systems.
	4. Problems in auxiliary heater.	4. See section on electric furnaces.
Pump goes on and off repeatedly	1. Coil blocked with dirt.	1. Remove dirt and debris from around coil.
	2. Filter dirty.	2. Clean or replace filter.
	3. Problems in distribution system.	3. See sections on electric furnaces and forced-air systems.

Power Interruptions. If a heat pump has been off for more than an hour because of a blown fuse, a tripped circuit breaker, or a utility power failure, the unit should not be put back into operation for about six to eight hours—especially if the temperature is 50° F or lower. The reason is that the lubricant in the pump's oil reservoir may be too cool to circulate properly. This can cause damage to the valves of the unit. Instead, set the pump on "emergency heat." This turns the pump off and keeps it from running. Leave the pump in this mode for about six to eight hours; then switch the pump to its normal heating setting. If little or no heat is generated at this point, call a professional service person.

Troubleshooting Distribution Systems

The way heat is distributed—through ductwork, by gravity or forced air, or through pipes—is as important as how it's generated. Whatever type of system you have, regular maintenance is essential to make the best use of the heat your furnace provides. Forced-air systems are probably the most common; radiant heat—steam or hot-water—is also in wide use. Gravity systems, the simplest of the three types, are not as efficient as forced-air and radiant heat, and are not used much to-

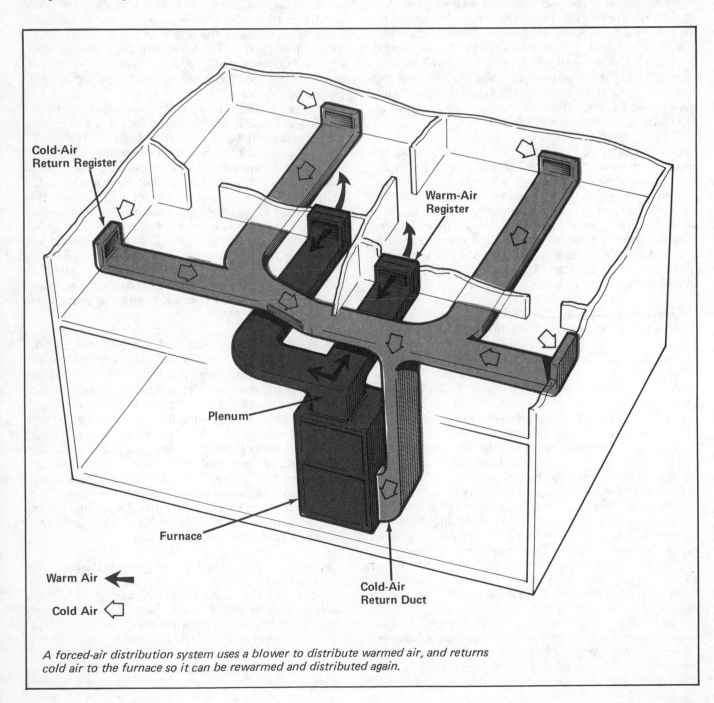

A forced-air distribution system uses a blower to distribute warmed air, and returns cold air to the furnace so it can be rewarmed and distributed again.

day. To maintain the ducts, registers, and returns of a gravity system, follow the procedures detailed for forced-air systems.

Forced-Air Systems

Fueled by gas, electricity, or oil, a forced-air distribution system is just what the name implies: air is forced from the furnace through ducts to registers in various rooms. Besides warming the air, the blower system that distributes the warmed air also returns the cold air to the furnace so it can be rewarmed and distributed to the rooms again. A forced-air system is also efficient for distributing cool air from a central air conditioner, with the same ducts, registers, and blower. There is little that can go wrong with a forced-air system. The big problems include noise and blockage of air flow, usually caused by dirt or by furniture or draperies blocking the registers. Forced-air systems should be cleaned and maintained as detailed earlier in this chapter; specific troubleshooting procedures follow.

Disassembly. Floor registers are slip-fit into ducts, or are held by retaining screws on the frame of the register. Wall and ceiling registers are held by retaining screws on the frame of the register. Duct joints are usually slip-fit, and held with sheet metal screws or duct tape. The ducts are supported by wire or metal strap hangers nailed or screwed to wooden framing members such as studs and rafters. All parts are easy to disassemble; lay them out in order as you work so you'll be able to reassemble them properly.

Filters and Blowers. See sections on specific furnaces, above, for cleaning and adjustment details.

Balancing the System. Forced-air systems often go out of balance, causing some rooms to be too hot or too cold. The furnace is usually not to blame; the cause of the problem is that ducts and registers are not properly set. Balance the system while the furnace is turned on.

To balance a forced-air system, open all the ducts and registers in the system. There may be dampers in various ducts; these are turned to open the ducts. The damper is open when it's turned parallel with the top and bottom of the ducting. Assemble six or seven thermometers and get them all to have about the same temperature reading. You can do this by laying the thermometers out together for about 30 minutes, and then noting any discrepancies. Tape the thermometers on the walls of various rooms—one thermometer to each room—so that each thermometer is about 36 inches up from the floor, away from the hot-air register or cold-air return. Then wait one hour.

Take a thermometer reading in each room. If one room shows a higher temperature than an adjoining room, close the damper or register slightly in the hotter room. Follow this procedure for each room, opening and closing dampers and registers, until the same tempera-

ture is maintained in each room, or the temperature balance you want is reached. During the balancing process, the thermostat to the furnace should be kept at the same reading. For the best results, balance the entire system.

Adjusting Blower Speed. An increase in blower speed can sometimes improve the flow of warm air through your home; a decrease can make the system quieter. You can increase the blower speed—or decrease it—by slightly adjusting the pulley on the blower drive motor. To increase the speed, slightly loosen the setscrew that holds the pulley to the drive shaft. Move or turn the pulley clockwise on the shaft one turn; then tighten the setscrew. If more speed is desired, turn the pulley clockwise two turns. To decrease blower speed, loosen the setscrew that holds the pulley to the drive shaft and move or turn the pulley counterclockwise on the shaft one turn; then tighten the setscrew. If less speed is desired, turn the pulley counterclockwise two turns.

The motor and blower pulley may also get out of alignment, causing the blower to be noisy and cutting down on the efficiency of your distribution system. To check alignment, place a carpenters' square against the outside of the motor and blower pulleys. The pulleys should be in a straight line, and at right angles to the motor shaft. If the pulleys are not lined up at right angles to the motor housing, loosen the setscrew holding the motor pulley, and move the pulley backward or forward as needed to align it properly. If the setscrew is jammed or rusted and won't loosen, or if the pulleys are a good deal out of alignment—more than about $\frac{1}{2}$ inch—loosen the mounting bolts on the motor and slide the motor backward or forward until the pulleys are properly aligned.

Noise Problems. Air forced through the ducts of the forced-air system can cause vibration and noise if the ducts are not firmly connected. The best way to stop this noise is to add duct hangers to the ducting system. The hangers are usually wrapped around or across the ducting and nailed or screwed to the stud or rafter framing. At the elbows of the ducts, where air moving through the ducts changes direction, the duct sections can become loose or separated. Push loose sections back together and tape the joints firmly with duct tape, available at most hardware stores and home centers.

Noise can also be caused by inadequate lubrication, worn or damaged belts, or too high a blower speed. Correct these problems as detailed above.

Heat Loss from Ducts. If ducts run through cold basements or exterior crawl spaces, they should be wrapped with fiberglass insulation, spiraled around the ducting and held with duct tape, wire, or heavy cord. Or wrap the ducts with aluminum-faced insulating tape, sold in wide rolls and available at heating supply stores.

Motors and Belts. See sections on specific furnaces, above.

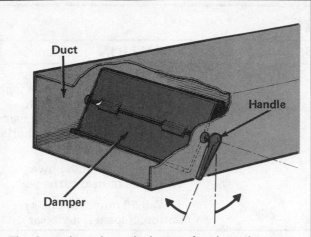

The ducts throughout the house often have dampers. The damper is open when it's turned parallel with the top and bottom of the duct.

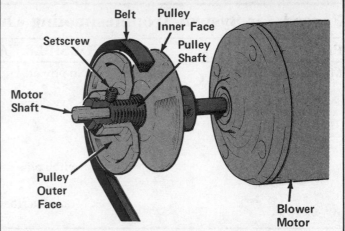

To adjust the blower speed, loosen the setscrew that holds the pulley to the drive shaft, and turn the pulley on the shaft.

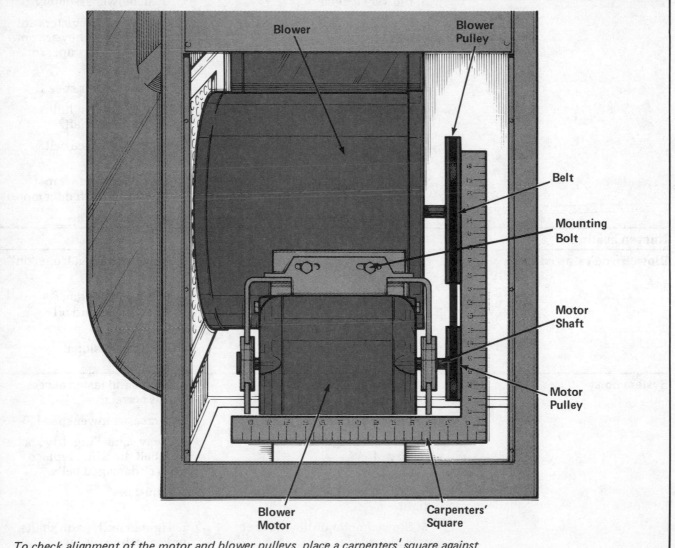

To check alignment of the motor and blower pulleys, place a carpenters' square against them. The pulleys should be in a straight line, at right angles to the motor shaft.

Forced-Air System Troubleshooting Chart

PROBLEM	POSSIBLE CAUSE	SOLUTION
Motor won't run	1. No power.	1. Check for blown fuses or tripped circuit breakers at main entrance panel, at separate entrance panel, and on furnace; restore circuit. Also see charts for specific furnaces.
	2. Switch off.	2. Turn on separate power switch on or near furnace.
	3. Motor overload.	3. Wait 30 minutes; press reset button. Repeat if necessary.
Not enough heat	1. Thermostat set too low.	1. Raise thermostat setting 5 degrees.
	2. Filter dirty.	2. Clean or replace filter.
	3. Blower clogged.	3. Clean blower assembly.
	4. Registers closed or blocked.	4. Make sure all registers are open; make sure they are not blocked by rugs, drapes, or furniture.
	5. Blower running too slow.	5. Increase blower speed.
	6. Blower loose.	6. Tighten nut that holds blower to drive shaft.
	7. Blower belt misaligned or broken.	7. Adjust or replace belt.
	8. Duct joints loose.	8. Trace ducts and wrap leaking joints with duct tape.
	9. Ducts losing heat.	9. Insulate ducts.
Uneven heating	1. System out of balance.	1. Balance system.
Blower won't stop running	1. Blower control set wrong.	1. Reset thermostat from "on" to "auto."
	2. Limit switch set wrong (gas or oil furnace).	2. Reset limit switch; see sections on gas and oil furnaces.
	3. Limit control needs adjustment.	3. Call a professional.
System noisy	1. Access panels loose.	1. Mount and fasten access panels correctly.
	2. Blower running too fast.	2. Decrease blower speed.
	3. Belts sticking, worn, or damaged.	3. Spray squeaking drive belts with belt dressing; replace worn or damaged belts.
	4. Blower belt too loose or too tight.	4. Adjust belt.
	5. Blower/motor pulleys loose or misaligned.	5. Tighten pulleys on shafts, and/or realign pulleys.
	6. Blower/motor needs lubrication.	6. Lubricate blower/motor.

Forced-Air System Troubleshooting Chart (Continued)

PROBLEM	POSSIBLE CAUSE	SOLUTION
System noisy (continued)	7. Ducting loose.	7. Make sure ducts are tightly fastened to framing with duct hangers; wrap joints with duct tape.

Steam Systems

Steam heat is not installed in modern homes, but it is such a durable heating system that many homes and apartment buildings are still heated by steam. Basically, a steam heat system works by gravity. A boiler in the basement of the building, usually powered by an oil or gas burner, heats water until it turns to steam. The steam rises, going up to radiators and warming the air in the rooms throughout your home. As the steam cools it condenses, and the water flows back to the boiler.

Slope. The steam system is a simple one, but for it to work properly, all pipes and radiators must slope back toward the boiler—if the water can't run back to the boiler, it collects and blocks the path of the steam. When this happens, there are hammering noises in the system, and one or more individual radiators may not function.

Correcting malfunctions caused by inadequate slope is easy. Place blocks of wood under the legs of the affected radiators to correct the angle of slope. If you suspect that the supply pipes are at fault, check their angle of slope with a level; these pipes may become incor-

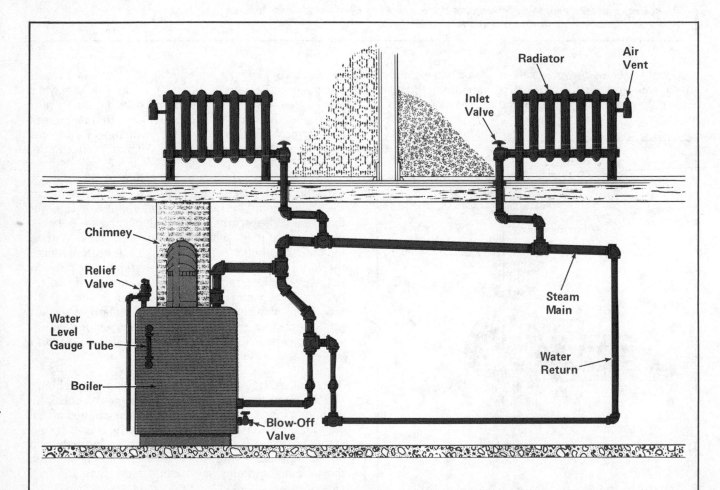

A steam heat system works by gravity. A boiler in the basement heats water until it turns to steam; the steam rises to the radiators and warms the air in the rooms of your house.

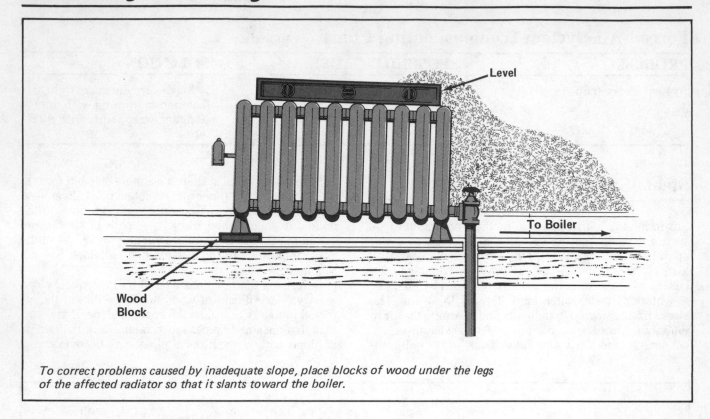

To correct problems caused by inadequate slope, place blocks of wood under the legs of the affected radiator so that it slants toward the boiler.

rectly tilted when the house settles. If you can get at the pipes, you can solve the problem by supporting the pipe with pipe straps to reestablish the proper slope.

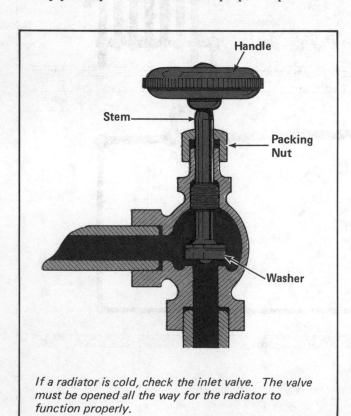

If a radiator is cold, check the inlet valve. The valve must be opened all the way for the radiator to function properly.

Water Level. If the heat throughout the system is inadequate, either the boiler isn't heating or the water level is too low. If the boiler isn't heating, the furnace may be malfunctioning, and you'll have to find and correct the problem there. Specific procedures for oil, gas, and electric heating systems are detailed earlier in this chapter.

The second possibility, a low water level in the system's boiler, is easier to handle. The level of water in the boiler should be maintained at about half full, and there should be an air space—called a chest—between the surface of the water and the top of the tank. Without the chest, the boiler can't work up a full head of steam; the water overfills the return lines, and may trip the relief valve. To correct this problem, add water to the boiler. If the water level in the boiler is consistently low, check the pipes for leaks. If you spot a leak at a pipe connection, try tightening the connection carefully with a pipe wrench. If the connection still leaks, call a professional service person.

Radiators. If an individual radiator is cold and both it and the pipes leading to it are tilted properly, check the radiator's inlet valve; this valve must be opened all the way for the radiator to function properly. If some radiators get warmer than others, the vents are probably not adjusted properly. Adjust the vents so that the ones farthest from the boiler are opened more than the ones closest to the boiler.

If air gets trapped in a radiator, steam may not be able to enter. When this happens, the radiator won't heat up. To purge the unwanted air, turn the air vent

Steam System Troubleshooting Chart

PROBLEM	POSSIBLE CAUSE	SOLUTION
System won't run	1. Problems in boiler/furnace assembly.	1. See sections on specific furnaces.
Not enough heat (entire system)	1. Thermostat set too low.	1. Raise thermostat setting 5 degrees.
	2. Boiler water level low.	2. Check boiler; if necessary, let boiler cool and refill half full.
	3. Problems in boiler/furnace assembly.	3. See sections on specific furnaces.
	4. Rust or scale in boiler and/or pipes.	4. Flush boiler system; add anti-scale preparation. If problem persists, call a professional.
	5. Problem in boiler.	5. Call a professional.
Not enough heat (individual radiator)	1. Radiator or pipes not sloping properly.	1. Check slope; prop radiator or adjust supply pipes to slope toward boiler.
	2. Inlet valve closed or only partially open.	2. Open inlet valve completely.
	3. Air trapped in radiator.	3. Open air vent valve to purge excess air.
	4. Radiator blocked.	4. Make sure radiators are not blocked by rugs, drapes, or furniture.
Uneven heat	1. Air vents not adjusted properly.	1. Adjust air vents so that those far away from boiler are open more than those close to boiler.
Leaks	1. Loose pipe connection.	1. Tighten pipe connection.
	2. Worn stem packing or washer on inlet valve.	2. Replace stem packing or washer on inlet valve.
Water level gauge unreadable	1. Rust or scale in system.	1. Flush boiler system; add anti-scale preparation. If problem persists, call a professional.
Pipes or radiators noisy	1. Water trapped in system.	1. Check slope; prop radiators or adjust supply pipes to slope toward boiler.

valve on the radiator until the hissing stops and water comes out; then close the vent. Use a screwdriver or the key furnished by the radiator manufacturer to open the vent; if you don't have the key, you may be able to buy one at a heating supply store. Some radiators are automatic; they don't have to be opened or closed to remove excess air.

Leaks. Leaks around inlet valves, radiators, and pipes are plumbing problems; you may or may not be able to correct them without professional help. There are special additives that you can put into the boiler's water supply to stop leaks. Pipe leaks are frequently due to loose connections, and can generally be stopped by tightening the connections with a wrench. Leaks around inlet valves are caused by deterioration of the stem packing or the washer in the valve; to correct this problem, the valve must be disassembled.

Radiator inlet valves are similar to faucets; the valve has a packing nut, a valve body or stem, and a washer assembly. To replace the valve packing or the washer, first shut off the boiler and let it cool. It isn't necessary to shut off the water; as the steam in the system cools, it will condense and flow back out of the radiator to the

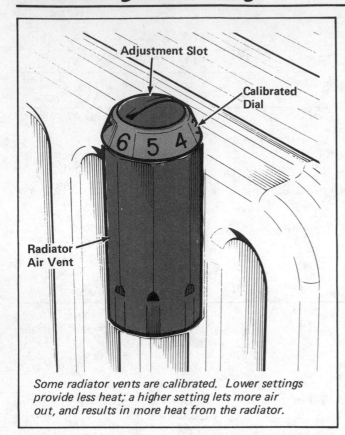

Some radiator vents are calibrated. Lower settings provide less heat; a higher setting lets more air out, and results in more heat from the radiator.

boiler. The handle to the valve is usually held by a screw; remove the screw. Unscrew the packing nut, remove the handle, and back out the valve stem or body. At the bottom of the stem is a washer, held by a screw. Remove the screw and the washer, and replace the washer with a new one of the same size and type. The packing nut may have a washer or may be filled with packing string; replace the washer or install new packing as you reassemble the valve. When all connections are tight, turn the system back on. For detailed instructions on faucet repairs, see the chapter on plumbing.

Flushing the System. Once a month, the entire heating system should be flushed to keep the pipes clear and the steam flowing freely. To flush the system, open the blow-off valve and let the water run off into a bucket until it runs clear. If the water remains rusty, or if the entire system is operating at less than optimum efficiency, the pipes are probably clogged with rust and scale. If you see any rust in the water level gauge tube, shut off the boiler and let it cool; then flush the system by draining and refilling it several times. Finally, add a commercial radiator preparation formulated to curb the buildup of rust and scale. These products are available at heating supply stores.

Boiler/Furnace Assembly. The boiler of a steam-heat system uses a gas or oil burner or an electric heating element to heat the water in the system. If there is no heat in the system, follow the procedures detailed

above for gas, oil, or electric furnaces, as appropriate. If problems occur in the boiler itself, follow the procedures above or call a professional service person.

Hot-Water Systems

Because water retains heat, it is used effectively to store and distribute heat in home systems. There are two types of hot-water systems: the gravity system and the hydronic, or forced hot water, type. Like steam systems, hot-water heating systems can be powered by gas, oil, or electricity.

Gravity systems depend on the upward flow of hot water to circulate heated water from the boiler through a system of pipes to radiators in the rooms of your home. The better radiators for hot-water systems are called convectors. These units employ a series of fins.

The heat from the water in the radiators or convectors is transferred first to the metal radiators and then to the air. As the water loses its heat, it sinks, and flows back to the boiler through return pipes. Most gravity systems heat the water to no more than about 180° F, and the cooled water that goes back to the boiler rarely falls below 120° F. Open gravity systems have an overflow outlet to let water escape, preventing a buildup of excess pressure in the system. Closed systems have a sealed expansion tank; when water pressure builds up in the system, the excess water flows into the expansion tank to prevent damage to the pipes or the boiler. Hydronic hot-water systems are much like closed gravity systems, except that a hydronic system uses a motor-driven circulating pump—called a circulator—to move the water. As a result, the water in a hydronic system moves more rapidly, and arrives at the room radiator with less heat loss, than the water in a gravity system.

Slope. Like steam systems, hot-water systems—especially gravity systems—depend on proper slope; all pipes and radiators must slope back toward the boiler. Hammering noises and failure to heat are indications of incorrect slope. To correct these malfunctions, check the slope of radiators and pipes, and prop radiators or fasten pipes so that all components are properly tilted.

Correcting malfunctions caused by inadequate slope is easy. Place blocks of wood under the legs of the affected radiators to correct the angle of slope. If you suspect that the supply pipes are at fault, check their angle of slope with a level; these pipes may become incorrectly tilted when the house settles. If you can get at the pipes, you can solve the problem by supporting the pipe with pipe straps to reestablish the proper slope.

Water Level. The water level in the hot-water system's boiler should be maintained, as with steam systems, at about half full; there should be an air space between the surface of the water and the top of the tank. Too low a water level can cause inadequate heating. In most cases, an automatic filling system keeps the boiler filled with the proper amount of water. If the water

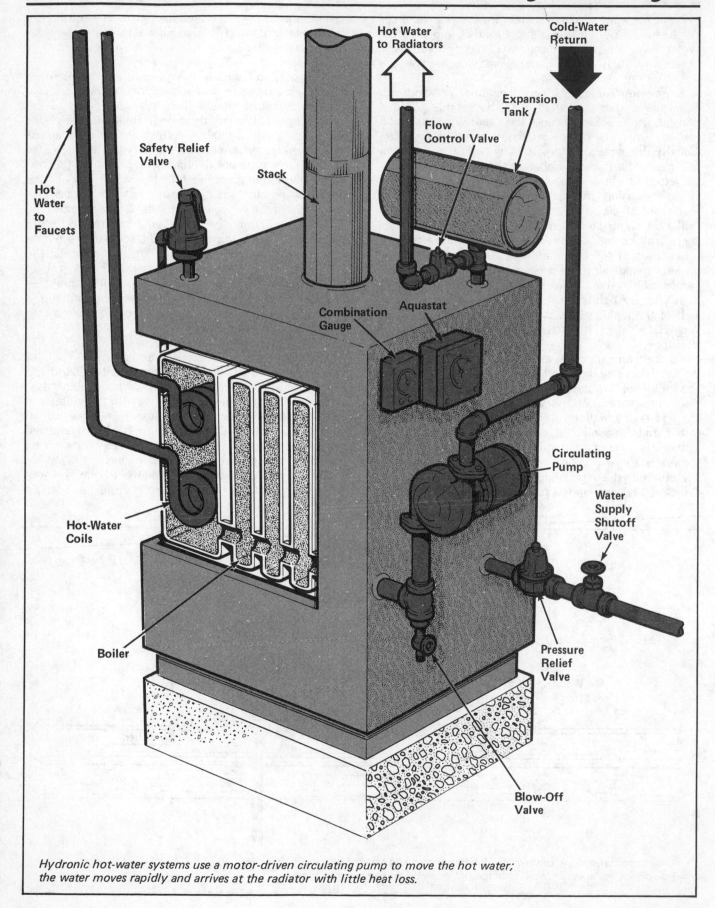

Hot Water
to Radiators

Cold-Water
Return

Expansion
Tank

Flow
Control
Valve

Safety Relief
Valve

Stack

Hot
Water
to
Faucets

Combination
Gauge

Aquastat

Circulating
Pump

Water
Supply
Shutoff
Valve

Hot-Water
Coils

Boiler

Pressure
Relief
Valve

Blow-Off
Valve

*Hydronic hot-water systems use a motor-driven circulating pump to move the hot water;
the water moves rapidly and arrives at the radiator with little heat loss.*

level of the system is consistently low, check the pipes for leaks. Close the water supply valve and note the water level for two or three days. If the level drops drastically, call a professional service person.

Expansion Tank. For efficient heating, the water in a hot-water system is heated well above boiling, but it doesn't turn to steam because the expansion tank and a pressure-reducing valve keep the water under pressure. Usually the expansion tank is hung from the basement ceiling, not far from the boiler; in older systems, look for the expansion tank in the attic. If there is not enough air in the expansion tank, the buildup of pressure will force water out of the safety relief valve located above the boiler. If water spurts from the pressure relief valve, there isn't enough air in the expansion tank—without enough air in the tank, the tank fills with water; the water expands as it heats up, and escapes through the safety relief valve. You can check for air in the expansion tank by lightly touching it. Normally the bottom half of the tank feels warmer than the top; if the tank feels hot all over, it has filled with water, and must be drained.

To drain an expansion tank, turn off the power to the boiler; then close the water supply shutoff valve and let the tank cool. On newer systems, a combination drain valve lets water out and air in when it is opened. If there is a combination valve, attach a garden hose to the valve, and remove about two or three buckets of water. If there is no combination valve, shut off the valve between the expansion tank and the boiler, and then completely drain the expansion tank. Turn the water supply back on, and turn on the power to the boiler to get the system running again. It isn't necessary to refill the expansion tank; it will fill up as part of the normal operation of the system.

Combination Gauge and Aquastat. The combination gauge—not the same as the combination valve—is an automatic control mounted on the side or top of the boiler. It generally has three indicators. On the upper part of the gauge, a moving pointer indicates the actual pressure in the system and a stationary pointer indicates the minimum pressure that has been preset for the system. If the moving pointer falls below the level of the stationary pointer, the system needs more water. The lower part of the gauge indicates the temperature of the water in the boiler. The maximum temperature for the system is preset by a pointer on the scale of a separate device called an Aquastat. The Aquastat controls the temperature of the water in the system. When it is set at a temperature, the boiler will heat the water until this temperature has been reached. Problems with either the combination gauge or the Aquastat should be taken care of by a professional service person.

Radiators and Convectors. If an individual radiator or convector is cold and both it and the pipes leading to it are tilted properly, check the radiator's inlet valve; this valve must be opened all the way for the radiator to function properly. If some radiators or convectors get warmer than others, the vents are probably not adjusted properly. Adjust the vents so that the ones farthest from the boiler are opened more than the ones closest to it.

Air trapped in a radiator or convector can prevent water from entering it and keep it from heating. To

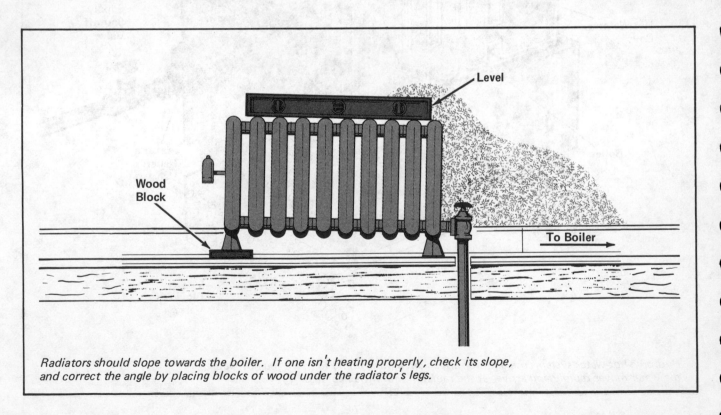

Radiators should slope towards the boiler. If one isn't heating properly, check its slope, and correct the angle by placing blocks of wood under the radiator's legs.

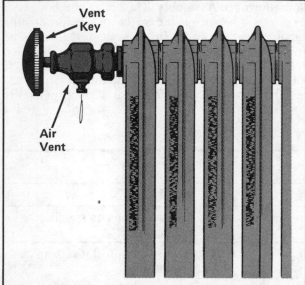

To purge air from a radiator, use a screwdriver or vent key to open the vent. When the hissing stops and water comes out, close the vent.

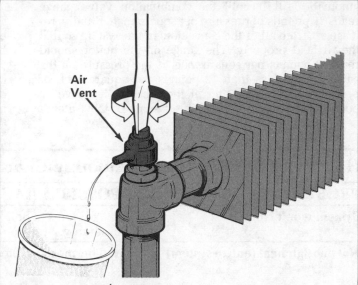

If a convector isn't heating properly, air may be trapped inside. Use a screwdriver to turn the vent until the hissing stops and water comes out; then close the vent.

solve the problem, turn the air vent valve on the unit until the hissing stops and water comes out; then close the vent. Use a screwdriver or the key furnished by the radiator manufacturer to open the vent; if you don't have the key, you may be able to buy one at a heating supply store. Some convectors and radiators are automatic; they don't have to be opened or closed.

Circulator. The circulator is a pump that forces the hot water to the radiators or convectors throughout the house. Problems with the circulator usually occur when the coupler that separates the motor from the pump breaks; this generally makes a lot of noise. Another source of trouble with the circulator is the pump seal; if water leaks from the pump, chances are the seal is damaged. If the circulator develops either of these problems, call a professional service person.

Leaks. Like steam systems, hot-water systems are prone to plumbing leaks, in the pipes and at inlet valves. You may or may not be able to fix leaks without professional help. There are special additives you can put into the boiler's water supply to stop leaks. Pipe leaks are frequently due to loose connections, and can be stopped by tightening the connections with a wrench. Leaks around inlet valves, however, are due to deterioration of the stem packing or the washer in the valve.

Radiator inlet valves are similar to faucets, with a packing nut, a valve body or stem, and a washer assembly. To replace the valve packing or the washer, first shut off the boiler and let it cool. It isn't necessary to shut off the water; as the system cools, the water will flow back out of the radiator or convector to the boiler. The handle to the valve is usually held by a screw; remove the screw. Unscrew the packing nut, remove the

handle, and back out the valve stem or body. At the bottom of the stem is a washer, held by a screw. Remove the screw and the washer and replace the washer with a new one of the same size and type. The packing nut may have a washer or may be filled with packing string; replace the washer or install new packing as you reassemble the valve. When all connections are tight, turn the system back on. For detailed instructions on faucet repairs, see the chapter on plumbing.

Flushing and Draining the System. Once a year, the entire heating system should be flushed to keep the pipes clear and the water flowing freely. To flush the system, open the blow-off valve and let the water run off into a bucket until it runs clear. If the water still looks rusty after the system has been flushed, call a professional service person.

Hot-water systems should be drained to prevent the pipes from freezing during a prolonged cold-weather power failure; it may also be necessary to drain the system to make repairs. To drain the pipes, turn off the power to the boiler at the main electrical entrance panel, by removing the fuse or tripping the circuit breaker that controls the circuit. Let the water cool until it's just warm. When the water has cooled, turn off the water supply valve, and attach a length of garden hose to the boiler drain. The hose should be lower than the boiler; position it in a laundry sink or at a floor drain. Open the drain valve and the air vents on all of the convectors or radiators. The water from the system will flow out through the hose; give it plenty of time to drain.

To refill the system, close the air vents on all of the convectors or radiators and shut the drain valve. Turn on the water supply to the boiler. If the boiler has an automatic shutoff, refilling is automatic. If the boiler isn't automatic, fill it until the combination valve gauge reads 20 pounds of pressure per square inch. Finally, release air from all of the convectors in the system so that they'll heat properly. The gauge on the boiler should read 12 pounds per square inch. If the pressure on the gauge shows less than 12 pounds per square inch of pressure, add more water; if the pressure is above 12 pounds per square inch, drain off some of the water.

Boiler/Furnace Assembly. The boiler of a hot-water system uses a gas or oil burner or an electric heating element to heat the water in the system. If there is no heat in the system, follow the procedures detailed above for gas, oil, or electric furnaces, as appropriate. If problems occur in the boiler itself, follow the procedures above or call a professional service person to make the repairs.

Hot-Water System Troubleshooting Chart

PROBLEM	POSSIBLE CAUSE	SOLUTION
System won't run	1. Problems in boiler/furnace assembly.	1. See sections on specific furnaces.
Not enough heat (entire system)	1. Thermostat set too low.	1. Raise thermostat setting 5 degrees.
	2. Boiler water level low.	2. Check boiler; if necessary, let boiler cool and refill half full.
	3. Problems in boiler/furnace assembly.	3. See sections on specific furnaces.
	4. Rust or scale in boiler and/or pipes.	4. Flush boiler system. If problem persists, call a professional.
	5. Aquastat faulty.	5. Call a professional.
	6. Combination gauge faulty.	6. Call a professional.
	7. Problem in boiler.	7. Call a professional.
Not enough heat (individual radiator or convector)	1. Radiator or convector not sloping properly.	1. Check slope; prop radiator or adjust supply pipes to slope toward boiler.
	2. Inlet valve closed or only partially open.	2. Open inlet valve completely.
	3. Air trapped in radiator or convector.	3. Open air vent valve to purge air.
	4. Radiator or convector blocked.	4. Make sure radiators or convectors are not blocked by rugs, drapes, or furniture.
Uneven heat	1. Air vents not adjusted properly.	1. Adjust air vents so that those far away from boiler are open more than those close to boiler.
Leaks	1. Loose pipe connection.	1. Tighten pipe connection.
	2. Worn stem packing or washer on inlet valve.	2. Replace stem packing or washer on inlet valve.
	2. Circulator seal or impeller faulty.	2. Call a professional.
Relief valve leaks	1. Air in system.	1. Drain expansion tank.
Pipes or radiators/convectors noisy	1. Cold water trapped in system.	1. Check slope; prop radiators/convectors or adjust supply pipes to slope toward boiler.
	2. Circulator coupler broken.	2. Call a professional.

Troubleshooting Cooling Systems

There are two types of home cooling systems: central air conditioning and individual room air conditioners. Both systems consist of the same basic components—a condenser, which uses electricity to cool a refrigerant liquid in a coil, and an evaporator, which cools the air in your home. The condenser unit of a central air conditioner is usually located outside; the evaporator is hooked to the distribution system of your home's heat source. Room air conditioners are much smaller; both condenser and evaporator are contained in one housing, and cooled air is vented directly into the room. Heat pumps, when operated in their cooling cycle, function as central air conditioners. Procedures for heat pump maintenance and repairs are detailed in the section on troubleshooting heating systems.

Central Air Conditioning

Central air conditioners are made up of two separate components: the condenser unit, usually located outside the house on a concrete slab, and the evaporator coil, which is mounted in the plenum—the main duct junction—above the furnace. Two coolant lines run from the condenser unit to the evaporator. When the air conditioner is turned on, the liquid refrigerant in the condenser coil is cooled. The cooled liquid flows to the evaporator coil through the first line. At the evaporator, warm air in your home is cooled by contact with the liquid-filled coil. As the warm air around it becomes cooler, the liquid in the coil becomes warmer, and is transformed to its gaseous state. The gas flows through the second connection line back to the condenser unit, where it is pressurized and cooled again to its liquid

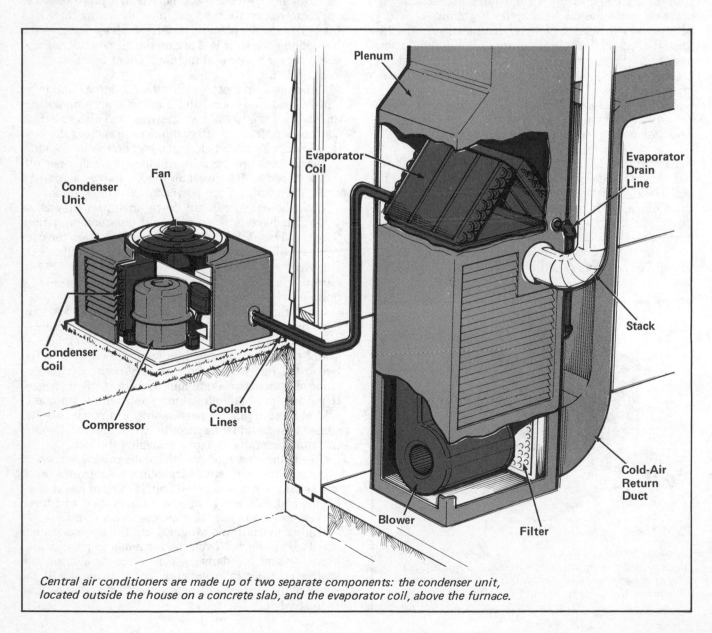

Central air conditioners are made up of two separate components: the condenser unit, located outside the house on a concrete slab, and the evaporator coil, above the furnace.

state. As it cools, the gas gives off heat, which is vented out of the unit by a fan located at the top or back of the condenser.

Most central air conditioners are hooked to a home's forced-air distribution system. Thus, the same motor, blower, and ductwork used for heating are used to distribute cool air from the air conditioning system. When a central air conditioner is operating, hot air inside the house flows to the furnace through the return-air duct. The hot air is moved by the blower across the cooled evaporator coil in the plenum, and is then delivered through ducts to cool the house. When the air conditioner works but the house doesn't cool, the problem is probably in the distribution system. In this case, refer to the section on troubleshooting forced-air systems.

Both the evaporator and the condenser are sealed, and a professional service person should be called for almost any maintenance other than routine cleaning. Central air conditioners should be professionally inspected and adjusted before the beginning of every cooling season, but don't let your maintenance go at this annual checkup—while there aren't many repairs you can make, there are specific maintenance procedures you can follow to keep your system operating at peak efficiency.

Caution: Before doing any work on an air conditioning system, make sure the power to the system, both condenser and evaporator assembly, is turned off.

Evaporator. The evaporator is located directly above the furnace in the plenum. The evaporator may not be accessible, but if it is, you should clean it once a year. If the plenum has foil-wrapped insulation at its front, you can clean the evaporator; if the plenum is a sealed sheet-metal box, do not attempt to open it.

To clean an accessible evaporator, turn off the power to the air conditioner. With the power off, remove the

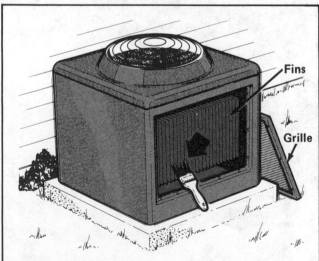

Clean the fins on the condenser with a soft brush to remove accumulated dirt; you may have to remove a protective grille to reach the fins.

foil-wrapped insulation at the front of the plenum; it's probably taped in place. Remove the tape carefully, because you'll have to replace it later. Behind the insulation is the access plate, which is held in place by several screws. Remove the screws and lift the plate off.

With a stiff brush, clean the entire underside of the evaporator unit; a large hand mirror can be very helpful in letting you see what you're doing. If you can't reach all the way back to clean the entire area, slide the evaporator out a little. The evaporator can be slid out even if it has rigid pipes connected to it, but be careful not to bend the pipes. Clean the tray below the evaporator unit; this tray carries condensation away from the evaporator. Pour a little liquid household bleach into the weep hole in the tray to prevent fungus growth. In extremely humid weather, check the condensate drain and pan every other day; if there's much moisture in the pan, the weep hole from the pan to the drain line may be clogged. Open the weep hole with a piece of wire.

When you've finished cleaning the evaporator, put the unit back into place, reinstall the plate, and tape the insulation back over it. Turn on the air conditioner and check for air leaks; seal them with duct tape.

Condenser. In most systems the condenser unit is located outside the house, and is prone to accumulate dirt and debris from trees, lawn-mowing, and airborne dust. The condenser has a fan that moves air across the condenser coil. You must clean the coil on the intake side, so before you turn the power to the air conditioner off, check to see which direction the air moves across the coils. Then turn off the power to the air conditioner.

With the power off, cut down any grass, weeds, or vines that have grown up around the condenser unit; they could be obstructing the flow of air. Clean the condenser with a commercial coil cleaner, available at refrigerator supply stores; instructions for use are included. Flush the coil clean with a spray bottle—not a hose—and let it dry.

Clean the fins with a soft brush to remove accumulated dirt; you may have to remove a protective grille to reach them. Do not clean the fins with a garden hose—water could turn the dirt into mud and compact it between the fins. Clean the fins very carefully; they're made of light-gauge aluminum, and are easily damaged. If the fins are bent, straighten them with a fin comb, sold at most appliance parts stores. Fin combs are designed to slide into the spaces between the fins. Use the fin comb carefully to avoid damaging the fins.

Check the concrete pad the condenser rests on to make sure it's level; set a carpenter's level front to back and side to side on top of the unit. If the pad has settled, lift the pad with a pry bar or a piece of 2×4, and force gravel or rocks under the concrete to level it.

During the fall and winter, outside condenser units should be protected from the elements to prevent leaf blockage and ice damage. Cover the condenser unit with a commercial condenser cover made to fit the shape of the unit, or with heavy plastic sheeting secured with sturdy cord.

Central Air Conditioner Troubleshooting Chart

PROBLEM	POSSIBLE CAUSE	SOLUTION
Condenser doesn't run	1. No power.	1. Check for blown fuses or tripped circuit breakers at main entrance panel or at separate entrance panel; restore circuit.
	2. Thermostat set too high.	2. Lower thermostat setting 5 degrees.
	3. Motor faulty.	3. Call a professional.
	4. Compressor faulty.	4. Call a professional.
Uneven cooling	1. Distribution system out of balance.	1. Balance system; see section on forced-air systems.
Inadequate cooling	1. Thermostat set too high.	1. Lower thermostat setting 5 degrees.
	2. Evaporator dirty.	2. Clean evaporator.
	3. Unit too small.	3. Replace with larger unit; call a professional.
	4. Problem in distribution system.	4. See section on forced-air systems.
Unit doesn't cool	1. Thermostat set too high.	1. Lower thermostat setting 5 degrees.
	2. Condenser dirty.	2. Clean condenser coil and fins; if necessary, straighten fins.
	3. Condenser unit blocked.	3. Remove debris blocking condenser; cut down weeds, grass, and vines.
	4. Evaporator dirty.	4. Clean evaporator.
	5. Problem in distribution system.	5. See section on forced-air systems.
	6. Compressor faulty.	6. Call a professional.
	7. Not enough refrigerant in system.	7. Call a professional.
Condenser unit turns on and off repeatedly	1. Condenser dirty.	1. Clean condenser coil and fins.
	2. Condenser unit blocked.	2. Remove debris blocking condenser; cut down weeds, grass, and vines.
	3. Evaporator dirty.	3. Clean evaporator.
	4. Problem in distribution system.	4. See section on forced-air systems.

Refrigerant. The coolant used in air conditioning systems is a refrigerant called Freon. If the system does not contain the proper amount of Freon, little or no cooling will take place. If you suspect a Freon problem, call a professional service person to recharge the system. *Caution:* Do not try to charge your system's Freon lines; Freon is volatile, and can be dangerous.

You can make one repair to the system's coolant lines. Examine the lines running from the condenser outside to the evaporator inside the house. If the insulation is damaged or worn, it will cut down on the cooling efficiency of the unit, and should be replaced. Replace damaged or worn coolant-line insulation as soon as possible, with new insulation of the same type.

Distribution System. In most cases, circulation problems and noisy operation are caused by problems in your home's heating/cooling distribution system. To correct distribution problems, see the section on troubleshooting forced-air systems.

Room Air Conditioning

Room air conditioners, also called window units, work the same way central air conditioners do. They are smaller than central systems, and they can be more expensive to operate. Depending on its size, a room unit may cool only the room it's located in or may be able to cool adjoining rooms too.

Both of the major components of a room unit—the condenser and the evaporator—are contained in one housing. The condenser coil faces outside; the evaporator faces the inside. Sandwiched between the coils are a compressor, two fans, a motor, and thermostat controls. Dirt is probably the biggest enemy of window air conditioners, because it can lower the efficiency of the evaporator coil, block the operation of the fan that blows out the cool air, clog filters, and block drain ports.

The coils, the compressor, and the motor of a room air conditioner are sealed components, so any repairs to them should be left to a professional service person. You can make minor repairs, though, and regular maintenance will keep your unit running well. When extensive repairs are needed, you can also save the cost of a service call by removing the air conditioner from its mounting and taking it to the repair shop.

During the winter, room air conditioners should be protected from the elements; either remove the unit from its mounting and store it, or cover the outside portion of the unit with a commercial room air conditioner cover or with heavy plastic sheeting, held with duct tape. Air conditioner covers are available at hardware stores, home centers, and appliance outlets.

Caution: Before doing any work on an air conditioner, make sure it's unplugged. Room air conditioners have one or two capacitors, located behind the control panel and near the fan. Capacitors store electricity, even when the power to the unit is turned off. Before you do any work on an air conditioner, you must unplug it and discharge the capacitor, or you could receive a severe shock.

First, unplug the air conditioner or turn off the power to the circuit. To gain access to the capacitor—there may be one or two—remove the unit's control panel. The capacitor is located behind the control panel and near the fan; it looks like a large dry-cell battery. To discharge the capacitor, use a 20,000-ohm, 2-watt resistor, an inexpensive wire unit available at most electrical supply stores. Fasten the clips of the resistor to the terminals of the capacitor; this discharges the capacitor. If the capacitor has three terminal posts, connect the resis-

tor to one outer terminal and the center terminal; then to the other outside terminal and the center terminal. After discharging the capacitor, you can proceed to make the necessary repairs.

Disassembly. Access to the filter, controls, thermostat, and evaporator coil of a room air conditioner is through the front grille, which is held to the housing of the unit by retaining screws or spring clips. Disassemble the control panel by removing the control knobs and lifting the panel off. The knobs may be friction-fit on shafts; pull them straight out and off the shafts. Or the knobs may have tiny setscrews at the base of the knob; loosen these screws and pull off the knobs. The escutcheon plate of each knob is screwed to the frame of the appliance. On some models, the working parts of the air conditioner can be removed from the housing shell by removing a series of screws. On others, the cabinet can be disassembled, sides and top. But for most repairs, only the grille and the control panel must be removed.

Filter. At the beginning of every cooling season, and once a month during the season, remove the front grille and clean or replace the filter. If you live in a very dusty area, clean or replace the filter more often. Most room air conditioners have a washable filter, which looks like sponge rubber. Clean the filter with a solution of mild household detergent and water; rinse well. Let the filter dry completely before reinstalling it. Some units have a throw-away filter, similar to a furnace filter. When this type of filter becomes dirty, replace it with a new one of the same type.

Power Cord. The power cord that connects the air conditioner to the wall outlet may become worn, and fail to supply electricity to the unit. To check the cord, remove the control panel. Unscrew the cord terminals and then attach a test wire across the bare lead wires. Hook the clips of a volt-ohm-milliammeter (VOM), set to the R × 1 scale, to the prongs of the cord's plug. If the meter reads zero, the cord is functioning; if the meter reads higher than zero, replace the cord. For complete testing and cord/plug replacement procedures, see the chapter on appliances.

Evaporator and Condenser Coils. Clean the evaporator and condenser coils at the beginning of the cooling season and every month during the season; if you live in a very dusty area, clean the coils more often. Use a vacuum cleaner on these components. If the fins on the coils are bent, straighten them with a fin comb, sold at most appliance parts outlets. Fin combs are designed to slide into the spaces between the fins. Use the fin comb carefully; the fins are made of light-gauge aluminum, and are easily damaged.

Switch. The selector switch, directly behind the control panel, turns the unit on. If the air conditioner does not run at any setting, and it is receiving power, chances are the switch is faulty. To correct the problem, remove

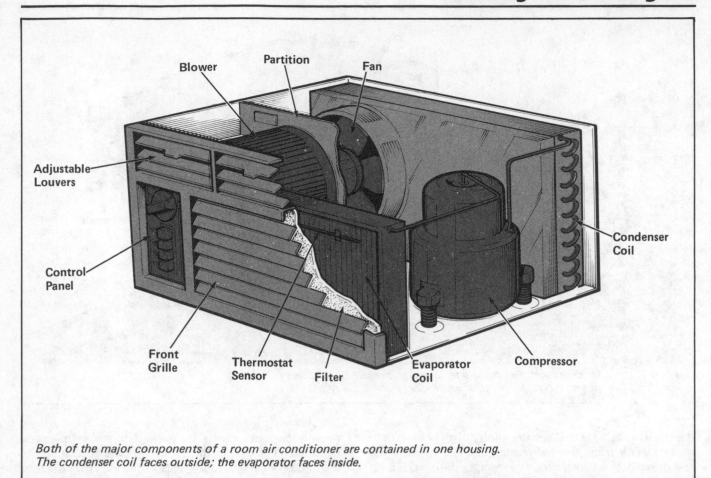

Both of the major components of a room air conditioner are contained in one housing.
The condenser coil faces outside; the evaporator faces inside.

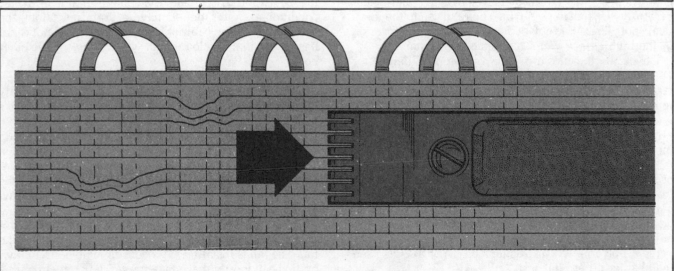

If the fins on the condenser coil are bent, straighten them with a fin comb.
Use the comb carefully; the fins are made of light-gauge aluminum, and are easily damaged.

the control panel and locate the switch. Check the switch terminals for burnt insulation or burn-like marks on the terminals; if you see any indication of burning, replace the switch with a new one of the same type. The switch is held to the control panel or frame with screws; unscrew it and connect the new one the same way. If,

after checking, you determine that the problem may not be the switch, call a professional service person.

Thermostat. The thermostat is located behind the control panel; to test and/or replace this component, remove the grille and the control panel from the unit. The

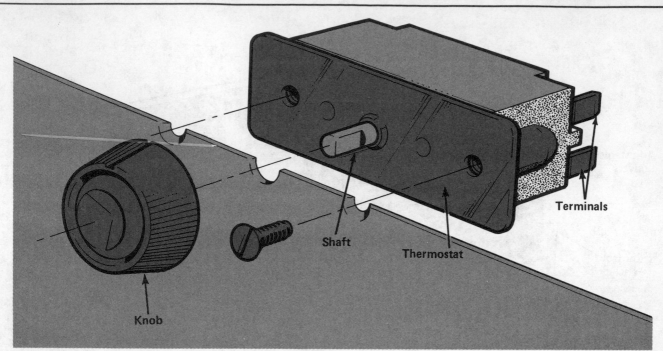

If the thermostat on a room air conditioner is faulty, remove the screws or clips that hold it in place, and replace it with a new one of the same type.

thermostat has a special sensing bulb attached to it; this part extends from the thermostat into the evaporator coil area. Its role is to sense the temperature, which is controlled by the thermostat. Remove the thermostat carefully; the sensing bulb must be returned to the identical spot. To make replacement easier, tag the location of the bulb before you remove the thermostat.

Check the thermostat with a volt-ohm-milliammeter (VOM), set to the R × 1 scale. Clip the probes of the tester to the terminals of the thermostat, and turn the temperature control dial to its coldest setting. If the meter reads zero, the thermostat is functioning properly; if the reading is higher than zero, replace the thermostat with a new one of the same type. The thermostat is held to the control panel or frame with screws, clips, or metal tabs; connect the new thermostat the same way the old one was connected.

If the thermostat has more than two lead wires connected to it—not counting the sensing bulb wire—do not try to test or replace it; call a professional service person. For detailed instructions on using a VOM, see the chapter on appliances.

Drain Ports. As the air conditioner operates, condensed moisture and water vapor from the evaporator coil are funneled through drain ports or an opening between the partition or barrier between the evaporator coil and the condenser coil. At this point, the fan blows the moisture against the condenser coil, where the water is dissipated. These drain ports can become clogged with dirt. The result is water leaking from the appliance, usually through the bottom of the grille. To prevent clogging, clean the ports with a short piece of clothes hanger wire or the blade of a pocket knife, at the beginning of every cooling season and every month during the season. Also check the condenser side of the air conditioner. Some models have a drain port along the bottom edge of the cabinet frame. If your air conditioner has this drain port, clean it out when you clean the other ports.

Fan. When a fan malfunctions, the problem is usually loose or dirty blades. If the fan doesn't work, or if it's noisy, cleaning and tightening will usually fix it.

First, open the cabinet and locate the fan. With a vacuum and/or a soft cloth, clean away any debris. Then check the fan blade on the motor shaft for looseness. The blade is fastened to the shaft with a setscrew at the hub of the blade; tighten the setscrew with a screwdriver or an Allen wrench. If the air conditioner has a round vent fan, tighten the fan on the motor shaft by inserting a long-bladed screwdriver through a port in the fan. The fan is installed in its housing with bolts, and vibration can loosen these fasteners. Tighten them with a wrench.

Most air conditioner fan motors are permanently lubricated and sealed at the factory, but some have oil ports for lubrication. If the fan has oil ports, apply several drops of No. 20 nondetergent motor oil (not all-purpose oil) to each port at the beginning of the cooling season.

If you suspect the fan motor is faulty, test it with a VOM. Disconnect the terminal wires from the terminals and clip the probes of the VOM, set to the R × 1 scale,

Room Air Conditioner Troubleshooting Chart

PROBLEM	POSSIBLE CAUSE	SOLUTION
Unit doesn't run	1. No power.	1. Check power cord, plug, and outlet. Check for blown fuse or tripped circuit breaker at main entrance panel; restore circuit.
	2. Motor overload or safety shutoff.	2. Wait 30 minutes; press reset button. Repeat if necessary.
	3. Switch faulty.	3. Check terminals and insulation; if burns are evident, replace switch. If switch looks all right, call a professional.
Fuses blow	1. Circuit overloaded.	1. Put on different circuit.
	2. Voltage low.	2. Call a professional or the power company.
Cooling inadequate	1. Thermostat set too high.	1. Lower thermostat setting 5 degrees.
	2. Filter dirty.	2. Clean or replace filter.
	3. Coils dirty.	3. Clean coils.
	4. Condenser blocked from outside.	4. Make sure outside of unit is not blocked.
	5. Motor faulty.	5. Call a professional.
	6. Compressor faulty.	6. Call a professional.
	7. Coolant leak.	7. Call a professional.
Fan runs, but unit doesn't cool	1. Thermostat set too high.	1. Lower thermostat setting 5 degrees.
	2. Thermostat faulty.	2. Test thermostat; if faulty, replace or call a professional.
	3. Coils dirty.	3. Clean coils.
	4. Motor faulty.	4. Call a professional.
	5. Compressor faulty.	5. Call a professional.
Unit cools, but fan doesn't run	1. Control switch set wrong.	1. Reset switch; try different settings.
	2. Fan clogged.	2. Clean and tighten fan blades.
	3. Fan blades bent.	3. Straighten fan blades.
	4. Fan motor faulty.	4. Replace fan motor or call a professional.
Unit turns on and off repeatedly	1. Coils dirty.	1. Clean coils.
	2. Filter dirty.	2. Clean or replace filter.

to the wires. If the meter reads between about 3 and 30 ohms, the motor is functioning properly; if the meter reads either zero or extremely high, replace the motor. To remove the motor, remove the fan, the power wires, and several mounting bolts; install the new motor with the reverse procedure. If the condenser coil must be moved to get the fan out, however, do not try to remove the motor; call a professional service person. For detailed instructions on using a VOM, see the chapter on appliances.

Motor and Compressor. If problems occur in the motor or compressor of the air conditioner, call a professional service person.

Furniture

Unlike most of the other components that make up your home, your furniture is movable—it goes with you when you move, it's rearranged or shifted periodically, and it may be handed down for generations. You add to your furniture collection gradually, and you may end up with more old pieces than new. Because it gets moved around, and because it takes a lot of abuse over years of service, your furniture needs regular care to keep it looking good. And when it needs repairing—whether the problem is in the finish or the wood, in the surface or the structure—you should know how to do the job yourself. Many people are afraid to do more to a finished wood surface than polish it, but this is a groundless fear. Once you know how your furniture is put together, you're equipped for anything—with patience and a little know-how, you can repair the finish, and then go on to repair the structure, too.

How Furniture Is Made

Like all the other components of your home, furniture is easy to work with when you know how it's put together. Essentially, all furniture is made to provide comfort and convenience, and judged on the basis of how well it succeeds in providing them. To function well, all furniture—no matter what type and age—must be sturdy, steady, and securely joined. Of course, there's more to good furniture than sturdy legs. Good wood and workmanship make good furniture; age enhances its value; and style is, if not essential, at least important. All of these factors affect the quality and usefulness of your furniture, and the techniques you need to know.

The Finish

The most common furniture problems involve the finish, the coating that protects the wood and gives it its glossy surface. Most furniture finishes are surface coatings; they protect the wood by forming a solid layer on top of it. Shellac, lacquer, and varnish, the most common furniture finishes, are all surface coatings. Other finishes, such as oil and penetrating resin, sink into the wood; they don't form a surface coating, but protect the wood by hardening inside the fibers. A damaged finish

coating can be repaired easily when the damage doesn't extend into the wood underneath it. When the damage goes all the way through the finish and into the wood, repairs will involve spot refinishing—an unpredictable technique, and not always a successful one, especially when the wood is stained. Whenever you work on the finish, bear in mind that the less finish you remove, the better your results are likely to be. If the surface is badly damaged, consider refinishing, and invest in a good book on the subject.

Many repair jobs, and most restoration projects, require a knowledge of the finish you're working with. If you don't know what the finish is, you could end up damaging a perfectly good finish, or wasting your time on a technique that won't work. This knowledge is also essential when you have to match one finish to another.

In most cases, the only distinction that really matters is the difference among the three basic natural, or clear, finishes: shellac, lacquer, and varnish. The pigmented finishes, such as paint or enamel, are easy to identify. The only other finishes you may encounter are oil, wax, and penetrating sealers, identifiable by touch and by the absence of a high gloss. On most furniture, a clear finish is one of the basic three—shellac, lacquer, or varnish. Modern furniture is often lacquered, but the finish on a piece made before about 1860 is usually shellac; lacquer and varnish were not developed until the mid-1800s. A varnish finish is rare on factory-finished pieces, because varnish is hard to apply and requires a long drying period in a dust-free environment. Very old furniture may be finished with oil, wax, or milk paint, and many fine furniture pieces are French-polished, a variation of the shellac finish. In general, old finishes are natural products; brand-new finishes, such as the polyurethanes, may be synthetics.

Before you make any extensive repairs to a finish, take a minute to identify it. First, test the finish with denatured alcohol; rub a little alcohol onto an inconspicuous finished area. If the finish dissolves, it's shellac. If it partially dissolves, it's probably a combination of shellac and lacquer. Test it again with a mixture of denatured alcohol and lacquer thinner; this should completely dissolve the finish.

If alcohol doesn't affect the finish, rub a little lacquer thinner on an inconspicuous finished spot. If the area turns rough and then smooth again, the finish is lacquer; if the finish crinkles and doesn't get smooth again, it's some type of varnish. If neither alcohol nor lacquer thinner affects it, the finish is varnish.

If the piece of furniture is painted, test the finish with ammonia; very old pieces may be finished with milk paint, which is dissolved only by ammonia. If the piece of furniture is very dirty or encrusted with wax, clean it first with a mixture of denatured alcohol, white vinegar, and kerosene, in equal parts. Then test it with the various solvents.

The Structure: Basic Joinery

All furniture is put together in a series of joints, and structural problems often involve joint weakening or failure. Some joints are simple, some complicated; some types are stronger than others. The joints used in good furniture are usually stronger than those in cheap pieces, but age and abuse can take their toll even when the original construction was good. To prevent more serious damage, all joints should be repaired as soon as possible when they loosen or separate.

Very old furniture is usually put together with mortise-and-tenon joints, which consist of a prong held in a hole. The dovetail joint is used in good-quality furniture; butt and lapped joints, the weakest types, are also the easiest to make, and are often used in cheap pieces. Other joints used in furniture manufacturing include blank or stopped mortise-and-tenon joints, dadoes, and stopped or dovetailed dadoes, miters, and doweled, rabbeted, or splined joints.

Mortise-and-Tenon Joints. In this type of joint, a prong or tongue of wood—the tenon—is secured in a hole—the mortise—in the joining piece. If the joint is blank or stopped, the mortise doesn't extend completely through the joining piece, and the end of the tenon is not visible on the outside of the joint. Mortise-and-tenon joints are extremely strong; they're used chiefly in chairs and tables.

Dovetail Joints. Dovetail joints consist of wedge-shaped openings, the dovetails, holding matching pins cut in the joining piece. These joints are the pride of cabinetmakers, in both old and new furniture. The through dovetail is the early version; in this joint, the dovetail goes completely through both pieces of wood. The pins in handmade dovetails are usually narrower than the spaces between the pins. On a real antique piece, only a few dovetails are used, and the tails and pins don't match exactly; with modern equipment, the tails and the pins are the same width, and more dovetails are used in each joint. Some dovetail joints are blind; the pins don't extend completely through the joining piece, and only the top or face of the joint is visible.

Dado Joints. A dado is a slot cut into the face or end of a piece of wood; the joining piece fits into this slot. In a simple dado joint, the slot goes completely across the

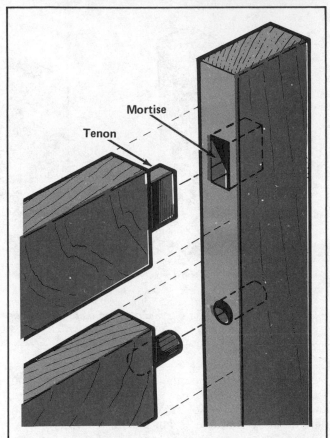

The mortise-and-tenon joint, used chiefly in chair and table frames, is very strong. Both square and round tenons are used in furniture construction.

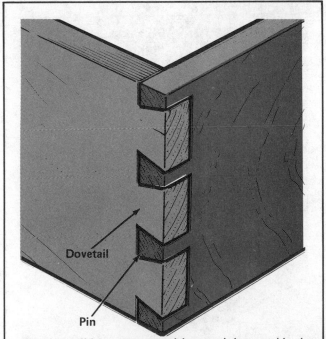

The dovetail is a strong, precision-cut joint, used in the best furniture. On antiques, dovetails were hand-cut; these dovetails are less even than machine-cut joints.

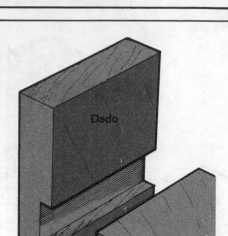
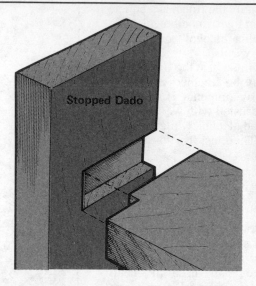
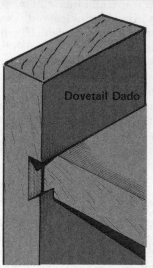

In the dado joint (left), a slot or groove is cut into one piece to hold the end of the joining piece. The groove of a stopped or blind dado (center) does not extend completely across the wood. The dovetail dado (right) is cut with a dovetail at the bottom for extra strength.

wood, and the edges of the joining piece are visible along the edges of the base piece. In a stopped or blind dado, the joint does not extend completely across the face of the wood, and is not visible from the edges.

Dadoes and stopped dadoes have considerable shear strength, and are used chiefly for shelving. The dovetail dado is a dado with a slight dovetail at the bottom; it's a fancy cabinet joint, strong and especially good-looking. In very old furniture, a dovetail dado joint is a real work of art because of the time the cabinetmaker had to spend to cut it.

Butt Joints. In this type of joint, the joining pieces are simply butted together—face to face, edge to edge, or face to edge—with no integral fastener. Butt joints are weak, and are sometimes fastened or held together with metal surface plates. Wood or metal butt joints held with a metal fastener such as a nail, screw, or mending plate, or a specially machined metal or plastic fitting, are called mechanical joints; they're used in chairs, tables, dressers, and cabinet pieces.

Lapped Joints. Lapped joints—cross-laps, half-laps, and sloped laps—are cut with both joining pieces notched or slanted to the same depth. Cross-laps are used to join crossing pieces; half-laps and sloped laps are used to join the ends of long pieces. Lapped joints offer a large glue area, but they aren't particularly strong; they're often used in drawer guide framing pieces, and may be pinned with nails or screws from the back. To strengthen lap joints, some cabinetmakers cut them with a dovetail configuration.

Miter Joints. In a miter, the joining pieces are cut at a 45-degree angle and joined to form a right angle. Miters are used for decorative molding and for frames; they are very weak, and are often reinforced with dowels, splines, or mechanical fasteners. Many cabinet-type pieces have mitered corner joints, almost always rein-

In the butt joint, the two joining pieces are simply butted together. Nails, screws, or metal mending plates are sometimes used for reinforcement.

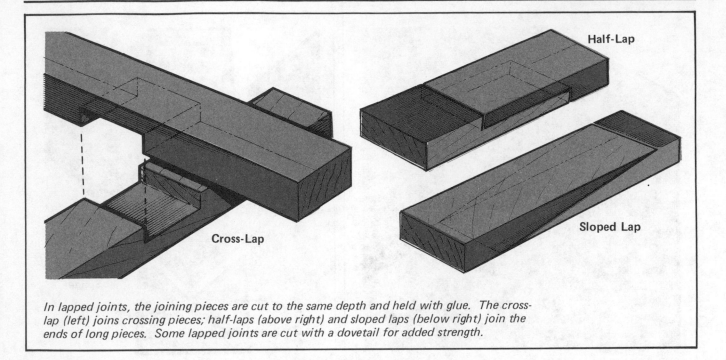

Half-Lap

Cross-Lap

Sloped Lap

In lapped joints, the joining pieces are cut to the same depth and held with glue. The cross-lap (left) joins crossing pieces; half-laps (above right) and sloped laps (below right) join the ends of long pieces. Some lapped joints are cut with a dovetail for added strength.

forced by dowels or by a plywood spline running the length of each joint. In less expensive furniture, miter joints may be supported with a strip of wood nailed or screwed to the inside corner of the joint. Sometimes triangular glue blocks are used for strength; the blocks may be reinforced by screws.

Doweled Joints. The doweled joint is a simple variation of the mortise-and-tenon joint, with dowels instead of a cut tenon holding the joining pieces together. Doweled joints require precision equipment. They are strong, and are common in chairs, tables, and cabinets, usually on stretchers and other framing pieces.

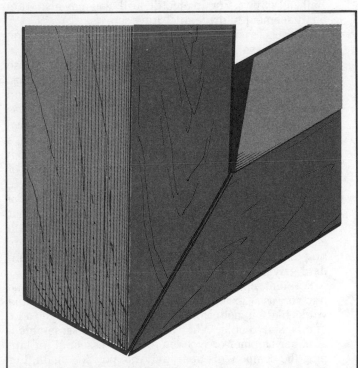

The miter joint, used for frames and molding, consists of two pieces cut at a 45-degree angle, joined in a right angle.

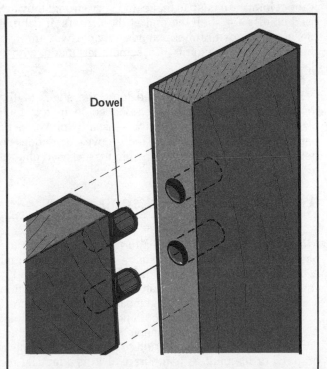

Dowel

The doweled joint is a variation of the mortise-and-tenon, with dowels holding the pieces together.

In the rabbet joint, one or both joining members are notched. Screws or nails are usually used for reinforcement.

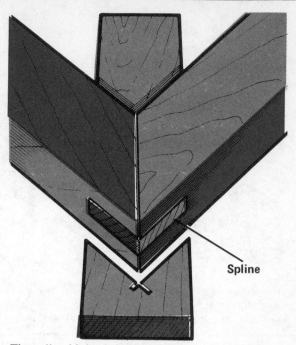

The splined joint is held together by a reinforcing spline, fitted into matching grooves in the joining members.

Rabbet Joints. The rabbet is a reinforced butt joint, with one or both joining members notched to fit together; it is usually reinforced with screws or nails. Rabbet joints are easy to make and very strong; they are used chiefly for shelving and at the corners of cabinet pieces. A stopped rabbet extends only partway through the wood. Rabbet joints are sometimes made with a dado variation.

Splined Joints. In a splined joint, the edges of the joining pieces are grooved or dadoed to match each other, and a reinforcing spline—usually plywood or hardboard—is inserted into the grooves or dadoes to hold the pieces together. Splined joints are used chiefly to join narrow boards.

The Furniture Workshop

Most of the tools required for furniture repairs are the basic tools of the home workshop—a claw hammer and a ball-peen hammer, screwdrivers, a hacksaw and a fine-toothed backsaw, a putty knife, a combination square, a steel rule and a tape measure, utility and craft knives, wood chisels, a smoothing plane, and a block plane. For matching components and marking cuts accurately, you'll also need friction-point calipers and a bradawl or ice pick. A hand-crank drill is adequate for most furniture jobs, but if your budget permits, buy a variable-speed electric drill; the variable speed lets you start drilling slowly and then increase the drill RPM as

the bit catches in the wood. With either type of drill, you'll need an assortment of drill bits, from 1/16 inch up to 1/4 inch, and small and medium-size countersinks for flathead screws. For an electric drill, you may also want an attachment to drive and draw screws.

The success of your structural repairs will depend on good clamping, so you must have a good selection of clamps. You'll probably use them more than you use any other tool. Start with half a dozen or so C-clamps, two each in small, medium, and large sizes. A strap clamp, a strap with a buckle device on the end of it, is required for holding irregular surfaces together; it is essential for joint repairs. Rope can be substituted for a strap clamp, but you can't get adequate pressure from rope unless you wedge a stick between two strands of the rope, twisting it firmly. This isn't always possible where space is tight. Other clamps that can be useful are wooden hand screws—which, unlike the other types, are expensive—and bar clamps, steel bars with clamping devices on each end. It's more economical to buy bar clamp fixtures, which fit on the ends of standard galvanized steel pipe.

For joint repairs, two other tools are useful. The glue injector, used to force glue into loose joints, looks and works like a hypodermic syringe, and can save you a lot of time and trouble. When a joint must be disassembled, a rubber hammer or wooden mallet is essential for tapping the components apart and into position again. For mending broken parts, you'll also need a doweling jig or dowel center points. The doweling jig is a clamp-like device that fits against the edge of a part; it has an ad-

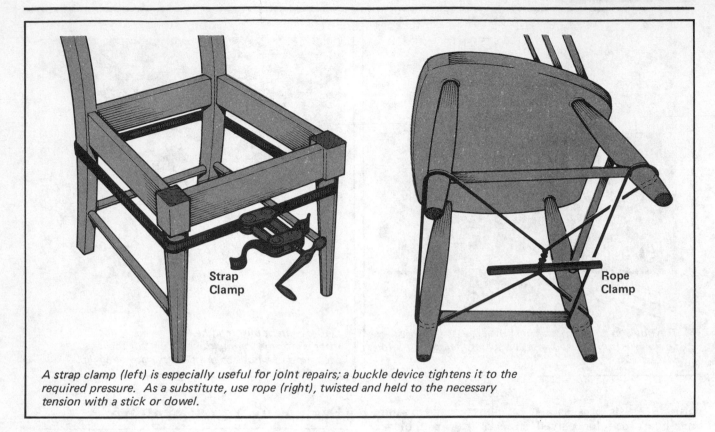

A strap clamp (left) is especially useful for joint repairs; a buckle device tightens it to the required pressure. As a substitute, use rope (right), twisted and held to the necessary tension with a stick or dowel.

justable sleeve to accept a drill bit. The doweling jig is used where dowel holes must be drilled into both joining parts. Dowel center points, small points used to mark the drilling location, can also be used, but they do not guide the drill bit; it's much harder to align the dowel holes. A doweling jig is more expensive, but if you'll be doing much repair work, it's worth the price. When you're working on the finish, you'll need paint-

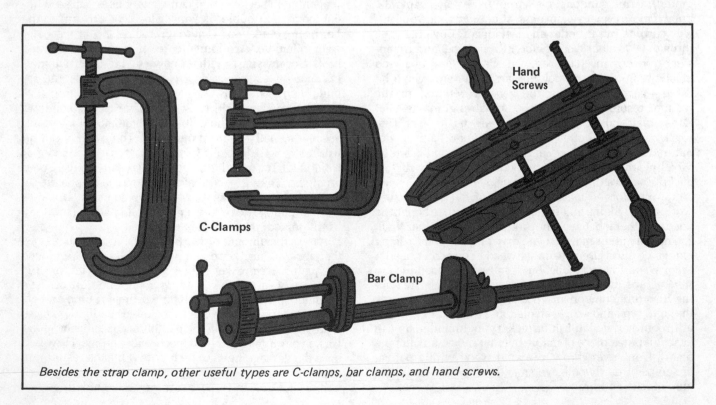

Besides the strap clamp, other useful types are C-clamps, bar clamps, and hand screws.

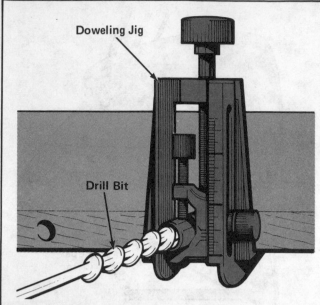

Doweling Jig

Drill Bit

The doweling jig clamps against the edge of the part to be doweled; an adjustable sleeve guides the drill bit into the wood.

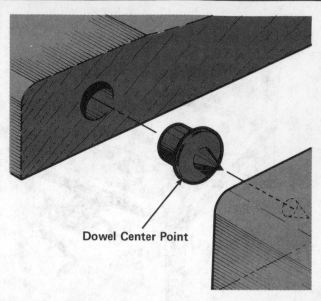

Dowel Center Point

Dowel center points can be used to mark the drilling location for the joining dowel hole, but they are less accurate and harder to use than the doweling jig.

brushes, artists' brushes, and sometimes a padded sanding block or—for curved surfaces—a foam block. Crack-filling may call for a plastic credit card, a palette knife, and sometimes an alcohol lamp to heat the filler.

The materials you'll need will vary with the repair job, but there are some basics you should have on hand. For stain removal and smoothing, you'll need several grades of fine sandpaper—garnet paper is acceptable, but the more expensive papers, aluminum oxide and silicon carbide, wear better and last longer. Buy grades 00 through 0000 steel wool, grade FFF pumice, and rottenstone powder for stain removal. Carpenters' glue and plastic resin or resorcinol glue are also items you'll be using—carpenters' glue for general repairs, plastic resin or resorcinol where structural strength is needed. Other materials to keep on hand are paste wax, fine black steel wire, boiled linseed oil, mineral spirits, denatured alcohol and lacquer thinner, and wood fillers—wood plastic, water putty, and putty sticks. Buy shellac sticks and wax scratch-mending sticks as you need them, in colors to match the finish of the piece you're working on. Stains and finishes should also be bought as you need them, because they may deteriorate over time.

The only other material you may need, if you're doing extensive furniture repairs, is wood. You won't need a lot of wood for most jobs, but it's always a good idea to save scraps, both hardwood and softwood. For replacing furniture components, use any piece of wood that's the right type and size—an old table leaf, a birch dowel or broom handle, an ash or hickory tool handle, an ash baseball bat, a piece of maple butcher block, an old pine board. Don't ever throw away old wood with a patina, or scraps of hardwood; even small scraps are useful for glue blocks and braces.

Evaluating Your Furniture

When your furniture is damaged, you must—as with any other repair—be able to assess the damage so that you can repair it properly. Is the finish disfigured by burns, scratches, or stains? This type of damage may affect only the surface, and can usually be repaired without too much trouble. Is veneer loose or broken? Is the hardware damaged? These problems too are usually easy to handle. Are joints loose, or is part of the wood broken or missing? With a knowledge of the basic joinery techniques, you can repair damaged parts and rebuild damaged joints.

When you're working with salvage or second-hand furniture, assessing the damage is even more important, because a really beat-up piece of furniture may not be worth saving. Most old furniture is fairly sturdy, or it wouldn't have survived; but it may also have some problems. Take a good look at it. Are the legs even? Is the piece sturdy? Does it wobble? Do doors and drawers work properly? Are the joints well made? Are they firmly joined, or have they separated?

Assess the amount of work you'll have to do to restore the piece. Is hardware complete and tight? Are hinges adequate? Are drawer guides or dust panels missing? If the piece of furniture is in fairly good condition, or if it's definitely an antique, it will be worth your time and effort to restore. If the wood is broken or badly damaged, there are parts missing, or the joinery is inferior, don't waste your time unless the piece is an antique. How bad does the damage have to be before it makes restoration impractical? This depends on how much work you're willing to do, but there are a few guidelines.

First, look for dry rot or insect damage. Dry rot cannot be repaired; the rotted component must be replaced, and this is a custom job. Insect damage, if the entire piece of wood is not affected, can sometimes be repaired; if this is the problem, restoration may be worth the effort. To check for dry rot and insect damage, push an ice pick or a knife blade into the wood. If there's little or no resistance, the wood is damaged.

Broken parts are sometimes repairable, but not always. If a part is split or wobbly, it can probably be repaired quickly. If it's broken off flush at the joint, the job is more difficult, because a replacement part must usually be custom-made to match the rest of the piece. This can involve expensive equipment or a professional woodworker, and the piece of furniture may not be worth the cost or the effort.

On veneered pieces, the condition of the veneer is very important. Has the veneer separated from the base, or is it damaged? Are there big pieces missing? Separated veneer is easy to reglue if it's intact, but replacing damaged or missing veneer can be expensive. If a large section of veneer must be replaced, the cost may be prohibitive.

If the piece is structurally sound, don't be discouraged by repairable problems. Wobbly joints can be reglued; missing hardware can be replaced. Coats and coats of old paint, lacquer, or shellac may be concealing beautiful wood; in this case, consider refinishing, and invest in a good book on the subject. If you like the piece of furniture, if it's worth saving, and especially if it's an antique, restoration is worth all the time and patience you'll put into it.

Making Surface Repairs

Old or new, furniture often shows evidence of hard service: stains, scratches, burns, and all the other signs of use and abuse. Veneer may be loose or broken; hardware may be missing; the wood may be discolored. Unless the damage is severe or extensive, most of these problems are easy to deal with. Surface repairs aren't difficult, but it can be hard to tell what you're getting into. If only the surface is affected, the damage is usually easy to repair; if the wood is damaged too, you may have to refinish part or all of the piece. In this case, consider refinishing, and invest in a book on the subject.

Stains and Discoloration

White Spots. Shellac and lacquer finishes are not resistant to water and alcohol; spills and condensation from glasses can leave permanent white spots or rings on these finishes. To remove these white spots, first try polishing the surface with liquid furniture polish; buff the surface firmly. If this doesn't work, lightly wipe the stained surface with denatured alcohol. Use as little alcohol as possible; too much will damage the finish.

If neither polishing nor alcohol treatment removes the white spots, the damaged finish must be treated with abrasives. For a very gentle abrasive, mix cigarette ashes to a paste with a few drops of vegetable oil, mineral oil, or boiled linseed oil. Rub the ash-oil paste over the stained area, along the grain of the wood, and then wipe the surface clean with a soft cloth. If necessary, repeat the procedure; stubborn spots may require several applications. Then wax and polish the entire surface.

If rubbing with ashes is not effective, go over the stained area with a mixture of rottenstone and linseed oil. Mix the rottenstone and oil to a thin paste, and rub the paste gently over the stain, along the grain of the wood. Rottenstone is a fast-cutting abrasive, so rub very carefully, and check the surface frequently to make sure you aren't cutting too deep. As soon as the white spots disappear, stop rubbing and wipe the wood clean with a soft cloth. Then apply two coats of hard furniture wax and buff the wood to a shine.

Blushing. Blushing, a white haze over a large surface or an entire piece of furniture, is a common problem with old shellac and lacquer finishes. The discoloration is caused by moisture, and it can sometimes be removed the same way white spots are removed. Buff the surface lightly and evenly with No. 0000 steel wool dipped in boiled linseed oil; work with the grain of the wood, rubbing evenly on the entire surface, until the white haze disappears. Then wipe the wood clean with a soft cloth, apply two coats of hard furniture wax, and buff the surface to a shine.

Black Spots. Black spots are caused by water that has penetrated the finish completely and entered the wood. They cannot be removed without damage to the finish. If the spots are on a clearly defined surface, you may be

Rubbing with oil and fine abrasives is often effective in removing spots and blushing. Rub along the grain of the wood, and then wipe the surface clean.

213

able to remove the finish from this surface only; otherwise, the entire piece of furniture will have to be refinished. When the finish has been removed, bleach the entire stained surface with a solution of oxalic acid, as directed by the manufacturer. Then refinish the piece.

Ink Stains. Ink stains that have penetrated the finish, like black water spots, cannot be removed without refinishing. Less serious ink stains can sometimes be removed. Lightly buff the stained area with a cloth moistened with mineral spirits; then rinse the wood with clean water on a soft cloth. Dry the surface thoroughly, and then wax and polish it.

If this does not remove the ink, lightly rub the stained area, along the grain of the wood, with No. 0000 steel wool moistened with mineral spirits. Then wipe the surface clean and wax and polish it. This treatment may damage the finish; if necessary, refinish the damaged spot as discussed below. If the area is badly damaged, the entire surface or piece of furniture will have to be refinished.

Grease, Tar, Paint, Crayon, and Lipstick Spots. These spots usually affect only the surface of the finish. To remove wet paint, use the appropriate solvent on a soft cloth—mineral spirits for oil-base paint, water for latex paint. To remove dry paint or other materials, very carefully lift the surface residue with the edge of a putty knife. Do *not* scrape the wood, or you'll scratch the finish. When the surface material has been removed, buff the area very lightly along the grain of the wood with

Spot-staining is tricky, but it is sometimes successful. Apply stain to the repair area with an artists' brush.

No. 0000 steel wool moistened with mineral spirits. Then wax and polish the entire surface.

Wax and Gum Spots. Wax and gum usually come off quickly, but they must be removed carefully to prevent damage to the finish. To make the wax or gum brittle, press it with a packet of ice wrapped in a towel or paper towel. Let the deposit harden; then lift it off with your thumbnail. The hardened wax or gum should pop off the surface with very little pressure. If necessary, repeat the ice application. Do *not* scrape the deposit off, or you'll scratch the finish.

When the wax or gum is completely removed, buff the area very lightly along the grain of the wood with No. 0000 steel wool moistened with mineral spirits. Then wax and polish the entire surface.

Spot Refinishing

Any repair that involves removing the damaged finish completely—deep scratches, gouges, burns, or any other damage—also involves refinishing the repair area. Spot refinishing is not always easy, and it's not always successful, especially on stained surfaces. If the damage isn't too bad, it's worth trying. If you'll have to touch up several areas on one surface, you're probably better off refinishing the surface or the piece of furniture completely.

To stain one area on a surface, use an oil-base stain that matches the surrounding stain; you may have to mix stains to get a good match. Test the stain on an inconspicuous unfinished part of the wood before working on the finished surface.

Before applying the stain, sand the damaged area smooth with fine-grit sandpaper, and wipe the surface clean. Apply the stain to the damaged area with an artists' brush or a clean cloth, covering the entire bare area. Let the stain set for 15 minutes and then wipe it off with a clean cloth. If the color is too light, apply another coat of stain, wait 15 minutes, and wipe again. Repeat this procedure until you're satisfied with the color; then let the stain dry according to the manufacturer's instructions.

Lightly buff the stained surface with No. 0000 steel wool, and wipe it clean with a tack cloth. Apply a new coat of the same finish already on the surface—varnish, penetrating resin, shellac, or lacquer—over the newly stained area, feathering out the new finish into the surrounding old finish. Let the new finish dry for one to two days, and lightly buff the patched area with No. 0000 steel wool. Finally, wax the entire surface with hard paste wax, and polish it to a shine.

Surface Damage

Scratches. To hide a small scratch quickly, break the meat of a walnut, pecan, or Brazil nut and rub it along the scratch. The oil in the nut meat will darken the raw scratch, making it less conspicuous.

When many shallow scratches are present, apply

hard paste wax to the surface with No. 0000 steel wool, stroking very lightly along the grain of the wood. Then buff the surface with a soft cloth. If the scratches still show, apply one or two more coats of hard paste wax to the surface; let each coat dry thoroughly and buff it to a shine before applying the next coat.

For one or two deeper scratches, wax furniture-patching sticks are usually effective. These retouching sticks, made in several wood colors, are available at hardware and sometimes grocery stores; choose a stick to match the finish. To use the wax stick, run it firmly along the scratch, applying enough pressure to fill the scratch with wax. Remove any excess wax with the edge of a credit card or other thin plastic card. Let the wax dry; then buff the surface with a soft cloth.

Badly scratched surfaces should usually be refinished, but to hide one or two very deep scratches, you may be able to stain the raw area to match, as detailed above. Apply oil-base stain with an artists' brush, drawing it carefully along the scratch; let it stand for 15 minutes and wipe it off. If necessary, repeat this procedure until the scratch matches the rest of the wood. Let the area dry completely, as directed by the stain manufacturer; then apply hard paste wax and buff the waxed surface to a shine.

Dings. Dings are tiny chips in the finish, usually caused by a sharp blow. The wood may not be affected. To repair a ding, use a sharp craft knife to remove any loose finish in or around the ding. Work carefully, scraping the damaged spot with the flat, sharp edge of the knife blade; do *not* scratch the spot. Then very carefully feather the edges of the ding with No. 0000 steel wool.

Clean the ding area with a soft cloth moistened in mineral spirits, and let it dry completely. Then, with an artists' brush, carefully apply new finish to the spot—varnish, shellac, lacquer, or enamel—to match the rest of the finish. The spot will be very noticeable at first. Let the finish dry; it will be glossy. Then lightly buff the spot with No. 0000 steel wool, and wax and polish the entire piece of furniture. The ding should blend perfectly when the job is complete.

Dents. Small, shallow dents in pine and other soft woods are usually easy to remove; large and deep dents, especially in hard wood, are harder to repair. Dents are easiest to remove from bare wood. Very large, shallow dents are probably best left untreated. Very deep dents should be filled, as detailed below for cracks and gouges.

On finished surfaces, you'll have to remove the finish around the damaged area. Using fine-grit sandpaper, carefully remove the finish for about 1/2 inch around the spot. To raise the wood in the dent, apply a few drops of water to the dent and let the water penetrate the wood for a day or so. Do *not* wet the entire surface. This treatment may be enough to raise the dent, especially if the dent is shallow and the wood is soft.

If this doesn't raise the dent, soak a cloth in water and wring it out. Place the damp cloth, folded in several layers, over the dent; then press the cloth firmly with a warm iron. Be careful not to touch the iron directly to the wood. This moist heat may be enough to swell the wood and raise the dent. If it isn't, apply a commercial wood-swelling liquid to the area and give it time to work—about a day or so, as directed by the manufacturer.

For deep dents that can't be raised with water, heat, or wood sweller, use a fine straight pin or needle to drive a series of holes in the dent. Pound the straight pin in about 1/4 inch, and carefully pull it out with pliers; the holes should be as small as possible. Then treat the dent as above. The pinholes let the water penetrate the wood's surface, and if you're careful, they won't show when the wood has been raised.

After the dent has been raised, let the wood dry for about a week, and then refinish the damaged area as above. Let the finish dry completely. Lightly buff the new finish with No. 0000 steel wool, and then wax and polish the entire surface.

Cracks and Gouges. Cracks and gouges should be filled so that they're level with the surface of the wood. For very small holes, like staple holes, wood-tone putty sticks can be used. If you can't match the wood, several colors can be mixed together. To use a putty stick, wipe it across the hole and smooth the surface with your finger. If you plan to finish or refinish the wood, let the putty dry for at least a week before proceeding further.

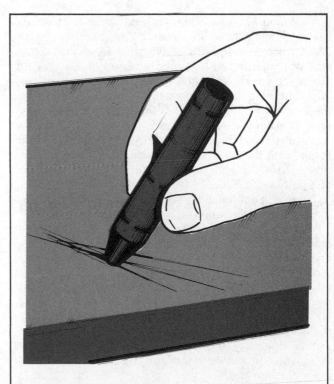

Wax patching sticks can be used to hide fairly deep scratches; press firmly to fill the scratch.

Use a fine pin or needle to drive a series of small holes in a stubborn dent; then swell the wood to raise the dent. The holes will not be visible.

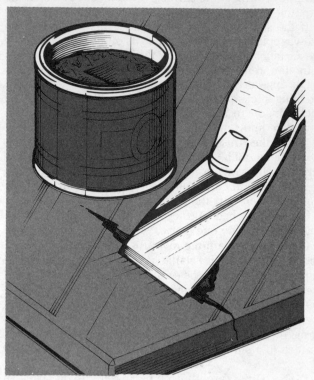

Fill deep cracks and gouges with wood plastic or water putty; leave the filler slightly high to allow for shrinkage as it dries. When the patch is dry, sand it smooth.

For larger holes, wood plastic and water putty are the easiest fillers. These fillers can be used on bare or finished wood; wood plastic is available in several colors, and water putty can be tinted with oil or water stain. However, wood plastic and water putty patches are usually noticeable, and may look darker than the wood. For the best results, test the patch on an inconspicuous surface to make sure the color is right.

To use wood plastic, carefully clean the crack or gouge with the tip of a craft knife, and then press the plastic firmly in with the tip of a craft knife or the edge of a putty knife. Wood plastic shrinks slightly as it dries, so press it in tightly and leave it mounded slightly above the surface of the wood.

Wood plastic dries fairly quickly, but let it set for at least two days. Then smooth the patch lightly with fine-grit sandpaper and buff the area with No. 0000 steel wool. If surrounding finish is involved, feather the edges so that the new patch blends in with it. Then, if necessary, stain the patch and buff it lightly with No. 0000 steel wool. Apply finish to match the rest of the surface, using an artists' brush and feathering the edges. Let the finish dry and then lightly buff it with No. 0000 steel wool; clean the area of any residue, and wax and polish the surface.

Water putty dries flint-hard, usually harder than the wood being patched. It's best used on bare wood. Water putty can be toned with oil and water stains, but you'll have to experiment to come up with a perfect match. To use water putty, mix the powder with water to the consistency of putty; then trowel it into the break with a putty knife, leaving the patch slightly high. Let the patch dry completely, and sand and steel-wool the area smooth and level with the surrounding surface. Finish the patch area as above, or finish the entire piece of furniture.

For the most professional patching job, use shellac sticks to fill cracks and gouges. Shellac sticks leave the least conspicuous patch, and are very effective on finished wood that's in good condition. Shellac sticks are available in several wood-tone colors; use a stick that matches the finish as closely as possible. Practice on scrap wood before working on a piece of furniture.

Carefully clean the crack or gouge with the tip of a craft knife. Shellac sticks must be heated and melted to fill the crack. The best heat source for this is an alcohol lamp or a propane torch turned to a low setting. Do not use a match to soften the stick; the smoke from the match may discolor the shellac. Do not use a range burner; liquid shellac could damage either gas or electric ranges. Hold the stick over the blade of a palette knife or a putty knife to prevent it from dripping.

To use a shellac stick, hold it to the heat source above the knife, until it has softened to about the consistency of glazing compound or putty. Then quickly press the softened shellac into the crack and smooth it with the

Heat the shellac stick over an alcohol lamp or a propane torch; hold a palette or putty knife between the stick and the flame to keep it from dripping.

When the shellac has softened to the consistency of putty, quickly press it into the crack, smoothing it in with the hot knife. Leave the patch slightly high.

hot knife. Make sure the soft shellac fills the break completely; it hardens quickly, so you'll have to work fast. Leave the patch slightly high. Then, with the heated putty knife blade, trowel the shellac smooth.

Let the patch set for one to two hours. When the shellac is hard, plane or sand the surface smooth and level. The finish surrounding the break usually doesn't have to be retouched, but the surface can be coated with shellac, if desired. To make the shellac match a satin-gloss finish, rub the surface smooth with No. 0000 steel wool and linseed oil.

To fill very deep holes, use wood plastic or water putty to fill the hole almost level. Let the filler dry completely, and then fill the indentation with a shellac stick. If a hole or split is very large, don't overlook the possibility of filling it with a piece of wood cut and trimmed to fit perfectly. If the patching wood can be taken from the piece of furniture in a spot that won't show, the repair may be almost impossible to detect.

Fit the wood patch into the hole or split; use carpenters' glue to bond it to the surrounding wood. Leave the patch slightly high. When the glue is completely dry, sand the plug smoothly level with the surface of the surrounding wood. Then refinish the piece of furniture.

Burns. Burns on furniture can range from scorches to deep char, but the usual problem is cigarette burns. Scorches from cigarettes or cigars are usually very easy to remove. Buff the scorched area with a fine steel wool pad moistened with mineral spirits until the scorch disappears. Then wipe it clean and wax and polish the surface.

More serious burns require the removal of the charred wood. Shallow burns, when repaired, will always leave a slight indentation in the wood, but this depression will not be conspicuous. Deep burn holes can be filled, as detailed above.

First, remove the damaged wood. With the flat sharp edge of a craft knife, very carefully scrape away the charred wood. For deep burns, use a curved blade. Do *not* scratch the burn area. Scrape away the char right to the bare wood, feathering out the edges. Any burned or scorched spots will show, so all the burn crust must be removed. Work carefully to avoid scratching the wood with the point of the knife.

If the surface is veneer, you must be *very* careful not to scrape through the veneer into the wood core. If the burn is deep enough to go through the veneer, the hole will have to be filled to the level of the core wood. The veneer will have to be patched, as detailed below.

When the charred wood has been completely removed, lightly sand the edges of the groove or trench to level it with the surrounding surface as much as possible. Press lightly into the groove with fine-grit sandpaper, removing only the char from the burned area; be careful not to damage the surrounding finish. If you're

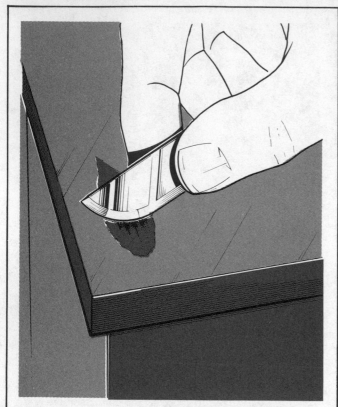

To remove a burn spot, scrape away the charred wood with a craft knife; feather the edges of the depression.

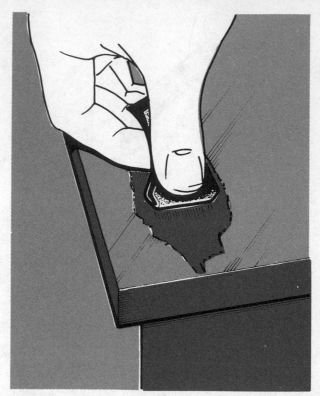

After removing the char, sand the burn area lightly to smooth it and level it out to the surrounding surface.

not sure all the burn has been removed, wet the sanded area. If water makes the burned area look burned again, you haven't removed all the char.

With deep burns, the groove left after the char is removed will probably be quite noticeable. Level the groove as much as possible with fine-grit sandpaper, but stay close to the edges of the groove. If you sand too far out from the burn area, the damaged area will be very visible as a wide saucer-shaped indentation. If the depression isn't too deep, try swelling the wood as detailed above for dents. If you're left with a deep gouge, the burn area can be filled with wood plastic or stick shellac, as above.

After smoothing out the burn, refinish the damaged area as above. Let the new finish dry for one or two days, and then lightly buff the patch with No. 0000 steel wool to blend the edges into the old finish. Finally, wax and polish the entire piece of furniture.

How to Repair Veneer

Because veneer is only a thin layer of wood, attached with glue to a solid base, it is very vulnerable to damage. On old furniture, the glue that holds the veneer is often not water-resistant. Prolonged humidity or exposure to water can soften the glue, letting the veneer blister, crack, or peel. Veneer is also easily damaged from the surface, and old veneers are often cracked, buckled,

or broken, with chips or entire pieces missing.

In most cases, as long as the veneer layer is basically in good shape, the thinness that makes it damage-prone also makes it easy to repair. Undamaged veneer can be reglued; chips and bare spots can be filled with matching veneer. If you're careful to match the grain, the repairs will hardly show.

Blisters. Small blisters in veneer can usually be flattened with heat. To protect the surface, set a sheet of wax paper and then a sheet of smooth cardboard on it, and cover the cardboard with a clean cloth. Press the blistered area firmly with a medium-hot iron; if there are several blisters, move the iron slowly and evenly back and forth. Be careful not to touch the exposed surface with the iron. Check the surface every few minutes or so as you work, and stop pressing as soon as the blisters have flattened. Leaving the cardboard in place, weight the repair area solidly for 24 hours. Then wax and polish the surface.

Large blisters must usually be slit, because the veneer has swelled. With a sharp craft knife or a single-edge razor blade, carefully cut the blister open down the middle, along the grain of the wood. Be careful not to cut into the base wood. Then cover the surface and apply heat as above, checking every few seconds as the glue softens; if the glue has deteriorated and does not soften, carefully scrape it out and insert a little carpenters' glue under the slit edges of the bubble with the tip of the knife. Be careful not to use too much glue; if necessary, wipe off any excess as the blister flattens. As soon as one edge of the slit bubble overlaps the other, carefully shave off the overlapping edge with a craft knife or razor blade. Heat the blister again; if the edges overlap further, shave the overlapping edge again. When the blister is completely flattened, weight the repair area solidly for 24 hours. Then wax and polish the entire surface.

Loose Veneer. Lifted veneer occurs most often at the corners of tabletops, on cabinet and dresser edges, legs, and drawer fronts. If the loose veneer is undamaged, it can be reglued.

First, remove the residue of old glue left on the back of the veneer and on the base wood. With a sharp craft knife or razor blade, carefully scrape out as much of the old glue as possible. Don't lift the veneer any further; if you bend it up, you'll damage it. After scraping out as much old glue as you can, clean the bonding surfaces with mineral spirits or benzene to remove any residue; glue left under the loose area will interfere with the new adhesive. If any glue still remains, sand the bonding surfaces lightly with fine-grit sandpaper, and then wipe them clean with a soft cloth moistened with mineral spirits. If more than one veneer layer is loose, clean each layer the same way.

The veneer can be reattached with contact cement, but you may prefer to use carpenters' glue because it sets more slowly and allows repositioning. To reglue the veneer, apply contact cement to both bonding surfaces and let it set, as directed by the manufacturer; if necessary, set a small tack or two between the layers to keep them from touching. Or apply carpenters' glue to the base wood, spreading it on along the grain with a small brush. Then, starting at the solidly attached veneer and working out toward the loose edge, smooth the loose veneer carefully into place. Contact cement bonds immediately, so make sure the veneer is exactly matched; if you're using carpenters' glue, press from the center out to force out any excess, and wipe the excess off immediately. If more than one veneer layer is loose, work from the bottom up to reglue each layer.

Reglued veneer, whatever adhesive is used, should be clamped or weighted. To protect the surface, cover it with a sheet of wax paper; make sure all excess glue is removed. Set a buffer block of scrap wood over the newly glued area, and use another block or a soft cloth to protect the opposite edge or side of the surface. Clamp the glued and protected surface firmly with C-clamps or hand screws, for one to two days. Then remove the clamps and the buffers, and wax and polish the entire surface.

Cracked or Broken Veneer. If the veneer is lifted and cracked, but not broken completely through, it can be reglued as above; large areas may be easier to repair if you break the veneer off along the cracks. Broken veneer can be reglued, but you must be very careful not to

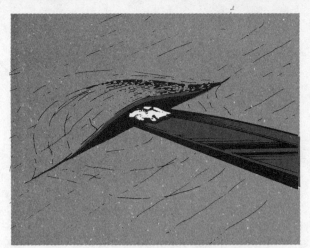

To repair a large blister in veneer, slit it and insert a little glue under the edges; then flatten it with heat.

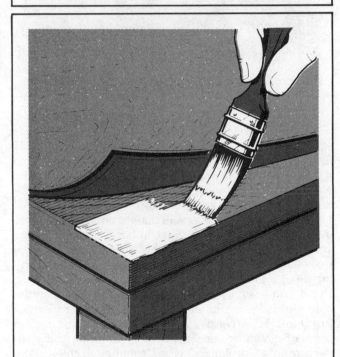

Loose veneer can be reglued. Apply glue to the base wood, press the veneer into place, and clamp it firmly.

damage the edges of the break. Do *not* trim ragged edges; an irregular mend line will not be as visible as a perfectly straight line.

Before applying glue to the veneer, clean the bonding surfaces carefully, as above. Fit the broken edges carefully together to make sure they match perfectly. Then apply contact cement to both surfaces, or spread carpenters' glue on the base wood. Set the broken veneer carefully into place, matching the edges exactly, and press firmly to knit the broken edges together. Clamp the mended area as above. Refinishing may be necessary when the mend is complete.

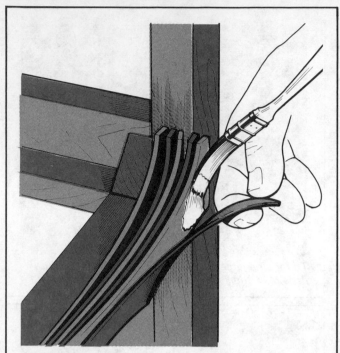

When more than one layer has separated, work from the bottom up, from the inside out, to reglue each layer.

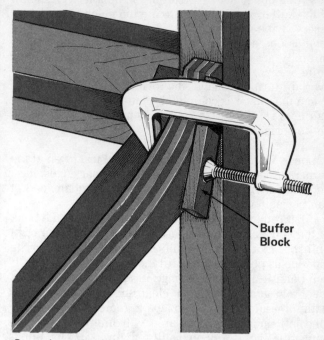

Buffer Block

Press the reglued layers together to align them properly; wipe off excess glue and clamp the mended part securely.

Chipped or Missing Veneer. Replacing veneer is easy, but finding a new piece to replace it may not be. If the piece of furniture is not valuable, you may be able to take the patch from a part of it that won't show. The patch area must be along an edge, so that you can lift the veneer with a craft knife or a stiff-bladed putty knife.

In most cases, patch veneer should not be taken from the same piece of furniture; you'll have to buy matching veneer to make the repair. If only a small piece is missing, you may be able to fill in the hole with veneer edging tape, sold at many home centers and lumberyards. Or, if you have access to junk furniture, you may be able to salvage a similar veneer from another piece of furniture. For larger patches, or if you can't find a scrap piece of matching veneer, buy a sheet of matching veneer from a specialized wood supplier, locally or by mail. National suppliers include:

Robert M. Albrecht
18701 Barthenia, Northridge, CA 91324

Constantine & Son
2050 Eastchester Rd., Bronx, NY 10461

Craftsman Wood Service
1735 W. Courtland Ct., Addison, IL 60101

Exotic Woodshed
65 N. York Rd., Warminster, PA 18974

M & M Hardwood
5344 Vineland Ave., N. Hollywood, CA 91601

Bob Morgan Woodworking Supplies
1123 Bardstown, Louisville, KY 40204

Real Wood Veneers
107 Trumbull St., Elizabeth, NJ 07206

H. L. Wild
510 E. 11th St., New York, NY 10009

The Woodworkers' Store
21801 Industrial Blvd., Rogers, MN 55374

To fit a chip or very small patch, set a sheet of bond paper over the damaged veneer. Rub a very soft, dull lead pencil gently over the paper; the edges of the damaged area will be exactly marked on the paper. Use this pattern as a template to cut the veneer patch. Tape the pattern to the patching wood, matching the grain of the new veneer to the grain of the damaged area. Cut the patch firmly and carefully with a sharp craft knife; it's better to make it too big than too small.

To make a larger patch, tape the patching veneer firmly over the damaged area with masking tape, with the grain and pattern of the patch matching the grain and pattern of the damaged veneer. Make sure the patch is flat against the surface, and securely held in place. Cut the patch in an irregular shape, as illustrated, or in a boat or shield shape; these shapes will be less visible than a square or rectangular patch would be. Cut the patch carefully with a craft knife, scoring through the patching veneer and through the damaged veneer layer below it.

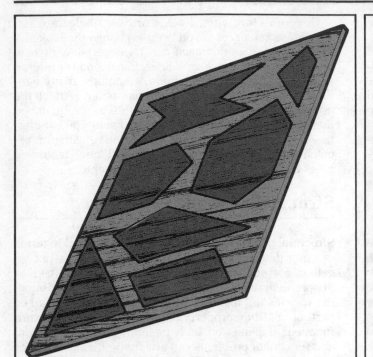

To mend veneer, cut a patch in an irregular shape; any of these shapes will be less visible than a square.

With the patch veneer held firmly, cut through the patching sheet and the veneer below it.

Untape the patching sheet and pop out the patch. With the tip of the craft knife, remove the cut-out patch of damaged veneer; if necessary, score it and remove it in pieces. Be very careful not to damage the edges of the patch area. Remove only the top veneer layer; do not cut into the base wood. Remove any old glue and clean the base wood as above.

Test the fit of the patch in the hole. It should fit exactly, flush with the surrounding surface, with no gaps or overlaps. If the patch is too big or too thick, do *not* force it in. Carefully sand the edges or the back with fine-grit sandpaper to fit it to the hole.

Glue the fitted patch into place with contact cement or carpenters' glue, as above, and clamp or weight it solidly. Let the repair dry for one to two days; then very lightly sand the patch and the surrounding veneer. Refinish the damaged area or, if necessary, the entire surface or piece of furniture.

Hardware Repairs

The hardware on old furniture—drawer pulls, handles, hinges, locks, protective corners, and decorative bands and escutcheons—often shows signs of long, hard use. Sometimes hardware is missing; sometimes it's loose, broken, or bent. Loose hardware can be repaired; missing or damaged pieces should be replaced. Replacement is also the solution if you don't like the existing hardware.

Many pieces of furniture are made with very common types of hardware; matching these basic designs is fairly simple. If the hardware is more distinctive or un-

Before gluing the patch in, test it for fit; it should fit flush with the surrounding surface, with no gaps.

usual, it may be easier to replace all the hardware than to find a matching piece; make sure the new hardware's bases are at least as large as the old. But if the piece of furniture is very valuable or an antique, or if the hardware is very attractive, the old hardware should not be removed. In this case, missing parts should be replaced with matching or similar hardware; a slight difference in design usually doesn't look bad.

Hardware stores, home centers, and similar stores offer a fair selection of furniture hardware; specialty hardware outlets and craft suppliers are usually better sources. The suppliers listed above for veneer woods also stock special hardware pieces.

Drawer Pulls and Handles. To tighten a loosely attached drawer pull, remove the pull and replace the screw with a longer one. If the screw is part of the pull, you'll have to make the hole in the wood smaller. When the hole is only slightly enlarged, you can tighten the pull by using a hollow fiber plug with the screw; for metal pulls, fit a piece of solid-core solder into the hole and then replace the screw. When the hole is much too big, insert wood toothpicks or thin shavings of wood, dipped in glue, into the hole; let the glue dry and carefully trim the shavings flush with the wood surface. Then dip the pull's screw into glue, replace the pull, and tighten the screw firmly. For a more substantial repair, enlarge the hole, glue a piece of dowel into it, and drill a new screw hole in the dowel.

Hinges. Hinges that don't work properly usually have bent hinge pins; in this case, replace the hinges. If the hinges are loose, try using slightly longer screws to attach them. When the screw holes are very much enlarged, adjust them by one of the methods detailed above. If the hinge leaves are damaged and the hinges cannot be replaced, glue the hinges into position with epoxy or a rubber- or silicone-base adhesive.

Locks. Locks on old pieces are often damaged, and keys are often missing. If the piece of furniture is an antique, or the lock is very unusual, have it repaired by a professional. Otherwise, remove the damaged lock and take it to a locksmith; order a matching or similar lock to replace it. Install the new lock the same way the old one was secured.

Loose Metal Bands and Escutcheons. Old bands and escutcheons often have an attractive design and patina; don't replace them unless they're badly damaged. To secure a loose band or escutcheon, squeeze adhesive caulking compound under the metal, and press it down to bond it to the wood. If this doesn't work, fasten the band or escutcheon with tiny metal screws, of the same metal as the hardware. You must match the metals— brass to brass, copper to copper, steel to steel, or whatever. If you don't match the screws to the metal plate, the metal will corrode. Use several screws, placing them to form a pattern; drill pilot holes before inserting them.

Coverup Hardware. If old hardware holes are impossible to repair, or if you want to change the look of a piece entirely, the damage can be covered with new wood or metal escutcheon plates. Escutcheons are used particularly under drawer pulls or handles; many handles are made with escutcheon-type backers. Attach the escutcheons with adhesive or with screws, matched metal to metal. If you're using escutcheon-type handles, no other treatment is necessary. If you're using an escutcheon under other hardware, drill new mounting holes as required. Keep your design simple.

Structural Furniture Repairs

Structural problems in furniture can be defined in terms of three things: the material itself, the way it's put together, and the way it functions. The material itself is the problem when a part is broken, warped, or missing; the way it's put together is involved when joints fail or parts aren't fitted properly. The way a piece of furniture functions depends on both material and construction, and functional problems can always be traced to one or both of these sources. Nothing can turn an all-around loser into a quality piece of furniture, but with a few basic repair techniques, you can handle most structural furniture problems. If you plan to refinish a piece of furniture, make structural repairs after stripping off the old finish and before preparing the piece for refinishing.

With extensive structural repairs, where parts are missing or support is inadequate, you'll probably need wood to match the piece of furniture. This can be a problem. Pine and oak are sold at most lumberyards and at home centers, but other furniture woods—walnut, cherry, mahogany, and other hardwoods—are harder to come by. Woodworking and millwork outlets usually stock and sell a variety of hardwoods, or can tell you where to find them. If you're looking for rare woods, the sources listed above for veneers may be able to help you. And don't overlook auctions, used furniture outlets, and wrecking contractors; you may be able to pick up some real bargains in wood or old furniture.

Whenever possible, repairs should be made with the same wood used in the piece of furniture. If you can't find the wood you need, use a light-colored wood— maple, gum, birch, or even pine. It's always easier to stain a light repair area than to refinish an entire piece of furniture to match one part or patch. You may also be able to borrow a piece of wood from a hidden part of the piece—a drawer bottom, a back leg, or any inconspicuous part. In this case, use the borrowed wood to make the repair and use the new wood to replace the borrowed wood.

Rebuilding Loose Joints

When a joint fails, you have two problems to deal with: the immediate functional problem and the long-term effect of the failure on the rest of the frame. A loose joint that's not repaired today may not break tomorrow, but it will put stress on other joints—and in a week's time, one wobbly leg may become two. To prevent simple structural problems from turning into more serious ones, loose or separated joints should be repaired immediately.

The basic joint repair techniques can be applied to all types of furniture, but each kind of frame has its own individual structural problems. Chairs are prone to broken rungs and split seats; tabletops warp; drawers stick or tip; caning and upholstery wear out. With common sense and a few particulars, you can keep all your furniture in good repair.

Gluing. The simplest solution is usually the best one, in repairs as well as surface work. When you discover a loose joint, first make sure the screws (if any) are tight; then try to repair it with an adhesive—plastic resin, epoxy, or resorcinol. Force the adhesive into the loose joint with a glue injector; if you can, wiggle the joint to distribute the adhesive. Clamp the joint for about two days, until the adhesive is completely cured. If possible, strengthen the glued joint with a glue block, as detailed below.

After gluing the loose joint, put the piece of furniture back into service. Check the joint again in a few weeks. If it has worked loose again, it can't be permanently repaired by regluing; you'll have to reinforce it, resecure it, or rebuild it completely.

Reinforcing: Glue Blocks and Steel Braces. Glue blocks, the original furniture braces, are solid pieces of wood used to reinforce joints and provide additional support. Steel corner plates and angle braces perform the same function, but they can also lower the value of a piece of furniture. For this reason, glue blocks are still an important part of furniture repairs. Valuable pieces of furniture, antiques, and good reproductions should always be repaired with glue blocks instead of steel braces when possible.

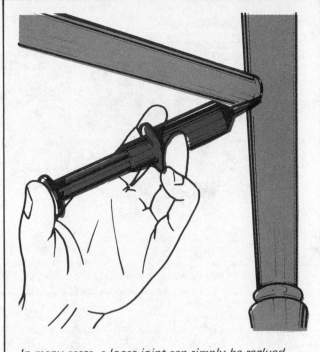

In many cases, a loose joint can simply be reglued. Force glue into the joint with a glue injector, and clamp the piece firmly until the adhesive is cured.

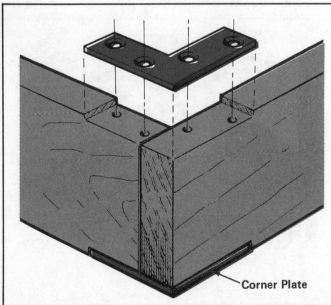

Corner Plate

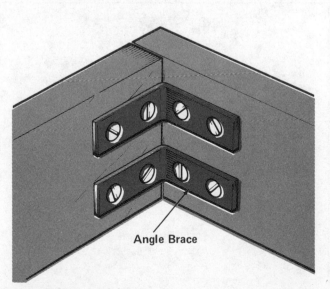

Angle Brace

Steel corner plates (left) and angle braces (right) are often used to reinforce weak joints, especially in inexpensive furniture. Because they can detract from the appearance of the piece, and can also lower its value, they should never be used on valuable furniture.

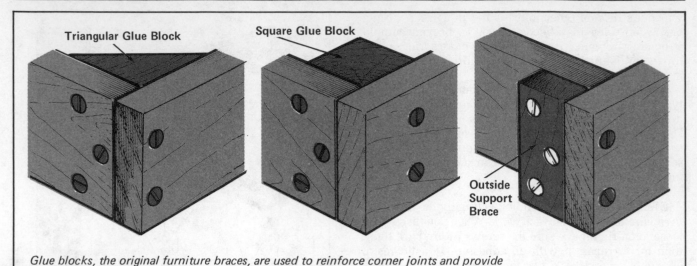

Glue blocks, the original furniture braces, are used to reinforce corner joints and provide additional support. Triangular glue blocks (left) are usually preferable for corner braces. Square glue blocks (center) are used on long joints and (right) as outside support braces.

Glue blocks for corner braces can be either square or triangular. Square blocks are used chiefly as outside support braces, or on long joints, such as the inside corners of drawers, where cutting a triangle would be impractical. In most cases, triangular glue blocks are preferable.

Glue blocks can be cut from any square stock, but hardwood is preferred. To make a glue block, cut a square piece of wood in half diagonally; the larger the piece of wood, the greater the gluing surface of the block. The length of the blocks will depend on the project; on the average, two inches is adequate. To strengthen chair and table legs, cut triangular braces

from one-inch nominal boards, as large as necessary. At the right-angle corner of the block, cut off a diagonal or make a notch to fit around the leg. For braces, 1×2 lumber works well.

To install a triangular glue block, spread adhesive on the two right-angle sides or edges. Set the block into the corner and twist it slightly to distribute the adhesive on the bonding surfaces. Small glue blocks can be strengthened by nails driven through the block into the furniture frame; drill pilot holes for the nails to make sure you don't split the wood. To strengthen chair and table braces, drive three screws through the block and into the frame: one screw straight into the corner and one

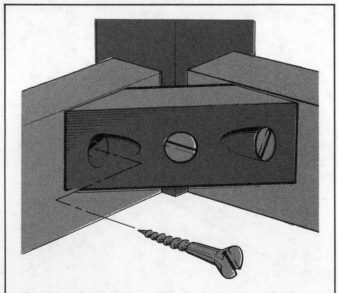

To strengthen a chair or table leg, cut a triangular brace, and cut off one corner to fit across the leg. Attach the block with glue and two or, if possible, three screws.

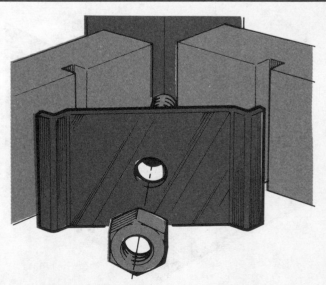

Some corner joints are held by steel brackets, set into notches in the frame. If a bracketed leg wobbles, tighten the bracket nut; if necessary, reseat the bracket.

straight into each side, at an angle to the inside block edge. Predrill the screw holes in both block and frame.

Sometimes a corner joint is held by a steel bracket instead of a glue block. If the leg wobbles, first make sure the nut that holds the bracket is securely tightened. If this doesn't solve the problem, and the bracket is set into notches in the frame, it may not be seated properly. Remove the nut and reseat the bracket; then replace the nut securely.

Resecuring: Screws and Glue. If a loose joint would be difficult to take apart, you may be able to solve the problem with a long screw. First, align the joint and drill a pilot hole for the screw. Then enlarge the top of the pilot hole so that a small piece of dowel can be installed over the screw head, as illustrated. Coat the screw with glue and drive it into the joint so that it pulls the joint tightly together. Before you tighten the screw, try to force adhesive into the loose joint; this will help strengthen the joint. Then tighten the screw firmly.

To cover the screw head, cut a piece of dowel to fit the enlarged hole; it should be slightly longer than the opening, so that the end of the dowel will protrude slightly above the surface of the frame. Insert the dowel plug with glue, making sure the end of the dowel is flush with the head of the screw, and let the glue dry completely. Then carefully cut the end of the dowel flush with the surface and sand it smooth. You'll probably have to refinish the frame so the dowel matches, and you may want to install false dowel plugs at the other joints in the frame so that they match. The dowels will give the frame a hand-made pinned or pegged look.

The screw/plug trick can also be used to repair loose rungs and backs, but the pieces involved must be large enough to accept the screw and dowel. Small parts such as turnings and slats may split when a screw is driven into them.

For the strongest screw-reinforced joint, the screw should be driven into a piece of dowel instead of into the frame itself. This isn't always possible, but if you can, disassemble the joint, drill a hole at the screw point, and plug the hole with a dowel, gluing the dowel into place. Then reassemble the joint with a screw and glue, as above. If you want to hide the head of the screw, enlarge the hole for a dowel plug; or countersink the screw slightly and fill the depression.

Rebuilding: Disassembly and Doweling. Rebuilding a joint—or a series of joints—is not as tough as it might sound, although it does require a good deal of patience. You must work slowly to make sure all the parts are in the right places and all parts fit tightly. To disassemble the joint, pull it carefully apart. If it doesn't come apart easily, use a rubber or wooden mallet to tap the frame pieces apart, but be careful not to damage the wood. Don't overlook the possibility that the joint was assembled with nails or screws as well as adhesive; in this case, you should remove the fasteners before you break the adhesive. If you can't remove them, break the adhesive bond and pry the joint apart very carefully. Don't

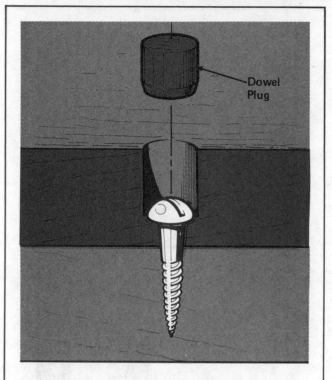

Dowel Plug

A loose joint can sometimes be resecured with a long screw, coated with glue and driven into the joint. Cover the screw head with a dowel plug.

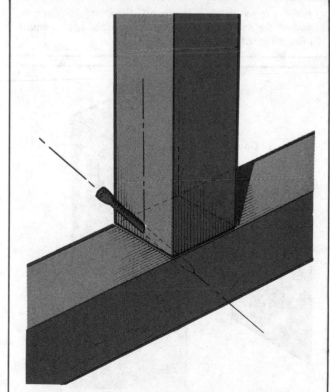

If a joint doesn't come apart easily, it may be held by nails or screws; these fasteners should be removed before the joint is disassembled.

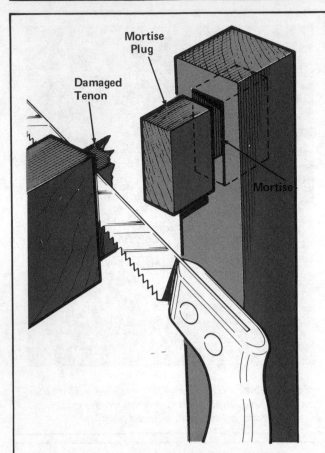

When a tenon is badly damaged, saw it off flush at the end of the frame piece. Close the mortise with a wood plug, glued in and trimmed flush.

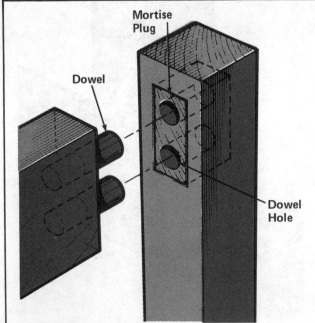

Use dowels to rebuild the joint. Drill holes in the end of the frame piece, where the tenon was, and in the mortise; then glue the dowels into place.

force the joint apart; if the nails or screws are embedded too firmly, you'll split or splinter the wood. If prying would damage the wood, consider sawing the joint apart. Use a hacksaw with a thin blade that will go through metal and not leave a wide cut.

After the joint is disassembled, it must be thoroughly cleaned. If the old adhesive is brittle or crumbling, scrape it off with a knife or a narrow chisel; if it's hard to remove, use sandpaper, hot water, or a hot vinegar solution. You must remove all dirt and old adhesive. Whatever method you use, be very careful not to damage the wood, or the joint won't fit together properly when you reassemble it.

Structural problems are most common in chairs and tables, and the joints involved are usually mortise-and-tenon. In most cases, the tenon is worn or broken. If the damage isn't too bad, you may be able to thoroughly clean the joint and then reassemble it with epoxy; this is a good joint filler as well as a bonding agent. Wipe off any excess epoxy after assembling the joint, and clamp the joint until the epoxy is completely dry. Keep the piece of furniture out of service for a week or so to make sure the glue has cured properly.

If the tenon is badly damaged, or if the joint was sawed apart, you'll have to rebuild the joint with hardwood dowels in place of the tenon—two dowels are adequate for most joints. Use dowels about the same width and about twice the length of the damaged tenon. Cut off the damaged tenon, and remove any broken wood from the mortise. Plug the mortise completely with a wood plug, glued in and trimmed flush with the surface. Then use dowels to connect the parts again.

To make the holes for the dowels—in the tenon base and in the plugged mortise—use a doweling jig, clamped to the edge of the wood and adjusted to center the dowel holes. Dowel center points can also be used, but they aren't as accurate as a jig. Drill the holes to a total depth of about 1/4 inch deeper than the length of the dowels, to allow for glue buildup under the dowels.

Score the sides of the dowels with pliers and round the ends slightly with sandpaper or a file. This improves glue distribution, and makes insertion easier and more accurate. Apply glue to the dowels and insert them into the holes in one side of the joint; then coat the edge of the wood with glue and slip the other joint piece onto the dowels. Tap the joint together with a rubber or wooden mallet, wipe off any glue that oozes out of the joint, and clamp the joint firmly for about two days, until the glue is completely set.

Repairing Chairs

Loose Joints. Seat frames are held by mortise-and-tenon or doweled joints supported by triangular glue blocks, notched to fit the legs. If you catch a loose joint in time, repair it with glue. If the joint is broken, you'll have to disassemble it and replace the dowels, as detailed above. The triangular glue blocks will probably be glued and screwed to the frame, and the dowel joint might even be supported with hidden nail or screw fasteners. Separate the joint carefully with an old screwdriver or a stiff-bladed putty knife; then replace the dowels. Make sure the joint is clean and dry before you reassemble it.

Sometimes you can use a mechanical fastener—an angle brace or a chair leg brace—to mend the frame. This, of course, really depends on the value of the furniture; do not lower the value of an antique with a piece of metal. Metal reinforcements are useless unless the joint is tightly fitted together, but they can be used to make a firm joint stronger. Fasten the braces with brass screws, and make sure the screws are long enough.

Fasten the metal angle to one side of the chair frame; predrill the screw holes. Insert a piece of thin cardboard under the opposite part of the angle; then drill the screw holes for that side. Drive in the screws fairly tight, remove the cardboard, and finish tightening the screws. When the screws are final-tightened, the angle will pull the joint tightly together to bridge the gap left by the cardboard.

Back Rails, Spindles, and Slats. On chairs with horizontal rails across the back, the rails are mortised into the side posts; on chairs with vertical spindles or slats, these parts are mortised into a curved or straight top rail. Rails, spindles, and slats can all be replaced easily, but replacement may be fairly expensive—don't bother if the chair isn't worth the investment. To replace a broken or missing part, have a millwork or woodworking shop custom-make a new part.

First, disassemble the chair back; it will probably be joined at the legs, seat, and rail. Carefully pry the joints apart, removing any nails or screws. Disassemble only the joints involved in the repair; it usually isn't necessary to completely disassemble the piece to get at the part. If you aren't sure you'll be able to reassemble the chair back, number the parts as you take them out.

Take the broken part, and a similar undamaged part, to the millwork or woodworking shop for duplication. When you have the new part, carefully clean the old adhesive from the joints. Then reassemble the chair with the new part, gluing each joint. Clamp the chair with strap clamps until the adhesive dries, and then refinish the chair completely.

Outdoor chairs made with wooden slats can be repaired the same way, but the slats can usually be replaced with wide moldings or thin boards. To replace a broken slat, cut and shape a piece of wide molding or a board to fit the frame. If the slats are fastened with screws, drill screw holes in the new slat and attach it with the old screws or matching new ones. If they're fastened with rivets, drill the old rivets out, and replace them with self-tapping or panhead sheet metal screws.

Loose Legs, Rungs, and Spindles. Loose rungs or spindles—and, where no bracing is used, loose legs—can sometimes be mended by forcing glue into the joints, but a part mended this way may work loose again. For a more permanent repair, carefully separate the part from the frame; if both ends are loose, remove

Insert a piece of thin cardboard under one side of an angle brace; remove the cardboard before final-tightening the screws on that side.

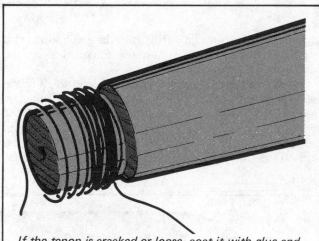

If the tenon is cracked or loose, coat it with glue and wrap it with silk thread. Let the glue dry; then glue the tenon back into its socket.

the entire piece. For very stubborn joints, twist the part slightly to break the glue bond; if necessary, use self-locking pliers. Pad the part to prevent damage to the wood from the pliers.

Remove the old adhesive completely from the part and from its socket; glue does not bond well to old glue. Be careful not to remove any wood from the end of the part, or it won't fit right. After removing the old glue, test each end of the part in its socket. If the ends fit snugly, apply glue to the sockets and reinsert the loose part. Clamp the reglued part and let it dry completely.

If the part is loose in its socket, you'll have to enlarge it to make a firm joint; if the tenon end is cracked, you'll have to reinforce it. Apply a thin coat of glue to the tenon, and wrap it tightly with silk thread; if necessary, apply more glue and cover the tenon with another layer of thread. Let the threaded tenon dry for a day and then

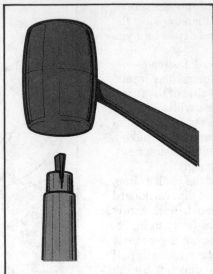

If the tenon is very loose, saw straight into the tenon and cut a thin wedge to fit the saw cut.

Tap the wedge carefully into the cut to enlarge the tenon slightly, and glue the enlarged tenon back.

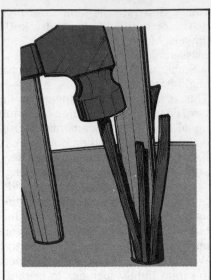

To wedge very loose joints, dip thin wedges in glue and pound them in around the loose part.

glue the reinforced end firmly into the socket; insert it carefully so you don't disturb the thread. Clamp the joint and let it dry completely.

Very loose legs or rungs can be wedged to fit if the tenon is sound. Clamp the part in a vise or have a helper hold it; then saw very carefully into the center of the tenon end, as illustrated. The cut must be square and centered, roughly the depth of the part that fits into the socket—about ¾ inch. For small parts, use a hacksaw

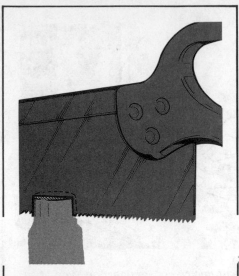

Where appearance matters, drill through the side of the joint into the loose part. Pin the joint with a nail through the drilled hole.

or a coping saw to make the cut; for thicker parts, use a backsaw or a combination saw.

From a piece of soft wood—pine quarter-round, if you have it—cut a thin wedge to fit the width and depth of the saw cut in the tenon. The object here is to spread the saw cut slightly with the wedge, thus enlarging the tenon to fit the socket. When you're satisfied that the wedge is the right size, very carefully tap the wedge into the saw cut. When the tenon is slightly enlarged, stop pounding and trim off any excess wood from the wedge with a utility knife or pocketknife. Be careful not to pound the wedge too far; excessive wedging will split the tenon. To test the wedge, insert the end of it into the saw cut and tap it down with a screwdriver handle. If you see the wood on both sides of the cut start to spread, the wedge is too wide. Finally, apply glue and reassemble the joint as above.

You may not be able to disassemble the piece of furniture for this wedging procedure. In this case, there are two more ways to do the job. If the joint is extremely loose, and appearance is not important, remove as much adhesive as you can. Make several thin wedges from molding—pine lattice is a good selection. Dip the ends of the wedges in adhesive and drive the wedges with a hammer around the loose part, between the part and the socket. Then, with a utility knife, trim the ends of the wedges flush with the surrounding wood surface. Equalize the pressure from the wedges as you drive them in; unless you place them carefully, the wedges can throw the part out of alignment, further weakening the joint.

Where appearance is more important, drill a ¹⁄₁₆-inch hole into the side of the joint through the loose part. Then make a pin from a 10d common or finishing nail. Cut off the head of the nail with a hacksaw; apply a drop or two of glue to the drilled hole and drive in the nail. Countersink the pin with a nail set or another 10d nail, and fill the hole with wood filler.

Broken Rungs and Spindles. Splits and breaks in nonstructural rungs and spindles can be repaired with glue. Separate the broken ends of the part and apply glue to each piece; or, if the part is only cracked, force glue into the crack with a glue injector. Join the pieces carefully, pressing them firmly together, and remove any excess glue. Wrap a piece of wax paper around the part, and then wrap the mended break firmly with a piece of cord, to keep the part aligned properly. Clamp the chair firmly with a strap clamp or a rope, and let the glue dry completely.

Broken Arms, Legs, and Other Structural Parts. Where strength is important, the broken part must be reinforced. The best reinforcement is a dowel pinning the broken pieces together. Use 1/8-inch to 3/8-inch dowel, depending on how thick the broken part is; drill the dowel holes with a bit of the same size.

Separate the broken ends of the part. In the center of one end, and at a right angle to the break, drill a one-inch-deep hole, the same diameter as the dowel. This hole marks the dowel location. Insert a dowel center point into the hole, point out. To mark the dowel location on the other piece of the broken part, match the pieces and press them firmly together to force the point of the dowel center point into the center of the matching piece of the broken part. Pull the pieces apart and remove the dowel center point; then drill straight into the second piece at the marked point, about one inch deep.

Measure the dowel holes, and cut a piece of dowel 1/4 inch shorter than their total depth, to allow for glue buildup. Score the sides of the dowel with pliers and round the ends slightly with sandpaper or a file; this improves glue distribution and makes insertion easier. Apply glue to one end of the dowel and insert it into the hole in one end; then apply glue to the protruding dowel and to the face of the break, and push the other piece of the broken part onto the dowel. Match the parts perfectly, wipe off excess adhesive, and clamp the mended part as above.

Where doweling isn't possible, or where you want to provide extra strength, use a steel mending plate to reinforce the break. Mending plates can be used on any flat surface. Glue the break as above, and let it dry completely. Then add a mending plate, long enough to span the break and narrow enough to be inconspicuous; use a plate with screw holes beveled to accept flathead screws.

Place the mending plate on the inside or least obvious face of the mended part. If appearance doesn't matter, secure the plate directly over the break, using flathead brass screws. For a less conspicuous repair, mortise the plate into the wood. Carefully trace the outline of the mending plate onto the wood with a scratch awl or a sharp nail. Score the wood along the outline with a series of straight-down chisel cuts, as deep as you want the mortise—about 1/4 inch for most plates, allowing

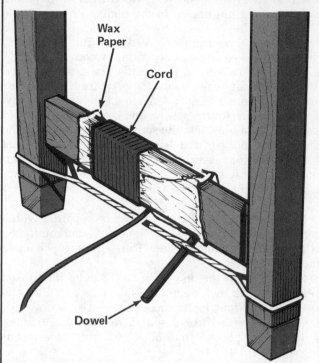

A split in a nonstructural part can be glued. Wrap a piece of wax paper around the glued part, bind it with cord, and clamp it firmly until the glue is dry.

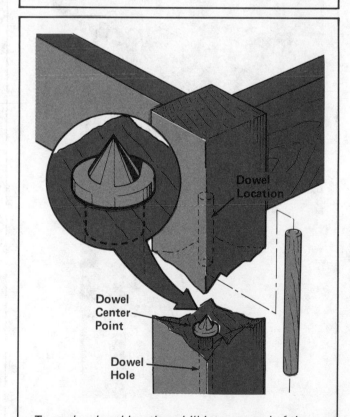

To mark a dowel location, drill into one end of the part and insert a dowel center point. Press the ends together to mark the drilling point on the second piece.

229

space to cover the plate with wood filler. Cross-score the wood at right angles to the outline; then turn the chisel over, bevel side down, and remove the excess wood in the scored outline, working with the grain of the wood and removing only a little wood at a time.

When the bottom of the mortise is as smooth and level as you can make it, test the plate for fit, and make any adjustments necessary. When the plate fits exactly, drill pilot holes for the screws and coat the mortise with a thin layer of glue. Dip the screws in glue, position the plate in the mortise, and drive the screws firmly in. Let the glue dry for several days, and then cover the mending plate evenly with wood filler or a veneer patch; finish the filler to match the wood.

Split Seats. Split chair seats can be repaired with a series of ⅛-inch dowels along the break, and reinforced with metal mending plates. The seat must be completely removed for doweling.

Drill holes for the dowels in each side of the broken seat, about one inch deep (or as deep as possible) and spaced about four to six inches apart. Use a doweling jig, clamped to the broken seat, to drill the dowel holes; dowel center points can also be used, but they aren't as

accurate. Cut and score each dowel as above, ¼ inch less than the total length of the dowel holes.

Apply glue to one end of each dowel, and insert the dowels into the holes along one side of the broken seat; then apply glue to the protruding dowel ends and to the broken edge, and join the two parts. Tap the pieces of the seat together with a rubber or wooden mallet, and wipe off any excess glue. Lightly clamp the glued seat, and let it dry for at least two days. For extra strength, you can add metal mending plates to span the break, as above—four plates should be adequate. Finally, reassemble the chair.

Insert Chair Seats. Chair seats set in or on frames are usually boards or plywood, covered with padding and cloth. These seats seldom split, but when they do, the simplest solution is to replace the seat with a new piece of plywood—⅜-inch thickness is best. If ⅜-inch plywood won't fit properly after the padding has been added, you may have to use ¼-inch plywood, but anything less than this will not provide the needed support. Use the old chair seat as a template or pattern to cut out the new one.

Padded chair seats are usually held to the frame with

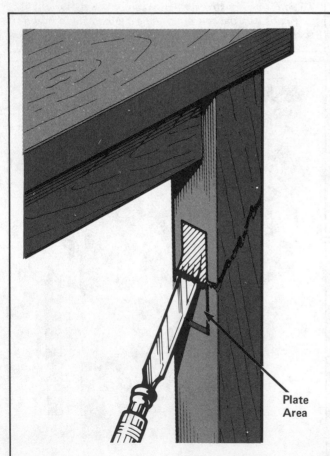

For extra strength, reinforce the break with a mending plate. Mortise out the plate area with a chisel, first scoring the outline and then cutting out excess wood.

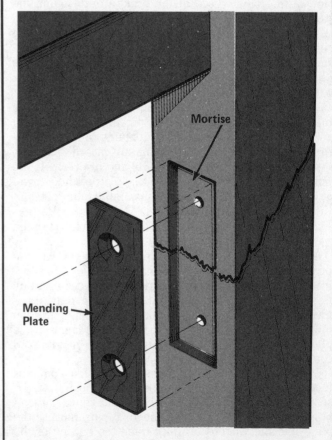

When the mortise is smooth and level, drill screw holes and glue the mending plate into place. Secure it with flathead screws, and cover it with wood filler.

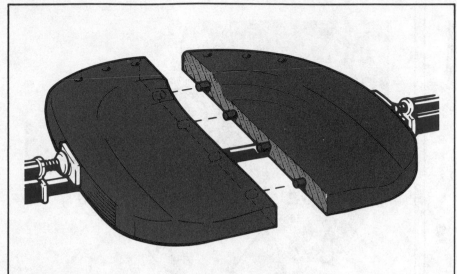

Repair a split chair seat with a series of 1/8-inch dowels, placed about 4 inches apart along the split. Clamp the seat firmly until the glue is completely cured.

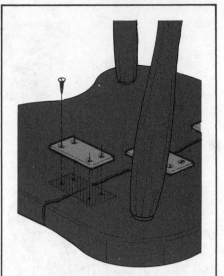

For a stronger repair, dowel the seat together; then reinforce the break with mending plates.

screws driven through glue blocks. Look carefully for these screws; the cloth covering the padding may hide them. Remove all fasteners, and replace them the same way to hold the new chair seat.

If the upholstery on insert seats is worn or damaged, it can easily be replaced. Dining room chairs are usually padded with cotton batting; some chairs have foam padding or a combination of foam and cotton. Both types of padding are available precut for chair seats. For most chairs, the padding should be about 3/4 inch to one inch thick.

To recover an insert chair seat, remove the seat from the chair. The seat is usually a piece of plywood, held to the chair frame by screws; the screws may be counterbored into the frame or may go up through the corner glue blocks. Remove the tacks or staples that hold the old upholstery fabric to the seat, and lift off the fabric. If refinishing is necessary, refinish the chair before proceeding further.

Using the old fabric as a pattern, cut the new fabric to fit. If the old padding on the chair seat is in good shape, it can be reused; if it's damaged, replace it with new padding. You may be able to fluff and smooth old cotton padding; if it's badly flattened, add a layer of foam padding to build the seat cushion up to 3/4 to one inch.

Lay the new fabric flat, wrong side up, and center the padded seat on it upside down. Fold the edges of the fabric up over the seat, stretching it firmly onto the plywood; if desired, tape the fabric firmly down with masking tape. Starting at the center of one side, fold the fabric under and attach it to the seat with heavy-duty staples in a staple gun. If the new fabric is very heavy, flatheaded upholstery tacks may be more secure. Set staples or tacks one to 1 1/2 inches apart along the side of the seat.

When the first side is completely attached, restretch

the fabric; then staple or tack the opposite side. Turn the seat over and smooth the padding; be sure the fabric is straight, with no wrinkles. Then turn the seat over again and fasten the other two sides. At the corners, fold the

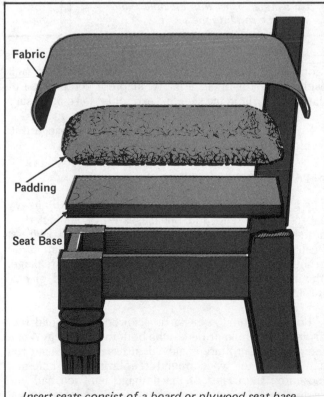

Fabric

Padding

Seat Base

Insert seats consist of a board or plywood seat base covered with padding and fabric. The seat rests in or on the chair frame, and is secured with screws.

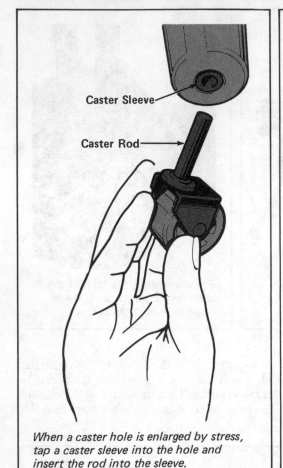

Caster Sleeve

Caster Rod

When a caster hole is enlarged by stress, tap a caster sleeve into the hole and insert the rod into the sleeve.

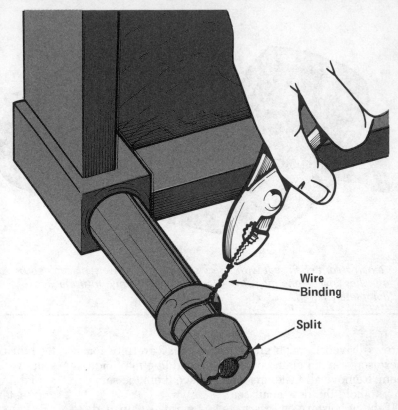

Wire Binding

Split

When the leg is split, remove the caster completely; glue the split together and bind the leg with wire to reinforce the break. Then bind the other legs to match.

fabric in to miter it neatly; if necessary, staple or tack each layer separately. Finally, staple a scrap piece of the new fabric to the seat, in case repairs are necessary in the future.

Replace the chair seat in the frame, and resecure it. Replace all the screws and tighten them firmly.

Repairing Legs and Feet

The legs and feet of furniture pieces—especially heavy cabinets, dressers, and bookcases—are subjected to both weight and, when they're moved, lateral stress. Pushing a heavily loaded piece of furniture can cause problems even if it doesn't cause immediate breakage, and these problems are very common in old pieces. Structural breaks should be repaired as above.

Loose Casters. A caster is secured by a metal rod, driven into a hole drilled in the bottom of the leg. When the piece of furniture is moved, stress on the caster rod can damage the wood around it, enlarging the hole and loosening the caster. If the damage isn't too bad, the casters may be loose; if it's been ignored long enough, the casters may fall out when the piece is lifted, or the ends of the legs may be split. Both problems can be solved.

To tighten loose casters, use metal or plastic caster sleeve inserts, available in several sizes. Remove the loose caster and tap the insert into the hole in the leg; no adhesive is needed. The sleeve should fit snugly; if it doesn't, use larger inserts. Insert the caster into the sleeve; this should solve the problem.

If the leg is split, remove all the casters on the piece. Apply glue along the split, and press the glued edges firmly together; wipe off any excess. To reinforce the break, bind the split with several wraps of fine black steel wire. On many pieces of furniture there's a ridge or a crevice at the caster point; if you wrap the wire around the leg at this point, the repair will not be obvious. If the leg doesn't have any carving or decoration at this point, you can notch the wood all the way around with a triangular file, and then wrap the wire in the notch. Treat all legs the same way so that they match.

One Leg Shorter Than the Rest. When this happens, you may be tempted to cut the other legs down to match the shorter one, but don't do it—instead, build up the short leg to match the others. Cutting usually results in serious mismatching, besides shortening the piece and ruining its design.

If the leg is only a little too short, use a metal leg cap to build it up. These caps, made in several sizes, have from one to three prongs on a metal base. To install a cap, just hammer in the prongs. To make sure you don't split the wood, center the cap on the leg and lightly tap it to mark the prong positions; then drill tiny holes to accept the prongs.

If a metal cap doesn't work, you may be able to add a wood extender to the leg. Cut the extender from the same wood as the piece of furniture, if possible; shape it to match. Fit the extender exactly and then glue and nail it to the bottom of the short leg; countersink the nails. You'll probably have to refinish the entire piece to blend the extender with the rest of the wood.

If the gap is really wide, you can V-notch the leg and the extender and glue the parts together, forming an A-shaped brace. This is a very strong repair, and will give the piece a real hand-made look, so you don't have to match the wood exactly. Assemble the joint with glue and countersink small nails; drive the nails where they won't show, and fill the holes with wood filler. Even if the holes are visible, the repair won't look bad.

Repairing Doors and Other Flat Parts

Splits. Split doors, panels, cabinet backs, and other flat parts should be repaired with glue and, if possible, with dowels, as detailed above. Very thin door panels and cabinet backs cannot be repaired, and should be replaced. Where appearance is not important, as on the back of a door that's always left closed, metal mending plates can be used for reinforcement.

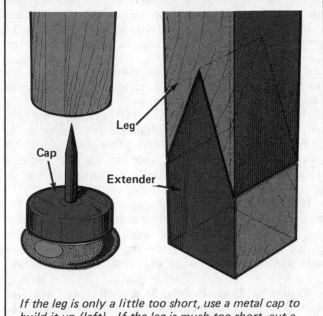

If the leg is only a little too short, use a metal cap to build it up (left). If the leg is much too short, cut a V-shaped extender piece from matching wood (right).

Sagging or Binding Doors. Sagging is usually caused by faulty hinge operation; make sure the hinges are working properly, as detailed above in the section on surface repairs. Binding can be caused by faulty hinges

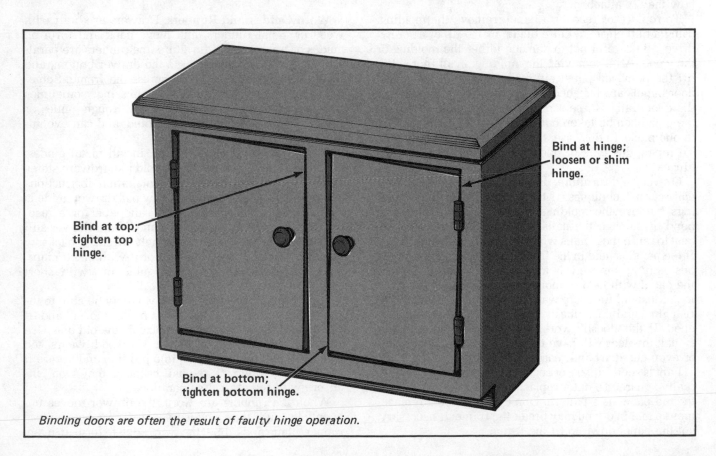

Binding doors are often the result of faulty hinge operation.

233

or by excess humidity. Swelling from humidity or moisture vapor is most common in spring and summer, and is most likely to affect wood that hasn't been properly sealed; in fall and winter, when the humidity is lower, the wood will shrink again.

Before you work on the wood, adjust the hinges. If the door binds at the top on the latch side, the top hinge is probably loose; tighten the screws, as detailed above. If the door binds at the bottom on the latch side, the bottom hinge probably needs tightening. If the door binds on the hinge side, the hinges may be too tight, or may be mortised too deeply into the wood. In this case, remove the affected hinge or hinges and add a shim of thin cardboard under each one; then replace the hinges.

If hinge adjustment doesn't work, you'll have to remove some wood at the binding points. Be very careful in removing any wood; use sandpaper rather than a plane. To prevent future swelling, seal the raw edge with shellac when the weather—and the wood—is dry.

Replacing Door Panels. Many cabinets have flat door panels, either veneered or covered with cloth, cane, metal, or glass. Split panels should be replaced. If the covering of one panel is damaged, all panels should be recovered, if necessary, to match.

Door and drawer panels are usually held in place by molding strips nailed around the edges, sometimes surface-mounted and sometimes set into a rabbet-type joint. These molding strips may be hard to see, but by carefully prying around the panel, you'll be able to see how they're attached.

To replace or recover a panel, remove the molding, using a butt chisel, a knife blade, or the tip of a screwdriver. Be careful not to damage either the molding or the wood. After removing the molding on all four sides, lift the damaged panel out of the frame. Some raised door panels are fastened with screws from the back of the door frame; these screws must be removed before the panel can be taken out. Raised panel doors may be in one piece; in this case, the panel cannot be removed. To repair this type of door, remove the door from its hinges.

On very old furniture, door panels often require special repair techniques. If the panels are held by moldings, remove the moldings very carefully. Try not to bend or damage the nails that hold the moldings; it's best to reuse these nails when you replace the moldings. If the panel is held in the frame in grooves (dadoes), the best way to remove it is to soften the adhesive around the panel with heat or moisture—a hot towel is a good tool. Most old furniture was put together with animal or fish glue, and this adhesive can usually be readily softened. If this doesn't work, take the piece to a professional; the door will have to be taken completely apart, or even cut apart and reassembled.

Panels set in square or rectangular frames are seldom really square. To cut a replacement for any panel, use the old panel as a pattern. Don't try to force a replacement panel in or you may break the frame; if necessary, cut the panel down to fit the frame.

Repairing Drawers

Loose Joints. Drawer frame construction is similar to chair construction, with dovetail joints in old or expensive furniture or butt joints, glued and held with corrugated nails, in newer furniture. Dovetail joints seldom separate; if they do, force adhesive into the loose joint and tap the joint together with a hammer. Butt joints are another problem. To tighten a loose butt joint, try gluing the joint and tapping it together as tightly as you can; clamp it firmly until the glue is dry. If this doesn't work, you may be able to nail the joint through the face of the drawer; countersink the nail heads and fill the holes with wood filler.

Binding. Problems with drawer frames are usually the cause of sticking and binding drawers. When a drawer sticks, it's jerked to get it open and slammed closed; this causes the joints in the frame to separate. First make sure the joints are tight. Then lubricate the drawer guides and the top and bottom edges of the sides with stick lubricant, wax from a candle, paraffin, or silicone spray. Do not use a petroleum lubricant; oil will collect dirt and dust, and cause more problems than the binding.

If lubrication doesn't solve the problem, carefully sand down the binding points. Remove only as much wood as necessary, and seal the raw wood with shellac to prevent future swelling. If sanding doesn't eliminate binding, examine the drawer's runners and guides.

Worn Guides and Runners. Drawers are built with wood or metal runners, and move back and forth on guides or tracks. In old furniture, the runners are parallel pieces of wood fastened to the drawer bottom, and the guides are strips of wood across the frame. Sometimes the runners or guides are missing; sometimes they're split, warped, or badly worn. Rough guides or runners can cause the drawer to bind, and can eventually damage the frame.

If the drawer guide is missing, install metal guides, available in several lengths and sold in hardware stores and home centers. Complete installation instructions are provided with the guides. If a wood drawer guide is rough, smooth it carefully with sandpaper or a rasp, or—as a last resort—a block plane. If the drawer still binds, remove the guide completely. Break a hacksaw blade in half and wrap one end of it with electricians' tape; wearing gloves, cut the guide out with short strokes of the saw blade.

After removing the old guide, you may be able to install metal guides, as above. For a neater job, cut and fit a new wooden guide, the same size as the old one. Use hardwood to make the guide; softwood wears too quickly. Glue the new guide into position and secure it with nails; countersink the nail heads so they won't interfere with the drawer's operation.

When the runners are worn, the drawer moves unevenly because the wood is uneven. To replace a worn runner, plane and rabbet the worn edge to form an even, smoothly mortised strip along the drawer edge. Glue a thin strip of hardwood into each mortised runner edge, building it up to its original height. Secure the runners with small nails, and countersink the nails so that they won't interfere with the drawer's operation.

If the drawer frame has a wood kicker above the sides, and the kicker is worn, smooth it and add a new hardwood strip to build it up again. Follow the same procedure used to replace worn runners.

Split Fronts. Split drawer fronts are usually the result of missing drawer guides. First, install drawer guides. Second, repair the split with glue forced into the break. Wipe away any excess glue and lightly clamp the edges with a strap clamp. Use only light pressure; too much pressure will buckle the wood at the split.

Split Bottoms. Drawer bottoms are not fastened into the drawer sides and ends; the bottom panel fits loosely into dadoes in the sides. This permits expansion and contraction of the wood, and prevents the joints from cracking. To replace a drawer bottom, just remove one end of the drawer and slide the bottom panel out. Replace it with a new plywood or hardboard panel cut to fit. Some drawer bottoms are lightly tacked to a piece of molding nailed to the inside edges of the sides and back, and some drawer bottoms are set on triangular glue blocks. Remove these fasteners or braces before disassembling the drawer. If the piece of furniture is an antique, the drawers were probably hand-fashioned. These drawers should *not* be repaired with plywood or hardboard.

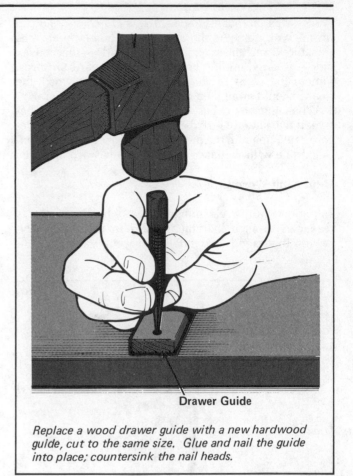

Replace a wood drawer guide with a new hardwood guide, cut to the same size. Glue and nail the guide into place; countersink the nail heads.

Straightening Warped Boards

Table leaves and other flat parts can warp unless they're properly sealed, and years of uneven humidity can leave them severely cupped. In most cases, unwarping them isn't too difficult.

To unwarp a board, work in summer; the traditional cure is exposure to wet grass and hot sun. Water a

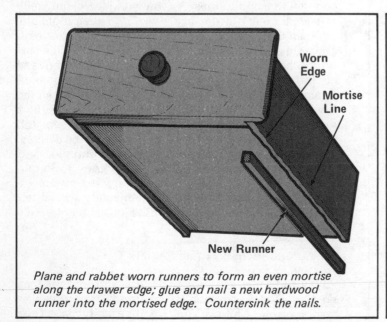

Plane and rabbet worn runners to form an even mortise along the drawer edge; glue and nail a new hardwood runner into the mortised edge. Countersink the nails.

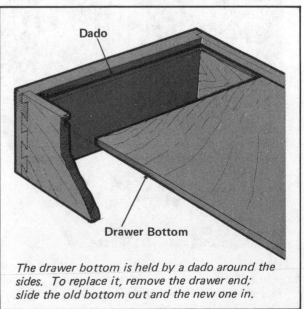

The drawer bottom is held by a dado around the sides. To replace it, remove the drawer end; slide the old bottom out and the new one in.

grassy area thoroughly and set the board convex side up on the wet grass. As the dry side of the board absorbs moisture from the grass, the moist side—the convex side—is dried out by the sun, and the board unwarps. Unless the warp is caused by stress in the wood, the board should straighten out within a day.

When the board has straightened out, clamp it between two straight boards so that it will dry evenly. Before replacing it in the piece of furniture, seal the unfinished side with shellac to prevent it from warping again.

Replacing Worn Caning

In antique furniture, caning is usually handwoven; it is threaded through individual holes in the frame, and woven in strand by strand. This type of caning should

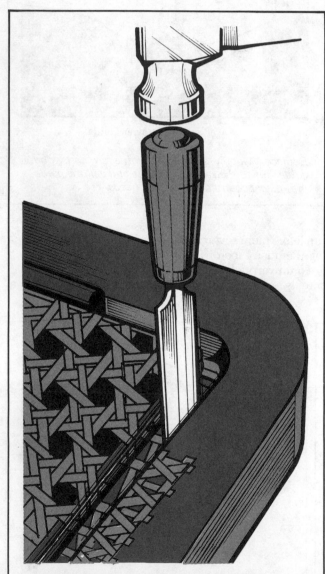

When the caning is firmly wedged around the opening, trim off the excess cane with a sharp chisel, set straight into the outside corner of the groove.

be replaced by a professional. In most newer furniture, the cane is prewoven; an entire sheet of cane is attached in a groove around the open frame. Sheet cane is easy to replace.

First, remove the old cane. If you can, pull the cane out of the groove, using a chisel to pry up the spline that holds it. If the spline is stubborn, you may have to soak the area with a towel soaked in very hot water and wrung almost dry. When the adhesive has softened, place a block of wood under the caning and tap the block with a hammer. This should dislodge the caning and the spline from the seat frame. After removing the cane, clean out the groove with a chisel. Make sure it's completely clean and dry before you install the new cane.

To replace the cane, buy a new spline and new prewoven sheet caning, about 1 to 1½ inches larger all around than the opening. Make sure the spline is the right width for the groove. Soak the cane and the spline in warm water for about 10 to 15 minutes to soften the fiber.

When the spline and the cane are pliable, blot them dry with a towel. Lay the caning over the groove, shiny side up. Starting at the center of one short side, pound the edge of the caning into the groove with a narrow wood wedge—cut the wedge from a 1×2 or a 1×3, and use a hammer to tap it along the caning. The bottom of the taper on the wedge should be slightly smaller than the groove. Work along the side of the frame toward the corners, wedging the cane firmly and squarely down into the groove; if it isn't securely wedged, it will come loose.

When the first side of the cane is in place, clamp the caned edge between two pieces of 1×2 or 1×3 to prevent the caning from popping out of the groove. Then stretch the sheet of cane across the frame and wedge the opposite side, starting at the center and working out. Repeat the procedure, clamping each side as you go, to secure the remaining sides. As you work, the caning may start to dry out; if necessary, rewet it to keep it pliable.

When the caning has been tapped into the groove all around the frame, trim off any excess at the outside corner of the groove; set a sharp chisel into the groove to cut the cane. Then lay a narrow bead of white glue all around the groove on top of the caning. Blot the spline dry and force it into the groove over the caning, using a wooden or rubber mallet to drive it into the groove. Pull the spline tight as you go, and ease it around the corners. You may have to install the spline in several pieces; if so, make sure the ends butt together tightly to form a continuous spline. Finally, wipe off any excess glue.

Let the glue and the cane dry completely; as it dries, the caning will become taut. Let the job set for at least a week before you use it.

Mirror and Picture Frame Repairs

Although frames are really not pieces of furniture, they do play a role in furnishing, and some frames can be very valuable. Antique frames were usually made from solid cabinet wood, such as walnut, cherry, or mahogany—wood that's both hard to find and expensive today. For this reason, most old frames are well worth repairing.

Loose Joints. The usual problem with frames is separating miter joints. There are several ways to fix open miter joints, but the easiest way is glue. Force glue into the open joint with a glue injector and clamp it with a corner or a strap clamp. Look for metal fasteners along the edges of the joint; if necessary, drive them back into the wood after the clamp closes the gap in the joint.

If the joint won't stay closed, it can be glued and nailed; drill pilot holes to prevent the wood from splitting. You can either leave the nails flush with the surface of the wood or countersink them and fill the holes. If you leave the nails exposed, use decorative nails such as brass.

If the frame is a valuable antique, and you don't want to use nails, close the joint with a corner spline. Clamp the frame in a vise, padding the wood with a piece of carpet or a thick layer of cloth. With a ripsaw, cut a notch into and across the corners of the joint along the edge of the frame, as illustrated. Cut a thin piece of matching wood to fit into the saw cut; test it in the cut and adjust it as necessary. Spread a thin coating of glue onto both sides of the spline, insert the spline into the cut, and pull the joint together with a strap clamp. Let the glue dry completely. Then, with a sharp block plane, trim the edges of the spline flush with the surface of the frame, and sand them smooth. Spot-finish the spline area to match, or refinish the entire frame.

Damaged Carvings. Chipped frames can be patched with a thick mixture of spackling compound or plaster of paris. Roughly form the design you want to duplicate with the patching compound. Position the rough patch material and lightly press it against the frame; then, with the tip of a craft knife or a toothpick, final-shape the compound so it blends in with the design. It will probably be impossible to match the design exactly, but the repair won't be noticeable.

Let the patch dry completely, and then spot-stain or paint it to blend it with the rest of the frame. Test the colors on a chunk of dried spackling compound or plaster of paris before you apply the mixture to the frame repair. You should be able to color-blend the patch perfectly.

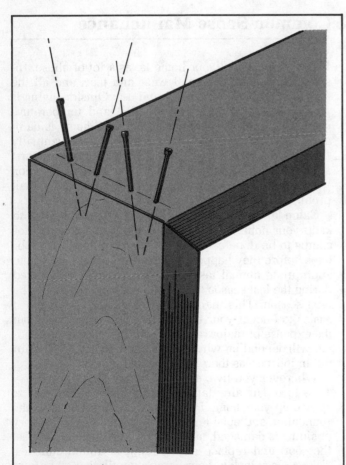

If glue doesn't hold a mitered corner, secure the joint with nails, driven into the wood at a slight angle. Drill pilot holes to keep the wood from splitting.

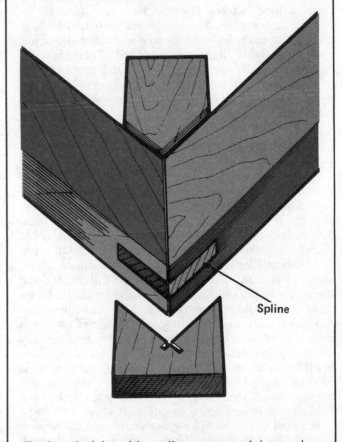

To close the joint with a spline, cut a notch into each joint edge; cut a thin spline from matching wood. Glue the spline in; when the glue is dry, trim it flush.

Structural Work

Until something goes wrong with their homes, most people don't know much about how they work. Home is where you live, where you keep your belongings and your friends come to visit; home is a place, not a physical object. But every home, whatever its size and shape, is also a physical structure, a collection of basic components that work together to provide you with an efficient shelter. It's a good shelter only as long as you keep it working properly, and when one of those components fails—the roof leaks, the stairs squeak, a window is broken, a wall is damaged—your home needs help.

Every homeowner and apartment-dweller has experienced these failures, from minor annoyances all the way to catastrophes. But while you're bound to have problems sometimes—things wear out, or break, or just don't work right—there's no need to be intimidated by the structure of your home. Structural problems are more likely to be a nuisance than a disaster, but even serious problems are easy to handle when you know how your home is put together.

How Your Home Is Built

Your home is made up of many separate parts: the foundation, the outside walls, the roof, the ventilation and drainage systems, the inside walls and floors, the window and door openings, even the decorations you add to your living space. When one of these parts fails, you have two problems to deal with: the immediate inconvenience or discomfort caused by the failure, and the stress it may put on other parts of the structure. Obviously, some problems are more serious than others, and can cause more eventual damage—cracked plaster is unattractive, but it doesn't threaten your home the way a cracked foundation wall would. But no matter how small the problem, you should take care of it as soon as you can. Even if the structural integrity of your home is not threatened, there's no reason why you should have to put up with problems in any part of your shelter.

The first step toward keeping your home in shape is learning how it works. This is not as difficult as it sounds, because each of the subsystems that makes up the structure is based on the same essential physical properties. Your home must be strong and solid; it must keep out hot and cold air, water, dirt, and insects; it must be comfortable and attractive. But when it comes to structural repairs, you don't have to know how to build your home so that it achieves these objectives; what you're concerned with is simply making sure it can continue to achieve them. You don't need any special training to do this: you're interested in trouble-shooting, not from-the-ground-up construction. What you do need is time, patience, a little basic know-how, and a lot of common sense.

Common-Sense Maintenance

Inside and outside, your home takes a lot of abuse. Inside, it's subject to normal wear and tear, and all the problems that come with age and use. Outside, aging is greatly accelerated by precipitation and temperature extremes. And when the outside of your home is damaged by severe weathering, the effects are eventually felt inside too. Weather, in fact, is your home's worst structural enemy, and you should take defensive action year-round to prevent weather damage and keep small problems from becoming worse.

Calendar maintenance is a very effective way to keep your home in shape. By setting up a schedule of chores to be done each season, you can head off problems before they happen. Each season, take care of the appropriate annual tasks; repair the damage incurred during the last season, and get your home ready for the next season. This maintenance schedule will make it easier to budget your time, and it will also spread out the expense of major repairs. Your maintenance schedule will depend on what part of the country you live in, but in most areas there are seasonal chores.

Wherever you live, spring is clean-up/fix-up time—time to repair any damage left by the winter, and to spruce up your home for a new year. First, inspect the foundation and outside walls of your home. If masonry or siding is damaged, take care of these repairs. Inspect the roof, and replace any missing or rotted shingles. Take a close look at your home's ventilation and drainage systems, and make sure they're in good order; open crawl space vents, check to make sure the chimney is clear, and clean and repair the gutters and downspouts.

Put the screens up and the storm windows away.

In summer, keep an eye on your home, and repair any new damage as it occurs. Summer storms can be severe, and repeated downpours can overload your gutters and downspouts. Make sure there's no standing water around your home, and keep the gutters clean and open. Inside, take care of plumbing problems.

Fall is the busiest season for preventive action. This is the time to check out your heating system, to caulk your home and install weatherstripping around doors and windows. Inspect the roof again, and make sure shingles, valleys, and flashing are in good repair. Clean the gutters and downspouts, cover crawl space vents, and turn off or protect outside water lines. Put the screens away and install the storm windows.

Winter is the season for rest, and for catching up. This is the time to take care of all the inside work you've been too busy to do—cracked walls, damaged tiles, carpet burns, squeaky floors. Take advantage of the cold weather to make the inside of your home comfortable.

Equipping Your Workshop

To keep your home in shape, you'll need a workshop—or a toolbox—equipped with an arsenal of basic tools and materials. For everyday projects, the most basic tools are sufficient: hammer, screwdrivers (slot and Phillips-head), pliers, measuring tape, drill, level, utility and craft knives, saws, files, wrenches, chisels, square. As you get involved in more repairs, add tools as you need them, and as your budget allows. The basic power tools are a drill with attachments, a saber saw and a circular saw; a sander—orbital or belt—is also useful. Other basic hand tools include a sledgehammer, a pry bar, a putty knife, wide and narrow scrapers, nail sets, a miter box, planes, tin snips, wire cutters, clamps, a caulking gun, and notched and pointed trowels. A propane torch also comes in handy.

With this selection of tools, you can handle just about any repair job, inside or out. For working up high, add a sturdy ladder and safety ropes; for painting, buy paintbrushes and rollers as you need them. Keep safety goggles and a breathing mask on hand for hazardous jobs. Whatever tools you acquire, buy the best tools you can afford. Good-quality tools are easier to work with, and, because they don't break or dull as readily, they're safer to use. And good tools will last a lifetime if you take care of them properly.

The materials you'll need will vary from job to job, but there are some basics you should have on hand. For everyday projects, build up an assortment of nails, screws, and other fasteners, in a range of sizes and types. Invest in various grades of sandpaper, in carpenters' glue and epoxy, in wood plastic and other fillers. Regular outside maintenance will require caulking and roofing compounds, glazing compound, concrete or blacktop patching mix; inside work will require spackling compound and paint. Buy replacement materials as needed for individual jobs—glass, wood, siding, weatherstripping. Save rope and sturdy cord, wire, scrap wood, and leftover materials from any installation or replacement; scraps of tile or carpeting, pieces of screening, bricks, and odd ceramic tiles will all come in handy when you need to make repairs. Save any material that's usable for repair purposes.

Inside Repairs

How attractive your home is, and how comfortable it is to live in, depends to a large extent on the condition of its interior walls and its floors. Every homeowner and apartment-dweller has seen the effects of age and use on these structural parts: walls crack, ceramic tile needs regrouting, stairs squeak, floors are damaged. All of these problems are easy to handle—you may even do a better job, because you care more about your home.

Patching Plaster

Everybody expects small cracks in plaster, but what do you do about the big ones? Fortunately, big cracks are much easier to fix than you might imagine. The trick is in using plaster of paris, which doesn't shrink.

To fill a large crack in a plaster wall, remove loose plaster; then wet the crack and pack plaster of paris in to its full depth. Smooth the surface with a scraper.

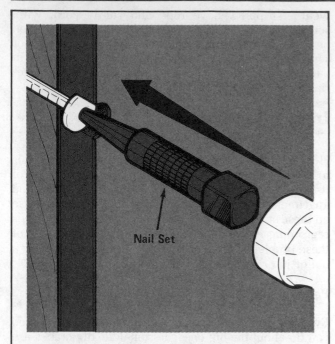

Nail pops in drywall are easy to eliminate. First drive the popped nail with a nail set as far as possible into the stud; then drive another nail above or below it.

Nail Set

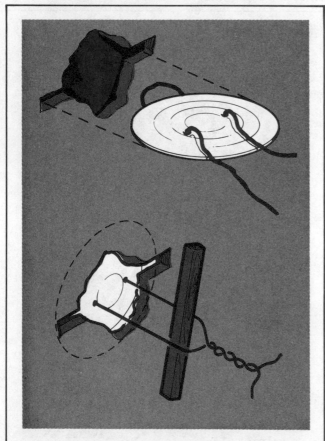

Cut slits out from the sides of the hole; thread a wire through a tin can lid and slide it in. Pull the lid flat on the inside, and hold it in place with a stick.

Before you can fill a large crack, you'll have to clean it. Use the pointed end of a beer can opener to cut out loose plaster; turn the opener to undercut and widen the opening. Then clean the loose plaster and dust from the crack with a vacuum cleaner. Mix a thick paste of plaster of paris and water, and wet the crack thoroughly with a paintbrush dipped in water. Pack plaster of paris into the wet crack to its full depth, and smooth the surface with a scraper. Let the filled crack dry until the plaster turns bright white—at least 24 hours.

Sand the patched crack lightly when the plaster is dry. If the crack was a wide one, you'll probably have to replaster it at least once to make the surface smooth. Wet the plastered area again with a wet paintbrush, and then smooth more plaster of paris over the crack. Let it dry for at least 24 hours after the final plastering; then sand the patch lightly and prime it with a thin coat of paint. When the primer is dry, paint the entire wall.

Mending Drywall

Most newer homes are built with drywall, not plaster; and drywall, like all building materials, has its own particular problems. One of the most common problems is the result of shrinking or warping in the framing behind the drywall; as the wood shrinks, nails loosen and pop out of the studs. These nail pops can be frustrating to deal with, because they'll show no matter how many times you patch over them. But they can be repaired permanently without too much trouble.

The first step is to redrive the popped nails. Hold a nail set over each popped nail, and hammer the nail as far as you can into the stud. The nail head will punch through the outside layer of paper and into the drywall. To make sure the nail stays there, drive another drywall nail to hold the drywall panel; set this nail about two inches above or below the old nail. Don't use a nail set on the new nail; pound it in flush with the wall and then give it one more light hammer blow to just dimple the surface of the drywall around the nail head. Cover the new nail head and fill the hole over the old nail with spackling compound, smoothed on with a putty knife or scraper. Let the compound dry and sand it lightly; if necessary, patch the nail heads once or twice again. Then touch up the patches or repaint the entire wall.

Holes in drywall can also be a problem, because this material can't withstand sharp blows the way plaster can—a door slammed into drywall can leave a neat doorknob-size hole. This kind of damage looks really bad, but even large holes are surprisingly easy to repair. For small holes, use a tin can lid to back a plaster patch; for large ones, cut a patch from scrap drywall.

To fix a small hole, remove any loose paper or plaster around the edges. Use a clean tin can lid, at least 1½ inches more in diameter than the hole, for a backer. Measure across the lid and cut a narrow slit out from each side of the hole with a keyhole saw, so that you can insert the lid sideways into the hole. Punch two holes in the center of the lid and thread a 12-inch piece of string or thin wire through them; then, holding the ends of the string or wire, slide the lid through the slit. Pull the lid flat against the inside of the wall, holding the string or wire firmly. To hold it in place, set a stick of scrap wood over the hole on the outside of the wall, and tie the string or twist the wire tightly over the stick. The tin can lid should be firmly held against the inside of the wall.

Mix plaster of paris with water to a thick paste, and pack plaster against the backer, and behind the stick, to fill the hole. Spackling compound doesn't work as well as plaster of paris, because it shrinks as it dries. Keep the plaster inside the hole; cover the backer and fill the slits, but don't spread plaster on the wall surface. Leave the patch slightly low; don't try to level it yet. Let the patch dry until the plaster turns bright white—at least 24 hours.

When the plaster is dry, cut the string or wire and remove the stick. You may be able to pull string out of the wall, but don't force it; if it won't come out, cut the ends flush with the patch surface. If you used wire, cut the ends flush with the patch. To finish the patch, fill it completely with more plaster of paris to cover the string or wire ends and make the patch level with the wall surface. Texture the plaster with a paintbrush to match the rest of the wall, and let the plaster dry. If the edges of the patch are obvious, sand the area lightly; then prime the patch with a thin coat of paint. When the primer is dry, paint the entire wall.

If the wallboard is badly broken, it requires a different repair procedure; instead of filling the hole with plaster, you'll have to use scrap wallboard to rebuild the damaged area. Cut a scrap piece of wallboard into a square or rectangle a little bigger than the hole or damaged area. Set the patch against the damaged area and trace around it; then cut out the outlined area of drywall with a keyhole saw. Keep your saw cut on the inside of the traced line so that the hole will be exactly the same size as the patch.

To hold the wallboard patch in place, you'll need a backing board, about six inches longer than the long dimension of the hole. Insert the board into the hole and hold it firmly against the inside of the wallboard. To keep it in place, fasten the ends of the board to the drywall with flathead screws driven through the wall at the sides of the hole; countersink the screws below the surface of the drywall. The board should be securely fastened, extending across the long dimension of the hole.

Use spackling compound or wallboard joint compound as glue to hold the patch in place. Spread compound on the exposed face of the backing board, and cover the edges of the wallboard patch with more compound. Set the patch into the hole, and adjust it so that it's exactly level with the surrounding wall; hold it in place until the compound starts to set. Let the compound dry—at least overnight. Then fill the patch outline and cover the exposed screw heads with spackling or joint compound; smooth the surface and texture it with a paintbrush to match the rest of the wall. Let the compound dry; if the patch outline still shows, sand it lightly and fill it again. Then prime the patch and repaint the wall.

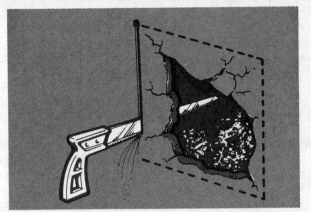

To mend a large hole in drywall, cut a square or rectangular patch piece; then cut out the damaged area to exactly the same size and shape as the patch.

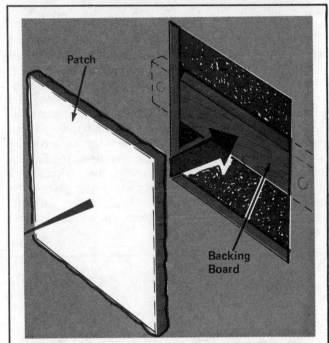

Patch

Backing Board

Secure a backing board on the inside of the wall to brace the patch; then coat the edges of the patch with spackling compound and set it into place in the hole.

Repairing Wallpaper

Although a papered wall is less likely to show cracks than a painted one, wallpaper is prone to several other problems—peeling, blisters, tears, and hard-to-remove dirt. All of these problems can age a room prematurely, but in most cases you can repair the damage. The repairs are easier if you plan ahead when the room is papered—save pieces of leftover wallpaper and a bottle of paste for patching, and coat the newly papered walls with a commercial protective coating. This transparent wallpaper coating can be used on most papers; test it on a scrap before you apply it to the entire room.

Loose seams in wallpaper can simply be repasted. Squeeze wallpaper paste under the loose edge with a squeeze bottle, or apply the paste with an artists' brush; then smooth the edge down and press it firmly with a seam roller. If the wallpaper is vinyl, use a special vinyl adhesive to reglue the loose edges.

Blisters can mar an otherwise perfect papering job. If the paper is newly pasted, the blister may be caused by a lump of paste that's still wet; when this happens, removing the lump is usually easy. Puncture the blister with a sharp needle or straight pin, and press the blister from the edges in toward the puncture, squeezing the excess paste out. Then wipe the excess paste off with a damp sponge, and press the area flat with a seam roller. If the paste is dry, or in old wallpaper, cut an X across the blister with a craft knife or a sharp razor blade. Bend the tips of the blister back and remove any dry lumps of paste; then apply a little new paste, smooth the edges back down, and press the reglued blister with a seam roller. The edges of the flattened blister may overlap slightly, but this won't be noticeable.

Wallpaper that's badly stained or torn can be patched with scraps of matching paper. If the paper is scratched or gouged, leave it in place; if it's loose around the tear, paste it down before patching. Don't try to remove damaged wallpaper before patching; instead, paste the patch directly over the damaged surface. To patch wallpaper, use a scrap of the same paper; match the pattern exactly to the damaged area. Tear out an irregular patch, a little larger than the damaged area; feather the edges of the patch as you tear it out, so that no hard edge will be visible on the wall. Apply wallpaper paste to the back of the patch and smooth it into place over the damaged area, pressing it down from the center out and aligning the pattern with the surrounding paper. Sponge off any excess paste.

Some wallpapers are washable, and can be sponged with a mild detergent solution. When nonwashable paper gets dirty, clean it with an artists' kneaded eraser; you may have to go over the entire wall to avoid spottiness. Or go over the walls with commercial wallpaper cleaner, as directed by the manufacturer. Before you use the cleaner on the entire wall, test it in an inconspicuous place.

Wallpaper that's worn all over usually can't be helped, but you may have only one or two worn spots to deal with. If you don't have any scraps of paper for patching, touching up the design is worth a try. Use felt-tip pens, carefully, to restore the rubbed or faded colors.

Ceramic Tile Repairs

Ceramic tile is very durable, but it can eventually show signs of wear—tiles crack or loosen, and the grout between tiles wears down and crumbles out. These are more than simple cosmetic problems, because unless you repair the damage, water can seep behind the tiles and cause more serious trouble. To keep the problem from getting worse, make the repairs as soon as you can.

Replacing a Tile. The hardest part of this job, especially if your bathroom is old, is finding a tile to match the broken one. If you can't find a new tile that matches, try looking in a junkyard for an old tile. With your replacement tile at hand, remove the cracked one. The easiest way to do this, without damaging the tiles around it, is to break up the old tile. Put a piece of masking tape at the center of the tile, and drill a hole into the taped spot with an electric drill and a carbide bit. Be sure to wear safety goggles while you do this; tile chips can do a lot of damage. After drilling a hole in the tile, peel off the tape and score an X across the tile with a glass cutter. Then, still wearing safety goggles, carefully break up the tile with a cold chisel and hammer, and remove the pieces.

After removing the old tile, you'll have to clean out the gap left by it. Use a scraper or a chisel to remove old adhesive and grout from the wall where the old tile was; if chunks of plaster have been pulled out of the wall, fill the holes with spackling compound, and let the compound dry. Make sure there's no loose grout around the opening.

To attach the new tile, you'll need ceramic tile mastic, sold at hardware stores, and ceramic tile grout. Spread mastic on the back of the tile with a putty knife or a notched spreader; leave the tile edges clean. Then carefully set the new tile into the opening on the wall. Press the tile firmly in, moving it slightly from side to side to distribute the mastic, until it's flush with the surrounding tile surface. The space around the tile should be even, and the tile should be perfectly aligned. To hold it in place while the mastic dries, tape it in place with masking tape or adhesive tape; if the tile is large, wedge pieces of broken toothpick around it to

To repair a blister in wallpaper, cut an X across it with a razor blade or craft knife. Apply paste to the loose tips and press them flat with a seam roller.

keep it from slipping. Let the mastic cure as directed by the manufacturer, and keep the tile dry during this curing period.

When the mastic has cured, remove the tape or toothpicks holding the tile in place. Mix ceramic tile grout to fill the joints around the tile; follow the grout manufacturer's mixing instructions, and make sure all lumps are removed. Use a damp sponge to apply the grout all around the new tile, filling the gaps completely. Grout is caustic, so wear rubber gloves. Let the grout set for about 15 minutes, and then wipe the wall with a clean damp sponge or towel to remove any excess grout. Be careful not to disturb the grout around the new tile. After removing the excess, let the grout dry completely, at least 12 hours—don't let the tile get wet during this drying period. Then rub the tile firmly with a damp towel to remove any remaining grout on the wall.

Loose ceramic tiles can be removed and then reattached with the same procedure. Scrape out the old grout around the loose tile with the corner of a putty knife, and then carefully pry out the tile; if it cracks, it will have to be replaced by a new one, as above. You can locate loose tiles by tapping carefully across the wall with the handle of the putty knife.

Regrouting Tile. Crumbling grout should be replaced as soon as possible to prevent mildew and water damage. Before you regrout, scrub the tile thoroughly with a strong household cleaner; rinse it well. If the old grout is mildewed, you must remove the mildew before you regrout; scrub the tile joints with a toothbrush dipped in chlorine bleach, and then rinse the wall thoroughly. When you're sure all the chlorine has been rinsed off, wash the wall again with ammonia to kill the mildew spores, and then rinse it with clean water. *Caution: Before you use ammonia, make sure there's no chlorine left on the wall; ammonia and chlorine combine to form a very dangerous gas.*

Let the wall dry, and then remove all the crumbling grout you can. Use the edge of a putty knife or a nut pick to scrape out the old grout. Then brush up any big chunks of grout and vacuum to remove the remaining debris. Rinse the wall again to make sure it's absolutely clean; it should be damp when the new grout is applied. Mix ceramic tile grout according to the manufacturer's instructions; make sure all lumps are removed. Apply the grout with a damp sponge, wiping it firmly over the wall to fill the joints. Wear rubber gloves while you work; grout is caustic. Smooth the newly grouted joints with a clean damp sponge; add more grout and smooth it again as necessary, to fill the tile joints completely.

When the joints are smooth and evenly filled, carefully wipe the wall clean with a damp sponge. Get the wall as clean as possible, but make sure you don't gouge the grout out of the joints. Let the grout dry for at least 12 hours; don't let the wall get wet during this period. Then scrub the wall firmly with a clean dry towel to remove any grout that's left on the tiles. Finally, to protect the new grout, seal the tile joints with a silicone tile grout spray.

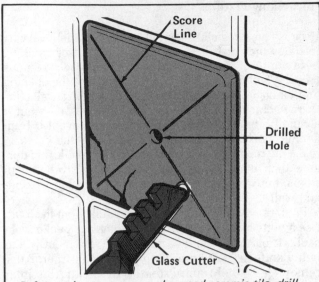

Before trying to remove a damaged ceramic tile, drill a hole through its center and score an X across it with a glass cutter. Then chisel out the pieces.

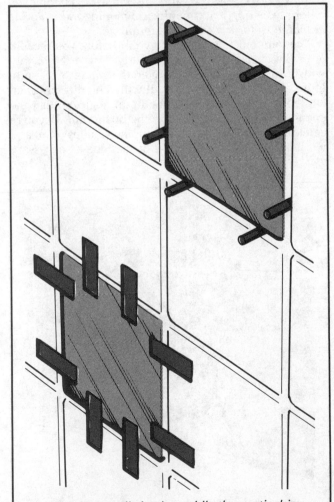

To hold the new tile in place while the mastic dries, tape it securely or wedge pieces of toothpick firmly into the open joints around it.

Recaulking Fixtures

Because tubs and sinks are subjected to widely varying loads as they're filled and emptied, grout or caulking between the fixture and the wall often cracks or pulls loose. When this happens, water seeps into the opening and damages the joint, and the surrounding wall, further. A cracked fixture joint may not look bad, but it should be fixed as soon as possible to prevent it from getting worse. Use silicone caulk or bathtub caulk to make the repair; these caulks are more flexible and durable than other types. Bathtub caulk is available in colors, but white caulk is suitable for any color fixture and wall.

First, remove all the old grout or caulk from the joint. Use a putty knife to pry out pieces of grout; peel out old caulk. If old caulk can't be peeled out, cut it out with a utility knife or craft knife to form a clean corner. After removing the old joint material, clean the joint thoroughly with a strong household cleaner. If the joint is mildewed, scrub it out with chlorine bleach, rinse, and then scrub it again with ammonia as above. Rinse it well. *Caution: Make sure all chlorine is removed before you apply ammonia; ammonia and chlorine combine to form a very dangerous gas.*

The joint must be completely dry before you recaulk it, or the caulk won't stick properly. Dry it thoroughly with a clean rag wrapped over the blade of a putty knife; if the joint is deep, dry it with a hair dryer. Then cut the nozzle of a caulk tube at an angle, so that the opening is a little larger than the open joint. If you're caulking several joints, start with the smallest joint and work up, recutting the nozzle of the tube as necessary

Squeeze the caulk evenly along the open joint; it must overlap both joint surfaces and fill the opening completely. Smooth the caulk with your finger.

for the larger joints. Bathtub caulk is simply squeezed out of the tube by hand; with a large cartridge of silicone caulk, use a caulking gun. Apply the caulk evenly all along the open joint, starting at a corner and working across the wall and around corners. Don't try to hurry the job; the bead of caulk must be firmly bonded to the joint surfaces all around the fixture. As soon as you finish applying the caulk, smooth it along the joint with your finger or thumb, pressing it evenly into the open joint. Very deep joints may require more than one application of caulk, because the first bead can be pushed all the way into the opening.

When the joint is completely filled and smooth, remove the caulk from your hands with a clean cloth or paper towel; it should come right off. Wash your hands as soon as you finish. Let the new caulk dry for several hours, and don't let it get wet during the drying period. Let the caulk cure completely, according to the manufacturer's instructions, before you touch it.

Eliminating Squeaks

Squeaky floors and stairs aren't serious structural problems, but they can be very annoying. If your floors are exposed hardwood, you may be able to stop the squeak by sprinkling talcum powder over the noisy boards and sweeping it back and forth to force it down into the cracks. On stairs, use packaged graphite powder or talcum powder in a squeeze bottle; apply the lubricant along all the joints in the problem area. The powder will lubricate the edges of the boards, eliminating the noise. For a more permanent repair, tackle the squeak with the procedures below.

Squeaky Floors. If there's a basement or crawl space under the noisy floor, work from this area to locate the problem. You'll need a helper upstairs to walk on the squeaky spot while you work. Watch the subfloor under the noisy boards while your helper steps on the floor above. If the subfloor moves visibly, or if you can pinpoint the noise, outline the affected areas with chalk. At the joists closest to your outlines, look for gaps between the joist and the subfloor; wherever there's a gap, the floorboards can move. To stop squeaks here, pound thin wedges into the gaps to stop the movement; shingles or wood shims make good wedges. If there are no gaps along the joists, or if the squeaks are coming from an area between joists, there's probably a gap between the floorboards and the subfloor. To pull the two layers together, drive wood screws up into the squeaky areas; drill pilot holes before inserting the screws. The wood screws must be long enough to penetrate into the floor above you, but make sure they aren't so long that they go all the way through the boards—if this happens, you'll end up with sharp screw points sticking up from your floor.

If you can't get at the floor from underneath, you'll have to work from the top, with spiral flooring nails. Locate the squeak and try to determine whether it's at a joist or between joists. To eliminate the squeak, drive

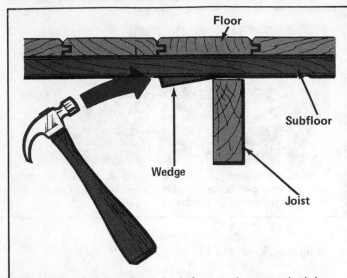

Working under the floor, look for gaps between the joists and the subfloor. Drive wedges into the gaps to keep the floor from moving, and to stop the squeaks.

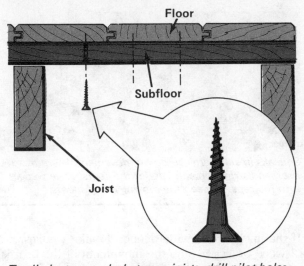

To eliminate squeaks between joists, drill pilot holes and drive wood screws up through the subfloor and the floorboards to pull the layers together.

two spiral flooring nails, angled toward each other in a V, through the floorboards and the subfloor; at a joist, use longer spiral flooring nails, and drive them through the floorboards and the subfloor and into the joist. Drill pilot holes before driving the nails; countersink the nail heads with a nail set, and cover them with wood filler.

If the floor is tiled or carpeted, and you can't get at the floorboards from above or below, you probably won't be able to eliminate the squeak without removing the floor covering. Before you do this, try to reset the loose boards by pounding. Using a hammer and a block of scrap wood as a buffer, pound the floor firmly over the squeaky boards, in an area about two or three feet square. The pressure of the pounding may force loose nails back into place.

Squeaky Stairs. Stairs are put together with three basic components: the tread, the riser, and the stringer (the side piece). In most cases, squeaks are caused by the tread rubbing against the riser or the stringer. If you can, work from under the stairs to fix the squeak; you'll need a helper to walk up and down the stairs while you work.

Watch the stairs from below while your helper walks on them; look for movement and for cracks in the wood, loose nails, or other problems. The simplest way to fix the squeak is to wedge the components—tread, riser, or stringer—that are moving. Cut small wedges from wood shingles or shims. To install a wedge, apply carpenters' glue to the side that will lie against the stairs. Drive the wedge into the squeaking joint, either tread-riser or tread-stringer. When the wedge is tight, secure it with small nails; be careful not to split the wedge. The nails must be long enough to hold the wedge securely, but make sure they don't go all the way through the stair component and stick out on the other side.

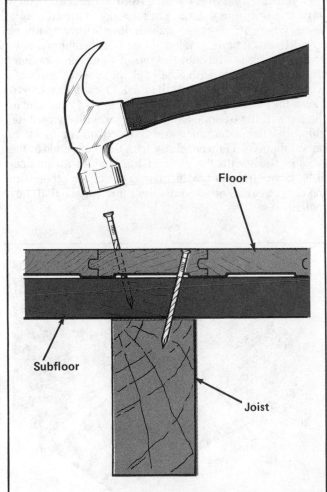

If there is no access to the floor from below, drive two spiral flooring nails, angled in a V, through the floor and the subfloor into a joist.

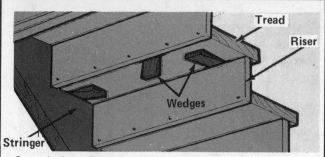

Squeaks in stairs are caused by movement where tread, riser, and stringer meet. Under the stairs, drive wedges into the gaps between the moving components.

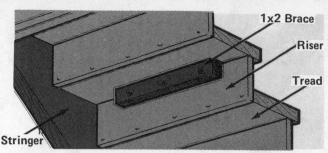

If the gaps between stair components aren't wide enough to accept wedges, brace the joints with 1x2 blocks to stop the movement of the stairs.

If the joints aren't wide enough to take wedges, use 1×2 wood braces to stop the movement of the boards. Use one long or two or more short 1×2 blocks for each stair-width joint. Apply carpenters' glue to the sides of the block that will lie against the stairs; then set the block into the squeaking joint and nail it into place.

If you can't get at the stairs from underneath, you'll have to work from the top. For squeaks at the front of a tread, where it meets the riser below it, drive pairs of spiral flooring nails, angled toward each other in a V, across the tread and into the top of the riser. Countersink the nail heads with a nail set, and cover them with wood filler. For squeaks at the back of a tread, where it meets the riser above, drive thin wedges into the joint at the back of the tread. Coat the wedges with carpenters' glue, and use a hammer and a wood buffer block to pound them in. Then carefully trim the wide ends of the wedges flush with the riser. If the wedges are noticeable, cover the joint with quarter-round or other trim molding; treat all other joints the same way so that they match.

Repairing Resilient Flooring

Today's resilient floors are a real boon, but they can lose their attraction very quickly when they're damaged. Fortunately, even the worst-looking damage is fairly easy to repair, whether the floor is tile or sheet vinyl or linoleum.

Tile Floors. Tile repairs are very simple, because only the affected tiles must be considered. If a tile is loose, it can be reglued with floor tile adhesive; if it's just loose at one edge or corner, there may be enough old adhesive left on the tile to reattach it. Cover the tile with aluminum foil, and then with a clean cloth. Heat the loose edges with an iron, set to medium heat, to soften the old adhesive and rebond it. When the adhesive has softened, weight the entire tile and let the adhesive cure for several hours or overnight.

If the old adhesive isn't strong enough to reattach the tile, use a floor tile adhesive made for that type of tile. Heat the tile as above, and carefully lift the loose edges

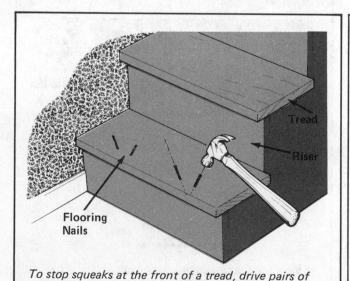

To stop squeaks at the front of a tread, drive pairs of spiral flooring nails, each pair angled in a V, across the tread and into the top of the riser below it.

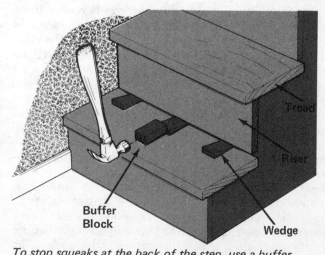

To stop squeaks at the back of the step, use a buffer block to drive thin wedges between the tread and the riser. Trim the ends of the wedges flush.

with a paint scraper or a putty knife. Scrape the old adhesive off the edges of the tile and apply a thin coat of new adhesive, using a notched spreader or trowel. Then smooth the tile firmly from center to edges, and weight the entire tile. Let the adhesive cure as directed by the manufacturer, and then remove the weights.

If a tile is damaged, you can easily replace it. To remove the tile, heat it with a propane torch with a flame-spreader nozzle; be careful not to damage the surrounding tiles. Then pry it up with a paint scraper or a putty knife. Or, instead of heating the tile, cover it with dry ice; wear work gloves to protect your hands. Let the dry ice stand for about 10 minutes and remove any remaining ice; then carefully chisel out the tile, from the center to the edges. The cold will make the tile very brittle, so that it shatters easily. After removing the tile, scrape all the old adhesive off the floor to make a clean base for the new tile. Fill any gouges in the tile base with spackling compound or wood filler, and let the filler dry completely.

Check the fit of the new tile in the prepared opening; use the same standard size as the old one. If the new tile doesn't fit exactly, sand the edges or carefully slice off the excess with a sharp utility knife and a straightedge. When the tile fits perfectly, spread a thin coat of floor tile adhesive in the opening, using a notched trowel or spreader. Warm the new tile with an iron to make it flexible, and then carefully set it into place in the opening, pressing it firmly onto the adhesive. Weight the entire tile firmly, and let the adhesive cure as directed by the manufacturer. Remove the weights when the adhesive is completely cured.

Sheet Flooring. Damaged sheet flooring looks even worse than damaged tile, but if you have a matching scrap of flooring, you can cut in a patch to replace the bad spot. You can also make a patching compound from scrap flooring, to fill deep scratches without patching. To make the compound, bend a piece of scrap flooring in half, right side out. Scrape the folded edge with a utility knife, making a fine powder; catch the scrapings in a small shallow pan. Rebend the flooring as you work to keep the scrapings the color of its top surface. When you have more than enough powder to fill the scratch, mix a few drops of clear nail polish with it; use only enough to make a thick paste. Cover the floor around the patch with masking tape, and then fill the scratch with your patching paste; smooth it along the scratch with a putty knife. Let the patch dry for about an hour, remove the tape, and buff the patch lightly with No. 000 steel wool.

When the floor is badly worn or damaged, use the scrap flooring to patch it; you'll need a piece of flooring a little bigger than the bad spot, with the same pattern. Position the scrap over the bad spot so that it covers the damage completely, and align the pattern exactly with the floor pattern. Tape the patch firmly in place on the floor, using package sealing tape all around the edges. Then, with a straightedge and a sharp utility knife, cut a rectangle through the scrap piece and through the floor-

To remove a damaged tile, soften it with a propane torch and a flame-spreader nozzle. Be careful not to damage the surrounding tiles.

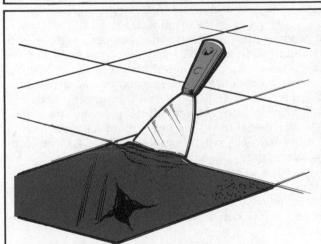

When the tile is soft, pry it up with a paint scraper or putty knife; then scrape the adhesive off the floor so the new tile will bond cleanly.

ing below it, to make a patch bigger than the damaged area. Cut along joints or lines in the pattern, if possible, to make the patch harder to see. You'll probably have to go over each cut several times to cut completely through the two layers of flooring; stay on the original score lines, being careful not to cut an uneven edge. Make sure the corners are cleanly cut.

When the flooring is cut through, untape the scrap piece and push out the rectangular patch. Soften the old flooring inside the cut lines by heating it with an iron, set to medium heat; cover the patch area with aluminum foil and then with a clean cloth, and press until the adhesive holding the flooring has softened. Carefully pry up the damaged piece with a paint scraper or putty

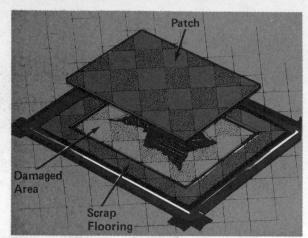

Use a piece of scrap flooring to cut a patch for damaged sheet flooring; tape the scrap piece down and cut through both layers.

knife. Scrape all the old adhesive off the floor to make a clean base for the patch; if there are any gouges in the floor, fill them and let the filler dry completely.

Try the patch in the opening; it should fit perfectly. If it binds a little, you can sand the edges slightly with medium- or fine-grit paper to adjust the fit. When the patch fits exactly, spread a thin coat of floor tile adhesive in the opening with a notched trowel or spreader. Set the patch carefully into the gap, press it firmly in, and wipe off any excess adhesive around the edges. Then heat-seal the edges to the main sheet of flooring. Protect the floor with aluminum foil and a clean cloth, as above; press the edges firmly but quickly with a hot iron. After bonding the edges, weight the entire patch firmly, and let the adhesive cure as directed by the manufacturer. Remove the weights when the adhesive is completely cured; don't wash the floor for at least a week.

Repairing Burns in Carpeting

Professional reweaving is expensive, but what else can you do when your carpeting is damaged by cigarette burns? Actually, with a little patience, you can usually repair the damage just as well yourself.

When only the tips of the carpet fibers are burned, carefully cut off the charred fiber with a small sharp scissors. Then sponge the area lightly with a mild detergent solution, and again with clean water. The low spot won't be noticeable when the carpet dries.

If the burn goes all the way to the backing, you can remove the charred fibers and insert new ones. Carefully cut out the burned fibers, and then pull the stubs out of the backing with tweezers. Clean out the entire burn area, so that you have a hole in the carpet with the woven backing exposed. To fill the hole, ravel fibers from the edge of a scrap piece of carpet; you'll need enough individual tufts of yarn to place one tuft in each

opening in the backing. If you don't have a scrap piece, use tufts from an inconspicuous area of the carpet, such as the back corner of a closet.

When you have enough fibers, apply a little latex adhesive to the exposed backing. Use a carpet tuft-setting tool, a small punch with a forked tip, to insert the new fibers, one fiber in each opening. Fold each fiber in half to form a V, and place the folded tuft into the tuft-setter. Set the tip of the tuft-setter into the opening in the backing and strike the handle lightly with a hammer. When you lift the tuft-setter, the fiber will stay in the carpet backing. Set fibers across the entire burn area, one at a time. The repair area should match the rest of the carpet in density and depth; if a tuft doesn't match in height, you can adjust by pulling it up a little with tweezers or tapping it down again with the tuft-setter. When the hole is completely filled, cut off any protruding fibers flush with the rest of the pile.

Retufting works well for small burns, but if the backing is burned through, or if a large area of carpet is damaged, you'll have to replace the burned area with a patch, cut from a piece of scrap carpet. Cut out a rectangle or square of carpet, a little larger than the burned area. The patch must match any pattern in the carpet, and the pile must run in the same direction as the damaged pile, or the patch will be very obvious. Press the patch firmly over the damaged area; holding it carefully in place, use a utility knife to cut around its edges and through the carpet under it. Cut completely through the backing, but don't cut into the carpet padding. When the entire damaged area is cut out, lift the burned piece out of the hole. Check the patch for fit, and trim the edges slightly, if necessary, so that it fits the opening exactly.

To install the patch, use double-faced carpet tape and latex adhesive. On each side of the hole, stick a piece of tape to the bottom of the carpet, leaving half its width exposed in the opening. Then apply a little latex adhesive along each piece of exposed tape. Position the patch and press the edges of the patch firmly onto the glued tape. The pattern and pile of the patch should blend with the surrounding carpet. Let the adhesive dry for several hours before walking on the patch, as directed by the manufacturer.

Replacing Baseboard Molding

Baseboard molding performs three functions: it hides the joint where floor and wall meet, it protects the base of the wall, and it adds a finishing touch to the room's decoration. In many older homes, years of abuse have left the baseboards cracked, split, or badly battered. They still function physically, but they look terrible. Fortunately, replacing the baseboards is not as difficult as it might seem. You can use the same techniques to replace damaged molding anywhere in your home.

Molding is generally installed in two pieces, the baseboard itself and the quarter-round or shoe molding. Either or both parts can be replaced, but if the quarter-round is not damaged, it can be reused. If you're replac-

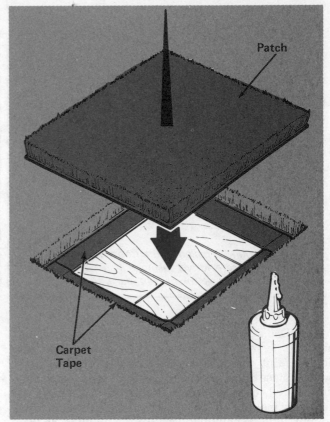

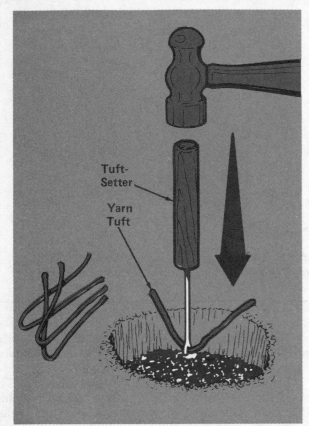

Retuft the burned area by inserting tufts of matching yarn into the carpet backing. With a tuft-setter, drive one tuft into each mesh in the backing.

Insert a patch of scrap carpet to repair a large burned area; cut out the damaged carpet and secure the patch with double-faced carpet tape and latex adhesive.

ing the molding around the entire room, buy new molding as nearly as possible the same height and thickness; if you're replacing only one section, bring the damaged section with you when you buy so you can match it exactly. Long strips of molding are more expensive than short ones, but they're much easier to install because there are fewer joints. If you can, use one long strip of molding for each wall instead of piecing short ones together.

The first step is to remove the old molding, first the quarter-round and then the baseboard itself. The quarter-round is usually nailed to the floor, not the wall. Insert the blade of a stiff putty knife between the quarter-round and the floor, and pry gently to loosen the quarter-round along the entire length of the wall. When the molding has loosened enough, use a screwdriver, a chisel, or a small pry bar, levering it on a block of scrap wood, to pry it up completely. Leave the nails in the quarter-round, and be careful not to break it—even if you're going to replace it, you'll need the old molding as a pattern for the new piece. When the quarter-round is out, carefully loosen the baseboard molding. Start with a putty knife inserted between the molding and the wall; then, as soon as the molding is loose enough to accept it, use the blade of a small pry bar. Work along

the entire length of the wall to avoid cracking the molding. As soon as the molding is loose enough, insert small wedges of scrap wood behind it, all along the wall, prying and wedging to remove the baseboard completely. Leave the nails in the molding, and try not to damage it.

After removing the old molding, check for nails left in the wall and floor, and pull them out. Then cut the new baseboard molding to fit. If possible, use the old molding as a pattern; otherwise, measure very carefully. It's better to cut a little long than too short. To make sure the pieces are all properly matched, measure and cut all the new molding before you nail it into place.

At outside corners, you'll need a miter box and a backsaw to make 45-degree cuts in the joining pieces. Hold the molding very firmly against the side of the miter box, and keep the miter box steady while you cut—brace it on the edge of your work table. The two 45-degree ends will fit together to form a perfect 90-degree outside angle.

At inside corners, you'll need a coping saw to cut a coped joint, with one piece of baseboard overlapped and curved over the other. First cut the baseboard for one side, making a straight cut to butt the molding firmly into the corner. Tack this baseboard into place near the corner with a small finishing nail driven part-

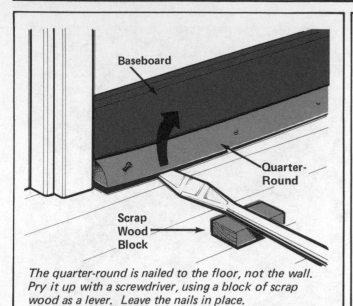

The quarter-round is nailed to the floor, not the wall. Pry it up with a screwdriver, using a block of scrap wood as a lever. Leave the nails in place.

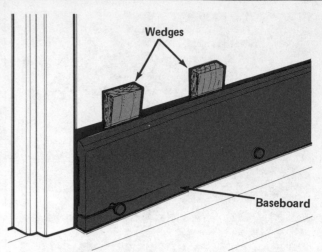

After removing the quarter-round, remove the baseboard, prying and wedging it gradually out from the wall. Work along the entire wall to avoid damaging the molding.

way in. Use a scrap of molding, also cut straight down the edge, to mark the outline of the joining piece of molding. Butt the scrap firmly into the corner against the first piece of molding. Then, with a sharp pencil or a scratch awl, carefully trace its outline onto the first piece of molding. Hold the pencil or scratch awl straight, with its point tight against the molding, so that your outline is exact. Remove the nail holding the long piece of molding in place, and then very carefully, with a coping saw, cut off the end of the molding along the traced outline. To make the joint, straight-cut a piece of

molding to fit the second wall; butt the molding firmly into the corner. Set the trimmed piece of molding over it; the outlined cut should fit exactly.

When all the molding is cut and fitted, you can nail it into place. Use two 2d finishing nails to fasten the molding at each wall stud; look for the nail holes left by the old molding. Sink the nail heads with a nail set. When the baseboard molding is in place, cut and fit the new quarter-round the same way you did the baseboard; or, if it's undamaged, reuse the old molding. If the end of the quarter-round is exposed at a door frame, round the

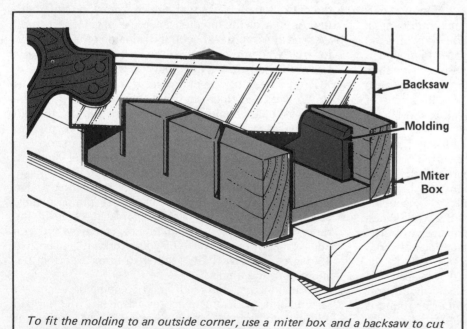

To fit the molding to an outside corner, use a miter box and a backsaw to cut each joining piece to a 90-degree angle; hold both box and molding steady to keep the cuts accurate. Join the miter-cut ends to make the corner.

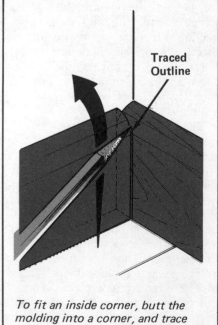

To fit an inside corner, butt the molding into a corner, and trace the outline of the joining piece.

cut end with a chisel so that it curves smoothly back from the door, and sand the curve smooth. Then nail the quarter-round into place, using 2d finishing nails about 12 inches apart; drive the nails into the floor, not into the baseboard. If you're reusing the old quarter-round, use the old nails if possible, driven through the same nail holes. Sink all nail heads with a nail set.

To finish the job, cover all exposed nail heads with wood plastic. When the filler is dry, finish the new molding as desired.

Windows and Doors

The openings in your home's walls—the doors and windows—are very often structural trouble spots. Windows and doors are the major heat loss areas in most homes; they may stick shut when they're painted or swell shut from humidity. Inside, shades and venetian blinds may not work right; outside, glass gets broken, screens get torn, and garage doors malfunction. Both inside and out, from weatherstripping to structural repairs, there's a lot you can do to keep your doors and windows working right.

Unsticking a Window

Double-hung windows, especially in older homes, often stick; they may be hard to open and close or they may refuse to open at all. The most common cause of this problem is that the window has been painted shut, and the paint has sealed it closed. The solution is usually simple: break the seal and clear and lubricate the sash tracks. The procedure takes strength, but it isn't difficult.

Before you start to work, make sure the window is unlocked. Then look for evidence of a paint seal between the sash and the window frame. The seal usually extends all around the window. To break the seal, push the blade of a stiff putty knife or paint scraper into the joint, cutting straight in through the paint. If necessary, tap the knife lightly with a hammer to force the blade in. Work all around the window to break the seal; if the window was also painted on the outside, repeat the procedure to break the seal on the outside. This should release the window.

If the window still doesn't open, look at the tracks in the window frame above the sash; they're probably blocked with built-up paint. Using a hammer and chisel, clean the excess paint out of the tracks; cut out the thickened paint, but be careful not to gouge the wood of the tracks. Smooth the cleaned-out tracks with medium-grit sandpaper on a narrow sanding block, and then spray them with silicone lubricant. The window should slide freely in the newly cleared tracks.

If the window still sticks, the paint in the bottom tracks is probably holding it. First, set a block of scrap wood against the sash at the window frame. Tap the block of wood with a hammer, very gently, to force the sash back from the frame. Don't exert too much force; all you want to produce is a very slight movement.

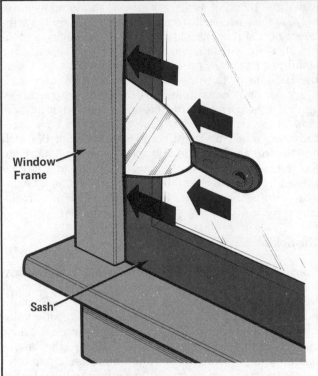

To free a window that's been painted shut, use a scraper or putty knife to cut the paint seal between the sash and the window frame.

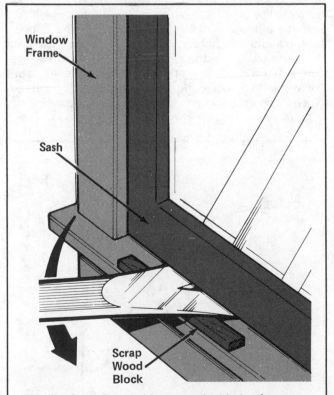

Working from the outside, insert the blade of a pry bar under the sash and pry gently from the corners in; lever the bar over a block of scrap wood.

Move the block of wood all around the window sash, tapping the sash back from the frame; then try the window again. If it opens, clean and sand the tracks, and lubricate them with silicone spray. If it doesn't open, use a small pry bar on it, preferably from the outside. Insert the flat end of the pry bar under the sash, and set a block of scrap wood under it for better leverage. Pry gently at the corners of the sash and then from the corners in toward the center. Use the pry bar very carefully; too much pressure could damage both the sash and the frame. If the window opens, clean and lubricate the tracks as above. If it doesn't, the sticking may be caused by extreme humidity, poor construction, or uneven settling. Don't try to force the window open; call a carpenter to fix it.

Unsticking a Door

Doors, like windows, stick for a number of reasons, from poor construction to extreme humidity. In most cases, it's easy to unstick the stubborn door. To diagnose the problem, close the door, watching it carefully to locate the binding point. If there's a gap between the door and the frame opposite the binding edge, the hinges probably need adjustment. If you can't see a gap anywhere between the door and the frame, and you had to slam the door to close it, the wood has probably swollen from extreme humidity. If the hinges and the wood are both all right, the door frame itself may be out of alignment; check the frame with a carpenters' square to see if this is the case.

If the binding is caused by poorly adjusted hinges, first examine the hinges for loose screws, both on the door and on the frame. Tighten any loose screws securely. If a screw doesn't tighten, the screw hole has become enlarged. When the hole is only slightly enlarged, you may be able to correct the problem by replacing the

screw with a longer one; make sure the head is the same size. Or use a hollow fiber plug with the old screw; spread carpenters' glue on the outside of the plug, insert it into the screw hole, and let the glue dry as the manufacturer directs. Then drive the screw into the hole. When the screw hole is badly enlarged, use wood toothpicks to fill it in. Dip the toothpicks into carpenters' glue and insert them around the screw hole; let the glue dry and then trim the toothpicks off flush with the surface. Drive the screw into the filled-in hole; it should hold securely.

If the screws are not loose, the hinges may have to be readjusted on the door frame. Close the door, watching to see where it sticks and where it gaps. If the door is tilted in the frame, it will stick at the top on one side and at the bottom on the other; there will be a gap between the door and the frame opposite each binding point. To remedy this situation, you'll have to shim out the hinge diagonally across from the binding point on the latch side—if the top latch edge sticks, shim the bottom hinge; if the bottom latch edge sticks, shim the top hinge. If the door has three hinges, shim the middle hinge as well as the top or bottom one.

Shimming the hinges is simple, but you must hold the door in place while you're working. Open the door as far as it will go, and push a wedge under it to hold it firmly. At the hinge to be adjusted, loosen the screws from the hinge leaf on the door frame; don't touch the screws in the door itself. Cut a piece of thin cardboard to the same size as the hinge leaf, and mark the location of the hinge screws on it. Cut horizontal slots in the shim to fit over the screws; then slide the shim over the screws behind the loosened hinge leaf. Keeping the shim in place, tighten the screws to resecure the hinge. Remove the wedge holding the door and close the door. If the door still sticks, but not as much as it did before, add another shim under the hinge. This should elimi-

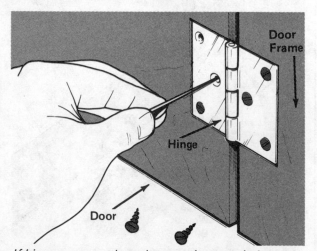

If hinge screws are loose because the screw holes are enlarged, fill the holes with wood toothpicks, dipped in glue, inserted, and trimmed flush.

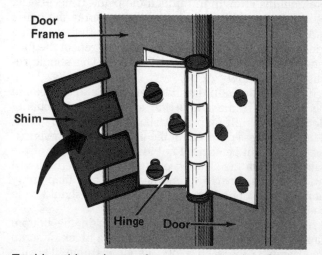

To shim a hinge, loosen the screws on the door frame side. Cut a shim from thin cardboard, with slots to fit around the screws, and slide it behind the hinge.

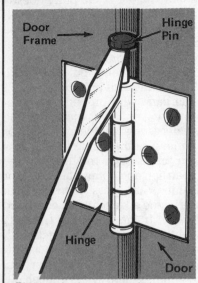

First at the bottom and then at the top, tap the hinge pin up and out with a screwdriver.

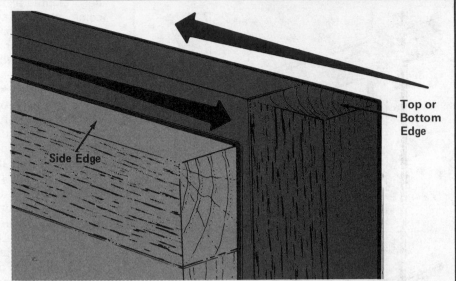

Plane the sides of the door (left) with a jack plane; cut from the center toward the ends. On the top and bottom edges (right), use a block plane; cut from the ends toward the center. Remove only a little wood at a time.

nate the gap between the door and the frame, and should also eliminate the binding.

If the door sticks even after shimming, or if there is no gap anywhere around the frame, you'll have to remove some wood at the binding points. Use a block plane on the top or bottom of the door, a jack plane to work on the side. If the door sticks at the sides, try to plane only on the hinge side; the latch side is beveled slightly, and planing could damage the bevel. Use the plane carefully, removing only a little wood at a time; keep your cuts even across the entire binding edge.

The top of the door can be planed without taking the door down. Wedge the door as far open as it will go, and work from a stepladder. With a block plane, cut carefully from the ends of the door toward the center. Don't cut from the center out; this could split the wood. Test the door after planing only a little bit; don't cut off any more wood than you have to.

If the bottom or side of the door needs planing, you'll have to take the door out of the frame. Close the door most of the way, but don't latch it. Door hinges are secured by long hinge pins; to take the door down, tap the hinge pins out, starting with the bottom hinge and working up. Using the tip of a screwdriver as a chisel under the pin's head, tap the pin up out of the hinge. If it sticks, tap a long nail up against the pin to dislodge it. Then tap out the middle and top hinge pins, and carefully lift the door out of the frame. Set the door on its side. If possible, have a helper hold it in place while you work; otherwise, clamp it to a large wooden crate to hold it steady. Then carefully plane the binding edge of the door. To plane the bottom, use a block plane, and cut from the ends toward the center. To plane the sides, remove the hinges and use a jack plane; cut from the center toward the ends. Never cut from the ends toward the

center on the side of the door; this could split the wood.

After planing evenly all along the binding edge, set the door back into the frame, and open and close it. If it still sticks, plane off a little more wood. Before you replace the door permanently, you must seal the planed edges; if you don't do this, the raw wood will absorb moisture and the door will stick again. Coat the raw edges with thinned shellac, and let the shellac dry for at least an hour. Then rehang the door.

If the door sticks because the frame is out of alignment, there's not much you can do to fix it. At the binding point, set a piece of 2×4 flat against the frame, and give it several firm hammer blows. This may move the frame just enough to solve the problem. If this doesn't work, you'll have to adjust the hinges or plane the edges to allow for the unevenness of the frame. The door may end up crooked, but it won't stick.

Replacing Broken Glass

A broken windowpane is one of the worst-looking and most immediate of emergencies—your protection from the weather is gone, and so is your security. But broken glass is also one of the easiest structural problems to fix. You can buy replacement glass, cut to measure, at lumberyards and hardware stores.

The first step is to remove the broken glass from the window frame. Wearing heavy gloves, work the pieces of glass back and forth until they're loose enough to pull out. Knock out any stubborn pieces with a hammer. Next, remove all the old putty from the frame, using a chisel or a scraper to pry it out. As you work, look for the fasteners that held the glass in place—metal tabs called glaziers' points in wood-frame windows; spring clips in metal frames. Set the points or clips aside; you'll

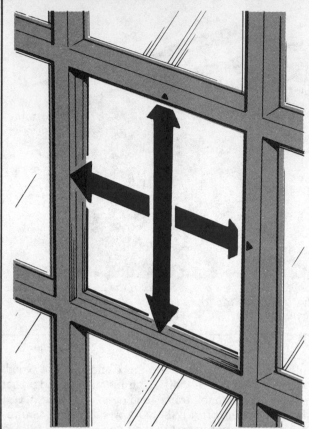

Measure the window frame from inside edge to inside edge, up and down and sideways. Have the new pane cut at least 1/16 inch smaller each way.

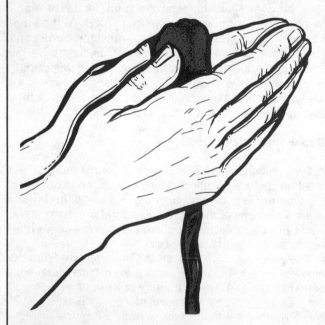

Use glaziers' compound or putty to install the new pane; roll the compound between your palms to make a long string about the diameter of a pencil.

need them to install the new glass. If the putty doesn't come out easily, soften it with a propane torch or a soldering iron; or paint it with linseed oil and let the oil soak in. Then scrape out the softened putty, being careful not to gouge the window frame.

When all the old putty has been removed, wire-brush the frame to take off the last traces of putty. Then paint the raw wood around the pane with linseed oil to prevent the new putty from drying out too fast; if the frame is metal, paint it to prevent rusting. Let the oil soak in or the paint dry, and then measure the frame for the new glass. The glass must be just enough smaller than the opening to allow for expansion and contraction, and for imperfections in the frame or the glass. Measure both ways across the opening, inside edge to inside edge, and subtract 1/16 inch each way. If the lip of the frame is very wide, it's best to subtract as much as 1/8 inch each way. Have double-strength glass cut to these precise dimensions. You'll need glaziers' points or clips every six inches or so around the pane; if there aren't enough old ones, buy new ones when you get the glass.

You can use either glaziers' compound or putty to install the new glass, but glaziers' compound is better. Roll a large chunk of compound between your palms to make a long string about the diameter of a pencil. Starting at a corner, press this cord into the outside corner of the window frame, where the glass will rest. Cover the entire diameter of the frame. With the compound in place, carefully set the new pane of glass into the frame, pressing it firmly against the cord of compound. Press hard enough to flatten the compound, squeezing out air bubbles and forcing some of the compound out around the frame. Then, to hold the glass in place, install glaziers' points or spring clips every six inches or so around the pane. Push the points partway into the wood with the blade of a putty knife, held flat against the glass; or, if the frame is metal, snap the spring clips into the holes in the frame.

When the glass is firmly held in place, seal the new pane with glaziers' compound all around the outside edge. Roll another cord of glaziers' compound, and press it firmly into the glass-frame joint, all around the pane. Then use a putty knife to smooth the compound all along the joint around the pane, to match the putty around the other windows nearby. Hold the putty knife at an angle to the lip of the frame, so that the knife cuts the compound off cleanly and evenly along the glass. If the putty knife sticks or pulls at the glaziers' compound, dip the blade into linseed oil and shake off the excess. Use long, smooth strokes to keep the joint even around the pane.

While the glaziers' compound is still fresh, carefully remove the excess from both sides of the new glass and the frame, with a razor blade or a glass scraper. Then let the compound dry completely—about three days. To finish the job, paint the new compound and the frame to match the rest of the frame. Lap the paint slightly over the edge of the compound and onto the glass, to seal the pane completely. Make sure the paint is dry before you clean the glass.

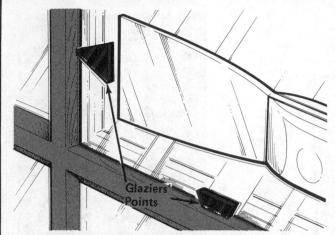

In a wood-frame window, glaziers' points hold the glass in place. Set one point every six inches around the pane; push the points in with the blade of a putty knife.

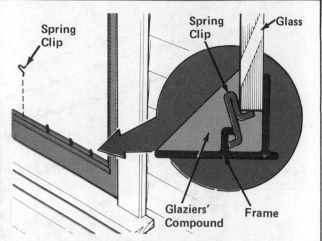

In a metal-frame window, the glass is held by spring clips instead of glaziers' points. Install the clips by snapping them into the holes in the frame.

Replacing a Broken Sash Cord

Double-hung windows, the kind found in most older homes, are still popular today in new home construction. Their most common problem—a broken sash cord—is still with us, too. Double-hung windows operate on a rope-and-pulley system. Each of the two window units, or sash, is held on each side by a rope or sash cord extending from the sash up to a pulley in the window frame, and over the pulley into the inside of the wall. A heavy weight at the end of each sash cord balances the weight of the window, and holds the sash in place when you open the window. When the sash cord breaks, the weight falls to the bottom of the frame, and there's nothing to hold the sash in place. You can replace the broken cord with a new cord, but to eliminate rope failure entirely, use sash chain, made for this purpose.

First, you'll have to remove the sash from the window frame. On both sides of the window, remove the inside stop molding along the side of the sash frame. If the molding has been painted over, cut the paint seal between the frame and the moldings; use a utility knife or a sharp single-edge razor blade. Then carefully pry off the molding strip with a stiff scraper or a flat pry bar.

After removing the stop molding, ease the sash out of the window frame on the side with the broken cord until you can get at the slot at the top of the sash where the cord is attached. Cut or untie the knot in the end of the cord, and pull it out of the sash frame. Then ease the other side of the sash toward you out of the frame—you may need help to balance the sash on the sill while you work. Untie the knot that holds the cord on this side, and pull it out of the sash frame—don't let go of the end, or it will be pulled into the window frame. Knot the loose end of the cord to keep it from being pulled in, and then lift the sash down out of the window frame. Set it aside while you work on the cord. If the broken cord operates

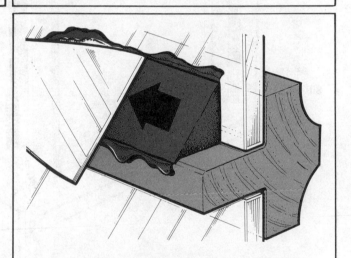

Seal the pane with glaziers' compound, using a putty knife to smooth the compound at an angle and cut it off cleanly along the glass.

the top sash, you'll have to remove the bottom sash and pry out the parting strip between the two sashes, then remove the top sash.

Many double-hung windows have access plates set into the sides of the frame, so that you can get into the window frame to replace the cord. Some old windows do not have access plates; with this type, the entire window frame must be disassembled to replace the cord. Look closely at the lower part of the window frame to find the access plate on the side with the broken cord; it may have been painted over. If the outline of the plate isn't clear, tap the track lightly with a hammer to show the edge; then cut around the plate with a utility knife or a sharp razor blade. Remove the screws that hold the plate and lift the plate out of the window frame; then reach into the opening in the frame and lift out the sash weight at the bottom. Remove the old cord from the

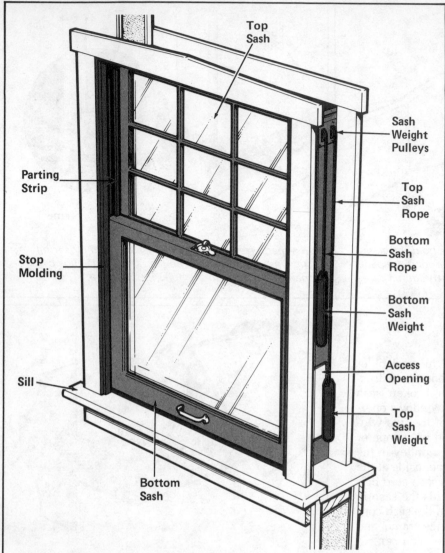

Top Sash

Parting Strip

Stop Molding

Sill

Bottom Sash

Sash Weight Pulleys

Top Sash Rope

Bottom Sash Rope

Bottom Sash Weight

Access Opening

Top Sash Weight

The top and bottom sash of a double-hung window operate on a pulley system, with weights inside the frame balancing the weight of the sash to hold the window open or closed.

Sash Pulley

Sash Chain

Before attaching the new chain to the sash, weight one end and feed it in over the pulley.

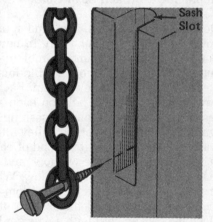

Sash Slot

Attach the free end of the chain to the slot in the side of the sash, where the cord was.

weight. Use the two pieces of the broken cord to measure a piece of sash chain to the correct length; leave several inches extra for fastening. Cut off the extra length with wire cutters.

Before you attach the new sash chain to the window, feed it over the pulley at the top of the frame. Attach a small weight to one end of the chain, and push it in over the pulley; don't let go of the other end. Let the chain down until you can see the end in the access plate opening. Then, being careful not to let the top end go, remove the small weight from the inside end. You may need someone to hold the top end while you work. Attach the sash weight to the inside end of the chain, looping the chain through the opening in the weight and binding the loop securely with sturdy wire. Pull the wire tight with pliers, and make sure the weight is firmly fastened—it must be able to support the entire weight of the sash. Set

the weight back into the access hole and pull the top end of the chain to eliminate slack, but don't replace the access plate yet.

With the weight secured to the chain, you're ready to install the sash. At this point, though, since the frame is already accessible, it makes more sense to replace the sash cord on the other side, too. Follow the same steps to remove the old cord, measure the chain, and attach the weight to the chain.

When both chains are secured to the weights, you can replace the sash in the window frame; you'll probably need help to balance the sash while you work. Before you lift the sash back, attach one chain to the slot in the sash on that side; use two ¾-inch wood screws to secure the chain through two links. Then lift the sash back into the window frame. With the sash in place, attach the chain on the other side to the slot on that side of the sash. To check the operation of the chains, raise the sash as far as it will go in the track; keep it braced against the parting stop as it moves. Have your helper look at the weights in the access holes at the sides of the window frame; the bottom of the weight on each side should be about three inches above the window sill. If a weight isn't the right distance from the sill, you'll have to adjust the chain at the slot in the sash to lengthen or shorten it as required.

When the weights are properly adjusted and the sash hangs evenly, let the sash down. While your helper holds the sash in place, replace the access plates and then the stop molding. If the sash is the top one, you'll have to replace the parting strip first, then the bottom sash and the stop molding.

Repairing or Replacing Screens

Screens are essential in summer to let air in and keep bugs out—especially to keep bugs out. When your screens develop holes, from abuse or just old age, it's time to take action—it isn't hard to repair the holes, or, when the screen is badly damaged, to install new screening.

Patching Holes. Pinholes in screening are very simple to fix. If the screening is metal, use an ice pick or a similar sharp tool to push the strands of wire back toward the hole; you may be able to close the hole completely. If there's still a hole, paint a little clear nail polish or household cement over it. Let the sealer dry and apply another coat; repeat, applying sealer sparingly, until the opening is filled. If the screening is fiberglass, you may be able to move the threads back into place; otherwise, fill tiny holes with clear nail polish or household cement. Be careful not to let the sealer run down the screen; blot any excess immediately.

Clean cuts and tears in screening can usually be stitched together; use a long needle and strong nylon thread, or, on metal screening, fine wire. Sew the edges of the tear together with a close zigzag stitch across the cut, and be careful not to pull the thread or wire so tight that the patch puckers. After stitching the tear closed, apply clear nail polish over the thread or wire to keep it from pulling loose.

To close a large hole, cut a patch from a scrap piece of screening, the same type—fiberglass or metal—as the damaged screening. Don't use metal screening made of a different metal; placing two metals together—steel to copper, for instance—can cause corrosion.

A fiberglass patch is very easy to install, if you can lay the screen flat. Cut a patch about 1/2 inch bigger than the hole all around, and set it over the hole. Place a sheet of aluminum foil over the patch area, shiny side down, and press the patch firmly with a hot iron—be careful not to touch the screen directly with the iron. The heat will fuse the patch onto the screening. If you can't lay the screen flat, sew the patch into place with a needle and nylon thread; use a firm running stitch, but don't pull the thread too tight. Apply clear nail polish

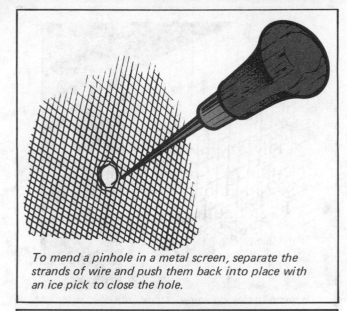

To mend a pinhole in a metal screen, separate the strands of wire and push them back into place with an ice pick to close the hole.

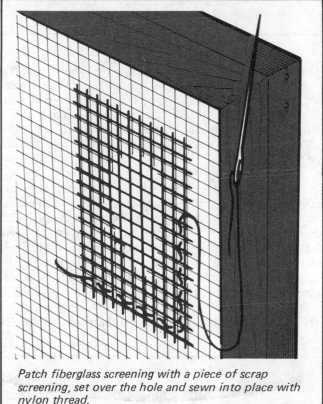

Patch fiberglass screening with a piece of scrap screening, set over the hole and sewn into place with nylon thread.

over the edges of the patch to keep it from fraying.

To patch metal screening, cut a square or rectangular patch about one inch bigger than the hole all around. Pull out the wires on all four sides to make a wire fringe about 1/2 inch deep all around the patch. Then bend the fringe wires down sharply at a right angle—use a block of scrap wood to make a clean bend on each side of the patch. When the fringe wires are evenly bent, set the patch over the hole in the screen and press it to insert

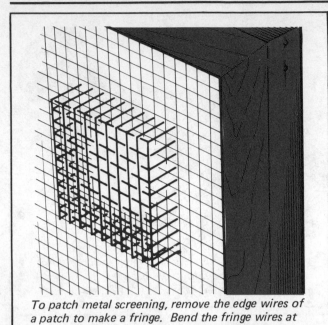

To patch metal screening, remove the edge wires of a patch to make a fringe. Bend the fringe wires at a right angle and press the patch over the hole.

you're working on an aluminum-framed screen, you'll also need plastic splining, a few inches longer than the diameter of the screen, to replace the old metal spline.

To replace a screen in a wood frame, use a stiff putty knife to carefully pry up the molding around the edges. Be careful not to crack the molding, and leave the brads in place to reattach it later. When the molding is off, pry out the tacks or staples that held the screening in place, and remove the screening. Pull out any staples or tacks left in the frame. If the new screening must be trimmed to fit, lay it over the frame and trace the outline of the opening on it with chalk. Then cut the screening to size, 1½ inches larger all around than the traced outline.

To stretch the screening into place in the frame, you must bow or arch the frame. There are two ways to do this, by weighting or clamping; in either case, the idea is to bend the frame into a pronounced bow. To use the weight method, set the frame the long way across two sawhorses, and hang a heavy weight from a rope around the center of the frame. To clamp the frame into a bow, set it on a workbench or a wide board across two sawhorses. Place a C-clamp at the center of each long side, holding the frame to the work surface, and set a long piece of scrap wood, such as a 2×4, between the frame and the work surface at each end. As you tighten the C-clamps, the frame will bow over the 2×4's.

the bent fringe wires through the screening around the hole. The patch should be flat against the screen, covering the hole completely. When it's properly positioned, fold the fringe wires down flat toward the center of the patch on the other side of the screen. Then stitch the patch down all around with a needle and nylon thread, or with fine wire.

Replacing Damaged Screening. When a screen has so many holes, or such big ones, that it isn't worth patching—or when metal screening becomes bulged and rusted—it's time to replace the screening entirely. As long as the frame is in good shape, this isn't as difficult as it sounds. If the frame is wood, you can use either fiberglass or fine-mesh aluminum screening; if it's aluminum, you must use aluminum screening. You may be able to buy the screening cut to size; otherwise, cut it about 1½ inches larger all around than the opening. If

When the frame is securely clamped, set the screening across it, aligned along one unclamped end. Use a staple gun loaded with heavy-duty staples to attach the screening to the frame; place the staples at right angles to the frame, about two to three inches apart. If you're using fiberglass screening, turn the cut edge under about one inch before stapling it down. When the first side is securely stapled, pull the loose screening over the clamped frame, and stretch it firmly and evenly across the opposite side. Holding it firmly as you work, staple the second side into place, setting the staples two to three inches apart at right angles to the frame. Then unclamp or unweight the frame; the screening should be pulled very tight as it straightens out. Staple the other two sides into place, and trim off any excess screening. To finish the job, replace the molding to cover the stapled edges of the screening.

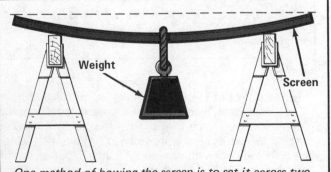

One method of bowing the screen is to set it across two sawhorses and hang a heavy weight from a rope at the center of the frame.

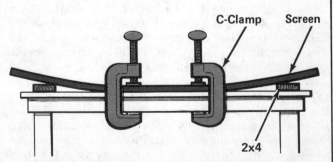

Another method is to clamp the frame; set a 2x4 under the frame at each end, and clamp the center firmly with C-clamps.

To replace a screen in an aluminum frame, you don't have to bow the frame, but you'll need a special splining tool to install the plastic spline. First pry up the metal spline that holds the old screening in place, using a screwdriver or a putty knife, and remove the old screening. Lay the frame flat, and position the new screening over it. Trim the edges so that the screening extends just to the outside edges of the frame. To keep the screening level with the frame, set scrap boards under it, the same thickness as the frame.

When the screening is trimmed correctly, position it so that one end and one side are lined up on the outside edge of the splining groove in the frame. Hold the screening carefully in place. Then, with the convex roller of the splining tool, force the edge of the screening into the splining groove; be careful not to let the screening slip out of place. Secure the other two sides the same way, stretching the screening taut as you work. When all four sides of the screening are in place, cut off any excess screening with tin snips. Then, using the concave end of the splining tool, drive the plastic spline into the groove to hold the screening in place. Start installing the spline at a corner and work around the frame; where the ends meet, cut off the excess splining. With the spline in place, your screen is as good as new.

Window Shades

Every homeowner and apartment-dweller who's ever used window shades is familiar with the many problems that beset them. There's the shade that's so tightly wound it snaps all the way up, the one that's so loose it won't go up at all, the one that binds at the edges or falls out of its brackets. In most cases, only a simple adjustment is needed to get your shades working properly.

A shade that binds is probably being pinched by brackets set too close together. When the brackets are mounted on the wall or on the outside of the window frame, this is easy to remedy; simply tap the brackets slightly outward with a hammer. This technique may also work on brackets mounted inside the window frame. If the shade still sticks, take it down; you'll have to remove some wood from the roller. Remove the round pin and the metal cap on the round-pin end of the roller, and sand the end of the roller down with medium-grit sandpaper. Badly binding shades may require further adjustment. When the brackets are outside-mounted, you can move one bracket out slightly; fill the old screw holes with wood plastic. When the brackets are inside-mounted, the shade will have to be cut down; have it professionally cut to fit the frame.

The opposite problem occurs when the mounting brackets are set too far apart; in extreme cases, the shade may even fall when you try to use it. When the brackets are mounted outside the frame, tap them gently together with a hammer; or, for a greater correction, move one bracket in closer to the other. When the brackets are mounted inside the frame, you'll have to adjust the space with cardboard shims. Take the shade

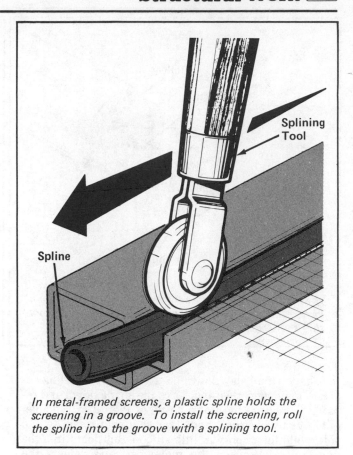

In metal-framed screens, a plastic spline holds the screening in a groove. To install the screening, roll the spline into the groove with a splining tool.

down and cut a piece of thin cardboard a little smaller than one bracket. Unscrew the bracket, set the shim behind it, and screw the bracket on over the shim. If necessary, add one or more shims to both brackets.

When the shade won't go up or down properly, the roller mechanism itself is usually at fault. Shades are operated by a strong coil spring inside one end of the roller. The pin that holds the shade up at this end of the roller is flat; this flat pin tightens or loosens the spring when you roll the shade up or down. At the flat-pin end of the roller, the spring is controlled by a pawl and ratchet, which stop the movement of the spring when the shade is released. If the shade is too tight or too loose, or if it doesn't stay in place when you release it, there is usually a problem with the spring or with the pawl-and-ratchet mechanism. Unless the spring is broken, this is easy to fix.

If the shade won't stay up, the spring is too loose. Pull the shade down enough to turn the roller a few times; if it's extremely loose, pull it down about halfway. Lift the flat-pin end of the roller out of its bracket; then roll the shade up by hand, keeping it tightly rolled. Set the roller back on the bracket and try the shade again. If it still doesn't stay up, repeat the procedure.

If the shade snaps up, and is hard to pull down, the spring is too tight. With the shade rolled up, lift the flat-pin end of the roller out of its bracket, and unroll it two or three turns by hand. Replace the roller on the bracket and test its operation; adjust it further if necessary. If

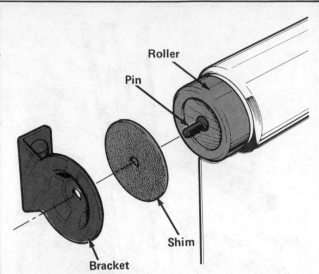

If the shade brackets are set too far apart, insert a shim at one end between the bracket and the roller; add more shims as needed at both brackets.

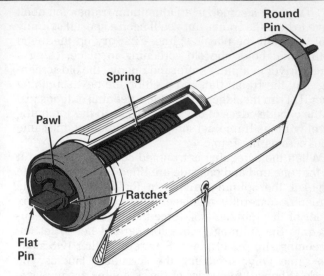

The shade is operated by a spring inside the roller; at the roller's flat-pin end, a pawl-and-ratchet mechanism stops the movement of the spring when the shade is released.

the shade won't stay down, the pawl-and-ratchet mechanism may need cleaning. Take the shade down and remove the cap at the flat-pin end of the roller. Vacuum out any obvious dust, and clean the mechanism with a soft cloth; then spray a little silicone lubricant into the mechanism. Replace the metal cap and rehang the shade; the mechanism should now catch properly.

A shade that works unevenly can also be repaired. If the roller rocks when the shade is raised or lowered, one of its pins may be bent. Take the shade down and examine the pins; if necessary, straighten them carefully with pliers. If the shade is crooked on the roller, it must be reattached. Take it down and unroll it completely onto a flat surface; pry out the staples that hold the shade to the roller. Reposition the roller so that it's exactly at right angles to the shade fabric, and, if there's a big difference, cut off any excess at the roller end of the fabric. With a staple gun and heavy-duty staples, reattach the fabric to the roller, setting the staples close together and parallel with the roller. Then carefully reroll the shade and rehang it. If necessary, adjust the spring tension as above.

Venetian Blinds

Venetian blinds are one of the most practical and long-lasting window treatments around, but they can eventually develop problems. When the cords break or the tapes look frayed and shabby, you can give your blinds new life by installing replacement cords and tapes, often sold in kits. It's a good idea to replace both cords—the lift cord and the tilt cord—at the same time; don't install only one new cord. If you're also replacing the tapes, make sure you buy tapes for the same width slats, and with the same number of ladders, as the old ones.

If the blind is clean and otherwise in good condition, and the old cord is not broken, you can install a new lift cord without taking the blind down. With the blinds down, tilt the slats to horizontal. The ends of the cord are secured to the bottom of the bottom rail. If the bottom rail is wood, the knotted ends of the cord are simply stapled under the ends of the tapes; if it's metal, remove the end caps and the clamps from the rail to expose the knotted cords. Untie the knot on the side opposite the lift cord, and butt the end of the new cord to this end. Tape the two ends firmly together with light adhesive tape.

Pull gently on the old cord to draw the new cord up through the slats on this side, across the top, and through the control pulley; leave a loop of excess cord for the new lift cord, and then continue to draw the cord down through the slats on the lift cord side. When the taped end of the new cord reaches the bottom rail, untape the old cord and discard it; cut off any excess cord at the starting end. Knot both ends of the new cord, and secure them the same way the old cord was secured—with staples if the bottom rail is wood; with the metal clamps if it's metal. Replace the end caps on the bottom rail, and slide the equalizer clip off the old lift cord and onto the new one. Adjust the cord with the equalizer until the blind works smoothly.

This procedure takes care of the lift cord, but not the tilt cord. To replace the tilt cord, untie the knots at the ends of the cord, and remove the pulls. The tilt cord is simply threaded over a pulley and out again; it doesn't connect with the lift cord. Remove the old cord by pulling it out; thread one end of the new cord over the pulley and feed it in until it comes out over the other side of the pulley. Slip the cord pulls over the ends of the cord and knot the ends to hold the pulls on.

When the lift cord is broken, or the slats need clean-

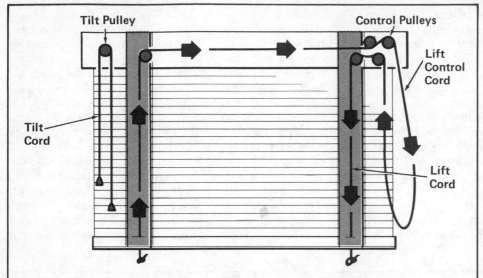

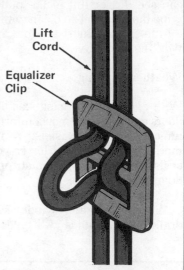

The lift cord is threaded up one side of the blind, over a pulley, across the top and through the control pulleys, and then down the other side; a loop of cord from the control pulleys forms the lift control. The tilt cord is separate.

The equalizer clip slides onto the looped lift cord; adjust the cord on the clip.

ing or painting, or you want to replace the ladder tapes, you'll have to take the blind down. Lay the blind out flat, all the way open, and untie both ends of the lift cord, as above—remove the staples if the bottom rail is wood; remove the clamps if it's metal. Pull the cord entirely out of the blind, and set the equalizer clip aside. Remove the blind's slats one by one, stacking them in order. If they're dirty, this is a good time to clean them; soak them in a bathtub, in a mild solution of liquid detergent, and then rinse and dry them thoroughly. The slats can also be repainted if you really want to spruce them up; use a fast-drying spray lacquer for this job.

When the slats are ready, pull out the hooks that hold the tapes in place at the top of the blind; one hook holds the tapes on each side. Position the new tapes in the top box and slide the hook into each pair of tapes, front and back, at the sides of the box. Slide the slats into place between the tapes; make sure they're all right side up, facing the right way. Fold the ends of the tapes under and fasten them to the bottom rail under the last slat.

With the slats in place, thread a new lift cord into the blind, starting at the tilt cord side and working up that side, across the top, through the control pulley, and down the other side. The tapes have woven strips—ladders—connecting the front and back pieces, on alternating sides. Insert the new cord right at the center of the tapes, so that these ladders are placed on alternate sides of the cord. At the control pulley, leave a long loop of cord for the new lift cord, and then keep threading the cord down through the slats on that side. When you reach the bottom rail, cut off any excess cord, knot both ends of the cord, and secure the ends to the bottom rail. To finish the job, slide the equalizer clip onto the lift cord and install a new tilt cord, as above.

Before you rehang the blind, check the control pulley mechanism to make sure it's working properly. If you

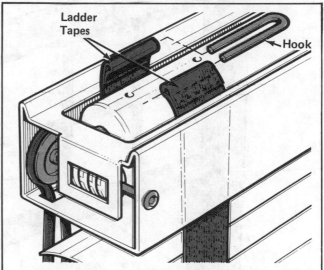

At the top of the blind, slide the hooks into the sleeves in the front and back ladder tapes at the sides of the box. One hook holds the tapes at each side.

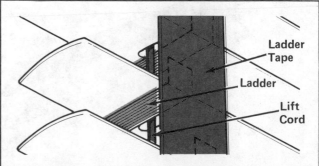

Woven strips—ladders—connect the front and back tapes. Insert the lift cord at the center of the tapes, passing the ladders first on one side and then on the other.

261

can see dirt or lint in the pulleys, vacuum it out and wipe the mechanism clean with a soft cloth. Then spray a little silicone lubricant into the pulleys to keep them working smoothly.

Weatherstripping

With energy costs rising steadily, drafty windows and doors are worse than uncomfortable: they're expensive, unnecessary fuel-wasters. You can keep your family more comfortable and lower your heating and cooling costs by installing weatherstripping around your home's doors and windows.

Windows. Drafty windows can be a real energy drain on your home. All types of windows should be weatherstripped, but double-hung windows are especially likely to need this treatment. Adhesive-backed foam weatherstripping is the least expensive and the easiest type to install, but it doesn't last as long as other types. For a job that will really stand up to the years, use hollow or sponge-filled tubular vinyl weatherstripping. Spring-metal weatherstripping is also available; it is both effective and durable, but it's more expensive and harder to install than the vinyl type. Whatever kind of weatherstripping you use, buy it in bulk; don't buy kits packaged for one or two windows. Measure one window to get a rough idea how much weatherstripping you'll need; it should cover every edge where two separate surfaces meet. If you're using tubular vinyl weatherstripping, you'll also need rustproof brads to attach it.

Weatherstripping is applied on the outside of the win-

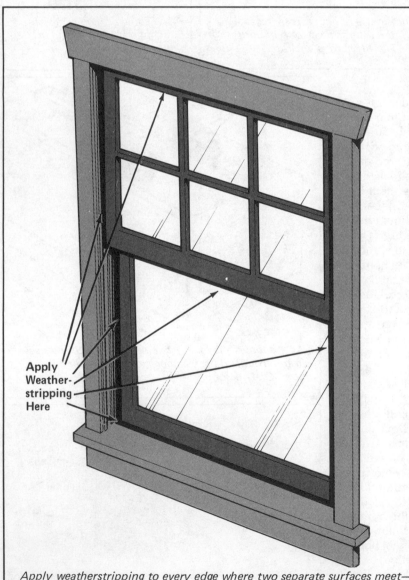

Apply
Weather-
stripping
Here

Apply weatherstripping to every edge where two separate surfaces meet— where the bottom sash meets the sill, where the top sash meets the frame, where the top and bottom sashes meet, and along every side joint.

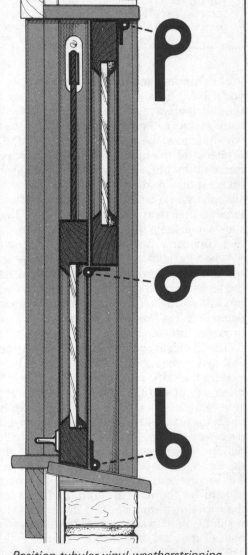

Position tubular vinyl weatherstripping with the flat part secured to the frame and the tubular part set into the gap.

dow. On double-hung windows, place a strip of weatherstripping—foam or vinyl—on the bottom edge of the bottom sash, where it meets the sill; on the bottom of the top sash, where it overlaps the bottom sash; on the top edge of the top sash, where it meets the frame; and along the side edges of both sashes, where they meet the frame. Foam weatherstripping should simply be stuck down on the sash frame so that it covers the gap; peel off the backing paper as you go, and cut a separate strip for each edge. Butt corners tightly together. Tubular vinyl weatherstripping must be nailed into place with rustproof brads. Before you work on each window, cut all the strips you'll need for that window.

To install tubular vinyl weatherstripping, set it along the edge to be sealed, with the tubular part in the gap and facing out, and the flat side flat against the frame. Place the vertical strips first, securing them with rustproof brads to the parting strips of the bottom sash. Most vinyl weatherstripping has prepunched holes for the brads. If there are no prepunched holes, drive brads every two inches along the weatherstripping. When all the vertical strips are in place, install the horizontal strips to seal the window completely. Follow the same procedure to seal each window.

Weatherstripping should not be painted. If you paint the house or the window frames, work around the weatherstripping, or remove it and then install new weatherstripping.

Doors. In many homes, drafty doors are accepted as a fact of life, and the rug folded across the bottom of the door is a winter institution. But it's an institution that doesn't have to be; the drafts are much better remedied with weatherstripping. You should make sure all exterior doors in your home—and all doors to unheated spaces, such as garages—are properly weatherstripped.

If you aren't sure a door needs new weatherstripping, have a helper direct a hair dryer around the closed door while you feel for air coming through to the other side. Anywhere you can feel the hot air, the weatherstripping is inadequate.

The top and sides of the door can be sealed with an adhesive-backed foam weatherstripping. Cut a piece of weatherstripping to cover each of these three edges. Wedge the door open, and clean and dry the door frame thoroughly; the weatherstripping must be installed over a clean surface or it won't stick. With the door frame clean and dry, apply the pieces of weatherstripping to the top and sides, on the narrow edge the door rests against when it closes. Butt the strips firmly together at the corners. On the hinge side, apply the weatherstripping directly over the hinges. On the latch side, cover the strike plate with the weatherstripping, and then cut away the foam over the plate with a sharp craft knife or utility knife.

If you don't want to use foam weatherstripping, you can seal the top and sides of the door with spring-metal weatherstripping, sold in rolls. The flat side of this weatherstripping is nailed to the door jamb; the flared-

Drive brads every two inches to attach vinyl weatherstripping; most weatherstripping has prepunched holes. Butt the strips firmly together at the corners.

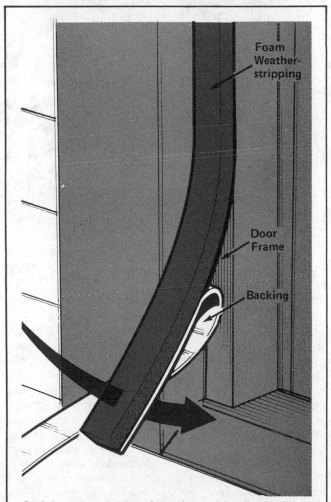

Seal the top and sides of the door with adhesive-backed foam weatherstripping. To install the foam, peel off the backing and stick the strip down.

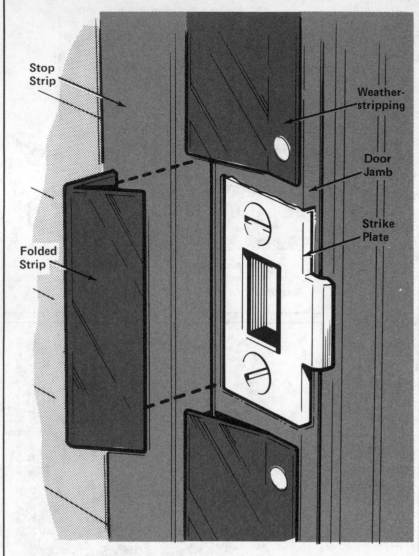

Stop Strip

Folded Strip

Weather-stripping

Door Jamb

Strike Plate

Install spring-metal weatherstripping with the flared side facing out. On the latch side, attach the folded strip to the edge next to the strike plate; then fasten strips above and below the strike plate.

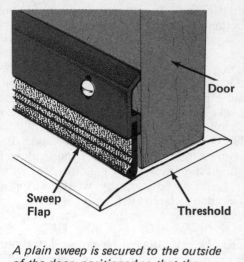

Door

Sweep Flap

Threshold

A plain sweep is secured to the outside of the door, positioned so that the bottom flap rests against the threshold.

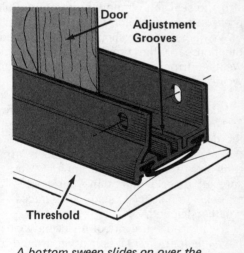

Door

Adjustment Grooves

Threshold

A bottom sweep slides on over the bottom of the door; adjustment grooves adapt it to any door.

out side should face the outside, and should almost touch the stop strip. Cut a strip to fit each of these three edges; you'll have to miter the corners with tin snips to fit them together. On the latch side, attach the folded strip provided next to the strike plate, and then fasten strips above and below the strike plate. If no special strip is provided for the strike plate, you can buy one separately. Nail each piece of weatherstripping into place with rustproof brads, set about two inches apart.

The bottom edge of the door requires more substantial treatment; foam or spring-metal weatherstripping is not adequate to seal the gap between the door and the threshold. To close this opening, you'll need an aluminum and vinyl sweep—a plain or flapped sweep, which covers the outside edge of the door, or a bottom sweep, which fits over the bottom to enclose it like a

sleeve. Either type can be installed without taking the door off its hinges.

To install a plain sweep, cut the sweep to exactly the width of the door, using a fine-toothed hacksaw. Close the door and place the sweep against the outside of the door, so that its bottom edge or flap fits against the threshold. Have a helper hold the sweep in place while you open and close the door; adjust the sweep as necessary so that the door opens easily. Mark the sweep's screw holes on the side of the door, and set the sweep aside. Drill starter holes at the marked points and then screw the sweep into place with the installation screws provided.

To install a bottom sweep, cut the sweep to exactly the width of the door; make sure your cuts are square. Open the door and slide the sweep over its bottom edge, like a sleeve. Most sweeps have adjustment grooves in the base, so that they can be adjusted to fit the thickness of the door exactly. Move the adjustable side of the sweep to the correct groove before you slide the sweep all the way onto the door. Close the door and, with a helper, adjust the sweep as above so that the door opens easily. Then mark the screw holes, drill starter holes, and screw the sweep into place on both sides of the door, using the installation screws provided.

Garage Door Repairs

Overhead garage doors, whether they roll up in sections or swing up in one piece, operate on spring tension; the door moves in metal tracks on the garage walls, and a heavy spring or springs provide the power. In most cases, repairs are fairly simple when the door doesn't work easily.

The first thing to check is the metal tracks inside the garage. Look at the mounting brackets that hold the tracks to the walls; if they're loose, tighten the bolts or screws at the brackets. With the garage door closed, and working inside the garage, examine the tracks for dents, crimps, or flat spots. If there are any damage spots, pound them out with a rubber mallet, or with a hammer and a block of scrap wood. If the tracks are badly damaged, they should be replaced; this is a job for a carpenter.

Next, check the tracks with a level to make sure they're properly aligned. Horizontal tracks should slant slightly down toward the back of the garage; with roll-up doors, the vertical sections of track should be exactly plumb. Both tracks must be at the same height on the garage walls. If the tracks are not properly aligned, loosen—but do not remove—the screws or bolts that hold the mounting brackets, and tap the tracks carefully into position. Recheck the tracks with the level to make sure they're in the right position; then tighten the screws or bolts at the mounting brackets.

When you're sure the tracks are straight, clean them out with concentrated household cleaner to remove dirt and hardened grease. Clean the rollers thoroughly, and wipe both tracks and rollers dry. Then lubricate both the tracks and the rollers—use spray garage door lubricant or powdered graphite in the tracks, household oil or silicone spray lubricant on the rollers. If there are any pulleys, lubricate them with the same lubricant you used on the rollers.

Binding or difficult operation can also be caused by loose hardware. On swing-up doors, check the plates where the spring is mounted to be sure the screws are tight, and tighten any loose screws. On roll-up doors, check the hinges that hold the sections of the door together; tighten any loose hinge screws, and replace any damaged hinges. Sagging to one side of the door can often be corrected by servicing the hinges. If a screw hole is enlarged, replace the screw with a longer one of the same diameter, and use a hollow fiber plug, dipped in carpenters' glue, with the new screw. If the wood is cracked at a hinge, remove the hinge and fill the cracks

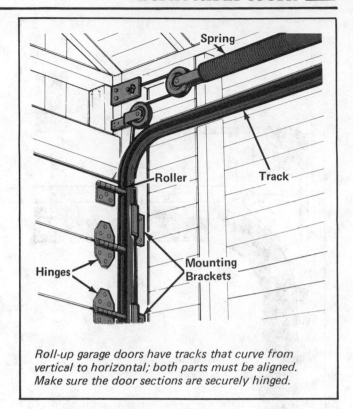

Roll-up garage doors have tracks that curve from vertical to horizontal; both parts must be aligned. Make sure the door sections are securely hinged.

and the screw holes with wood filler; let the filler dry and then replace the hinge. If possible, move the hinge onto solid wood.

If the tracks and the hardware are in good condition but the door still doesn't work right, the problem may be in the springs. *Caution: If a roll-up door has only one torsion spring, at the center of the door, do not try to repair it; the tension is so great that the spring could injure you. For doors with this type of spring, call a professional repair service.*

On swing-up doors, the spring on each side is hooked

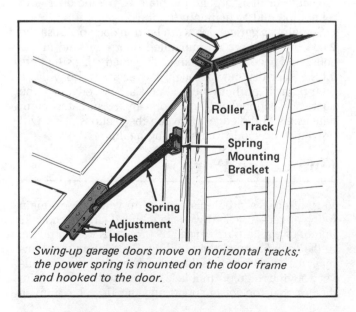

Swing-up garage doors move on horizontal tracks; the power spring is mounted on the door frame and hooked to the door.

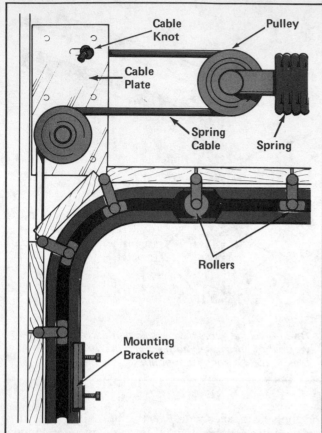

On roll-up doors, the spring tension is controlled by a cable on a pulley. To adjust the tension, pull the cable and reknot the end to shorten or lengthen the cable.

into holes or notches; to adjust the tension, move the spring hook to the next hole or notch. On roll-up doors, the spring on each side is controlled by a spring cable on a pulley. To adjust the tension of this type of spring, pull the cable farther through the plate above the door, and reknot the end to maintain the tension.

Sometimes garage doors are hard to open because the wood has swollen; an unpainted door can bind at the edges and become very heavy. To remedy this situation, let the door dry out thoroughly, over several dry days; then paint it on both sides. Paint all the edges of the door; on sectional roll-up doors, make sure the paint penetrates to the edges between the sections. This will prevent the wood from swelling again.

Foundation Work

Very often, the problems you see in your home's main living areas—cracked walls, sticking doors, even leaks in roof or walls—are caused by problems farther down, in the foundation of the building. Foundation problems may make themselves known in several ways. One very obvious sign of trouble is a sagging floor, which indicates that the joists supporting the floor have given

way. The classic trouble spot is the basement, which may be damp all the time or may flood during heavy rains. If you don't have a basement, your first indication of trouble may be a crack in the foundation wall, sudden cracks in inside walls, or gaps at door and window frames. Most problems of this type can be traced to poor drainage of stormwater away from the house. Whatever the problem, there's a good chance that you can fix it. You can't make major structural repairs yourself, but if you act promptly, you can take care of most foundation maintenance and repair work.

Leveling Sagging Floors

Sagging floors can be caused by uneven settling, but severe localized sags on the ground floor are usually the result of problems in the floor joists. If you can get at the beams under the sagging floor, the problem is fairly easy to deal with. Before you start, check your local building code to make sure your repair is in conformance with code. You'll need a jackscrew—a screw-type house jack—to make this repair; jackscrews are available from rental outlets.

Before you start working, you should have a good idea where the sag is; look for the low spot in the floor. In the crawl space or basement under the sag, examine the exposed floor joists to locate the low point and determine the extent of the sag. At the lowest point of the sag, set a 4×8 timber flat on the floor under the sagging beam. This timber will serve as a footing or support base for the jackscrew. Measure across the entire sag area, from the sagging beam out past several sound beams in each direction. Cut a 4×6 timber to this measurement, and nail the 4×6 flat across the center of the sag with long spikes. The 4×6 should cross the sagging joist, extending past it across several sound beams on each side. Drive nails through the 4×6 into every joist it crosses.

Set the jackscrew on the 4×8 timber under the 4×6, adjusted to its lowest position. It should be centered directly under the low point of the sagging joist. Measure the distance from the top of the jackscrew to the bottom of the 4×6, and cut a 4×4 timber to this length; make sure the ends are square. Then set the 4×4 on end on the jackscrew, forming a post between the jackscrew and the 4×6 beam. The 4×4 must be solidly set and exactly plumb; check it with a level to make sure it's accurately placed.

With the post in place, turn the handle of the jackscrew just until you feel resistance, and then stop. *Caution: Do not turn the handle of the jackscrew after you feel resistance, or you could cause serious structural damage to your home.* Wait a full 24 hours, and then turn the handle one-quarter turn further—no sooner, and no more than one-quarter turn. Wait another 24 hours and again turn the handle one-quarter turn; repeat this procedure as necessary until the sagging beams straighten out. Before you make each adjustment, check the beams with a level to see how far they've changed position. *Caution: You must wait at* least 24 hours between adjustments; don't worry if you miss a day. Do not turn the jackscrew handle any more than one-quarter turn a day; if you try to hurry the process, you could do serious structural damage.

As you continue to jack them up, the sagging beams will eventually level out. When all the beams in the sag area are even, stop jacking up the brace beam. To hold it in place, you'll have to install a post at each end of the beam; leave the jackscrew in place for the time being. Steel Lally columns or adjustable jack posts are the best supports; the jack posts are easier to install. Jack posts are available at building supply outlets. They must be left in place permanently, so you'll have to buy them instead of renting. The posts work the same way the jackscrew does.

Whether you use jack posts or Lally columns, you must provide a concrete footing for each one; the concrete of the basement floor is not strong enough to support them. Set the posts in place at the ends of the brace beam and mark the position of each one on the floor; then set the posts aside while you prepare the footings. Leave the jackscrew in place while you work.

Break up a two-foot-square section of the floor, centered on the marked post area, for each footing. Wear safety goggles for this job, and use a brick chisel and a heavy sledgehammer to break up the old concrete. Break through the old concrete to a depth of at least one foot; the opening doesn't have to be perfectly level, but it must be at least one foot deep at its shallowest part. Then remove the debris, clean out the hole, and flush it thoroughly with water.

While the opening is still wet, mix ready-mix sand concrete mix according to the package directions. A wheelbarrow is the best mixing container, because you can also use it to pour the concrete; use a shovel as a mixing tool. When the concrete is ready, spray the hole lightly with water; it should be wet but not streaming. Then paint all exposed surfaces of the opening with liquid concrete bonding agent—without this step, the footing will not bond properly to the old floor. Use a stiff throwaway paintbrush to apply the bonding agent. While the bonding agent is still wet, pour the prepared concrete into the hole. Spread the concrete with the shovel, making sure there are no gaps. It should be roughly level with the surrounding floor.

To finish the job, strike off the footing with a long piece of 2×4. Set the 2×4 on the edge across the new concrete, and pull it back and forth over the footing in a firm zigzag stroke. This smooths and levels the surface of the footing. After striking off, use a wood float—a concrete tool that looks like a large trowel—to final-smooth the surface. As you smooth the footing, a sheen of water will appear on the surface of the concrete. Wait until this film of water disappears, about 45 minutes to an hour; then smooth the footing again with a flat steel trowel. This second smoothing will make the surface harder. A sheen of water will again come to the surface during this step; wait until the water disappears and then cover the footing with a sheet of heavy plastic to keep it from drying out too fast. Weight the edges to

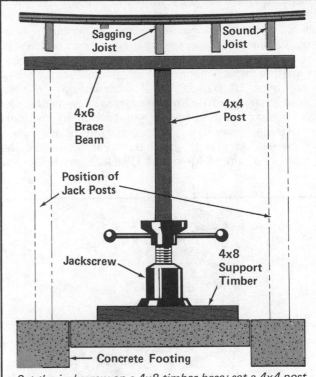

Set the jackscrew on a 4x8 timber base; set a 4x4 post on it, and use a 4x6 as a brace beam. Install a jack post at each end of the brace beam.

hold the plastic in place. Let the concrete cure for a week. During this period, remove the plastic and spray the concrete lightly, two or three times a day.

When the new footings are completely cured, you can set the jack posts in place permanently. Set each jack post into place, centered on its footing under the brace beam. With a level, adjust each post to exact plumb. Then set the posts so that they meet the brace beam exactly—stop turning as soon as you feel resistance. Finally, with the jack posts in place, remove the jackscrew. The sagging floor is now permanently leveled.

Preventive Maintenance: How to Keep Your Foundation Healthy

Foundation damage can be caused by poor construction, but the problem is far more likely to be poor drainage, which leads to shifting and uneven settling of the soil under and around the house. There isn't much you can do once settling has occurred—if the damage is slight, you can live with it; if it's extensive, you'll have to call in a professional engineer. But there is something you can do, no matter how old your house is, to prevent uneven settling from becoming a problem.

Essentially, preventive maintenance is based on keeping water away from the house. Fix all plumbing leaks immediately. Walk around the house and look at the ground near the foundation; the soil should always slope away from the house. If the ground is level or slopes in toward the house around the foundation, you'll have to regrade the soil to slope it properly. Water should never be allowed to collect around the foundation. Go outside again during a heavy rain and watch the course of the runoff around the house; there should be shallow runoff channels in the ground to carry water away from the foundation. If these natural drainage routes have been filled in, open them so rainwater can flow away from the house. If you have to dig channels or regrade, reseed or sod to prevent erosion.

The next step is to see that vegetation around the house is properly maintained. Check flower beds near

Downspout

Splash Block

Stormwater must be routed away from the foundation. Clean downspouts regularly, and install concrete splash blocks to break the force of runoff water.

the house to make sure they slope away from the foundation; if they're curbed or edged, make sure the edging doesn't trap water. When you plant trees or shrubs, keep them away from the foundation. Any large plant draws water out of the soil, and can cause areas of unequal moisture, which may cause shifting of the soil. When you water grass and flowers, water evenly all around the house—even where there are no plants—to keep the soil evenly moist all around the foundation.

Next, look at any walks, drives, or patios that butt directly against the house. All paved areas should slope away from the house, and paving should meet the foundation wall in a smooth, rounded joint. If this joint is cracked, or if it tends to hold water, you should cut it out and remortar it. Use packaged mortar mix, available at hardware and building supply stores.

Cut out the joint with a hammer and chisel, undercutting it so that it's wider at the bottom than at the top. Wear safety goggles as you work. Wire-brush the joint to remove the debris, and flush it thoroughly with water. Mix the mortar as the package directs; then, while the joint is still wet, fill the joint firmly with mortar. Use the back of an old spoon to shape the mortar into a smooth curve, so that the joint curves up from the pavement to the foundation wall. Let the mortar cure for two to three days, or as directed; during this period, spray it lightly with water two or three times a day to keep it from drying out too quickly.

Your gutter and downspout system is another important factor in foundation moisture control. Clean the gutters and downspouts regularly to make sure they're open and flowing freely. Runoff from the downspouts must be kept away from the foundation; if the downspouts empty directly at the foundation, install long drainage sleeves or concrete splash blocks to break its force. If your gutters are not adequate to handle stormwater drainage, you should extend the system or have new gutters installed.

When uneven settling does occur, deal with the problem immediately. If cracks in the foundation wall are serious or if they're getting noticeably worse, call a professional to do the work. Otherwise, you can fill the cracks with mortar, as detailed in the section below on masonry repairs. Deepen each crack to a depth of one to two inches, using a hammer and chisel; wear safety goggles to protect your eyes. Undercut each crack so that it's wider at the bottom than at the top. Wire-brush the widened crack to remove loose debris and then flush it thoroughly with water. Mix the mortar as the package directs; then, while the crack is still wet, pack the mortar firmly in with a small, sharp trowel, to fill the crack completely. Let the mortar cure, as above.

If uneven settling has caused gaps or spaces around doors and windows, seal the gaps immediately with caulking compound; follow the procedures outlined later in this section in "Caulking." Caulk around all windows and doors, and wherever pipes go through the foundation wall. If the foundation is a different material than the siding, also caulk along the joint where the foundation ends and the walls of the house begin.

Drying Out a Basement

For many people, keeping a basement livable is a constant struggle. Humidity builds up in both basements and crawl spaces; the original waterproofing may not be adequate to keep the foundation wall dry. In wet climates, the soil may be so wet that water is forced up through the joint between the basement floor and the walls. And in really severe cases, there may be water actually flowing through an opening in the wall. If the foundation wall is badly damaged, or if the entire foundation is inadequately waterproofed, professional repairs are required. In most cases, you can do the job.

The first step in drying out the basement is preventive maintenance, as detailed above. Unless you take these preventive measures, any repairs you make will only be effective temporarily. Before you do any further work on your basement, make sure the soil is graded to slope away from the foundation, vegetation is properly planted and cared for, paved areas are properly joined to the house, and the gutters are in good working order.

If humidity is the problem, water in the basement may be just condensation. You can lower the humidity and reduce condensation by installing a dehumidifier, an exhaust fan, or an air conditioner; by using dehumidifying crystals in damp areas; and by wrapping cold-water pipes with insulating tape.

Seepage. Where seepage through the entire foundation wall is occurring because the original waterproofing was inadequate, you may be able to eliminate moisture in the basement by painting walls with waterproofing paint. Several types of basement paint or waterproofing compound are available. Some must be mixed, as the manufacturer directs; some must be applied to a wet surface. Before applying the compound, scrub the walls down with a wire brush to remove dirt and chips. Wear safety goggles to protect your eyes. After cleaning the walls, mix the compound and wet the walls, if necessary, as directed by the manufacturer. Apply the compound to the walls with a stiff masonry brush or even a scrub brush; work it in well to fill all rough and uneven surfaces. Let the compound dry as directed. A second coat is usually required; apply it the same way.

If the problem is seepage through the wall-floor joint, you can seal the joint with epoxy mortar, sold as a two-part mix. This can be done only when the floor is dry. First, cut the joint open with a hammer and chisel, deepening it to a depth of one to two inches and undercutting it so that it's wider at the bottom than at the top. Wear safety goggles to protect your eyes. Wire-brush the joint to remove all debris, and then vacuum it thoroughly. Mix the epoxy compound as directed on the package, and pack it firmly into the open joint with a small trowel. Then, with the back of an old spoon, shape the epoxy into a smooth curve all along the joint. The epoxy must cure for at least 24 hours.

Cracks. Leaks through cracks in the foundation wall are also easy to repair. If the damage is serious, of

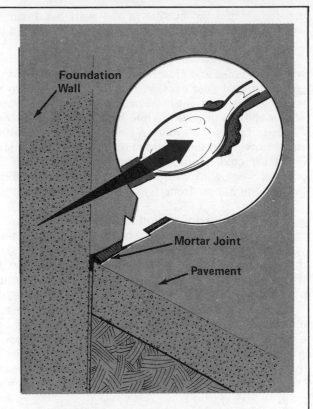

To keep water from collecting where a paved area meets the foundation, undercut the joint and fill it with mortar; shape the mortar into a smooth curve.

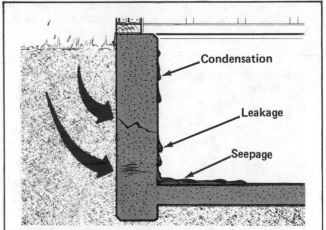

Water in the basement may be coming from any or all of three sources: condensation, leakage, and seepage through the wall-floor joint.

course, or if the cracks are widening visibly, you should call a professional. But you can repair less serious damage yourself. First, before you work on the basement walls, inspect the outside of the foundation wall, and make all necessary repairs outside, as detailed above in "Preventive Maintenance." If the foundation wall has large cracks that extend much below the surface of the ground, it should be professionally repaired and waterproofed. When the outside of the wall has been repaired, you can work on the inside to stop leaks in the basement.

To repair cracks inside, deepen and undercut them with a hammer and chisel, as above; wear safety goggles to protect your eyes. Wire-brush the cracks to remove debris, and flush them thoroughly with water. Mix mortar as directed. While the cracks are still wet, fill them tightly with mortar, smoothing it level with a small trowel. Let the mortar cure for two or three days, or as directed. During the curing period, spray the patched area lightly with water two or three times a day to keep the mortar from drying out too quickly.

Wet Cracks and Constant Leaks. Even when water comes in constantly through a crack or hole in the wall, you can repair the damage with hydraulic cement. Hydraulic cement, unlike mortar, hardens even in flowing water. It's sold as a mix, in hardware and building supply stores.

Hydraulic cement is not applied with a trowel, as regular mortar is. Instead, it's formed into a long plug and inserted into the hole. If there is a long open crack, it should be filled gradually, top to bottom, with plugs of hydraulic cement. This gradually reduces the flowing crack to one open hole, which is then filled with a final plug.

First, deepen and undercut the crack or hole with a hammer and chisel; wear safety goggles to protect your eyes. Remove debris with a wire brush. Mix the hydraulic cement as directed. Then, wearing rubber gloves, shape a long, carrot-shaped plug of cement, the same diameter as the hole (or the same width as the

To fix a constant leak, use hydraulic cement, formed into a plug and inserted into the hole. Hold the plug until it's set; then trowel the surface smooth.

crack). Let the plug set briefly, as directed; as soon as it starts to harden, push the plug into the hole. Hold the plug in place until you can feel that it's firmly set, and then trowel the surface smooth. If you're repairing a crack, work from top to bottom with plugs of cement to close the entire opening.

Frame Repairs

Your home is built to withstand wear and weather, and if you don't look at the outside too closely, it's easy to assume that everything is in good shape—until one day it's too late, and all the little problems have become big ones. To prevent this kind of structural deterioration, it's a good idea to make a periodic tour of inspection around the outside of your home, so that you can repair the damage before it's serious. One of the most important of the routine jobs is caulking. When siding or porch flooring is damaged, you can forestall more serious problems by taking care of the repairs immediately.

Caulking

No matter how well your home is built, it must also be well caulked if it is to function properly. Caulking serves three important purposes: it finishes the joints where outside surfaces meet; it prevents drafts and heat loss; and it prevents water, dirt, and insects from entering and damaging your home. Caulking is important everywhere two outside surfaces meet. To make sure your home is sealed against the elements, you should inspect it yearly for missing or damaged caulking, and recaulk as necessary to repair the damage.

There are several types of caulking compound. Oil-base caulks are the least expensive, but also the least durable; for most applications, acrylic latex or silicone caulk is better. Acrylic latex, an all-purpose caulk, can be painted over. Silicone caulk is far more durable, and is very easy to work with, but it's also very expensive, and it usually can't be painted over. For masonry-metal joints—where pipes go through the foundation wall, for instance—use butyl rubber caulk. Polyvinyl acetate (PVA) caulk is also available, but it's less durable and less widely used than other types. For caulking wall-to-roof or chimney-to-roof joints, use roofing compound. All of these types of caulk are sold in bulk tubes, to be used with an inexpensive caulking gun. Many caulks are available in white, gray, black, and clear forms. When you buy caulking compound, read the label to estimate how much you'll need; it's a good idea to buy one or two tubes extra.

Plan routine caulking for dry, warm weather; caulking should not be done when it's very cold or very hot. If you must work in very cold weather, warm the caulk to room temperature before you start. If you must work in very hot weather, chill the caulk briefly in the refrigerator to keep it from getting runny. All surfaces should be dry when you apply caulking compound.

Caulking is not a difficult procedure; all it really requires is patience and attention to detail. When you're ready to work, inspect your home carefully to find the places that need caulking. In general, there should be caulking along every joint where two outside surfaces meet—around windows and doors, at the point where the house walls meet the foundation, where porches or steps are attached, around air conditioners, pipes, and vents. Every corner seam should be caulked, and every seam between sheets of siding. On the roof, there should be caulking where the chimney meets the roof and along every flashing edge, at the chimney surface and at the roof surface. If caulking is missing or damaged at any of these points, you should recaulk the entire joint.

Before you can apply new caulk to a joint, you must remove the old caulking. Sometimes you can peel the old caulk out in long strips. If you can't, and if it's hard to dislodge the caulk with a putty knife, use a sharp utility knife to cut the old caulk out, forming a clean, square joint. Be careful not to damage the joint surfaces. For joints along glass, carefully scrape the glass with a single-edge razor blade or a glass scraper, and then clean and dry the glass. After removing the old caulk, go over the joint with a dry paintbrush to remove dust and other debris.

Once you get the feel of it, caulking is very simple. With a sharp utility knife, cut off the tip of the caulk tube's nozzle, cutting at an angle. Most tubes have cutting guidelines marked on the nozzle. The open tip of the nozzle should be roughly the same diameter as the width of the narrowest cracks to be caulked; the bead of caulk must be wide enough to overlap both sides of the joint. For larger cracks or joints, you'll have to recut the nozzle to make a wider bead of caulk. With the nozzle

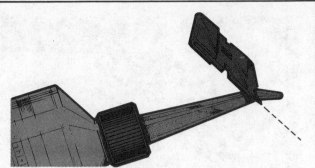

Cut off the tip of the caulk tube at an angle, to the width of the narrowest joint to be filled. Most tubes are marked with cutting guidelines.

cut to the correct width, pull out the plunger of the caulking gun and set the tube of caulk into the gun, base first, so that the nozzle of the tube sticks out through the slot on the end of the gun. Then turn the plunger of the gun to point up, and push it in just until it engages. Finally, break the seal between the tube and the nozzle; push a piece of stiff wire or a long nail into the nozzle to puncture the foil or plastic seal.

To use the caulking gun, hold the nozzle at a 45-degree angle to the joint you want to fill. With the plunger of the gun engaged and the seal of the tube broken, squeeze the handle firmly. In a few moments, caulk will begin to flow out of the nozzle. The caulk is forced out of the tube by the pressure of the plunger; as you squeeze the handle of the gun, the plunger moves in, notch by notch, and the caulk flows out. Draw the nozzle of the tube slowly along the open joint, with the tip slanted in the direction you're caulking. The caulk

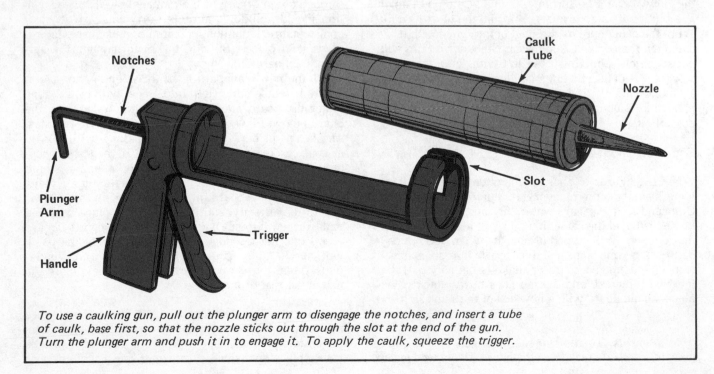

To use a caulking gun, pull out the plunger arm to disengage the notches, and insert a tube of caulk, base first, so that the nozzle sticks out through the slot at the end of the gun. Turn the plunger arm and push it in to engage it. To apply the caulk, squeeze the trigger.

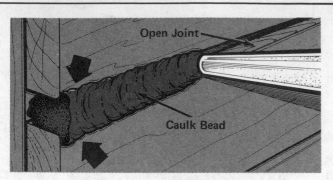

Fill each joint smoothly and evenly; the caulk should overlap both surfaces, with no gaps or bubbles. Hold the gun so the caulk flows behind the nozzle.

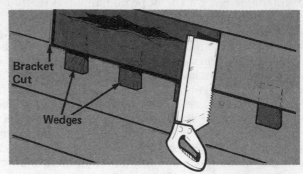

To remove a damaged clapboard, drive wedges to pull it away from the house, and pry out the nails. Then cut out the damaged section with a backsaw.

should flow out behind the nozzle as you go; don't try to push it ahead of the nozzle. As you work with the caulking gun, let the caulk flow at its own rate; don't try to hurry it. The gun releases caulking compound at a steady rate, one click at a time. You can't speed it up by squeezing the handle harder—all you can do is adjust your rate of movement to use it well.

Fill each joint with one steady movement from end to end, adjusting your speed as necessary to the flow of caulk. The caulk should fill the joint completely, overlapping both side surfaces, with no gaps or bubbles. At the end of the joint, twist the nozzle out and turn the gun nozzle up to minimize the flow of caulk. Don't expect the caulk to stop flowing instantly; the caulk released by the last click will keep coming. If caulk builds up on the nozzle between joints, wipe the excess off the nozzle with a paper towel. When you're finished caulking, stop the flow of caulk by turning the plunger to point down and pulling it out to disengage it from the tube of caulk.

Let the caulk cure as directed before you touch it. To clean up, remove as much excess caulk as you can with paper towels, and finish the job with the appropriate solvent. Fresh acrylic latex caulk can be removed with soap and water; dried silicone caulk will peel off your hands like rubber cement. Use leftover caulk as soon as possible; it will eventually harden in the tube.

Replacing Damaged Siding

When clapboards or shakes are rotten or broken, your home's siding can no longer do the job it's meant to do. Damaged siding lets air, water, dirt, and insects through to the inside; at the same time, it leads to decay and further damage in the wood around it. When you notice a bad spot in your home's siding, repair it as soon as you can—the damaged board or shake is the only part that must be replaced, and the job goes fairly quickly. Replace the old board with a new one of the same size and shape.

Clapboards. To remove the damaged board, you'll have to wedge it away from the house. Drive wedges up

under the damaged board to pull it out from the sheathing below it. Look for the nails in this section of clapboard, and pull them out. If you can't remove them with a claw hammer or pliers, cut them off flush with the sheathing with a hacksaw. To release the top of the board, drive wedges under the clapboard that overlaps the damaged board, and remove the nails from the top of the board.

Once the siding has been released, you can cut the damaged section out. Leave the wedges in place under the clapboard. Cut through the board on each side of the damaged area, using a backsaw or a hacksaw. If you don't have enough room to use a saw conveniently, use a hacksaw blade with one end wrapped with electrical tape. Cut all the way through the board to bracket the damaged area; if necessary, move the wedges to make room for the saw. When the board is completely cut through on both sides of the damage, the damaged section should pull down and out fairly easily. If it won't come out, break it up with a hammer and chisel, and remove it in pieces. Be careful not to damage the surrounding boards.

Cut the new clapboard to fit the opening, and test it for fit; it should slide right into place, with its top edge under the board above and its bottom edge over the board below. Plane the edges for an exact fit, if necessary.When the new board fits well, paint it with a primer coat; make sure both sides and all edges are covered. Also paint the raw edges of the opening, where the old siding was cut out. Let the paint dry completely. Then set the new board into the opening, and adjust it so that it fits perfectly. Nail the board into place with 16d nails, driven through the bottom and through the board above into the top edge. Caulk the edges of the patch with acrylic latex caulk, as detailed above in "Caulking." When the caulk is dry, paint the new siding to match the rest of the house.

Shakes or Shingles. Damaged shakes or shingles are replaced the same way clapboards are. If they're natural unstained cedar, however, it's a good idea to take your replacement shakes from an inconspicuous area of

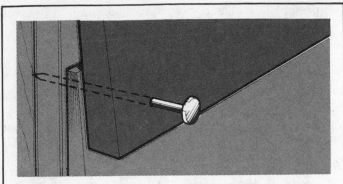

Slide the new clapboard into the gap, with its top edge under the board above and its bottom edge over the board below.

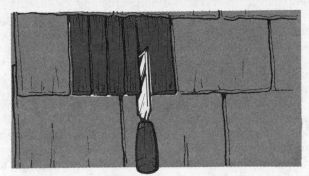

If a damaged shake doesn't come out easily, split it into several pieces with a hammer and chisel; remove the pieces and pull out the nails.

the house, and to use the new shingles on that spot. This trick eliminates a new-looking unweathered patch in the repair area.

Wedge each damaged shake or shingle out, driving wedges under the damaged shake and under the shakes that overlap it. Pull out or cut off all nails, as above. Then remove the damaged shake. If it doesn't come out easily, split it into several pieces with a hammer and chisel, and remove the pieces. Insert the new shake and nail it into place with 16d aluminum nails; do not use steel nails. If the shake doesn't have predrilled nail holes, drill pilot holes for the nails to keep the wood from splitting.

Replacing Damaged Porch Flooring

Wooden porches are a pleasure to live with, but they are also subject to heavy wear and damage. If you live in an older home, the porch floor may be the first thing to go. When porch flooring breaks or wears out, more than the looks of the porch are involved—a weak spot in the floor is dangerous, and it can lead to further damage. Unless the whole floor is weakened, you can easily replace the damaged boards.

Porch flooring is nailed directly to the joists of the framing; to repair the damaged area, you'll have to replace the boards in a square or rectangle from joist to joist. Look at the boards to see where the joists are; you'll see a line of nails along each joist. Using a carpenters' square, draw an outline around the damaged area—from board edge to board edge, from the inside of a joist to the inside of another joist. If the boards are damaged where they cross a joist, draw the outline out to the joists on either side of it. The boards in this outlined area will be replaced.

Bore a hole inside two diagonally opposite corners of the outline, using a hand brace and a ³/₄-inch bit. Position each hole so that it touches the marked outline on both sides, but does not touch the sound boards outside the repair area. With a saber saw or a keyhole saw, cut across the damaged boards, working from the hole at one outside board across the damaged boards to the

other side of the marked outline. You should have to cut only across the boards; the long edges are joined by tongue-and-groove edges, and should pull apart. Carefully pry out the damaged boards with a pry bar. At the outside board edges, be very careful not to damage the tongue or the groove of the sound board outside the outline. You may have to use a chisel to remove the last pieces of the old boards.

Cut new tongue-and-groove flooring strips, the same width and thickness as the old ones, to replace the old ones. Test them for fit in the opening; they should fit exactly in the gap left by the old boards. On the last board, you'll have to cut off the bottom part of the groove to make the board fit flat. Cut the groove piece off with a hammer and a sharp chisel; be careful not to damage the rest of the board. Then sand the raw surface lightly.

To brace the boards at each end, you'll have to install 2×4 cleats along the inside faces of the joists at the sides of the hole. Cut a piece of 2×4 as long as the hole for each joist. Before you install the cleats, paint all of

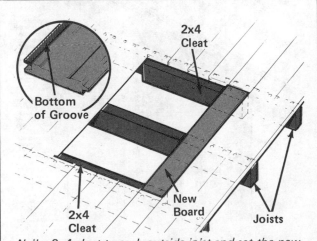

Nail a 2x4 cleat to each outside joist and set the new boards into the opening; cut off the bottom of the groove on the last board.

the patching materials—floorboards and 2×4 cleats—with two coats of wood preservative, on all sides. Make sure all surfaces are covered. Let the preservative dry as directed, and then nail the 2×4 cleats flat to the side joists, with their top edges flush. The top edges of the cleats must be exactly level with the top edges of the joists.

With the cleats in place, set the new floorboards into the opening, one by one, with their ends resting on the cleats along the joists. Set the first board in tongue first, and insert each board to lock its tongue into the groove of the previous board. Nail each end of each board to the cleat with two or three 16d finishing nails. At the last board, lock the tongue in and set the groove side flat over the tongue of the adjoining board. It won't lock to the joining board, but with the bottom of the groove removed, it will fit into place. When all the nails are in place, countersink them with a nail set, and fill the cracks and cover the nail heads with water putty. Do not use wood plastic; it isn't strong enough. Water putty dries rock-hard.

To finish the job, let the water putty dry and then sand the patch lightly. Paint the patched area with a primer coat of porch and floor enamel, and let the paint dry. Then repaint the whole porch.

If the old boards were rotten, you should take steps to prevent further decay. Cover the ground under the porch with heavy plastic, lapping the plastic about six inches up at the sides. Set a few stones or bricks on the plastic to hold it in place. For the most effective rot preventive, paint all exposed wood under the porch—framing, joists, and floorboards—with a coat of wood preservative. These preventive measures will keep your porch strong and healthy for years to come.

Roof and Gutter Repairs

Structural damage is always disturbing, but as anyone who's gone through it knows, few things can make you feel as helpless as watching water pour through your ceilings as the rain pours down outside. The leak could be anywhere—in the roof itself, in the chimney flashing, in the seal around a vent pipe. If the gutters aren't running freely, water could be backing up at the downspouts and forcing its way in. But the situation isn't hopeless. While it's raining, you should—besides mopping up the mess, of course—try to locate the problem. Once the rain stops, you can usually repair the damage.

Fixing a Leaky Roof

The average lifetime of an asbestos shingle roof is about 15 to 20 years. If your roof is old, leaks may be the result of overall deterioration, and there isn't much you can do to remedy this except have a new roof put on. Usually, though, leaks are caused by localized damage somewhere on the roof—cracked or missing shingles or shakes, or, on a flat roof, a blistered or cracked area. The hardest part of repairing this kind of damage is locating it. You should *never* work on your roof while it's wet or windy, but spend some time while it's still raining to locate the leak. This will greatly simplify the actual repairs.

If there's an unfinished attic or crawl space below the leaky roof, finding the leak shouldn't be too difficult. Climb into this space, and look around with a flashlight—don't turn a fixture or trouble light on; it's easier to see a leak in the dark. Water coming in through the roof at one point often runs down the beams or along the ceiling joists before dripping into the space below, it may travel quite a distance from the actual point of entry to the apparent leak point. Watch for the gleam of water in your flashlight beam, and try to trace the water to its highest point on the roof, where it's coming into the house. When you find the leak, outline the wet area with chalk. If you can, push a piece of stiff wire up through the bad spot, so that it sticks out on the roof above. This will make it easier to find the bad spot when you're working outside.

If there's a finished ceiling directly under the leak, it will be harder to locate the problem, but you can make an educated guess. Draw a rough plan of the roof in that area, and mark chimneys, vent pipes, ridges, and wall intersections on it. Every place where two surfaces meet, or the roof changes pitch, is a potential trouble spot; any one of these spots anywhere close to the leak is a good place to start looking.

Caution: Never work on the roof while it's still wet; it must dry out completely before you can fix the leak. When you do work on the roof, wear rubber-soled shoes and old clothes. On gentle pitches, tie a rope to

Water leaking in at one point may travel quite a distance before dripping into a room below. While it's still raining, use a flashlight to trace the leak.

Actual Leak

Inside Leak Point

the chimney for use as a safety rope. On a steep roof, you'll need an anchor hook or framework for the ladder; don't try to make repairs unless the ladder is secured to the ridge of the roof. Use an extension ladder to get up to the roof; brace the ladder firmly against the house, with the top of the ladder extending above the roof. If possible, don't rest the ladder on a gutter. Always work away from power lines.

Asbestos Shingle Roofs. Shingle roofs are usually easy to fix. At the marked leak point, or where you think the leak might be, look for damaged, curled, or missing shingles. At every place where two surfaces meet, and around every chimney or vent, look for breaks in the flashing or caulking, or gaps in lines of roof cement. If you can't see any damage to the shingles or flashing in the leak area, you'll have to call a professional roofer; the problem may be inadequate flashing or simply deterioration of the shingles.

If you do find evidence of shingle problems, the repairs are fairly simple. Curled-back shingles can be reattached with asphalt roof cement or compound—use the troweling-consistency cement, or buy roof cement in tubes for use with a caulking gun. In warm weather, you can easily straighten out the curled shingle. In cold weather, asbestos shingles become very brittle, and must be softened before they can be flattened out. To soften a brittle shingle, use a propane torch with a flame-spreader nozzle. Apply the flame carefully to the curled edges of the shingle; it should get just warm enough to soften, but not hot enough to catch fire. Then flatten the edges of the shingle. To reattach the shingle, apply roof cement generously to the bottom; a good dollop of cement at each corner is usually enough. Then press the shingle firmly into place.

If shingles are torn, rotten, or missing, they should be replaced with new ones. Any shingle that lifts right off the roof with no effort is rotten, and should be replaced. If you find a large area of rotten shingles, you may need a whole new roof; in this case, you should call a professional. Otherwise, replace the damaged shingles—flat or ridge—with shingles left from the installation of the roof. If you can't get matching shingles, you can make do with nonmatching ones; or, in an emergency, cut shingle-size patches from sheet aluminum or copper. To make it easier to slide the new shingle up into place, round its back corners slightly with a sharp utility knife (or, on sheet-metal patches, tin snips).

First, remove the damaged shingle. Lift the edges of the surrounding shingles and carefully remove the nails with a pry bar. Slide the old shingle out; if there's loose or brittle roof cement left under it, scrape the opening clean. When shingles are blown off by a storm, remove any protruding nails left in the roof; nails that don't stick up can be left in place. With the old shingle removed, slide the new shingle into the gap, with its front edge aligned with the shingles on each side and its back edge under the shingles in the row above it. If you're using a piece of sheet aluminum or copper, coat the back of the patch with roof cement before you slide it into place.

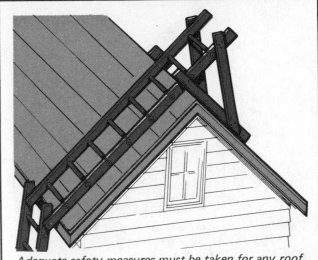

Adequate safety measures must be taken for any roof repairs. Always use safety ropes; on steep roofs, use a ladder framework to provide secure anchoring.

Lift the corners of the overlapping shingles and fasten the top of the new shingle with a 6d galvanized roofing nail driven through each corner. Cover the nail heads with roof cement, and then smooth down the overlapping shingle edges.

If you're replacing rows of shingles, it isn't necessary to round the back corners, except where the top row meets the row above. Ridge shingles, the tent-shaped shingles along the peak of the roof, can be replaced the same way; overlap them along the ridge and over the shingles on both sides. Do not try to use flat shingles; you must use new ridge shingles. Cover the back of each new ridge shingle with roof cement before setting it into place; secure each corner of the shingle with a roofing nail, and cover the nail heads with roof cement.

After replacing the damaged shingles, or if the shingles are undamaged, inspect the chimney flashing, the flashing around vents or vent pipes, and any line of roof cement where two surfaces meet. If the metal flashing

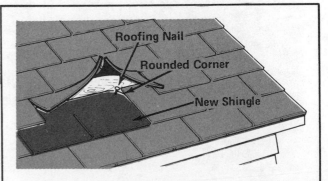

Round the corners of the new shingle and slide it up into the gap. Lift the corners of the overlapping shingles and drive a roofing nail at each corner.

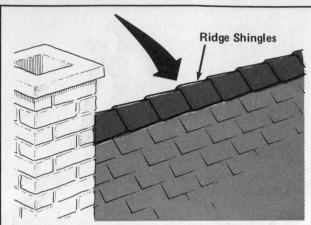

For repairs on the peak of the roof, use ridge shingles, overlapping along the ridge and over the shingles on both sides of the peak.

around a chimney or dormer is not thoroughly caulked, fill the joints with roof cement in a caulking gun. Along joints sealed with a line of roof cement, apply roof cement with a putty knife to areas that look worn or cracked. Apply the cement liberally; cover the questionable areas completely. If there are any exposed nail heads in the flashing, cover them with roof cement. Make other flashing repairs as detailed below.

Flat Roofs. Flat roofs are built up of layers of roofing felt and tar; leaks usually occur at low spots, or where the roofing felt has been damaged. In most cases, the leak is directly below the damaged spot, and the damage to the roofing felt is easy to see. If there's still water pooled in the leak area, mop it up or soak it up with rags, and let the surface dry. Brush off any gravel. Look for cracks in the felt, or for large blisters where the top layer has separated.

To mend a blister, use a sharp utility knife to slice it open down the middle. The cut should penetrate to the full depth of the blistered layer, but should not reach the sound roofing felt beneath it. Lift the cut edges of the blister. If there's water inside the blister, press from the edges in toward the center to squeeze the water out from between the layers of roofing. If there's water under a large area of the roof, the problem is more than a simple blister; water may be running in from an adjoining pitched roof surface. In this case, it's best to call a professional roofer.

Before you can repair the blister, the inside layers of roofing felt must be dry. If there was water inside the blister, soak up all you can; then prop the edges up to let the layers dry. In cold weather, or if the layers are thoroughly saturated, you'll have to use a propane torch to dry out the felts. With a flame-spreader nozzle on the torch, play the flame carefully over the inside layers of the blister. Roofing felt and tar are very flammable; don't let the layers get hot enough to burn or bubble. When the layers of roofing are dry, spread a thick coating of roof cement on the bottom edges of the loose felt, and press the sides of the blister down firmly. Close the blister permanently with a row of 6d galvanized roofing nails along each side of the slit, and then spread roof cement over the entire blister; make sure the nail heads are well covered.

When a flat roof has a hole in it, you'll have to patch each damaged layer of roofing felt. With a sharp utility knife, cut out a square or rectangle of roofing around the hole; keep the edges as even as you can. Cut through each damaged layer of roofing felt, one by one, to the depth of the hole, but don't cut any more than you have to. When all the damaged layers have been removed, you should have an evenly cut-out square or rectangle. If there's water between the layers, soak up what you can and then very carefully dry out the roofing felt with a propane torch.

When the surrounding roofing is dry, fill in the hole with pieces of 15-pound roofing felt—not paper—cut to the same size as the hole. The idea here is to rebuild

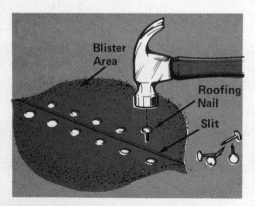

Slit the blister open and dry it out; then cement the loose felt down. Secure both sides of the slit with roofing nails.

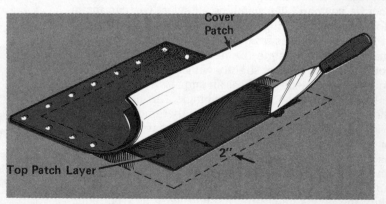

Cut out the damaged layers of roofing and rebuild the cut-out area with layers of roof cement and roofing felt. Spread more roof cement over the top, and cover the patch with a final layer of felt.

the damaged area to the same level as the rest of the roof. Cut the patches with a utility knife, one patch for every layer of roofing you removed. Spread roof cement thickly on the bottom of the hole, set a patch into the hole, and press it into place; then spread more roof cement over the patch. Fill the entire hole this way, building up layers of felt and roof cement, until the top patch is flush with the surrounding surface. Finish the job by cutting a larger patch, two inches bigger all around than the filled-in hole. Spread roof cement over the top patch, extending it at least two inches out onto the roof all around, and then set the large patch over this coating. Nail this cover patch down with 6d galvanized roofing nails, set about one inch apart, and coat the nail heads with roof cement.

After patching the damaged area, take a look at the entire roof, and especially at flashing and joints finished with roof cement. Caulk flashing joints with roof cement in a caulking gun; make other flashing repairs as detailed below. Spread new roof cement on any joint that looks worn or damaged. If the whole roof is in bad shape—if you can see thin spots or cracks all over it—it should be recoated with liquid asphalt (not roof cement). This won't solve the problem permanently, but it will extend the lifetime of an old roof. Paint the liquid on with an old broom—wear clothes you don't mind getting rid of, because this is a messy job. Clean your hands and your tools with mineral spirits, and be sure to dispose of waste materials properly.

Wood Shake or Shingle Roofs. Repairing a shake roof is similar to repairing an asbestos shingle one, although it may be a little more difficult. Use the same type of shakes or shingles to replace the damaged ones; if a ridge shingle is damaged, use a new specially cut ridge shingle instead of trying to make do with regular shingles.

Damaged wood shakes or shingles must usually be split before they can be removed. Use a hammer and a sharp chisel to split the damaged shake; slant the chisel up into the shake at the same angle as the pitch of the roof. Be careful not to gouge the surrounding shakes. Pull the pieces of the shingle out, and cut off the nails that held it in place—since shakes aren't flexible, like asbestos shingles, it isn't possible to pry the nails out. Use a hacksaw blade, wrapped with electrical tape at one end, to cut off the nail heads, as far down the nail shaft as you can. If you can't reach the nails without damaging the other shakes, you'll have to work around them.

Measure the gap left by the old shake, and cut a new one about ³/₈ inch less than this measurement, using a fine-toothed hacksaw. You must allow this ³/₈-inch clearance, because the first time it rains the shake will swell. If you were able to cut off the nails that held the old shake, you can just slide the new one up into place, with its top edge under the overlapping shingles, and nail the shake down with two galvanized roofing nails, one at each side of the exposed top edge. If you weren't able to cut off the nails, you'll have to notch the new

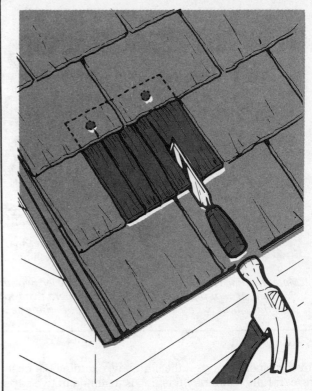

Remove a damaged shake by splitting it with a sharp chisel, slanted up into the shake along the roof pitch. Then cut off the nails with a hacksaw blade.

shake to fit around them. Push the shake up into the gap, hard enough so that the edge is marked by the two old nails. Then carefully cut slots at the marked points with a coping saw; if possible, clamp the shake in a vise so it doesn't split. Slide the notched shake into place, and nail it with two roofing nails. To finish the job, set the heads of the nails with a nail set, and seal them with caulking compound.

Flashing and Valley Repairs

The metal seals around chimneys and dormers, called flashings, can eventually pull loose, collecting water instead of shedding it. Chimney flashing that's pulled out of place can channel water down into your home, with disastrous results. Flashing is also used where two roof pitches meet; this is called valley flashing. When flashing is badly damaged, or when a leak is severe, you need a professional repair job; but in many cases you can repair the damage yourself. Use ladders and safety ropes to get at the roof, as detailed above; make sure the roof is dry.

To prevent leaks at the flashing, it's a good idea to inspect it every spring. If you can see thin spots or gaps along a flashing joint—at a chimney or along a valley—spread roof cement over the entire joint, applying it generously with a trowel. The flashing edge should be

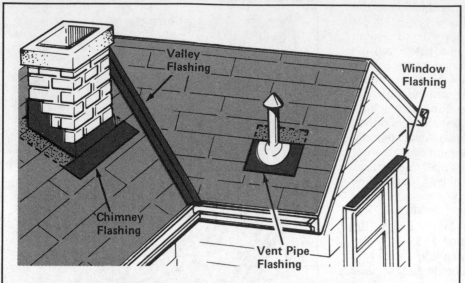

Metal flashing is used to seal out water wherever two surfaces meet—around the chimney, at vent pipes, along the valleys where two roof pitches meet, and sometimes over exposed windows. Inspect flashing yearly.

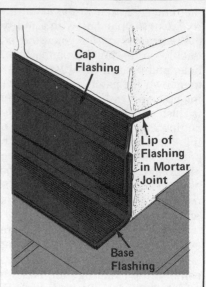

Chimney flashing has two parts, the base and the cap. The lip of the cap is embedded in mortar.

covered completely. At the chimney, examine the flashing carefully. Chimney flashing is installed in two parts: the base, which covers the bottom of the chimney and extends onto the roof; and the cap, which is mortared into the chimney bricks. If the mortar holding the cap flashing is crumbling or the flashing has pulled loose, you'll have to resecure the flashing.

Pull the lip of the cap flashing out of the mortar joint, only as far as it comes easily. Do *not* yank the entire flashing out, or pull it completely away from the chimney. The less you have to separate it, the easier it will be to fix. With the flashing out of the mortar joint, clean out the old mortar with a hammer and chisel; wear

safety goggles to protect your eyes. Then, being careful not to damage the flashing, wire-brush the joint to clean out the debris. Use cement mortar mix to fill the open joint; mix the mortar as directed. Wet the joint with a paintbrush dipped in water. Then, with a small trowel, fill the joint firmly with mortar. When the joint is full, press the lip of the flashing into the mortar, in the same position it was in before. Press the flashing in firmly, but don't push too far or it may pop back out, and you'll have to start all over again. Let the mortar dry as directed. When the joint is completely cured, caulk all around the joint, over the lip of the cap flashing, with butyl rubber caulk.

In an open valley, the flashing strip is exposed; a strip of metal is visible along the joint where two roof pitches meet. Repair this type yourself.

In a closed valley, the flashing is covered by shingles; no exposed metal is visible. This type should be professionally repaired.

At vent pipes or metal chimneys, make sure the joint at the base of the pipe or chimney is sealed. If you can see gaps at the roof line, caulk around the base of the pipe or chimney with roof cement in a caulking gun. Vent pipes on pitched roofs usually have a protective collar; if the collar is loose, tap it back into place, and then caulk the collar-base joint with roof caulk.

Valley flashings are not always repairable. If you see a strip of metal all along the joint where two roof pitches meet, the valley is open; if the joint is shingled over, it's closed. Open valleys are easy to get at; you can see the damage and you can repair it. Because closed valleys aren't visible from the roof, the only sign of damage is usually a leak directly under the valley. This kind of valley must be repaired by a professional roofer.

To repair an open valley, inspect it for holes all along the joint. You can patch small holes with sheet metal, the same metal—either copper or aluminum—the valley is made of. Do not use a different metal to patch the valley; this would cause corrosion. First, clean the surface of the valley with a wire brush. Cut a sheet-metal patch about two inches bigger all around than the hole. Spread a thick coating of roof cement on the damaged area and press the patch into place, bending it to the shape of the valley. Spread more roof cement over the edges of the patch to seal out water.

If you can't see any holes along an open valley, but it has leaked, look for loose shingles along the edges of the valley. Working from the bottom up, reset any loose shingles with roof cement; then apply more roof cement to cover the shingle edges all along the valley. If you can't find any loose shingles, the problem may be that the valley is too narrow, and simply isn't adequate to seal the joint. This situation should be handled by a professional roofer, because the entire valley will have to be replaced.

Replacing Vent Pipe Flashing

Vent pipes and appliance chimneys are sealed with metal flashing to prevent leaks, but the flashing may eventually need replacement. Pitched-roof vents are usually flashed with a flat metal sheet cut to fit around the pipe, and a protective collar that fits around its base. Flat-roof flashing usually covers the entire vent, with a flat base and a pipe casing that slides on over the chimney. Replacing either type of flashing is fairly easy—just make sure your replacement flashing is exactly the same type and diameter as the old one. Follow the roof safety procedures detailed above.

Vents on Pitched Roofs. On a pitched roof, the base of the flashing is covered with shingles on the side above the chimney, and left exposed on the side below it. To remove the old flashing, you'll have to remove the shingles on the up-roof side. Lift the shingles with a pry bar, but be careful not to damage them; they must be replaced to cover the new flashing. If you break a shingle, you'll need a new one to replace it. To remove the flashing itself, insert the blade of the pry bar under its edge,

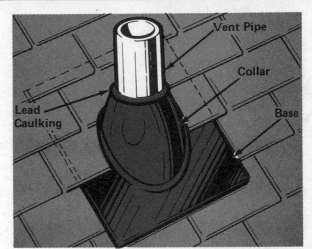

Pitched-roof vent pipe flashing consists of a flat base and a protective collar that fits around the pipe.

and lever the bar on a block of scrap wood to lift the flashing. Wear work gloves while you do this; the edge of the flashing is sharp. Lift the flashing up over the vent pipe, being careful not to knock the pipe out of place. Then pull out any nails left around the pipe, and fill the holes with roof cement.

Set the new flashing over the pipe, with its protective collar aligned the same way the old one was. Nail down the flashing with 6d galvanized roofing nails, and cover the nail heads with roof cement. Apply more roof cement to seal the base of the protective collar. If the top of the collar is loose around the pipe, tap the lead caulking in against the pipe with a screwdriver. Then, with the flashing secure, replace the shingles over the top of the flashing. Starting with the bottom row and working up, nail each shingle into place at the top; use two 6d galvanized roofing nails for small shingles, four nails for large ones. As you work, cover the nail heads with roof cement. Slide the top edges of the top row of shingles under the overlapping bottom edges of the row above.

Vents on Flat Roofs. On a flat roof, the base of the flashing is embedded in the roofing material; to replace it, you'll have to cut a hole in the roof and then rebuild it. If there's gravel on the roof, sweep it away from the vent pipe to clear a four-foot-square area. Locate the edge of the flashing base and, with a sharp utility knife, cut a slit through the roofing felt along one side of it. Wearing work gloves, insert the blade of a pry bar into the slit and under the edge of the flashing. Lever the bar over a block of scrap wood, working along the slit in the roofing, to release the flashing. Cut around the remaining three sides to free the flashing completely. Then, being careful not to knock the pipe out of place, lift the old flashing out and over the pipe. You should now have an evenly cut-out square in the roof.

The new flashing is not built into the same hole, but

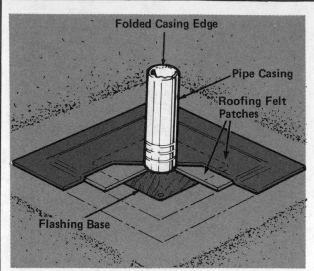

Flat-roof vent pipe flashing has a casing pipe that covers the entire pipe; the edge of the casing folds down to seal it. The base is covered by roofing.

set on top of the roof; your first step in installing it, therefore, is to fill the hole. For each layer of roofing that you can see in the hole, cut a patch of 15-pound roofing felt. Use the base of the old flashing as a pattern to cut the felt. On each piece of roofing felt, mark the location of the vent pipe, and cut a hole at that point so that the patch will fit snugly over the pipe. When all your patch pieces are ready, spread roof cement thickly on the bottom of the hole. Set the first patch over the pipe and press it firmly into the hole; then spread more roof cement on top of it. Fill the entire hole this way, building up layers of roofing felt and roof cement, until the top patch is level with the surface of the roof. Spread a thick layer of roof cement over the top patch, and fill any gaps around the vent pipe with more cement.

Set the new flashing carefully into place over the vent pipe. Wear work gloves while you do this; the edges of the flashing are sharp. Press the new flashing down firmly, so that the vent pipe is encased in the flashing pipe and the base is aligned the same way the old one was. Nail down the flashing with 6d galvanized roofing nails, and cover the nail heads with roof cement. Using pliers, fold the top edge of the casing pipe down over the top edge of the vent pipe to seal the new flashing.

To finish the job, cover the base of the flashing with two more layers of roofing felt, the first three inches larger and the second six inches larger all around than the flashing. As you did with the first patches, cut a hole in the center of each piece so that it will fit over the vent pipe. Spread roof cement thickly over the base of the flashing, extending it three inches onto the roof all around. Set the smaller piece of roofing felt over the pipe and press it into place. Cover this piece of felt with another layer of roof cement, again extending it three inches onto the roof all around, and set the larger patch into place. Press this final patch down and nail it into place with 6d galvanized roofing nails, about one inch apart; cover the nail heads with roof cement. If you removed gravel from the patch area, you can now spread it back over the bare spot, but this isn't necessary.

Maintaining and Repairing Your Gutter System

Good drainage is very important to your home's structural well-being. Gutters and downspouts, the primary components of your drainage system, must be kept clear to prevent stormwater from overflowing or backing up; blocked gutters can cause erosion around the house, damage to the exterior walls, basement leaks, and, eventually, uneven settling of the foundation. To prevent these drainage problems, you should give your gutters and downspouts regular periodic maintenance, and repair them at the first sign of trouble. When you work on your gutters, follow the roof safety procedures outlined above.

At the minimum, you should clean your gutters twice a year, in late spring and late fall; if you live in a wooded area, more frequent cleaning is advisable. A plastic scoop is an ideal gutter-cleaning tool. To clean the gutters, shovel out leaves and other debris with the scoop; wear work gloves to protect your hands. Work from a ladder that's tall enough to let you reach the gutters comfortably. As you work, move the ladder frequently; don't bend out to reach to either side. After cleaning out all the loose debris, flush the gutters with a garden hose.

Even when the gutters look clear, a downspout may be blocked. Check your downspouts by flushing them with the hose. If a downspout is clogged, you can break up the clog with a plumbers' snake, fed down through the opening in the gutter; then clear out any remaining debris with the hose. To keep the downspouts clear, use a wire leaf strainer at each one—copper wire for copper gutters, stainless steel for all other types. Insert a leaf strainer into each downspout opening along the gutters; push it in just far enough to hold it steady. The strainer will keep sticks and other debris from entering the downspout.

Many people use plastic or metal screening leaf guards on their gutters, to keep leaves from building up in the gutters. Leaf guards are not usually as effective as they're made out to be, though—they do keep large leaves out of your gutters, but leaf fragments, leaf cases, and other small debris go right through the screening. Gutters covered by leaf guards must still be cleaned regularly, and leaf guards make the cleaning much more difficult.

After cleaning out the gutters, let them dry thoroughly, and inspect them for signs of damage. Rust spots and holes can be mended with scrap wire screening and asphalt roof cement. First wire-brush the damaged area to remove dirt and loose rust; then clean the area well with a rag soaked in mineral spirits. If the hole is small, or if the metal isn't rusted all the way

Clean gutters at least twice a year to prevent clogging. Shovel out the leaves and other debris with a plastic scoop; then flush the gutters with a garden hose.

To keep downspouts clear, flush them with the hose; if necessary, remove clogs with a plumbers' snake. Use a wire leaf strainer at each downspout.

through, a screening patch isn't needed; just spread roof cement over the damaged area. To repair an open hole, cut a piece of scrap wire screening, 1/2 inch to one inch bigger all around than the hole. Spread roof cement around the hole, and press the patch down into it; spread a thin layer of cement over the screening. Let the patch dry; then, if the holes of the screening are still open, spread another layer of cement over the patch to close it completely.

If the gutter is extensively damaged, or has a large hole in it, patch it with sheet metal instead of wire screening. If the gutters are copper, be sure to use copper for this repair; use sheet aluminum for other types of gutters. Cut a piece of sheet metal big enough to cover the inside of the gutter completely and wrap around over the outside edges. The patch must extend at least one inch beyond the damage each way along the

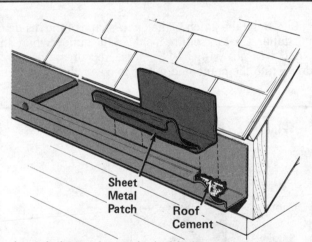

Large holes can be patched with sheet metal, bent to the shape of the gutter. Spread roof cement on the damaged gutter before installing the patch.

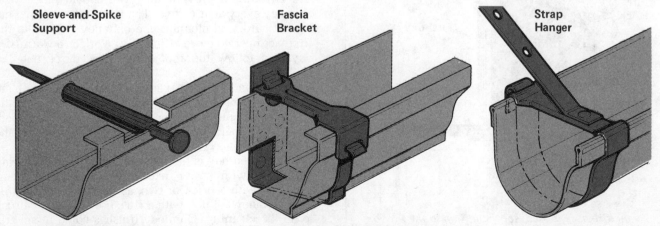

There are three types of gutter hangers: sleeve and spike supports (left), fascia brackets (center), and strap hangers (right). Gutter hangers should be used about every 2 1/2 feet.

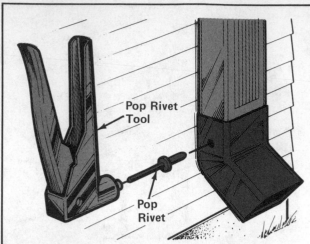

Reattach loose sections with pop rivets. Drill through the overlapping sections; then set one rivet through each exposed side of the loose section.

gutter. Bend the patch to the exact shape of the inside of the gutter. Coat the entire inside of the gutter, where the patch will go, with roof cement, and press the patch down into the cemented gutter to cover the hole. Bend

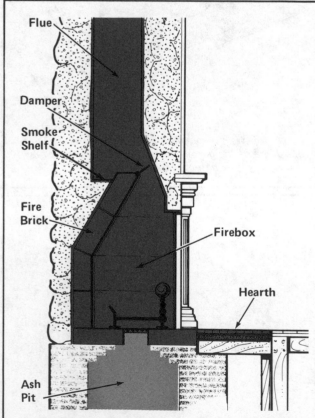

As the fireplace is used, soot builds up in the firebox and on the sides of the flue. To prevent problems, clean the chimney and the ash pit regularly.

the edges back over the gutter lips with pliers, and then coat the entire patch inside the gutter with roof cement. Make sure the edges of the patch are well covered.

Besides patching obvious damage, inspect the gutters for sags, loose sections, and loose hangers. Gutters are held by any of three types of hangers: sleeve-and-spike supports, the simplest; fascia brackets, which are nailed to the face of the wall; and strap hangers, which are nailed to the roof. Loose sleeve-and-spike supports can be adjusted or renailed. Loose fascia brackets and strap hangers can also be renailed; use 6d galvanized roofing nails to reset them. Cover the nail heads with roof cement to prevent leaks. If you can't get at a fascia bracket to renail it, or if the gutter sags even though all its supports are solid, you'll have to add supports; there should be a support about every 2½ feet along the gutter. Make sure you cover all nail heads on the roof with roof cement.

If a section of downspout or an elbow is loose, it should be reattached. You can do this temporarily with duct tape, but duct tape should not be left in place permanently. For a sturdier repair, reattach the loose section with pop rivets; you'll need an inexpensive pop rivet tool for this job. Pop rivets can be installed from the outside, so it isn't necessary to take the sections of downspout apart. Hold the loose section up in the proper position. With an electric drill and a bit of the correct size for the pop rivets you're using, drill through the overlapping sections—make one hole on each exposed side of the downspout. Then set a pop rivet through each drilled hole: set a rivet in the pop rivet tool, insert the tip of the tool into the hole, and squeeze the handles of the tool until the rivet pops off. Pop rivets will hold the section of downspout in place permanently.

Cleaning a Chimney

If you have a wood-burning fireplace, you know how much soot is produced by a fire. Over years of use, soot can build up in a chimney, blocking it and creating a fire hazard. To prevent this, you should clean your chimney every year or two. The job is a messy one, but it's not hard, and cleaning the chimney will make the fireplace operate more efficiently. Work on a warm, dry day, and follow the roof safety procedures detailed above.

First, open the damper to the fireplace. Seal off the fireplace opening from the room with a heavy plastic sheet, taped into place, or a piece of scrap plywood. Make sure there are no leaks or cracks around the edges.

If your chimney is not lined with a flue, use a burlap bag filled with straw, excelsior, or wadded paper, weighted with a brick or two, as your cleaning tool. If your chimney is lined with a flue, use a chimney brush to do the cleaning. Chimney brushes come in several sizes—either round or square—to completely fill the flue opening.

Fasten the bag or brush securely to a rope; if you're

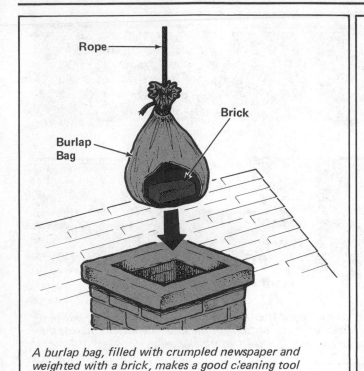

A burlap bag, filled with crumpled newspaper and weighted with a brick, makes a good cleaning tool for unlined chimneys.

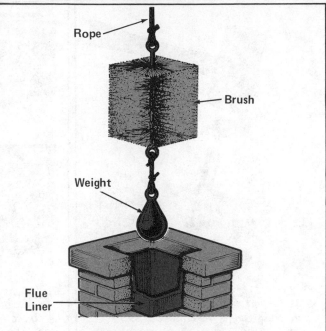

For chimneys with flue liners, a chimney brush is the best cleaning tool. Use a brush the same shape, round or square, as the flue liner.

using a brush, attach a weight below the brush to provide a little added pull. Working from the roof, lower the bag or brush down the chimney until it hits the bottom. A chimney brush fills the entire flue opening; lower and raise the brush several times to dislodge caked soot. If you're using a bag, start at one corner of the chimney. Lower the bag, pull it up, and repeat, lowering and raising it, several times. Now move the bag around the perimeter of the opening, moving it about a foot each time, and repeat this procedure until you've cleaned the entire chimney area. This takes care of your work on the roof.

If the fireplace has an outside door, open it and remove the soot that's fallen through. Wait an hour or so for the dust to settle; then remove the plastic sheet or plywood from the fireplace opening. With the opening uncovered, take a large hand mirror and a flashlight and hold them so you can inspect the chimney. Look for any obstructions. If there are any, you will have to go back on the roof and repeat the cleaning procedure described above. If there are no obstructions, put on gloves and reach over the damper to the smoke shelf. Gently clean away the debris. Finally, vacuum out the fireplace and the smoke shelf.

Masonry Repairs

More than any other structural part of your home, the masonry—concrete, blacktop, brick, or concrete block—is supposed to be permanent. Wood rots; glass breaks; shingles tear; other components wear out or

break; masonry, theoretically, endures. But what happens when the driveway cracks, the steps crumble, or a brick falls out of the chimney? You may be hesitant to tackle masonry problems, even if you've worked on all the other components of your home. But masonry, like every other structural component, is easy to deal with when you know the right techniques. With a little basic know-how, you can handle almost any masonry problem.

Patching Concrete Slabs

Cracks and holes in concrete should never be ignored, because temperature changes and water penetration, especially in cold weather, can very quickly break up the sound concrete around them. To keep the damage from escalating, patch cracks and holes as soon as weather permits. Buy liquid concrete bonding agent and ready-mix sand concrete mix to repair the slab. For large or deep cracks or holes, use gravel concrete mix.

Cracks. Before a crack can be filled, it must be deepened and undercut so that the patch will bond properly. Use a cold chisel and hammer to enlarge the crack and deepen it to a depth of one to two inches. Wear safety goggles to protect your eyes as you work. Angle the chisel into the crack to make the bottom of the opening wider than the top; this will lock the patch concrete into the gap. Then remove all chunks of concrete, and brush the remaining debris out of the crack with a stiff broom or whisk broom. Flush the cleaned crack thoroughly with a garden hose, turned on full-force, and then

Enlarge and deepen the crack with a cold chisel; angle the chisel out to undercut the crack.

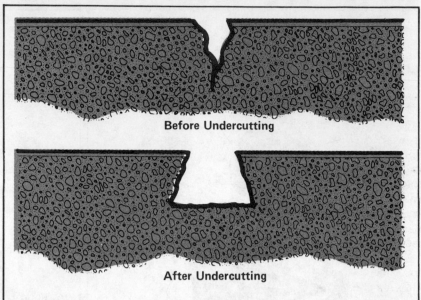

Before Undercutting

After Undercutting

A crack that isn't enlarged (top) is wider at the top than at the bottom. A correctly undercut crack (bottom) is wider at the bottom than at the top. The patch concrete is locked into the opening.

sponge out any standing water. If the crack goes all the way through the slab, and the ground underneath is eroded, pour sand into the crack just to the bottom edge of the slab. Dampen the sand thoroughly with the hose.

While the crack is still wet, mix the concrete as directed. A sturdy wheelbarrow is the most convenient container; use a shovel to mix the concrete. When the concrete is mixed, pour liquid concrete bonding agent into the crack to coat the inside surface entirely. Spread the bonding agent with a stiff paintbrush, and clean the paintbrush immediately when you finish. Then quickly fill the crack with the wet concrete. Pack the concrete in with a trowel, and make sure there are no air spaces along the bottom of the crack. Smooth the concrete along the surface of the crack with the trowel. If the crack is very wide, the surface of the patch should be leveled with the surrounding surface. Set a piece of 2×4 on edge across one end of the crack, and pull the 2×4 in zigzags along the entire length of the crack. This will level the patch and remove excess concrete.

Let the concrete set for about 45 minutes. When the sheen of water has disappeared from the surface, smooth the concrete again with a steel finishing trowel or a clean piece of 2×4—a trowel will give the concrete a denser, more polished finish. Then let the concrete cure for about a week. During this time, spray the crack two or three times a day with the hose to keep the concrete from drying out too quickly. If the crack is very wide, cover it with a sheet of plastic during the curing period. Lift the plastic two or three times a day to spray the crack.

Holes. Before you can fill the hole, you must undercut it; if it's shallow, it must be deepened to at least one inch. Remove all loose concrete. Then, wearing safety goggles to protect your eyes, deepen the hole with a cold chisel and hammer. Cut all the way down to sound concrete, and angle the chisel out at the edges so that the bottom of the hole is wider than the top. Remove the broken concrete and sweep out the debris with a stiff broom or whisk broom; then flush the hole thoroughly with a garden hose, turned on full-force. Sponge out any standing water left in the hole. If the hole extends all the way through the slab, and the ground underneath is eroded, pour sand into the hole to the bottom edge of the slab, and moisten the sand thoroughly.

While the hole is still wet, mix the concrete in a wheelbarrow, as directed. Then quickly cover the inside surface of the hole with the concrete bonding agent. Spread the bonding agent with a stiff paintbrush; pay particular attention to the undercut edges. Clean the paintbrush immediately. As soon as you've spread the bonding agent, shovel the new concrete into the hole; pack it into the undercut edges with a trowel. Mound the concrete slightly above the surface of the slab, and then pound it down with the back of the shovel. Cut through the concrete with the blade of the shovel to make sure there are no air spaces, and then pound the patch down again. Leave the new concrete slightly higher than the surrounding surface.

Use a piece of 2×4 to level the patch. You can do this by yourself if the patch is small; you'll need a helper to level a large patch. Set the 2×4 across the filled hole, and pull it in zigzags over the new concrete; the 2×4 will remove the excess and bring the concrete level with the surrounding surface. The new concrete will have a sheen of water on the surface. Let it set for about 45 minutes to an hour, and then, when the surface water has disappeared, smooth the concrete with a wood float until the surface is filmed with water again. Use long, smooth strokes and press lightly so you don't mark the new concrete; stop smoothing as soon as the water sheen reappears.

Let the concrete set again until the water sheen has disappeared. If you want to match a dense, highly polished concrete surface, smooth the patch again with a steel finishing trowel, using long, even strokes and working until the film of water appears again. If you want a rougher, nonskid texture, finish the surface of the patch with a push broom. Set the broom on the old concrete to one side of the patch, and then push it slowly and evenly across the patch and onto the old concrete on the other side. Don't push the broom hard enough to dig into the concrete; what you want is an even brushed look. After this final texturing, let the concrete cure for at least a week. To keep it from drying out too quickly, cover the patch with a sheet of plastic. Two or three times a day during the curing period, remove the plastic and spray the patch lightly with the hose.

Mending Concrete Steps

When concrete steps start to crumble along the edges, they usually go fast. More concrete is broken off as people use the steps, and the crumbling edges can be hazardous as they deteriorate further. Fortunately, repairing the steps isn't as hard as you might think; you can recast the edges with sand concrete mix, using the same techniques described above. Use liquid bonding agent to bond the new concrete properly.

As with any concrete repair, the first step is to chisel out and undercut the damaged area with a cold chisel and sledgehammer. Wearing safety goggles to protect your eyes, cut into the crumbled edge at least one inch, or down to solid concrete. Cut a deep open V all along each damaged edge, with one arm of the V straight into the riser and the other arm angled into the tread of the

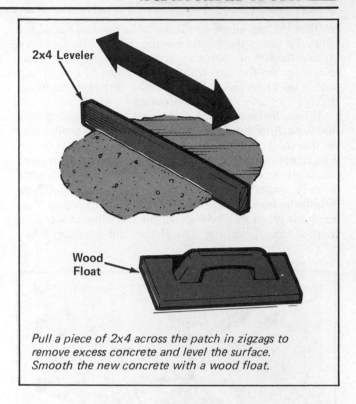

Pull a piece of 2x4 across the patch in zigzags to remove excess concrete and level the surface. Smooth the new concrete with a wood float.

damaged step. Even if only one end of the step is crumbling, chisel out the entire edge. Clean out the debris with a stiff whisk broom, and flush the open V thoroughly with a garden hose, turned on full-force.

For each damaged step, build a form to recast the open edge. For the front of the form, use a board as long as the step and as wide as the step is high, so that the top edge of the board is flush with the top of the step. Set the board against the riser under the broken edge, and hold it in place with several bricks. Complete the form by closing in the ends of the step with a board set against each side; if you can, use boards just tall enough

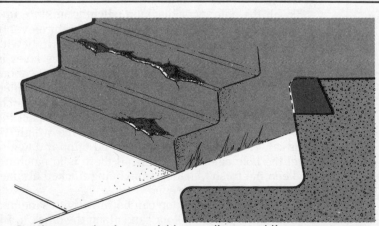

Good preparation is essential in mending crumbling concrete steps. To ensure good bonding of the new concrete, undercut the damaged edges with a cold chisel, forming a deep open V.

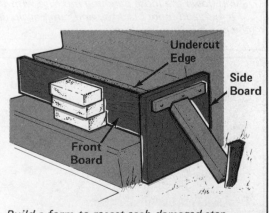

Build a form to recast each damaged step. Set a board against the front of the step; use another board to close each open end.

so that the top edges are flush with the surface of the step. To brace these side boards, nail a piece of 2×4 across the top of each one, and wedge each board into place against the step with another piece of 2×4 placed under the cross-piece. Drive a stake at the bottom of the wedge 2×4 to keep it from slipping.

When the forms are in place, wet the steps again with the hose. Mix the concrete as directed—a wheelbarrow is the most convenient container. With a stiff paint-brush, spread liquid concrete bonding agent over each chiseled-out edge; make sure the corner of the V is completely coated. Clean the brush immediately. Then, while the bonding agent is still wet, fill the open V on each prepared step with concrete. Pack the concrete in with a trowel, forcing it well into the undercut edge.

Chop out loose blacktop and clean out the debris; keep the hole dry. Then pour blacktop patching mixture directly into the hole.

Tamp down the loose patching mixture with the end of a 4x4; add more blacktop and tamp again until the patch is firm and level.

To prevent further damage, coat the entire driveway—patch and all—with liquid blacktop sealer, spread with a push broom.

Make sure there are no air spaces in the concrete; cut through it with the point of the trowel to fill any gaps. Then smooth the surface of the concrete roughly level with the surface of the step. The front and side of the new edge are shaped by the forms.

To finish the step, smooth the top surface of the edge with a wood float to level it. Let the concrete set for 45 minutes to an hour, until the water sheen disappears from the surface; then smooth it again with the wood float, so that it matches the texture of the old concrete. If you want to match a denser, more polished texture, let the concrete set for another 45 minutes until the water sheen disappears again, and then final-smooth it with a steel finishing trowel. Stop smoothing as soon as the water comes to the surface again.

Let the concrete cure for at least a week, and leave the forms in place during this time. To keep the concrete from drying out too quickly, cover the steps with a sheet of plastic. Two or three times a day during the curing period, lift the plastic and spray the concrete lightly with the hose.

Patching Broken Blacktop

As anyone who has a blacktop driveway knows, asphalt deteriorates much more quickly than concrete, and once it starts to crumble, the process accelerates. But black-top is as easy to patch as it is quick to break down. Blacktop patching mixture, sold in bags, requires no mixing or heating, and you can prolong the life of the whole driveway with liquid blacktop sealer. Make all your blacktop repairs in warm weather; blacktop is brittle and slow to bond when it's cold.

Unlike concrete, blacktop must be dry when it's repaired. With a shovel or a trowel, chop out all the loose blacktop from the damaged area. Cut down and out on the sides to solid blacktop. Remove the crumbled black-top and clean out the hole with a stiff broom or whisk broom. If the hole is very deep, fill it with gravel to within three or four inches of the surface. Pound the gravel in with the back of the shovel.

To fill the hole, pour blacktop patching mixture into it, right from the bag. Spread the patch mixture evenly to just below the surface, and then tamp it in firmly with the end of a piece of 4×4 timber. When this layer is firm, pour in more blacktop patch, mounding it to about 1/2 inch above the surrounding surface. Tamp the patch again to level it with the surface. For a firmer patch, drive over the filled hole several times to compact the new asphalt; the patch may sink under the weight of your car. Add more patching mix and tamp it down to level the hole again, and that's all there is to patching. To keep the fresh blacktop from being tracked around, sprinkle the patch with sand.

Small cracks in blacktop can be filled with sand and liquid blacktop sealer. Pour sand along the crack to fill it partway, and then pour the blacktop sealer into the crack over the sand. The sand will absorb the sealer quickly; if necessary, add more sealer to fill the crack completely. To fill large cracks, mix sand and blacktop sealer to a thin paste, and pack this paste in with a trowel. Force the patching paste in to the full depth of each crack, and smooth the surface level. Sprinkle sand along newly patched cracks to keep the sealer from being tracked around while it dries.

To prevent further damage to the driveway, you may want to coat the entire surface with liquid blacktop sealer. Applied every two or three years, the sealer can really prolong the life of an asphalt drive. If you seal the driveway after patching it, do not sprinkle sand on the newly patched areas.

Spread the blacktop sealer with a push broom, coating one section of the drive at a time. Throw the broom head away when you finish the job. Block the driveway off until the sealer is completely dry, as directed by the manufacturer.

Tuckpointing Loose Mortar Joints

Brick and concrete block don't deteriorate as quickly as wood, but they do need regular maintenance. Over the years, and especially in very cold or wet climates, the mortar between bricks can loosen or crumble. This can result in further damage, both inside and out, as water seeps through the open joints; interior walls may be damaged, and the mortar outside will crumble even more. Professionals charge a lot to repair loose mortar joints, but the repair work, called tuckpointing, requires very little skill—just strength and patience. You can save yourself a lot of expense and aggravation by tuckpointing loose mortar joints yourself, as soon as possible. Buy mortar mix and, if the old mortar is colored, mortar coloring. If the mortar joints are rounded, you'll also need a tool called a jointer, or a piece of pipe or rod the same diameter as the joints, to smooth the mortar.

The first step is to clean out the damaged mortar. Wear safety goggles to protect your eyes while you work. With a cold chisel and hammer, cut out the crumbling mortar to a depth of at least 1/2 inch, or down to sound mortar. Work on the vertical joints first, and then on the horizontal ones. Brush the debris out of the joints, and flush them with a garden hose, turned on full-force. Keep your safety goggles on until the joints are completely cleaned out.

After cleaning out the joints, mix a small amount of mortar, as the package directs. Use a scrap of corrugated cardboard to test the color. Spread a little mortar on the cardboard; it will dry very quickly. If the dried mortar doesn't match the color of the old mortar, add mortar coloring as necessary—test the colored mortar on the cardboard with each mixture. When the test mortar is the right color, mix and color as much mortar as you'll need to repair the wall.

Mortar should be applied to a wet surface, so it won't dry out too quickly. Spray the wall lightly with the hose, so that it's wet but not streaming. Then, with a small, sharp trowel, press the mortar firmly into the cleaned-out joints. Fill the vertical joints first, then the horizontal ones. Force the mortar in to the full depth of the open joints; make sure there aren't any gaps. As you finish

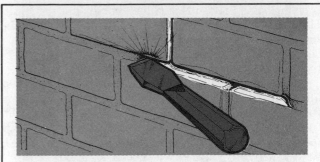
Cut out crumbling mortar to a depth of at least 1/2 inch, first in vertical joints and then in horizontals.

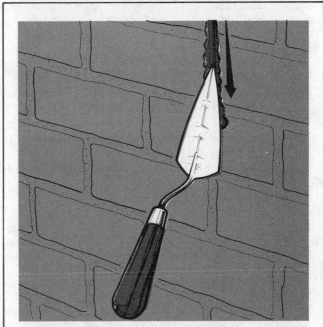
Press mortar firmly into the cleaned joints to fill them completely, with no gaps in the mortar.

Mortar Jointer

Remove excess mortar and finish the joints—verticals first—with a mortar jointer or the point of a trowel.

each joint, go back over it to remove excess mortar and make the joints look like the old ones. For V-shaped joints, use the point of the trowel to shape the mortar. For a smooth, concave U-shaped joint, use a mortar jointer; or finish the joints with a piece of metal rod or

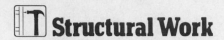
pipe the same (or a little smaller) diameter as the joints. Holding the trowel or jointer at a steady angle to the mortar, draw it smoothly and firmly along the newly filled joint. At the end of the joint, remove the excess mortar. Then go on to the next joint.

Scrape excess mortar off the wall as you work. After all the joints are filled, the mortar must be kept damp for several days while it cures. Spray the wall lightly two or three times a day during this curing period. If there's still excess mortar on the wall, you can remove it with a stiff brush when the mortar is cured.

Replacing a Brick

On old buildings, where tuckpointing has been neglected—and especially on chimneys—there may be loose or broken bricks. This situation is obviously more serious than damage to the mortar; besides causing further damage, it can also be hazardous. Particularly when a chimney is involved, you should replace loose or damaged bricks as soon as you can. Use mortar mix, coloring as needed, and, to replace broken bricks, new bricks of the same type and color.

First, remove the brick. If it's very loose, you may be able to pull it right out. Otherwise, cut out the old mortar around the brick with a cold chisel and hammer; wear safety goggles to protect your eyes. Be careful not to damage the surrounding bricks or, if it's not broken, the loose brick. If the loose brick is damaged, or if you can't get it out by removing the mortar, break it up with the hammer and chisel, and remove the pieces. Then chisel out all the mortar left in the hole, and wire-brush the

hole to remove all traces of the old mortar. If the old brick is not damaged, also chisel off any old mortar adhering to it. Flush out the hole with a garden hose, turned on full-force, and put the old brick or the replacement brick in a bucket of water.

After cleaning out the hole, mix a small amount of mortar according to the package directions, and spread a little on a scrap of corrugated cardboard to test it for color, as detailed above for tuckpointing. When you have a good color match, mix enough mortar to replace the brick. Spray the hole lightly with the hose, so that it's wet but not streaming. Spread a thick layer of mortar on the bottom of the hole, but not on the back, sides, or top. Then remove the brick from the bucket of water, shake it to remove excess water, and spread a thick layer of mortar on the top and the ends of the brick. Don't spread mortar on the back of the brick; as the brick is pushed into the hole, the mortar on the bottom will be forced behind the brick.

Set the mortared brick into the hole, pushing it firmly in so that its face is flush with the surrounding bricks. With a small, sharp trowel, press in the mortar that has squeezed out around the brick; if the brick is crooked, add more mortar as necessary to even it out. Then scrape off any excess mortar and finish the mortar joints, as detailed above for tuckpointing.

The newly replaced brick should be kept moist for several days while the mortar cures. Spray the brick lightly two or three times a day during the curing period. If there's still excess mortar on or around the brick, remove it with a dry, stiff scrub brush when the mortar is fully cured.

Clean the hole in the wall and flush it thoroughly; wet the cleaned hole and the brick. Spread a thick layer of mortar on the bottom of the hole, and on the top and ends of the brick; then push the mortared brick firmly into the hole.